A HISTORY OF MODERN LEEDS

DEREK FRASER editor

A history of modern Leeds

MANCHESTER UNIVERSITY PRESS

Published by MANCHESTER UNIVERSITY PRESS
Oxford Road, Manchester M13 9PL

British Library Cataloguing in Publication Data

A history of modern Leeds.
   1. Leeds, Eng. – History
   I. Fraser, Derek
   942.8'19   DA690.L4

   ISBN 0–7190–0747–X *cased*
        0–7190–0781–X *paperback*

Photoset in Plantin by
Northern Phototypesetting Co., Bolton
Printed in Great Britain
by Butler & Tanner Ltd., Frome and London

CONTENTS

LIST OF TABLES

LIST OF ILLUSTRATIONS

PREFACE

In 1837 a young visitor to Leeds commented scathingly on the town he was entering for the first time:

> This amongst all others is the vilest of the vile. At a mile distant from the town we came under a vast dingy canopy formed by the impure exhalation of a hundred furnaces. It sits on the town like an everlasting incubus, shutting out the light of heaven and the breath of summer. I pity the poor denizens. London is a joke to it. Our inn was consistent with its locality; one doesn't look for a clean floor in a colliery or a decent hotel in Leeds. [R. L. Brett (ed.), *Barclay Fox's Journal* (1979), p. 110].

The disparaging tone of his remarks could hardly, in all fairness, be employed today, for Leeds is now a clean, attractive and relatively prosperous modern city. How and why Leeds became 'the vilest of the vile', and how and why it ceased to be so, comprise one of the major themes in this book.

The writing of the book grew out of a strange paradox. During the last quarter of a century Leeds has been a popular quarry for historians interested in urban development, particularly in the nineteenth century. Scholars from many universities, especially Leeds itself, have pursued research on the history of the town. This accumulation of knowledge has been impressive and has illuminated many aspects of the town's history. In historical terms Leeds has emerged from the Dark Ages. Yet on the other hand it has remained one of the few contemporary cities without an authoritative modern civic history. Before the second world war Manchester commissioned an exhaustive municipal history, and since the war Birmingham has completed a history which runs up to 1970. Both ventures ran to three volumes. Among smaller cities Nottingham, Leicester, Lincoln and Middlesbrough have had their story told, but Leeds has remained an untrodden field. Nor were the prospects at all encouraging of this deficiency being remedied by the Victoria County History. Some city volumes have been produced, notably on Birmingham, Coventry and Hull, but there has not yet been even the first glimmerings of an organisation to mount a Leeds volume, and experience suggests that such studies have a gestation period of at least ten years. So there is hardly the prospect of a definitive large-scale history of Leeds before the end of the century and the research work mentioned earlier remains in university theses, academic monographs and learned articles, remote from the wider public.

To bring that scholarly research to a broader audience is the main aim of this book and its original motivation. Every contributor to the volume has pursued original research on some aspects of the city's history. All have been encouraged, however, to write for the intelligent layman rather than the academic specialist. While each chapter is based upon meticulous historical scholarship it has been composed with the general reader in mind who has some interest in the growth and development of one of our most important provincial cities.

A word is required to explain the structure of the book. It would hardly have been sensible to have divided the history of Leeds into equal chronological compartments, for the city's development has been uneven. The arrangement of chapters has been based upon the belief that the crucial period of history was that which felt the impact of industrialisation. It was from c. 1780 to c. 1914 that Leeds became a great commercial and industrial city and it was during this period that change was most rapid. Correspondingly it is this period where there has been the most heavy concentration of historical research. The main part of the book is therefore devoted to thematic chapters on that crucially important period, sandwiched between chronological surveys before and after. Thus Chapters I and II cover the early history of Leeds up to the late eighteenth century, while Chapters XVI and XVII trace the sixty years from 1914. Chapters III to XV analyse important themes in the social, economic, political and cultural history of a rapidly changing town during what has been called 'The Age of Great Cities'.

In a co-operative venture such as this, the work of many hands, effective teamwork is essential and I am happy to record my thanks to my colleagues who worked so harmoniously together. They bore with patience and forbearance the editorial tribulations I heaped upon them and I congratulate them on accepting the collective responsibility for a task which has not been attempted since 1846. Though spread across the land from Exeter to Edinburgh, the contributors all shared the general desire to see the city on which they had worked placed on the historical map. I thank all the authors for their efforts and I hope that my editorship has been worthy of their talents.

We have been fortunate in dealing with so sympathetic a publisher. Martin Spencer has been a source of support and encouragement and his senior editor Ray Offord devoted great skill and care to the task of copy editing. We are most grateful to them both. Two others deserve mention, for they contributed much to the book. I thank Ron Jones who drew the maps, and Ruth Fraser, who compiled the index. When I first considered the writing of this book I was much encouraged by Gordon Forster, who sustained my hope that such a book was possible. He has been more than simply one of the contributors, and I am grateful for his aid.

I hope the book will be a source of pleasure and enlightenment to all readers, but particularly to those who live and work in the city of Leeds today. To them the book is respectfully dedicated.

D.F.
University of Bradford,
January 1980

ACKNOWLEDGEMENTS

The publication of this book would not have been possible without generous financial support from many quarters. The editor, contributors and publishers are pleased to record sincere thanks for the subventions which were provided.

Mr Stanley H. Burton, despite some reservations, made the first offer of subsidy at a very early stage in the book's preparation. Mr Raymond M. Burton most generously supported the project, and it was his subvention which made the idea of the book a viable proposition. We are most grateful to the Burton family for this initial support at a crucial time. The major financial commitment was made by Leeds City Council, and thanks are due to Lord Bellwin, the former leader of the council, and to Mr K. H. Potts, the former Chief Executive, for their interest and support while the book was being written. Negotiations between editor, publisher and the council were handled with understanding and tact by Mr J. Rawnsley, the Director of Administration, and in the later stages of production his help was invaluable. It is important also to record our thanks to Mr Stuart Johnson, the Director of Education, and Mr A. B. Craven, the City Librarian, for their encouragement and support. The Leeds City Council has been a most sympathetic benefactor.

The book has also benefited from grants for specific purposes. We are most grateful to the University of Leeds for making a contribution towards the cost of illustrations; to Yorkshire Television for subsidising the cartographic expenses; and to the Leeds Civic Trust for covering the cost of preparing an index. All three bodies materially assisted in improving the quality of the finished product, and we thank them most sincerely.

The Thoresby Society freely made its materials available to us, for which we thank them, and thanks are due to those who granted permission for the reproduction of illustrations. Specifically, the Brotherton Library of the University of Leeds, Special Collections, figs. 74, 75; the *Illustrated London News*, fig. 43; Leeds City Council, pp. ii–iii; its Department of Leisure Services, Central Library, the front and rear endpapers, p. 409, and figs. 35, 36, 66, 67, 70; the City Archives, figs. 13, 68, 69; the City Art Gallery, fig. 72; Leeds City Transport, 44; the Thoresby Society, figs. 2, 5, 6, 37, 59, 60, 61, 62, 63, 64, 71; Wakefield Metropolitan District Libraries, Department of Archives and Local Studies, Goodchild Loan MSS, p. 45; Dr R. G. Wilson, p.1; Yorkshire Post Newspapers Ltd, figs. 76, 77. All other illustrations are from the authors' own collections.

To all those who have given a practical vote of confidence to this project we express our sincere thanks and hope that the book demonstrates that such confidence was well placed.

THE EARLY
MODERN TOWN

G. C. F. FORSTER

The foundations: from the earliest times to c. 1700

I

I   Leeds as a human settlement may well be fifteen hundred years old, for it is possible that it originated in the British kingdom of Elmet during post-Roman times.[1] 'Loidis', from which Leeds is derived, perhaps perpetuated the Anglian pronunciation of the British name of the river Aire and was at first the name of the people living by that river; later it was applied to a region of the principality of Elmet and ultimately to a single important place within it. Leeds may even have been the last independent capital of Elmet, before that British kingdom was overwhelmed by the advancing Anglo-Saxons early in the seventh century. From that time we are on surer ground in thinking of Leeds as an area with continuity of habitation down to the Norman Conquest and beyond. It lay on the border between British territory in the north-west and the Anglo-Saxon, and later the Norse-Danish, kingdom to the east and south. Carved stones still preserved at the parish church and the city museum suggest the existence of an important church, possibly a missionary centre, from the eighth century if not earlier, and it seems reasonable to suppose that a small settlement of farmers and craftsmen would be found in the vicinity of such a church. 'A territory coextensive with the medieval parish of Leeds,' Professor G. R. J. Jones has argued, 'had formed one large British estate,' a 'multiple estate', perhaps, of a kind traced elsewhere in the north.[2] In order to accommodate Anglo-Saxon and, later, Scandinavian settlers, this area, served by its mother church, was subdivided into lesser estates many of which emerged in the Domesday survey as small manors. These comprised the neighbouring hamlets subsequently described as the parochial out-townships (which are beyond our present concern) and above all the most important township in the parish, the in-township of Leeds itself (fig. 1).

At the time of Domesday Book Leeds was a fair-sized and flourishing vill, occupied by thirty-five families and a priest, with a church and a mill. It had the characteristics of a small 'multiple

B   Buslingthorpe   H   Hillhouse
CB   Cat Beeston   K   Knowsthorpe
GW   Great Woodhouse   NH   North Hall
                            S   Sheepscar

ARMLEY   Manor in 1086

Hunslet   Berewick or Sokeland
          in 1086

Wortley   Later name

•   Main medieval settlements

———   Leeds parish boundary

- - - -   Other parish boundaries

———   Township and hamlet boundaries

- - - -   Municipal boundary in 1967

0   1   2   3   4
              Miles

1   Boundaries of the constituent medieval townships and hamlets within the county
borough of Leeds up to 1974. (*Leeds and its Region*, fig. 25, p. 122)

estate', with several outlying hamlets dependent upon two significant
focal settlements. One of these, the religious focus, lay round the
parish church; the other, the secular focus, which may have been the
more important, lay half a mile to the west and became the capital
messuage, or headquarters, of the medieval manor. Before the
Conquest, as a further consequence of the fission of the original large
estate, the in-township of Leeds had been parcelled among seven lesser
landlords – 'seven thegns for seven manors', as Domesday Book states
– but manorial unification had more recently been imposed under the
lordship of Ilbert de Lacy, a powerful Norman baron possessed of the
extensive property which came to be known as the honour of
Pontefract. About the same time more men and plough teams seem to

have been concentrated in Leeds, a step which probably accounts for
the rise in the recorded value of the manor between 1066 and 1086,
when that of most places in the West Riding fell. Not long afterwards,
certainly by 1100, de Lacy granted the property to Ralph Paynel,
another wealthy Norman baron, to be held as a sub-tenancy of the
honour.

2   Kirkstall Abbey from the east

These measures were part of the new military arrangements
established by the Norman overlords. They increased the importance
of Leeds, which stood at a river crossing, and strengthened the
position and influence of the Normans in the locality. One sign of the
place of Leeds in the new Anglo-Norman connection was Ralph
Paynel's grant of the parish church with its revenues to Holy Trinity
priory, York, which was a dependency of the great Benedictine abbey
of Marmoutier, a wealthy monastery much favoured by Norman
dukes and barons. Another contact between the Leeds district and
the wider European world was made in 1152, with the establishment
of Cistercian monks on a site said to have been formerly occupied by
hermits in the out-township of Headingley. The monastery, soon to be
known as Kirkstall Abbey, was founded 'at the moment when the

Cistercian order had reached maturity and the height of its fame', and the abbey was designed and erected at the time when Cistercian building was at its 'most original and influential'.[3] The monks were also responsible for the clearance of woodlands and waste, the establishment locally of granges and the promotion of sheep and cattle grazing. Although the immediate impact of these pursuits on local farming and trade can hardly have been negligible it is at present impossible to assess the effect that the activities of Kirkstall's monks and lay brethren had on the development of the district, which at the end of the twelfth century remained rural in character.

II　　The beginning of Leeds as a town is marked by the borough charter of 1207.[4] Maurice Paynel (sometimes called 'de Gant'), lord of the manor, gave the charter, hoping to create thereby a 'new town' within the bounds of his manor. This was a speculative undertaking at a time when innumerable lords all over Western Europe were embarking on similar town plantations. It was only a modest charter and a modest scheme, providing the opportunity for a town to develop by granting the essential liberties and privileges to some of those who dwelt in Leeds, or to any who might thereby be persuaded to dwell there.

Maurice's charter stipulated that the burgesses should be personally free, paying a fixed rent for their tenements (or burgages), which could be built upon, divided, bought and sold. It instituted a borough court with a more flexible procedure than that of an ordinary manorial court to cater for the needs of a trading or industrial, rather than a purely agricultural, community. Finally, it allowed the burgesses such economic facilities as the right to build workshops, to disregard a summons to the borough court if absent on business and to enjoy a very limited exemption from tolls. But the charter gave no rights of self-government, created no guilds or markets and granted no extensive trading privileges. Leeds was to be a 'manorial borough' in which the lord reserved to himself a number of customary rights, notably to exact certain financial dues, to appoint the reeve and to force the burgesses, like other tenants on the manor, to bake bread in the seignorial oven. In short, the charter simply offered 'personal freedom, free tenure and a borough court with a somewhat freer procedure ... the lowest conditions precedent for urban development'.[5]

Moreover, just as Leeds was not a manor transformed into a borough but became a borough *within* a manor, so also it was not physically co-extensive with the manor, but consisted of a group of tenements within it, occupying only a small part of the manorial area.

This new town of the early thirteenth century was laid out along the line of a street, wide enough to hold a market and later to be called Briggate. On each side of the street there were approximately thirty burgage plots, the truncated remains of which have been convincingly identified by Mr G. Woledge with the narrow yards depicted on nineteenth-century maps and still partly in existence.[6] These burgage plots were the sites on which houses and workshops were built. Near the south end of this street there was already a river crossing, and soon afterwards there may have been a bridge, but of this there is no documentary evidence until 1384. Thus the borough of Leeds was planted on virgin soil adjacent to the river but standing on rising, better-drained ground.

Leeds in the thirteenth century, however, was not compact but, as an old 'multiple estate', consisted of several distinct areas of habitation and activity. There was the old settlement around the parish church of St. Peter. The newly founded borough lay between the village to the east and the dwellings, capital messuage, park and mills of the manor of Leeds to the west, on Castle Hill, later to be known as Mill Hill. Because of the discrete structure of the manor the demesne was cultivated by bondmen living in the outlying hamlets, notably Woodhouse and Knowsthorpe, where there were open fields and commons, while each of the burgage holders had, along with a plot in Briggate, half an acre in the fields at Burmantofts (i.e. 'borough men's tofts'). Finally, still within the parish, were the hamlets of the out-townships. The gradual coalescing of these different settlements forms an important strand in the subsequent history of Leeds.

The institutions of local government were equally various. The 'new town' had its own court, but there were separate courts for the rest of the manor of Leeds (which reverted to the de Lacys by 1248, merging in 1311 into the great Lancastrian inheritance). Since the late eleventh century there had existed the separate Church manor of Kirkgate-cum-Holbeck, a dependency of Holy Trinity priory, York, and the out-townships were individual centres of manorial jurisdiction. Kirkstall Abbey too had its own courts and officials for its tenants and property. This complex organisation was not rationalised until after 1626, when the whole parish came under the jurisdiction of the new Corporation.

During the remainder of the Middle Ages, therefore, links between the 'new town' and the traditional manorial organisation were necessarily strong. The manor was larger in area and value than the borough, and farming was the primary occupation of most of the inhabitants. To some extent the townsmen were fed on the produce of the manorial fields, for clearly the limited amount of cultivation possible on the small holdings at Burmantofts could only marginally supplement the burgesses' main income from trade or industry. No doubt the borough's craftsmen and traders in their turn satisfied the needs of the smaller, scattered settlements. It is also probable that bondmen took advantage of the economic opportunities and legal privileges of the borough to secure personal freedom for themselves, so that by 1400 the conditions of other tenants had largely approximated to those of the burgesses. Furthermore, by the early fourteenth century income from what may broadly be termed burghal, industrial and commercial sources formed almost half the manorial revenues and bears witness to the 'new town's' importance in the economy of the wider area.

The substantial increase in these revenues between 1258 and 1341, and their stability for another three decades (when manorial incomes elsewhere were often falling), provide solid evidence of local development and prosperity. This is reflected too in the building of a court-house, in the contemporary extensions to the twelfth-century parish church and in the erection of chapels of ease in certain out-townships. The poll tax of 1377 suggests that the population of the whole parish before the Black Death was about 1,000 people, of whom 350 to 400 lived in the central area, including the 'new town'. Furthermore, tax returns of 1334 and 1377 show that the significant degree of relative affluence enjoyed earlier by the villages on the magnesian limestone belt had spread along the valleys of the Aire and Wharfe and into the Aire Gap, and that in wealth and population Leeds then ranked with these larger, richer places to the east, south and north-east, rather than with the smaller, poorer settlements of the Pennine uplands.[7]

To some extent this prosperity was due to trade. In this connection Leeds had certain geographical advantages, for it not only stood on the York to Chester road and near the Wharfedale–Skipton route through the Pennines, but it also had an important river crossing and lay at the converging point of several tracks through the hills to the west. Before 1258 the Monday market was established in the borough, presumably in Briggate; during the next 120 years more stalls were erected, and eventually there were also several shops at the northern end of the market. By 1322 Leeds had a fair and within twenty years a second fair, but there are no signs of any spectacular development in commerce, which was probably still of only local importance.

Of much greater significance was the growth of local industry, first sustained by the circumscribed liberties granted in 1207. Before 1300 there were weavers, fullers and dyers in Leeds, and the accounts of

1322–27 mention a fulling mill, a coal mine and a forge: the later fortunes of the industrial town were to be built on cloth, coal and iron. Records of the first three quarters of the fourteenth century reveal further industrial activity. There were new tenters and more fulling mills; these, with the dye vats, became increasingly valuable as cloth manufacturing was slowly but steadily establishing itself in the district. New quarries were being worked in the in-township, as were two new coal mines; licences were granted for small intakes from the waste; the rents of certain properties rose. The prosperity of fourteenth-century Leeds can be largely attributed to this extension of local industry, and the cloth manufacture in the Aire valley may have been stimulated at this time by the sale locally by Kirkstall and other Cistercian abbeys of their annual wool clip, which they had hitherto exported. During the closing years of the century, however, Leeds (like many other places) seems to have suffered a measure of economic stagnation, due in part to severe outbreaks of the plague: the records reveal lapsed holdings, reduced values and a fall in manorial income. Nevertheless, from the end of the fourteenth century the signs are that the local economy was remarkably stable, at a time when there was sharp decline in many places, and that its recovery began earlier than elsewhere. Thus by the mid-fifteenth century local gentry families – the Dyneleys, Nevilles and Manstons, the Scargills, Danbys and Mauleverers, for example – had begun to take an interest in local property or in leases of manorial assets. At the same time there were more new intakes, tenters and fulling mills, and more dwellings in the 'new town' and the central area of the in-township.[8]

III   The century from *c.* 1450 to *c.* 1550 was a period of great expansion in the textile industry of the West Riding,[9] where those engaged in cloth manufacturing enjoyed certain advantages over York and Beverley, the old centres of the Yorkshire industry: easier access to wool supplies, cheaper food and labour, opportunities for agricultural by-employment, a multiplicity of fast-flowing streams, and the absence of guild restrictions. With its local industry already well established, if comparatively modest, Leeds was well placed to participate in this advance, although for long on a less spectacular scale than Halifax or Wakefield. During this period, therefore, fulling mills and tenter frames proliferated, the output of cloth, especially broadcloth, increased rapidly, and there was already some degree of specialisation in the finishing processes. Moreover, by the 1520s the growth of the textile industry had spread wealth through the valleys and uplands west and south of Leeds, which thus no longer stood on the western periphery of a thriving agricultural district but at the junction of prosperous farming and textile areas. This position subsequently enhanced the commercial importance of the town, in whose market the clothiers of the Aire valley could readily sell their pieces of cloth and buy wool or foodstuffs grown in the Vale of York.[10]

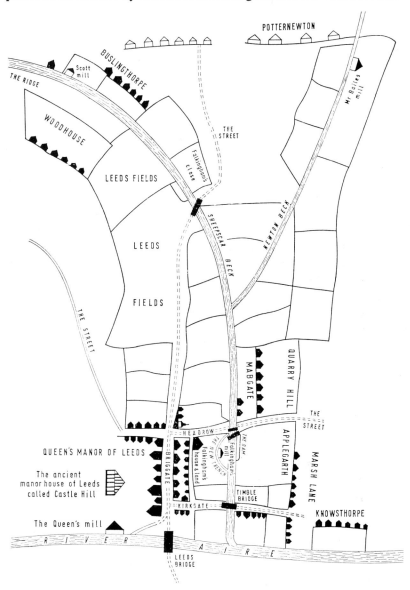

3   The first surviving plan of Leeds, 1560. This crude plan, which shows houses in the manor of Leeds, was produced as evidence in a lawsuit over mill rights and has been redrawn: see *Thoresby Soc.*, X (1899). (*Leeds and its Region*, fig. 32, p. 138)

Industrial development was reflected in growing wealth and a degree of physical expansion paralleled by a rising population. By the mid-sixteenth century the whole parish probably had rather more than 3,000 inhabitants, living partly in the out-townships but mainly in the central area. During the next two generations, thanks partly to immigrants in search of opportunities, the population seems to have doubled, a rate of increase which was probably not maintained in the first half of the seventeenth century, partly because of sporadic outbursts of the plague. However, the resultant demand for housing and food put great pressure on building sites in the central area and on the capacity of the manorial mills to grind the tenants' corn. Despite litigation, such as gave rise to the first plan of Leeds in 1560, private mills were erected, but it is clear that the town was now rapidly outgrowing its manorial framework.

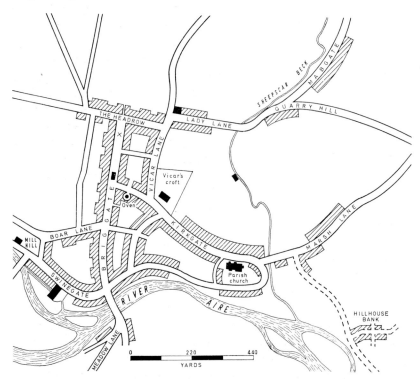

4   Leeds in 1612. This plan is based on the written survey of the manor of Leeds in 1612 and other material, reconstructed in map form in D. Ward's thesis cited in note 19. (*Leeds and its Region*, fig. 33, p. 139)

The crude plan of 1560 shows that there was already some expansion from Briggate, the nucleus of the medieval 'new town', for by then buildings had spread into Marsh Lane, Vicar Lane, Quarry

Hill and Mabgate to the east, as well as along the Headrows to the north. By this time the village round the church and the 'new town' in Briggate had coalesced. Surveys of 1612 and 1628 reveal a further stage in this development.[11] In addition to the spread of buildings along Boar Lane, in Mill Hill and around the bridge on both banks, the growth of the built-up area also involved the infilling of vacant land behind the facade of dwellings on each of the main streets; the resulting yard property housed much of the growing population. At the time of the 1628 survey Briggate was

> a large and broad streete (paved with stone) . . . The houses on both sides thereof are verie thicke, and close compacted together, beinge ancient meane and lowe built; and generallie all of Tymber; though they have stone quarries frequent in the Towne, and about it.

The multiplication of cottages and workshops in those parts of the town away from 'close compacted' Briggate did not, however, mean that the whole central area was built up, for there were still numerous gardens, orchards and tenter grounds (where cloth was stretched and dried on tenter frames). There were tenters too, and woolhedges, on the common land known as Woodhouse Moor; here, and at Knowsthorpe, there were also coal mines. No common fields survived, but the open land north and south of the town was broken up into small holdings where the cottagers engaged in farming as well as in cloth production, and numerous fulling mills stood on the lesser streams flowing into the river Aire. The only notable building was the parish church, 'a verie faire church built after a Cathedrall structure, and having one side thereof double-Iled', but the whole town stood 'pleasantlie in a fruitefull and enclosed vale'.

Leeds now played an important dual role in the West Riding textile industry: as well as manufacturing in general, finishing processes in particular were carried on in the town, cloth from the villages to the south and west being funnelled into Leeds for dressing, cropping and dyeing. The growing number of clothworkers, like those elsewhere in the Riding, carried on their craft in workshops attached to their own homes; some were helped merely by their families, others were employers of labour with large stocks and extensive premises. The cloth was marketed by local merchants. Their expanding business aroused complaints from York and Hull, where the old established merchant houses found themselves being slowly ousted from their once dominant position in the increasingly lucrative export trade in cheap kerseys and northern dozens. These Leeds merchants and merchant-manufacturers, some of whom became wealthy, were seldom former clothiers. Instead, for the most part they seem to have been descendants of substantial yeomen and smaller landed families – such as the Wades and the Sykeses – attracted to the district during the sixteenth century by the active land market which resulted from disposal of the estates of Kirkstall Abbey and other ecclesiastical property.[12] These newcomers sought business and wealth, and the social standing which matched them. But their fortunes depended upon steady trade and reliable products, and during the reign of James I trading fluctuations, together with abuses in manufacturing which lowered the quality of the cloth, caused problems. Consequently the merchants and cloth finishers were eager to regulate the wool supply and to control cloth manufacture, in order to uphold standards.

Difficulties in the economic life of Jacobean Leeds were accompanied by a remarkable ferment in its public life. First, its inhabitants secured exemption from tolls throughout the realm. Then, following a dispute about the right of presentation to the vicarage of Leeds, a body of trustees was appointed for that purpose. Thirdly, a bitter controversy about the alleged mismanagement of local charities resulted in the institution of a committee for charitable uses to administer the funds. Again, in 1619 Leeds was made a staple town for wool dealing (which proved to be only a short-lived privilege). Finally, about the same time, the moot hall was rebuilt and enlarged for the transaction of more public business. In all these activities a small group of men predominated; they were in the front rank of local trade and industry and were supported by Sir John Savile of Howley, a neighbouring landowner, courtier and champion of the 'cloth interest' in the West Riding. They clearly wished for a more influential part in local affairs and for a more elaborate system of local government than that provided by the traditional manorial organisation which the town had undoubtedly outgrown.[13]

IV   The need which the leading townsmen perceived for closer regulation of cloth manufacture, and their personal ambitions, combined with the results of the public activities just mentioned and the fame and prosperity already enjoyed by early seventeenth-century Leeds, enabled them, with the influential support of Sir John Savile, to claim a charter of incorporation for the town.[14] On 13 July 1626, therefore, King Charles I granted a charter of incorporation to the borough of Leeds as 'a free Borough' and 'a body corporate and politic'. The preamble to the charter set forth the need to stamp out abuses in the manufacture of cloth, thereby emphasising the basic objective of the charter and its progenitors. The corporate borough of Leeds was granted the right to possess property, to plead and be impleaded at law, and to have a common seal for the transaction of public business; these were the usual privileges of any chartered corporation. The government of the town was placed in the hands of one alderman, nine principal burgesses and twenty assistants. The first office-holders were named in the charter itself, and they were to hold office for life; vacancies were to be filled by co-option, and fines were to be imposed on those refusing to serve, once chosen. The corporation was granted specific powers to institute guilds and to frame regulations about the making of cloth as well as about other matters affecting good order in the town; these regulations were to be enforceable at law. The alderman, the nine principal burgesses and the recorder were to act as Justices of the Peace within the boundaries of the borough, whilst the corporation was to choose lesser officers: two sergeants at mace; a coroner; a clerk of the market; and constables. Tuesday was declared to be market day, and the corporation secured the right to receive tolls.

The Leeds charter of 1626 was very typical of town charters in general, but one should perhaps note four particular features of it. There was in the first place no mention of the borough created in the early thirteenth century, and one is left to assume that the functions of that early manorial borough had lapsed later in the Middle Ages, though there seems to be no evidence one way or the other. Secondly, the corporate body secured jurisdiction over the entire parish of Leeds, and although the manorial rights were preserved they were purchased in the 1630s by a group of local men who subsequently put the major part of them in trust for the corporation. Thirdly, the town was not granted the right to return members to the House of Commons, although Savile and members of the local oligarchy had clearly hoped that it would be; later attempts to secure parliamentary representation met with no success, except in the Cromwellian parliaments of 1654 and 1656. Fourthly, the charter was the work of a small group of local men who dominated the new corporation as they had dominated the public life of Leeds for a generation: Skelton, Hilary, Cooke, Sykes, Harrison, Hopton, Marshall, Casson, Metcalf; all these men and their families, most of them first or second generation incomers, were prominent in Leeds during the seventeenth century. Moreover, no fewer than eight of the charity commission were numbered among the first members of the corporate body which owed so much to their initiative.

Opposition to the new corporation quickly developed among the humbler clothworkers, who feared, with good reason, that the dominant merchants and wealthier clothiers intended to use municipal powers for their own ends by controlling the work of the ordinary craftsmen in an attempt to raise standards of production. Agitation against the formation of guilds for this purpose continued for many years without success, guilds being founded before 1640 and reorganised in 1662. Moreover, during the 1650s a company was created to control the methods and materials of the broadcloth workers of both Leeds and the West Riding. This too was a contentious scheme, for the men of Leeds could justifiably argue that cloth manufacture had to be regulated not only within the boundaries of the town but in the wider cloth-producing area as well, in order to uphold standards and incidentally to ensure that the Leeds clothiers were not placed at a disadvantage. The company might also have strengthened the regional importance of the town's cloth market, but in practice it achieved little or nothing, although its shadowy existence was renewed by statute in 1662.

The local rivalries described and the national political upheavals of the Civil War and Interregnum form the backcloth for the charters granted to Leeds after the Restoration. In 1661 complaints from members of the corporate body ousted earlier for Royalism led to the dismissal of their Parliamentarian supplanters and to the issue of a new charter of incorporation in November 1661. No change was made in the essential structure of local government: the oligarchic constitution was retained in this charter, which vested the government of the borough in a mayor, twelve aldermen and twenty-four assistants. The original powers granted to the corporation were defined more closely and confirmed, with the addition of the right to hold Quarter Sessions, appoint a common clerk and levy rates. This charter remained the basis of the government of Leeds until the reforms of 1835, except for the period 1684–89, when, as part of the royal attack on borough liberties, it was superseded by a charter similar in most respects but empowering the king to nominate and remove members of the corporation. Lists of the aldermen and assistants show that, in the later seventeenth century as before, membership of the town's governing body was largely confined to a number of families – about a dozen at any one time – of prosperous merchants and merchant-manufacturers, who formed a closely knit, self-perpetuating group and admitted to their circle a rather larger number of local merchants as occasion demanded. After 1661 the new generation of governors – Wade, Hick, Killingbeck, Busfield, Iveson, Fenton among them – included some families who continued to be important in the town well into the eighteenth century. With others they formed a local merchant society, bound by links of commerce, marriage and social activity, an oligarchy of urban gentry which controlled the town.

Much of the work of Leeds Corporation after 1661 was humdrum and stereotyped, dealing with the co-option of new members, appointments to local office, entertainment of distinguished visitors and the issue of bye-laws on various matters.[15] One has to ask, which of the town's activities were affected by the work of the corporation? The aldermen acted as JPs, with the duty of preserving law and order and of punishing malefactors in their court. They also accepted some of the responsibility for the relief of the poor and for the care of the parish church. Guild and apprenticeship restrictions had some effect on local economic activity. The corporation defended its own jurisdiction, and for some twelve years it engaged in a lawsuit to ensure that the privilege of freedom from toll for its townsmen was enjoyed at both Wakefield and Hull. In 1677 the corporation petitioned for the establishment of a post office and a postmaster in Leeds. Furthermore, it upheld the interests of local clothiers and merchants against outsiders, or against rivals in Wakefield or Gomersal, and it fought their battles in dealings with the corporation of London, which managed Blackwell Hall, the market for provincial cloth in the City. It also displayed a certain civic pride in its processions and public ceremonial, as well as in its acquisition of a new mace in 1694. About the same time the corporation commissioned Sorocold's waterworks. Finally, in 1699 members of the corporation played a leading part in the Aire and Calder navigation scheme and later in the plan to erect the first cloth hall: in both undertakings they clearly identified themselves with the developing interests of the town.

V   An important element in the growing public activity which had led to the charter of 1626 was religious zeal, stimulated by the changes of the Reformation. At that time Kirkstall Abbey and the parochial chantries were dissolved without causing a stir, and, although in Elizabeth's reign Leeds stood on the edge of a strongly Romanist area in the lower Wharfe and Aire valleys, there was little recusancy in the town itself. But during the closing decades of the sixteenth century moderate Puritan teaching spread rapidly throughout the textile district and was embraced by many notable parishioners in Leeds.[16] In their desire for the propagation of Puritanism some of them bought the right of presentation to the vicarage about 1588 and appointed an energetic Puritan to the living. Differing religious opinions underlay the dispute about the choice of another vicar in 1615; this resulted in the establishment of a trust, dominated by leading Puritan townsmen who thus secured an influential voice in the ecclesiastical affairs of the town. Religious differences also played a part both in the controversies

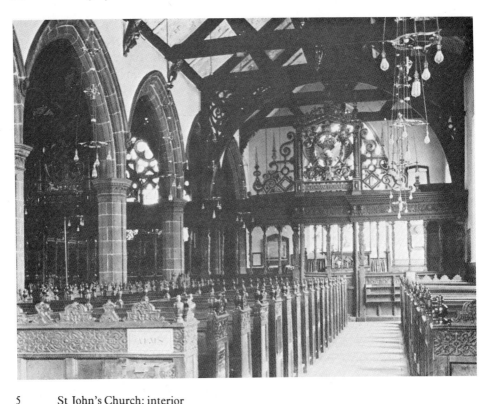

5   St John's Church: interior

about the town charities and in the violent clash between Vicar Cooke and the manorial underbailiff. Moreover the Puritan vicars were supported by a succession of Puritan curates in the chapels of the out-townships, and from time to time clergy and laymen alike were presented in the ecclesiastical courts at York for opposition to ceremonies and disaffection to the Book of Common Prayer. In this religious ferment the building and consecration in 1634 of St John's church takes its place. The gift of John Harrison, a prosperous merchant, St John's, with its splendid contemporary plaster and woodwork, was intended to cater for the spiritual needs of the growing population of upper Briggate and the Headrows, and its first minister was a Puritan controversialist of some repute.

The well established Puritan tradition of Leeds made a fertile seedbed for Nonconformity after 1660. Several conventicles flourished and were visited by respected preachers like Oliver Heywood, while the Quakers too were active. The growing support for Dissent is witnessed by the establishment in 1674 of a Presbyterian chapel in Mill Hill, but the Congregationalists and Quakers had to wait another twenty years before they too secured permanent meeting places, in Call Lane and Meadow Lane respectively. All these sites were some way from the principal streets of the town, in situations which symbolise the exclusion of their supporters from the mainstream of civic life.

VI   Like the Puritans before them, Nonconformists – such men as John Thoresby, William Milner and Samuel Ibbetson – nevertheless played their part in the town's business and industrial activities after the Restoration.[17] Leeds then had to recover from the dislocations of social and economic life during the revolutionary period arising notably from the prolonged industrial depression, local fighting and the brief, successful siege by the Parliamentarians in January 1643 (almost the only occasion when the town figured in national politics), as well as the severe outbreak of the plague in 1645. As industry slowly revived Leeds shared in the recovery and eventual expansion of the cloth trade between Hull and the north European ports, especially the trading towns of Holland, which many Leeds merchants, including for a short time Ralph Thoresby, visited on business. During the last decade of the seventeenth century a marked upsurge in exports of West Riding kerseys and the newer, lighter bays brought more prosperity to the important merchant houses of Leeds (some thirty in number) and enabled them to secure a tighter hold on the cloth trade of the region. In Leeds itself clothiers and merchants had continued to throng the huge cloth market held on or near Leeds bridge and, to relieve the pressure, it had been removed in 1684 into Briggate, where its bustling activity never ceased to arouse the interest and admiration of visitors. The 'great multitudes' who attended Leeds market were not only interested in cloth but came to buy a variety of goods made by numerous local craftsmen or imported by retailers in the town, some of whom – such as the tobacconists, upholsterers, vintners, grocers, goldsmiths and booksellers – were catering for the increasingly ambitious needs of a thriving community.

Prosperity was paralleled by the multiplication of social amenities of various kinds. Provision for the poor included a number of charities and almshouses endowed by substantial townsmen, notably John Harrison, who established his 'hospital' (an almshouse) near St John's church. From 1662 the corporation took a measure of responsibility for the poor. It drew up an elaborate scheme for the prevention of begging and for the provision of relief: a regular poor rate was to be assessed; a clothier was named as master for the house of correction, in which the inmates could be taught one of the textile crafts; the town was divided into six wards, in each of which aldermen and others were ordered to supervise parochial officers in the discharge of their duties for the relief of the poor. Pauper children were apprenticed by the magistrates, and after 1705 there was a charity school for forty poor boys and girls. The grammar school, possibly founded during the fourteenth century but reorganised in the mid-sixteenth, had long provided a few fortunate boys with a traditional grammar education, though perhaps without much distinction. Not the least of Harrison's benefactions was to rehouse the school on a pleasant site at Town End. There were also several 'petty' schools teaching elementary subjects.

The growing number of townsmen with literary habits were able to take advantage of the library established by Alderman Godfrey Lawson at the grammar school in the 1690s. Among its many readers was the famous Ralph Thoresby, FRS, who gathered round him a small literary coterie, made a collection of scientific and archaeological objects and wrote a number of antiquarian works, including the first published history of Leeds, *Ducatus Leodiensis* (1715), which supplies much information about the seventeenth-century town. Unfortunately Thoresby's museum was dispersed after his death, but by this time various other diversions were established: there were race meetings on Chapel Allerton moor, inns, coffee houses and occasional plays, not to mention the numerous alehouses and the athletic pastimes which helped to make life more bearable for ordinary townsfolk. Finally, a different amenity of enduring importance was the waterworks, built in 1694 by George Sorocold: a waterwheel pumped river water up Briggate to a reservoir, whence it was distributed by gravity feed in lead pipes to consumers in the principal streets.

The number of people living in Leeds in the later seventeenth century was between nine and ten thousand, of whom about two-thirds dwelt in the central area (or in-township), the remainder in the villages and hamlets of the out-townships, of which Holbeck and Hunslet were the most populous. The hearth tax returns of 1664 and 1672 provide some evidence of the distribution of wealth in the in-township.[18] Leeds (unlike York) seems to have had few complete paupers, but about two-fifths of the householders, taxed on only one hearth, lived close to the level of bare subsistence: these were probably the humblest journeymen, servants and dependent labourers. A further two-fifths of the householders, taxed on two or three hearths, enjoyed greater comfort and no doubt comprised the average craftsmen and shopkeepers. Only the remaining fifth – substantial clothiers, retailers, merchants, with a few resident gentry and professional men – were assessed at a higher rate and had attained a range of wealth rising in some cases to considerable affluence.

In all parts of the town mean and good property was intermingled, for rich and poor still lived in close proximity, and houses and workshops were jumbled together.[19] But at this time the poorest dwellings were mainly to be found amidst the fulling stocks and dyehouses on the eastern side, from Mabgate to Marsh Lane, and to a lesser extent in Kirkgate, where there was a mixture of substantial and modest housing. Humbler dwellings preponderated among the finishing shops in Mill Hill, but here and south of the river there was much medium-sized building as well. The most substantial houses were largely concentrated in Briggate and the adjoining part of Kirkgate and the Headrows, where there were several impressive residences, such as Red Hall and Wade Hall, built of timber, brick and stone in the traditional style.

At the end of the seventeenth century Leeds remained a compact town, still centred on overcrowded Briggate and Kirkgate, but the houses, workshops and warehouses were surrounded by open spaces for gardens, orchards and tenter grounds. Moreover in recent years wealthy merchants had begun to require more exclusive residences on the outskirts of the existing built-up area, away from the noisy market and the crowded yards. New, impressive houses were therefore being built for the 'wealthier sort' in the potentially fashionable Boar Lane and in the salubrious open country around St John's and the Town End, already known as 'Hightown'. Thus from its modest beginnings Leeds had become the busy, thriving town admired by Celia Fiennes in 1698, when she wrote:

> Leeds is a large town, severall large streetes cleane and well pitch'd and good houses all built of stone, some have good gardens and steps up to their houses and walls before them; this is esteemed the wealthyest town of its bigness in the Country, its manufacture is the woollen cloth the Yorkshire Cloth in which they are all employ'd and are esteemed rich and very proud; they have provision soe plentifull that they may live with very little expense and get much variety . . .[20]

NOTES

The author wishes to acknowledge the helpful comments on an earlier version of this chapter by Emeritus Professor J. Le Patourel, Mr G. Woledge and Mrs J. W. Kirby.

[1] This section is largely drawn from: G. R. J. Jones, 'To the building of Kirkstall Abbey', in M. W. Beresford and G. R. J. Jones (eds.), *Leeds and its Region* (1967), 119–30; G. R. J. Jones, 'Leeds – the beginnings of the city', *University of Leeds Review*, XI (1968), 114–18; G. R. J. Jones, 'Early territorial organization in Gwynedd and Elmet', *Northern History*, X (1975), 16–17, 21.

[2] Jones, *Leeds and its Region*, 124.

[3] J. Le Patourel, 'Medieval Leeds: Kirkstall Abbey – the parish church – the medieval borough', [*Publications of the*] *Thoresby Soc[iety]*, XLVI (1963), 5.

[4] For what follows in this section see: *Documents Relating to the Manor and Borough of Leeds, 1066–1400*, ed. J. Le Patourel, *Thoresby Soc.*, XLV (1957), *passim*; J. Le Patourel, 'Medieval Leeds', *Thoresby Soc.*, XLVI, 1–21; H. Heaton, *The Yorkshire Woollen and Worsted Industries* (1920, repr. 1965), 1–44.

[5] Le Patourel, *Thoresby Soc.*, XLVI, 14.

[6] G. Woledge, 'The medieval borough of Leeds', *Thoresby Soc.*, XXXVII (1945), 288–309.

[7] G. C. F. Forster, 'From the foundation of the borough to the eve of the industrial revolution', *Leeds and its Region*, figs. 29, 30.

[8] For information about later medieval and Tudor Leeds I am indebted to one of my research students, Mrs J. W. Kirby, who has kindly made available material from her forthcoming edition of documents relating to the manor and borough of Leeds, 1400–1640.

[9] For what follows see: Heaton, *Yorkshire Woollen and Worsted Industries*, 45–123; W. G. Rimmer, 'The evolution of Leeds to 1700', *Thoresby Soc.*, L (1967), 91–129.

[10] Forster, *Leeds and its Region*, fig. 31.

[11] Thoresby Society Library: MS Box V (Survey of the Manor of Leeds, 1612); City of London Record Office: Royal Contract Estates, Rental 6.16, 1628, now edited and published in M. W. Beresford, 'Leeds in 1628', *Northern History*, X (1975), 126–40.

[12] R. G. Wilson, *Gentlemen Merchants: the Merchant Community in Leeds, 1700–1830* (1971), ch. 2.

[13] G. C. F. Forster, 'Jacobean Leeds', *University of Leeds Review*, X, 143–7.

[14] *Leeds Corporation and the First Charter, 1626–1661* (1952); J. W. Wardell, *The Municipal History of the Borough of Leeds* (1846), *passim*; G. C. F. Forster, 'The early years of Leeds Corporation', *Thoresby Soc.*, LIV (1979).

[15] *The Court Books of the Leeds Corporation, 1662–1705*, ed. J. G. Clark, *Thoresby Soc.*, XXXIV (1936), *passim*; R. Thoresby, *Ducatus Leodiensis* (1715), ed. T. D. Whitaker (1816).

[16] See G. C. F. Forster, 'Parson and people – troubles at Leeds Parish Church', *University of Leeds Review*, VII (1961), 241–8; R. A. Marchant, *Puritans and the Church Courts in the Diocese of York, 1560–1642* (1960), 31, 33–5, 111–12, 115–17, 319–22.

[17] For this section see: Thoresby, *Ducatus Leodiensis*, *passim*; *The Diary of Ralph Thoresby*, ed. J. Hunter (2 vols., 1830) *passim*; Heaton, *Yorkshire Woollen and Worsted Industries*, 248–58; Wilson, *Gentlemen Merchants*, 15–18, 41–2.

[18] J. D. Purdy, 'The hearth tax returns for Yorkshire', unpublished M.Phil. thesis, University of Leeds (1975), *sub.* Leeds; Forster, *Leeds and its Region*, fig. 34.

[19] D. Ward, 'The urban plan of Leeds', unpublished M.A. thesis, University of Leeds (1960), chs. 1–3.

[20] *The Journeys of Celia Fiennes*, ed. C. Morris (1947), 219–20.

BIBLIOGRAPHICAL NOTE

There is no major monograph on the history of Leeds before 1700. For the period from the earliest times up to *c.* 1200 see the important, pioneering writings of Professor G. R. J. Jones, cited in note 1. The main surviving records of the manor of Leeds, and of the borough created in 1207, have been edited, with an introduction, in *Documents relating to the Manor and Borough of Leeds, 1066–1400 (Thoresby*

Society, XLV, 1957), by Professor J. Le Patourel, who has also published some reflections on 'Medieval Leeds', *Thoresby Soc.*, XLVI (1963); Mr G. Woledge's paper 'The medieval borough of Leeds', *Thoresby Soc.*, XXXVII (1945) is an interesting and convincing piece of urban topography. For Leeds in the period from *c.* 1400 to 1640 very little has appeared in print, but Mrs J. W. Kirby's forthcoming edition (for a Leeds University M.Phil. thesis) of manorial and burghal records should fill an irritating gap in our knowledge. Unfortunately some of the early records of the corporation chartered in 1626 have failed to survive, but the earliest extant minute books of the corporation are accessible in *The Court Books of the Leeds Corporation, 1662–1705*, ed. J. G. Clark (*Thoresby Soc.*, XXXIV, 1936). Leeds is placed in the wider context of the textile industry of Yorkshire by H. Heaton, *The Yorkshire Woollen and Worsted Industries* (1920, repr. 1965), and Professor W. G. Rimmer's stimulating paper 'The evolution of Leeds to 1700', *Thoresby Soc.*, L (1967) discusses the economic development of Leeds and its changing regional position relative to that of Wakefield. The sixteenth- and seventeenth-century roots of some of the notable mercantile families have been traced in R. G. Wilson, *Gentlemen Merchants: the Merchant Community in Leeds, 1700–1830* (1971). Little large-scale work has been done on the ecclesiastical history of Leeds, but there is useful material about the post-Reformation clergy in R. A. Marchant, *The Puritans and the Church Courts in the Diocese of York, 1560–1642* (1960) and in the late Canon R. J. Wood's 'A Leeds "Crockford" *c.* 1550 to 1836' (Thoresby Society Library, microfiche, 1973). Much of our knowledge of the families, social life and topography of Stuart Leeds is based on the work of a notable contemporary, Ralph Thoresby: his *Ducatus Leodiensis* (1715), ed. T. D. Whitaker (1816), and *The Diary of Ralph Thoresby*, ed. J. Hunter (2 vols, 1830), contain a great deal of information which has yet to be fully analysed. Abundant topographical detail is to be harvested from the editions of medieval documents already mentioned, as well as from the surveys of 1612 and 1628 cited in note 11 and depicted in fig 4, and from John Cossins's well known plan of 1725; D. Ward's thesis cited in note 19 is an invaluable survey of the town's historical geography. Finally, this chapter is a revised version of the present writer's paper, 'From the foundation of the borough to the eve of the industrial revolution', in M. W. Beresford and G. R. J. Jones (eds.), *Leeds and its Region* (1967).

6   Cossins's plan of Leeds, 1725

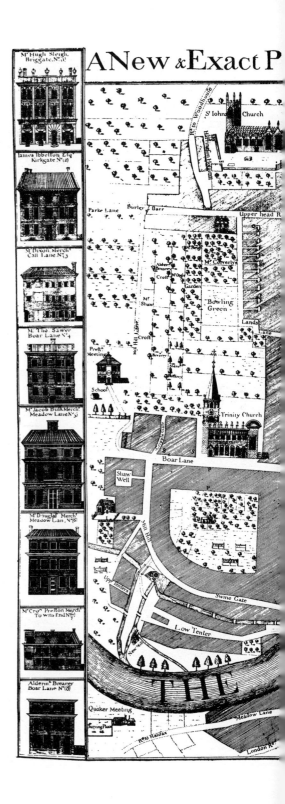

R. G. WILSON

II   *Georgian Leeds*

The historian of eighteenth-century Leeds has a difficult task. The trouble is that the Victorian city, like its great Town Hall, casts such a deep shadow that the life of the town in the previous century stands dimly in the shade. All the action in the city's drama appears to occur in a great second act that encompasses the 1830–1914 period. And since the town was largely rebuilt between these dates those interested in its past have difficulties in imagining how it appeared before 1820. To entitle a chapter 'Georgian Leeds' invites wry disbelief. For the two words as understood in the popular imagination are not easily brought together. In fact the history of Leeds in the eighteenth century represents a crucial watershed in the town's development. It also illuminates central themes in Britain's industrial evolution: in its population growth (the subject of Chapter III) and in its conversion from a small, primarily market town in 1700 into an industrial city a century later. Of course the two themes are closely related and the conversion was not completed with scientific precision. In this chapter I want to concentrate upon the second theme to uncover the springs of action that allowed the town to develop in the way it did. For there was nothing automatic about this transformation. The town might easily have stagnated in terms of size and economic development, like York, Southampton and a dozen other prominant pre-industrial towns, or expanded more slowly, like its near-by market rivals, Wakefield and Halifax.

I   Some visitors to the town in 1700 were puzzled. With 6,000 inhabitants it came well down the league table of provincial towns. Yet the parish of Leeds, coextensive with the borough, covered 21,000 acres – an enormous area by southern standards – and contained thirteen villages and a conflicting number of hamlets besides the central township itself.[1] In these outlying villages possibly as many as a further 5,000 souls were collected. Most were concentrated in Holbeck and Hunslet, Armley and Bramley, busy villages to the south and west and all archetypes of the organisation of rural industry in the pre-factory era. On its northern extremity Leeds ran out into pleasant, undulating country that was scattered with the houses of the minor landed gentry and those merchants who could afford a rural retreat. Even in Leeds township this diversity of landscape was evident. Within the space of little more than half a square mile there were similar contrasts. Industry was largely confined to two areas: cloth finishing along Swinegate and the Calls, within a stone's throw of the river Aire, which became lined with warehouses after 1700; eastwards across the two bridges over Sheepscar beck, itself crowded with a variety of water-driven mills in the last mile of its course, the town's clothiers gathered in Marsh Lane and Mabgate.[2] But except in Briggate, Call Lane and Kirkgate there were open vistas of the country, and the pleasant smell of horses, cattle and hay pervaded all but those areas most crowded with workshops or when a cold east wind carried the noisome stench of urine and dyeing liquors across the town. Everywhere behind the half-dozen definable streets were closes of pasture, orchards and gardens which provided the more well-to-do inhabitants and the town's inns and carters with a supply of hay and grass, vegetables and fruit. In 1741 Christopher Topham was offering the lease of a 130 acre farm, with its land conveniently gathered in a ring fence, within the *township* of Leeds. Forty years later, when there had been much infilling of the central area, John Elam was offering 'summering for 12 head of cattle' in Park Lane.[3] Yet neither the township nor the parish was noted for its farming, and very few inhabitants earned their living solely from the land. Visitors to the town – then eager to explore the urban scene – always came to view its market and industry.

And they were invariably impressed. Those twin gospels for historians of the early eighteenth century, Celia Fiennes's and Daniel Defoe's *Tours*, both testify to the wealth and vigour of enterprise of the town in the 1690s and 1720s. Celia Fiennes held no brief for thatch, half-timber and olde England but singled out for praise any town that mirrored the virtues of the London she so much admired — new architecture and opportunities for money-making. Such criteria led her to place Leeds in a list of urban front-runners. And Defoe, even when his hyperbole is discounted at a generous rate, conveys that he was much impressed not only by the size of the West Riding cloth industry and its principal market at Leeds, but also with the drive of the men who had lately thrust both into national consideration.[4]

But it is difficult to take the brief observations of these intelligent and seasoned travellers, with their ready eye for a sharp comparison, much further. Our knowledge of Leeds and those who lived there over two centuries ago does not allow us to recreate its economy and society in a way that entirely satisfies the reader of the 1980s, used to a diet of

surveys and statistics. Any picture of its growth must, at least before
the censuses after 1841 open up a whole new range of precise social
observation, be impressionistic. Yet until recently its focus seemed
sharp enough, in that writers invariably held that the prosperity of
Leeds depended upon the growth of the wool textile industry. Celia
Fiennes ascribed it in the 1690s simply to 'the Yorkshire cloth in
which they are employed'. And the figures produced annually after
1726 for woollen cloths milled in the West Riding indicated to
contemporaries some rough measure of the rate at which the industry
and its chief production centres expanded.[5] Recently, however,
historians – cutting away at this monolithic explanation – have shown
the town's economic expansion to have been more complex. They have
uncovered three, not one, main arteries: that expansion depended
upon the growth of other industries besides wool textiles, although the
latter remained central until the 1820s; that all industries developed
not by the rapid spread of a capital-intensive factory system so much
as by the extension of the ubiquituous craft shop; that the town
increasingly evolved as the commercial centre of the West Riding
textile region as its communications improved in the course of the
eighteenth century. Let us examine briefly each of these developments
in turn.

Table 1 Proportion of workforce in textile and non-textile industries after 1740

	Occupied population	Woollen manufacture	Other textiles industries	Non-textile industries
1740s	4,000–5,000	3,000–4,300	200	500–800
1790s	10,500–13,000	5,200	1,750	3,500–6,000
1841 (census)	59,715	13,338	9,473	37,090

Source. W. G. Rimmer, *op. cit.*, 138.

Fifteen years ago Professor Gordon Rimmer, working from a
variety of sources – all in various ways incomplete and unsatisfactory
but ingeniously utilised – demonstrated that the *proportion* of both
the town's employed workforce and firms engaged in textiles declined
after 1740. On the other hand the number of other trades increased
sharply. In the 1720s he was able to locate about fifty, a figure which
had increased threefold by the time of the first reliable town directory
in 1797. Of course, much of this increase simply reflects the natural
trend of increasing specialisation of occupational function as
population and wealth increased. But it is evident that there were
major new developments by the 1790s. Not only was there a much

larger preoccupation with transport and the handling of coal but new industries were becoming strongly rooted – pottery-making, linen manufacture, soap-boiling, sugar refining and chemical manufacture. Others, long established, were expanding: brick manufacture, woodworking, and the increasing number of building firms reflected the growth of the town and of the prosperity of many of its inhabitants; dressmaking, shoemaking, tailoring and printing responded to similar consumer pressures.[6] On the supply side, cheap coal, cheaper transport and good marketing facilities encouraged industries to expand in the borough. This broadening of the economy is apparent throughout the eighteenth century. Its pace – reflecting the general prosperity of the wool textile industry in the West Riding – was somewhat irregular, especially in the 1775–83 period. But it is necessary to stress continuity, the essential gradualness of development because it produced no hiatus, no 'revolution', no great leap forward – events that are so unlikely in reality.

Many of these developments occurred without significant changes in the size of economic organisation before the 1790s. The majority of the 150 trades in the town at the end of the century were carried on in craft shops that employed a master and perhaps no more than a dozen journeymen or women. By this time such 'shops' filled the streets and yards of every road except the new Parks area, and even that was not long clear of the appendages of cloth-finishing. Before 1790 the largest enterprises in terms of capital investment, with the exception of a handful of giants like the Aire and Calder Navigation, the Leeds Pottery and Middleton colliery, were the establishments of the big cloth export merchants. The seventy-five or so firms involved in the foreign and home markets in 1781 varied considerably in size, but even the largest employed no more than half a dozen packers, pressers and clerks, besides at the most thirty cloth dressers, some of whom were irregularly employed on a commission basis.[7] It was these finishing establishments, some owned direct by the merchants and others by independent cloth dressers and dyers, that increasingly became the centre of the Leeds cloth industry in the eighteenth century. For production of the traditional Leeds broadcloth declined after the mid-century, and clothiers – always small-scale in this branch of the industry – were driven south to the out-townships of the parish as property prices in the inner town rose sharply. Only in the 1790s when yarn-spinning and the preparatory processes of woollen cloth manufacture were successfully mechanised was the exodus reversed, for then factory production, in some instances eventually absorbing the entire processes of manufacture, was established in all the textile industries in the town, wool, worsted, cotton and linen alike.[8] Yet these late developments should not obscure the fact that before 1830 Leeds remained the predominant marketing and finishing centre of the West Riding wool textile industry. The fame of the Leeds trade abroad reflected its skills in the final stages of manufacture. For in the days before complete factory mechanisation many of the shortcomings of domestic manufacture were concealed during the completion of the finishing processes. Most of this know-how was practised in the town's dyehouses and cropping shops – themselves unmechanised before the general introduction of dressing machinery after the Napoleonic wars.

In other industries the craft shop also predominated. Here the scale of organisation was similar to that found in the finishing shops of the smaller merchant firms. We cannot be certain about numbers and comparable sizes because insurance registers, which have in recent years given historians such valuable insights into the scale of industrial organisation in the half-century before the coming of the factory system, include little material for the West Riding before the 1770s. Insurance came relatively late to Yorkshire. In the West Country and Norwich cloth industries, however, the insurance records trace the very gradual growth of industrial units in the sixty years after 1720.[9] If a similar trend occurred in Leeds – and there is no reason to think that the scale of developments was very different – then a few of the merchants' insurance valuations on their houses, warehouses and finishing shops would approach levels that were similar to those of early factory insurance valuations. By the 1780s this meant sums of two or three thousand pounds. These were, to use the jargon of the economic historian, the proto-factories of the pre-industrial period. The majority of industrial premises were smaller, valued before the great inflation of the French wars (1793–1815) at a few hundred pounds each. There were hundreds of these small establishments by the early nineteenth century. Professor Rimmer reckoned there were 1,076 firms in the town in 1797, 2,546 in 1817 and over 7,000 in 1842. Of course many were small retail outlets, inns and corner shops which render somewhat meaningless his figure of ten persons employed by the average firm in 1842. Factories were important, especially in the textile industries after the 1790s. In 1800 there were fewer than twenty; by 1842 this figure had increased tenfold. But the big factory of the textbook was still the exception that caught every visitor's eye. As late as 1842 only one in four of the town's occupied population worked in factories, and a high proportion of these were children. Four out of five additional workers in the town's labour force in the first forty years of the nineteenth century found employment outside the factory and mill.[10]

The central role of the craft shop in the industrial maturation of Leeds in the century before 1830 had important implications for capital requirements. Study of underdevelopment in the Third World since 1945 has placed crucial stress upon the importance of capital to stimulate growth. In our first industrial revolution its role was different and perhaps less crucial. In two respects the history of Leeds illustrates this point. Firstly the analysis of old insurance records has shown that fixed capital requirements were less than was once thought, except in the construction of the largest, fully integrated factories like those of Benjamin Gott and John Marshall. Secondly, the central role of the craft shop in a variety of industries, introducing some machinery but in no way measuring up even to a contemporary's concept of a factory, meant again that capital requirements during the first phase of industrialisation were generally not large. Both features make for continuity in that, clearly, few masters were suddenly crushed by the competition of great factories and forced to find impossibly large sums to expand. There were areas where substantial amounts of capital were necessary: that required to float a large firm exporting cloth to the Americas after the 1790s was calculated in tens of thousands of pounds, and the biggest mills were eventually built up on a comparable scale. But these were exceptions, invariably financed by the big merchant families or those manufacturers who had done well in the initial stages of mechanisation and ploughed back an appreciable proportion of their profits in the generally good years that extended from 1783 to 1808.[11] The majority of enterprises were much smaller. It would be misleading, however, to suggest that Leeds was a Smilesian paradise on earth for the small capitalist. In one sense it was. The scale of industrial organisation gave the overlooker, the small master, the young man of initiative his chance during boom conditions. Yet at the first onslaught of a trade recession he often disappeared from the pages of the trade directories as rapidly as he had found a place there.

The third aspect of the town's economic development is its rise as a commercial centre. Again the point of departure is the cloth industry, for the hub of commercial life was the cloth market, once held on Leeds bridge and removed, by reason of the fog that hung along the river, into Briggate itself. Then in the course of the eighteenth century the merchants and the leading clothiers and dealers built and extended a series of cloth halls which kept the trade of broadcloths for the region firmly in Leeds itself.[12] This was achieved, in the face of considerable opposition from other market centres in the industry, because the merchants in Leeds controlled an increasing proportion of West Riding cloth-finishing. And, as the growth of the West Riding wool textile industry accelerated – much faster than its competitors in the West of England and Norwich – Leeds devoured a lion's share of this prosperity. It did so because growth was in no small measure due to hard selling by its salesmen abroad and throughout the British Isles.[13]

The great twice-weekly cloth markets – one of the seven wonders of Georgian industrial England – had a wide magnetic field. For those who earned their living by making and selling cloth, those who came weekly from the neighbouring towns and villages, did not mount their galloways as soon as the market closed. They refreshed themselves, sometimes very liberally, in the leisurely manner of the eighteenth century, in the inns that crowded along Briggate, and bought necessities for their trade and families on the stalls and shops of Briggate and the Headrow. There was nothing new in this. Leeds had long been the market centre of the eastern half of the West Riding textile region, an exchange not only for cloths but also raw materials and foodstuffs, for nearly all the inputs for the cloth industry were imported into the region, and the uplands of the West Riding had long since been unable to meet the cereal requirements of its population.

But Leeds was more than a market for industrial raw materials and foodstuffs. As the textile industry grew and others, especially coal mining, developed, and agriculture itself witnessed a new era of prosperity after 1750, wealth generated in this area gave it a prosperity which few other regions in England exceeded. The wealth was very unequally divided. In Leeds its cream was skimmed by the merchants and a growing professional class of doctors, attorneys and bankers who provided essential services for an expanding, well-to-do community. These people and those of similar standing in the villages and towns around spent much of their income in Leeds. The growing variety of shops is one indication of the range of this consumer expenditure. Few of the early newspapers were without notices that a grocer, wine merchant, mercer, milliner or general dealer in Briggate or the Headrow had received a parcel of goods from London that was guaranteed to tickle the palate or arouse the fashion consciousness of the town's elite. Then there were shops that retailed a more standard fare: drapers and ironmongers, who in Leeds as elsewhere were often wholesalers over a wider region and among the wealthier members of urban society. And drysalters, wholesale tobacconists and wool staplers kept shops and warehouses that serviced the entire broadcloth region.

Much of the wealth acquired in the expansion of trade, industry and agriculture found its way into building. The middle and upper classes of Georgian England enjoyed a new comfort. It was by no

means confined to the landed classes, for evidence of house-building
and the inventories of merchants, etc., show that the more prosperous
urban classes shared the same greatly improved standards of
construction and a much wider selection of furniture, upholstery,
china, silver and general household goods. Most was manufactured
locally, save for silver and the finer china. Taste percolated down to
the provinces from London and in the process the sillier, more
expensive excesses were filtered out. Pattern books that spread the new
fashions were simplified by local architects, builders and craftsmen.
Unfortunately we know little about provincial urban taste before
1800. We do know a great deal about the fitting up of country houses
and those of the gentry who kept houses in London, Bath or
Edinburgh. But knowledge on such matters in towns like Leeds is
limited. What we can be certain about is that in Leeds, a town visitors
found prosperous throughout the century, the houses of its merchants,
leading professional men and few rentiers were well fitted simply
because their occupants shared a wealth that placed them at least on a
parity with the smaller landed gentry. Certainly sale notices,
when they begin to appear in the newspapers after 1800, and
the occasional inventory before, confirm this.[14] Leeds always
possessed cabinetmakers, upholsterers – so important in fitting up
Georgian rooms – and painters who could meet the requirements of
the region's elite. And as all commentators on eighteenth-century
taste noticed, there was always an army of people lower down the
social scale eager to adapt fashion to their more modest incomes.

Moreover Leeds developed as a social centre in the eighteenth
century. It is easy to dismiss the town as a monument of industrial
grime that no one visited unless they had business to transact. Chapter
VIII shows how lively interest in the arts was among the business elite
in the first half of the nineteenth century. A hundred years earlier it
was equally so. Of course, patronage had a largely local flavour then.
A small handful of merchants like Sir Henry Ibbetson and William
Denison had such deep purses that they could afford to adorn their
walls with old masters and employ the north's leading architect, John
Carr, on their building projects.[15] But most of those with pretensions
in such matters were content to have their spouses, children and pets
commemorated on canvas by artists who seldom had much claim to
celebrity in London. Nevertheless they were well aware of changing
fashions in architecture and taste, and their ample means allowed
them to indulge their interest.

Certainly the town's organised social life possessed vitality in the
eighteenth century. As a centre it compared favourably with most
county towns. Its social round was not regulated in any formal way

like that of York, Bath or Bury St Edmunds, but there was a constant round of cock-fighting – that brought toughs of every social class into Leeds before 1770 – horse racing on Chapel Town moor, theatre-going, dancing and card assemblies. When new assembly rooms, attached to the rebuilt White Cloth Hall, were opened in June 1777 'the company in general were very agreeably surprised at the neatness and elegance of the different apartments, which are allowed on all hands, to be as complete and highly finished as any set of rooms of that kind in the whole Kingdom'.[16] In the winters that followed there was a regular programme of concerts and assemblies. The musical festival, established in the 1780s, and the theatre both brought London performers to Leeds. The Leeds Circulating Library, built in 1810 at a cost of £5,000, would, claimed the pompous Rev. T. D. Whitaker in his new edition of Thoresby's *Ducatus Leodiensis*, 'not disgrace a College Library'. There are several reasons why a ritualised social life developed among the elite by the 1770s. Leeds possessed an affluent merchant and professional class that had numerous connections with the neighbouring gentry through marriage, business and county administration. The corporation gave a civic dignity and an excuse for celebration that few other towns in the West Riding possessed. Moreover eighteenth-century rural society was dull and restrictive for the educated and well-to-do. They welcomed the diversion of busy clamour that a large town provided. Only in the nineteenth century did all this change when the town became oppressively industrial, when the old merchant elite was submerged among a race of new industrialists and increasing prosperity and eventually the railways opened up a new world of social distractions in London, at the seaside and abroad. Then the old social forms of the eighteenth century, under real pressure from 1800 onwards, collapsed.

II   In the last decade there has been a great revival of interest in social history. Its exponents have shown that it requires precision no less than economic history. But with a dearth of systematically recorded information before the census of 1841 it is difficult to recreate the society of a town like Leeds in the eighteenth century in any total, continuous way that will satisfy the much more exacting criteria of the new social historians. The days when all a historian need do was collect a *pot-pourri* of quotations to illustrate social class and conditions have passed. Now the difficulty is that reconstructions of aspects of social life are infinitely time-consuming and the materials themselves – parish registers, newspapers, poor rate books and directories – are in many ways incomplete sources. Yet they are all we have. From them and others we know something about the elite in Leeds, its merchants, clergy, attorneys and bankers, but as yet too little about small masters, shopkeepers and even less about journeymen and the poorest classes.[17] At one level we require findings from systematically observed data about their origin, education, prospects, religion, some idea of their life cycle, if we are to understand the key relationship between social change and industrialisation; at another, more knowledge about the social recreations and customs of these groups. Now we have only a restricted view of that strange, harsh world obtained from the narrow cracks that the Quarter Sessions records and newspapers occasionally open up. Completeness in reconstructing the world of the various classes in pre-Victorian society is an elusive goal, but this exciting field is wide open to the enquiries of the demographic and social historian.

In Leeds the picture is not entirely blank. For although the knowledge we require about social organisation and composition in pre-industrial towns is limited, our understanding of its formal social institutions – the organisation of education, religion and politics – is more complete. Again, there are limitations in that we tend to view the activities only of the more well-to-do. It is partly a consequence of surviving source material, much more that social organisation than usually excluded the rest. Here I want to say something about religion and politics. Chapter IX discusses the relationship between education and the changing economic and social structure.

The milestones of eighteenth-century religious history are well known. Even when we narrow the focus to Leeds the road has long been marked: Thoresby's diary provided, when it was first published in 1830, a close view of the religious life of the elite and the sharp divisions between the High and Low Church parties that racked the town between 1680 and 1715; the physical confines of church and chapel life are again well known, particularly the building of Holy Trinity in the 1720s and St Paul's (now demolished) in the 1790s; there is a good deal of biographical information about the clergy, the patronage system that operated to fill the main livings and the infrequent but sharply contested elections to the vicarage of Leeds.[18] Similar details are known about at least the two chief Dissenting meeting houses in Mill Hill and Call Lane. All this is familiar territory, and the way parts at this point. On the one hand it is possible to pursue the path of doctrinal issues that divided congregations and supposedly gave their spiritual lives some meaning. It is by and large a murky, uncertain track. The other is to pursue the congregations themselves further.

The Anglican is in some ways the least rewarding. Always

comprehending, in theory, a large majority of the town's population, congregation here is a nebulous phenomenon in that so much of the Church's authority was vested in the clergy. Clearly the annually elected churchwardens were involved, but the evidence of the vestry meetings before the 1790s suggests that participation of large numbers of the congregation was minimal. This was largely because it was in no way responsible for payment of the clergy.[19] Therefore involvement in church affairs was not necessarily practical and was all too frequently passive. It is always hazardous to measure the intensity of the spiritual life of a congregation, since faith has a private face. But the outward signs are that between 1720 and 1780 it was in poor shape in the Anglican Church. At least, this is the impression conveyed by the diary of the Evangelical curate of Hunslet in the 1750s. When the vicar and parish curates met at their monthly club at the Angel Inn they were, perhaps not surprisingly in these surroundings, 'all clergymen and yet not one word of spiritual things among us'. By the 1790s the pendulum of Anglican religious conformity had begun to swing back again. It was partly the work of a popular Evangelican minister, the Rev. Miles Atkinson, who built St Paul's church in Park Square in 1791. When John Russell came to Leeds in 1799 to paint its worthies he noted, 'I do not hear the evil language in the streets of Leeds as in London. I have not heard an oath, nor have I been witness to an immoral action. This place is very remarkable in respect to religion, and what is more so, that amongst the rich and great a very considerable body are devout, approve and receive the gospel.'[20] These are impressions, real enough, but they can tell us little about the membership of the congregation and the way in which Church membership affected the lives of the individuals who composed it.

When we turn to the Dissenters – Unitarians, Baptists, Quakers, Congregationalists and eventually Methodists – it is clear that the congregation was the life blood of the chapel in a way that it never was in the Anglican Church. The latter could in the last resort function without one, a Dissenting chapel had no existence beyond the payment of the next quarterly subscription. All these places of worship were run by a caucus of merchants, shopkeepers and small masters. Some – the Unitarians and Congregationalists especially – were more socially discriminating than others, but none was egalitarian, for all were controlled by a dozen or so of the more prosperous members of their congregation. They paid the piper and they called the tune. In all cases religious nonconformity entailed civic disabilities. This meant the congregations were both cohesive and inward-looking in the face of Anglican political supremacy. Sometimes they provided educational facilities for the less affluent children in the congregation and were always the social basis of that particular community. And because the minister was paid by a public subscription of the faithful the financial standing of members was well known. Such a mutual knowledge of each other's worth and capabilities meant that men like John Marshall and Edward Baines owed some of their early success to help they had received from considerate chapel elders.[21] It is this sort of cohesion that gives these Dissenting congregations an importance in the history of Leeds that is disproportionate to the numbers of their members.

The political life of Leeds in the eighteenth century mirrored the organisation of its economy and society. But it did so in an extreme way. The merchant oligarchy, itself carefully recruited by an expensive system of apprenticeship and the high cost of buying partnerships, never entirely controlled the economic life of the town in spite of owning most of the property in it and reaping the largest profits in the cloth industry. For there were always other industrial interests outside wool textiles and clothiers in the region, especially the larger worsted manufacturers, who asserted some independence. Yet through their control of the corporation, given to them in the seventeenth-century charters, the merchants were able to exert a tight hold on political power down to 1835. Let us see how this situation developed and what implications it had.

In theory there were no restrictions to debar any male residing within the borough from becoming a member of the corporation, since the attempt to form a class of freemen was never successful. Yet in practice because the common councillors were elected by the corporation itself on its own nominations recruitment was narrowly restricted. What criteria of selection did it adopt? The evidence suggests that kinship, wealth and leisure were primary considerations. Education, so significant in determining the composition of twentieth-century English elites, was unimportant in the eighteenth-century selection process, since although all merchants possessed a sound basic education the status of different schools was largely ignored. Much more important was occupational training.

Leeds was incorporated as late as 1626. That first charter had been granted at the request of the merchant community – 'the ablest men of Leeds for their owne ends', as their opponents identified them – to secure political and economic control of the town.[22] Chapter I shows that the municipal history of Leeds, like that of every other borough, was stormy in the seventeenth century. In fact the cloth merchants' manipulation of the corporation was never relaxed. After 1705, when occupations of the common councilmen are given for the first time, we can measure quite accurately the merchants' presence. Sixty-three per cent of those elected between 1706 and 1795 were woollen merchants. An even greater predominance of merchants occupied the more prestigious office of alderman (71 per cent were merchants between 1710 and 1835) and mayor (73 per cent in the same period).[23] Except for a sprinkling of surgeons, attorneys and bankers – a related, satellite group – the corporation was drawn from the merchant community who controlled the town's premier trade. The Municipal Corporation Commissioners summarised the position exactly:

> the close constitution of the Corporation is obvious, all vacancies in each branch of it being filled by the Select Body, gives to that body absolute and uncontrolled self-election ... Family influence is predominant. Fathers and sons and sons-in-law, brothers and brothers-in-law, succeed to the offices of the Corporation, like matters of family inheritance.[24]

If family relationship and wealth were the principal guidelines for selection, there were others. The elite was never confined to the dozen or so families that formed its core. Between 1700 and 1780 twelve leading families within the corporation provided about thirty out of the seventy-three members elected to the aldermanic bench.[25] How were the rest chosen? Even among cloth merchants selection was necessary. For the twenty-four or so merchants who were on average at any time members of the corporation (there were twenty-four common councilmen, twelve aldermen and the mayor) never formed a higher ratio of all the merchants than one in two in the 1720s or one in six in the 1790s. Therefore when vacancies occurred, if there was no obvious candidate from the leading families in the corporation, the town elders looked among junior partners in the larger merchant firms. These young men had served their apprenticeship with merchants who were themselves aldermen and common councilmen. Even if they possessed no family ties they were known to the elite from serving their apprenticeship and, when it was completed, purchasing a partnership. They were then able to pass the tests of respectability, proper acquaintance and acceptable views which the inner caucus of the corporation informally set.[26] Surgeons, attorneys, bankers after 1770 and all wealthy newcomers were admitted on similar conditions. Because the activity of the Leeds trade attracted many thrusting young men, the corporation extended membership to those who could conform to its principles of civic worth.

What of those merchants and others who remained outside? On what grounds were they excluded? The face of the coin that the corporation ignored was lack of wealth and connection — for the merchant class was not uniformly rich. Extremes of income varied from those few great export merchants returning several thousand pounds a year to those scarcely surviving with annual profits in the home trade of a few score pounds. These latter, often advanced from the finishing and manufacturing sectors of the cloth industry, were bereft of the benefits that an expensive training and prestigious partnership conferred. Besides these there were Dissenters throughout the eighteenth century who remained outside the corporation solely on the grounds of their religion and political opinions. In terms of wealth and connection there were at least half a dozen Dissenting families who were the equal of the inner oligarchy of the corporation.[27] The economic elite therefore never entirely coincided with the political elite. But for most of the century this did not lead to impossible tensions. At times, however — between 1680 and 1715, again after 1775 and especially 1793 – the cut-and-thrust of national politics exposed the fact that the political and economic elites failed to fit.[28] It is well known that the political and sectarian clash between the corporation and the Whig Dissenters attempting to gain control of the improvement commission and the vestry were so fierce that government in the town was threatened with paralysis.[29] Real prolonged tension was evident only after 1800. It had its roots in the fact that the corporation never entirely contained the town's economic elite.

It is not sufficient to cite the number of merchants active in the corporation as sole testimony of the homogeneity of this elite. Sociologists analysing the structure of elite groups isolate two sorts of integration – 'social' and 'moral'. The former means the frequency of contacts – social, marital and economic – within the group: the latter examines whether it shares common ideas and ethos, whether it is aware of overall solidarity, whether in Meisel's words it possesses 'consciousness, coherence and conspiracy'.[30] Clearly both types tend to be closely related. Were they very evident in the corporation of Georgian Leeds?

Since it was composed of large numbers of merchants the degree of economic interrelationship was high. Some common councilmen and aldermen were partners in the same firm, and all merchants attended the cloth halls, throughout the West Riding. They were also involved in improving the transport facilities of the region, especially the Aire and Calder Navigation and after 1740 the turnpike roads. Social relationships were at two levels. Even at the formal level the corporation was a convivial body. It did not meet regularly in the eighteenth century – on average four times a year – but it would be a mistake to imagine that socialisation stopped here. In the year that William Wilson was mayor (1762–63) the corporation met four times, he and the aldermen attended four Quarter Sessions and five Petty Sessions. But most of the £98 he expended in office was spent at the King's Arms, where he found a pretext to submit bills for seventeen separate occasions.[31] No election to office was ever concluded without a 'treat' at one of the leading inns. At an informal level members of the corporation were thoroughly integrated socially: initial selection ensured this. Mrs Benjamin Gott's diaries, which record little besides the innumerable times she and her husband dined with or entertained the Leeds aristocracy – the Becketts, Bischoffs, Blayds and Dixons – are at least good testimony to the social cohesion of the leading merchant families.[32]

An analysis of the degree of 'moral' integration is more difficult. This stems from the types of document which have survived, for the minutes of the corporation are highly succinct. They are in reality order books that briefly summarise decisions and make no attempt to record discussions. Occasionally another source illuminates a debate, but the sense of harmony we now derive from the records is probably much exaggerated. Moral solidarity seems to have been better preserved than in other corporations. This arose for three reasons. Firstly the corporation shared common religious beliefs and did not have to make any attempt to contain within itself the Dissenting *v.* Anglican rift that was evident in the economic elite. After the great divisions of 1680–1715 the corporation presented a remarkably united front. Baines could detect no chinks in its moral armour between 1800 and 1834. Secondly Leeds returned no M P before 1832 (except very briefly during the Commonwealth), hence — especially since there was no contested election for Yorkshire between 1741 and 1807 — there was no attempt by local political grandees to drive a wedge into the corporation.[33] Thirdly the corporation – and this was very exceptional in Georgian England – owned no property.

For this last reason the power wielded by the corporation was limited. Not only did it own no property but it collected no rates. Revenue came entirely from fines paid on admission to and especially resignation from office. In 1796, by which time the fines had become onerous, sums accumulated from this source were no more than £1,800. Of course, this explains why the corporation met so infrequently and why its reputation was better than that of most closed corporations in the early nineteenth century. But power extended beyond the corporation in important directions. The aldermen, as Justices, were responsible for administration of the law, the highways and oversight of the Poor Law, a task always — and rightly — considered onerous. When John Hardy, the Recorder of Leeds, resigned in 1833 he wrote:

in these days of jealous but laudable scrutiny into the concerns of public bodies that of the Corporate Magistrates of Leeds will come out of the ordeal leaving no other impression on the minds of the Inquirers than that of astonishment at their great and gratuitous sacrifice of private comfort and convenience to the laborious and too often thankless performance of public duty.

The Municipal Corporation Commissioners exactly underlined Hardy's views.[34] Regulation of the town's cloth industry, which the charters vested in the corporation, was handed over to the county magistrates in the Stamping Acts of 1725, so its right to supervise the woollen industry – only fitfully enforced before this date – was not exercised thereafter. It was much more concerned with the administration of justice at the Quarter Sessions and frequent Petty Sessions.[35] This was an important activity in many towns, and one neglected by historians too busy looking at the work of their country counterparts.

The influence of the corporation was not restricted to its judicial functions. It would be highly misleading to antedate the division in Leeds, by the Webbs, between 'the Tory Corporation and Whig commissioners, Dissenting Churchwardens and church overseers – in the background a turbulent Vestry confronting an obstinate Bench of Magistrates' before the 1790s.[36] All the records make it clear that the activities of the corporation elite were paramount in a whole variety of institutions up to that date. Certainly it kept control of the vestry and improvement commission. Vestry meetings before 1790 were poorly attended.[37] At these the elite easily controlled events. Corporation members were frequently churchwardens, and it seems to have been usual in this period for young men to have served the office of overseer before election to the corporation. The aldermen supervised the overseers and constables from the bench, and they had the power to amend the Poor Law and stock assessments of the overseers. This right was much abused between 1715 and 1740. Only after the 1770s did the elite drop out of active vestry participation. The same pattern of involvement is apparent in the improvement commission, enacted in 1755 to relieve the corporation of cleansing, paving and lighting the streets. The 1790 Act introduced an important constitutional change which allowed the vestry to elect thirteen commissioners (it came into effect to fill vacancies after 1795).[38] But until 1800 the corporation elite firmly controlled the commission: indeed, the mayor and aldermen were constitutionally members of it. What seems to have happened is that as the leading merchant families which dominated the corporation grew wealthier they were drawn into county society. They lost as a result their taste for routine administration of the Poor

Law and trivial town business as an increasing amount of their time was consumed in the Volunteer Corps of the town and county after 1793 and, as the game licence lists amply testify, in rural pursuits. Relinquishment of interest in town affairs at the level of vestry and Poor Law administration was for these reasons frequently voluntary.

There were also a number of committees which except in a legal sense are best viewed as sub-bodies of the corporation, since they were again dominated by its members before 1800. These included the committee of Pious Uses, which administered the town's charities, the grammar and charity school trustees and the patronage of the town's three churches. The advowson of the parish church was held by twenty-five trustees drawn entirely from the Anglican elite that ran the corporation. There was no more exclusive body in Leeds. It did not prevent bitter contests when vacancies arose – patronage was a vicious, highly personal system – but it explains why the Anglican clergy were so closely related to the corporation oligarchy during the eighteenth century both in fact and in spirit.[39]

But because its formal power was limited by lack of economic resources, when the town expanded rapidly after the 1770s the corporation possessed little real strength. It could still make a grand show, its town clerk rattling off splendid, empty petitions when George III's family suffered one of its frequent calamities, but the reality of its power was becoming increasingly hollow. That is why the Whig Dissenters could so easily get well within reach of authority from the stalking horses of the vestry and improvement commission. And the power of all eighteenth-century corporations was limited in a more general sense. All suffered the same tendency to inactivity because the ruthless pursuit of interest and patronage greatly narrowed the range of ability recruited. Moreover there was only a small bureaucracy of clerks and officials to translate formal power into real action.

In Leeds the corporation – closed in nature and thoroughly integrated to the end – possessed in the final analysis little real strength. Before 1780 it had informally pushed its interests everywhere in the town, and from the bench the aldermen had striven to control developments. After 1783 when the town grew rapidly and new industries sprang up and others altered in size the corporation was overwhelmed by the scale of expansion and the rise of a new well-to-do manufacturing class whose outlook, politics and religion were often very different from its own. It might still inhibit the progress of political and religious reform and cling to its old privileges, but in the economic and social development of the borough its actions had a minimal effect. It had abandoned serious attempts to control either by the 1780s.[40] There was over half a century of *laissez-faire* before the new corporation introduced controls in numerous directions after 1835.

NOTES

[1] Population estimate from W. G. Rimmer, 'The industrial profile of Leeds, 1740–1840', *Thoresby Soc.*, L, Part 2 (1967), 130.

[2] See J. Cossins, *A New and Exact Plan of Leeds* (1725).

[3] *Leeds Mercury*, 14 April 1741, 26 March 1782.

[4] C. Morris (ed.), *The Journeys of Celia Fiennes* (1947), 219–20, and D. Defoe, *A Tour through England and Wales* (Everyman edition, 1930), II, 204–8.

[5] The figures were published annually in the newspapers and are to be found together in many places; see especially B. R. Mitchell and P. Deane, *Abstract of British Historical Statistics* (1962), 189. For a discussion about their validity see the author's *Gentlemen Merchants: the Merchant Community in Leeds, 1700–1830* (1971), 38–41.

[6] *Ibid.*; see also the long series of articles written on Leeds and its industrial growth in *The Leeds Journal* during the 1950s by Rimmer and other authors. A useful checklist of these articles appears in *Thoresby Soc.*, L, Part 2 (1967), 179.

[7] Wilson, *op. cit.*, 71–3, 239–40.

[8] D. T. Jenkins, *The West Riding Wool Textile Industry, 1770–1835: a Study of Fixed Capital Formation* (1975), *passim*; also his 'Early factory development in the West Riding of Yorkshire, 1770–1800', in N. B. Harte and K. G. Ponting (eds.), *Textile History and Economic History* (1973), 247–80, and his forthcoming article on the Yorkshire cotton industry.

[9] For Yorkshire see Jenkins's work and M. Dickenson, 'The West Riding woollen and worsted industries, 1689–1770: an analysis of probate inventories and insurance policies', unpublished Ph.D. thesis, University of Nottingham (1974). Dr S. D. Chapman kindly gave me access to the details of the Sun Office policies which he has transcribed for the Norwich and West Country industries. Professor M. W. Beresford has also used the insurance registers extensively for his study of housing in Leeds.

[10] Rimmer, *op. cit.*, 146–57.

[11] Wilson, *op. cit.*, 111–34.

[12] The best account of the cloth halls is to be found in H. Heaton, 'The Leeds White Cloth Hall', *Thoresby Soc.*, XXII (1913), and in his *The Yorkshire Woollen and Worsted Industries*, 359–404.

[13] R. G. Wilson, 'The supremacy of the Yorkshire cloth industry in the eighteenth century', in Harte and Ponting, *op. cit.*, 225–46.

[14] The inventory of the contents of Walter Stanhope's house (Spencer–Stanhope MSS, 1214), William Denison's (Denison Papers, University of Nottingham) and the sale of Wade Browne's furniture (*Leeds Mercury*, 28 November 1807) provide examples.

[15] Wilson, *op. cit.*, 214, and *id.*, 'Ossington and the Denisons', *History Today*, XVIII (1968), 164–72.

[16] *Leeds Intelligencer*, 17 June 1777.

[17] Summarised in the author's *Gentlemen Merchants*, the research for which was completed before the new interest in social history and detailed demographic studies. The newspapers, parish registers, Quarter Sessions records and the vast amount of miscellaneous material collected in the city archives provide a rich seam for the new techniques.

[18] The fullest modern account is to be found in C. M. Elliott, 'The economic and social history of the principal Protestant denominations in Leeds', unpublished D.Phil. thesis, University of Oxford (1962).

[19] Leeds Parish Vestry Minute Books, 1716–1844, now deposited in the Leeds city archives.

[20] Quoted in the Calender of the Clark MSS (diary of the Rev. Henry Crooke, 1757–1769) in Leeds city archives; G. S. Williamson, *John Russell, R.A.* (1894), 66.

[21] W. G. Rimmer, *Marshall's of Leeds, Flax Spinners, 1788–1886* (1960), 40; Sir E. Baines, *Life of Edward Baines, late M.P. for the Borough of Leeds* (1851), 45–7.

[22] W. G. Rimmer, 'The Evolution of Leeds to 1700', *Thoresby Soc.*, Vol. L, Part 2, 91–129 at 117–25, and H. Heaton, *The Yorkshire Woollen and Worsted Industries* (1920), 220–42, provide a good account of Leeds's incorporation. The charters are printed in the appendices of J. Wardell, *The Municipal History of the Borough of Leeds* (1846).

[23] Wardell prints the names of mayors, aldermen and common councilmen after 1660 (pp. clii–clxxv). Occupations are found in the Court Books themselves, LC/MI-3, and the town's directories.

[24] P.P. (1835), XXV [116] *Municipal Corporations*, I, 620.

[25] I.e. Atkinson, Blayds, Cookson, Denison, Hall, Ibbetson, Kitchingman, Lodge, Milner, Preston, Rooke and Wilson.

[26] John Wormald (mayor, 1776), Joseph Fountain (mayor, 1777) and Whittell Sheepshanks (mayor, 1795 and 1815) provide illustrations of this type. Other newcomers advanced very quickly in the corporation by intermarriage into the town elite: John Beckett (mayor, 1775) is a good example. In Leeds there was no regular advancement of common councilmen. The inner elite proceeded to the office of alderman often within a year or two of election. Therefore it was possible to be mayor in Leeds very soon after first joining the corporation.

[27] Of course many leading Dissenting families at the end of the seventeenth century could not resist the pressure to conform in religion over the next fifty years. Social and political forces were too strong to resist. But there was a core who did not: the Busks and Bischoffs at Call Lane; the Oates, Wolrichs and Stansfelds at Mill Hill; the Elams in the Leeds Quaker meeting.

[28] Divisions in the corporation were most bitter between 1685 and 1715 because sectarian differences were initially contained within the corporation itself. Thoresby's diary provides a good personal account. But after 1705 all pretence of unity was abandoned when the High Church party purged the corporation of Low Church Whigs and Dissenters. No fewer than sixty elections to the corporation were made in the nine years after June 1705 to fill gaps created by wholesale resignation. A comparable number of elections was made in the last thirty years of the unreformed corporation's existence.

[29] S. and B. Webb, *The Manor and the Borough* (1908), 415–23, present the collision in its starkest terms. More recent extended accounts are found in E. P. Hennock, *Fit and Proper Persons*, 179–201; D. Fraser, *Urban Politics in Victorian England* (1976), *passim*; R. J. Morris shows the way it infiltrated and undermined the effectiveness of the voluntary societies in Leeds in his 1970 Oxford D.Phil. thesis 'The organisation and aims of the principal secular volutary organisations of the Leeds middle class, 1830–1851'.

[30] See G. Parry, *Political Elites* (1969), 31–3.

[31] 'William Wilson, Mayor of Leeds, 1762–3', *Thoresby Soc.*, Miscellany, Vol. 2, Part 4 (1956).

[32] Gott MSS, Brotherton Library, University of Leeds.

[33] Attempts by the Irwins of Temple Newsam and Lowthers of Swillington to interfere in Leeds politics were evident only between 1710 and 1730. Since neither

family owned much property in either the parish or the township of Leeds they had little success except briefly in 1715.

[34] LC/M3, entry for 22 March 1833.

[35] Leeds city archives, LC/Q5 2–6.

[36] S. and B. Webb, *op. cit.*, 423.

[37] Leeds Parish Church vestry Minute Books, 1716–1844.

[38] The improvement commission minute books have not survived, although the Webbs claimed to have seen them. The Acts of 1755, 1790, 1809, 1815, 1825 (each time extending the role of the improvement commission), the newspapers and J. Wardell, *Municipal History*, provide material about the powers and composition of the commission.

[39] Lists of the trustees of the advowson appear in many manuscript collections, especially those of Thomas Wilson and John Lucas, both deposited in Leeds city archives. See also J. R. Wood, 'Leeds Church patronage in the eighteenth century', *Thoresby Soc.*, XLI, Part 2 (1948), 103–13.

[40] The Quarter Sessions books reveal that all serious attempt to regulate industry or the apprenticeship system had been given up by 1780. And the volume of work handled by the justices did not increase in relationship to the population expansion.

BIBLIOGRAPHICAL NOTE

There is no good modern single account of eighteenth-century Leeds. W. G. Rimmer, who worked extensively on the town's economy in this period, went to the University of the West Indies in 1961 and then to Australia. His research was never published in the monograph all those interested in the history of Leeds eagerly awaited. But at least we are fortunate to have his *Marshall's of Leeds* (1960) and his three papers published by the Thoresby Society in 1967. They are invaluable. So are the many articles of a more general nature that he contributed to the series on 'Leeds and its Industrial Growth' in *The Leeds Journal* in the 1950s (see note 6). M. W. Beresford has researched in great detail aspects of housing in Leeds and the town's physical development and he has encouraged a generation of research students to work in this and related fields (see the notes to Chapter IV). Of course the Thoresby Society has been publishing material on Leeds's history for nearly a century now. Its volumes are an essential starting point for anyone interested in the city's past. The author's *Gentlemen Merchants* (1971) traced the history of the merchant community and touched on the history of the woollen industry and the town at various points. It provides a reasonably up-to-date bibliography that indicates the variety and richness of the printed materials and manuscript sources that are available to all those who would delve deeper into aspects of Leeds's history in this period.

THE AGE
OF GREAT CITIES

C. J. MORGAN

Demographic change,
1771–1911

III

O smoky city, dull and dirty Leeds,
Thou may'st be well for trade and eke for wealth,
And thou may'st cleanse thyself at times by stealth,
Like men who do, but never own, good deeds.[1]

Hazlitt's rather undistinguished verse, written in 1824, sums up one important feature of Leeds in the nineteenth century. At one and the same time the city generated great wealth and widespread filth and squalor. The growth of industry was fundamental to both these developments, but it was not the sole cause — the smoke came from domestic fires as well as from factory chimneys. The unprecedented rise in the number of people living in Leeds provided industry with its workforce but put enormous pressure on the social capital of the town. It was the upsurge in population as well as the expansion of industry that caused the appalling problems of environmental health and quality, of dirt and disease that disfigured the history of the town during the nineteenth century.

I   The outstanding feature, therefore, of the population between 1771–1911 was rapid growth (see table 2). Between the first census of 1801 and that of 1911 Leeds grew from a town of just over 50,000 people to a great city of nearly 450,000. The 1801 census provided the first reasonably accurate population figures for many parts of the country, but fortunately two earlier enumerations of the inhabitants of Leeds, taken in 1771 and 1775, have survived.

Both these local censuses were taken to supply evidence in a controversy then in progress as to whether the population of the country was increasing or declining. The first, in 1771, was organised by Dr Joseph Priestley, the eminent scientist and, between 1767 and 1773, minister at Mill Hill chapel. He and interested friends carried out their canvass on behalf of one of the protagonists in the debate, Dr

Richard Price, and arrived at a figure for the Leeds township of 16,380. Subsequently, in 1775, Price's friends carried out another canvass and recorded an increase to 17,121 in the township. Price's principal opponent, William Wales, also had friends and supporters in Leeds, and they carried out a canvass of the ten out-townships shortly after the 1775 survey. Wales, in fact, published the results for only eight of the townships, omitting Chapel Allerton and Potternewton, but a total for these townships combined which clearly derives from this survey was given by James Lucas, a Leeds surgeon, in his work on parish registers. Lucas also gave somewhat higher figures for Holbeck and Hunslet which have been used to arrive at a borough population figure for 1775 of 30,609. The efforts of Priestley and his friends have given us a most valuable indication of the population of Leeds before the onset of rapid industrial change. It shows that between 1775 and 1801 the town grew by about three-quarters and by a massive 1,356 per cent between 1775 and 1911.

This increase was part of two wider demographic movements. The population of Britain was rising rapidly in this period, and England and Wales increased from about 9 million in 1801 to 36 million in 1911. This represented an increase of about 300 per cent, but in Leeds it was more than twice as much. This indicates the other important demographic change with which the town was closely associated – the process of urbanisation. In 1801 about 34 per cent of the population of England and Wales lived in urban areas; by 1911 it was 79 per cent. The nineteenth century has been aptly described as the age of great cities, and Leeds was certainly one of them. However, it should be remembered that Leeds had already established itself as a major town during the eighteenth century. By 1775 it was probably the seventh largest in England, in 1801 it was the sixth and in 1851 the fifth, having overtaken first Norwich and then Bristol. Only London, Liverpool, Manchester and Birmingham were larger. In 1911 the position was complicated by the extension of the boundaries of some cities while those of Leeds remained unchanged until 1912, when Roundhay, Shadwell, Seacroft and Crossgates were incorporated. However, Leeds probably retained its fifth position.

It was therefore not a town that rose suddenly to eminence during the nineteenth century. Its rate of growth could not match that of Middlesbrough, which had four houses and twenty-five inhabitants in 1801 and numbered 91,302 a hundred years later. Nor could it rival neighbouring Bradford's staggering annual rate of increase of 5·9 per cent in 1821–31. Indeed, the growth of Leeds, though rapid, was relatively even (see table 2). Only in 1841–51 did the annual rate of increase fall below 1·5 per cent, and only in 1811–31 did it rise above

Table 2 Population of Leeds borough, 1775–1911[a]

Year	Total	Average annual % rate of increase	% of increase due to:	
			migration	*natural increase*[b]
1775	30,609			
1801	53,276	2·2	59·0	41·0
1811	62,665	1·6	20·4	79·6
1821	83,943	3·0	46·8	53·2
1831	123,548	3·9	66·5	33·5
1841	152,054	2·1	38·2	61·8
1851	172,270	1·3	25·1	74·9
1861	207,165	1·9	34·3	65·7
1871	259,212	2·3	40·2	59·8
1881	309,119	1·8	12·0	88·0
1891	367,505	1·7	29·0	71·0
1901	428,968	1·6	24·0	76·0
1911	445,550	0·4	[c]	100·0

Notes

  [a] The hamlets of Coldcotes and Osmondthorpe in the parish of Whitkirk and in the townships of Seacroft and Temple Newsam respectively were incorporated in the parliamentary borough of Leeds in 1832 and were subsequently included in the borough's census figures. Osmondthorpe was also included in the 1775 enumeration and so totals for the two hamlets have also been incorporated in the borough totals for 1801–31.

  [b] See note 2 for the assumptions on which this calculation is based.

  [c] Between 1901 and 1911 there was out-migration of over 30,000, 83·8 per cent more than the growth in population.

2·5 per cent. However, a pattern can be discerned. The rapid increase of the last quarter of the eighteenth century was followed by a decade, 1801–11, which represented a relative pause before thirty years of hectic growth. Between 1811 and 1841 the population more than doubled, and then again there followed a relative pause in 1841–51, a decade of social and economic crisis. Growth then resumed at a steady, though slowly declining, rate for the rest of the century. The first ten years of the twentieth century heralded a new phase, with the end of the city's rapid expansion. In future population increase could be sustained only by the extension of the borough boundaries.

II   The rise in Leeds's population over this period derived from two sources: natural increase of births over deaths within the city and net in-migration from other parts of the United Kingdom and, towards the end of the period, from eastern Europe. There are a number of problems in calculating the relative importance of these two factors, and the proportions given in table 2 should be treated as reasonable approximations only.[2]

It is generally agreed that before the middle of the eighteenth century towns maintained or increased their population only by in-migration, because deaths persistently outnumbered births. Leeds shared this experience, with burials generally outnumbering baptisms from the 1640s to the early eighteenth century. After a period of fluctuating fortunes baptisms finally established a permanent superiority over burials in the 1760s and natural increase became a significant factor in the growth of the borough for the first time. The reason for this change is not clear. The death rate probably fell, and it seems likely also that the birth rate rose, but the relative importance of, and the reasons for, these developments are a matter for continuing debate.

Nevertheless during the two periods of very rapid growth in-migration continued to make the major contribution of at least 60 per cent during 1775–1801 and at least 53 per cent in 1811–41. In the decade of fastest growth, 1821–31, at least two-thirds came from in-migration. As one might expect, the two decades of somewhat slower growth, 1801–11 and 1841–51, experienced much lower levels of in-migration. When higher levels of population growth resumed after 1851 the pattern changed. Migration never again assumed the importance it had had, and in the last half of the nineteenth century natural increase provided about three-quarters of the borough's growth. The opening years of the twentieth century heralded a new trend, with net out-migration of over 30,000. In the 150 or so years covered by this review, therefore, Leeds passed through three significant phases which form part of the wider pattern of urban development. It began as a major in-migration centre, then grew primarily by natural increase, and finally net out-migration began.

The importance of the massive migration into Leeds cannot be expressed only by statistics. The economic, social and political life of the town in the nineteenth century owed much to men who were not natives of the borough. Important industrial innovations were carried out by Benjamin Gott (from Calverley), Matthew Murray (Stockton), Peter Fairbairn (Kelso) and John Barran (London). The investigation and improvement of sanitary conditions owed much, as we shall see, to Robert Baker of York. Perhaps the most striking illustration is that of the Baines family, who dominated the political life of Leeds for so long. The founder of this local dynasty, Edward Baines, arrived in 1795, having walked from Preston 'with a bundle on his arm and very little in his pocket'.[3] Baines made his fortune but the thousands of other migrants had to be content at best with more modest success.

A more typical experience was probably that of Robert Spurr, who, in his autobiography, left us a rare glimpse of a working man's life in the first half of the nineteenth century. Particularly, he illustrates the frequent movement from place to place that lay behind the statistics for net migration. People were constantly on the move in the nineteenth century even within a town, shifting from house to house as their economic circumstances altered: Spurr lived in five different parts of Leeds during the six years 1825–31. His account also emphasises the importance of the family as a unit in helping its members when times were hard.

Robert Spurr was born at Ossett in 1801. His first wife died in 1825, and in that year of economic crisis he was unemployed. He and his brother walked to Liverpool and back, but found no work; later he had more success in Hunslet and then Leeds before falling ill with typhus and then another complaint which kept him off work for a year. By this time he was in desperate straits and had to sell two chairs to buy a new hat.

> I then went off with a very heavy heart to seek work. I worked 3 months at Gildersome, making mens' boots at 2s. per pair. After that, i came to work for Brother John again for some short time. But i wished again to try my weel of fortune else where, so i went to work at Leeds, up at bank, and lived with Brother David but i slept at another place. I had not been there long before my master removed to meanwood and all the shopmen went with them – 5 in number. This was a very pleasant place and i enjoyd the working days very well. It is a very healthy country in that land scape. There was parks, woods and groves. It was full of beauty. But when Sunday after noon came i was left alone because my shop mates went to the publick house to enjoy them selves. But i could not do that and support my self and my son.[4]

The son, Joshua, was his child by his first marriage, and was brought up by Spurr's mother and sister. The pleasant life at Meanwood did not last, because the master went bankrupt, owing Spurr 50s in wages. He moved to Rodley, where again he enjoyed his work:

> In this Rodley shop there was 11 men in number. We had plenty of work and plenty of pastimes, such as sing, dance and drink and all kinds of folly from morning till night. So time passed away when at our work very well – except that profane swearing that i never did practice, nor did i like to hear it. But when Sunday came i found it was all vanity and vexation of spirit. All my shop mates went to their own homes and i was left alone.

This master too went bankrupt, and Spurr's travels finally came to an end in 1831 when he settled in Bramley. There he became a member of the Zion Baptist chapel and married for a second time.

This union lasted for thirty-four years, and they had eight children.
Life was hard. He tried to start a boot shop of his own but it failed and
he had to borrow money to bury his fourth child, who died three weeks
old. Christmas 1837 was especially bleak, with only one shilling to
spend:

> we was as clear from money as a toad is from feathers. Our table was very
> scanty; we had plenty of poverty, because the people was feasting on our
> money. And so we was from year to year, working and trying to get our
> bread day by day.

Three more attempts to start a shop failed, and it was not until his
children had grown up and were earning that life began to improve. At
last, in the improved economic conditions of the 1850s and with the
help of a loan of £5, a boot shop was successfully launched. Spurr now
succeeded in keeping out of debt, and looking back on his life in 1867
reflected with some pride on his achievements:

> After i left Ossett i went from town to town, from shop to shop, working
> for different men and living and lodgin with other men for near ten years.
> Some times it was very unpleasant to me. Then i got married to a poor
> hard working woman. She was faithfull to her trust. We where united to
> gather near 34 years before she Died. During our pass through life we
> have had births and deaths, times of sickness and of health; we have been
> in poverty and in plenty; we have had poor trade and good trade. But i do
> not remember at any time putting a price upon my goods to extortion
> from a customer that which was not right. I have often had too little for
> my labour and i might have a good conscience, beliving it would be better
> for us at the end. We have had 8 Children (as well as Joshua) but lost 4 of
> them by Death. So now, as a working man, i think after all my poverty, if
> any one has reason to be thankfull, it is me. For there his a deal of people
> in poverty and in debt, but all my debts is paid and all my Children is
> sober hard working Children . . . (and i hope they are all resting on the
> faith of the Gospel of Christ).

Robert Spurr died two years later at the age of sixty-eight.

III   So far we have examined trends in the borough of Leeds as a whole,
a large area containing diverse economic and social features. An
analysis of developments within the borough will therefore reveal
important trends in the economic and social structure of Leeds. The
ancient division of the borough into the in-township and the ten out-
townships provides a convenient basis for this analysis (see fig. 7
and table 3).

The in-township dominated the others. In 1775 about 56 per cent of
the borough's inhabitants lived there, and this rose to a peak of 58 per

Comparative populations and
growth rates of the townships in
Leeds, 1775–1911. The curves are
logarithmic to indicate growth rates

7   clearly

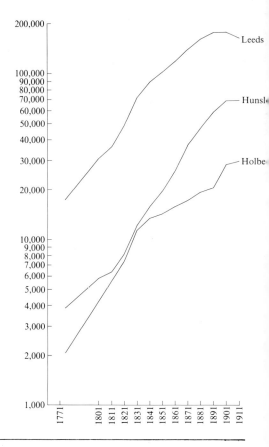

Table 3 Population of the townships, 1775–1911

	1775	1801	1811	1821	1831	1841	1851	1861	1871	1881	1891	1901	1911
Leeds	17,121	30,669	35,951	48,603	71,602	88,741	101,343	117,566	139,362	160,109	177,523	177,920	163,552
Armley	1,715	2,695	2,941	4,273	5,159	5,676	6,190	6,734	9,224	12,737	18,992	27,521	28,645
Beeston	862	1,427	1,538	1,670	2,128	2,175	1,973	2,547	2,762	2,928	2,962	3,323	7,618
Bramley	1,378	2,562	3,484	4,921	7,039	8,875	8,949	8,690	9,882	11,055	14,787	17,299	19,729
Chapel Allerton	(833)[a]	1,054	1,362	1,678	1,934	2,580	2,842	3,083	3,847	4,324	4,377	5,841	8,809
Farnley	540	943	1,164	1,332	1,591	1,530	1,722	3,064	2,964	3,608	3,590	4,351	4,208
Headingley-cum-Burley	667	1,313	1,670	2,154	3,849	4,768	6,105	9,674	13,942	19,138	29,911	41,561	46,434
Holbeck	2,055[b]	4,196	5,124	7,151	11,210	13,346	14,152	15,824	17,165	19,150	20,630	28,249[c]	29,970
Hunslet	3,825[b]	5,799	6,393	8,171	12,074	15,852	19,466	25,763	37,289	46,942	58,164	69,064[c]	69,795
Potternewton	(419)[a]	509	571	664	863	1,241	1,385	1,878	3,457	5,107	9,269	26,004[e]	40,589
Wortley	894	1,995	2,336	3,179	5,944	7,090	7,896	12,058	18,923	23,530	26,854	27,456	25,488
Coldcotes and Osmondthorpe	—[d]	114	131	147	155	180	247	284	395	491	446	379[e]	703

Notes

[a]Lucas gave a combined total of 1,352 for Chapel Allerton and Potternewton townships, I have distributed this figure between them in the same proportions as they consistently followed in 1801–41, i.e. Potternewton 31 per cent.

[b] Lucas gave alternative and higher figures for Holbeck and Hunslet than Wales, which I have used. Wales's figures were: Holbeck 2,045 and Hunslet 3,367.

[c] In 1896 the boundaries of Holbeck and Hunslet were altered by an exchange of territory. This made little difference to the population figures. In 1901, using the old boundaries, the figures were: Holbeck 28,179 and Hunslet 69,134.

[d] Osmondthorpe was included in the Leeds township total; Coldcotes may have been included with Potternewton.

[e] In 1894 Coldcotes was incorporated into Potternewton and is included with that township in 1901 and 1911. It made little difference to the totals – in 1901 Coldcotes had seventeen inhabitants.

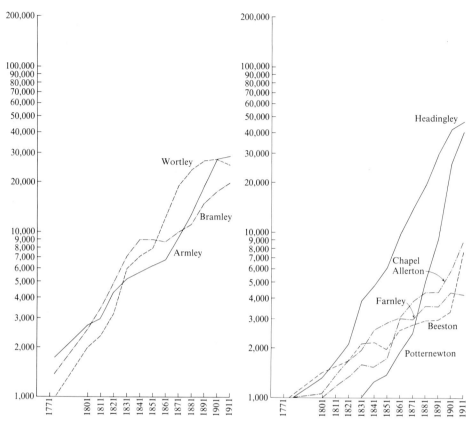

cent of the greatly increased population in 1851 (see fig. 7). Although there was a surplus of baptisms over burials from the 1770s, the township's growth was mainly sustained by in-migration before 1851. About two-thirds of the growth before 1801 was due to this factor, and calculations suggest that the proportion was maintained until 1841, the high death rate limiting the contribution of natural increase. This movement of people into the township clearly reflected the attraction of workers to its expanding industrial and commercial base. Other industrial townships also generally expanded. Holbeck grew particularly rapidly until *c.* 1831 as the centre of the flax industry. In the 1820s, the decade of fastest growth, in-migration accounted for over 80 per cent of the increase. Wortley and Bramley also expanded as centres of textile production, but Hunslet, the largest of the out-townships, experienced rather mixed fortunes. Until the 1820s it was in relative decline, and in 1831 it was nearly toppled from its primacy by Holbeck. From this point, however, Hunslet again expanded rapidly. These trends reflect the relative lack of water-power resources and good transport links there in the early nineteenth century. The advent of steam power and the opening of new roads and bridges enabled the textile and engineering industries to expand and confirmed Hunslet's position as the largest out-township.

This close spatial association of industrial expansion and population growth was the norm in nineteenth-century cities. Home and work were often physically tied by three factors. Hours of work were long, and there was no public transport; walking was the main means of getting about, as both Edward Baines and Robert Spurr illustrated. Another important reason was that many workers had only casual jobs and so had to live near the places where such jobs were available. All this meant that the industrial townships were also the main residential areas, and the basic distribution of population in the borough changed little in the period 1775–1851 (fig. 8). In 1775 the industrial townships contained 88 per cent of the population, and this rose to 92 per cent of the greatly increased population of 1851.

The agricultural townships of Farnley, Chapel Allerton and Potternewton experienced only modest growth, with some degree of out-migration and in Farnley's case a net loss of population in the 1830s. Beeston too declined relatively, despite the presence of coal mines in the area; the major pit at Middleton then lay outside the borough boundary. One township showed the pattern of the future – Headingley. In every decade after 1821 Headingley increased its share of the borough population. This was partly due to the expansion of Kirkstall as a textile and ironfounding centre, but the main explanation lay in the position of Headingley village to the north of Leeds, above and away from the smoke and squalor of industry. As the 1861 census report put it, 'The sanitary position of Headingley with Burley has induced a large portion of the mercantile community of Leeds to reside in the township.'[5] Headingley had become a middle-class suburb. By 1851, therefore, Leeds was becoming socially segregated, with the middle classes escaping to the suburbs and leaving the workers behind in the industrial areas.

A major development of the second half of the century was the relative decline of Leeds township. By 1891 just under half the borough's population lived there, in-migration having ceased to be an important factor in the 1870s. Of the industrial townships Hunslet continued to grow rapidly, although mainly by natural increase after *c.*1871. Two other major growth areas were Armley and, especially between 1851 and 1871, Wortley. The railways and engineering were important employers in all three townships. Bramley, and especially Holbeck, experienced relative decline until *c.* 1891 because of the decline of the textile industry, especially flax in the case of Holbeck.

The other townships maintained the trends of the earlier part of the

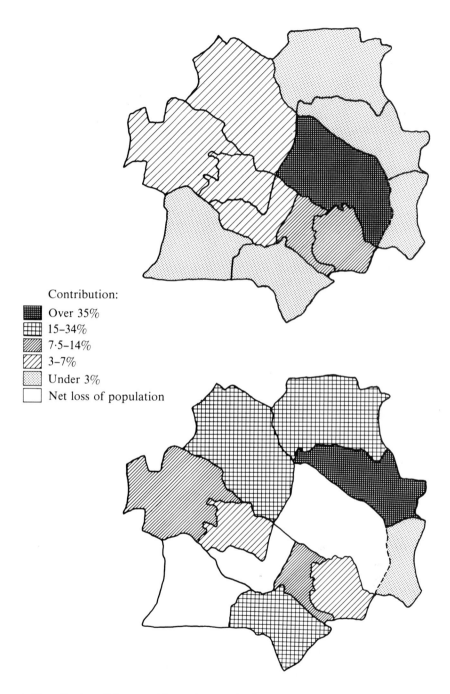

Contribution:

- ▓ Over 35%
- ▦ 15–34%
- ▨ 7·5–14%
- ▨ 3–7%
- ░ Under 3%
- ☐ Net loss of population

8   Contribution of the townships to the growth of Leeds borough in (*above*)
      1811–41 and (*below*) 1901–11

century. There was a brief expansion in Farnley in the 1850s when the ironworks were opened but this was followed in later decades by small absolute falls in population. Chapel Allerton and Potternewton experienced modest growth, with some suburban development reflected in net gains from in-migration. However, the only true suburb continued to be Headingley, whose role was strengthened by the development of a public transport system of horse buses and trams aimed at a middle-class clientele. About 60 per cent of Headingley's growth between 1851 and 1891 was due to in-migration. Once again it is clear that the basic pattern of population distribution established in Leeds at least as early as 1775 remained unchanged. The six industrial townships, despite their varying fortunes, retained their dominance, with 89 per cent of the borough's population in 1891 as compared with 92 per cent in 1851.

This well established pattern was obvious to a government inspector in 1871:

> To the north and north west the borough includes a tract of agricultural country among the pleasant valleys of which a ready escape is found from the unpicturesque appendages and murkey atmosphere of the town. Here, and on the elevated ground north west of the town, from which an extensive view of Airedale and of the bold ridges of moorland, which divide the valley of the Aire from Wharfedale is obtained, the wealthy merchants and tradesmen of Leeds have thrown out a thick fringe of luxurious mansions and country seats. To the west, south west, and south of the town, along the course of the river, lie the large and teeming villages of Kirkstall, Armley, Wortley, Bramley, and Farnley, with continuous hamlets. ... The different trades which constitute the principal industries of the town are here predominant. Tall columnar chimneys, great piles of buildings, and the smoke-blurred atmosphere, characteristic of manufactories and their activities in those villages. So thickly chequered in this part of the borough with mills and workshops that it is hard to escape from the sound of sharp-driven shuttles and the whirr of machinery.[6]

The next twenty years saw the beginnings of a transformation in this long-established pattern of distribution. By 1911 the share of the six industrial townships had fallen to 76 per cent. The most spectacular change occurred in Leeds township, where a net out-migration of over 40,000 took place between 1891 and 1911. Hunslet also experienced out-migration in this period, and in 1901–11 Armley and Wortley followed suit. These developments indicate the onset of a new phase in the development of all industrial cities — that of the growth of suburbs. Higher real incomes, shorter working hours and an expansion of public transport enabled the lower middle class and the better-off members of the working class to join the middle class in the suburbs. By the end of the nineteenth century the process of urbanisation in Britain was virtually completed, and most towns and cities ceased to grow much faster than the country as a whole. Urban expansion took the form of physical extension as the crowded, compact industrial city became the dispersed city of the twentieth century.

In Leeds the absolute or relative decline of the industrial township was matched by the expansion of the suburbs (see fig. 8), aided by the development of a quick and cheap electric tramway system from the 1890s. The decline of Holbeck and Bramley was halted by residential development, while Headingley lost its select middle-class status as terraced and even back-to-back housing was built there. Chapel Allerton and Beeston also expanded, but the spectacular transformation took place in Potternewton, which quadrupled in size between 1891 and 1911. Over 80 per cent of that growth was due to in-migration. In 1881 Potternewton ranked eighth in size of the eleven townships; in 1911 it was fourth. The growth of suburbs extended beyond the city's boundaries, with Roundhay expanding by about 170 per cent between 1891 and 1911, and this was recognised in the boundary extension of 1912.

IV   This discussion of population distribution within the borough would not be complete without a more detailed analysis of Leeds township, which until the 1880s contained over half the borough's population. The divisions or wards of the town form a basis for this analysis, but a change in their boundaries in 1835 makes comparison before and after that date difficult (see fig. 9).

A detailed breakdown of the 1775 enumeration permits a reasonably accurate analysis for that year. The ancient core of the town covered by Upper, Mill Hill and Kirkgate divisions contained about 50 per cent of the inhabitants, and another third lived in the North East and East divisions on the roads radiating out in those directions. The remainder was divided evenly between South division and North West division, which included the hamlet of Woodhouse. The next fifty years or so to 1831, during which the township population more than quadrupled, saw considerable modifications in this pattern (see fig. 10).

By 1831 the old core of the town contained only 16 per cent of the population. It had grown modestly to 1811, mainly because of the development of the Park estate, but stagnated thereafter. Meanwhile the major expansion took place in the immediate suburbs. North East and East divisions now contained half the population, crowded into the back-to-back housing to the east of Vicar Lane, the Leylands and the Bank. North West division grew still faster with the expansion of industry along the river and in Woodhouse.

This pattern of the township's population became still clearer between 1841 and 1881. The population of the new Mill Hill and Kirkgate wards fell after 1851 as they developed as commercial districts and rising land values forced out residential users. Further signs of this process can be seen in the decline in the 1870s of North and South wards, which impinged on the central district. The resulting out-migration and the overall expansion in the population (80 per cent) was absorbed by the steady advance of back-to-back terraces to the north and west.

By 1881 the township's period of growth was nearly over, and yet another set of boundary changes makes analysis difficult. However,

Ward boundaries in Leeds township. (*Below*) Pre-1835: *1* Upper division, *2* Kirkgate division, *3* Mill Hill division, *4* South division, *5* North West division, *6* North East division, *7* East division. (*Right, above*) 1835–81: *1* Kirkgate ward, *2* Mill Hill ward, *3* South ward, *4* West ward, *5* North West ward, *6* North ward, *7* North East ward, *8* East ward. (*Right, below*) Post-1881: *1* Mill Hill ward, *2* Central ward, *3* South ward, *4* West ward, *5* Brunswick ward, *6* North ward, *7* North East ward, *8* East ward

9

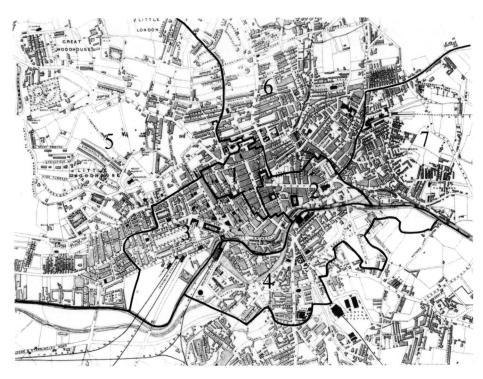

Comparative populations and growth rates of the wards in Leeds township,
1775–1911. 1771–1831 core: Upper, Mill Hill and Kirkgate divisions; 1841–81
10   core: Mill Hill and Kirkgate wards

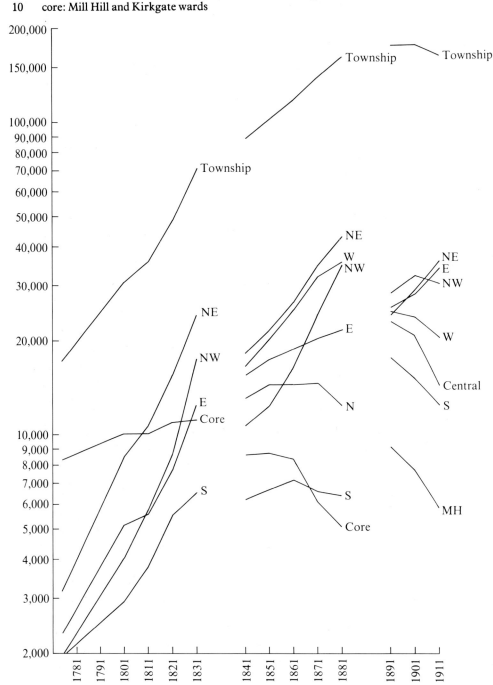

some points can be made. The central area continued its decline, and some signs of the out-migration to the suburbs can be seen in the population falls in Central, West, South and North West, which covered areas developed by cottage property earlier in the century. Only East and North East wards now expanded, growing by over one-third, as the only parts of the township where suburban development could occur along the York Road. Nevertheless the pattern established earlier in the century remained substantially intact in 1911: a central business district with few permanent inhabitants surrounded by a ring of factories and working-class cottages. Beyond that, in the burgeoning suburbs, was the pattern of the future – the flight from the inner city.

V   The importance of in-migration in the growth of the borough has already been stressed, and it accounted for at least a third of the nineteenth-century increase. Unfortunately we know little about the origins of these migrants. Birthplaces were not recorded by the census until 1841, and only in 1851 was a distinction made between Leeds and the rest of Yorkshire. In 1841 10 per cent were recorded as having been born outside the county, a figure which rose to 13 per cent in Leeds township. Obviously this figure has limited value because it is generally thought that migrants travelled relatively short distances and the bulk of them would come from Yorkshire. A study of Preston in 1851 suggests that 70 per cent of its migrants had travelled less than thirty miles. This view is confirmed by the figures from Leeds in 1851, which show that 55 per cent of its migrants had been born in Yorkshire. The proportion of migrants in the Leeds population in 1851 was, however, relatively low – 31 per cent. Bradford recorded 55 and Preston 53 per cent. Unfortunately it is not possible to continue this analysis because the census does not again distinguish between Leeds and the rest of Yorkshire as a birthplace until 1911.

Two in-migrant groups obviously require closer examination – the Irish and the Jews. The Irish settlement dated from the early nineteenth century, and in 1841 there were about 5,000 Irish in the Leeds township (where the bulk of them lived), some 6 per cent of the population. The great influx occurred between 1841 and 1851, especially after 1846 as the great exodus to escape the Famine began. By 1851 the number of Irish had doubled to over 10,000, and in 1861 a peak of nearly 15,000 was reached. This represented an eighth of the township's population and it was much the largest Irish community in Yorkshire. Between 1841 and 1861 Irish in-migrants accounted for well over half the total migration into the township. They were concentrated in the Kirkgate and Bank districts.

The Jewish community was also long established, dating back into the eighteenth century, and it was estimated that there were about five hundred families in 1877. An estimate of 1841 gave only ten families, so there was some influx in the middle of the century. The major immigration came after 1881 to escape the Russian pogroms. The *Lancet* put the position graphically:

> ... the greater part came from the province of Knovo; and at starting they are often acquainted with but one word of English, and that word is Leeds ... It seems evident that, as a whole, they readily earned their living at Leeds, and to the Russian jew, in dread of obligatory military service, and suffering from religious persecution, the name of Leeds was but a modern term for an El Dorado.[7]

The census does not specifically distinguish Jews, but in 1871 the number of foreign-born in Leeds was over 900, by 1891 it was nearly 6,000, and it reached a peak of 7,500 in 1901. Not all were Jews, but those born in Russia and Russian Poland formed the bulk of this group – just over 83 per cent. This does not give us the total size of the Jewish community, as the existing population and children born in Britain would not be included. An estimate for the late 1880s was 6,000 and for 1909 as much as 25,000. This seems rather high, and perhaps 20,000 would be the upper limit. Like the Irish before them the Jews concentrated, initially in the Leylands district, where some streets were 85 per cent Jewish. Given that the bulk of them lived in Leeds township, the Jews represented about 12 per cent of the population there in 1911. In 1905 restrictions were placed on immigration and by 1914 it had virtually ceased.

VI   Important though migration was to the growth of Leeds, the excess of births over deaths accounted for roughly two-thirds of the borough's nineteenth-century growth. There are a number of problems associated with the compilation of the vital statistics, and two points in particular should be noted. Firstly, figures for the period before 1841 are of baptisms and burials, and they underestimate, to a varying extent, the number of births and deaths. The figures can be used only to indicate broad trends.[8] Secondly, the rates quoted in succeeding paragraphs are crude rates only, that is, they do not take into account the age structure of the population. Obviously a population containing many young adults could be expected to have a high birth rate; equally, because child mortality was high, a high death rate would also be likely.[9] Industry attracted many young adults to Leeds in the nineteenth century, and its high birth and death rates partly reflected this factor.

The birth rate does not require much detailed discussion. The civil registration statistics show a high birth rate fluctuating around thirty-eight per thousand in the 1840s and 1850s, and the baptism figures suggest a similar pattern for the period 1775–1841. The rate reached a peak of about forty-three per thousand in 1874–78 but then fell steadily until the second world war. In all this, Leeds followed the national trends but always at a higher rate because of the age structure of its population.

VII   The analysis of mortality is also hampered by the lack of reliable figures for deaths before 1841. It would appear that the death rate in the township fell in the second half of the eighteenth century (see table 4) and then stabilised at around thirty per thousand between *c.* 1800–75 (see fig. 11). The reasons for the eighteenth-century decline are not clear. One suggestion is that smallpox mortality was greatly reduced by inoculation. The disease was endemic, with occasional epidemics, as in 1721–22, 1773 and 1781. In the latter year nearly 400 people were inoculated, but the efficacy of occasional inoculations (the next one was in 1788) must be doubted.

Table 4 Burial rates (five-year averages) in Leeds township, 1700–90

	Population^a	Burial rate $(^o/oo)^b$
1700	7,000	43·0
1720	8,500	39·1
1740	10,638	39·6
1754	14,000	33·7
1771	16,380	33·8
1775	17,121	32·4
1790	24,000	34·8

Notes

^{a} The population figures are estimates except in 1771 and 1775 when the local enumeration occurred.

^{b} Burial figures compiled from all surviving registers.

Whatever their imperfections, the figures do show a death rate for Leeds that was persistently higher than the national average or that for rural areas. The difference can be illustrated even within the borough by comparing the industrial Leeds township with rural Chapel Allerton and Potternewton. In Leeds township there was a marked contrast between the North registration district, 86 per cent of whose inhabitants were working-class in 1841, with the West district, with only 58 per cent working-class residents (see fig. 11). Such contrasts reflected variations in living standards and conditions in the different areas.

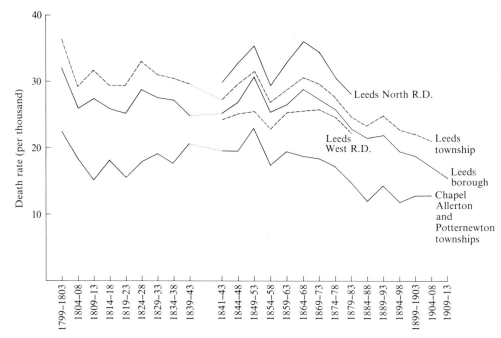

11   Death rates[a] (five-year averages) in Leeds borough,[b] selected townships,[c] 1799–1913[d]

    a Between 1799 and 1843 the rates are based on burial totals from Anglican and Nonconformist registers plus a 7 per cent allowance for unregistered infants. Between 1841 and 1913 the Registrar General's figures for deaths have been used.

    b Between 1799 and 1843 the rates are for Leeds parish; between 1841 and 1868 for the registration borough (see note 2) and between 1869 and 1913 for Leeds borough

    c Between 1799 and 1843 the rates are for Chapel Allerton and Potternewton but between 1841 and 1861 they were combined with Roundhay and Shadwell and between 1861 and 1908 with Roundhay and Seacroft.

    d The rates for Leeds, Chapel Allerton and Potternewton townships end in 1908 because the Registrar General's districts were changed in 1911.

    Inevitably, public concern with diseases tended to focus on occasional dramatic epidemics, notably the two serious cholera outbreaks of 1832 and 1848–49. Leeds suffered in these, and at least 700 people died in 1832 and over 2,000 in 1849. But these appalling visitations were less important statistically than the continuous presence above all of tuberculosis, but also of other infectious diseases like typhus, typhoid and dysentery. These spread easily among the inadequately fed workers who crowded into the insanitary districts of the industrial towns. Robert Baker's analysis of the situation was clear:

> In the manufacturing towns of England, most of which have enlarged with great rapidity, the additions have been made without regard to either the personal comfort of the inhabitants or the necessities which congregation requires. To build the largest number of cottages on the smallest allowable space seems to have been the original view of the speculators. ... Thus neighbourhoods have arisen in which there is neither water nor out-offices, nor any conveniences for the absolute domestic wants of the occupiers.[10]

Overcrowding was a major problem. One study suggests that the number of persons per built-up acre in Leeds township reached a peak of 390 in 1780 and then fell to 341 in 1815 and less than 200 by 1841 as the town expanded physically. This improvement, however, did not remove particular cases of appalling overcrowding like the notorious Boot and Shoe Yard, where 341 people living in fifty-seven rooms were reported in 1839. Even the majority who lived in houses built since the 1780s had only two rooms in which families of five or more lived. Parents, and children of both sexes, had to sleep in one room. The situation of these overcrowded houses served only to worsen the picture. Baker described the experience of Thomas Rooley, his wife and unemployed son, who lived in a house situated in a courtyard:

> The water in front of the house has accumulated from various sources. The yard has never been dry since he came to it. There is a sump hole, a great depth, in one corner . . . but it is full of deposit. The stench is often so bad, and especially after rain, that he and his wife cannot bear it. The fire-place of his house has a small place under it for ashes, but he has been forced to remove the grate and put down an oven-plate to cover it with, in the consequence of the stench coming under the house . . . Last week, in consequence of much rain, he would have been up to the knees in wet but for baling the water out . . . He worked five hours at it . . . The necessary above drains into this water through the partition wall . . . Then there are suds and dirty water also . . . for there is no drain nor means of throwing them elsewhere.[11]

The water supply in Leeds seems to have been reasonably good after 1842. Until then the only piped water came from the river Aire, which was also used as a sewer, so it was as well that only 2,000 houses were thus supplied and the rest of the inhabitants relied on wells, boreholes and water carriers. The arrival of a new supply from Eccup in 1842 and subsequent augmentations meant that by 1870 the quantity of water provided was considered ample for domestic use. Its quality was criticised, as, more significantly, was the failure to provide sufficient for the flushing of the sewerage system. This pointed to the greatest sanitary deficiency – the sewering and cleansing of the town. In 1832 Baker described in Fleece Lane 'a surface of privy soil, as near as the eye can judge of 10 yards by 4'.[12] Forty years later, despite a costly sewerage scheme, J. Netten Radcliffe wrote of a middenstead in Wellington Yard 'which measures 21 feet long by 5 feet 10 inches broad, and which is 6 feet deep below the surface of the ground. Into this middenstead fell not long ago a half tipsy man, plunging deep into the revolting filth, and there, suffocated, he lay until, days afterwards, discovered by the scavengers.'[13] Before the 1850s the only sewers were the private property of those who constructed them for their own houses. In 1832 Baker found only four such sewers in the whole of the Lower North East ward and only three streets that were paved and cleansed. The sewerage scheme of 1850–55 did not affect most of the side streets, especially the enclosed yards and courts, where most people lived. Refuse, domestic and human, was deposited in common middensteads and ashpits which were situated in the streets or even under the houses. In theory the deposits were cleared by scavengers but often they were missed. In 1832 seventy cartloads of manure were removed from Boot and Shoe Yard; in 1865 Dr Hunter reported the removal of twenty tons of filth from one receptacle. Such deposits as were cleared were taken to a central depot whence they were removed by rail or canal. A breakdown in this system in 1865 confronted Dr Hunter, a government inspector, with 'thousands of tons of midden stuff needlessly accumulated'.[14]

In 1871 Netten Radcliffe summed up Leeds's sanitary progress over the previous forty years and found little to commend. The localities that Baker had depicted on his map of 1832 as seats of cholera continued to be notoriously unhealthy in the 1860s. The death rate of the borough told the same tale – it had changed little since the 1840s (see fig. 11). This stagnation of the death rate at a high level was not, however, unique, and appalling environmental conditions could be found in every industrial town. Comparisons with other cities are not easy; much depends on the boundaries of the areas from which statistics were gathered. Leeds borough contained rural areas and so could be expected to have a lower rate than Liverpool, which was entirely built-up. Nevertheless, even if we use the urbanised Leeds township only for the purposes of comparison, Leeds does not come out at all badly. Despite this it was a focus of government attention in the 1860s, and three reports were published which secured Leeds's reputation as a particularly unhealthy town. The reason for the concern was the high rate of deaths from diarrhoea, which was undoubtedly due to the notorious middens and the failure of the town council to cleanse or abolish them (see table 5).

Table 5 Comparative death rates, 1855–62 (⁰/oo)

1. *Crude death rates, 1855–62*

England 21·8

Chapel Allerton	17·0	Leeds West	26·3
Ripon	19·1	Leeds township	26·7
Hunslet	24·3	Sheffield	27·2
Bradford	25·0	Leeds North	29·5
Leeds borough	25·2	Manchester	31·9
Birmingham	26·3	Liverpool	32·3

2. *Crude death rates from respiratory diseases and consumption, 1855–62*

England 5·7

Ripon	4·3	Sheffield	7·9
Bradford	5·9	Leeds township	8·8
Birmingham	7·3	Manchester	9·2
Leeds borough	7·4	Liverpool	10·2

Source. E. R. Braithwaite, *An Inquiry into the Causes of the High Death Rate in Leeds* (1865), pp. 8, 11, 16, 18.

The 1870s were a turning point, both nationally and in Leeds: the death rate at last began to decline. One important factor in this decline was an improvement in the life chances of young children. In Leeds between 1851 and 1860 on average 19 per cent of children died before the age of one, and this horrifying level of mortality lasted for the rest of the century. A peak of nearly 21 per cent was reached in 1893, but a decline began in 1907, and by 1909–13 the average was 13 per cent. The position of children aged one to four years improved earlier. Between 1851 and 1860 their death rate averaged 5·4 per cent, but by 1901–10 this was halved to 2·2 per cent.

The fall in the death rate also reflected a reduction in the incidence of infectious diseases. Diagnosis of disease was uncertain in the nineteenth century, but it appears that tuberculosis declined by about a half, typhoid fell very considerably, while cholera and typhus (nearly) disappeared completely. Leeds, however, continued to suffer higher than average mortality from diarrhoea; its average figure for

1882–91 was over a quarter higher than that for twenty-eight other large towns.

Improvements in the diet of working people were the main cause of the death rate's decline. Sanitary reform also played a positive role. Overcrowding was reduced by the regulation of house-building and the construction of larger houses after 1874. The development of suburbs later in the century also reduced the pressure on central areas. The 1901 and 1911 censuses indicated that between 10 and 11 per cent of the population were living in overcrowded conditions, that is, with more than two persons to a room. But appalling slums remained. The Quarry Hill area, where 10,500 people lived in 2,200 houses, had a death rate nearly twice that of the borough in 1893–95. Metcalfe Yard still had privies and ashpits, while one house contained a slipper maker, a resident family and a herring-curing establishment in the cellar. Nevertheless sanitary arrangements had improved. Augmentation of the water supply, the extension of the sewerage system and above all the slow removal of the middensteads were responsible for the decline in cholera, typhoid and bowel infections.

Although the diagnosis of disease improved in the second half of the century, medicine could do little to cure patients. The success of smallpox vaccination was the only exception to this. Leeds Infirmary, which was moved to its present site in 1869, would not accept infectious cases. The most important provider of medical help was the Poor Law, and an infirmary, now St James's Hospital, was built in 1874. Later in the century the council built isolation hospitals at Seacroft (1896) and Killingbeck (1898).

Lung diseases continued to be a major cause of death, responsible for about a quarter of the mortality in the whole of the period 1851–1911. The effects of industry played their part here. Visitors all agreed that Leeds was a smoky town, and in 1842 Baker contrasted weekdays and Sunday, when 'the eye may traverse from an elevated station over the whole edifices and see from hill to hill'.[15] Domestic fires added to the outpourings of dyehouses, potteries and steam engines. (See fig. 70.) Little effective action was taken, and in 1888–89 measurements of sunshine indicated that Leeds enjoyed the sun for only about 20 per cent of daylight hours when the average for England and Wales was nearly 30 per cent. Central Leeds averaged only 16 per cent.

Industry also affected the health of its employees. A Leeds surgeon, Charles Thackrah, published a pioneering study of occupational health in 1831. In evidence given to a select committee on child labour chaired by a Leeds alderman, Michael Sadler, flax workers spoke of the dry and dusty atmosphere of the carding room and the humid conditions in the spinning shop, where they were wet to the skin. Unfenced machinery resulted in accidents: one girl had her finger screwed off below the knuckle. Later, Edward Greenhow pointed out the high rate of pulmonary disease in textile towns, especially Leeds, though it was hard to differentiate between the effects of factory employment and those deriving from the general environment of the town. Nevertheless, too much attention can be given to factories, where, in 1842, only a quarter of the workforce was employed. Braithwaite's analysis of tuberculosis deaths in 1860–64 found the highest incidence among printers and clerks, and other craft trades were high on the list. In 1904 Jewish schoolchildren were found to be in better physical condition than gentile children, but those same children, on entering the crowded tailoring workshops, showed a high incidence of tuberculosis. In 1910 Jewish cases formed a fifth of the Leeds total.

VIII   By the end of the century the great wealth generated by Leeds industry was, to some extent, improving the lives of the workers in the town. For some, escape to the more salubrious suburbs was now possible, and the worst features of an insanitary environment had been removed for the majority. Nevertheless, the overall verdict must rest with a tireless campaigner for reform in mid-nineteenth-century Leeds, James Hole, who in 1866 wrote, 'Few towns are so advantageously situate as Leeds for securing the health and comfort of a large population and in few localities are these advantages so sacrificed.'[16]

NOTES

[1] Cited in J. Toft, 'Public health in Leeds in the nineteenth century: a study in the growth of local government responsibility *c*. 1815–80' (unpublished M.A. thesis, University of Manchester, 1966), p. 103.

[2] *Migration and vital statistics.* Before 1841 the main data source is totals of baptisms and burials performed in Anglican churches in Leeds parish. These underestimate the number of births and deaths, because an unknown number of Dissenters and young children were omitted, and so an esimate of these omissions has to be made. Between 1775–1801 Yasumoto's estimates of births have been used, but for 1801–41 no worthwhile estimate has proved possible. Figures for deaths are more reliable because I have totalled burials at the Dissenting chapels and so reduced the number of omissions. To my totals I have added 7 per cent to allow for the omission of young children, bringing the proportion of infant deaths to the average level of the 1840s.

Migration figures before 1801 have been calculated using Yasumoto's totals of births and deaths to obtain a figure for natural increase. After 1801 a totally different method has been used. We know the size of the natural increase in each decade for the country as a whole, and this rate can be applied to Leeds. It assumes that the rate in Leeds was the same as that nationally, which it was not; the rate was higher, except in Leeds township. This method, therefore, overestimates the importance of migration, possibly by 10 per cent.

After 1841 the Registrar General's figures for births and deaths permit the calculation of accurate birth and death rates and figures of natural increase. The drawback is that the districts from which the figures were collected did not coincide with the borough boundaries. All the statistics after 1841 therefore relate to the registration borough, which between 1841 and 1861 included Churwell, Gildersome, Horsforth, Roundhay and Shadwell and between 1861 and 1911 included Churwell, Roundhay, Seacroft and Shadwell.

³ R. V. Taylor, *Leeds Worthies* (1865), 435.

⁴ R. J. Owen (ed.), 'The Autobiography of Robert Spurr', *Baptist Quarterly*, XXVI (1976), 282–8. The text is as in the original, with punctuation supplied by the editor.

⁵ 1861 *Census Report*, Vol. 1, 613.

⁶ *Report on the Sanitary State of Leeds*, P.P. (1874), XXXI, 33.

⁷ *Lancet*, 9 June 1888.

⁸ See note 2 for the assumptions on which the figures for births and deaths are based.

⁹ The birth rate indicates the number of live births as a proportion of the population, usually expressed as a rate per thousand. The death rate expresses the same proportion for deaths.

¹⁰ *Sanitary Condition of the Labouring Population . . . Local Reports (England and Wales)*, P.P. (1842), XXVII, 351–2.

¹¹ *Ibid.*, 354–5.

¹² R. Baker, *Report to the Leeds Board of Health* (1833), 13.

¹³ *Report on the Sanitary State of Leeds*, P.P. (1874), XXXI, 46.

¹⁴ *Ibid.*, 43.

¹⁵ *Sanitary Condition of the Labouring Population . . . Local Reports (England and Wales)*, P.P. (1842), XXVII, 406.

¹⁶ J. Hole, *The Homes of the Working Classes* (1866), 123.

BIBLIOGRAPHICAL NOTE

There are two invaluable studies of Leeds population, both dealing mainly with the period before 1812: M. Yasumoto, 'Urbanisation and population in an English town', *Keio Economic Studies*, X (1973), and F. Beckwith, 'The population of Leeds during the industrial revolution', *Publications of the Thoresby Society*, XLI (1945). Beckwith deals in detail with the 1771 and 1775 enumerations.

No comparable studies of the nineteenth century exist. Population totals can be found in the decennial *Census Reports*; the 1851 report usefully summarises the figures for 1801–51. Birth and death statistics are less easily available. The *Census Reports* of 1801–31 contain baptism and burial totals for Leeds parish for every ten years between 1700 and 1780 and then annually between 1780 and 1830. The totals in the 1841 *Census Report* relate to the 'Registration Borough'. All these figures derive mainly from Anglican church registers, some of which have been published. Leeds Parish Church registers for the period 1572–1776 can be found in *Publications of the Thoresby Society*, I (1891), III (1895), VII (1897), X (1901), XIII (1909), XX (1914) and XXV (1922). The society has also published the registers of the chapels in the parish for the period 1724–1812 in volumes XXIII (1916), XXIX (1927) and XXXI (1931). The original registers of the parish church can be consulted at the vestry and many of the chapel registers have been deposited at the Leeds Archives Department. The department also has some Nonconformist registers but the bulk are at the Public Record Office; for details consult the *List and Index Society*, vol. 42. My forthcoming thesis on 'The burial problem in Leeds' will contain burial totals derived from all these registers.

After 1841 the *Annual Reports of the Registrar General*, and especially the decennial summaries, give much more accurate information on births and deaths. Care is needed with changes in registration district boundaries, which are outlined in the reports. After 1890 the *Annual Reports* of the medical officer of health are very useful.

Public health conditions and policy have been the subject of two unpublished theses. J. Toft's 'Public health in Leeds in the nineteenth century: a study in the growth of local government responsibility, *c.* 1815–80' (M.A., University of Manchester, 1966) contains much information. B. J. Barber, in 'Leeds Corporation, 1835–1905: a history of its environmental, social and administrative services' (Ph.D., University of Leeds, 1975), analyses both environmental conditions and the impact of sanitary policies. Our major source of information for the 1830s and 1840s is Robert Baker's series of reports: *Report to the Leeds Board of Health* (1833); 'Report upon the condition of the town of Leeds and its inhabitants' in *Journal of the Statistical Society of London*, II (1839–40) and 'Report on the state and condition of Leeds' to be found in the *Local Reports* of Chadwick's *Sanitary Inquiry* (P.P. (1842), XXVII). The reports of three government inspectors can be consulted in the *Second, Eighth* and *Thirteenth Reports of the Medical Officer of the Privy Council* (P.P. (1860), XXIX, 133–40; P.P. (1866), XXXIII, 648–67, and P.P. (1874), XXXI, 33–71). Two local reformers added to our knowledge. J. Hole, *Homes of the Working Classes* (1866), contains an appendix on Leeds, and J. Braithwaite, *An Inquiry into the Causes of the High Death Rate in Leeds* (1865) is particularly concerned with occupational health. The latter part of the nineteenth century is covered intermittently by the surviving medical officers of health's *Reports* for 1867–77 and 1890–1914 and those of the borough council's sanitary committee for 1883–93 and 1899–1913 (in Leeds Reference Library).

One important source remains largely unexploited, and this is reflected in my chapter. The census enumerators' returns for the censuses of 1841–71 are now available. Only one study has so far used these – T. Dillon's 'The Irish in Leeds, 1851–61' (*Publications of the Thoresby Society*, LIV (1973)). Our knowledge of the social and occupational structure and of migration patterns could be transformed by an analysis of the returns, which are available on microfilm in Leeds Reference Library.

MAURICE BERESFORD

IV
The face of Leeds, 1780–1914

'I should say, Sir,' observed Mark Tapley, 'that that's a state of things as opens one of the jolliest look-outs for domestic architecture that ever I heard tell on.' [Charles Dickens, *Martin Chuzzlewit*, 1843]

I   In 1780 nearly half the houses of the borough lay compactly at the centre of the four square miles of the urbanised in-township, the others in the ten villages and hamlets of the forty square miles of the rural out-townships. The in-township contained nearly half the hundred thousand houses built between 1780 and 1914, extending streets from the original compact area of no more than eighty acres to obliterate the fields except for the former township commons at Woodhouse moor and the Ridge.

Within this period the data enable two periods of exceptional growth to be identified: 4·8 per cent per annum in 1772–93 and almost the same rate in 1821–31 (table 6). In the first period new houses were built in the centre of the old town, in the new East End that was being created in a fit of absence of mind, and in the more deliberate West End; by the second period this West End was lost to industry and smoke, and a second West End started out in Little Woodhouse was being ceded as its inhabitants made a knight's move to the new suburb of the northern townships. In the fields over which they had jumped the terraces of new working-class houses were in progress. Individual streets of the out-townships were built to a style and a density identical with urban Leeds, especially to the south of the river, but even there agricultural land was to be found in 1914 alongside such vestigial commons as Holbeck and Hunslet moors.

This pace of growth created public health problems discussed in Chapters III and XII. Just over half the houses standing in 1801 had been built since 1780 (table 7) so that the rawness of the red brick in houses, factories and warehouses was an essential aspect of the industrialising townscape that map and engravings cannot convey. The camera came too late: its role, especially in the fine series of photographs associated with slum clearance proposals, was to record in sombre black and white the wrinkled face of an old town centre. Half the houses standing in 1914 had been built before 1841, and a fifth were more than a hundred years old; two-thirds of them were the pride and despair of Leeds, its back-to-backs.

Table 6 Houses in Leeds township, 1672–1901

Year	Houses	Average annual growth (%)
1672	1,194	
		1·4
1740	2,364	
		1·2
1772	3,347	
		4·8
1793	6,691	
		0·4
1801	6,882	
		1·9
1811	8,187	
		3·6
1821	11,191	
		4·3
1831	16,065	
		2·4
1841	19,986	
		1·1
1851	21,215	
		2·0
1861	25,650	
		2·1
1871	31,085	
		1·4
1881	35,499	
		0·9
1891	38,522	
		0·5
1901	40,623	

Note. Boundary changes make the 1911 figure non-comparable.
Sources. 1672: hearth tax; 1740: LCA, DB 204/3; 1772: *Pub. Thoresby Soc.* XXIV (1919), p. 34; 1801–1901: census reports.

Table 7 Houses less than twenty years old, Leeds township, 1793–1911 (%)

Year	Whole in-township	Kirkgate Division	North East Division	North West Division
1793	50	—	—	—
1801	50	28	74	63
1821	39	17	38	53
1831	49	11	53	66
1841	44			
1851	24			
1861	22			
1871	32			
1881	28			
1891	29			
1901	28			
1911	27			

Sources. 1793: F. M. Eden, *State of the Poor*; census reports.

II In the beginning – and for a long time after – there was only the centre, for had Leeds been a walled city it could scarcely have remained more compact. No new street was built between 1613 and 1767, and the 'carefully collected' private census[1] of 1775 assigned six out of every ten of the 4,096 families to the central medieval streets and the extension over Leeds bridge; two out of ten lived in the ribbon of houses on the other approach roads and the remainder in the scattered hamlets of the in-township, principally at the Bank and Far Bank (366 families) and Great Woodhouse (270 families), all clearly delineated in Tuke's 'actual survey' of 1781.

The small-scale plan of Leeds on Jefferys's county map of 1768–70 shows that other merchants were following the pioneers whom Cossins's map of 1725 had shown breaking from tradition to build detached houses in fields along the road to Sheepscar; and when the bar was built on the Otley turnpike in 1758 it is significant that it lay not at the bar marking the old limits of the town on the Headrow but near the present Parkinson Building of the university, leaving movement to and from the merchants' houses on Woodhouse Lane toll-free. Deeds, insurance policies and press advertisements confirm that the Georgian houses of Woodhouse Lane resembled those on Meadow Lane, Hunslet Lane, Park Lane and North Street, with residences facing the street and finishing shops for the merchants' daily workforce at their rear alongside the warehouse, counting house and stables.

Neither Jefferys's nor Tuke's maps were on a scale large enough to show what had happened since 1725 to the gardens, orchards, crofts, tenter grounds and inn yards that Cossins showed behind the frontage houses on the main streets of the town, but there is much evidence that in these very years they were accumulating piecemeal small houses and workshops lying 'backsides', as conveyances and leases put it. A croft behind the Boot and Shoe inn, Kirkgate, with only a warehouse in 1767 had twelve new one-room cottages advertised for sale in 1770 and seventeen low-value 'tenements' insured against fire in 1782; five

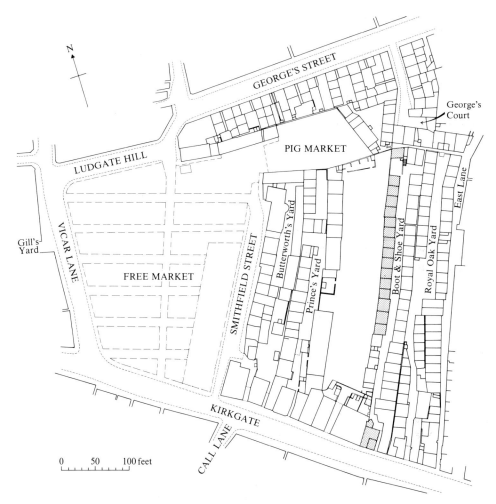

12 The north-west side of Kirkgate, before demolition for extension of the municipal market, 1843. Yards ('folds' or 'garths') have been in-filled piecemeal with blind-back cottages set against the yard walls. The houses of one proprietor (John Dufton) in the notorious Boot and Shoe Yard are indicated by shading. (After the original in Leeds City Archives, LC Eng. Box 10)

more were added by 1795, and three more by 1805. When it achieved notoriety in the years of the cholera and the sanitary inquiries of 1839 and 1842 there were thirty-six of these 'cottages' in the yard, none with sanitation or water supply.

The cholera's first victim in Leeds on 28 May 1832 was a child of an Irish woollen weaver living in Blue Bell Fold at the Bank in a cottage of the same size as those in the Boot and Shoe Yard (five and a half yards square), having a first-floor bedroom but set back-to-back with a similar house, sharing a party wall. The Blue Bell Fold represented a second type of encroachment during these years of population growth, occupying not inn yards but the fold yards of older farmsteads along Marsh Lane and Mabgate. Some of these little roadside clusters, irregular in frontage, can be studied in detail on the surveys made for the trustees of the town's charities in 1793. If the cholera struck hard here and in the Kirkgate yards it was not because houses were ancient and decayed: none dated from before 1750, and most had been built in the last quarter of the eighteenth century (tables 8 and 9).

Table 8 New houses built, Leeds town divisions, 1740–1831

| Division | Initial stock in 1740 | New building | | Stock in 1801 | New building | | |
		1740–72	1772–1801		1801–11	1811–21	1821–31
East	280	211	723	1,214	132	665	995
Middle and Kirkgate	617	10	239	866	35	144	−28
Mill Hill	387	33	102	522	7	43	22
North East	362	136	1,454	1,952	641	1,221	1,769
North West	154	179	577	910	351	676	1,811
South	211	181	255	649	179	311	196
Upper or Hightown	353	233	183	769	−48	−50	9
Total	2,364	983	3,535	6,882	1,305	3,004	4,874

Sources. As table 6. The house count of 1772 has been preferred to the more detailed private census of 1775, since it – like the Rate Books and the first four censuses – employed the seven ancient Divisions of the town: these are defined in LCA, DB204/3, 149. Cf. fig. 9(a).

Yard and fold developments were economical in their high densities and the absence of water and sanitation. Nor were the proprietors put to the charge of road construction, pavage and drains, since the houses were sited behind thoroughfares. The Improvement Act of 1755, mainly concerned with lighting and paving the central streets, described Leeds as 'inhabited by great Numbers of Tradesmen,

Table 9 Average annual rates of growth, Leeds town divisions, 1740–1831 (%)

Division	1740–72	1772–1801	1801–11	1811–21	1821–31
East	2·4	5·1	1·1	4·9	4·9
Middle and Kirkgate	—	1·3	0·4	1·6	−2·7
Mill Hill	0·3	0·8	0·1	0·8	0·4
North East	1·0	10·1	0·1	4·7[a]	4·6[a]
North West	3·6	6·0	3·9	5·4	9·3[b]
South	2·7	2·2	2·8	3·8	2·5
Upper or Hightown	2·1	1·1	6·2	−7·0	0·1
All town	1·2	3·6	1·9	3·6	4·3

Notes
  [a] 1811–21: North East Upper 4·8 per cent, Lower 4·6 per cent; 1821–31: Upper 4·2 per cent, Lower 4·9 per cent.
  [b] 1821–31: North West Upper 5·5 per cent, Lower 14·4 per cent.
Sources. As table 8. Comparisons with years after 1831 (table 6) are possible only for the township as a whole, owing to boundary changes from divisions to wards. In 1841–51 the North West, the fastest growing, had a rate of only 2·1 per cent per annum.

Manufacturers Artificers and others . . . obliged to go early and late with great Burdens'. Noise, smells, human congestion and this traffic in the central area were no doubt repulsive forces driving the better-off westwards, but there was attraction in a new fashion of living in terraces and squares that crept in from Bath, Bristol and Bloomsbury.

Jefferys's plan of 1768–70 was in time to catch Park Row, the first West End terrace, running north from the end of Boar Lane past Mill Hill chapel to Park Lane. In January 1768 the chapel trustees took a forty-year building lease from Richard Wilson and erected a minister's house next to their burial ground, three months after the merchant Thomas Barstow had taken a thirty-year lease of the next plot northward, on which he built a house, office, stables and coach house that he afterwards insured for £770. The West End had been initiated.

Its progress was uneven, being interrupted by the outbreak of the American war and the dislocation of cloth exports, and then again by the Napoleonic wars. More fatal, and relieved by no peace treaties, was an attack from within, like Jacobin sedition. The town's older dyehouses lay east of town on the Timble beck, their smoke shown frankly on Lodge's *Southern Prospect*, engraved in 1715 for Thoresby's *Ducatus*, but the prevailing south-westerly winds took this smoke away from the residential area. In 1767 John Close converted a group of farm buildings at Drony Laith, half a mile west of town, into a dyehouse with adjoining finishing shops; near by Wormald and Gott first took a lease and then bought the field known as Bean Ing. The dyeworks flourished, steam engines and a gasworks were installed at Bean Ing, and the smoke blew eastwards. Attempts to prosecute the town's leading chimney owners for nuisance in 1811 and 1824 produced no relief, but long before then the blight had settled. In August 1822 the *Intelligencer* reported that one of the three factories that had lately crept into the area was installing a steam engine: 'this, we doubt not, will put the finishing stroke to the [house-building] business in that quarter'. It did. In 1824 the town's second gasworks was built in Park Street, and when the 'building ground' of Fowler's 1821 plan found purchasers it was in order to build working-class streets which were as much hosts to the cholera in 1832 as the older cottages of the east. With unintended irony the preacher's text at the consecration of St Paul's church in April 1794 was Genesis xxvii, 17: 'And he was afraid and said, "How dreadful is this place!" ' The virtual absence of new building in Mill Hill division can be seen in table 8.

St Paul's church in Park Square was demolished in the 1930s, eight Georgian houses at the south-west corner even earlier for Ambler's Moorish warehouse (1878), but there is enough left of the other frontages to savour the original character of a private domain with the proprietors' central garden. Park Place (1778–94) also has fine houses, despite some deplorable laxities in planning permission, while in East Parade (1779–89) past disasters are invoked to discredit current preservation. South Parade (1776–78), like the parent Park Row (1767–76), has long since been rebuilt as offices. Albion Street (1792) – 'perhaps the pleasantest street in the town', according to the *Leeds Guide* of 1806 – was poised between the Wilson's West End and the old town centre and one of its earliest houses, built for the surgeon William Hey, has survived as the Law Society offices, now on the corner of the later Albion Place.

The termination of development on the Park estate in 1797, with less than ten of its fifty fields disposed of, was no temporary wartime blockade of traffic in bricks and mortar. Already there were signs that the well-to-do were preferring not only another quarter of town, a new West End on the slopes of Little Woodhouse, but another style. This was more greedy of land than the Georgian streets. The widest frontage in Park Place was sixteen yards, and the central houses on the north and east sides of Park Square were no more than twenty-two yards wide. But the merchants whose new mansions were dotted across the northern slopes from Belle Vue through Denison Hall, Claremont, Springfield House and Beech Grove (naming only the survivors) had each purchased a complete field or more. 'Could

Thoresby return to survey the environs of his native town,' wrote Whitaker[2] in 1816, 'no change perhaps would more attract his notice than the numbers of commodious and cheerful villas which dread of smoke and a desire for comfort have drawn about it. A rood of land about a country house is a little landscape.'

In 1799 an advertisement for Springfield House (1792), which still stands in the university precinct, spells out the mixture of domesticity and industry in its little landscape.[3]

To be SOLD AT AUCTION

A newly erected Mansion-House with every requisite Outbuilding, and also an excellent Garden with a Wall Four Yards high, in which there is a large Basin well supplied with fine Water, and which Garden, and an Orchard adjoining, are stocked with the choicest Fruit Trees together with two pleasant Dwelling-Houses [i.e. the gardeners' cottages at the foot of the field,] and a large well-built Warehouse Twenty-seven Yards by Twelve properly divided, for Dressing, Packing-Shops etc. . . . The Estate commands a most extensive and delightful View over the Town and the adjoining Country. The House consists on the Ground Floor of a Dining Room (26 ft by 28) – Drawing Room (22 ft by 18) – and Kitchen fitted up with Stoves (24 ft by 18) (and all $12\frac{1}{2}$ ft high) together with a Store Room (18 ft by 12), Back Kitchen, Pantry, and Brewhouse (with every requisite Utensil for Brewing, and a Pipe to convey the Liquor into the Cellars) under which are excellent arched Cellars, Laundry (24 ft by 18) with Stoves etc, Dairy and Larder. There are Nine spacious and airy Lodging-Rooms with commodious Dressing-Rooms, and Water conveyed into a Closet for the use of the Rooms; and the House is well supplied with hard and fast Water. The Estate has Right of Common upon Woodhouse Moor, and is very valuable for building upon. By the lower Field is a Spring of Water that has never failed when all the Springs in the Neighbourhood have been dry, and the water is conveyed through the Dressing-Shops and is of the first consequence to any Merchant who wishes to dye his own Grain Colours, as it gives a superior softness in the finishing of Cloth.

III   The changes in the face of the East End already described – yard and fold infill – produced no new streets. These appeared quite suddenly in 1785 and 1786 through two quite different types of enterprise, although the type of house produced by each is not easily distinguishable. In both the continuous street lines were made up of two-storey back-to-back terraces on each side of a street, the dimensions and character of the houses being those already encountered in the Blue Bell and other folds. The back half of each house was usually reached through a narrow tunnel built integrally with the houses rather than take up valuable space by running a back lane or alley behind the whole terrace and, should the depth of the plot permit, a complete court would be erected at the rear, approached through the same or a further tunnel. Under some of the terraces one-room cellar dwellings were excavated, and passers-by had the protection of a railing to prevent them falling down the steep steps which led from the street. On parts of Cavalier and Quarry Hills the slope allowed the front cellar to be at the street level and only the back cellar excavated; and a wooden gallery ran along the front of the terrace to give access to the house proper.

When new, and with open field ground still behind them, these houses may well have been seen as superior to the village cottages from which migrants were coming to Leeds or even to older houses in yards and folds, and it must be remembered that in 1785 the factory chimney, the gasworks, the railway engine sheds, the overcrowded burial grounds and other features of the classic East End were yet to come. Proper appreciation of this age of innocence is easier if we ask, who were the developers of these first East End streets? They were terminating building clubs which drew on an artisan membership in steady employment with an income large enough to afford a monthly subscription for up to fourteen years. The subscriptions formed a common fund from which the trustees were recompensed for interest on the mortgaged building land, and then – as the fund allowed – house after house was built, the order of possession being decided by a prior ballot; houses could then be mortgaged in the usual way. The lucky member continued to contribute to the fund but when all the houses were completed the club terminated. The typical member occupied the front house of his back-to-back pair and found a tenant for the back house and for the cellar, if there was one; and since members could subscribe for more than one share or plot the venture was an opportunity for artisan and shopkeeper investment.

Innocence of the imminent deterioration in the environment is perhaps best exemplified by the two building clubs of 1786, the Lesser and the Greater, whose trustees bought Boggars (or more politely Boggard) Close, next to the Methodist chapel and burial ground on Quarry Hill. In this close the Lesser Society laid out High Street, made up of back-to-backs, courtyards and cellar dwellings, while, immediately adjoining, the Greater Society laid out St Peter's Square, complete with proprietary garden in the centre like its exact contemporary in the West End, Park Square.

In the same area and almost at the same date, close to employment in the town workshops, the markets, the warehouses and the wharves, Richard Paley began in 1787 what was to be a more enduring tradition than the clubs, the acquisition of land for division into lots for freehold sale to developers who then erected groups of houses for rent or resale. Paley himself built and retained houses for renting, 275 of them at the time of his bankruptcy in 1803, and 290 others had been erected by developers on his other plots.

There could have been no feeling that these houses were inimical to the club streets: Paley himself had a share in the Greater Society, and his plots for back-to-back development on the north side of York Street adjoined the garden of his house on the south side of St Peter's Square. But within a few years the serpent was in Eden.

Paley himself was the first to bring the steam engine and the factory chimney to these East End fields (1790), but he was not interested in providing homes for his factory labourers: it is significant that even in 1815, twelve years after his bankruptcy, there was no street yet built in the actual fields where his two largest mills stood, any more than Marshall or Gott had built streets by their mills. Even so, it would seem that there was over-provision of land at prices that builders for low-income tenants could afford. Fowler's 1821 plan of *Leeds . . . with the Recent Improvements* had 'building ground' printed across three groups of fields, two of them in the east once Paley's, and the third in the west, the plots of the Wilson estate as laid out 'for sale' twenty-four years earlier.

Yet elsewhere there had been development, with 3,000 houses added between the censuses of 1811 and 1821. Some of it was in progress by 1815, especially in the fields between Lady Lane and Templar Street known as the Leylands, where the Giles plan shows Nile and Trafalgar Streets in mid-progress, names matched by Waterloo Street, the one new street in the South division, but still void in 1821.

IV The next decade, 1821–31, witnessed the greatest building development of any in the century, whether measured by rate of increase or by the absolute number of new houses erected. In the course of answers to questions posed by the Home Secretary the mayor wrote in 1823:[4]

> The Increase of the Buildings has been Considerable. Owing to the reduced profits of Trade many Individuals Chusing to sink their Capital in Building rather than the risking it in Trade. The Increase has principally been in Cottages, and by the influx of labourers and Strangers from the Country and from Ireland they are generally occupied, but Houses of a Superior description have not been built in proportion, and rents are generally lower.

It was characteristic of Leeds that this greater ambit was made up

not of a continuous stream of building flowing in one particular
direction but of scattered invasions of field land, like a rising tide
seeking out rock pools. On each edition of Fowler's maps between
1821 and 1844, as on the large-scale Ordnance Survey maps published
in 1850, there were scores of fields half occupied by unfinished streets;
neighbouring fields still open ground (and to remain so for several
decades); and other fields where only the highway frontage had been
occupied.

There was clearly no shortage of land on offer: the problem lay
elsewhere. Its plot of land made up only one-eighth of the cost of a
back-to-back, but land was steadily rising in value; so were many
building costs. There was no significant improvement in building
efficiency, and in the 1870s back-to-backs were still costing the £70 or
£80 of the 1820s. If investors were to get the 7 or $7\frac{1}{2}$ per cent net that
all contemporaries believed minimal to induce them to put their
savings into houses then a rent of £5 a year or more made heavy
incursions into the pockets of a labouring class with low levels of
income. The ordinary seasonality of work and the chance incidence of
sickness and mortality in the family further reduced effective demand
in any year, and each commercial crisis was marked not only by
bankruptcies but by an abrupt termination of building projects in
progress.

The sporadic development indicated on all Fowler's maps was not
simply the consequence of uneven demand. There had obviously been
over-optimism in supply, and this was related to an important aspect
of land ownership in Leeds that also had a clear cartographic
expression. Very many long, narrow fields measuring some 220 yards
long and 40 yards wide abutted short-side-on to the principal roads
fanning out from town, whether country lanes turnpiked, like
Sheepscar Lane and York Road, or minor footways like Long Balk
Lane (Camp Road). The latter name indicates that these fields owed
their shape to their origin: they were simply bundles of open-field
selions gathered together at enclosure and distributed among the
numerous freeholders owning common rights. The narrow fields were
not only numerous – seventy of them can be counted undeveloped in
Fowler's 1831 map – but largely in single ownership: very little
agglomeration into petty estates had taken place, probably because
the fields had considerable value for their merchant and craftsmen
owners as tenter grounds and grazing.

But the multitude of proprietors ensured that the decision whether
or not to develop did not lie in the hands of a few. In any season of
constructional optimism there would be some who felt that the time
had come to cash the dividends of rising land prices, especially those

whose social path was leading them to cease active involvement in business and to reside away from Leeds. Fifty-three such fields were designated as 'building ground' and not farm land in the tithe award of 1846.

The shape of such fields, five times as long as they were broad, proved well adapted to replication of the terraced back-to-backs and courts that we have seen evolve from the inn yards into the larger fields of Crackenthorpe Gardens (Union Street), Boggard Close (High Street and St Peter's Square), and McAndrews' Gardens (Paley's first estate). Indeed, Paley, innovator as ever, may have shown the way in 1792 when he laid out Skinner Lane and built two merchant's houses but planned to utilise the remainder of the field to the full by placing a line of single-roomed two-storey cottages, blind back against the northern wall of the field, just as the inn owners, the Northouses, had lined the walls of the Boot and Shoe Yard.

A row of back-to-backs demanded a building plot at least thirteen yards deep, even with the narrowest rear yard; the streets themselves were commonly from ten to thirteen yards wide; and the facing houses on the other side required another thirteen yards: some forty yards' width for a complete ribbon. These fields, a furlong in length and so often forty yards wide, were fertile ground into which to transplant the back-to-backs from their East End origins, especially since one of the short sides of each field already abutted on a public thoroughfare.

Conducive as these fields were to easy – perhaps over-easy – development, the piecemeal character of their development had heavy social costs. 'Irregularity' was a common adjective used critically by sanitary reformers when they contemplated Leeds; they could not mean irregularity of frontage, for nothing was more characteristic of a terrace street, whether of through houses or back-to-backs, than a regimented building line. The courts beyond the tunnels were often irregular, it is true, fitting into the last square yard of a plot, but the burden of the reformers' complaints was that single-field development by small proprietors weighted the scales against any provision of common services in water, paving, drainage and sewerage — and not simply through anxiety to save money; it was quite uneconomic to provide services that would not be taken beyond the end of a short street, usually no longer than the furlong of the parent field. The short street ending up against a stone boundary wall was a familiar sight, and some still survive in north Leeds, a monument to fragmented development. 'There have not been a dozen streets of any length laid out in Leeds within the last thirty years,' wrote James Hole[5] in 1865; 'the result is the greatest confusion.' 'Indeed as to arrangement,' said the *Mercury*[6] in 1852, 'the whole town might have had an earthquake for an architect.'

In Little Woodhouse and along Woodhouse Lane Fowler's maps reveal a series of other small developments and frustrated projects of the 1820s and '30s that together illuminate a quite different process, for here the new streets were not the first invaders. The fields had been first commandeered in the 1790s to make the 'rood of land' around the villas that Whitaker had noted in 1816 as their 'little landscape', although in fact the area was rather larger than the romantic rood. Now the willingness to cede these little landscapes to a street builder was ominous for the fall of the second West End.

A key point in this retreat was the development of Springfield Place as a street of two facing terraces of through houses, commencing in 1833. These were engineered by Newman Cash, owner of Springfield Lodge, one of those houses of refuge from the smoke of the first West End, built in 1783. His small houses sold well, and in 1836 he bought land for a second venture for rather superior houses in Springfield Mount (1839), but this was not completed until 1890; the first back-to-backs came to Little Woodhouse in Driffield Place by 1844, and when the adjoining Lyddon estate came out of its long wrangle in Chancery (1828–45) the heirs sold it off in 145 lots of terrace-house size, and Mrs Lyddon's Georgian houses at Preston House, Lyddon Terrace and Beech Grove Terrace were marooned for ever. Seven years after the first Lyddon sale the *Mercury*[7] commented, 'no quarter of the town exhibits worse arrangements of streets, a worse principle in the internal construction of houses or a greater feebleness of built than this area *which is almost entirely new*'.

A compromise solution was to create a square, modelled on the three Georgian squares. This was attempted in the grounds of Denison Hall (Hanover Square, 1828) and Little Woodhouse Hall (Woodhouse Square, 1829) and at Blenheim Square (*c.* 1830) on the other side of Woodhouse Lane, the last of the Leeds squares. Yet all three failed to be completed, as their present appearance shows, simply because their projectors underestimated the reluctance to live so near to industry. John Atkinson commented on the failure to the Commons Committee on Smoke Prevention[8] in 1845: 'the body of smoke that comes across the side of the hill where I live is vastly large ... there is a place called Woodhouse Square near me into which the smoke used to pour'. 'A large part of the mercantile community of Leeds' had gone to reside in the more sanitary Headingley since 1851, according to a footnote in the 1861 census, and by the end of the '70s there were back-to-back streets in late-developed fields next to every one of the middle-class terraces initiated in the 1820s and '30s: Blenheim Terrace, Brunswick Place, Grove Terrace, Brunswick

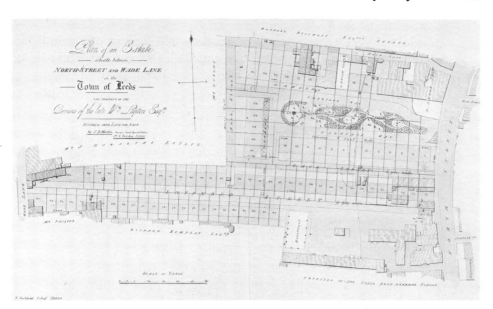

13   Intended street and square in the grounds of the Lupton house (shaded, lower right), North Street, 1830. William Lupton died in 1828, leaving his widow with ten children and extensive debts from his worsted manufacturing business. The land sales were part of an attempt to rescue the family from financial difficulties; in the south-east corner of the area was the family house (illustrated as No. 11 Town End in the margin of Cossins's map of 1725), with warehouses and workshops behind. The plots around the ornamental Belgrave Square were not taken up but sold for Belgrave chapel (1836); plots in Merrion Street began to be sold in 1832. (From the coloured original by S. D. Martin, Leeds City Archives, DB Map 365)

Terrace and Portland Place.

One portent of disillusion with the second West End was the proclamation of two 'New Leeds' in 1825. That term had already been used by Edward Baines in the 1817 directory: 'The buildings to the east of Briggate may properly be termed the *Old Town*, those to the west the *New Town*, the latter forming the residences of the more respectable part of the inhabitants, the former that of the lower orders', but even as he wrote the lower orders were being accommodated in the west, and the respectable were seeking novelty elsewhere. In 1825 Griffith Wright sold plots between Dolly Lane and the Sheepscar beck, to make Cambridge Street, Tiger Street and Mushroom Court, an area marked on Fowler's 1831 plan as *New Leeds* but an unattractive, low-lying and inaccessible quarter. There was more publicity for a second New Leeds just over the boundary in Chapel Allerton, its 'elegant and appropriate Designs for Villas and Fancy Cottages' intended for a different clientele.[9] 'Without manufacturing smoke,' commented the *Mercury*,[10] 'this Utopia would indeed be a *New Leeds*.' Both ventures date from the heady days of speculation in 1825: Lion Street and the others were achieved, but Earl Cowper's venture foundered in the same bankruptcy of Hurst Hurst and Robinson that ruined Sir Walter Scott, and its later progress is really part of the history of the residential suburbs created in the out-townships.

V   In terms of houses and population the ten out-townships cannot be neglected, although there is as yet little serious published work on which to draw. In numbers, whether of houses or of people, they accounted for a substantial part of the borough. The private census of 1775 assigned nearly half the population of the borough to the out-townships, and when the census of 1801 made the first count of houses the proportion was only slightly smaller, as table 10 shows. But perhaps the most remarkable feature was the maintenance of that proportion virtually unchanged until the decade 1861–71: that is, the number of new houses built in the out-townships, even during the decades of fastest overall growth, kept pace with those in the central town area. Only after 1871 did the central area grow less rapidly as some of its former residential streets were given over to retail shops, warehouses, banking, insurance and commerce, the new housing being increasingly suburban.

Growth did not come to all the townships at the same date, nor did their housing all take the same form. A broad distinction can be made between the three northern out-townships, predominantly residential, and the southern townships where industry and housing were found side by side. Between 1801 and 1851 three times as many new houses were built in Holbeck and Hunslet as in the combined northern townships, and this earlier growth claims first attention for the south bank of the Aire, leaving the more exclusive residential areas of the north and north-west until the next section.

Table 10 Development of the out-townships, 1775–1911: houses in the ten out-townships as a percentage of the whole borough

1775 (population)	44	1861	43
1801	42	1871	46
1811	43	1881	48
1821	42	1891	52
1831	42	1901	59
1841	42	1911	63
1851	41		

Sources. B.L. Add. MSS, 33770; W. Wales, *An Inquiry* ... (1781); and census

14   An early merchant residence: Red Hall, built in 1628 for Alderman Thomas Metcalf, reputedly the first brick house in central Leeds and the place of Charles I's imprisonment, 9 February 1647; demolished for the extension of Schofield's department store

A lawyer's residence: Barstow's House and Yard, Nos. 50, 51 and 52 Kirkgate, opposite the parish church – three Georgian houses across the width of a medieval garth, with access to the garth (sixty yards long) by an archway under the central house, similar to houses illustrated in Cossins's map of 1725. Thomas Barstow lived here as town clerk in 1781 and 1792 but then moved to Park Row. In 1773 an advertisement for this house praised the uninterrupted view from the back windows to

15   Gledhow and Chapeltown

16   The town workhouse on the corner of Lady Lane and Vicar Lane, instituted in 1726 and enlarged at intervals until 1830, when 250 paupers were accommodated

Leeds 'backsides': single-room cottages against the wall of York Yard, between York Street and Marsh Lane, erected in 1820; part of a group of fourteen that 17   included cellar dwellings. (Cf. Boot and Shoe Yard, fig. 12)

18   Leeds 'backsides': a timber-
framed house with jettied
storeys in Lambert's Yard on
the east side of Lower Briggate,
probably the oldest surviving
house in central Leeds; *c*. 1600

    Yard housing imitated within
a field: Cooper's Court behind
Kendall Row, Bowman Lane.
The joiner John Kendall erected
eighteen back-to-backs in
Kendall Street and sold the
remainder of the field to the
cheesemonger James Cooper in
1793: Cooper erected sixteen
blind-back houses, some of
which are seen in the
photograph, those in the
distance being set against the
wall of industrial premises in
19   Dock Street

Building-club houses: St James Street, Woodhouse Lane, 1793–95. The larger
house behind the lamp was built in 1793 by Richard Kendall, shoemaker, on one of
the plots that he acquired by virtue of his eleven shares in the St James Street
Building Club, which began operations at the Woodhouse Lane end of the street in
1788; he built the two adjoining smaller houses in the same year, and the corner
20   shop (left) was built by another member in 1795

21   Building-club houses: Alfred Place, off Camp Road. The wall in the foreground
marks the southern end of Brick Close, purchased for the thirty-three members of
the club in January 1826; four houses were completed that year, but when the club's
secretary fled to America with the funds in 1843 only twenty-nine houses had been
built, the latest being shown here

22   Croft's Buildings, a group of retail shops erected between 1815 and 1818 by the joiner Abraham Croft on Pasture Close, between Water Lane and Meadow Lane. At that time, before Victoria bridge, Water Lane was the main artery from Leeds to Marshall's mill, Murray's foundry and the industrial village of Holbeck

The workshops behind a merchant's house erected by Richard Paley at Skinner Lane in 1792; they were later converted to dwellings and other houses built
23   alongside, creating Brown's Square

24   The north side of Charles Street, two-storey blind-back houses, built 1813–15 with tunnel (left) leading to Johnson's Square (fig. 25) at a lower level, owing to the falling slope of Quarry Hill

25   Johnson's Square: fifteen single-room houses below the level of Charles Street, approached by tunnel and steps (centre); cf. Line Fold, fig. 27

High-density housing, 1806: Camp Field, off Water Lane, an isolated position near the flax mills of Marshall and Benyon – ninety-two pairs of back-to-backs occupied a field, Bar Croft, measuring 70 yards by 125 yards. The corporation attempted amelioration in 1898: to reduce the density alternate rows were cleared, 26 as shown here

27 Line Fold, erected *c.* 1830: the rising slope of Quarry Hill allowed three pairs of two-storey back-to-backs to be erected over three single-room cellar dwellings; the cellars were entered from the lower level of the fold (foreground), the south side of the back-to-backs from the wooden gallery coming from the higher level of Billet Street, traffic in which was prevented from falling into the fold by a wall (right); the other side of the back-to-backs lay in Billet Yard, a closed court reached from Charles Street by a tunnel

Piecemeal development of houses and industry in adjacent fields, 1830: Plane Square, off York Street, an incongruous name for a cul-de-sac of four houses filling a space between Plane Street and the gasworks (1818); the photograph, one of those taken to support the corporation's case in 1901, shows a sanitary inspector with a roll of plans.

28

29   Piecemeal development of terrace houses in the West End: Bedford Place, 1825. Newman Cash, stuff merchant, laid out 6,000 sq. yds in forty-two building plots north of Park Lane: different purchasers built in different styles, as can be seen; they were bound by covenant to rise to at least two storeys and 'to erect iron palisades', the protective railings between pavement and area basements. No. 13, with ill luck threatened further by the ladder, was built with No. 15 on a double plot and Nos. 19–21 on another; the three-storey No. 17 on a single plot. All were through houses with two rooms on the ground floor but no garden; Chorley's woollen mill lay immediately behind

30   A deceptive facade: a line of seven houses made up the south side of Stamford
        Place, a cul-de-sac off Skinner Lane, *c*. 1860; as the isolated chimneys suggest and
        fig. 31 confirms, they were built one room deep, blind-back

31   The cliff-like wall formed by the blind backs of Nos. 9–15 Stamford Place (cf. fig.
        30)

*(Photographs from the author's collection; the building history of the town is
magnificently illustrated by photographs in the Local History Collection, Leeds
Central Library, and those from the former City Engineer's Department now in
Leeds city archives)*

These residential areas eventually monopolised the word 'suburb', at least in the language of estate agents and house advertisements, but at the beginning of the nineteenth century Holbeck and Hunslet were frequently spoken of as 'industrial suburbs'. When a parliamentary committee of 1806 examined Robert Cookson, a master clothier of Holbeck,[11] he described both Hunslet and Holbeck as 'villages adjoining each other' but also as 'joining to Leeds like the suburbs of the town'. What he had in mind was the development along Water Lane, Meadow Lane and Hunslet Lane in towards the streets of the small South division, that part of the in-township proper that lay beyond Leeds bridge, where these three arteries converged, an area that was 'suburban' in an older sense.

The contribution of this South division to the early growth of housing (table 8) was not maintained. The older merchants' houses became unattractive to their owners as residences once flax mills, foundries, gasworks and railway yards clustered round them, and they quickly passed to non-residential uses or were demolished for more factory space. The low-lying vacant fields behind them, like those of Holbeck and Hunslet, were taken more for industry than for new housing, although in Camp Field, near Marshall's mill off Water Lane, congested housing reached degradation not surpassed in Boot and Shoe Yard, and without the excuse of a constricted central site.

The convoluted and even intermingled boundaries of Holbeck, Hunslet and the South division were symbolic of their close economic links with Leeds and with each other: even when Leeds bridge was the only crossing the journey to work was short from one to another, and even before mills and heavy industry the labour force for the potteries and the collieries was drawn from all areas. There was a Hunslet ferry to the mills of the Bank before South Accommodation bridge, and Gott built a footbridge from Bean Ing for his workers from Holbeck and Armley twenty years before Wellington bridge. The close ties of these two out-townships are also indicated by the Leeds directories that included their streets in the single alphabetical sequence of 'Leeds' but treated the other out-townships separately as late as 1861.

When in 1791 the surgeon James Lucas took some of the data from the 1775 census to illustrate the deficiencies of parish registers he selected Holbeck, Hunslet and Bramley as typical 'manufacturing villages'. At that time very little of these 'manufactures' would have been produced outside domestic workshops. Tuke's map of 1781 shows the physical form of the villages, although the only large-scale plan that is known is for Hunslet (1791). None of the villages then had buildings aligned along the straight type of frontage that always suggests a constructed street: all lay on winding lanes or straggled

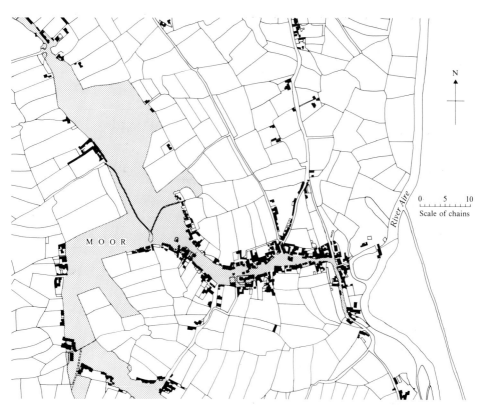

32　The industrial village of Hunslet, 1791, gathered around the still extensive
township moor merging into a village green that ended near the water mill on the
river (centre right). Hunslet was virtually by-passed by the Wakefield turnpike from
Leeds (right). (After the survey by J. Johnson and J. Sidgwick, copied in 1817 and
now in Leeds City Archives, Farrer Add. 316)

around the greens and unenclosed township moors. The main street of
Hunslet was longer and wider than Briggate, but it denoted the green
of a semi-pastoral Pennine village and not a market thoroughfare; the
only thoroughfare, the Wakefield turnpike, cut across it near the river
just as the railroad from the colliery at Middleton was laid over and
across the fields and the moor on its way down to its staithe by Leeds
bridge. The village of Holbeck was smaller and less compact than
Hunslet, but it too had its central green and many cottage
encroachments on the town moor, and before the end of the eighteenth
century both townships had begun to accumulate factories alongside
their watercourses and on the Aire. When houses were built for the
industrial population of these townships they followed the pattern of
central Leeds in first filling up the fold yards and then turning to short
new-built streets. In form these were identical with the terraced streets

of back-to-back houses engendered in central Leeds. At the end of a decade of exceptional population growth, Charles Fowler extended the 1831 edition of his plan southwards to include part of Hunslet and Holbeck, when a few short streets were shown near the two villages but with many more near the boundary of the townships on the Elland and Wakefield turnpikes.

In the next eighty years some 17,000 houses surrounded the factories, railway yards, gasworks and brickyards, and the absence of villas and other middle-class housing gave a fearful monotony to acres of brick-built back-to-backs which also spread up the slopes of Beeston Hill into that township. This monotony and the close proximity of industrial smoke and waste have always given travellers from the south by road or rail a thoroughly depressing introduction to Leeds, not much improved by the motorway clearances. If there was some good quality of life engendered, as Richard Hoggart argues, then it had to be below the surface, for it could hardly be at the visible level.

'Holbeck is, and Hunslet is nearly, now united to Leeds in unbroken continuity,' wrote Baker in 1858.[12] At that time it was a broken discontinuity that distinguished the four other southern townships where village was separated from village by green fields, and even Armley, the nearest, was not continuously built up on the side separating it from Leeds. Wellington bridge (1818) and Monk bridge (1827) took turnpikes out of town on the south-western side and relieved the ancient congestion at Leeds bridge, but their turnpikes were aiming for Huddersfield, Halifax and Elland, making sites in Holbeck accessible to Leeds more by accident than by design, and they did not pass through the village itself. Armley was also by-passed, and the terrace invasion was postponed until the '70s. It was in Armley that Gott took over the manorial mills to supplement the output of Bean Ing, but it was also at Armley that he built his country mansion and laid out his park.

For the third of his 'manufacturing villages' Lucas had chosen not Armley but Bramley, the westernmost township. Bramley was in form a second Armley, a farmers' and weavers' village cluster, but more remote until the last two decades of the century, when streets were built near the railway station, along the Bradford tramway, and on the borough boundary at Rodley and Stanningley. The two remaining out-townships, (Old) Farnley and (Lower) Wortley, were hardly touched by residential development before 1914. Farnley's rusticity was emphasised by its hall and park, although industry and accompanying housing had created a New Farnley and a New Wortley on the Holbeck and Armley side of these townships, but distant from the original hamlet clusters, which remained very much as Tuke's map had depicted them in 1781.

Despite the leafier surrounds, the housing in these south-western townships was as solidly working-class as that of Hunslet and Holbeck. If the face of the communities seemed different, the leafiness no doubt contributed to the more favourable impression; chimneys had certainly come to the textile mills but there was an absence of heavy industry; and the local quarries made stone available as a cheap building material even for working-class terraces, giving them at least some affinity with the vernacular architecture of stone farmhouses, shops and cottages that still stood in the village centres.

VI In 1845 Darnton Lupton, mayor of the town, accompanied John Atkinson to London to give evidence before the Select Committee on Smoke Prevention.[13] The Luptons had once lived alongside their warehouse and workshops in North Street, and the Atkinsons had tried to develop Clarendon Road on their Little Woodhouse estate in the West End. 'Every one who can, is going out of town,' Lupton now told the committee; and Atkinson added: 'as they now have the means of omnibuses they can do it'.

It is clear that neither witness had in mind the development of the industrial suburbs on the south bank: at that date the movement to the leafier northern residential suburbs was selective of the social class that it involved; the migrants were not Everyman but 'Everyone who Can', and it was a movement led by the same families who had peopled the first West End before its fall. Any time after 1838 one could catch the omnibus from Paradise Lost to Paradise Regained, with a choice of northbound vehicles, one on the Otley turnpike to Headingley village and the other on the Harrogate turnpike to Potternewton and Chapel Allerton. One must hurry; the town's leading citizens cannot be kept waiting: they dine early. 'Time brings about strange changes,' wrote the *Mercury* in 1863: 'how different is the merchant of to-day with his ornate warehouse in town; "his genteel villa residence in the country;" his carriage and pair; and his luxurious dine at six.'[14]

The three northern out-townships were not devoid of industrial building, since the Hawksworth and Adel becks had always been important sources of water power, but the small number of mill chimneys that they sprouted were virtually concealed in the ravines, and by the end of the nineteenth century the former leats and millponds of the upper Meanwood valley had been landscaped within the grounds of large houses on the east of Weetwood Lane. It was the absence of industry on the plateaux above the valleys that made these townships so attractive as a refuge from Leeds smoke. Some of the refugees had left early, to occupy existing country houses. The banker John Beckett came to Meanwood Hall in 1801, and John Marshall, the flax magnate, left his house in Meadow Lane in 1805 and took a lease of New Grange (now Beckett Park), where industry was visible only as the romantic skyline glow of Kirkstall forge, admired by Dorothy and William Wordsworth when they came to stay with the Marshalls. These were mansions with park land, equivalent in size to Denison Hall in the first West End. There was a considerable demand for something rather less magnificent, sometimes met by converting a farmhouse, more frequently by finding a landowner who would sell a field for a villa, equivalent to Claremont, Belle Vue and Springfield Lodge in Little Woodhouse.

More than half Headingley was owned by the Earl of Cardigan, and the total acreage belonging to the Earl of Mexborough and Earl Cowper made up more than half the area of Potternewton. None of these earls occupied residences in the Leeds area, and all in turn were willing to augment their rent roll with building leases or, when their agents advised, to realise increased land values by sales. In 1819 his agent wrote from Leeds to the fifth Earl Cowper in Hertfordshire:[15]

> the elegancies and comforts of life are more sought after. This, I conceive, will continue to increase and introduce a disinclination for residence in so dirty a town. Of course, land proper for country houses will increase in value.

To find the right moment, the right area, the right price and the right type of building project was not so easy: the partnership that paid Earl Cowper £29,860 for fifty-five lots in Leeds New Town in 1825 was bankrupt by 1828, and the earl ignominiously but profitably repurchased the empty lots for £20,000. The fifth earl's names are commemorated in Louis and Francis Streets, but the land sales dragged on through the time of the sixth and seventh earls, being completed only in 1873. The whole Mexborough estate came on the market in 1845 but in ten-acre lots, too large to find many takers. Smaller landowners at Headingley Hill were making building sites available with frontages on the Otley turnpike from 1829 but some of these remained unsold twenty years later. The Cardigans were limited to leasehold dispositions by the terms of their family settlement, and their first freehold sales were of the land at Burley assigned to them on enclosure of the commons in 1831. The enclosure of the moor at Far Headingley set off development there also, and by 1839 there were two rival proprietors offering 'the means of omnibuses' from Leeds to Headingley.

In short, the northern out-townships showed not only the same

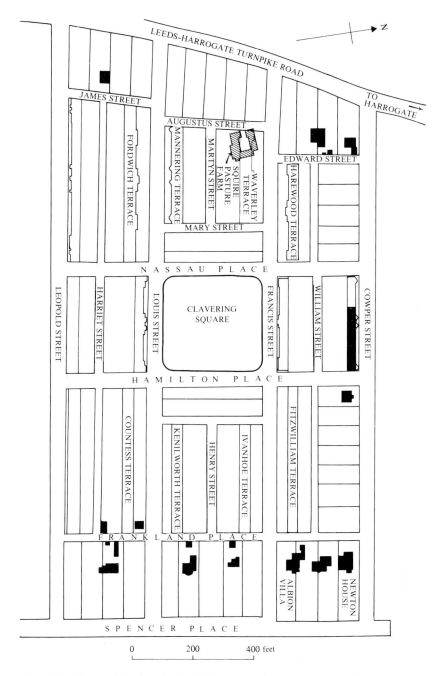

33   The New Town of Leeds at Squire's Pasture on the Cowper estate, Potternewton, as intended in 1828. The failure of this venture, which contributed to Sir Walter Scott's insolvency, is indicated by the small number of houses (shaded) actually built by 1847. (After a map by Dr Colin Treen)

progression from mansions to villas as the old West End but many of the same chance forces (a death, a bankruptcy, a decision to live in the south) that determined when land came on the market; the ups and downs of trade punctuated the chronology in the same way; and there was the same tale of misjudged opportunities, abortive schemes and long-drawn-out projects, the strategies of which have now been laid bare by Dr Colin Treen's microscopic study.

Nor does the parallel end there, for terraces were to follow the villas. The former common of Burley village was near the riverside mills at the most industrial corner of the large township, and the first houses that it bore after its enclosure in 1831 were working-class cottages; the edge of the moor at Far Headingley already had an array of cottages before the enclosure, and although some of the newly enclosed land was taken for houses as large as Castle Grove, the home of a linen manufacturer (1831–34), four-roomed stone terrace houses were erected *c*. 1838 in what was appropriately named Cottage Road, and not all the enclosures were built over by 1846.

By that time there were signs of a transformation on the south-eastern boundary of Headingley and Leeds proper, along the west side of Woodhouse moor and almost within sight of the earlier villas at Headingley Hill. Kensington Terrace, Finsbury Place and Torquay Terrace mark this significant invasion. The Leeds–Harrogate–Thirsk railway had its station at Headingley by 1850, raising the hopes of estate agents, but its viaduct from Armley to Kirkstall did not enhance that part of Burley, and in the fields between it and the Leeds boundary back-to-backs made their appearance – not the first back-to-backs, for they existed already in Burley village – but their first appearance in brick in a predominantly stone-built township. These developments were due to the Uptons, a solicitor's family who had already sold the New Gas Company an adjoining site for its gasometer.

It was the census report for 1861 that found it necessary to explain the fifty per cent increase in Burley and Headingley since 1851 by the presence of 'a large part of the mercantile community of Leeds', fearful perhaps that readers might imagine a misprint or a miscount. In fact the mercantile element was not so numerous as to account for the 800 new houses.

The lesson was clear, and those who valued seclusion were driven yet farther from town to the northern fringe of the borough, and beyond it into Roundhay and Adel. In 1861 William Brown built Bardon Grange in Weetwood Lane, and the banker Henry Oxley came at the same time to build 'The Elms' (now Oxley Hall); the brewer, F. W. Tetley, commissioned George Corson to design 'Foxhill' in the

Small-scale street development on three estates in Lower Burley, 1846–74, mainly in back-to-backs. The firm lines show plots purchased by different developers and the heavy lines the boundary between the estates of T. W. Lloyd (bottom), Beckett (centre) and T. E. Upton (top), which lay between Kirkstall and Burley Roads and between the township boundary and the railway viaduct. (After a map by Dr Colin Treen)

34

B   Beckett estate
L   T.W. Lloyd estate
U   T.E. Upton estate

0   200   400 feet

next year, and Corson's 'Spenfield' near the reservoirs was designed in 1875 for another member of the Oxley family, perhaps the most remarkable expression of tasteful opulence in Victorian Leeds.

As promptly as a fugue, the older villas in Headingley itself experienced the same development as the villas of Woodhouse a generation or more earlier: their owners departed either to Morecambe or the next world, and the legatees hastened to find a surveyor to parcel out the building lots or an estate agent to find some developer who would purchase. The fate of the Headingley House estate was untypical: the Marshalls abandoned it for the Lake District in 1888, expecting it to be sold to 'capitalists or a syndicate', but it was bought for his own residence by the clothing manufacturer Joseph Hepworth, who used his new wealth to move from Cromer Terrace in Woodhouse; but by 1900 he had moved to Torquay, and Headingley House came on the market, this time finding its 'syndicate' purchasers, and the rest of the pattern of history was reasserted.

An oddity also became available, more extensive than any villa grounds: the park land of the former Zoological and Botanical Gardens, the 'Royal Park', bankrupt and hopefully put up for sale in 1859, 1863 and 1866. Like Victoria Road in the Fawcett estate at Headingley Hill (1838) it was necessary for a long new access road to be built before interest was displayed. This was Cardigan Road, still lined by the large villas of the '70s, with the zoo bear-pit mysteriously surviving, and with George Corson's 'Clareville' on the corner of Spring Road, built for the auctioneer and estate agent John Hepper; eight large villas were erected by 1879, but there was then a pause. Building land to the east and west of these villas was offered for sale in 1869 and 1872 in smaller plots, but Cardigan Road retained its attraction for some: 'Sandholme' and 'Wallingfen', with their chateau towers, are an identical pair of villas built in the '90s for their own residences by the builders Benjamin and William Walmsley, by which time the park grounds farther east were almost completely covered with terraces of through and back-to-back houses.

The Walmsleys themselves developed 224,000 square yards of building plots in the northern townships between 1883 and 1892, and Charles Stott, a retired builder from Armley, nearly twice that area between 1883 and 1903; they were matched by the developments of the partnership of H. H. Hodgson, an estate agent, and W. S. Arnold, a contractor (1893–1903). These large developers (and others) were active in all three northern townships, the same progress of villas, terraces and villa infill being completed in the central part of Potternewton by 1914 and substantially in progress in the more distant fields of Chapel Allerton which played Farnley to

Potternewton's Bramley.

Landowners such as the three earls had used the fixed building line, the minimal ratable value, the designated house size and other restrictive covenants to preserve the social character of the new streets and maintain the value of unsold land adjoining them: from the late '60s the corporation building inspectors were able to use bye-laws to impose minimum standards on new houses in a very different part of the social spectrum. Nothing could be more significant of the change in the type of customer expected by the larger developers at the end of the century than the conditions imposed by J. W. Archer, woollen manufacturer, when selling to builders the parcels that he and the surveyor-architect, John Hall, had carved from 148,000 square yards of the former Cowper estate between Roundhay and Harehills Road, purchased in 1888 and 1889 for a sum near £26,000. The restrictive covenant[16] went to the very limit of amiability: it permitted 'any class of dwelling houses approved by the Corporation of Leeds'. One might as well have been in Hunslet or Holbeck.[17]

VII   While the out-townships were developing these differences, echoes of those that had separated the first East and West Ends, the centre of the town was also changing. In some central streets, particularly Albion Street, Park Row and South Parade, Georgian merchant houses were demolished for banks and office building; in Park Lane Park House was taken for the site of the Town Hall in 1858; Mount Pleasant and Sunny Bank for the new Infirmary site in 1863–68, and, a little farther out, Beech Grove for the Yorkshire College of Science in 1877. In the East End the notorious Boot and Shoe Yard was demolished for market extensions in 1844, and 222 houses in the eastern part of Union Street for municipal baths and Mill Garth police station (1876); other houses had been compulsorily purchased and demolished under Improvement Act powers for street widening, as in Boar Lane (1866). With these subtractions and with little space remaining for new housing the population of the in-township levelled and then fell, as table 3 shows.

Everywhere houses aged, and the face of the town became wrinkled; the first generation of working-class streets had survived the publicity and criticism of the '30s and '40s, and when there was a second stirring of the public conscience after James Hole's prize essay of 1865 the same streets were again named. All but a handful of the streets that won notoriety at the time of the cholera in 1832 survived to 1914.

The public discussions of the '60s achieved little in the way of clearances, and private efforts also failed. There were pressure groups like the Leeds Ladies' Sanitary Association (1865), and Hole's essay when published was illustrated by plans of Victoria Terrace, Beeston, and Albert Terrace, Burley, both the work of a Model Cottage Building Committee (1861) with its motto 'As the Homes, So the People'; and it also built in Langham Street, New Wortley, and in Meadow Lane. A Society for the Erection of Dwellings for Working Men was responsible for forty-two other houses at Wortley (1866), and the Leeds Industrial Dwellings Company built twenty-four tenements in four-storey galleried flats in Shannon Street before it became moribund for a decade. Then it adopted a new policy of purchasing existing terrace property as model landlord, paying a regular 4 per cent dividend to its shareholders, and owning nearly a thousand houses by the end of the century.

Model housing schemes engendered by interest in Hole's proposals and by philanthropy foundered, as elsewhere in England, on the economics of high costs and the low wages of tenants. In a town addicted to back-to-backs, tall tenement buildings were unacceptable: the thirteen three-storey tenements in Marsh Lane for which plans were approved in 1900 were miniatures compared with those in Glasgow and London, and the chairman of the Unhealthy Areas Committee, F. M. Lupton, agreed that they were 'barracks'.

The work that Lupton reported in his pamphlet *Housing Improvement* (1906) was not initiated before 1895, and arbitration was still in progress in 1903. By 1906 the corporation had demolished nearly 4,000 houses in York Street and Quarry Hill, the heart of the first East End; in Holbeck fifty-nine of the hundred back-to-backs crammed into Camp Field were cleared to give light and air; and at the Bank the 104 houses of the Hill House Building Club (1790) were demolished soon after they had been visited by Sidney and Beatrice Webb on a visit of historical inquiry in 1891.

Cellar dwellings began to be closed from 1873, but apart from those in the designated Unhealthy Areas the back-to-back terraces remained inviolate, and indeed multiplied. In 1858 Baker had emphasised the monotony of housing in the borough: 82 per cent of the houses were rated at under £10 a year, and between 1886 and 1914 the building clauses committee approved plans for 57,029 houses, nine-tenths of them in terraces; and nearly two-thirds of the houses completed in the same period were back-to-back. The affection of Leeds builders and house owners for the back-to-back always surprised sanitary reformers, especially those in northern cities such as Manchester and Bradford which had banned them long before. The furthest official intervention in Leeds was bye-law 11 of 1866, which compelled builders of new back-to-backs to provide a privy-and-ashpit yard between each block of eight. Although simple one-up-and-one-down houses continued to be provided, the size and style of the back-to-back began to be elaborated in the '70s, with attics and dormers, porches, gardens, double fronts, bay windows and individual privies in a sub-area. An Act of 1909 banned further back-to-backs of any kind except in streets already approved, but this escape clause allowed them to be built in Leeds until 1937.

VIII The face of Leeds in 1914 was not made up entirely of houses, although they were everywhere the architectural feature that dominated the townscape and managed to survive even in the centre. If the pavements of the central streets seemed to be a mere foyer to shop windows, those who rode on the top deck of trams along Briggate, Boar Lane and Kirkgate were still face to face with the first-floor facades of former private houses. If in Park Row the grandiose architecture of banks and insurance offices had destroyed the Georgian houses, others in East Parade, Park Place and Park Square were preserved (as Blenheim Terrace and Queen Square in our own day) by the needs of professions like medicine, the law and accountancy in the absence of purpose-built office blocks. Insurance companies and banks often rented spare accommodation as private offices, but was there, one wonders, an independent purpose-built office block in Leeds before 1914? Questions of this sort are a reminder of how little is yet known about commercial buildings, although Pevsner and Linstrum have commented on a small number of outstanding warehouses, banks and insurance offices.

In 1813 the new Court House in Park Row, erected under the Improvement Act of 1809, enabled the magistrates and councillors to meet in their own premises for the first time. The magistrates had previously rented rooms in a house in Kirkgate shared with the circulating library and the chief constable, while the council met in the Moot Hall above the butchers' shambles. Now perhaps the Moot Hall could be pulled down, the blood and offal go somewhere else, and Briggate return to its full width? But there were questions of compensation, and it did not happen until 1825. 'What would the town of Leeds have been, but a small hamlet,' mused John Cawood, Tory businessman and improvement commissioner, in 1822, 'if private interest had not sometimes given way to public good?'[18] 'This is an age of combined effort for public purposes,' wrote the Whig newspaper proprietor Edward Baines a year later when the new commercial buildings of Chapter VII were under way.[19]

Asa Briggs's study of the Town Hall, opened in 1858, was subtitled *An Essay in Civic Pride*:[20] although temporarily unnerved at the sight of the bill, that pride lasted well beyond 1858, and it also had a prehistory, as Baines's and Cawood's comments show; it gave a public as well as a private face to Leeds, although by 1914 public houses and buildings for public worship greatly outnumbered public buildings in the civic sense. The Municipal Buildings were erected next to the Town Hall in 1876 but in a concealed position behind houses on the north side of Park Lane, and neighbouring School Board offices were built to match in 1880; the Poor Law guardians had their own offices in East Parade (1860). By quantity the ratepayer as patron of architecture was more evident in the out-townships: in the prison at Armley (1847), the new workhouse (1858) and Poor Law infirmary (1874) at Beckett Street, the waterworks at Headingley and Woodhouse moor, and in elementary schools, branch libraries, police stations, tram depots, gasometers, public conveniences and burial grounds.

As late as 1858 there was as yet no street or square that could be regarded as a civic focus, although the conjunction of the Infirmary, the Coloured Cloth Hall, the Court House and the town's principal Dissenting chapel made the junction of Boar Lane, Park Lane and Mill Hill approximate to one, even if the open space was irregular and in no sense a square. Before Wellington Street was cut to Wellington bridge (1818) there was only a cul-de-sac westwards: traffic to the Bradford turnpike and Kirkstall bridge had to go up Infirmary Street. A large projected open space, with Park Row, South Parade and East Parade as its sides and open to the Cloth Hall and Infirmary at the south, was lost when the land was sold for development in 1805. Nevertheless the western side of Park Row was thought fitting for the new Philosophical Hall in 1829, and Charles Fowler, who liked to decorate the emptier spaces on his plans, chose a view of the hall for his 1821 map; for the 1826 revision he chose the Commercial Hall, on the corner of Boar Lane and Park Row; and for 1831 a vista of the 'western entrance to Leeds', looking past the Infirmary from the end of West (now St Paul's) Street.

Like the authors of introductory matter to directories, cartographers were always aware that Leeds had a public as well as a private face. Cossins used merchant houses for his marginal embellishments but did find room for an elevation of the Moot Hall. In 1781 Tuke gave twenty-three references to 'all the Public Edifices of the Township'; in 1815 the Giles plan numbered forty-nine, nearly half of them being churches or chapels; Fowler's plan of 1821, 'with the Recent Improvements', increased the list of fifty-four, to eighty-two in his revision of 1826, to 124 in 1831 and 181 in 1844, grouped under 'churches, chapels, charitable buildings, law commercial and other, fire engines, gasworks, newspaper offices, newsrooms, public offices, railway offices' and – as an addendum – the new borough goal at Armley. It could hardly demonstrate better how many of the activities falling within other chapters of this book had involved buildings.

Of these the places of worship were naturally the most scattered. No new Anglican church was built in the centre of town after 1780 and with the departure of many of the first residents the new church at Park Square had poor congregations; a small Dissenting chapel in a Kirkgate yard that had fallen into bankruptcy was converted into St James's church in 1801. Otherwise new churches followed new streets into the suburbs, notably with the four Million Act churches (1826). Dissenting chapels were equally scattered, finding a building to rent, seeking a vacant plot to build when congregations prospered, and then with the decline of inner-city population fostering offshoots in the suburbs.

After the demolition of the Moot Hall, Leeds's principal street, Briggate, had no public buildings. The old corn exchange lay beyond the Cross in New Street and the new exchange of 1862 lay in Vicar Lane. It is not known which was the first shop window to pass from being a source of daylight inward to a place of display outwards, but with the multiplication of shops in Briggate and Boar Lane their windows became public places. The gradual movement of open-air markets robbed Briggate of sights and smells but gave Vicar Lane its Kirkgate Market (1857, exterior rebuilt 1904).

The covered market site had been won by demolition, first of the 1717 vicarage house for the Free Market (1824) and then the Boot and Shoe and adjoining yards in 1843 for its extension. There was demolition also to widen the approaches to Leeds bridge after the 1842 Improvement Act, and there were other clearances to make way for Crown Point bridge (1840), where the elevated approach roads have incongruously preserved the Georgian house of the master dyer John Chadwick; other street widening proposed in the 1842 Act was postponed for economy. Briggate had been laid so wide in 1207 that there was no need to widen it, and Park Row, like the other Wilson estate streets, had been generously provided with space, but Boar Lane was narrow and its south side was set back in 1866 under powers conferred by the 1866 Improvement Act. Photographs of this reconstruction survive.

The Town Hall had been built on the Blayds estate in Park Lane, beyond the end of the Headrow. Even by 1914 this area lacked the feeling of a civic centre. The long south facade of the Library was hidden by a line of warehouses where the Memorial Gardens now are, and Victoria 'Square' was little more than a pavement. The removal of the corn exchange to its present site next to the White Cloth Hall and Assembly Rooms in 1863 might have created another focus for public buildings near the markets had not the Cloth Hall and Assembly Rooms been in decline by that date. The West End cloth hall was also in decline, although its courtyard was used for public assemblies before 1858.

The new Town Hall housed the council and law courts as well as public meetings and music festivals, and the Court House was then released for use by the Post Office. The plans for a new post office on the Cloth Hall site, freed by the Act of 1885, gave an opportunity, usually credited to Colonel Harding, to make the space in front of it something more than a turning place for trams and create City Square (1896) to greet passengers emerging from the town's largest railway station, although, as photographs show, the railway had not bothered to give it a dignified facade, and until the coming of the Queen's Hotel (after 1914) the south side of City Square was distinctly shabby.

The central railway stations had made a late entrance; the first terminus (1834), for the Selby line, was at Marsh Lane, set in one of the few East End fields that had not been developed in the '20s. This was soon superseded by the North Midland terminus in Junction Street, off Hunslet Lane (1839), originally intended to be nearer to Leeds bridge alongside the South Market and near the original staith of Brandling's railway from Middleton colliery. The first central terminus, in Wellington Street, was under construction when the Ordnance Survey maps were being drawn in 1847–48 and some sheets of the first edition were revised to include it. The other central station – now the sole survivor – had a more profound effect on the face of Leeds: in its construction in 1852 it obliterated the ancient manorial water mills, the King's Mills, and straddled the weir and their goits; its later junction line to Marsh Lane (1864) was the first intrusion of a railway over existing streets and provided a late and small example of the destructive power of railway viaducts. It gave Briggate a second bridge, enveloped much of the parish church's New Burial Ground, and added further smoke and gloom to Paley's courtyards between York Street and Marsh Lane.

A few streets were added to the town centre after Albion Street (1792). For the making of Bond Street and Commercial Street in 1804 two burgage plots were cleared to give access to Briggate at the east end, and a house in Park Row was demolished for a western extension in 1823. Boar Lane had not extended beyond Briggate before the making of Duncan Street in 1787; and Duncan Street then ended in a high wall with no access through the Kirkgate yards to Vicar Lane until 1868. Both Upper and Lower Headrow maintained their medieval narrowness until the 1930s but the eastern side of Vicar Lane was set back on a new frontage when the market buildings were erected; Maurice Paynel's modest failure to take Briggate any farther north than the Headrow in 1207 was remedied in 1868 by the construction of New Briggate, with the Grand Theatre (1877–78) and the arcades (Chapter VII).

Besides clearances, public squares and road widening another augmentation of open space, the public parks, gave the face of Leeds a character denied to many northern industrial towns. The two private gardens and park at Headingley were financial failures but the near-by commons of Woodhouse moor and ridge, on the township boundary, survived attempts by the lords of the manor to enclose them in 1801 and 1854. The moor was purchased by the corporation in 1857 and the ridge in 1876: a third area of common, the Carr, was lost to cottage encroachment. The 1856 Improvement Act also gave powers for the purchase of Hunslet and Holbeck moors for public recreation, but these remained privately owned until 1879 and 1900 respectively. Meanwhile the 1873 Improvement Act sanctioned the purchase of 773 acres that comprised the Roundhay Hall estate, even though it lay outside the borough. Smaller acquisitions took place between 1864 (Lemon Street playground) and 1899 (Burley Recreation Ground), bringing the total area in 1900, excluding Roundhay Park, to 443 acres. Leeds was then second to Liverpool (and then only by a decimal point) in *per capita* acreage of open space.[21]

These open spaces are as integral to the face of urban Leeds as silences are to the sound of music. Except for losses to the motorway at Hunslet and Holbeck moors, they have succeeded in keeping open space inviolate as field land all around was submitting to the invasion of bricks and mortar. They helped to prevent the face of Leeds from being a monochrome, and among them the four pieces of township moor are the survivors of community land that has existed as long as there have been houses to be called Leeds.

NOTES

[1] B.L., Add. MS 33770, 56–8.
[2] T. D. Whitaker, *History of Loidis and Elmet* (1816), 87.
[3] *Leeds Mercury*, 17 May 1799.
[4] Leeds city archives, LO/M6, 281, 17 February 1823.
[5] J. Hole, *The Homes of the Working Classes* (1866), 125.
[6] *Leeds Mercury*, 25 September 1852.

[7] *Ibid.*

[8] *S.C. on Smoke Prevention*, P.P. (1845), XIII, 560.

[9] *Leeds Intelligencer*, 28 July 1825.

[10] *Leeds Mercury*, 30 July 1825.

[11] *S.C. on the State of the Woollen Manufacturers*, P.P. (1806), III, 75.

[12] Robert Baker, 'On the industrial and sanitary economy of the borough of Leeds in 1858', *Journal of the Statistical Society*, XXI (1858), 428.

[13] *S.C. on Smoke Prevention*, 560 and 577; see also James Holdforth's evidence to the Committee on the Leeds Improvement Bill, 1842: House of Lords Record Office.

[14] Cited in J. Mayhall, *Annals of Yorkshire* (1875), II, 192.

[15] Hertfordshire Record Office, Cowper MS T. 4951.

[16] Leeds Corporation Deeds, 15469.

[17] Section VI draws on Colin Treen, 'Building and estate development in the northern out-townships of Leeds, 1781–1914', unpublished Ph.D. thesis, University of Leeds (1977).

[18] *Leeds Intelligencer*, 5 August 1822.

[19] *Leeds Mercury*, 18 September 1823.

[20] A. Briggs, *Victorian Cities* (1963), ch. IV.

[21] This paragraph is based on J. G. Branston, 'The development of public open spaces in Leeds', unpublished M.Phil. thesis, University of Leeds (1972).

R. W. UNWIN

Leeds becomes a transport centre

V

The development of Leeds from a landlocked town of the seventeenth century into a major centre of road, water and railway communications by the mid-nineteenth raises a number of questions. When, how and why did the transformation take place? What were the main effects and consequences? Who were the principal personalities involved, and what were their motives? The relationship between transport improvements, industrialisation and urbanisation is complex and can best be understood within a regional topographical, geographical and economic context. Changes need to be related to costs, and the general proposition may be accepted that, other things being equal, the transport requirements of a community tend to be met with a minimum expenditure of resources.

I   Situated at a crossing point on the river Aire where the Pennine highland zone meets the lowland zone, the position of Leeds on a geographical and economic frontier had a marked effect on its transport role. The usefulness of roads before waterways were developed has been considerably underestimated, and in the seventeenth century landlocked Leeds was dependent on land carriage, 'the very medium of our inland trade' according to Defoe.[1] In 1686 a census of inn accommodation ranked Leeds fifth in Yorkshire in terms of stabling. (Table 11.)

The principal route passing through Leeds was the trans-Pennine Chester–Manchester–Elland (Halifax)–Leeds–York road (fig. 35). To the west and south-west the hills around Halifax necessitated the use of packhorses rather than waggons to convey the raw materials and agricultural produce which passed through Leeds into the manufacturing districts. Cloth, carried down the valleys in exchange, was not merely finished and marketed in Leeds; it could be transhipped to a cheaper, more efficient and higher-quality carrier system of waggons, which operated to the inland ports of Tadcaster, York, Selby and Knottingley, where it was again transhipped into sloops and keels for Hull. At the end of the seventeenth century one Leeds merchant explained to his correspondent in Hamburg that waggons to Selby were in much demand at certain times of the year but that to use packhorses was likely to take 2 per cent off the value of exported cloth.[2] For small quantities of cloth, particularly if carried over long distances, packhorses may have had the edge over waggons, and the use of the former continued well into the eighteenth century.

Table 11 Accommodation and stabling at inns in Yorkshire market towns, 1686

Market town	Stabling for horses	Guest beds	Market town	Stabling for horses	Guest beds
York	800	483	Hull	349	199
Wakefield	543	242	Halifax	306	130
Malton	543	205	Sheffield	270	119
Beverley	460	182	Pontefract	235	92
Leeds	454	294	Thirsk	234	110
Doncaster	453	206	Richmond	228	99
Ripon	422	118	Scarborough	114	74

Source. P.R.O., W.O. 30/48, Abstract of a Particular Account of all the Inns, Alehouses ... in England with their Stable-Room and Bedding in the Year 1686.

Leeds was also well placed to benefit from the wool trade with the northern counties via the Chapeltown–Harewood–Knaresborough–Ripley–Ripon route. On the other hand, Wakefield, which still rivalled Leeds as the principal clothing town in the West Riding, was better placed for the wool trade from the Midlands and Lincolnshire. South of Leeds bridge, Meadow Lane and Hunslet Lane opened up the routes to Halifax in the west, Wakefield in the south and Pontefract–Ferrybridge to the south-east. This latter route was also the 'news' and post road, Leeds being only a branch office subsidiary to Ferrybridge on the main London–Edinburgh route. The roads south of the bridge were also used by passengers who wished to travel by coach from Wakefield or Ferrybridge to London, a regular service having been established by the end of the seventeenth century.

Pressure on Leeds bridge and the roads around the town increased in the decades after the Restoration, and the congestion of packhorses, cloth waggons and coal carts contributed to the removal of the cloth

The road from York to West Chester surveyed by John Ogilby for *Britannia*
(1675). Note the distances in miles, furlong subdivisions and compass direction. The
principal landmarks are shown, including coal mines at Seacroft and the leading
35   inns. Today there is a White Horse Inn near the position shown on the map

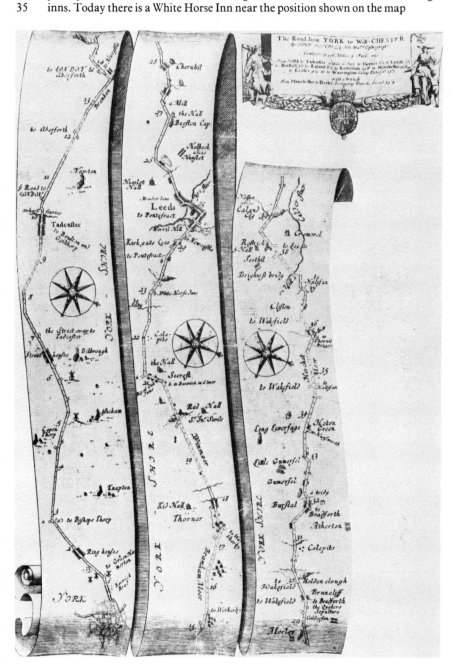

market into Lower Briggate in 1684, Thoresby recording that:

> the new cloth–market ... by order of the Mayor and Aldermen, is removed from off the bridge to the broad street above, to prevent the inconveniency from the cold air of the water in winter, and the trouble of carts and carriages in summer.[3]

The increasing use of wheeled traffic on the roads to the Ouse and Aire ports occasioned a growing volume of complaints about repairs and upkeep. Between 1640 and 1700 the West Riding magistrates levied more than £500 for the repair of different stretches of the Leeds–Selby road. In 1658 – five years before the first turnpike Act – the JPs urged parishes on the route to petition either the Lord Protector or the next Parliament 'for the setting a Toll upon the Carriages of Straingers' (*sic*) but no action was taken. Local petitions for the repair of the Leeds–Selby road were heard at the Leeds or Pontefract Quarter Sessions.[4] The Leeds–Pontefract–Ferrybridge road also had a high proportion of wheeled traffic and in 1679–87 the corporation spent upwards of £170 defending lawsuits occasioned by the bad state of repair of Pontefract Lane. Such difficulties figured prominently among the factors prompting a growing ·interest in alternative forms of transport.[5]

II   By the later seventeenth century the transport network was inadequate to cope with the growing demands of the manufacturing districts. Although carriage by waggon was cheaper than by packhorse, both forms were expensive in comparison with water transport, which was between a quarter and a half the cost of land carriage. An unimproved transport system could be a barrier to economic growth, with high costs curtailing markets and fostering regional economic insularity.

The Aire and Calder Navigation schemes of the later seventeenth century were a revival of the earlier proposals of 1621 and 1625, which had been defeated by the determined opposition of York, whose corporation, under a charter of 1462, had been appointed conservator of the river Ouse and its tributaries. Commercial jealousy as much as conservancy seems to have prompted York, and rivalry between the northern capital and the 'upstart' clothing towns of the West Riding was both bitter and protracted.

William Pickering, cloth merchant, author of *Marrow of the Mathematicks* and mayor of Leeds in 1679, was the only member of the corporation with the foresight to revive the Aire and Calder scheme in the face of costly litigation over the repair of Pontefract

Lane and in anticipation of the benefits of cheaper transport. Nevertheless, although Pickering's *Reasons* (1685) claimed that the proposed waterway would provide a stimulus for trade and save upwards of £1,000 per annum on land carriage his scheme remained only on paper.

Confidence, capital and engineering skill are the prerequisites for major transport undertakings, but it was not until the mid-1690s that several factors combined to make a determined effort to secure a navigation Act worth while. The Aire and Calder Navigation, as finally conceived, was the creation of the wealthiest woollen merchants in Leeds, who were leading members of the town corporation, together with a number of landowners in the Leeds and Wakefield area who hoped to open up extended markets for coal mined on their estates. It was clear that the reduction of transport costs was likely to prove advantageous at a time when many of the overseas markets for English woollen cloth were becoming saturated. At the same time the tax on seaborne coal, imposed in 1695 to help finance the protracted war against France, created market conditions favourable to the growth of the inland coal trade. That similar river navigation schemes were being developed elsewhere also encouraged a degree of emulation.

To the confidence and capital investment propensity of the Leeds merchants was added the engineering skill of John Hadley of West Bromwich, the one-time partner of George Sorocold, who had installed the first waterworks in Leeds. Hadley estimated that £5,200 would be necessary to make the river Aire navigable for vessels of up to fifteen tons between Leeds and Weeland on the lower reaches of the river and that it could be accomplished by building seven locks and deepening several stretches of the waterway, particularly below the port of Knottingley.

The passage of the Aire and Calder Bill through Parliament provides an insight into the politics of transport. Support came mainly from the manufacturing districts of the West Riding and the neighbouring counties of Lancashire and Westmorland. Opposition was strongest from interests dependent upon the Yorkshire Ouse — York, Selby and Tadcaster, the transhipment ports. Mercantilist ideas assumed that there was a more or less fixed volume of economic activity, and that if one trading community prospered another must in consequence decline. The Aire and Calder controversy marked the final stage in the struggle for commercial supremacy between York and the West Riding towns. The navigation Bill was also opposed by the coal interests of the north-east, from Newcastle and Sunderland.

The various economic interests exerted their influence to secure a political 'interest'. The two Yorkshire MPs, who received electoral support from the corporation of Leeds, favoured the Bill, together with Lord Irwin of Temple Newsam and a number of members who were currently promoting a similar Bill to extend navigation to Sheffield. However, in 1698 the first Bill was 'counted out'. When it was reintroduced in the following parliamentary session the promoters came to a private agreement with one of the MPs for Pontefract, promising to lease his water mills and to permit coal from his estate to pass downstream free of lock dues, together with concessions for his constituents. This 'bought' ally helped to pilot the second Bill through the House of Commons.

More important in the final passage of the Bill were two reports prepared by Trinity House on the instructions of the House of Lords, which had sought advice from various quarters – including a 'Dr. [Isaac?] Newton' – about the likely effects of the navigation on the tidal Ouse. As in the case of other opposed transport schemes, numerous petitions had been presented, printed *Reasons* circulated, counsel employed and MPs solicited, but private Bill legislation of the period provides few examples of recourse to an independent opinion.

Although the Trinity House officers were 'treated' by both sides, it is doubtful if the final report was unduly biased. The benefits likely to accrue to the West Riding woollen industry were set out, but so too were the likely detrimental effects on Selby. York had lost for ever its prominence in cloth manufacture, and failure to maintain the Ouse had led to a decline in the city's trading position. On the other hand Knottingley, which had upwards of 900 tons of shipping, had become increasingly important for transhipment between Hull and the West Riding.[6]

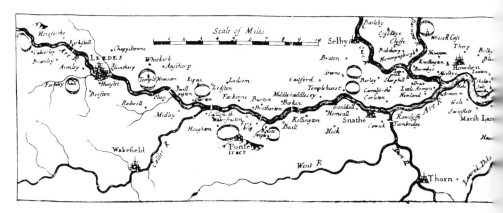

36   The Aire and Calder Navigation in the early eighteenth century, from the map of Sutton

Under the terms of the 1699 Act eighteen 'undertakers' were empowered to make the Aire and Calder navigable from Leeds and Wakefield to Weeland, near which the Aire flowed into the Ouse. In November 1700 the navigation was open to Leeds bridge, and small boats could come up to the newly erected 'Towns Warehouse' on the north bank. Cloth could now be packed directly into vessels in Leeds en route for Hull and so to London, the Baltic and the Low Countries. (Fig. 36.)

Born in hope, the waterway was beset in its early years by engineering, financial and legal difficulties. Disputes arose between the separate groups of Leeds and Wakefield undertakers concerning their respective costs, capital outlay and tolls, but in 1705 these were resolved and the two concerns united. The total capital invested in the Aire and Calder Navigation rose from £11,300 to £26,700 by 1720, but dividends were low and seldom paid.

From the first decade of the eighteenth century the navigation became less a corporation concern than a private company whose business affairs were known only to shareholders, and whose dividends – disappointing at first – were not legally restricted. Relations between the company and other trading interests in the region were often strained, and from the 1720s the suspicion grew that, although the navigation was an invaluable asset and the artery of the West Riding waterway system, its monopoly position benefited merely a few families – mercantile in origin but *rentier* by descent. By the second quarter of the eighteenth century the navigation had surmounted its teething troubles and was entering a period of sustained prosperity, due less to its tardy efforts at technical improvement than to favourable economic factors such as the growing

Nicholls (1712). The oval rings represent a number of the principal parks and landed estates

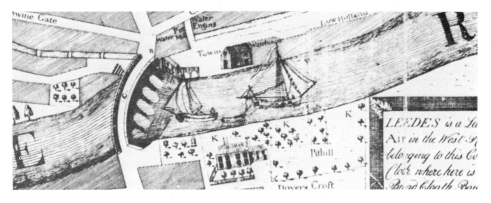

37   The port of Leeds (1725): a section from Cossins's map. Note the Town
         Warehouse near the bridge and the river vessels

population, wealth and industry of the region. Dividends rose from 6
per cent in 1720 to 12 per cent by 1740. Although water transport
provided the basis for the transition to an industrial economy, costs of
carriage – 10*s* per ton in summer and 16*s* in winter – were high, and
the search for cheaper alternatives continued.[7]

III   Road improvement by means of turnpikes, though undertaken on a
piecemeal basis, was much more systematic than was once believed. At
first attention was focused on the trans-Pennine routes between the
growing manufacturing districts of Lancashire and Yorkshire. The
Chester–Manchester–Leeds–York route was part of Ralph Allen's
system of cross posts, and in 1734 the first Yorkshire turnpike Act
covered the Manchester–Saddleworth and Rochdale–Halifax–Elland
roads.

The promotion of turnpikes – like the development of waterways –
was marked by rivalry between neighbouring towns. Commercial
competition between Leeds and Wakefield had been exacerbated over
the building of the early cloth halls, and in 1739–40 it was proposed to
extend the Calder navigation to Elland and by other streams to
Halifax. When the necessary Bill was aborted at committee stage by
the riparian landowners an alternative road scheme was promoted for
the Wakefield–Elland–Halifax route, which would meet the
Blackstone Edge turnpike and establish a complete trans–Pennine
waggon route. The Wakefield designs aroused the suspicions of several
Leeds merchants, and in response it was decided to promote Bills to
improve the roads west of Leeds and also to develop the old routes
eastwards to the inland ports. The schemes for the Halifax–Leeds–

Selby road and the Wakefield–Pontefract–Knottingley–Weeland road were designed to by-pass the Aire and Calder Navigation, the shortcomings of which were highlighted by the most severe winter for a generation.

In public the navigation trustees answered their critics by pointing out the early difficulties the company had had to surmount and asserting that the statutory powers granted to them had never been exceeded. In private the navigation 'interest' preferred not to oppose the road Bills openly. Rather they chose to work behind the parliamentary scene to draw off opposition and to insert clauses into the Bills which would render the proposed turnpikes east of Leeds and Wakefield financially ineffective, particularly by the exemption of coal from toll, a ploy which received support both from cloth manufacturers and from local colliery landowners. Although six Yorkshire road Bills were passed in 1741, the Halifax–Leeds–Selby scheme was badly mauled in the House of Commons, and clauses were introduced to exempt coal from toll and to ensure that no turnpike gate was fixed nearer to Leeds than West Garforth bridge. It was not until 1751 than an Act for the Halton Dial–Tadcaster road (the only stretch of the Chester–York route not yet turnpiked) also made provision for the effective repair of the route to Selby. Both roads were partly promoted to provide alternative outlets to the navigation, and both connected with the Great North Road.

The turnpike network developed around Leeds during the mid-eighteenth century was designed largely to meet the growing demands of a region whose population, manufactures and trade were placing a growing strain on the existing transport system. Facilitating intra-regional dealings in wool and agricultural produce between the North and West Ridings was the prime object of the Leeds–Harrogate–Ripley–Boroughbridge–Ripon Act (1753), and evidence of the extension of domestic woollen manufacture to new districts was provided by promoters of the Leeds–Otley–Skipton Act (1755). Complaints about the damage done by heavy vehicles – particularly coal carts – on the Leeds–Wakefield road finally led to an Act being passed in 1758, with pressure from as far afield as Barnsley and Sheffield. That action was not taken sooner was probably due to the opposition of interests in the vicinity of Leeds who were apprehensive about the setting up of turnpike gates on a well frequented road and claimed that repairs could be effectively carried out under the existing parish system.

While some had sufficient influence to frustrate the intentions of turnpike promoters by subtle manipulation of the legislative process, others felt compelled to take more direct action. For example, in 1753 several people were wounded in an affray over the siting of turnpike gates at Harewood bridge, but whether this was part of a concerted move against road tolls is not clear. Shortly afterwards the refusal to pay toll led to several arrests at Beeston, the outcome of which was a serious riot centred upon the King's Arms in Briggate, where the magistrates were sitting to deal with the offenders.[8]

The Leeds cloth merchants were the guiding interest behind the development of the turnpike network. Although dividends were limited in law to 5 per cent, the capital investment propensity of the merchant community in the town was also paramount. The importance of turnpike trust development before 1770 has often been underestimated, and it is apparent that the trustees were relatively successful as administrators and road repairers. That trust finances were in a chronic state is explicable partly by the slow rate of economic growth in the mid-eighteenth century and partly by the statutory restrictions on the incidence of tolls and siting of gates.

At first the turnpike solution was regarded as an expedient of limited duration but it soon became apparent that the renewal and extension of statutory powers would be necessary. By 1773 a total of £5,709 was outstanding upon the credit of the Leeds–Selby road tolls, and interest had not been paid for five years, a situation which was partly alleviated in the renewal Act (1786) which stipulated half-toll for coal vehicles and ended many of the winter exemptions. The Leeds–Elland renewal Act (1777) ended the practice whereby loads of coal and lime passed several times on some stretches of the sixteen-mile road under cover of a single toll payment, an essential expedient for a trust indebted for £7,137 and in which no interest had been paid for several years. Such measures were not untypical of the way in which many West Riding trusts were able to increase rates and to end exemptions. At national level more general turnpike legislation attempted to restrict the use of narrow-wheeled or exceptionally heavy vehicles which did so much to damage surfaces.

The onset of more sustained economic growth in the textile and associated industries after 1783, and a boom in passenger traffic and the carrying trade, led to a decided upturn in turnpike business which was reflected in the annual rents paid by the toll farmers. Increases in toll rates and the increased powers of trusts in successive renewal Acts must be taken into consideration, but it is clear that the financial position of the turnpikes around Leeds had improved by the closing years of the eighteenth century.[9] (Table 12.)

IV   Although coach services between London and York or Wakefield had been developed by the end of the seventeenth century, another generation elapsed before the north–south operators regularly touched Leeds, and it was not until the 1750s that a well integrated network of stagecoaches was established in the region. As roads were improved, vehicle traffic flourished and travelling times between Leeds and London were reduced from four days in the early 1750s to twenty-six hours in 1785. By the latter date daily coaches were also operating from Leeds to York, Hull, Sheffield, Birmingham, Manchester and Carlisle, and in 'the season' to Scarborough and Harrogate. The town now had its own post office independent of Ferrybridge, and when the first Leeds to London mail coaches started in 1785 the fare was £3 3s for each of the five inside passengers but half-fare for the sole outside passenger, with an average travelling speed of under ten miles an hour[10]

Table 12 Toll leases on the principal turnpike roads around Leeds (£ per annum)

	1778	1789	1798	1804	1810	1820
Leeds–Selby	571	635	600	1,270	1,565	1,800
Leeds–Tadcaster	640	885	890	1,460	1,755	2,380
Leeds–Wakefield	800	945	1,350	2,105	2,300	
Leeds–Elland			1,880	1,965	2,040	1,775
Leeds–Bradford–Halifax	852	1,025	2,843		4,445	4,725

Source. R. G. Wilson, 'Transport dues as indices of economic growth, 1775–1820', *Ec.H.R.*, 2nd ser., XIX (1966), p. 115.

By 1800 about forty horse-drawn coaches were entering or leaving Leeds daily, and the following generation saw the town grow into an important coaching centre. By 1830 about half a dozen inns centred on Briggate and adjacent streets controlled the coaching business: for example, between five in the morning and five in the evening no fewer than forty coaches left the Bull and Mouth, twenty-two the Rose and Crown, and eighteen the White Horse. In the evolution of public transport the stagecoach, in operation and organisation, bridges an important gap between the pre-industrial period and the railway age.[11]

The structure of the freight transport services of Leeds was largely determined by the town's geographical position and by its growing commitment to the finishing and marketing of cloth. Defoe described a set of travelling Leeds merchants who operated with a drove of packhorses to the fairs and markets up and down the land. Although packhorse transport probably lingered on longer in the West Riding than in other counties, it was increasingly superseded by the cheaper waggon services. In the 1750s the cumbersome broad-wheel waggon could take up to ten days for the Leeds to London journey; by the 1830s a fly van took thirty hours.

The growth years for freight transport were from about 1780 to 1840. In 1781 about twenty-five carrier firms were centred on Leeds, operating more than sixty services a week. Local land carriage predominated but the town also had important freight links with London, Manchester, Liverpool, Newcastle, York and Sheffield. By the 1820s 'main line' freight services had increased fourfold, and these were supplemented by numerous local services, particularly on market days. The complex network was operated by over 180 local and long-distance carriers using a variety of vehicles – including waggons, caravans and fly waggons – and based on inns and warehouses in Water Lane, Lands Lane, Boar Lane, Meadow Lane and the Calls whence there were regular links with the waterside wharves.[12]

For the most part, passenger and freight routes followed the lines of the old parish roads – now turnpiked – and before 1800 few trusts attempted to do more than straighten or divert very short stretches. John (Blind Jack) Metcalf is often credited with the improvement of the Leeds–Harrogate road via North Street, Chapeltown Road and Harewood; and for converting the Park Lane–Kirkstall Lane–Stanningley route to Bradford into a practicable coach road. John McAdam, the leading road engineer of the turnpike age, improved the Leeds–Stourton–Methley–Pontefract route to the Great North Road. On the other hand the Leeds–Wetherby road, the Kirkstall road and the Leeds–Armley–Bramley–Bradford road were practically new constructions. (Fig. 38.)

V   Despite some shortening of communication axes, road transport remained expensive, and wherever possible it was combined with other, cheaper forms of carriage. By 1760 river navigation had been extended to Elland and Halifax, while west of the Pennines seminal transport developments were taking place centred on Liverpool and Manchester. The transition from the canalisation of rivers to the building of canals was decisive in breaking away from the rigid pattern of water transport dictated by nature and made possible the linking of the eastern and western industrial areas. Although inspired in Bradford, Blackburn and Liverpool rather than in Leeds, the trans-Pennine canal to Liverpool placed the town astride a main waterway across the industrial north. In the first years after the passing of the 1770 Act for a canal between Leeds bridge and Liverpool, work was concentrated on those sections where a maximum return on capital investment was expected. By 1777 a stretch between Leeds and Gargrave had been completed, but then money ran out and it was not until 1790 that a further Act authorised the raising of additional capital and a variation of the original route of John Longbotham and James Brindley. Initially authorised with a capital stock of £260,000, the canal was finally completed in 1816 at a total cost of £1,200,000.[13]

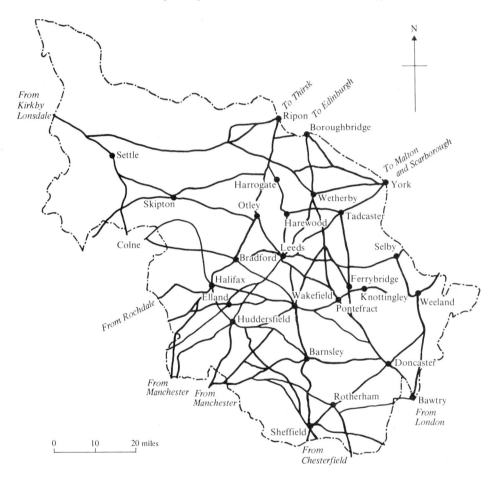

38   Leeds and the West Riding: the turnpike network in the early nineteenth century (*c.* 1830)

The provision of cheaper carriage for the foreign trade of south Lancashire and the West Riding – whose textile industries were attaining a position of world renown – was also facilitated by two other trans-Pennine canals, the Rochdale and the Huddersfield. In the early nineteenth century a number of east–west freight services integrated land and water carriage – for example, by road from Leeds to Halifax or Huddersfield and then by canal to Manchester.

East of Leeds, the volume of traffic on the Aire and Calder Navigation rose about seven times between 1700 and 1770 but the inadequacies of the waterway were the subject of a growing number of complaints. The Leeds and Liverpool Canal scheme, and the improvement of the river system above York, encouraged many merchants and landowners to promote a waterway from Leeds to the Ouse which would be independent of both the lower Aire valley and the monopoly of the navigation and its lessees. The route was surveyed by James Brindley and Robert Whitworth, and support came from many Yorkshire towns, but the navigation interest – whose shareholders were now enjoying 25 per cent dividends on initial capital – aborted the Leeds–Selby canal Bills in 1771-73. The descendants of the original merchant shareholders now derived most of their income from land, rents and investments. They regarded their navigation stock increasingly as inherited property and successfully defended it in a property-conscious Parliament.

The threat of more effective competition compelled the navigation to rectify the worst defects of the waterway. In 1771 John Smeaton, the Leeds engineer, pointed out in a detailed report that the original undertaking had been planned on too small a scale, although in the 1690s few could have foreseen the extent to which trade would grow. Faced in the 1770s by the prospect of a rival Leeds–Selby canal, the navigation virtually stole its opponents' thunder by successfully obtaining its own Selby Canal Act, which also empowered extensive rebuilding on the main line of the waterway. Although the navigation reached agreement with most of the riparian proprietors, a number of corn and fulling mill owners opposed the new scheme, as Henry Baynes of Knostrop bitterly complained to Viscount Irwin:

> ... since I have seen the Proprietors' new Bill I think they have the impudence of highwaymen ... I think if the Parliament suffer such an Act to pass, they deserve to have another Guy Fox [*sic*] under their houses to blow them up. We choose Members for the Security of our properties and instead of answering that end, they act quiet [*sic*] the contrary and put them in the power of a parcel of Wolves ...[14]

By 1778 a new set of locks had been installed throughout the line, five new cuts made and the Haddlesey–Selby canal constructed to by-pass the lower Aire. Equally important, the system of farming the waterway, which had led to continuous allegations of unfair practices, was ended, and a professional manager appointed. Administration improved and dividends rose even more rapidly as the navigation benefited from the sustained growth of the regional economy after the 1780s (table 13). Out of a total dividend of £70,000 in 1826 the two largest proprietors, Richard Fountayne Wilson and Sir William Milner – a direct descendant of the leading promoter of the original undertaking – earned £9,322 and £7,843 respectively from their navigation stock.

Table 13 Dividends and toll revenue on the Aire and Calder Navigation, 1794–1826 (£)

			Toll revenue			
Date	Dividends	*Miscel-laneous*[a]	Coal	Corn	Stone and lime-stone	Total
1794–96	32,666	20,950	11,569	6,611	5,305	44,435
1797–99	34,000	21,770	14,520	7,671	4,361	48,322
1800–02	38,000	26,299	18,253	10,522	7,193	62,267
1803–05	43,333	27,060	20,301	8,886	9,001	65,248
1806–08	48,000	24,670	20,721	8,408	9,991	63,790
1809–11	48,000	25,431	22,020	9,641	10,815	67,907
1826[b]	70,000	43,226	27,816	19,849	19,447	116,441

Notes
[a] Wool, cloth, foodstuffs, dyestuffs mainly.
[b] Figures for years after 1816 were accounted on a different system from those for 1775–1816 and are not strictly comparable.
Sources. Average figures from R. G. Wilson, 'The Aire and Calder Navigation', Part III: 'The Navigation in the second half of the eighteenth century', *Bradford Antiquary*, N.S., Part XLIV (1969), table II; Part IV, 'The Navigation in the first half of the nineteenth century', *Bradford Antiquary*, N.S., Part XLV (1971), table 1.

Between 1778 and the 1820s Selby served once again as the port for Leeds, but it soon became apparent that the Selby canal, like the original navigation, had been planned on too diminutive a scale for the growing volume of traffic, while the Ouse port lacked docks and was too far up the river for the growing quantities of south Yorkshire coal exports. To provide a transhipment port as near as possible to the West Riding coalfield and industrial hinterland, the Aire and Calder Navigation built the Knottingley–Goole canal under an Act of 1820 and created the new port of Goole. Once again opponents of the navigation complained against:

the overweening influence of such an opulent body as the Proprietors of the Aire and Calder, who had half a dozen Members of Parliament amongst themselves, and a great influence with the County Members.[15]

Originally designed by Rennie, the Knottingley–Goole canal was built by George Leather and completed in 1826.

39   The Aire and Calder Navigation in Leeds in 1829. Note the seven-storey warehouse at Leeds bridge, built 1827–28

In Leeds itself extensive waterway improvements – particularly dock and warehouse rebuilding – were undertaken in the late 1820s and then, in the face of the prospect of another alternative canal, it was decided to canalise much of the navigation above Castleford. Eventually, after the expenditure of almost £1 million, vessels of 100 tons were able to reach both Wakefield and Leeds. Today many of the wharves and quays above and below Leeds are disused, and business has largely turned its back on the river. How different the scene when the water approach to the town was taken at the zenith of the canal age:

> The principal improvements . . . on this line of water communication . . . render this approach to Leeds worthy of a large metropolis . . . The long vistas of water, wide and straight, bounded by graceful elliptical bridges . . . the lock houses, ornamental buildings, the solid masonry at the sides . . . altogether form a perfect specimen of modern art and excellent taste.[16]

It was fitting that the secretary and manager of the navigation during its great expansionist phase should have been the foremost canal historian of the nineteenth century, Joseph Priestley.

The significance of canals in industrial development can be seen in the contrasting experiences of East Anglia and the West Riding, for by the early nineteenth century there was a marked disparity between the transport systems of the two regions, contributing to the relative failure of one textile manufacturing centre and the more rapid industrial development of the other. Effective waterways helped to reduce the costs of raw materials and the price of manufactured goods, so assisting in the development of the ever-increasing markets that factory production and the application of steam power demanded.[17] Less dramatic in terms of wider markets was the flow of stone, sand, flour, bricks, tiles and other heavy goods in and out of the area, which had considerable impact on the economy of Leeds and its region. Above all, it was the ready transport of fuel supplies that permitted sustained urbanisation. (Fig. 40.)

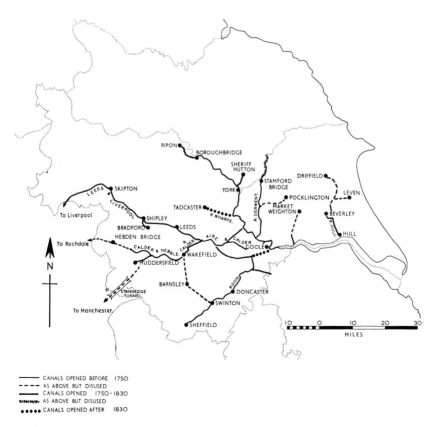

CANALS OPENED BEFORE 1750
AS ABOVE BUT DISUSED
CANALS OPENED 1750–1830
AS ABOVE BUT DISUSED
CANALS OPENED AFTER 1830

40   The Yorkshire waterways in the early nineteenth century (*c.* 1830)

VI   Few towns could have developed so rapidly without continuous supplies of relatively cheap coal, and the tapping of fresh resources was invariably greeted with corporate congratulation. When the first boat freighted with coal from Rothwell Haigh colliery reached Leeds bridge in 1735 it was greeted by an artillery salute; and when the Middleton waggonway was opened in 1758 'the bells were set a ringing, the *Cannons* of our Fort fired, and a gereral joy appeared in every face'.[18] Middleton waggonway has an important place in early railway history, being the first in which the wayleaves acquired by a colliery proprietor were safeguarded by a private Act. A native of Tyneside – cradle of the mineral railway – Charles Brandling, owner of the Middleton estate, had already laid a coal waggonway to waterside staithes at Thwaite Gate for river trade. The Middleton waggonway to a coal staith immediately south of Leeds bridge was specifically built to supply the town with coal, the corporation being guaranteed 23,000 tons per annum at 50·3*d* per ton, a fixed rate with which other local collieries at Beeston, Halton and Rothwell could not easily compete – dependent as they were on packhorse, waggon or river boat and subject to turnpike or navigation tolls. Subsequent Acts increased the tonnage of Middleton coal sold in Leeds and advanced the price to 84*d* per ton. By the end of the eighteenth century the colliery had closed its distant sales in the river valley markets and sent its whole output to the town.[19]

During the French revolutionary and Napoleonic wars several factors encouraged colliery landowners to develop new forms of traction on their waggonways. Fodder prices increased rapidly, and the average price of horses purchased for the Middleton line rose from £14 in 1771-89 to £26 in the early nineteenth century. Increasing road costs contributed to the mounting interest in railway development. In 1807 the rails of the Middleton waggonway were replaced throughout with iron. Five years later the first commercially viable steam locomotives were used at Middleton when John Blenkinsop, the colliery viewer, commissioned Matthew Murray to build rack-and-pinion engines, which proved capable of drawing 110 tons at a speed of $3\frac{1}{2}$ m.p.h. Middleton exerted considerable influence on early railways, often being acknowledged as the first place in England where steam locomotives were used. By the 1830s the absence of further locomotive development – due perhaps to inertia from being first in the field – gave the Middleton locomotives a decidedly antiquated appearance:

> The rail-road and locomotive steam-engines are curious and worthy of observation, being of the earliest manufacture in the country . . . A wheel on one side of the engine works upon a line of cogs, with which the rails on

41   Middleton Colliery railway (1829). (Behind is R. D. Chantrell's Christ Church, then three years old, one of the Million Act churches for workers in the new industrial suburbs mentioned in Chapter IV)

the same side are furnished, so that, though her motion is slow, her purchase is that of the rack and pinion. This crazy, rickety, old engine continues to trundle along day after day at the rate of about five miles an hour, and affords an extraordinary instance, by comparison, of the improvements in machinery that have taken place within the last fifteen or sixteen years.[20]

Advocated by one Leeds merchant as early as 1802, proposals for a Leeds–Selby railway were not taken seriously until the 1820s. Early attempts foundered in the 1825 financial crisis, when only the Liverpool–Manchester scheme survived from major proposals for an east–west (Liverpool–Hull) rail link. By the later 1820s the financial situation had improved and the east–west schemes were revived in Hull, apprehensive of the growing competition from Goole. In 1829 a company was formed to promote a Leeds–Selby railway, with an associated steam packet service to the Humber port. Although George Stephenson had surveyed the Leeds–Selby–Hull line in 1825, there was some criticism of his plans, which were modified by James Walker.

The Bill was opposed by existing carrying interests, but the Aire and Calder Navigation was unable to defend its monopoly position any longer and in Leeds the railway was supported by the principal inhabitants, including Benjamin Gott, John Marshall and Edward

Baines, all of whom were directors of the company. About 50 per cent of the initial share capital (£177,600) was raised in Leeds, where merchants, flax and linen manufacturers, wool staplers and dyers figured prominently – including the Gott family (£10,000) and the Marshall family (£6,000).[21]

At first, lack of capital and an anxiety to see some return on initial outlay drove railway companies to establish termini in the outskirts of towns. In Leeds the siting of the earliest station at Marsh Lane avoided interfering with the wharves and warehouses of the navigation, which was forced to reduce its freight charges almost immediately after the opening of the Leeds–Selby line in 1834. In 1840 the rail route was extended to Hull, but of the initial capital of £340,000 Leeds interests – including the Gotts and the Marshalls – contributed only £17,500. The facility of the east–west route was diminished for some years when George Hudson leased the Leeds–Selby line and, to ensure the interests of his York and North Midland company, compelled passengers to take a roundabout route via Milford junction.

For a time it seemed possible that Leeds might become the hub of Yorkshire's railway system. (Fig. 42.) The grand design for a London–Birmingham–Leeds–Newcastle–Edinburgh line would have linked up the principal centres of industry – hardware, pottery, textiles and coal – but when George Stephenson began construction through the Midlands it was decided to make York and not Leeds the pivot of the north-eastern route. By forming a junction with the North Midland (Derby–Leeds) line at Normanton the York railway interests (among whom George Hudson figured prominently) hoped to gain a central position on the network of lines rapidly developing between London and the north.

The Derby–Leeds line (1837-40) put Leeds into direct communication with the Midlands and London but ventured no further within the outskirts of the town than Hunslet. Dividends on this high-cost line – £40,000 per mile – were low, and the shareholders, ignoring heavy capitalisation, demanded an inquiry in 1842 from which the ubiquitous Hudson emerged once more with the initiative.[22]

Virtually by-passed at Normanton, businessmen in Leeds sought to turn the tables on the York interests by promoting the Leeds–Thirsk line (1845–49), from which it was hoped to tap the main-line traffic to the north. Such plans were largely thwarted by Hudson, who anticipated that a Newcastle–Thirsk–Leeds axis would deprive the York and North Midland and the Great North of England companies of much of their through traffic. It was not until 1854 that an Act recognised the North Eastern Railway, which had emerged from private agreements between the York and North Midland, the Leeds–Thirsk and the York–Newcastle–Berwick companies and was thus able to control almost all the lines of Yorkshire, Durham and Northumberland.[23]

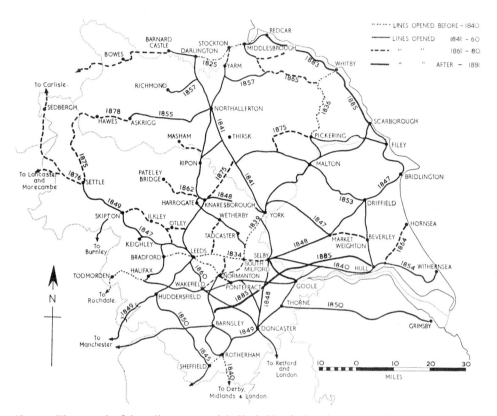

42   The growth of the railway network in Yorkshire during the nineteenth century

Westwards of Leeds the Manchester–Leeds line (1836-41) did not run directly into the town at first but made a junction with the North Midland at Normanton. In 1846 the Hunslet Junction–Leeds (Wellington Street)–Bradford line was opened, a local enterprise promoted by Bradford traders, supported by George Hudson and engineered by George Stephenson. Five years later this company passed into the hands of the Midland Railway, for which Leeds was the main northern centre.

By the mid-nineteenth century railway companies had gained in strength. Their potential was being more fully realised and growing confidence was manifested in efforts to establish termini of a more central character and to connect up lines converging on towns from different quarters. City-centre land was expensive and its value rose even further when the nature of the market became better understood. Solicitors and engineers who devised schemes for the extension of railways and termini within cities could play on the fear of railway companies that a rival might get a more favourable site and cream off the market. Railways were a powerful agent of change in Victorian cities, but the cost of new termini put a crippling burden on the companies, which usually failed to penetrate the heart of the business district but had a marked effect on the inner areas trapped between central commerce and suburban fringe.

The station confusion in Leeds provides an example of the results of the lack of central direction in the most important phase of railway growth. Between 1846 and 1856 railway accommodation was greatly extended by the formation of Wellington Street Station, Central Station and the Great Northern Station, which were on the south side of Wellington Street and from which all passenger trains departed, except those from Marsh Lane. By the early 1860s Wellington Street Station was bursting at the seams in trying to cater for five railway companies (the Midland, the York and North Midland, the London

43   Holbeck Junction (1868). (*Illustrated London News*, 30 May 1868, pp. 532–3)

and North Western, the Leeds Northern, formerly the Leeds and Thirsk, and the Lancashire and Yorkshire, the nucleus of which was the Manchester–Leeds line), a situation that was not alleviated until the opening of Leeds New Station in 1869. Owned jointly by the London and North Western and the North Eastern Railway companies, this station was erected on the 'Dark Arches' over the river Aire. It served the Leeds Extension line (1865-69), which commenced in Holbeck and crossed the city – Briggate, Kirkgate, Duke Street – by a series of viaducts and bridges; then via an embankment, specifically designed not to disturb the graves, through St Peter's church burial ground to Marsh Lane. To satisfy ecclesiastical susceptibilities the 1865 authorisation Act provided for the laying of rails on 'India Rubber'; for the use of semaphore signals instead of whistling, to minimise sacrilegeous noise; and for the replacing of gravestones on the slopes of the embankment.[24]

To some extent the existence of effective waterways, turnpike roads and railways – often paralleled along the same trade routes – allowed the free play of the forces of market competition in order to achieve a pattern of services and charges that would stimulate continued demographic and industrial growth, particularly through

the supply of food, coal and raw materials. Apart from being important direct employers of labour the railways also stimulated a range of associated industries, particularly engineering. During the mid-nineteenth century Hunslet became one of the most concentrated locomotive building centres in the world. The decline of the old trade in cloth could be economically compensated for by the rise of the clothing trade, due partly to the network of radiating railways which helped to transport the new and cheap cloths of shoddy and mungo from the textile districts lying to the west. Railways and industry grew hand-in-hand.

When the steam engine had first taken to the rails it had been expected that other forms of transport would suffer. Dividends on the Aire and Calder Navigation reached a peak in 1825-27 but then declined for the rest of the century. Freight rates on the navigation were greatly reduced – for example, from 7s to 2s 3d a ton on general goods – and the survival of the Aire and Calder as an independent concern offering an alternative mode of carrying bulky goods probably kept rail freight charges down.

Even before the coming of the railways many turnpike trusts centred on Leeds were hopelessly in debt. Despite a degree of overlapping trustee control, and some attempt to adopt a common policy for the different trusts, efforts to appoint a central co-ordinating authority had met with little success. By the 1830s there were forty-six miles of turnpike roads and thirty toll gates within the municipal boundaries which belonged to eighteen different trusts and controlled in all 178 miles of road. Toll gates lingered for another generation after the advent of the railways, although they were cleared from the streets of Leeds itself in pursuance of the 1842 Improvement Act. In 1866 the town's highways passed under municipal control.

By 1830 the railways had scarcely affected the coaching and freight networks. Indeed, the following decade marked the heyday of coaching, with fierce competition between rival companies over times and fares. When change did come, it was often swift in the case of inter-regional routes. In 1835 the Leeds–Selby railway was carrying 3,500 passengers a week during the summer months, compared with 400 who had previously travelled by coach. The opening of major rail links such as Leeds–Derby–Birmingham–London, Leeds–York–Newcastle and Leeds–Manchester rapidly destroyed long-distance coaching. Toll income for stagecoaches on the Leeds–Elland road fell from £369 in 1846 to £73 in 1850. In 1851 the Midland Railway operated excursion trains to the Great Exhibition from Leeds at 5s return fare; not to be outdone, the Great Northern advertised at 4s 6d.[25] No other form of transport could compete with such rates. In the 1840s a growing number of road haulage firms transferred to the railways, and long-distance road freight services gradually faded away. Toll income from common carriers on the Leeds–Elland road fell from £181 in 1846 to £40 in 1850. Yet, far from displacing horses, the railways created new and expanding demands for horse labour.

VII   The growing towns and railheads acted as a focus for the reception and distribution of goods and passengers, with concurrent increases in market and suburban flows. The outward expansion of Leeds stimulated the demand for improved local and feeder transport, but development south of the river placed a severe strain on the bridging facilities. Until the early nineteenth century Leeds bridge, at the foot of Briggate, was the only dry communication between the northern and southern parts of the town; between 1818 and 1870 the Aire was bridged at five other points. Waterloo (Wellington) bridge (1818-19) was built by John Rennie, the eminent civil engineer, at a cost of £7,000, to improve communications with Holbeck, Armley and Wortley. Ten years later two suspension bridges were fixed over the river: Monk bridge, a 'bow and string' construction, was cast at the Bowling Ironworks and built at a cost of £4,800 to improve communication with Holbeck; and a bridge from South Accommodation Road in Hunslet to the south-east of the town was built at a cost of £4,200. The early Victorian years were marked by further bridging works: Victoria bridge (1837-39), which formed the principal means of communication between Leeds and Holbeck, cost £8,000; and Crown Point bridge (1842), cast at Park Ironworks, Sheffield, cost £8,750 and formed a link between Hunslet and the East End of Leeds. Under the Improvement Acts of 1866 and 1869 extensive street rebuilding was authorised, and the corporation was empowered to improve Leeds bridge. Despite the funnelling of much traffic to the other bridges the old crossing was still busy, and it was estimated that 4,000 vehicles and 55,000 foot passengers passed over it each Saturday, the principal market day. The entire cost of replacement (1870-73) was more than £50,000. In 1871 all the bridges were freed from tolls.

Like most other major towns, Leeds had some form of urban passenger transport from at least the early nineteenth century. At first private hackney carriages were used, but fares were high. Short-stage coaches were also used, and a 'neat coach' operated from Bramley, Town Street, to Leeds in the early nineteenth century at 9d per head for the four miles. The horse omnibus was cheaper, and there was a regular service to Marsh Lane Station in 1835:

> from the centre of the town to the station in an omnibus, one of the most prepossessing carriages of that description ... It was a well-finished vehicle, fitted up within side with glazed pink lining, neatly plaited in festoons, a large looking-glass at the end for the benefit of ladies; and, what was better than all, – it was carefully driven.[26]

A regular horse-bus service to Far Headingley was running by 1839, with five return trips daily at a single fare of 6*d*. Soon other services were operating to Chapeltown, Kirkstall and Hunslet, and this initial horse-bus network persisted largely unchanged until the 1860s. Less frequent services operated to Whitkirk, Meanwood, Wortley, Scarcroft and Roundhay, and market buses ran to sizeable villages a few miles out.

The opening of tramways in Liverpool and London in 1869–70 set off a spate of tramway promotions and the boom of the 1870s. Horse tramways were less costly to operate than horse omnibuses because two horses could pull a vehicle twice as large on a smooth rail than on a relatively rough road. In Leeds there is little evidence (apart perhaps from the area around Dewsbury Road) of suburban transport 'pioneering' the development of an area; rather the omnibus and tram networks followed development and catered for a known or carefully calculated demand. Under the Leeds Tramways Order (1871) powers were granted for the construction of five tramway routes. Shortly afterwards, under the Leeds Tramways Act (1872), the requisite powers were transferred to the Leeds Tramways Company, which rapidly developed horse tramway routes to Far Headingley, Chapeltown, Hunslet, Kirkstall and Marsh Lane. This network was supplemented by other horse omnibus routes, while a second Leeds Tramways Act (1877) authorised a new route to Upper Wortley and a branch along Meanwood Road.

Although cheaper than horse omnibuses, the horse trams were still costly to operate, and various attempts were made to develop alternative forms of traction. Steam trams were introduced in Leeds in the 1880s but caused damage to the lines. The breakthrough came with electrification, pioneered in Europe and first exploited on a large scale in the United States. In 1891 an electric tram service was started between Roundhay and Sheepscar, probably the first electrically operated public tramway using the trolly system in England. The Leeds tramways were transferred to the corporation in 1894, and cheaper fares and increased services rapidly followed, so that, by the early twentieth century, corporation trams were running from 4.30 a.m. to 12.30 at night.[27]

The substitution of electric power for horse power led to a big reduction in operating costs and fares. Because of the greater speed of trams, towns could grow outwards along routes which often extended beyond existing built-up areas, enabling more people to migrate to the suburbs. When workmen's cars were introduced in Leeds in 1889 electrification was already being pioneered, and the development of new forms of traction in the 1890s made regular urban travel possible for the working classes. The electric tram began a public transit revolution, with social effects that were perhaps no less significant than the earlier mechanisation of inter-urban transport.

44   Horse tram (n.d.) No. 58 outside the Woodman Hotel in Otley Road, Headingley

NOTES

[1] J. A. Chartres, 'Road carrying in England in the seventeenth century: myth and reality', *Economic History Review*, 2nd ser., XXX (1977), 73.

[2] Bodleian Library, MS Eng. misc. c. 260, Letter Book of a Leeds merchant, 1686–88, signed J[oseph] K[itchingman].

[3] J. Hunter (ed.), *The Diary of Ralph Thoresby*, II (1830), 433.

[4] West Yorkshire Record Office, Quarter Sessions Order Book, E. 179, Pontefract Sessions, April 1658. Carriages in this instance means carts and waggons.

[5] 'The Court Books of the Leeds Corporation, 1662–1705', *Thoresby Soc.*, XXXIV (1936), 63, 65, 67, 93, 101, 118.

[6] R. W. Unwin, 'The Aire and Calder Navigation, Part I: The beginning of the Navigation', *Bradford Antiquary*, N.S., Part XLII (1964), 53–85.

[7] R. W. Unwin, 'The Aire and Calder Navigation, Part II: The Navigation in the Pre-canal Age', *ibid.*, Part XLIII (1967), 151–86.

[8] T. Bradley, *The Old Coaching Days in Yorkshire* (1889), 142–4.

[9] R. G. Wilson, 'Transport dues as indices of economic growth, 1775–1820', *Economic History Review*, 2nd ser., XIX (1966), 110–23.

[10] H. W. Hart, 'Some notes on coach travel, 1750–1848', *Journal of Transport History*, IV (1959), 149.

[11] For the zenith of coaching see G. C. Dickinson, 'Stage-coach services in the West Riding of Yorkshire between 1830 and 1840', *Journal of Transport History*, IV (1959), 1–11.

[12] E. Baines, *History, Directory and Gazetteer of the County of York* (1822).

[13] J. H. Farrington, 'The Leeds and Liverpool Canal: a study in route selection', *Transport History*, III (1970), 52.

[14] Temple Newsam MSS, TN/LA5/1/31, quoted in B. F. Duckham, 'Selby and the Aire and Calder Navigation, 1774–1826', *Journal of Transport History*, VII (1965), 88.

[15] T. Hill, *The Old and New Rates of Tonage [sic] . . . upon the Aire & Calder Navigation from Selby, Weeland and Goole to Leeds and Wakefield* (1826), 4.

[16] Sir G. Head, *A Home Tour through the Manufacturing Districts of England, in the Summer of 1835* (1836), 230–1.

[17] J. K. Edwards, 'Communications and the economic development of Norwich, 1750–1850', *Journal of Transport History*, VII (1965), 98.

[18] *Leeds Intelligencer*, 26 September 1758.

[19] W. G. Rimmer, 'Middleton Colliery, near Leeds (1770–1830)', *Yorkshire Bulletin of Economic and Social Research*, VII, No. I (1955), 41–57; M. J. T. Lewis, *Early Wooden Railways* (1970), 130–1.

[20] Head, *op. cit.*, 170.

[21] D. Brooke, 'The promotion of four Yorkshire railways and the share capital market', *Transport History*, V (1972), 246.

[22] M. Robbins, 'The North Midland Railway and its engineers, 1842–43', *Journal of Transport History*, IV (1959), 180. Normanton Station (1841) was designed as the junction for three companies: the York and North Midland, the North Midland, and the Manchester and Leeds. M. J. Minett, 'The railway stations of George Townsend Andrews', *Journal of Transport History*, VII (1965), 44.

[23] D. Brooke, 'Railway consolidation and competition in north-east England, 1854–80', *Transport History*, V (1972), 5.

[24] W. W. Tomlinson, *The North Eastern Railway* (1914), 634–5.

[25] D. Joy, *A Regional History of the Railways of Great Britain*, VIII, *South and West Yorkshire* (1975), 44.

[26] Head, *op. cit.*, 202.

[27] G. C. Dickinson, 'The development of suburban road passenger transport in Leeds, 1840–95', *Journal of Transport History*, IV (1959), 214–23.

BIBLIOGRAPHICAL NOTE

Waterways. C. Hadfield, *The Canals of Yorkshire and North East England* (2 vols, 1973), has continued the tradition of J. Priestley, *Historical Account of the Navigable Rivers, Canals and Railways* (1831, repr. 1967), in tracing the history of individual waterways, and commences with the Aire and Calder Navigation. In addition to collating the published material which has appeared over the past generation, the histories of some undertakings not previously written up are provided. For the Leeds and Liverpool Canal, C. Hadfield and G. Biddle, *The Canals of North West England* (2 vols., 1970) provide detailed information. The Ouse and Humber have been written up by B. F. Duckham, *The Yorkshire Ouse* (1967), a scholarly account of the inland and estuarine waterways which for many centuries provided an outlet for the West Riding and the Vale of York. In *The Company Town of Goole* (1969), J. D. Porteus has written of the origins and early development of the Aire and Calder port on the Ouse.

Roads. Two general books will prove useful. In *The Turnpike Road System in England, 1663–1840* (1972) W. Albert demonstrated that turnpikes were not built haphazardly but in an economically rational manner, radiating at first from London. E. Pawson, *Transport and Economy: the Turnpike Roads of Eighteenth Century Britain* (1977) attempts to explore the relationship between transport and economic growth during the industrial revolution. The individual turnpikes centred on Leeds have not been fully written up in the manner of W. B. Crump, *Huddersfield Highways Down the Ages* (Tolson Museum Handbook No. 12, 1949, repr. 1968), and the original manuscript material is located at the West Yorkshire Record Office and in the John Goodchild Collection at Wakefield Metropolitan District Library. Coaching in Leeds and the turnpike riots are included in another reprinted work, T. Bradley, *The Old Coaching Days in Yorkshire* (1889), but the numerous drawings of the author provide a Dickensian – if over-roseate – view of coaching life. For the changing pattern of services the commercial directories, beginning with *Universal British Directory* (1792–95), can be used, but a compilation for one year has been made by A. Bates, *Directory of Stage Coach Services 1836* (1969). Urban transport in more recent times is the theme of A. Young, *One Hundred Years of Leeds Tramways* (1970), which, besides details of vehicles and routes, has a useful tramways map.

Railways. The most useful recent work, which is particularly helpful on Leeds stations, is D. Joy, *A Regional History of the Railways of Great Britain*, VIII, *South and West Yorkshire* (1975). For individual companies and amalgamations, W. W. Tomlinson, *The North Eastern Railway: its Rise and Development* (1914, repr. 1967), should be consulted; and J. Marshall has written up *The Lancashire and Yorkshire Railway*, the financial accounts of which have been used in S. Broadbridge, *Studies in Railway Expansion and the Capital Market in England, 1825–73* (1970). There has been a dearth of studies of locomotive workshops, but *The Railway Foundry, Leeds, 1839–1969* by R. Redman is a sumptuously produced account of the progress and products of a firm of which the town had every right to be proud.

E. J. CONNELL
M. WARD

Industrial development, 1780–1914

VI

Leeds will be a Town of Trade and Commerce as Long as the River and Coals Last.[1]

We may have some cause to doubt now the accuracy of an anonymous advertiser in the *Leeds Mercury* of 1783, but the diversity and pace of development of the town's manufacturing industries in the nineteenth century bore out this optimistic prognosis. Cloth and yarn, steam engines and railway locomotives, caps and clothing, glass and pottery, all kinds of machinery – for these products and many more Leeds at one time enjoyed a national and even international reputation. To understand why, we should have to seek an explanation in the basic natural advantages of local coal and other minerals, a good location, and the skills and enterprise of those entrepreneurs who weathered financial crisis to amass (sometimes) considerable fortunes – men like Benjamin Gott and John Marshall, early textile pioneers, James Kitson and James Fowler, engineers, or John Barran and Montague Burton, two of the leading names in the clothing industry.

This chapter aims to give an impression of the course of industrial development during a critical phase in the evolution of Leeds, at a time when manufacturing industry was the principal driving force in the economy. It is divided chronologically into two sections, 1780-1850 and 1850-1914.

Throughout the late eighteenth and nineteenth centuries the town's prosperity rested firmly on a foundation of textiles, never more so than during the first phase of the industrial revolution, which may be said to have lasted roughly to 1850. 'The trade of woollen cloth,' it was said in 1816, 'has raised Leeds to its present consequence.'[2] To which we might add the output of flax yarn and of worsted cloth, as well as a significant trade in carpets, linen and even cotton yarn. Founding and engineering also emerged as major industries in the first half of the nineteenth century but are more associated with a second phase of development which lasted from the middle of the nineteenth century to the eve of the Great War. Though in terms of employment engineering never became the leading sector of manufacturing until after 1914, in terms of value of output and as an economic base for the borough its importance was second to none in the second half of the period under consideration.

By 1914 Leeds could boast of its 'enormous variety of industries . . . which furnish a unique stability to its trade'.[3] Quite how this complex of industries emerged is easier to describe than to explain. Why Leeds and not, say, Wakefield should have grown to become the chief industrial and commercial centre of the West Riding cannot be said with certainty. Undoubtedly both the river and coal played their part, as did the fact that other raw materials were either close at hand or brought to the town at relatively low cost by a developing transport network. Such advantages were repeatedly emphasised by contemporary writers. 'We are,' wrote one observer in 1858,

> close to valuable beds of limestone, an open valley, a navigable river, canals accommodating vessels of 120 tons, and communicating with the Mersey at Liverpool, the Ouse at Goole, and thence with the Humber . . . and railways branching off in every direction . . . These advantages give every possible facility for bringing raw materials, sending away manufactured goods, and for the access of men of business.[4]

He might also have mentioned the abundance of the local water supply, most of it relatively soft, a factor of considerable benefit to the textile industries.

The Aire was rendered navigable downstream to Goole and the Humber by improvements commenced in 1699, whilst to the west the Leeds–Liverpool canal was completed by 1816. The railway came in 1834, the line from Selby (linked via the river Ouse with the port of Hull) terminating in Marsh Lane, slightly to the east of the town. Much of the local traffic, however, consisted of carts and pack animals which followed the turnpikes and other roads and tracks that radiated from Leeds.

Both waterways and railways (including the pioneering line linking the Middleton collieries with the town) were instrumental in bringing large quantities of Yorkshire coal to fuel the boilers and furnaces of the Leeds factories. 'The neighbourhood,' Langdale wrote in 1822, 'abounds with coal, the very soul of steam engines,' whilst thirteen years later Sir George Head reckoned that 'in no manufacturing town in England . . . is more coal consumed, in proportion to its extent, than in Leeds'.[5]

Carboniferous coal measures underlie most of the borough, and coal has been worked in the district since Roman times. It acquired its greatest importance after 1780, when new sources of power were introduced in the textile industries and there was a burgeoning demand from the fires and furnaces of the dyers and metalworkers. The agreement negotiated between the mayor and corporation of Leeds and the proprietors of the Middleton collieries in 1758, renewed at intervals until the 1820s, guaranteed the supply at moderate price levels, and consumption grew steadily to around 300,000 tons per annum by 1830.[6] John Marshall, greatest of the flax spinners, considered that manufacturing prosperity rested upon security of property, good machinery, and a plentiful supply of cheap coal, and certainly the Yorkshire coal industry responded to the rise in demand. Output doubled between 1830 and 1850, and by 1877 the Leeds area contained 102 collieries together producing $2\frac{1}{2}$ million tons of coal. Within the borough there were pits to the east along the York road and in the southern out-townships, and by 1911, around which time production reached a maximum, there were almost 5,000 miners recorded in the census.[7]

If coal and transport were the cornerstones of the town's success as an industrial centre in the nineteenth century, due credit must also be given to its inhabitants, who comprised the entrepreneurial skill and labour force. Fertile soil means but little without skilled farmers, and such basic advantages as Leeds possessed played a primarily passive role. The story of the industrial revolution owes much to the men of vision and enterprise who risked capital in the pursuit of profit and wealth.

I   The industrial revolution in Leeds, however, began with a man of endless enterprise but apparently limited vision. Richard Paley, soap boiler, ironfounder, potash manufacturer, textile manufacturer and property developer, introduced the modern factory to the borough by erecting two cotton mills at the Bank, in the eastern part of the in-township, in 1790. The story of Paley, his financial adventures and ultimate bankruptcy, has been related elsewhere,[8] and it will suffice to note that he it was who introduced the cotton industry and the steam engine as a source of motive power to Leeds. Steam engines had previously been installed in other works, for example at Pym Nevins's Larchfield Mills, but were used merely to pump water back up to waterwheels. Paley's engine, which was built for him by Sturges and

Co. of Bradford – another firm in which he was a partner – supplied power direct, if inefficiently, to the spinning machinery, a development which became more widespread after the introduction of Watt's rotary engines.[9]

Others attempted to emulate the success of Paley and his Lancashire counterparts, and by 1800 Leeds formed a minor outpost of the cotton industry, with perhaps ten factories employing around 2,000 workers. As the traditional centre of the woollen industry it may be that Leeds felt a little ill at ease with the less familiar cotton, however. In any case, cotton spinning soon declined as attention turned to the woollen industry, and by 1810 the former had all but disappeared from the borough. Some cotton concerns went bankrupt, but others displayed that adaptability which was characteristic of Leeds manufacturing throughout the nineteenth century by turning to other activities. Gowland and Clark, an odd alliance of a Whitby sea captain and a Leeds ropemaker, developed the scribbling side of their business, for instance.[10]

The overriding feature of Leeds industry up to the middle of the nineteenth century was the dominance of textiles, notably the manufacture and finishing of woollen cloth. As the leading sector of the borough's economy, textiles dictated the course and pace of industrial change and were the principal focus of innovation. Engineering and many other trades which expanded in the early part of the century looked principally to textiles for their market, and expansion in the woollen and flax industries attracted an expanding workforce whose everyday needs were met by the introduction and expansion of other trades. For instance, an increase in the workforce of the textile mills of, say, 1,000 would draw in perhaps 3,000 new inhabitants, a large enough market for perhaps one new corn mill, or ten new tailors. In this way industry became more diversified, and change was both causative and cumulative, but trade and the general level of prosperity depended squarely upon the situation in textiles.

By the middle of the eighteenth century it was becoming increasingly clear that as a centre of cloth-making Leeds in-township was losing out on account of its higher rents and labour costs. Most of the twenty-six stages in cloth-making were undertaken in the out-townships and outside the borough, which remained, however, the centre of marketing and finishing and dyeing. The development of the factory woollen industry, initially focused upon Leeds, temporarily reversed this decline, at a time when demand for Yorkshire cloths was reaching new heights. Output of the coarser narrow cloths and the higher-quality broadcloths (superfines) in the West Riding doubled between 1770 and 1790 in response to a buoyant export market, rising prosperity at home, and the military demand occasioned by the French wars. Up to 1792 expansion in demand was maintained by expanding the workforce and some improvements to the machinery employed. Water provided power for some stages of manufacture, fulling for example, but in the main cloth remained a handicraft industry. Cloth produced outside Leeds was marketed in the town, where the merchants also concerned themselves with the dyeing and finishing processes. Finishing shops and dyehouses were not uncommonly attached to the substantial residences of the merchants, frequently located on the fringes of the town. In his 'capital mansion house, with gardens and stabling, and warehouses and dressing shops attached'[11] the merchant enjoyed a comfortable existence.

A conservative group in the main, certain of their number nevertheless reacted to the challenge of an expanding market in a very positive fashion, a fashion which to the clothworkers represented a distinct threat:

> Some merchants have commenced in the Erection of immense Buildings in which all the Machinery and Contrivances they [i.e. the clothiers] have invented for facilitating Labour, are consolidated and connected in such a Manner, and in such Quantities, as to be worked by a much less number of Hands, for the sole Advantage of the Merchants, some Individuals of whom are likely to sequester at Once the Profits of Two or Three Hundred Master Clothiers and their Families.[12]

The first step in this direction was taken by Benjamin Gott, the youngest partner in the mercantile house of Wormald Fountain and Gott of Park Row. To meet the rising demand for blankets and army cloths Gott constructed a large complex of factory buildings, later known as Park Mills, on sixteen acres of land to the west of Leeds purchased from the owners of the Drony Laith estate. From the outset this project was conceived on a scale hitherto unknown in the woollen industry – 1,200 workers performing all the processes of cloth manufacture and turning out 4,000 broadcloths a year by 1797.[13]

Despite the undoubted success of the enterprise Gott had few imitators. Other merchant houses which entered the field of manufacturing and erected factories were J. and E. Brooke, Pym Nevins, and Fisher Nixon and Co., and by 1805 there were said to be five factories in the borough, together responsible for 6 per cent of all the cloths produced in Leeds. The precise number may in fact be disputed, since there was no agreement as to what constituted a factory. One contemporary definition was a place where 'perhaps two hundred hands in one building' toiled, 'under the immediate surveillance and superintendence' of their masters.[14] Certainly the advent of the factory in the Leeds woollen industry was the manifestation of organisational change rather than technological progress, and it was this against which the domestic clothiers protested:

> And whereas the Trade of Merchant or Dealer in Cloth hath hereto before been carried on separately and distinctly from the Trade of Maker of Cloth, but of late years sundry Merchants and dealers in Cloth, possessing large Capitals, have established extensive manufactories of Woollen Cloth, intending to manufacture Cloth therein . . .[15]

Though the woollen manufacturers were amongst the first to install steam engines in their mills in Leeds, until the 1820s most processes continued to be performed by hand. Moreover the domestic branch of the industry also adopted new machinery and applied power wherever possible. The distinction between the domestic and factory branches of the industry was primarily in terms of organisation. Nor should it be assumed that their courses ran entirely separately. Gott, like many other manufacturers, continued to buy from the clothiers in the Leeds cloth halls, whilst the development of factory machine spinning after 1820 was primarily to serve the domestic weaving industry.

45   Benjamin Gott's Bean Ing Mills, Wellington Street: front wing, *c.* 1826. Probably the first integrated woollen mill, combining steam-powered spinning and hand-loom weaving with other processes in the one plant. Note the bell

That so few factories were established in the years 1800 to 1815 may be attributed to the shortage of capital and more restricted demand of the home market in a period of war. Upon the cessation of hostilities several new factories sprang up in Leeds, but even in 1822 domestic output was of much greater significance than factory production in the West Riding woollen industry. Baines devoted the main part of a brief account of the industry to domestic production:

> The first stages of the manufacture are carried on in the villages and hamlets of the surrounding country, where the wool goes through the respective operations of spinning, weaving, and finishing,

mentioning factory production only as an afterthought:

> Of late years, however, manufactories of cloth have been established on a larger scale, and the use of machinery has much increased.[16]

In another, less well established branch of textiles factory-based production was the norm from the very beginning. In spite of the spinning mills of the Knaresborough area and some linen-weaving in the Leeds and Barnsley areas, the flax industry may be regarded as a new introduction to Leeds in the 1790s. Ure was later to observe that 'the energy of two or three capitalists will sometimes determine the rise of a manufacture round their residence though apparently not the most congenial soil for its growth'[17] and perhaps nowhere is this more true than for the Leeds flax industry. Without John Marshall, son of a Briggate linen draper, Leeds might never have become the premier centre of the British flax industry in the first half of the nineteenth century. After a brief period of experimentation at an isolated water mill at Adel, where he was aided by that most able engineer Matthew Murray, Marshall sank his capital into an enormous factory in Holbeck, equipping it with the machinery he and Murray had developed and a twenty-horse engine from Boulton and Watt. Upwards of a thousand workers were engaged, and production started in 1792.[18] Once the success of this venture was proved other new mills were established, many of them – Benyon's in Holbeck, for example – by former partners and employees of Marshall.

Leeds flax factories benefited from easy access to both locally grown and imported Baltic flax, landed at Hull and shipped via the Aire and Calder Navigation, and from cheap coal. The number of mills rose to nineteen by 1821 and to thirty-seven by 1855, the trade dominated from the outset by a small number of very large concerns.[19] A clear distinction may be made between a handful of factories, each employing more than 500 hands and housing by 1842 more than 10,000 spindles, and the large number of small businesses which frequently survived through hire spinning.[20] In times of industrial prosperity the capacity of the latter was much in demand, but lack of

46   Marshall's flax mills. The two earliest mills were demolished about a century ago. Mills C (1817), D (1826) and E (1830) still stand. (From the Leeds Chamber of Commerce *Directory*, 1910)

      Marshall's Temple Mill and offices, 1840–43, designed by Ignatius Bonomi, represent the zenith of the flax trade in Leeds. By 1886 the mill was a clothing works. The People's Flour Mill (fig. 54) stood on the opposite side of Marshall Street

47   until 1979

capital often proved fatal when times were hard. In the depression of the late 1830s eighteen firms, one in three in the Leeds flax trade, foundered.

At its peak in the 1850s the town's flax industry employed 9,500 workers, many of them children, the majority female and Irish, and accounted for a tenth of the gross output of British flax mills. Marshall's alone consumed 10 per cent of the country's total import of raw flax at one stage, an estimated 50,000 acres of land being needed to maintain their supply of raw material.[21]

Yet at no stage was flax able to challenge the supremacy of the woollen industry in Leeds. In 1851 there were twice the number of woollen and worsted workers as in flax, and Leeds remained the principal centre for the dyeing, finishing and marketing of cloth until at least the middle of the century. As we have already noted, progress in factory cloth production after the initial impetus in the 1790s was slow, for a variety of reasons. The poor state of trade ensured that few new mills were constructed before 1815, and despite a brief burst of activity in that year the main development did not take place until the mid–1820s. By then the technical difficulties inherent in spinning wool, a relatively weak fibre, at speed were being overcome, and organised opposition to machine finishing was waning. In 1825, when money was cheaper and trade prospects were bright, woollen mills sprang up all over Leeds, though particularly in the west. 'Spring Gardens and North Hall were but a short time ago in the country,' a contemporary account commented; 'the scene is now completely changed. Large dyehouses and immense factories line the northern side of the river.'[22]

The quantity of steam power employed expanded accordingly. Lindley's survey of 1824 revealed a total of 739 h.p. at work in Leeds woollen mills. By 1830 the figure had risen to 1,884 h.p., reaching 2,265 h.p. in 1838, a striking advance even if some allowance is made for possible inaccuracies.[23] The actual output of cloth must have risen at an even swifter rate, since this period witnessed advances in both the efficiency of steam engines and the productive capabilities of the textile machines. The substitution of mules for jennies, for example, enhanced spinning productivity fivefold.

Two features of the woollen industry deserve special attention. First, like other towns of west Yorkshire, Leeds specialised in certain types of cloth and certain branches of manufacture. It was justly renowned for its fine-quality broadcloths and was the principal centre for dyeing and finishing, and cloth marketing. The second feature is that right up to the 1840s many workers in the woollen industry continued to be employed on a domestic basis. Though Leeds had a number of fully integrated mills, after the pattern of Gott's factories, the specialist scribbler and slubber or cloth finisher were more characteristic until the middle of the century.[24] Wool was commonly prepared and spun in Leeds, the yarn then sent out of the town to country clothiers, the woven cloth being returned for dyeing and finishing. The domestic and factory systems were thus complementary rather than opposed, and although many mills incorporated extensive weaving rooms their owners often continued to buy and market cloths from the surrounding countryside. Gradually, however, production, particularly of woollen cloth, became more centralised, and by 1850 the independent dyers and finishers were looking more to the worsted stuff trade for their business. Though Bradford was the undisputed capital of the worsted industry, Leeds had a useful interest in stuff dyeing and finishing. Such locational specialisation was probably born more out of behavioural conservatism than hard economic fact, as is illustrated by the almost wholesale desertion of Leeds for Bradford by the worsted yarn spinners and stuff weavers in the 1840s and 1850s, 'on a sudden panic, during which they supposed that Bradford was about to absorb the whole stuff trade'.[25] Leeds in fact had at one time formed a minor centre of the worsted industry, with more than 2,000 factory workers in 1838 and perhaps 1,000 stuff weavers operating from their cottages on an outwork basis.

A handful of carpet factories, a solitary silk mill and a little cotton spinning complete the picture of Leeds as one of the country's foremost centres for the production of textiles throughout the first half of the nineteenth century. In a period when industrial growth was the basis of urban growth, textiles lay at the heart of the town's industrial economy, accounting for one in three of the workforce in 1851, one in two of every worker in manufacturing. The textile mills and dyehouses required 4,500 h.p. to drive their machinery in 1858, more than for all the remaining industries put together.[26]

Such a well developed textile industry generated a demand not only for coal, labour and transport but also for machinery and utensils, bricks, wood and iron. 'The necessities of the woollen trade involving the replacement of hand labour by machinery may be said to be the foundation of the Engineering business now carried on at Leeds,' the chamber of commerce stated in 1910.[27] Beginning with steam engines, hackles and gills, combs, gears and slays, and many other machines and utensils for work in the flax and woollen mills, produced originally in small workshops, the industry graduated to machine tools, locomotives, cranes, boilers, and a whole host of products. The beginnings of large-scale organisation and new methods of production could be discerned as early as 1795, when Matthew

48   (*Right*) Croft Street mill – typical of the 1830s, brick-built, fireproof, with cast iron girders, columns and window frames and 'Yorkshire' sash windows on the third floor

Whitechapel Yard, the first Congregational chapel in Leeds (1758), had become a small tannery
49   by 1817 with four tan pits in the yard outside

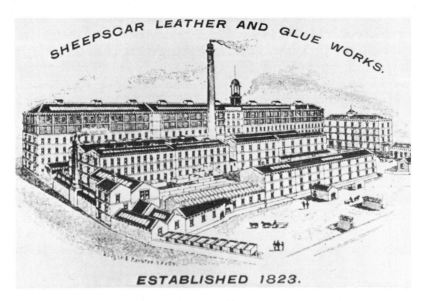

50   Charles F. Stead began tanning in 1823 and is still in business, but this view is now unusual, since Scott Hall Road runs at the rear of the site. (From the Leeds Chamber of Commerce *Directory*, 1910)

Murray, the father of Leeds engineering, left the employ of John Marshall to set up in business on an adjacent site in Water Lane. Fenton Murray and Wood's Round Foundry was immediately to the east of Marshall's mills, whilst immediately to the west Taylor Wordsworth and Co. also commenced as machine makers, one year later than Murray. Both companies specialised in textile machinery, as did two other prominent engineers who both started in the early nineteenth century – Samuel Lawson of Hope Foundry (1812), the inventor of the screwgill, and Peter Fairbairn of the Wellington Foundry (1826).

Initially the manufacture of machinery was a skilled handicraft. Machines were constructed from wood and cast iron, usually on a commission basis for the millwrights whose function it was to equip and maintain mill machinery. Early machines had almost as much wood as iron, and in addition to its foundries and machine shops Leeds housed sawmills and wood-turners, their workshops scattered throughout the industrial quarters. Engineering premises were generally small, harbouring a single master and a handful of journeymen and apprentices. Power was rarely employed, except in larger concerns such as Fenton Murray and Wood, which managed to find work for 120 hands even in 1806. Lindley's survey of 1824 showed that, whereas 110 of the 129 steam engines then installed in Leeds workshops and factories had been constructed by Leeds firms (two-thirds of them by Fenton and Co.), the machine makers together employed only 107 h.p., a fraction of the power used in textile mills.[28]

Many of the engineering firms prospered on the ingenuity of their owners. Fairbairn as well as Murray worked in close conjunction with John Marshall, and Samuel Lawson was responsible for a string of patents for flax machinery in the 1820s and 1830s. Murray inaugurated the construction of locomotives in Leeds, an activity carried on by the Hunslet Engine Company, which formed a major nucleus of engine-building throughout the nineteenth century. The specialisation in textile machinery remained a feature during the whole of this period, but the range and variety of products were being extended all the time. Markets widened and employment grew, and by 1851 one in twelve males found employment in metalworking and engineering; in 1858 there were 4,140 boilermakers and engineers, 2,630 making flax and tow machinery, and 2,250 in the manufacture of iron.[29]

Growth in textiles gave impetus to other trades besides that of machine-making, certain of which emerged as industries of national importance. The modern leather industry in Leeds began with the erection of a tannery in Kirkstall Road by James Rhodes and Richard

Nickol in 1828. What was a 'small-scale neighbourhood trade' at the beginning of the nineteenth century became by 1870 the leading centre for the production of sheepskins and the second centre for the tanning of hides.[30] Favourable conditions for the leather industry were provided by the institution of the South Market Leather Fair in 1827, the increase in slaughtering in an expanding town, improvements in transport, and the use of new tanning agents. Rhodes and Nickol replaced traditional oak bark with gambier and shumac, a development which speeded up the tanning process considerably. The abolition in 1835 of the duty on English leather gave further encouragement to the industry, and by mid-century there were a dozen or so quite extensive tanneries and skinworks, many of them in the Buslingthorpe neighbourhood.

The leather industry serves as a good example of the complexity of inter-industry associations which characterised manufacturing in Leeds throughout the nineteenth century. The principal raw materials were cattle and horse hides, calfskins and sheepskins, obtained in large measure from the town's slaughterhouses. Besides gambier and shumac and other tanning agents, cod oil, acid, lime, various dyewares, sometimes even shredded rabbit skins and dog dung were also required! By-products of the trade included refuse hair, used in the manufacture of cheap carpets and blankets, and scrapings for the glue industry, whilst the spent lime and solids from the tanpits were sold to local farmers for manure. In all some 20,000 people were said to depend directly or indirectly upon the trade by the 1860s, including perhaps the queues of small boys who lined up outside the works each morning with their bucketfuls of street dung.[31]

The chemical industry served not only the woollen industry and other textiles but also the glassmakers of Hunslet and later the leather industry. One of the major products was vitriol (sulphuric acid), of which there were twenty producers in Leeds by 1826. This was combined with salt to make soda, an important industrial material of particular use to soap and glass makers. The soap was used principally by the woollen industry, which in turn yielded lanolin and other greases which were used as lubricants. Glycerine, a by-product of soap making, was used in the production of explosives, and thus were the linkages extended.

Finally mention must be made of the dyestuffs trade. Before the development of synthetic dyes in the second half of the century the production of dyestuffs was a separate trade from the chemical industry, although there were many points of contact. Copperas, for example, was manufactured at several works in Hunslet from iron pyrites extracted from local mines. As well as its use as a dye copperas went into the production of vitriol, which was reacted with magnesian limestone from to the east of Leeds to form Epsom Salts and Venetian Red, a paint pigment and a starter for Prussian Blue dye. The Epsom Salts were used as a mordant in dyeing. For the main part the sources of the dyewares were natural products, principally indigo (blue), cochineal (red) and a range of lichens and logwoods. Lichens were macerated with ammonia to yield a colour range from blue to red, whilst the rasping and chipping of logwoods was a common activity in various small water mills.

After mid-century such industries altered considerably in character. Technological progress and organisational change extended the industrial revolution into new sectors of activity, and the basis of the Leeds economy broadened out from its narrow dependence upon textiles and allied industries.

II   Between 1851 and 1911 the importance of manufacturing to Leeds declined slightly; the proportion of the workforce engaged in manufacturing falling from 74 to 68 per cent. At the same time the structural composition of the workforce changed remarkably. (Table 14.) The staple trades of 1850, cloth and flax, suffered decline, and in the latter case almost total eclipse. They were replaced by expansion in engineering, leather and chemicals, and by the emergence of three new industries – clothing, footwear and printing. The result was that by 1914 Leeds had a much more diverse economy, with the dress trades and engineering dominant.

Decline in textiles was occasioned by a precipitous fall in the numbers employed in flax spinning, and by a shift in the location of cloth and worsted production away from Leeds. The woollen industry reached a stationary position by the late 1870s, and despite demonstrating flexibility and a praiseworthy ability to adapt its production to market demand Leeds was only fourth by size of workforce in importance among the towns of the West Riding by 1901.[32] In 1859 the principal products were broadcloths and fancy woollens and coatings, but by 1914 these had been supplanted by suitings and serges (for the clothing trade), union cloths (with cotton warps) and shoddy cloth.[33] Worsted spinning deserted Leeds for Bradford in the wake of the stuff trade in the mid-1850s but revived again towards the end of the century when changing demand favoured the production of worsted coatings. Employment in woollen and worsted fell slightly in the second half of the century, as did the number of mills (a response to greater integration as much as anything else), but output expanded. According to one source, there were 102

Table 14 Occupational structure of Leeds, 1841–1911

	1841	%	1851	%	1861	%
I Agriculture	1,543		2,247		2,650	
Ib Animals	22	2·6	66	2·8	79	2·8
II Fishing...........................	3		1		1	
III Mines and quarries.............	1,082	1·8	1,798	2·1	3,439	3·5
IV Bricks, glass and pottery	885	1·5	1,281	1·5	1,630	1·6
Total I–IV.........................	3,535	5·9	5,393	6·4	7,799	7·9
V Chemicals and oils	347	0·6	748	0·9	927	0·9
VI Engineering	3,741	6·3	7,415	8·8	12,208	12·4
VII Precious metals	111	0·2	190	0·2	299	0·3
VIII Textiles	22,625	37·8	28,889	34·4	28,311	28·7
IX Skins and leather	615	1·0	1,023	1·2	1,767	1·8
X Dress............................	4,995	8·3	9,184	11·0	9,822	10·0
XI Food, drink, tobacco and lodging	2,545	4·2	4,727	5·7	5,752	5·8
XII Woodworking	968	1·6	1,546	1·9	2,078	2·1
XIII Paper, books and printing	572	1·0	783	0·9	1,222	1·2
XIV Building........................	3,148	5·3	4,179	5·0	5,665	5·8
Total V–XIV	39,667	66·3	58,680	70·0	68,051	69·0
XV Gas, water, electricity and sanitary	34	0·1	158	0·2	310	0·3
XVI Transport......................	1,756	2·9	3,483	4·1	3,910	4·0
XVII Commerce	1,073	1·8	806	1·0	1,578	1·6
XVIII Government (local and national)..........	238	0·4	369	0·4	466	0·5
XIX Defence	370	0·6	559	0·7	418	0·4
XX Professional	1,049	1·8	1,966	2·3	2,454	2·5
XXI Domestic and other service ...	6,229	10·4	7,347	8·8	9,214	9·3
Total XV–XXI	10,749	18·0	14,688	17·5	18,350	18·6
Total I–XXI	53,951	—	78,761	—	94,200	—
XXII Others occupied	5,833	9·8	5,128	6·1	4,407	4·5
Total I–XXII.....................	59,784	100	83,889	100	98,607	100
XXIII Unoccupied..................	91,842	—	87,918	—	108,783	
Total I–XXIII	151,626	—	171,807	—	207,390	—

factories in 1855 containing 118,637 spindles; by 1904 the number of factories had fallen to 74, but spindles were up to almost 150,000.[34] Most of the mills were located in the out-townships to the south, though offices ('counting houses') and warehouses were frequently maintained in the Park Square–East Parade area.

Leeds remained a centre of finishing and dyeing, but competition from elsewhere and the increasing tendency for the large, integrated mills to undertake their own dyeing and finishing forced the survivors to associate. The cloth finishers formed the Leeds Dyers' and Finishers' Association (1900), whilst the shift in the worsted trade was indicated by the number of Leeds firms who joined the Bradford Dyers' Association (1898). In general the dyers did not adapt well to an age of synthetic dyes and German competition. Indeed, other Leeds industries were also facing up to the fact that they were not the sole producers on the world market, and, coupled with the effects of the

[over 20] 1871	%	1881	%	1891	%	1901	%	1911	%
1,789		1,801		2,068		1,675		1,838	
86	2·1	110	1·4	75	1·3	—	0·9	—	0·8
4		1		4		1		—	
2,764	3·0	4,063	3·0	3,210	1·9	3,829	1·9	4,897	2·3
1,294	1·4	2,053	1·5	2,482	1·4	3,507	1·8	3,244	1·5
5,937	6·5	8,028	5·9	7,839	4·6	9,012	4·6	9,979	4·6
944	1·0	938	0·7	1,578	0·9	2,024	1·0	2,545	1·2
13,082	14·4	18,149	13·4	21,558	12·7	28,090	14·2	33,156	15·2
367	0·4	565	0·4	806	0·5	1,149	0·6	1,430	0·7
17,506	19·3	22,786	16·9	22,313	13·2	18,330	9·3	20,257	9·3
2,339	2·6	3,400	2·5	3,874	2·3	3,778	1·9	3,846	1·8
9,315	10·2	16,790	12·4	30,172	17·8	34,612	17·5	39,721	18·3
6,439	7·1	8,122	6·0	10,608	6·3	13,765	6·9	16,609	7·6
1,957	2·2	2,638	2·0	3,063	1·8	4,117	2·1	4,501	2·1
1,196	1·3	2,639	2·0	4,484	2·6	6,715	3·4	8,131	3·7
6,768	7·4	9,138	6·7	10,525	6·2	14,725	7·4	10,189	4·7
59,915	65·9	85,165	63·0	108,981	64·3	127,305	64·3	140,385	64·6
487	0·5	618	0·5	1,009	0·6	1,755	0·9	2,025	0·9
4,782	5·3	8,108	6·0	11,400	6·7	16,102	8·1	17,083	7·9
1,746	1·9	4,719	3·5	6,287	3·7	9,088	4·6	12,215	5·6
636	0·7	961	0·7	1,317	0·8	1,891	0·9	3,204	1·5
509	0·6	534	0·4	297	0·2	519	0·3	398	0·2
2,494	2·7	4,258	3·1	5,580	3·3	6,676	3·4	7,765	3·6
8,369	9·2	13,575	10·1	14,820	8·7	15,452	7·8	15,250	7·0
19,023	20·9	32,773	24·3	40,710	24·0	51,483	26·0	57,940	26·7
84,875	—	125,966	—	157,530	—	187,800	—	208,304	—
6,077	6·7	9,212	6·8	12,011	7·1	10,046	5·1	8,944	4·1
90,952	100	135,178	100	169,541	100	197,846	100	217,248	100
49,211	—	174,657	—	196,588	—	230,898	—	228,543	
140,163	—	309,835	—	366,129	—	428,744	—	445,791	—
+119,053	—								
under 20									
259,216	—								

Source. W. G. Rimmer, 'Occupations in Leeds, 1841–1951', *Thoresby Soc.*, L (1967), 158–78. Reproduced by courtesy of the society.

'Great Depression', the period 1870–90 was a difficult time. Many of the great names in textiles disappeared from Leeds. Gott and Sons closed down in 1870, whilst Marshall and Co. transferred their business to New England.

Fortunately there were new names waiting in the wings, and by the beginning of the twentieth century firms such as Nussey's and Lupton and Co. were the leaders of a revived cloth industry which by 1913 was said to be in a 'healthy state'.[35] With a labour force trimmed to 20,000 by 1911 and new machinery, output at the turn of the century was probably about 50 per cent up on 1850, though it must be remembered that national output rose even more rapidly, by more than 200 per cent, and that, relatively speaking, Leeds's importance as

51   Victoria Mills, Holbeck. A cloth-finishing mill dating from 1840 but extensively
rebuilt and enlarged by Thomas Boyd in 1873 during the revival of the finishing
trade in Leeds

a cloth-making centre was therefore declining.

Decline in the flax industry during the 'Great Depression' was more
precipitous, leaving Leeds with no more than a foothold in the
industry. Competition from Belfast and abroad proved too much for
many firms, and the census recorded the worsening fortunes of the
trade: 8,461 workers in 1861, 3,540 in 1881, down to 975 in 1901.
The survivors concentrated upon linen weaving – heavy canvas and
tarpaulin in the main – and relied upon government and railway
contracts. The causes of the sharp contraction in flax spinning are
complex but are certainly to be found somewhere in the failure of
Leeds firms to adopt new machinery and adapt their production at a
time when they were facing higher labour costs and stiffening
competition. They were slow to adopt power-loom weaving (there
were fewer than 1,000 power looms even at the end of the 1860s) and
to become vertically integrated. Belfast mills could pay lower wages,
whereas in Leeds the emerging clothing industry also competed for
unskilled and semi-skilled female labour, forcing wages rates up.
Additionally Leeds's advantage of cheap coal, which William Brown
had considered critical in 1821, was by now of less importance,
transport and machinery being that much more efficient.[36]

The greatest of all the flax spinners, Marshall and Co., were forced to let their new power-loom shed in 1876, only thirteen years after it was built, to a firm of clothing manufacturers, a sign of the changing times. The collapse of the flax industry left many empty mills but caused the town no lasting harm, as once again its economy displayed an admirable adaptability to changing circumstances. Few former flax mills remained vacant for long, as the old spinning rooms and loom sheds were divided into workrooms for the emergent dress trades.

Though factories for the production of caps and hats had been established earlier, a small factory in Alfred Street, set up by John Barran in 1856, ushered in a new era for the clothing industry. Of particular significance to the trade was the development, at Barran's suggestion, of the band knife by the engineering firm of Greenwood and Batley. The knife was capable of cutting through several layers of cloth at the same time, introducing mass production and standardisation to one stage of manufacture. The American sewing machines and score or so of workers in Barran's factory concentrated initially on the production of boys' clothing, but the ready-made trade soon extended into uniforms, suits and outerwear.[37] The market for this output was to be found among the prospering labouring classes and in the demand for uniforms occasioned by the Crimean war and the expansion of the railways and the police force. Scarlet tunics, navy serge trousers, heavy boots, all were mass-produced in Leeds for the rank-and-file soldiery.

Much of the skilled labour required by the clothing trade was provided by the influx of Jewish immigrants after 1881, whilst the decline in the flax industry released thousands of unskilled girls and women on to the labour market. Both played their part. Many Jews started their own clothing business, often with a minimum of capital, in rented rooms with hired equipment. The giant business of Montague Burton and Co. was founded in Sheffield in 1900 with a capital of only £100.[38] Though the conditions in such small workshops were said to be substantially better than in the East End of London, still many of them were overcrowded and unhygienic, the labour force often toiling long hours for scant reward.[39] There were a great many such 'sweatshops' in Leeds by the 1890s, some operating independently, others acting as outworkers for the fifty or so large factories in which the labour force was predominantly female. Clothing accounted for one in four of the jobs for female workers by 1911, by which time the total labour force in the industry exceeded 30,000. From its initial nucleus in the Park Square area the industry had spread to all parts of the town, located in former textile mills and other old industrial premises for which the rents were low, and in newer purpose-built factories in the suburbs where land was cheaper and the developing urban transport system allowed firms to assemble their workforce.[40]

Leeds in 1914 was the home of 100 wholesale clothiers, with perhaps eighty factories, and a host of small tailoring concerns housed in any available space.[41] One such sweatshop was housed in 'the little front room of a cottage, where two machines and some four or five people might work'.[42] Certain of the major concerns had by this time attained national status and their factories were the largest in the country. Barran's factory in Park Lane, for example, housed over 2,000 workers, and the average factory gave work to 250–300 hands. With certain exceptions most of the larger firms had extended their activities into retailing by the beginning of the twentieth century. First Joseph Hepworth, who had started as a tailor in Wortley in 1868, then Blackburn's, Price's, J. May and Co. and finally, of course, Montague Burton's, whose operation was removed to Leeds in 1906.

Leeds benefited from its proximity to the woollen industry, the availability of female labour and Jewish skills, the readiness of local engineers to develop machinery for the trade, but perhaps above all to the fortuitous concentration of enterprising individuals whose willingness to innovate and initiate placed the town in the forefront of the clothing industry. Specialising in men's and boys' outerwear, ladies' mantles and costumes, and hats and caps, the trade served a national market, one recommendation for the Leeds product apparently being its freedom from infection and disease![43]

Sewing machines and the band knife also constituted the basic equipment of an important footwear industry, the materials for which were close at hand. The town's leather industry supplied heavy leathers for boot soles and lighter leathers for the uppers; from the linen industry came the sewing thread, whilst the soles were often nailed on with Hunslet-made rivet nails. And if the soles were beginning to wear thin there were Blakey's famous boot protectors, produced by the thousand at their factory in Lady Lane.

There were further parallels between the clothing and footwear industries. Both emerged during the 1850s, in time to take advantage of the military contracts generated by the Crimean war. Both took over premises left vacant by the textile industries. Both employed primarily female labour. One difference, however, was that large-scale organisation in the footwear trade existed before the introduction of machine sewing. The most eminent Leeds firm in the trade, Stead and Simpson, started life as curriers and leather factors in 1834. Some time during the 1840s they began the manufacture of ready-made boots; the uppers and soles were cut at their premises in

Kirkgate and then put out to journeymen for hand stitching. In 1851 the firm was said to employ 120 workers, though whether this refers solely to the cutters at the central factory is not known.[44] The other main concern in the industry, Joseph Conyers and Sons, also began as curriers, then started production of boots at a factory in Boar Lane. Together these two produced an average 10,000 pairs of boots a week by 1858, two-thirds of the Leeds output.[45]

Even when production mounted to 40,000 pairs a week by 1880, then to almost 100,000 a week in 1890, many of the 8,000 or so workers remained outside the factory and in their own homes.[46] From this peak the labour force shrank somewhat to around 5,000 in 1914, partly in response to increasing centralisation in the industry – Stead and Simpson, for example, concentrated all their Leeds production at Sheepscar in the 1880s – but principally because many of the eighty-five to ninety wholesale manufacturers were slow to adapt to changes in demand. Leeds continued to specialise in heavy boots when the market was demanding shoes made from lighter leathers. The number of firms was pruned to around fifty after a series of bankruptcies which affected smaller concerns mainly. As with the clothing trade the amount of capital necessary to set up in the footwear business was not very great: many firms operated with a total capital of under £500 and were unable to weather even minor financial setbacks.

Reduced demand from a declining footwear industry adversely affected the town's leather trade, which for a time was almost the largest in the country. The leather industry served other markets, but unfortunately there were more serious problems than a dip in demand from the local boot industry to be faced by the 1880s. The halcyon days of the Leeds leather industry were 1850 to 1880, after chrome tanning was popularised. New tanneries and skinworks were constructed throughout this period, many of them in the 1850s, Buslingthorpe, Meanwood and Kirkstall emerging as the chief localities. The advantages to the industry were similar to those which favoured the town's other trades – local raw materials, plenty of water, and a ready-to-hand market. As the industry expanded, dependence upon imported hides and skins increased, and when the exporting countries, principally India, began to tan the 'kips' themselves the Leeds tanneries were hard hit. Contemporaneously the light leather trade faced increasing competition from Continental producers, with the Germans to the fore, and all told the years 1880 to 1900 were troubled ones. Even the largest concerns were affected. Wilson Walker and Co., whose tannery at Buslingthorpe was the largest in the country, and whose registered capital in 1893 was

£400,000, collapsed in 1901. Having fallen slightly in the previous decade, employment rose again slightly to just under 4,000 in 1911, but Leeds never recovered its position in the trade.

It has already been noted that Leeds manufacturing during the nineteenth century was marked by the strong inter-association of its different industries. Engineering, which developed initially to serve the textile trades, held a basic position in this complex. In the second half of the century new branches of engineering reflected a developing technology, and as more industries underwent their own revolution the demand for machinery expanded. From an early specialisation in steam engines and textile machinery Leeds became a metalworking district second only to the Black Country in importance. By the time of the first world war the town could lay claim to more than fifty branches of engineering products ranging between rat traps and dynamos, perambulators and railway locomotives. Instructively, the chamber of commerce devoted twelve out of twenty-seven pages on manufacturing in its 1913 yearbook to fifty-one categories of metal and engineering goods.[47]

Originally the basic raw material for the engineering trades was supplied by an important local iron industry. Though Leeds itself was never more than a minor centre – there were only two blast furnaces in the borough in 1871 – the coal measures of the surrounding district yielded blackband ores which were smelted for pig iron, which was then wrought into 'Yorkshire Best', using sulphur-free coal from adjacent pits and a cold blast. In Leeds itself there were, however, a great number of foundries, Griffiths recording 174 puddling furnaces in 1871.[48] Most of these were south of the river, in Hunslet mainly, whilst the blast furnaces were located at Farnley and along the York Road. Production of wrought iron fell towards the end of the century as local ores were exhausted and steel replaced iron, but the engineering industries continued to prosper, using material brought from Cleveland and Sheffield among other sources.

It is possible here to give only the barest indication of the nature and extent of a group of industries which together employed more than 33,000 workers in 1911, accounting for one in five of all occupied males. Certain points are worth emphasising, however. Again we must stress the contribution of the entrepreneur and the role of the individual firm in industrial development. For example, Leeds firms made some of the earliest hydraulic machinery. The Kirkstall Forge produced a 1,250 ton forging press in 1863. Tannett Walker built the largest hydraulic press in England for John Brown's of Sheffield in the 1890s, as well as one for the Krupp steelworks at Essen in Germany. Other presses were turned out for cotton baling, oilseed crushing, and for dock machinery. Leeds was also in the forefront of the development of the steam locomotive. Apprentices from Murray's Round Foundry went on to set up their own works, and locomotive building flourished in Hunslet from the 1840s onwards. The leading firms were complementary rather than competitive, and as the British railway companies set up their own locomotive works they either turned, like the Hunslet Engine Company, to export markets or, like Hudswell Clarke, to narrow-gauge engines. Besides industrial locomotives Leeds also produced all kinds of rolling stock. Samuel Fox invented and manufactured the pressed-steel bogie and wagon underframe; the Leeds Steel Works introduced manganese steel rails; and wheels and axles of 'Yorkshire Best' were turned out at Kirkstall Forge.

Traction engines, steamrollers and steam waggons were all made in south Leeds and Hunslet after John Fowler began designing traction engines and steam ploughs in 1850. His first models were made up at Kitson's Airedale Foundry, but later Fowler set up on his own at adjacent premises in Hunslet Road. His tractors, adapted to burn straw or wood, were exported to the United States before the civil war and a 20 ton Fowler engine hauled Prussian guns to the siege of Paris in 1870. One 40 ton crawler even found its way to the Yukon in 1901.

The western out-townships of Rodley and Stanningley led the country in the construction of cranes, from which were developed steam excavators and diggers. The early production of 'haystack' boilers for 'fire engines' paved the way for the development of marine boilermaking. As steam replaced sail and ships became larger, boilers and engines grew bigger and operated at higher steam pressures. Marine boilers were made at Leeds, initially with Yorkshire iron, later from steel, shaped by Leeds-built hydraulic presses and flanging machines. Linked to this was the manufacture of gasholders and storage tanks.

The specialisation in textile machinery continued to be a feature of Leeds engineering. Fairbairn and Lawson continued to manufacture flax and tow machinery long after their local market had been extinguished. Other firms constructed machinery for the woollen industry; cardmaking was an important trade, and when the shoddy industry arose some firms turned to manufacturing garneting machines whilst others diversified into various branches of wireworking – corn sieves, fencing, machinery guards and even rat traps.[49] Nail-making began in Leeds about 1800 as a domestic trade but grew most rapidly after James Roberts introduced machine cutting in 1820 at his Hope Street works. The industry reached its zenith in the 1860s but even in 1900 there were still six nailmakers in

Leeds, four of them located in Hunslet, together producing 250 tons per week.

Leeds engineering firms also turned out bolts, screws and other standardised parts, spades and shovels, pressed steel holloware, oilcans and oil lamps, gas burners (the firm of George Bray and Co. at one time dominating the national market), copper tubes, brass fittings and a host of other small products as well as the machine tools, locomotives and boilers already mentioned. From Kirkstall Forge to Thwaitegate both banks of the Aire were lined with engineering works, with rarely more than four or five firms in exactly the same line of business.

Whilst it must have been gratifying to note the continual advance in engineering employment in the period after 1850, from 7,415 in 1851 to 33,156 in 1911, and though the chamber of commerce affirmed that its members were 'fully alive to the situation',[50] there were certain disquieting features of the local engineering industry by 1914. Leeds was still a centre of wrought iron rather than steel, of machinery rather than machine tools, of steam rather than electrical engineering. In 1914 mechanical engineering firms outnumbered those in electrical engineering by almost two to one, and the dominant concerns were nearly all old-established. New industries were failing to develop in the borough. Although Job Day began building a 10 h.p. four-cylinder light car in 1910 Leeds never became a centre for the motor industry. The Blackburn Aeroplane Company began in Hunslet in 1909 and moved to the Olympia Works, Roundhay, in 1913 but this was an isolated development, and in any case the firm left soon after for Brough on Humberside.

Leeds has remained an important centre of mechanical engineering and the manufacture of machinery, but in this critical period it failed to attract a fair share of the newer engineering industries and had to withstand the decline of its old established iron industry. As early as 1857 50,000 tons of pig iron were being imported into the district annually, and although a few concerns changed to steelmaking, many ironfounders went out of business.[51] Whitham's of Kirkstall Road, for instance, at one time the largest firm of re-rollers in Leeds, went into liquidation in 1891.

Before turning to those industries which could be found in any large provincial centre in the second half of the nineteenth century and which served a predominantly local market, mention must be made of the printing trade, for which Leeds was said to be second only to London. Leeds firms specialised in quality colour printing of everything from postcards to calendars and posters, on tinplate as well as card and paper. One or two large concerns dominated. Alf Cooke

52 Richard Kilburn made fulling stocks from 1810 onwards at various sites in south Leeds. The Perseverance Works in Elland Road dates from 1865

'Soapy Joe's' began as skin and hide dealers *c.* 1830, then turned to soap in 1848. Now Elida-Gibbs, part of the Unilever group. (From the Leeds Chamber of Commerce *Directory*, 53 1910)

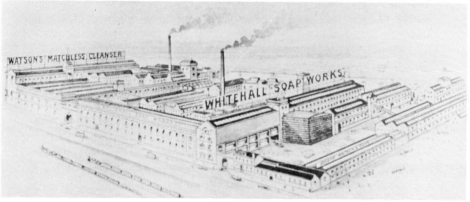

started the Crown Point Works in 1872, and former employees of his went into business on their own as Chorley and Pickersgill of Cookridge Street and Charles Lightowler of Joseph Street.[52] An interest in the stage led Waddington's to become specialist printers to the theatrical world, then from posters and programmes they went on to become, almost by chance, the largest manufacturers of playing-cards in Britain. The letterpress printers, such as E. J. Arnold and Son, expanded business on a basis of long runs of railway timetables, HMSO work, and school books for the post-1870 school boards. Such a large concentration of printing activity warranted specialist engineers and suppliers. A nationally known printing-press maker moved into south Leeds to be nearer its customers, and a firm of printers' lead casters moved into the town 'to meet the requirements of the trade'.[53] There were other type foundries and also one printing-ink maker.

Despite the importance of Leeds colour printing the great majority of printers catered for a more restricted local market. They were 'jobbing printers', working to commission and located in small workshops near the centre of the town so as to be accessible to their clients. As such they were typical of 'those trades which are common to all congregated populations whose wants have to be supplied'.[54] The organic development of the town and the surrounding industrial area demanded building materials, foodstuffs and a variety of industrial products to satisfy local needs. Nevertheless some firms in such industries managed to achieve national status. The majority of companies in the chemical industry, for example, manufactured dyestuffs, acetic, nitric and sulphuric acids, greases, stearines, disenfectants and pharmaceuticals for local consumption, but the Yorkshire Dyeware and Chemical Company (founded 1900) and Joseph Watson and Sons were two concerns which built up a national and international market for their products. The latter began life as dealers in skins and hides and leather dressers in the 1830s, then branched out into soaps and fats when they moved to Whitehall Road in 1861. Concentrating upon soap, production jumped from 100 tons per week in 1885 to 500 tons a week by 1906.[55]

At one time Leeds was renowned for its pottery, especially the creamware made by Humble Green and Co. at their Leeds Pottery in Hunslet before 1830. More typical of the town's earthenware industries, however, were Wortley fireclay products, terracotta and faience from Burmantofts, and sanitary ware, bricks and gas retorts. The growth in the population required an extensive programme of house building, for which the brickworks of east Leeds, Holbeck and Farnley provided the basic material. The surface clays of the lower coal measure series were made into low-grade bricks much favoured by the speculative builders of working-class housing. Higher-quality products – firebricks, faience work and terracotta – were made out of the finer, more plastic clays deposited in a 3 ft band beneath the smelting coal of the Low Moor Better Bed. This clay had to be mined, but the higher cost of extraction was justified by the higher price and the wider market it achieved. Terracotta from Burmantofts was used widely by late Victorian and Edwardian architects to face prestige buildings and may be seen to this day on the front of the Opera House at Manaos, in the heart of the Amazonian jungle.[56] For the most part, however, clay was extracted at the surface and made into bricks which were sold to local builders. Sometimes a firm of brickmakers such as J. and C. Boyle would lease the mineral rights to a parcel of land at the edge of the town, establish clay pit and brickworks, and then use the bricks to build houses on near-by land. In this way transport costs were kept to a minimum.

54   The five-storey brick-built mill which became the original Leeds Co-op flour mill in 1848. The nearer, stone building was built in 1840 as part of Matthew Murray's Round Foundry and became the Co-op flour mill in 1905

The growing population required basic foodstuffs as well as housing. Before 1838 all corn was ground at the soke mill in Swinegate, an obligation only removed when the reformed corporation bought out the rights of soke for £13,000 by private Act of Parliament. This soke had applied to most of the in-township; the out-townships had their own mills. Beeston soke mill was at Hunslet, that for the manor of Potternewton was at Scott Hall on the Adel beck. New steam mills were built in the out-townships from the 1820s onwards and in the in-township after 1840. One such mill was established by the Leeds Flour Mill Society in Holbeck in 1847 – the 'People's Mill', an early venture in co-operation.[57] Here as in other Leeds corn mills rollers replaced stones in the 1880s, and in 1884 one firm was boasting that it could produce flour 'equal to that prepared on the continent, and at a cheaper rate'.[58] However, this development did not protect the industry from the growing competition of coastal mills after 1870, when imported wheat began to replace home-grown grain, and many firms went out of business, in spite of attempts to increase profitability by some concerns who 'stretched' their flour with plaster of paris. The Leeds Industrial Co-operative Society, as the Flour Mill Society had become, survived and was still grinding a daily ten stone in 1914, but other mills had to either close down or turn to provender milling for horse fodder. Crown Point Mill was rebuilt in 1868 with a horse's head carved on the keystone of the main entrance arch.

After bread the main staple of the working class was beer, and Leeds was a major centre of the malt trade. Initially the maltsters supplied the vast number of publicans in Leeds who brewed their own beer, but as time passed the common (wholesale) brewer, with his own malting, took an increasing share of the trade. One of the early maltsters was Joshua Tetley of Armley, who took over Sykes's brewery in Hunslet in 1823 to start what was to become one of Yorkshire's most famous breweries.[59] The number of common breweries rose to a peak of thirty-three in 1886, from which it has now fallen (1978) to two, the trend of consolidation and amalgamation having started in the 1890s. This consolidation derives from both technological and marketing changes, and indirectly from the influence of the temperance movement, founded in Bradford in 1830 and established a year later at Leeds. The movement encouraged the consumption of beer, as being preferable to spirits, and take-away bottled beer rather than endless rounds in the bar. Breweries of a different and less threatening kind produced black (spruce) beer or vinegar. Leeds in fact had one of only two vinegar breweries in Yorkshire, the Cambrian Vinegar Company, a Birmingham offshoot of which was later to become the HP Sauce Company. Other food and drink products emerging from the town's factories by the beginning of the twentieth century included jam, aerated waters and the famous 'Yorkshire Relish' made by Goodall and Backhouse, all of which were sold in jars and bottles made by the local glass and stoneware industries.

III   Significant though such trades were, it must again be emphasised that the strength of the industrial economy of Leeds rested on a foundation of prosperous staple industries. Though the chamber of commerce stated that

> Its continuous industrial prosperity has been maintained by the enormous variety of industries which flourish within its borders and which furnish a unique stability to its trade,[60]

it should be noted that in 1911 43 per cent of the borough's workforce (one in two of all manufacturing workers) was employed by the engineering, clothing, footwear and textile industries. (See table 14.)

During the first phase of industrial development, when textiles were dominant, local supplies of raw materials – notably cheap coal – and a developing transport network were of critical importance.

> It owes its commercial importance and its prosperity to its position on the confines of the great Yorkshire coalfield, its proximity to one of the most important agricultural areas in the kingdom, and the variety of natural resources of the country.[61]

The initial advantage thus gained was put to good effect, and in the second half of the nineteenth century the industrial complex was extended to embrace a host of iron- and clay-based trades as well as leather, footwear and clothing industries. The rich variety of manufacturing industry formed a complex system of interrelated activities and firms from which few industries were completely independent. Inter-industry linkages were encouraged by, among other factors, the flexibility and adaptability of the entrepreneurial class. Not untypical was Joshua Buckton, first a woollen merchant, then a cloth manufacturer, and finally a founder and machine maker specialising in anchor-chain testing equipment; or Joseph Simpson, who started out making brick-making machinery but later became the largest manufacturer of perambulators in the world;[62] or Benjamin Pullan, one-time dyer, cloth manufacturer and later steam engine manufacturer; or the firm of Thackray's, which began as butchers in premises opposite the Infirmary, went on to make butchers' knives, and eventually became surgical instrument manufacturers.

Capital too was fortunately mobile. The study of the sources of capital suggests that it came from a diverse cross-section of the community. In the early period of industrial development especially, partnerships were often complex and an individual might invest in several enterprises. Richard Paley had financial interests in ironfounding, potash manufacture, several cotton-spinning enterprises and soap boiling.[63] Joshua Bower was involved in glass and chemical manufacture, glue boiling and coal mining. Francis Tetley, the brewer, also extended his interests into coal mining – he headed the group which bought out the Middleton Colliery estate in 1867. Investment in manufacturing offered the prospect of substantial reward and attracted money from a variety of sources.

Benjamin Gowland, partner in the firm of Gowland Boyne and Co., cotton spinners, was a sea captain from Whitby. Titley Tatham and Walker, flax spinners, were a partnership of a Leeds gentleman, a Staffordshire Quaker and a Nottingham brassfounder.

Later on much of the capital for industrial expansion came by ploughing back the profits, or from loans from banks and other institutions. In general the average quantity of capital invested in an individual concern expanded as time progressed, and the size of

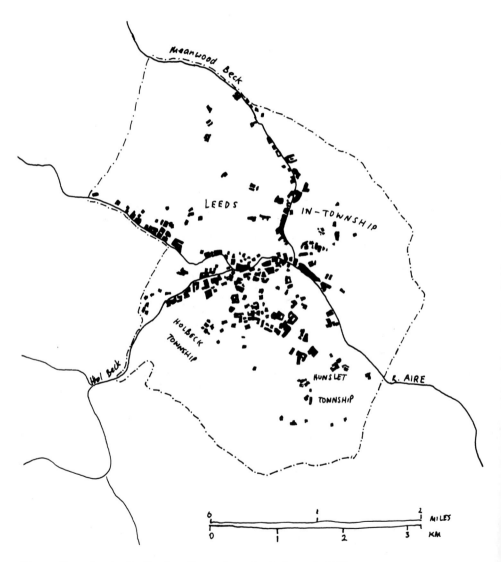

55   Inner Leeds: distribution of manufacturing industry in 1850

factory units followed suit. As firms expanded their business they were forced either to extend their premises or to relocate. In this way industrial expansion contributed to the extension of the town, and there is evidence to suggest that at certain times its role was a leading one. The development of the built-up area westwards towards Kirkstall, for example, was initiated by factories congregating alongside the left bank of the river Aire.

The valley of the Aire and that of the Adel (or Meanwood) beck,

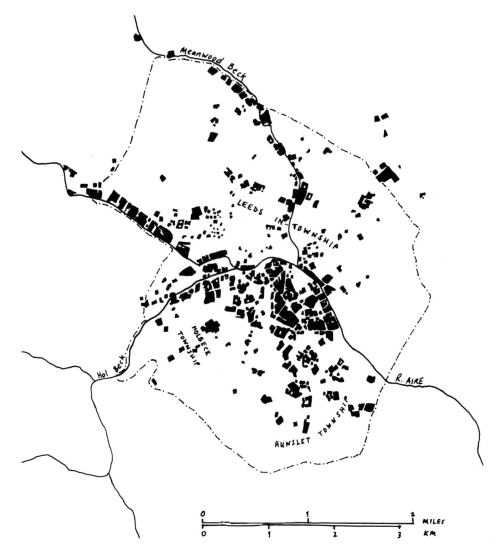

56   Inner Leeds: distribution of manufacturing industry in 1914

along with south and east Leeds, remained the principal industrial districts (see figs. 55 and 56). Such areas, usually low-lying and flat, had the best access to water and transport facilities, and, being surrounded by areas of dense back-to-back working-class housing, to labour also. Of importance also to the location and timing of industrial land development was the influence of the property market. Although the Leeds land market was primarily freehold, consisting of a multitude of holdings, the development of one or two larger estates had a profound effect upon certain districts. The Larchfield estate, for example, only came on to the market in 1835, before which it helped to maintain a quasi-green belt between south Leeds and Hunslet. Within a few years of its being offered on the market the fields were covered with foundries, engineering works and a glassworks.

The availability of land, infrastructural development, cheap raw materials and water, a mobile labour force, the spirit and enterprise of individual entrepreneurs, all played their part in the industrial development of the town. Between 1780 and 1914 Leeds industry underwent a transformation, one that was not always welcomed:

57   Banklow Mills. In the foreground the original mill, *c.* 1800, dwarfed by a spinning mill of *c.* 1890, and in the background extensions built *c.* 1830. The many names on the walls indicate how redundant mills found new uses, with multiple occupancy

The demoralizing effects of crowding together promiscuously the labourers in factories have in large towns been materially aided by the nature of their habits, and the vices which large towns afford facilities for pursuing.[64]

Demoralising perhaps, economically successful certainly. New industries, new developments in technology, a revolution in industrial organisation helped transform the economy and the landscape of Britain in the nineteenth century. Leeds was at the forefront of these developments, playing a particularly prominent role in textiles, engineering and the clothing trade, justifiably claiming the title of 'the commercial metropolis of Yorkshire'.[65]

NOTES

[1] *Leeds Mercury*, advertisement, 15 March 1783.

[2] S. Pigot, *Commercial Directory of Leeds* (1816), 13.

[3] Leeds Chamber of Commerce, *Commercial Yearbook* (1910), 35.

[4] T. Fenteman and Co., *An Historical Guide to Leeds and its Environs* (1858), 25.

[5] T. Langdale, *Topographical Dictionary of Yorkshire* (1822), 341. Sir G. Head, *Home Tour through the Manufacturing Districts of England in 1835* (1836), 172.

[6] W. G. Rimmer, 'Middleton Colliery, near Leeds, 1770–1830', *Yorkshire Bulletin of Economic and Social Research*, 7 (1955), 41–58; 'Coal', *Leeds Journal*, 25 (1954), 3–7.

[7] T. Baines, *Yorkshire Past and Present* (1877), 102–4.

[8] M. W. Beresford, 'The making of a township: Richard Paley in the East End of Leeds', in C. W. Chalklin and M. A. Havender (eds.), *Rural Change and Urban Growth* (1974), 281–320.

[9] Paley in fact scrapped the Low Moor engine in favour of a 36 h.p. engine from Boulton and Watt, in 1797. This latter was relatively expensive – £665 initially – but much more efficient, consuming less than half the coal. See the correspondence between Paley and Boulton and Watt in the Boulton and Watt Papers, Box 261, Birmingham Public Libraries.

[10] 'Scribbling' is a preparatory process in the spinning of wool whereby the knots and lumps are eliminated by means of rotating spiked cylinders.

[11] *Leeds Intelligencer*, advertisement, 3 July 1791.

[12] Leeds city archives, DW 986E, *Petitions of the Woollen Manufacturers in the West Riding of Yorkshire* (1794), 2.

[13] The history of Park Mills and the story of the Leeds woollen industry in this period are ably told in W. B. Crump (ed.), 'The Leeds woollen industry, 1780–1820', *Thoresby Soc.*, XXXIII (1931), and in two articles by Professor H. Heaton: 'Benjamin Gott and the industrial revolution in Yorkshire, '*Economic History Review*, III (1931), 45–66, and 'Financing the industrial revolution', *Bulletin of the Business History Society*, XI (1937), 1–10.

[14] *Report of the Select Committee appointed to Consider the State of the Woollen Manufacture*, P.P. (1806), III, 268.

[15] A Bill to enable the Trustees of the Two Cloth Halls in Leeds . . . to make Byelaws and Regulations for the Preservation of the Ancient Mode of Carrying on the Trade Between the Cloth Merchants and the Cloth Manufacturers, and for other purposes, 34 Geo. III (1794), 2. (Leeds city archives, D W. 986E).

[16] E. Baines, *History, Directory and Gazetteer of the County of York* (1822), 29–30.

[17] A. Ure, *The Philosophy of Manufacturers* (1861 edn.), 70.

[18] An excellent, exhaustive account of the business may be found in W. G. Rimmer, *Marshall's of Leeds, Flax Spinners, 1788–1886* (1960).

[19] W. Brown, 'Information regarding Flaxspinning in Leeds', (1821), unpublished MS, Dundee Public Libraries. R. Baker, 'On the industrial and sanitary economy of the borough of Leeds in 1858', *Journal of the Statistical Society*, XXI (1858), 427–53.

[20] H. C. Marshall, 'List of Spinners and Spindles' (1842), Marshall Papers, MS No. 20, Brotherton Library, University of Leeds.

[21] A. Warden, *The Linen Trade, Ancient and Modern* (1864), 377–8.

[22] E. Parsons and W. White, *Annals of Leeds, York, and the Clothing District of Yorkshire* (1830), 299.

[23] W. Lindley, 'Number of Steam Engines . . . in Leeds and its Immediate Vicinity . . . March 1824', University of Leeds, Brotherton Library, MS No. 18. Parsons and White, *Annals* (1830) 326. *A Return of the Number of Persons Employed in . . . Factories in the United Kingdom*, P.P. (1839), XLII.

[24] 'Slubbing', like 'scribbling', is a preparatory process in the spinning of wool.

[25] A. Ure, *Philosophy* (1861), 707.

[26] Baker, 'Industrial and sanitary economy', 432.

[27] Leeds Chamber of Commerce, *Commercial Yearbook* (1910), 36.

[28] Lindley, 'Number of Steam Engines'.

[29] Baker, 'Industrial and sanitary economy', 438.

[30] W. G. Rimmer, 'Leeds leather industry in the nineteenth century', *Thoresby Soc.*, XLVI (1960), 119–64.

[31] *Third Report of the Commissioners Appointed to Inquire into the Best Means of Preventing the Pollution of Rivers*, P.P. (1867), XXXIII, Vol. II, 202–5.

[32] *Return of the Number of Woollen, Worsted, and Shoddy Factories*, etc., P.P. (1904), LXXXVII, 1109.

[33] E. Baines, 'On the woollen manufacture of England, with special reference to the Leeds clothing district', *Journal of the Statistical Society*, XXII (1859), 1–34. Chamber of Commerce, *Yearbook* (1913), 54.

[34] Fenteman, *An Historical Guide*, 26–7. *Return of the Number of Woollen, Worsted, and Shoddy Factories*, etc., P.P. (1904), LXXXVII, 1109.

[35] Chamber of Commerce, *Yearbook* (1913), 54.

[36] Brown, 'Information'.

[37] J. Thomas, 'The Leeds clothing industry', *Yorkshire Bulletin of Economic and Social Research*, Occasional Paper No. 1 (1955), 8–10.

[38] See J. F. Fraser, *Goodwill in Industry* (1925).

[39] *Report by the Labour Correspondent of the Board of Trade on the Sweating System in Leeds*, P.P. (1888), LXXXVI, 561.

[40] G. C. Dickinson, 'The development of the suburban road passenger system in Leeds, 1840–95', *Journal of Transport History*, IV (1960), 214–23.

[41] Thomas, 'Leeds clothing industry', 48.

[42] Anon., 'The sweating system in Leeds', *Lancet*, I (1888), 1209.

[43] Chamber of Commerce, *Yearbook* (1913), 68.

[44] *Census Enumerators' Returns* (1851), P.R.O. H.O. 107/2320.

[45] Baker, 'Industrial and sanitary economy', 442.

[46] J. Dodgson, *Guide to Leeds* (1879), 40. British Association, *Handbook, Leeds Meeting* (1890), 122.

[47] Chamber of Commerce, *Yearbook* (1913), 53–80.

[48] S. Griffiths, *Guide to the Iron Trade of Great Britain* (1873), 279.

[49] See Proctor Brothers, *During Nine Reigns, 1740–1940* (1941).

[50] Chamber of Commerce, *Yearbook* (1913), 54.

[51] W. G. Rimmer, 'Engineering: the nineteenth century', *Leeds Journal*, 26 (1955), 229–31.

[52] See A. J. Turner, *The Crown Point Story, 1866–1966* (1966).

[53] London Printing and Engraving Co., *The Century's Progress* (1893), 188.

[54] Baker, 'Industrial and sanitary economy', 442.

[55] W. G. Rimmer, 'Men who made Leeds – Joseph Watson', *Leeds Journal*, 32 (1961), 143–6.

[56] Anon., 'Burmantofts Works (Leeds Fireclay Co.)', *Annual Report of the Yorkshire Philosophical Society* (1915), 9–11.

[57] G. J. Holyoake, *Jubilee History of the Leeds Industrial Co-operative Society* (1897), 27.

[58] *Leeds Express*, 16 February 1884, 'Peeps into Leeds works – Moorhouse & Co.'.

[59] See J. Tetley and Sons Ltd., *Reviewing a Century of Progress, 1823–1923* (1923).

[60] Chamber of Commerce, *Yearbook* (1913), 35.

[61] *Ibid.*

[62] *Leeds Express*, 14 April 1883, 'Peeps into Leeds works – Joseph Simpson's'.

[63] See Beresford, 'The making of a township'.

[64] P. Gaskell, *Artisans and Machinery* (1836), 30.

[65] Chamber of Commerce, *Yearbook* (1913), 35.

BIBLIOGRAPHICAL NOTE

A cursory examination of the notes to this chapter indicates the great variety of sources available to the historian of Leeds industry during the industrial revolution. Manuscripts, Parliamentary Papers, local directories, maps and plans, property deeds and estate documents – these and many other sources have something to tell us. If the reader is interested in following up such lines of inquiry perhaps we may immodestly refer him to two theses, both housed in the Brotherton Library, University of Leeds: M. F. Ward, 'Industrial development and location in Leeds north of the river Aire, 1775–1914' (unpublished Ph.D. thesis, 1972), and E. J. Connell, 'Industrial development in south Leeds, 1790–1914' (unpublished Ph.D. thesis, 1975). For the more general reader the series of short articles published in the *Leeds Journal* by W. G. Rimmer and others under the title 'Leeds and its Industrial Growth' is recommended. A full list of these articles may be found in Volume L, part 2, of the *Publications of the Thoresby Society*, which contains three longer articles by Rimmer on the industrial evolution of Leeds from 1700 to 1951. The chapters by E. M. Sigsworth and J. Buckman in M. W. Beresford and G. R. J. Jones (eds.), *Leeds and its Region* (1967), also provide a good introduction to the history of Leeds industry.

For individual industries coverage varies from exhaustive to barely adequate. Rimmer has written an excellent account of the leather industry in 'The Leeds leather industry' (see note 30), and we are indebted to the same author for the account of the flax industry contained in his book on the firm of Marshall's (note 18). The woollen and worsted industries are well documented in the articles by Heaton and Crump (see note 13) and also Professor Heaton's *The Yorkshire Woollen and Worsted Industries* (1965). M. T. Wild provides a useful account of the industry from the viewpoint of the historical geographer in his contribution to J. G. Jenkins (ed.), *The Wool Textile Industry in Great Britain* (1972), pp. 185–234. New methods and new sources are employed by D. Jenkins in his *The West Riding Wool*

Textile Industry, 1770–1835 (1975), but we are still reliant upon J. H. Clapham's *The Woollen and Worsted Industries* (1907) or E. Lipson's classic of the same title (1921) for an account of the industry after 1835. Finally in this category there is the excellent paper on the Leeds clothing industry by Joan Thomas, already refered to in note 37. We are still waiting, however, for any account of the vitally important engineering industries.

Other useful published works, which are, however, perhaps lacking a little in objectivity, are the yearbooks published by the Leeds Chamber of Commerce (1910, 1913, 1920), and the portraits of individual firms contained in the London Printing and Engraving Company's *The Century's Progress* (1893) and the Historical Publishing Company's *Industries of Yorkshire*, Part 1 (1888). More reliable contemporary accounts are contained in Baker's article (see note 19) and the *Handbooks* issued by the British Association for their meetings in 1856 and 1890. Finally for those who feel that any such writings invariably concentrate upon the stronger sex, Clara Collett's 'Women's work in Leeds', *Economic Journal*, I (1891), 460–73, should help to redress the balance.

KEVIN GRADY

VII   Commercial, marketing and retailing amenities, 1700–1914[1]

Earlier chapters have described the growth of population, trade and industry during the period from the industrial revolution to the first world war. In conjunction with other factors the activities of the merchant community, and transport developments, were major forces accounting for this growth. The supply of housing expanded to cope with the rapid rise in numbers. In addition people had to have places where they could buy the necessities of life, producers and middlemen needed somewhere to sell their wares, merchants and manufacturers required financial services and access to business information.

In 1700 there were no banks, no formal meeting places or associations for businessmen, and no commercial information services; there were no impressive complexes of shops, and markets were held in the streets, where they were subject to disturbance from traffic and the weather. By 1914 the town could boast nineteen banks, a stock exchange, a businessmen's exchange, and a chamber of commerce; it had an outstanding shopping centre, with five notable arcades; and its marketing facilities were amongst the best in the country. Without these developments Leeds could not have retained its dominance in the cloth trade let alone taken advantage of the opportunities offered by the growth of the national and international economies. How and why did such a range of services spring up, and what impact did they have? The question can be answered in terms of four broad phases of provision. The first, 1700–c. 1820, was dominated by the needs of the cloth trade. The second, c. 1820–c. 1840, was noteworthy for bursts of intense activity and a shift in emphasis to the requirements of a broader range of economic activities – in particular general marketing and the corn trade. Before the 1840s commercial, marketing and retailing amenities were provided almost solely by private enterprise; in the third period, c. 1840–c. 1860, the town council assumed a much greater degree of responsibility in this sphere. By the late 1850s the basic framework had been completed; in

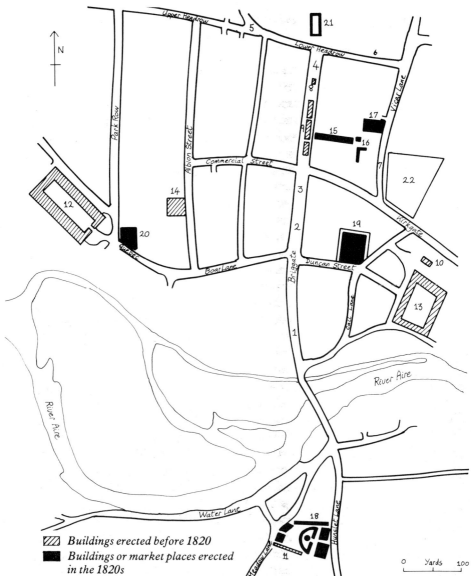

58   Markets and commercial amenities, 1700–1845. *Street markets* (*c. 1715*): *1* Cloth Market, *2* General Market, *3* Fish Market, *4* Corn Market, *5* Horse Fair, *6* Pig Market, *7* Cattle Market. *Buildings erected before 1820*: *8* Market Cross (1619), *9* Old Shambles (*c.* 1615), *10* First White Cloth Hall (1710–11), *11* Second White Cloth Hall (1755–56), *12* Coloured Cloth Hall (1756–58), *13* Third White Cloth Hall (1775–76), *14* Irregulars' Cloth Hall (1792–93). *Buildings or market places erected in the 1820s*: *15* Bazaar and Shambles (1823–25), *16* Fish Market (*c.* 1824), *17* Leadenhall Wholesale Carcass Market (*c.* 1830), *18* South Market (1823–24), *19* Central Market (1824–27), *20* Commercial Buildings (1826–29), *21* Corn Exchange (1826–28), *22* Free Market (Vicar's Croft) or Kirkgate Market (1826–27)

the final era, *c.* 1860–1914, it was consolidated and improved.

I   The visitor in 1700 could not fail to be impressed by the great activity in the town's markets. On Tuesdays and Saturdays most of the streets in the centre were appropriated for their purposes.[2] (See fig. 58.) Considerable commotion surrounded the livestock pens in the Headrow and Vicar Lane, but Briggate was the focal point of market days. This long, broad street saw dealings in a variety of commodities, from corn, fish, fruit and vegetables to dairy produce, wool, drapery, shoes and hardware. In the middle of the upper end of Briggate was Middle Row, a group of buildings, including the town hall, which housed the meat shambles. Contemporaries suggested that, with the possible exception of Halifax, Leeds was the greatest market for provisions in the north of England. Yet it was most famous for its cloth market, held in lower Briggate on trestle tables early in the morning. The markets were said to be one of the marvels of the age. Clothiers came from miles around and, in almost total silence, cloth worth ten or twenty thousand pounds – enough to build four large churches – changed hands in little more than an hour.

During the century and more from 1700 to *c.* 1820 there were no significant alterations in the general markets. The only changes were the improvement of the butchers' shops on the ground floor of the town hall when it was rebuilt in 1710–11, and the reconstruction of a small shelter known as the Market Cross in 1776.[3] However, the story of the cloth markets was very different. On several occasions during the eighteenth century neighbouring towns enviously sought to attract the trade away from Leeds by building large halls to house their own cloth markets. In response, and to accommodate an ever-increasing volume of business, a succession of cloth halls were constructed in Leeds.[4] The first challenge came from a new hall at Wakefield in 1710. The White Cloth Hall, so named because it was used for the trade in undyed cloth, was erected in Kirkgate in 1710–11. In 1755–56 it was superseded by a larger one in Meadow Lane. Two years later the needs of dealers in dyed cloth prompted the building of the Coloured Cloth Hall at Quebec (now City Square). In 1776 the second White Cloth Hall was superseded by an even larger one in the Calls. Finally, in 1793, another was opened in the basement of the new Music Hall in Albion Street. Known as the Irregulars' Cloth Hall or the Tom Paine Hall, it was for clothiers who were barred from the other halls because they had not served a seven-year apprenticeship.

The first and third White Cloth Halls were financed by the

merchant community, the remaining ones by the clothiers. By contemporary standards they were all exceptionally large buildings: the third White Cloth Hall, costing some £4,000, held 1,210 stalls; the Coloured Cloth Hall, at over £5,000, accommodated 1,770. Because of their size, the courtyards were often used for public meetings – the Coloured Cloth Hall Yard could hold 20,000 people. (See figs. 59 and 60.) The importance of the halls cannot be overstated: contemporaries thought them the foundation of Leeds's commercial success in the eighteenth and early nineteenth centuries.[5] All that remains today of these once imposing buildings is the shabby and decaying facade of the third White Cloth Hall.

Apart from the cloth halls, perhaps the most important arrivals in this first period were the banks. There were only about a dozen in provincial England in 1750, and in Leeds there were none.[6] The town's first, Lodge and Arthington, was established in 1758. In 1770 John Beckett joined the firm as a partner, and in the ensuing years he assumed control. Beckett's, as it became known, was to become one of the country's leading banks. It was followed by the Leeds New Bank in 1777 and Leeds Commercial Bank in 1792. The Commercial Bank failed in 1812, but the gap was soon filled by the foundation of the Union Bank in 1813. They were a welcome repository for savings and valuables, but it was their services to commerce and industry that were of primary importance. By 1781 the total value of Leeds merchants' trade at home and abroad was over a million pounds.[7] The banks assisted the commercial and industrial community in three main ways.[8] In an age of recurrent shortages of coin they provided a regular supply of cash, or substitutes for it, making the payment of wages and the settlement of transactions easier. They extended credit to merchants and industrialists, whose liquidity frequently suffered from the need to do the same for their customers, and from slow payment from overseas. (Credit normally took the form of discounted trade bills or overdraft facilities.) Finally, they also backed manufacturers with working capital.

Their value is demonstrated by the extent to which they were used. John Micklethwaite, for example, who held a typical merchant's account with Beckett's in the 1790s, resorted to the bank for drafts almost daily. In 1796 he recorded 444 separate transactions for drafts and cash totalling £10,647.[9] The banking houses not only provided financial services but tended to be a good deal larger than the average provincial partnership banks. In 1814 the Union Bank was able to allow the merchant firm of Rhodes Clapham and Glover an overdraft of £37,000 – an enormous sum by contemporary standards.[10] Moreover, Leeds bankers were experienced in handling foreign trade

59   The Coloured (or Mixed) Cloth Hall, built in 1756–58

60   The Coloured Cloth Hall yard

bills; as early as the 1780s Beckett's dealt with numerous bills drawn on various European cities.[11]

Although cloth marketing and financial facilities grew stronger during the eighteenth century, the means for commercial information to circulate and businessmen to meet were poor and slow to improve. They developed in a haphazard way, and even by 1820 Leeds had nothing on the scale of the merchants' exchanges at Liverpool and Manchester.[12] In the early eighteenth century men of business gathered at public houses such as the Griffin Inn and the Three Legs of Man in Briggate, or the Coffee House. These establishments offered refreshments and a small range of newspapers and periodicals.[13] By the end of the century the Coffee House was the most popular. The *Leeds Directory* for 1806 commented, 'The Coffee House – Briggate is frequented by the gentry, merchants and principal inhabitants in the centre. Which renders it in great degree the rendezvous of the mercantile part of the town.'[14] The growing need for a wider range of commercial information was catered for to some extent by the establishment of a newsroom in Briggate *c.* 1768 and two substantial subscription libraries in 1768 and 1793.[15] By 1778 the first of these, the Leeds Library, was building up a considerable section of books on law, politics and commerce. In 1785 the first Leeds chamber of commerce was formed – a merchants' association for discussion and agitation on matters of mutual interest. The chamber discussed topics such as the speed and efficiency of the post mails, transport, commercial treaties, and the encouragement of inventions. For unknown reasons it appears to have been disbanded in 1790.[16] The early years of the new century saw the first really significant and permanent improvement with the founding of the Commercial News Room and Leeds Exchange, opened in Briggate in 1806. A large newsroom was furnished with maps, gazetteers, directories and all the national and provincial newspapers and periodicals of commercial importance. Adjoining it, a suite of rooms with desks was provided where merchants could transact business in private.[17] Exactly three years later the Union Newsroom, catering for those with commercial and political interests, was opened in the lower storey of newly erected premises for the Leeds Library in Commercial Street[18] (now occupied by W. H. Smith and Son Ltd).

By 1820 Leeds was a thriving, expanding town. Although the cloth halls had declined as the factory system reduced the ranks of the independent clothiers and by-passed the halls in the marketing process, its importance as the centre of the trade remained undiminished.[19] Despite the failure of the Commercial Bank, the banking community was respectable and stable. On the other hand, general marketing facilities had not significantly improved during the eighteenth century, while the population had grown eightfold. Moreover the town still lacked a proper merchants' exchange. The 1820s were to provide a spectacular solution to these problems.

II   Complaints became louder in the early nineteenth century, and there were frequent calls for improvement. Rapidly rising prosperity from 1822 to 1825 stimulated a building boom, and from the numerous schemes that were put forward emerged the Bazaar and Shambles, built in 1823–25; the South Market, built in 1823–24; the Central Market, built in 1824–27; the corn exchange, built in 1826–28; the Commercial Buildings, built in 1826–29; and the Free Market, laid out in 1826–27.[20] (See figs. 58 and 61–64.) With the exception of the corn exchange, all were open every day except Sunday.

The Bazaar and Shambles, situated between Briggate and Vicar Lane, solved the problem of butchers' shops being dispersed around the town which had resulted from the inadequacy of the old meat shambles. It also solved a traffic problem by permitting the demolition of Middle Row. The premises consisted of some sixty shops, arranged in two rows, fifty of which were occupied by butchers. In addition there was a hall over the central block which was used as a bazaar for the sale of fancy goods, millinery and clothes. A fish market was also provided at the east end of the Shambles. About 1830 slaughterhouses and facilities for wholesaling meat were added at this end. The latter became known as the Leadenhall Wholesale Carcass Market.[21]

The Central Market, in Duncan Street, consisted of a market hall surrounded on three sides by rows of shops. The interior and exterior were lined with shops intended principally for butchers and fishmongers. The central area contained stalls for fruit and vegetables, and dairy produce, and a balcony which served as a fancy goods bazaar. In all, the place housed sixty-seven shops, fifty-six stalls, six offices and an hotel.

The South Market, between Hunslet Lane and Meadow Lane, was essentially a market place with extensive covered facilities. It had a 'cross' where dairy produce was sold, and shops and stalls for meat, farm products, manufactured goods and other merchandise. The whole area included twenty-three butchers' shops and stalls, twenty-six miscellaneous shops, eighty-eight stalls, nine slaughterhouses and eighteen dwellings.

The corn exchange, at the top of Briggate, was used for the sale of corn by sample. Its principal feature was a colonnaded quadrangle divided into compartments or stands. It also incorporated warehouses and offices for the corn factors and dealers, an hotel and a tavern, and four large shops.

The Free Market, which occupied the site of the present-day City Markets, was used for cattle, pigs, and fruit and vegetables on market days, and for hay, straw and teazles on every day except Sunday. Its opening led to a partial removal of the markets from the streets and, with the demolition of Middle Row, relieved the congestion in Briggate.

Finally, the Commercial Buildings, at the junction of Park Row and Boar Lane, sought to offer a focal point for commercial activity. On the ground floor was a large circular vestibule which served as the merchants' exchange. The business community were invited to meet there between twelve and one o'clock on business days to discuss commercial affairs. In addition to providing a new home for the Commercial News Room the premises contained a coffee room, a restaurant, a concert room/meeting hall, offices for solicitors and brokers and the West Riding Insurance Company, a committee room, and a fourteen-bedroom hotel.

All but one of the projects were due to private enterprise. The South and Central markets, the corn exchange and the Commercial Buildings were financed by unincorporated joint-stock companies, and the Bazaar and Shambles by two butchers. The exception was the Free Market, paid for out of a rate levied by the improvement commissioners. The size of the expenditure was unprecedented for a Yorkshire town; the total of well over £120,000 would have been enough to build almost 2,500 working-class houses. The Bazaar and Shambles cost some £20,000, the South Market £22,000, the Central Market £30,000, the Commercial Buildings £34,000, the corn exchange £12,500 and the Free Market over £8,000.

Such an impressive achievement can be attributed to a combination of factors. The expectation of profits, the desire to exploit land holdings, and hopes of protecting and promoting business interests were particularly influential. Inter-town rivalry, public spirit and civic pride also played a part. The high profits and public value of similar buildings in Liverpool and Manchester were frequently referred to, and the Central Market and the Free Market were in fact modelled on counterparts in those towns. But there had been too much optimism. At the end of 1825 the boom collapsed. In the succeeding years there was sufficient demand to ensure the success of the Bazaar and Shambles, the corn exchange and the Free Market, but the other ventures were less fortunate. The South Market failed to attract the public retailers in any numbers, and its only measure of success came

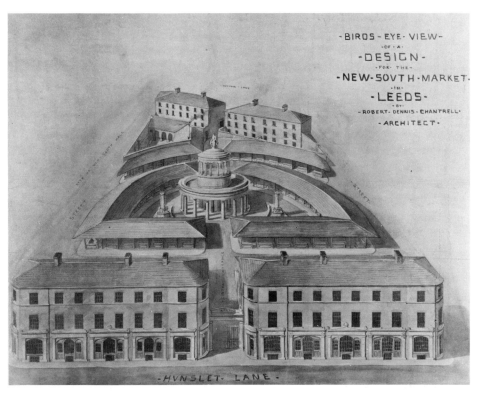

61   The South Market, built in 1823–24

62   The Central Market, built in 1824–27

with the establishment of quarterly leather fairs in 1827. For the first few years of its existence the Central Market did little better. Likewise, the patronage and income of the Commercial Buildings were disappointing; by 1849 the building was shabby and the hotel closed.

The boom of the mid-1820s affected financial institutions as well as marketing and commerce. Its collapse led to a banking crisis in which sixty-three provincial houses went under. Most of the Leeds banks weathered the storm. In fact the townspeople were so gratified by their performance that the procession to the foundation ceremony of the Commercial Buildings in 1826 halted twice to sing 'God Save the King' and give three cheers in honour of the banks of the town, which had 'supported its credit, afforded relief, and given stability to its commercial pursuits, during the season in which trade and commerce in general had experienced such a serious depression'.[22] The Leeds New Bank failed in 1827, but no more succumbed in the next few years. The one newcomer was a branch of the Bank of England; its opening in 1827 caused considerable controversy in local financial and business circles.[23]

Demands for commercial improvements had been more than satisfied, and the 1830s saw no new developments in this sphere. Banking, however, was another matter. The crisis of 1826 had induced the government to pass an Act permitting the establishment

63   The Commercial Buildings, built in 1826–29

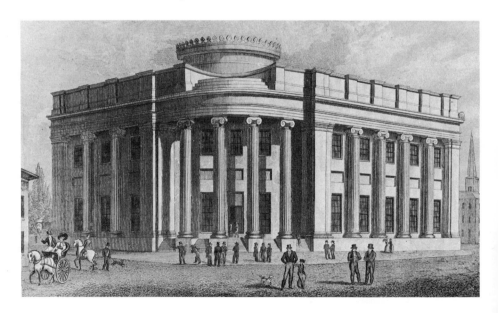

of joint-stock banks outside a sixty-five-mile radius of London. The impact of the legislation was felt in Leeds during the 1830s with the foundation of six such enterprises between 1832 and 1836. The problem was that, like the markets of the 1820s, they were borne on a wave of euphoria. In 1837 this boom too collapsed, and with it one of the new banks, the Northern and Central Bank of England.

III   Like the period just examined, the years 1840–60 were distinguished by the number of new amenities provided in a comparatively short space of time. They were also noteworthy in the extent to which the town council now became involved, and it was in the middle years of the century that the basic framework of commercial, marketing and retailing amenities was completed.

The early 1840s brought another sharp reminder of the difference between short-term and long-term growth with the closure of all but one of the five joint-stock banks that had survived the collapse of 1837. The Yorkshire Agricultural and Commercial Bank failed in 1842, and was soon followed by the Yorkshire District Bank in 1843. The others were sheltered for a while by the return of prosperity in the mid-1840s, but the collapse of the boom brought the failure of the Leeds and West Riding Joint Stock Banking Company in 1846 and Leeds Commercial Joint Stock Bank the following year. The private

64   The corn exchange, built in 1826–28

banks, particularly Beckett's and the Union Bank, stood firm.

Although the levels of economic activity reached in the boom years of the 1820s and 1830s were abnormally high, the underlying trend had always been one of steady growth. By 1840 the town's marketing facilities were again becoming inadequate. In 1840 *Leeds Mercury* noted, 'It is notorious to all our readers, that for fair and market accommodation there is not a town in the kingdom in so bad a condition as Leeds, . . . we feel assured that new accommodation of this kind is much wanted and must be supplied before many more years have passed away.'[24] The corn and cattle trades in particular needed better facilities. The answer to these demands represented the beginning of a new era in the history of Leeds markets. In 1842 the reformed corporation established a committee which took over responsibility for Kirkgate Market (the former Free Market) and the remaining street markets.[25] Virtually all the improvements of the ensuing years were undertaken by this committee under the auspices of the council, rather than by private enterprise.

In 1842 the committee decided to enlarge Kirkgate Market by purchasing some adjoining land. The extension would provide more room for the sale of livestock, and there were to be shops around the perimeter.[26] As the committee pointed out, an additional merit of the scheme was that the redeveloped land included the most insanitary property in the town, notably the notorious Boot and Shoe Yard.[27] In 1843, while the scheme was in progress, a privately owned pig and calf market was opened in King Charles' Croft. (See fig. 65.) At first it was successful, but with the completion of the Kirkgate extension in 1846 it seems to have been driven out of business.[28] The enlarged Kirkgate Market now provided room for the normal livestock markets, but it was not intended to cope with the huge volume of business at the annual horse and cattle fairs held in July and November. In 1845, after an unsuccessful attempt to obtain the use of St Peter's Square, the market committee solved this second problem by establishing a fair ground on a one-and-a-half-acre site in Woodhouse Lane leased from the trustees of Potter's Almshouses.[29]

The most striking project of the 1840s was the stock exchange.[30] In 1836 there had been only two share brokers in Leeds but, as a result of the glut of railway promotions, the number had risen to over a hundred by 1845. This rapid growth created a demand for formal and efficient organisation of the share market. In December 1844 the Leeds Stock Exchange Association was formed, and opened for business in January 1845. The event was greeted with great optimism and pride. The *Leeds Intelligencer* commented:

There can be no doubt that this establishment will tend to increase the importance of the Leeds share business, by facilitating transactions, and thus centering in Leeds that portion of the share trade which the opulence and situation of the town have a right to claim, but which hitherto has (for want of an Exchange in Leeds) been transacted in other marts.[31]

When the Association began trading it had two rival organisations, but these quickly disappeared as share prices tumbled in 1846. By 1850 the stock exchange had about fifty members, and membership remained around that level for many years. The institution was rather more status-conscious than its provincial counterparts, and in 1846–47 it erected its own premises in Albion Street at a cost of

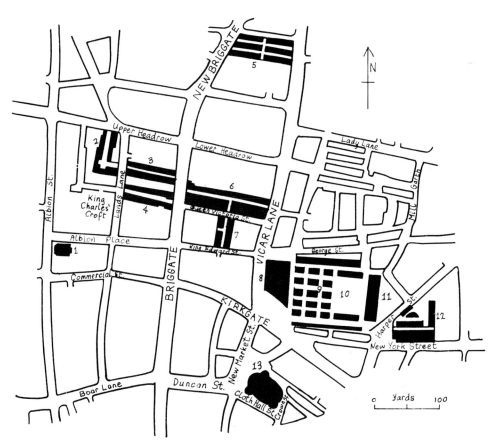

65   The principal marketing and retailing amenities built in 1846–1900. *1* Stock Exchange (1846–47), *2* Victoria Arcade (1898), *3* Thornton's Arcade (1877–78), *4* Queen's Arcade (1888–89), *5* Grand Arcade (1896–98), *6* County Arcade (1898–1900), *7* Cross Arcade (1898–1900). *Kirkgate Market: 8* Covered market (1855–57), *9* Shops (1875), *10* The open square, *11* Fish market (*c.* 1875), *12* Wholesale Meat Market and Abattoir (1898–99), *13* Corn Exchange (1861–64)

£12,500. Leeds was for long the only provincial town with a purpose-built stock exchange.

The years between 1851 and 1864 witnessed the most radical developments since the 1820s. The first was the establishment of the second chamber of commerce[32] in 1851 under the stimulus of the Great Exhibition. Its objects, an annual report pointed out, were 'finding new markets, resisting encroachments upon us from all sides, and agitating for laws to protect us from dishonesty, and removing restrictions in the way of our business'. Delegations were sent to foreign exhibitions, and lectures on commercial and economic subjects were frequently arranged. Among the speakers on opportunities abroad was the 'intrepid African explorer', the Rev. Dr Livingstone, who in 1857 addressed the members on 'the commercial bearing of his recent discoveries in Africa'. The chamber also provided a commercial and business information service catering specifically for local needs. In essence it represented the collective voice of commerce and industry, the town's leading merchants, manufacturers, lawyers and bankers. Membership rose from 87 in 1851 to 228 in 1898, and it still thrives today.

In the 1850s discontent grew with the shortage of covered market accommodation. In 1853 the proprietors of the Central Market, seeing the possibilities of the situation, applied to Parliament for an Act incorporating their company and permitting them to enlarge the market.[33] The council, alarmed by the threat of interference with its rights, opposed the Bill.[34] Although the legislation was rejected, the council's victory was soured by a sharp rap on the knuckles. The Commons committee expressed the view that a new covered market was urgently required, and implied that the council should remedy the situation, or a renewed application by the Central Market proprietors might not be rejected.[35] The committee's comments had their effect; in addition to embarking on a scheme to erect a covered market, the council decided to investigate the provision of improved accommodation for the sale of cattle.[36] In July 1853 the market committee was empowered to purchase a site between Camp Road and North Street, and to lay it out as a cattle market. Smithfield Cattle Market, as it was known, opened in 1855 at a cost of approximately £14,000. Sales of cattle were removed from Kirkgate Market and the sale of horses in the streets was prohibited. A centuries-old practice, the sale of livestock in the streets, had been brought to an end.

Meanwhile the plans for a covered market were under way.[37] In December 1853 the council accepted the market committee's recommendation that a covered market should be erected on the Kirkgate Market site, and voted £14,000 for the purpose. The market

66   Kirkgate Covered Market in 1901 on the eve of its demolition

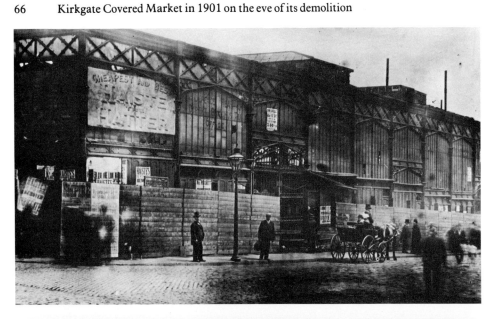

67   Kirkgate Covered Market: interior

was opened in May 1857. Its design was manifestly inspired by the Crystal Palace, in fact the plans were submitted to Sir Joseph Paxton for his comments. (See figs. 66–7.) The 1858 guide to Leeds describes the new hall and its surroundings:

> The building is of iron and glass, covering an area of 4,040 yards, and is situated at the junction of Vicar Lane and Kirkgate. The style of architecture is Gothic. . . . It has 44 convenient shops on the outside, and 35 inside, where there are also four rows of iron stalls. At night this beautiful crystal market hall is well illuminated by 200 gas lights, arranged round handsome cast iron pillars. Altogether it is the most complete structure of its kind in England. . . . At the east side of this market there remains about 5000 square yards of open market ground, where an extensive variety of fruit and vegetables are exposed for sale on Tuesday and Saturday; besides which there are several shops with fruit, poultry, fish, and other goods.[38]

Perhaps the covered market's greatest claim to fame is that it was the birthplace of Marks and Spencer, for in the 1880s it housed Michael Marks's first Penny Bazaar.[39] From the 30 November 1857 the placing of stalls, benches, goods, wares or merchandise in Briggate was prohibited.[40] The Briggate street market too had become a thing of the past.

By the 1850s perhaps the most neglected of all Leeds traders were the corn factors. There had been no improvement since the building of the corn exchange in 1825–27, and farmers selling grain in sacks were still trading in the open air in Kirkgate Market. In 1859, after repeated petitions, the council decided to erect a building to house both the sack market and the sale of corn by sample.[41] This oval-shaped Corn Exchange, which still survives, was built in 1861–64 at a total cost of £32,000. Although the council rejected the idea of an additional storey, the exchange was still substantial enough to accommodate fifty-nine offices and an open area with space for 170 stands. The building is a reminder that although Leeds was a hive of industry it was still a major centre for the marketing of agricultural produce.

The Corn Exchange, although one of the council's most notable early achievements, was not an innovation. Essentially, innovation before 1914 came to an end with the opening of Kirkgate Covered Market in 1857. The facilities provided in subsequent years replaced or extended existing ones. However, there was still plenty of scope for activity.

IV   So comprehensive were the changes from 1860 to the first world war that almost all the buildings which existed in 1860 had been demolished or replaced by 1914. One of the most significant factors, particularly in the earlier years, was the need for street and transport improvements. In 1868 the White Cloth Hall in the Calls was partially demolished for the extension of the North Eastern Railway and replaced by a smaller building in King Street.[42] Soon after, the old corn exchange and the Commercial Buildings were also demolished, in 1869 and 1871 respectively, to permit the extension of Briggate and the widening of Boar Lane and Duncan Street.[43] In the process of buying up land to widen Duncan Street the council also acquired the Central Market, but apart from losing a portion of its forecourt the market survived for another thirty years under the council's management.[44] The town evidently felt the loss of the Commercial Buildings, for in 1872–75 they were replaced by the Royal Exchange, erected on part of the original site. Costing £61,000, it incorporated an exchange room, a newsroom, offices, shops, a club and a restaurant.[45] In 1889 the Coloured Cloth Hall was demolished to make way for City Square and the new Central Post Office, and, shortly after, the White Cloth Hall in King Street suffered the same fate. By this time little business was being transacted in the halls, and in commercial terms they were no great loss. The South Market outlived all these buildings by over fifty years; in 1914 it was hardly more than a warehouse, but it was not demolished until after the second world war.[46]

While street widening played an important part, the principal force at work was the growth of demand. Despite the extensive improvement of Kirkgate Market in the 1850s, it was necessary to add another ninety shops to the lower end of the market hall in 1875. These were used mainly for wholesale purposes. About the same time a wholesale and retail fish market, situated at the lower end, replaced the old and inadequate premises near the Shambles.[47] These improvements sufficed for another twenty years. Meanwhile increases in the livestock trade had made the five-acre Smithfield site too small, and in 1886 the council provided a new cattle market on a sixteen-acre site in Gelderd Road, south of Leeds. Known as the Victoria Cattle Market, it cost £43,357.[48] The next development was a wholesale meat market and abattoir in 1898–99. The meat trade had grown with the increase in population and the Shambles, now almost eighty years old, were cramped and insanitary. As the celebratory brochure pointed out, 'Under these circumstances it was obvious that the provision of premises adequate in area, centrally situated, and conveniently constructed could not be delayed, if Leeds was to retain its position as the important meat centre of the North.'[49] The new premises, adjoining the lower part of Kirkgate Market, cost £25,809.[50]

The most spectacular addition of the period was the City Markets, built in 1902–04. In 1893 the Central Market had been severely damaged by fire and, although the building remained partially in use, it was resolved to demolish it in the near future.[51] Around the same time the need for widening Vicar Lane had become urgent. This conjuncture and an increasing volume of trade resulted in a scheme for rebuilding Kirkgate Covered Market. In 1898 the council authorised the erection of a new market hall.[52] The shops and 'open square' at the back of the existing hall were covered over, then in 1902 the hall was demolished and work began on its replacement.[53] The City Markets were opened in 1904 and consisted of a hall with eighteen shops fronting the main roads and an open area inside occupied by stalls and surrounded by small shops. Its upper storeys housed a hotel, a restaurant and billiard, coffee and club rooms. The cost of the project was £116,750.[54] The City Markets survive to the present day, but the additions of 1875 and 1898–1900 were destroyed by fire in 1975.

Concurrently, major developments were taking place among the banks. Only six had survived the crisis of the mid-1840s, and in the following decade there had been no further attempts at expansion. However, in 1859 a new wave of growth was ushered in by the formation of the Yorkshire Penny Savings Bank (now the Yorkshire Bank). Nine new banks or branches of non-Leeds banks were established between 1859 and 1869. Although several of the newcomers were short-lived, by 1870 there were twelve banks. Between 1870 and 1900 the numbers remained largely unchanged, despite periodic entries and exits, but thereafter they rose sharply as branch banking underwent rapid growth.

Prior to 1860 there were few retail developments, apart from shops built in new streets. For the most part, those which lined the main streets were old and drab. However, the situation altered dramatically in the years leading up to the first world war. Rising real incomes and increased food imports,[55] among other factors, led to the building of five impressive shopping arcades and the virtual redevelopment of the shopping centre.

The arcades originated from the shortage of vacant land fronting the main streets and, amazingly, the layout of the medieval borough of Leeds.[56] The ancient system of burgage plots had created a series of yards linking Briggate to the streets which ran parallel to it. Earlier in the century, burgage plots had been utilised in the planning of Commercial Street and the Bazaar and Shambles, and in the 1870s

Charles Thornton was the first person to extend the idea to the construction of arcades. In 1877–78 he built Thornton's Arcade on the site of the Old Talbot Inn and Yard. Its success encouraged emulators. Armistead and Procter built the Queen's Arcade on the site of the Rose and Crown Yard in 1888–89. This was followed by the Grand Arcade, promoted by the New Briggate Arcade Company in 1896–98, and the Victoria Arcade of 1898. The largest and most sumptuous, the County Arcade and its adjunct the Cross Arcade, were built in 1898–1900 by the Leeds Estates Company.

The arcades and the new City Markets formed the central features of what amounted to a complete transformation of the shopping centre between 1875 and 1909. A shoppers' guide to Leeds claimed in 1909:

> No city in England can boast a more wonderful transformation than that witnessed in Leeds during the past two or three decades. . . . The centre of Leeds had been practically re-carved and polished. Nearly the whole of the ramshackle property that skirted the east side of Briggate has been demolished, and on the site had been erected a class of shop property that would do credit to any city in the country. With the offices in Park Row, East Parade, and South Parade almost equal improvements have been made, while for some time past there seems to have been a wholesome rivalry amongst the owners of shop property in Commercial Street to remodel their premises in the most up-to-date and withal artistic lines. Boar Lane, Duncan Street, and Vicar Lane reveal equally amazing individual enterprise.[57]

V   In conclusion, two general points may be made. While all the amenities provided between 1700 and 1914 were a response to the growth of population and trade, the major influence on their timing was the economic climate. Most of the eighteenth-century developments came in bunches coinciding with notable periods of prosperity: the Coloured Cloth Hall, the second White Cloth Hall and Beckett's Bank in 1755–58; the third White Cloth Hall, the Market Cross and Leeds New Bank in 1775–77; the Irregulars' Cloth Hall and Leeds Commercial Bank in 1792–93. The correlation is particularly striking in the market developments of the mid-1820s, the joint-stock banks in the mid-1830s, and the Stock Exchange in the mid-1840s. It occurs later, too, not least in the years when the Wholesale Meat Market, several of the arcades, and the City Markets were projected and built – the chamber of commerce described trade as 'good' in 1898 and 'exceptionally good' in 1899.[58] The second general point is that a major factor in helping Leeds to secure its position as a commercial and marketing centre was the alertness of the business community and the council to what was happening elsewhere, and their willingness to take action when serious competition appeared. The story of the cloth halls and the markets in the 1820s demonstrates the point. The quotations in preceding pages about the Stock Exchange and the Wholesale Meat Market reveal that throughout the nineteenth century considerable importance was attached to maintaining the town's position as a regional centre. Although much-needed improvements were effected slowly in the absence of external pressures, the provision was handsome when it came.

It remains to evaluate the overall contribution to the development of the town. We have suggested already that it was of considerable importance in permitting the growth of population, trade and industry, but it can also be argued that it went substantially beyond this. In the first place, the availability of good amenities would have encouraged businessmen to set up in Leeds and so promote its prosperity. Secondly, the rapid expansion of industry relied on growth in the market for its products. The existence of amenities which assisted trade and promoted contact between sellers and potential buyers was therefore crucial. Finally, and perhaps most important, the amenities played a vital role in securing the capital essential for economic growth. Clearly, the banks and the Stock Exchange stimulated the flow of funds into local commerce and industry, but in fact all the amenities played a part. Much of the wealth produced in the passage of goods from producers to consumers accrues to middlemen. Because Leeds was equipped with the facilities to handle the trading and marketing of local products, the capital of the middlemen stayed in the town and was available to create further wealth. Equally, the attraction of Leeds's amenities, particularly its markets, brought in many outsiders, enabling local middlemen to tap the wealth of neighbouring areas and enlarging the market for local products. Much more research on the impact of commercial, marketing and retailing facilities needs to be undertaken before we can attempt to quantify their contribution to the development of the town. Nevertheless, it is safe to conclude that it was substantial.

NOTES

[1] I wish to thank Professor M. W. Beresford for his comments and advice on the original draft of this chapter, and J. C. Lucking for drawing the drafts of figs. 58 and 65. I owe a special debt to the staffs and assistants of Leeds city archives, Leeds Reference Library, the Brotherton Library, Leeds Civic Hall, the Thoresby Society and the Yorkshire Archaeological Society for the help they gave me in my research. The Thoresby Society and Leeds Reference Library were kind enough to permit the reproduction of illustrative material from their collections – figs. 59–64, Thoresby

Society; figs. 66–7, Reference Library.

² Contemporary descriptions: R. Thoresby, *Ducatus Leodiensis* (1715), 14–15; D. Defoe, *A Tour through the Whole Island of Great Britain* (1971 edn.), 500–2.

³ Pious Uses Committee Minutes, Leeds city archives, DB/197/1, Part 1, 151–5 (1710–11); Part 2, 521, 26 February 1776.

⁴ H. Heaton, *The Yorkshire Woollen and Worsted Industries* (1965), especially ch. 11. H. Heaton, 'The Leeds White Cloth Hall', *Thoresby Soc.*, XXII (1931), 131–71.

⁵ Wakefield Public Rooms Committee, *Public Library and Newsroom* (1 July 1820).

⁶ For the history of Leeds banks see: H. Pemberton, 'Two hundred years of banking in Leeds', *Thoresby Soc.*, XLVI (1963), 54–86; W. C. E. Hartley, *Banking in Yorkshire* (1975), especially 132–7. Except where otherwise stated, the details about Leeds banks in this chapter are drawn from these works.

⁷ J. Singleton, 'Extracts from an old Leeds merchant's memorandum book, 1770–86', *Thoresby Soc.*, XXIV (1915), 36–7.

⁸ W. G. Rimmer, *Marshall's of Leeds, Flax Spinners, 1788–1886* (1960), 37, 96–7. R. G. Wilson, *Gentlemen Merchants* (1971), 153–9.

⁹ Wilson, *op. cit.*, 158.

¹⁰ R. G. Wilson, 'The fortunes of a Leeds merchant house, 1780–1820', *Business History*, IX (1967), 81–3.

¹¹ L. S. Pressnell, *Country Banking in the Industrial Revolution* (1956), 365.

¹² E. Baines, *History and Gazetteer of the County Palatine of Lancaster* (1824), I, 164; II, 135.

¹³ *Leeds Mercury*, 30 December 1729, 13 January, 7 April 1730.

¹⁴ A. Mattison's notes on the 1806 Leeds Directory (held at Leeds Reference Library).

¹⁵ F. Beckwith, 'The beginnings of the Leeds Library', *Thoresby Soc.*, XXXVII (1940), especially 147, 162.

¹⁶ M. W. Beresford, *The Leeds Chambers of Commerce* (1951), 11–22.

¹⁷ *Leeds Intelligencer* 16 December 1805.

¹⁸ *Ibid.*, 2 January 1809.

¹⁹ E. Baines, *History, Directory and Gazetteer of the County of York* (1822), I, 20–1.

²⁰ The provision of these enterprises is discussed fully in K. Grady, 'Profit, property interests, and public spirit: the provision of markets and commercial amenities in Leeds, 1822–9', *Thoresby Soc.*, LIV (1976), 165–95.

²¹ E. Parsons, *The Civil, Ecclesiastical, Literary, Commercial and Miscellaneous History of Leeds . . .* (1834), II, 253.

²² *Leeds Intelligencer*, 18 May 1826.

²³ *Ibid.*, 6 September 1827.

²⁴ *Leeds Mercury*, 5 September 1840.

²⁵ Leeds Improvement Act, Market Committee Minutes (hereafter Mkt. Com. Mins.), 3 August 1842 (Leeds Civic Hall).

²⁶ *Ibid.*, 16 September, 23 December 1842.

²⁷ Report Book, Leeds Improvement Act, I, Report of the Market Committee, 18 January 1843.

²⁸ Mkt. Com. Mins., 14 June, 16 November 1943; 2 May 1844.

²⁹ *Ibid.*, 28 August–16 October 1845.

³⁰ The following details about Leeds Stock Exchange are drawn from: T. Fenteman, *An Historical Guide to Leeds and its Environs* (1858), 45; W. A. Thomas, *The Provincial Stock Exchanges* (1973), especially 50–4, 99–102; and J. R. Killick and W. A. Thomas, 'The provincial stock exchanges, 1830–70', *Economic*

History Review, 2nd ser., XXIII (1970), 96–111.

[31] *Leeds Intelligencer*, 18 January 1845.

[32] Fenteman, *op. cit.*, 46; Beresford, *op. cit.*, especially chs. 3, 5, 8.

[33] *House of Commons Journal*, 16 Vic. (1852–53), 10 February 1853.

[34] Mkt. Com. Mins., 28 December 1852.

[35] Leeds Corporation Report Book, Municipal, III, Report, 9 May 1853.

[36] Mkt. Com. Mins., 20 May, 7 July, 11 August 1853; 10 May 1855. Fenteman, *op. cit.*, 44.

[37] Mkt. Com. Mins., 26 September, 22 December 1853; 19 April 1855; 2 July 1857.

[38] Fenteman, *op. cit.*, 43.

[39] G. Rees, *St. Michael – a History of Marks and Spencer* (1969), 1–22.

[40] Mkt. Com. Mins., 2 July, 30 September 1857.

[41] *Ibid.*, 31 March 1856; 15 January, 30 September, 1 December 1858; 5 January–31 March 1859; 8 August 1860; 8 May 1861; 4, 10 April 1862; 1 February 1864. Leeds City Council, *City of Leeds Markets and Corn Exchange – the Official Handbook* (1951) (hereafter, *Markets Handbook*), 39.

[42] Heaton, *op. cit.* (1965), 390.

[43] Leeds Corporation Deeds Nos. 217 and 216, respectively.

[44] Leeds Corporation Deed No. 225.

[45] *Kelly's Directory of Leeds, 1914* (London), xxxiii.

[46] Cloth halls: Heaton, *op. cit.* (1965), 390–2. South Market: Leeds Corporation Deeds Nos. 898, 1126 and 12716.

[47] *Markets Handbook*, 33–5.

[48] *Ibid.* 41.

[49] City of Leeds, *Opening of the New City Meat Market and Slaughterhouses 24 July 1899* (1899), 6–8.

[50] *Markets Handbook*, 43.

[51] Mkt. Com. Mins., 22 September 1893, 3 January 1894.

[52] *City of Leeds, Council Proceedings* (1898–99), meeting 7 December 1898, 13.

[53] Leeds City Council, *Annual Reports of Committees* (1897–98), Market Committee Report, 2.

[54] City of Leeds, *Opening of the New Market Hall, 1st July 1904. Markets Handbook*, 33–5.

[55] J. B. Jefferys, *Retail Trading in Britain, 1850–1950* (1954), 1–9.

[56] For the information about the arcades I am indebted to Jane Hatcher, who allowed me to consult her unpublished article on the subject, which is based on research sponsored by Leeds Polytechnic School of Architecture.

[57] Leeds Traders' Special Show Week, *Shopping in Leeds* (1909), 27.

[58] Beresford, *op. cit.*, 184. For details of economic fluctuations in the period 1700–1914 see: T. S. Ashton, *Economic Fluctuations in England* (1959); D. H. Aldcroft and P. Fearon (eds.), *British Economic Fluctuations, 1790–1939* (1972).

BIBLIOGRAPHICAL NOTE

The principal secondary sources for this chapter have already been referred to in the notes. However, especially worthy of note are the works of Wilson and Heaton on the development of the merchant community and the cloth halls. Likewise, the works by Pemberton on Leeds banks, and Thomas on the Stock Exchange. Until recently the development of retailing and markets in Leeds has been almost totally neglected. As yet there is no study of retailing in Leeds, but the gaps in our knowledge about markets and commercial amenities have been partially filled by two works: K. Grady, 'Profit, property interests, and public spirit: the provision of markets and commercial amenities in Leeds, 1822–9', *Thoresby Society Publications*, LIV (1976), 165–95; and K. Grady, 'The provision of public buildings in the West Riding of Yorkshire, *c.* 1600–1840' (unpublished Ph.D. thesis, University of Leeds, 1980). The latter has the advantage of comparing developments in Leeds with those in the other principal West Riding towns.

With respect to primary sources, town guides, directories, and newspapers were especially useful. These are available at the City Reference Library and the Brotherton Library. Miscellaneous documents held by the Thoresby Society and the Yorkshire Archaeological Society were also of considerable value, but the most valuable archival material is held at Leeds City Archives, Leeds Civic Hall, and the Brotherton Library. This was as follows: *Cloth Halls.* Brotherton Library, The White Cloth Hall Papers; Leeds City Archives, DB 24, The Coloured Cloth Hall Papers. *Markets and commercial.* Amenities in the 1820s: Leeds City Archives, FW 211; Leeds Civic Hall, Leeds Corporation Deeds Nos. 216, 217, 225, 1189, 12716. Stock Exchange: Leeds City Archives, Records of Leeds Stock Exchange. Markets after 1842: Leeds Civic Hall, Minutes and Reports of Leeds City Council and its Committees. In particular, the minutes of the Market Committee, which give detailed information from 1842 onwards. The Arcades: Leeds City Archives, documents relating to two of the arcades have recently been put on deposit.

R. J. MORRIS

VIII

Middle-class culture, 1700–1914

Leeds like all the great manufacturing cities in England is a dirty smoky, disagreeable town ... Leeds is perhaps the ugliest and least attractive town in all England. [J. G. Kohl, 1844]

I always hope that a museum will be retained on that site [Park Row], as witness of something non commercial in the middle of an absolute materialistic neighbourhood [E. Kitson Clark, 12 May 1916, 49 West Riding Division B.D., Camp 16]

I   Much of this book is about the way in which the people of Leeds sought power and wealth through politics, commerce and industry. This chapter is about the way in which they used some of that power and wealth to enjoy and promote science, art, music, literature, the theatre and others of those cultural activities directed 'to the improvement of the human mind and spirit'.[1] The majority wanted little more than entertainment and the status derived from taking part in activities highly regarded by others. A small portion of those who made up the middle classes of Leeds made a considerable creative contribution to the cultural activities they took part in and brought to themselves and others a deeper understanding of the world around them. By 1832 over a fifth of the population could claim middle-class status. Most of them were shopkeepers, master manufacturers and moderately wealthy professional men, but they were led by an elite of merchants recently joined by the major manufacturing families and linked to their wealthy professional aides. This elite became increasingly conscious of the need for culture. By the nineteenth century, culture was not only a matter of personal pleasure but a defence against those who criticised them as the money-makers of mucky Leeds; after all, Lord Ashley compared them unfavourably with Sodom and Gomorrah. When the Philosophical and Literary Society established itself the satisfaction was evident.

Leeds has long both in the number of its inhabitants and in its commercial importance ranked as the metropolis of the West Riding of Yorkshire . . . we shall no longer hear the inhabitant complain that there is nothing to show the visitor nor the stranger, that Leeds contains no object of interest, save dirty and smoky manufactories.[2]

The cultural achievement of this middle class complemented their economic status. The achievement was a mixed one. In the main it was that of collectors and borrowers. In this they represented much of the British middle class, at least in the manufacturing towns of the north. They were in the very best way the 'philistines' of Arnold's *Culture and Anarchy*. When they wished to decorate and extend the meaning of their lives and the life of the communities in which they lived, they went out and purchased what they wanted. They drew on the inspiration of London, its books, music, its art market and scientific societies. They plundered world history. They plundered the cultures discovered by their trade, and the results still lie scattered in the museums, libraries and architecture of modern Leeds.

II   The eighteenth century was the period which laid the foundations of the cultural life of the industrial revolution. Thoresby's diaries showed how narrow and bleak that life was around 1700. His own pioneering interest in antiquities was shared by a few men only, and they were scattered across the north and Midlands of England. Reading and listening to sermons was the major cultural activity he shared with others. The weekly record of the sermon was a feature his diary shared with those of Mrs Elizabeth Gott 120 years later, but there the similarity ends. Experience of art and literature was limited to the private possessions of the wealthy merchants' houses; contact and discussion only came from the visits of friends and relatives.

Throughout the period music was a major form of entertainment and expression. Public performances had their beginning, like so much else, in the church and public house. Leeds Parish Church installed an organ in 1713, and an organist was appointed a year later, though Thoresby felt that the organ voluntaries were merely an excellent time for reading pamphlets and sermons. There were occasional concerts in the Assembly Rooms in Kirkgate in the 1720s. In 1741 Leeds was included in the musical tours of Mr Parry, domestic harper to Sir Watkin Williams Wynn, who played pieces by Handel, Corelli and Vivaldi, including the 'Cuckow Extravaganza'. These visits and the music which accompanied the dancing assemblies that were held each winter were the staple diet until the appointment of Crompton as organist at the parish church. He promoted a series of concerts in the Assembly Rooms and by 1762 was ready to advertise a series of subscription concerts. The price of a double ticket for a lady and a gentleman was 15s. These concerts, like the sporadic efforts which had gone before, were a mixture – Handel, Arne, Bach and Avison, with the harpsichord, French horn and violin as the favourite solo instruments. Overtures, a concerto, parts of longer works, orchestral and oratorio were mingled with popular songs and even short plays and recitations. By the 1760s there was a concert room in the Rose and Crown in Kirkgate, and music was played in the churches for entertainment rather than as part of an act of worship. In 1767 Purcell's *Te Deum* and *Grand Coronation Chorus* were performed in the chapel in Holbeck, a success which was followed at Christmas with the appropriate parts of the *Messiah*. By 1768 the *Messiah* had arrived on the West Riding scene, and that winter was performed eighteen times in the Assembly Rooms, tickets 1s, or 15s for the season. Oratorio, often performed in one of the churches, became a major part of music in Leeds. Unlike the concerts, they were not followed by dancing. Leading vocalists often came from other towns, and Leeds singers would travel elsewhere to help other performances. After 1772 the new organist Jobson maintained the activity generated by Crompton, helped by the opening of the New Assembly Rooms over the north side of the White Cloth Hall in 1777. By the 1780s the musical entertainments of earlier years were becoming more differentiated. There was oratorio. There was lighter music at Mr Hindle's Great Room in the Rose and Crown, and the old mixture of orchestral selections with songs, airs and glees but fewer recitations. The subscription concerts, like the assemblies, were places to see and be seen, a way of identifying with and being identified with the elite of Leeds and the surrounding countryside. When the New Assembly Rooms were opened the dancing was led by Sir George Saville and Lady Effingham. Thirty years later these events were still an important part of elite entertainment. In January 1810 Mrs Gott recorded, '. . . took Miss Clifton, John Dixon, John, William, Susanna and Anne to the concert, staid to see the dancing, the little girls joined a young party and danced two dances'.[3]

The subscription concerts continued, with gaps during the economic distress in 1781–83 and the years after 1798. Handel increased in popularity. In 1784 Leeds had its own Handel commemoration festival in Trinity Church, and the subscription concerts included more and more choral music. In 1794 the Music Hall was opened in Albion Street, and promptly became the venue for these concerts as well as for many public meetings, travelling entertainments and lectures. In the 1790s music became a part of demonstrations of loyalty. The subscription concerts had the patronage of the Volunteers, and the military bands played and provided instruments for many different kinds of performances. In the winter of 1797 the opening concert began with *Rule Britannia*, complete with a special verse written by the Duke of Leeds to celebrate the victory of Camperdown.

The scattered concert programmes of the 1820s showed a revival of the old mixture and an increase in the charity concerts which had been a feature of Leeds music since the 1760s, in aid of Harrison's Hospital, the General Infirmary and other causes. After 1800 an increasing number were held to collect money for the poor in times of economic slump. The concert in aid of the 1832 relief fund included a sinfonia by Mozart, a grand overture by Rossini, many glees and songs, and a hymn, tune by Haydn, words by Michael Thomas Sadler:

> Music in the best of causes,
> Sinking deeper than the ear
> ... Hark, yon objects of compassion
> Thus their grateful feelings pour.
> Lord, a rich remuneration
> On this generous audience shower ...

The performances of the 1820s were not concerts in the modern sense but still selections from longer orchestral pieces interspersed with songs and short instrumental pieces. Even the so–called oratorio rarely contained a full work. There was still Handel and Haydn, with the addition of Rossini, Mozart, Romberg and Weber. The songs included more Italian lyrics, the 'Favourite Strains of the Scottish Bards' by Sir Walter Scott and a never-ending selection of sentimental ballads – 'Lo, here the gentle lark', song by Bishop; 'See the chariot at hand here of love', glee from Morsley; 'O, thou art the lad of my heart, Willy, There's love and there's life and glee', Scotch air; in other words the popular music of the day. It was a vast and formless profusion suiting a variety of tastes which prospered with the commerce and industry of Leeds.

III   Small groups of men discussing literary and scientific interests must have been part of urban society since the seventeenth century. For Leeds the years around 1770 were again a turning point. Between 1769 and 1775, when Joseph Priestley, the theologian and experimental scientist, was minister at Mill Hill chapel, he enjoyed the company of a group which included Smeaton the engineer, and William Hey, surgeon, a devout Tory Evangelical, a Methodist turned

Anglican and a founder of the Leeds General Infirmary. Priestley's own work on air and Hey's on the blood, which earned him the fellowship of the Royal Society in 1775, were both a part of the most advanced scientific work of their generation. The Leeds meetings were a prototype of the better known Lunar Society which flourished in the Midlands when Priestley moved to Birmingham in the 1780s. The textile economy of the town could not support an active scientific culture in the manner of Newcastle, Manchester or the Midlands, despite several attempts. Between 1783 and 1786 a small philosophical society, with Hey as first president, met privately. Hey looked back with pride on what he believed was valuable scientific work done by this group. In his paper 'On the arched aurora borealis', submitted to the Royal Society in 1787, he began, 'One advantage resulting from the institution of philosophical societies is thus: an increase in the number of observers: an advantage of greatest moment with respect to those phenomena of nature which are local and transient . . .'[4] When Baines wrote the introduction to his Leeds directory in 1817, he looked back on several unsuccessful efforts. 'With the exception of those arts which have an immediate reference to commerce and manufactures, philosophical researches are not much cultivated in Leeds; still less do literary pursuits engage the attention of its inhabitants.' One society founded in 1793 failed after six years. Two others, founded since then, had also failed, as had the Northern Society's art exhibition in 1809–11. One reason was hinted at in an earlier guide to Leeds:

> An attempt was made in the year 1793 with a partial degree of success, to establish a society for the discussion of literary and moral subjects, but the temper of the times was so adverse to everything which suggested the idea of debate, that the number of its members was never considerable and after being continued for several years with various success, it was entirely given up.[5]

The bitter political and religious divisions of Leeds produced a lively political life and, in the form of Baines's *Mercury*, a major cultural innovation in newspaper content, but this was of little help in promoting open scientific and literary discussion. Nor did the economic needs of the town, unlike those of the mining industry of north-east England, provide much encouragement.

The Leeds Library was the most enduring of the results of the cultural renaissance which began like the expansion of the textile industry around 1770, and encompassed music and the theatre as well as books. The library was founded in 1767 under the influence of Joseph Priestley. It was a proprietary library, following a pattern of organisation developed in Liverpool. In 1808, financed by its wealthy shareholders, it emerged from 'a dark and incommodious garrett in a back yard' to the elegant building which it still occupies in Commercial Street. The Rev. Whitaker regarded circulating libraries as 'equivocal institutions'. They diffused '. . . a mediocrity of information'. 'They afford materials for general conversation, they make agreeable men, and thus the middle ranks of society in large towns, through the influence of these institutions meet on a general level.'[6]

By the 1800s the number of subscription libraries had grown in variety and number. The New Subscription Library, for which one of the Unitarian Dissenting Lupton family was treasurer between 1805 and 1811, had a Whiggish flavour to counter the mild Tory Anglican nature of the Leeds Library. The *Monthly Repository*, the *Edinburgh Review* and biographies of Washington, Priestley, Franklin and Fox were the staple of the alternative elite culture which the Whig Dissenters were building with their new-found wealth.[7] The Wesleyans had a large library of their own in St Peter's Square, and other, smaller ones were run by several booksellers to serve an insatiable and growing taste for novels and other popular works.

Of all the cultural activities, reading was the most popular and all-pervasive. The early newspapers advertised books when notices of other amusements were sparse. By the 1760s there were frequent notices of books and periodicals, *The Monthly Melody*, *The Royal Female Magazine*, *Christians Magazine* and the *Universal Review*, sold by men like G. Copperthwaite, who also offered histories, sermons, the *Universal Dictionary of Arts and Sciences* (eight volumes), *The Spectator* and *The Tatler* (see *Leeds Intelligencer*, 8 July 1760). By the end of the century the book advertisements, almost always from London publishers, included many more novels, and the reading habit was supported by public readings, like those given by the Rev. C. Vincent in the Music Hall in March 1801. This was family entertainment; 'the lover of jest and ribaldry would have been out of his element . . .'.[8]

The bookshops of late eighteenth-century Leeds were social and intellectual centres for a middle class which had yet to develop the clubs, newsrooms and philosophical societies of the next half-century. When John Heaton, a clothier's son, was apprenticed to the Briggate bookseller John Binns in the 1780s he found, 'It was here [the bookshop] that the clergy met on Monday morning to discuss together perchance the sermons of the previous day, more probably the last pamphlet from London, or the contents of the new number of the *Gentleman's Magazine*.' This habit survived into the 1820s, when

John Heaton junior, who became a leading medical man of the mid-nineteenth century, recalled, 'my father's shop was a common resort for several gentlemen of leisure in the town, who spent their spare time there, looking over books or chatting together on public and social affairs'.[9] Already the place of bookshops was being taken by the other institutions. Books were so much part of the fabric of the culture of the middle and other social classes that they pass almost unnoticed. For Mrs Gott, with the wealth of Bean Ing to support her life at Armley, books were presents for the family at New Year, and a reason for trips into Leeds to change a library book. For the less wealthy they were treasured possessions to be carefully bequeathed in wills, and for many clerks, shopkeepers and artisans they were a reason for joining the new Mechanics' Institution in the 1830s and 1840s. The borrowers' register clearly showed where taste lay. In 1846 42,501 books were issued, of which 13,758 were fiction and only 303 were politics and statistics. The bulk of the rest were history, biography, travel and the fine arts. Some members at least shared surgeon Thomas Nunneley's belief that 'the reading of trashy novels was a great waste of time'.[10]

IV   Tate Wilkinson, who built the town's first theatre in Hunslet Lane in 1771, experienced in full the difficulties of those who sought to promote the cultural life of Leeds. In the early eighteenth century Leeds had occasional visits from travelling players who performed in the Great Room of the Rose and Crown, or on a stage set up in the yard. Such performances became increasingly common. They were advertised as concerts, and the plays were performed with music during the interval, a device which avoided the need for a licence. Tate Wilkinson was an outstanding entrepreneur. He created a theatre circuit based on York which included Leeds, Pontefract, Wakefield, Doncaster and Hull. In this way he was able to amass a vast stock of painted scenery and keep his actors fully employed. He had an ability to select, when they were relatively unknown, players like Mrs Jordan and Charles Matthews who later became famous on the London stage. Wilkinson rarely got large or appreciative audiences in Leeds, which became known as 'the Botany Bay of actors'. On one side were the Methodists and other Dissenters who preached against the 'devil's children' and stayed away. The very titles of the plays must have made them uneasy – *The Clandestine Marriage, The Virgin Unmasked, School for Scandal* and, perhaps worst of all, the new masquerade *A Methodist Parson*. When Charles Cummins, one of the stock actors of the company, died on stage in 1817 the Evangelical churchmen moralised with solemn glee and recommended attending '. . . Bible Societies, Missionary Societies, Tract Societies, and Sunday School Unions', where 'without injury to your morals' could be seen 'not the painted cheeks and seducing smiles of the actress . . . but a far more lovely sight – the features of modest beauty, lighted up with a glow of sacred rapture'.[11] The offerings in Hunslet Lane were harmless enough – musicals, light comedy and a little Shakespeare – but for those who escaped the Methodists there were the Leeds croppers, a self-confident group of skilled men with a great capacity for enjoying rather than respecting their theatre. As Mrs Siddons languished on stage preparing to drain the poisoned cup one night a strident voice called from the back row, 'That's right, Molly, soop it oop, ma lass!' At about the same time another young actress was unwisely strolling by the canal and was seized by the croppers with the cry, 'I've caught a laker.' She was wrapped in brown paper, soaked in canal water and chased towards the town 'with yells of delight'. Leeds was hard work. Tate Wilkinson and his company loved York, especially in race week, and the location of subscribers to his memoirs showed how comparatively weak interest was in Leeds – the largest town in the list. There were 576 subscribers, of which York had 112, Leeds 35, Hull 32, Wakefield 21 and Doncaster 15.

The fortunes of painting and sculpture were better. There was a small but growing community of artists from the 1790s. The place occupied by the camera and the photographer in many lives now was taken by the sketch book and the portrait and landscape painter, those artists who gained the everyday patronage of the provinces, 'those who chronicle our faces or perpetuate the remembrance of our dogs and horses . . .'.[12] Schwarnfelder was probably the most outstanding of the group in the 1820s, if only because he was animal painter to the Prince Regent, and his pictures sold for the highest prices at the exhibitions – up to £50 or £60. He began painting clock faces and tea trays and became best known for painting the pets, horses and dead game of the wealthier families of the area. More typical were Charles Cope and Joseph Rhodes. The demand for paintings was inadequate, so they made their living by teaching painting and drawing to the young ladies of the middle class. Rhodes ran an evening class which attracted the sons of local merchants and shopkeepers. Cope was 'an enthusiastic artist . . . a water colour painter in landscape pure and simple', who left his son a collection of 'fine engravings of Turner's "South Coast" and Northern series'. Rhodes had begun his working life apprenticed to a house painter, but after a spell in London, where he attended evening classes at the Royal Academy under West and Fuseli, he returned to Leeds about 1811, where he taught for forty years and built up a reputation as a careful and painstaking artist of landscape and conversation pieces. They were not great artists but they made a comfortable and friendly living and gave a great deal of pleasure to customers like Joseph Rogerson, the Bramley scribbling miller, who wrote in his diary for 15 September 1812, 'Got my portrait taken at Leeds.' It was a quick and satisfactory job. A week later he wrote, 'At Leeds to-day. Flatt Market. Corn lower'd 25/- Pr Ld – Got my portrait home to-day; they say it is a very good likeness.'[13]

Industrial and commercial wealth created a series of major art collections in the big houses on the hills above the Aire. The most important was without doubt that of Benjamin Gott at Armley. The house had been rebuilt by Smirke in 1803 and landscaped by Repton. He bought carefully and thoughtfully through London dealers and the local exhibitions which he helped to sponsor. By 1819 he had two paintings attributed to Claude, and in the 1820s he exhibited paintings attributed to Caravaggio, Claude, Poussin, Murillo and several Dutch painters. In 1828 his portrait and that of his wife Elizabeth were painted by Sir Thomas Lawrence, and in 1829 Schwarnfelder paid several visits to the house to paint the dog Juno. The early death of Gott's son Benjamin in 1817 during a visit to Athens had an important influence on his patronage. Benjamin junior had already completed a major tour of the Low Countries in 1814, and reported back on the art galleries and local importers of woollen cloth with equal precision. His next trip through Italy to Greece in 1817 ended in his death from fever in Piraeus and his burial in the Temple of Theseus at Athens, having died, as his epitaph said, 'In the ardent pursuit of knowledge and in the full vigour of his life'. The memorial in Armley church was commissioned by his father from a distant cousin, Joseph Gott, who chiselled several statues and medallions from the marble of north Italy for the Gott family and their friends, and in 1822 Gott commissioned a view of Athens from the Edinburgh artist Hugh William Williams.[14]

For those who wanted to look at pictures rather than own them the situation around 1800 was tantalising. There were many rich country house collections like that of the Ingrams at Temple Newsam and the collection of Turner watercolours and oils being built up by Fawkes of Farnley Hall, but they and the others were notoriously difficult of access for the general public. The exhibitions of the Northern Society for the Encouragement of the Fine Arts in 1809-11 and 1822-30 were a major innovation. These exhibitions began as a selling point for the products of local and London artists. They were organised by the local eccentric and collector F. T. Billam, in conjunction with his friends among the Leeds artists and a committee of gentry, merchant and manufacturing patrons, including Gotts, Marshalls, Blaydses and Becketts. The exhibitions were typical of many held in provincial English towns in the first thirty years of the nineteenth century, but they were far more successful in terms of attendance and sales than those in Norwich or Liverpool, and far more harmonious than those in Newcastle, whilst Manchester and Birmingham found it hard to sustain any run of exhibitions at all. The Leeds success as a marketing centre for modern paintings was probably due to the happy relationship between the Tory merchant elite and their county gentry, who, after all, were in many cases only a generation away from merchant wealth and still used Leeds as a social and political centre. These men bought the pictures whilst the rest of the middle-class population paid their 1s to see them.

The pictures on show were mainly landscapes and portraits, with some animal paintings and religious themes. The early exhibitions included only 'modern paintings'. Despite the contributions of men like Schwarnfelder and Cope, London was the dominant source of supply. (Table 15.) When the exhibitions revived in the 1820s they included 'Ancient Masters', thus serving the wider interests of collectors and visitors as well as those of the artists. The paintings shown again indicated the manner in which the gentlemen collectors of the area were able to indulge their taste. (Table 16.) The landscapes, seascapes, interiors and conversation pieces of the

Table 15 Source of paintings at the Northern Society's exhibitions, 1809–10

Source of paintings exhibited	No. of artists		No. of paintings	
	1809	*1810*	*1809*	*1810*
Leeds	4	6	44	29
London	14	26	61	78
Rest of Yorkshire	17	19	74	57
Rest of Britain[a]	5	8	18	15
Total	40	59	197	179

Note
[a] Edinburgh, Newcastle, Liverpool.

seventeenth-century Dutch masters dominated as one commercial community avidly collected the artistic products of the trading elite they had supplanted in world trade. The eighteenth-century British painters like Richard Wilson were sought for their landscapes, and the

Table 16 Origin of paintings at the Northern Society's exhibition, 1824

Origin of paintings	No. of artists	No. of paintings
Dutch, sixteenth-century	3	5
Dutch, seventeenth-century	47	72
British, mainly eighteenth-century	22	37
Italian, sixteenth-century and earlier	9	18
Italian, seventeenth-century	17	37
Spanish, sixteenth- and seventeenth-century	5	6
German, seventeenth-century	4	10
French, mainly seventeenth-century	7	14

seventeenth-century Italians for classical as well as religious subjects.

Many of these pictures were again shown at the Public Exhibition of Works of Art, Science, Natural History and Manufacturing Skill organised by a joint committee from the Mechanics' Institution and the Philosophical and Literary Society in 1839, and at two similar exhibitions in 1843 and 1845, all of which raised money for the Institution's hall. Fawkes again lent the complete run of his Turner watercolours, which were always given a special cheer at the public dinners and were welcomed by the *Leeds Mercury* in 1843 as 'unequalled in truth, power and brilliancy'. These exhibitions had a mood of moral and social purpose quite distinct from the earlier ones. There was defensive urban pride in the comments of George Goodman, wool merchant and former mayor: 'The splendid paintings . . . showed that a high degree of civilization and improvement was taking place in the town'.

The social purpose was twofold. Dr Pyemont Smith felt that the exhibition provided 'a rational evening's amusement drawing the working classes to the Exhibition with their wives and families, instead of spending their hours rioting in the public houses'. Costs were low because of the free loan of exhibits and the voluntary administrative work done by the committee. Admission was 6*d*, or 2*s* 6*d* for a season ticket. Edward Baines junior hoped that 'the exertions and sacrifices made by gentlemen of property . . . [would] . . . knit together the different classes of society in bonds of kindness'.[14] The industrial middle class were becoming acutely aware of the dangers of class conflict, in the form of violent trade unionism, anti-Poor Law disturbances, Chartist and short-time agitations. They hoped that this sharing of cultural products would help bridge the gap. The books and classes of the Mechanics' Institution, founded in 1824, the gardens of the Zoological and Botanical Society, and the railway excursions in the 1840s to Chatsworth and the Lake District were all part of this movement.

The exhibitions were among the few occasions when the industrial products and skills of the West Riding were brought into association with creative culture. Visitors were entertained by the displays of a glass blower from the Hunslet works of Joshua Bower and by textile machinery driven by a small steam engine. There was little interaction between the two sides of the exhibitions. There was an ill attended School of Design in the 1840s inspired by Henry Cole's Arts–Manufactures movement in London, but the purpose was educational rather than creative. In Leeds, as in the rest of Europe, the middle classes and the artists they patronised were reluctant to use their industrial achievements as a source of inspiration or of materials for their art.

V   Industrial wealth meant that an increasing number of Leeds people began to travel for recreation. Benjamin Gott's ill fated trip has already been mentioned. He had been following in the footsteps of one of the younger Becketts. In the 1840s John Heaton, the bookseller's son, now a young physician, visited Paris, toured Italy and with his new wife travelled up the Rhine on what was the traditional marriage tour of his class and generation. More typical were the journeys of Edward Baines junior in the 1820s to London, Portsmouth, Edinburgh and the Lake District. They were enough to make him return to Leeds in 1824 feeling

> I quitted it [London] therefore with feelings of regret as departing from the seat of power and grandeur, the high parliament of genius and learning, the museum of art, the emporium of wealth, to reside in a comparatively small mean and empty place . . . my fellow townsmen must pardon this libel on my native Leeds.[16]

This dissatisfaction with Leeds and the wider range of experience of the younger men who came to control the town after 1815 was one factor in the successful foundation of the Philosophical and Literary Society in 1819. This society, based on the Philosophical Hall in Park Row, became the focus of the most important cultural activities of the elite over the next seventy or eighty years.

'The energy and knowledge of Leeds people,' wrote the young surgeon Charles Turner Thackrah, was 'too exclusively devoted to the acquisition of wealth.'[17] This dissatisfaction with Leeds as a place of profit mingled with other influences to produce the Phil. and Lit. The medical profession, with its scientific interests, had increased fourfold since the 1780s.[18] Willian Hey senior had been an isolated if inspiring figure. The generation of doctors who worked in Leeds between 1820 and 1850 produced several men with the same initiative and scientific interest. Adam Hunter studied fever. Thackrah himself was to publish the first work on industrial medicine. James Williamson combined medicine with an interest in education, and Robert Baker quarrelled with him over who should have the credit for their work on sanitation and public health. The eighteenth-century Infirmary had been joined by the House of Recovery, a fever hospital, in 1804 and the Public Dispensary in the 1820s, all of which provided a basis for practice, teaching and the exchange of ideas.

The Phil. and Lit. was inspired by the example of other successful provincial societies in Manchester and Newcastle. There was a firm rejection of aristocratic patronage. The first committee insisted that it had 'little assistance from the patronage of rank and power . . . a fact highly honourable to the promoters of the society'.[19] This was quite different from the promoters of music and fine arts, who had delighted in such patronage. There was a careful consciousness of middle-class identity and independence in the early Phil. and Lit. which combined easily with the utilitarian and scientific interests of the Unitarian congregation at Mill Hill. Their minister, Philip Wicksteed, was an active member in the 1830s and 1840s:

> . . . it [the society] was a source of keen interest and enjoyment to him. It brought him into contact with many interesting people, and furnished him with the occasion for formulating and extending his own studies and opinions in matters not immediately connected with his professional work . . .[20]

Although the Marshall family was making the genteel transition from chapel to church, its interest in education, in geology and in the collection of statistical information all betrayed the intellectual influences of the Unitarians, a religious group which was the basis of Lit. and Phils. in many other provincial towns.

Another source of the broadening intellectual, especially philosophical, interests of the middle class came from the Edinburgh education which many preferred to Oxford or Cambridge. Both the older Gott boys had spent a year or so in Edinburgh, not taking a degree but listening and attending classes. Several of the doctors had also come south. Given this, and the other cultural links with Scotland – *Blackwood's* and the *Edinburgh Review* were eagerly read in Leeds – it was not surprising that many of the titles of papers read at the Phil. and Lit. had the broad humanistic expansiveness of the essay topics given to Edinburgh students in the early years of the nineteenth century: 'On Personal Identity' by the Rev. R. W. Hamilton, March 1825; 'On the physical modes of matter' by Alexander Taylor, MD, December 1828; 'The philosophy of music' by William Hey junior; 'The application of mathematical reasoning to metaphysical and moral science' by the Rev. James Acworth.

The hints of middle-class independence which the Society carried with it did not hinder a deep interest in classical literature and learning which the elite had imbibed with their aspirations to emulate if not replace the aristocracy. Knowledge of the authors of ancient Greece and Rome would, wrote Thackrah, '... enlarge our acquaintance with the dispositions and manners of men'. The discussion of politics and religion was forbidden, so as to prevent the disunity which had ruined some of the earlier societies, but such contentious issues might be tackled in a calmer manner in the context of Greek and Roman civilisation. Thus Baines junior, talking on 'The Elgin Marbles and the causes of the excellence of Grecian Sculpture', found the cause in '... the almost unlimited freedom of their government [and] that spirit of competition which their institutions encouraged among the Athenians ... competition furnishes the greatest stimulus to excellence of almost any kind'.[21] From a man who had witnessed Peterloo, opposed the corn laws and advocated free trade and the free spread of machinery this was a code which hardly needed breaking.

For the intellectually active portion of the Leeds elite the Philosophical and Literary Society became an important sounding board for new ideas and a basis for social action. When the Mechanics' Institution was founded in 1824, thirteen of the twenty members of the first committee were members of the Phil. and Lit., including Benjamin Gott. In the early years the Institution had frequent loans of the Society's hall for its meetings. In 1826 Dr James Williamson talked on infant education, no doubt reflecting the views of James Wilderspin, published in London two years before, that children should be in school from the age of five. The same year saw the foundation of the Leeds Infant School Society, with many members of the Phil. and Lit. active. During the 1820s F. T. Billam gave several papers on art and art history to stimulate interest in the Northern Society exhibitions. M. T. Sadler provoked much discussion with his paper 'On the best means of improving the condition of the poor in large towns' and gave an account of his anti-Malthusian ideas, which were later to be published in two volumes. William Osburn, the wine and spirit merchant, gave several papers on the recent discoveries and speculations on Egyptian antiquities. J. I. Ikin, the surgeon, spoke on political economy and the effects of machinery on wages in the early

1830s, a period of violent trade union influence in Leeds. In 1837 J. G. Marshall promoted the formation of a statistical section which was one influence behind Baker's 1839 pamphlet, which also appeared as a paper to the Society in the same year. In later years the Phil. and Lit. took an active part in the building of the Town Hall and the creation of the university.

Despite this wealth of activity the Society rapidly lost sight of one of its original aims, that of promoting active scientific research. Even the number of scientific papers at meetings declined from thirteen out of sixteen in 1822 to some three or four per year in the 1840s, when philosophy, art and literature attracted most attention. Many members had so far forgotten William Hey's original intentions that science had become a form of amusement. The Rev. William Sinclair introduced the programme of the annual *conversazione* in 1848 as one designed 'to salve the miseries of the man of business in quest of suitable amusement'. The programme included a demonstration of the electric clock by J. P. Cox, Esq., the Electric Telegraph Company's superintendent, and experiments with gas light and the cycloidoscope by William West, Esq.

One of the most enduring contributions the Society made to Leeds was its museum, which still forms the basis of the city collection.[22] Here the talents of the middle class as collectors and borrowers showed to perfection. The bulk of the objects were donated by friends and members, and all were acknowledged in the annual reports. They were a celebration of wealth, of travel, of the anxiety to possess, control and understand creation. The rich profusion of objects were collected, classified and labelled, almost as a form of worship; 135 specimens of British birds from Mr John Atkinson, surgeon, specimens illustrative of the geology of Yorkshire by Edward Sanderson George, gentleman. Minerals, birds, mosses, plants and antiquities came in from all corners of the British Isles, and from all points touched by the trade, tourism and empire-building of the men of Leeds and their friends – a smoking pipe from Athens by George Goodman, 117 lavas from Vesuvius from George Banks, stuff merchant, and a specimen of an Indian dress from Obediah Brook, Esq., surgeon – collecting, possessing, displaying, the barbaric joy of a class of men just beginning to feel their power and success in war and industry. Pride of place was taken by the Egyptian mummy which was presented to the Society by John Blayds, the banker, in 1824. It appears to have been purchased in Trieste from J. Passalacque, a native of Egypt and 'a most successful spoliator of the tombs of the ancient Egyptians'.[23] Notable by its absence from the collection was any reference to the economic activities upon which the wealth of members was based. As with their art, the middle classes turned their back on the mills, forges and workshops from which their wealth came.

The instinct for collecting and borrowing showed in the architecture of the middle years of the nineteenth century. In the building of Park Square the merchant and professional men of Leeds had taken the pattern books of London architects and then relied on the nature of local materials, mellow red brick and yellow sandstone, to develop the elegant lines of the eighteenth-century West End. This habit faded with the nineteenth century. Marshall's new single-storey mill in Holbeck was the most advanced design possible in terms of production and working conditions, but it was encased in the splendour of ancient Egypt. When Mill Hill chapel was rebuilt in 1843 the simple lines of the old building were abandoned for squat decorated Gothic, whilst the Anglicans built one Gothic church after another, using a revival of medieval styles to make a statement about the nature of worship, and about the link between the town and God, which came from the architect's pattern book and the ideas expressed by Pugin in the 1840s. Armley gaol, built in 1847, was not content with the functional lines of the Benthamite panopticon but used the image of the medieval castle for an aggressive statement of power to terrify the captive and assure the strong of their safety. Across the river, Cuthbert Broderick's Town Hall, in some ways the last of the classical tradition, imported the civic splendour of Italy and Germany, whilst upon the facades of the growing number of office blocks in what was once the residential West End appeared bits of Italian, oriental and classical facades. There was little attempt to use the material of the industrial revolution except in the iron-framed girder arches across the railway stations and in some of the arcades, and the Minton tiles which encrusted the interior of the Town Hall. Industrial skills were concealed in the frame of the building and in the keen edge of the stone-cutting and brick-making machinery of the contractors.

This account of culture relies on the records of public activities, but it must not be forgotten that for most people reading and discussing books, playing and listening to music were something enjoyed in private with small groups – family, friends, church, chapel, public house or institution. Records of this exist only in the brief mention in diaries and biographies. Mrs Gott notes 'the young people' dancing reels, her pleasure at the musical abilities of a house guest and the visit of Mr Muff 'to put the instruments in tune'. The enjoyment behind Joseph Rogerson's cryptic diary entry is evident. 'Opened our new organ today; there was a very grand sing, the chapel so crowded as I never saw it. Text preached by Mr. Humphreys from 8 chap Romans 1 verse. A collection was made for the general infirmary at Leeds' (19 September 1813). There was the list of book purchases carefully entered in the household account of the Quaker merchant John Jowitt in the 1830s, and Charles Cope's memory of his father: 'He was never so happy as when listening to reading aloud in the evenings while drawing . . . On Sunday afternoon he had a doze, with a yellow silk handkerchief thrown over his head. In the evenings of Sunday, my sister and I had to read aloud grave books such as Hannah Moore, till the weekly arrival of his friend F. T. Billam.'[24]

The Leeds directories show a steady increase in the number of retail outlets for books, music and pictures between 1814 and 1870, an expansion which was a response to the demand of ordinary people for cultural activities. Some of the fluctuations must reflect the quality of the directory, and none of the figures can indicate the increasing size of shops or businesses, but several trends do emerge. There was an expansion in the number of bookshops in the 1820s and 1850s, whilst libraries increased in the 1830s and late 1850s, both periods of stagnation for the bookshops. There was a period of difficulty for all in the 1840s, as might be expected from the state of trade in that decade. There was a steady and sustained increase in landscape and portrait painters from 1820 to 1837, and another increase in the 1850s before the expansion faltered in the face of the development of the photographer's studio. The state of music is hardest to read, as the quality and practice of each directory varied. After establishing themselves at around fifteen in the 1820s the number of music sellers varied little; music teachers showed a clear increase in the 1850s as the middle class spent some of the prosperity of the mid-Victorian boom on teaching themselves music as well as on books and having their pictures painted. The fall in the number of booksellers in the late '50s and '60s was due to the increased specialisation between booksellers and stationers, the move of many shops to the suburbs and the increased size of outlets. W. H. Smith had arrived in Leeds by 1871.

Music increased in both quality and quantity, with a slow development in organisation and content. There was a growing world of professional musicians, some based on London and touring, the virtuosi who dominated concert life, like Paganini, who played in the Music Hall in 1832. There were others based in Leeds and the West Riding who supplemented an income from performances by teaching or by a post as organist in church or chapel. Amateur musical societies grew in number and variety — many hired professionals for lead and solo parts if necessary. As the expansion in the number of music teachers suggests, there was an increase in playing among family and friends. The violinist George Haddock recalled that in mid-century 'there were at least a dozen houses of our first and most influential families at which weekly quartet meetings were held, these being the principal recreations for the winter months'.[25] There was no sharp dividing line between the worlds of family, amateur and professional music. The Leeds Musical Soirées, started in 1848, were organised by a select society which included Heatons, Marshalls, Kitsons and Heys among its members. They met in members' houses and occupied the intervals between selections from Handel, Mendelssohn and Wesley with refreshments, including sherry and port.[26]

Table 17 Economic history of books, music and pictures in Leeds, 1814–70

	Booksellers and stationers	Libraries	Music		Artists	Photographers
			Sellers	Teachers		
1814	14	—		3	—	—
1816	13	—		6	—	—
1817	13	—		10	4	—
1822	21	10		13	4	—
1826	24	10		12	9	—
1830	28	10		15	10	—
1834	26	16	11	12	10	—
1837	28	21	14	10	14	—
1842	33	19	17	15	11	1
1847	39	16	14	12	12	1
1849	30	13	10	16	14	1
1851	35	11	12	21	15	1
1857	54	26	18	37	14	18
1861	51	35	15	53	11	25
1870	54	22	13	53	22	33

Source. Leeds directories, 1814–70.

Concerts like those which had revived in the 1820s contained the familiar mixture of operatic overtures, popular airs, and songs and extracts from larger oratorio and orchestral works. In the 1830s and 1840s the string quartet had an important place in public as well as private playing. When Walton's Music Saloon was opened in 1837 in South Parade, Thomas Haddock, another violinist, promoted a series of chamber concerts dominated by the quartets of Mozart, Haydn and above all Beethoven. Walton had to sell in the slump of the early 1840s and the saloon eventually became the Mechanics' Institution.

The 1850s established Leeds as a major centre of choral music. The foundations had been laid by the eighteenth-century enthusiasm for Handel and by the fact that choral singing was one of the few forms of cultural expression over which Anglican, Methodist and Dissenter did not fall out. A new standard was set by the appointment of Dr Samuel Sebastian Wesley as organist to Leeds Parish Church, a part of the Rev. Walter Hook's campaign to revitalise Anglicanism in the town. By his playing and composing Wesley made the parish church famous for its voluntaries, fugues and choral services. Wesley inspired the Leeds Choral Society, which continued under his successor, R. S. Burton. Despite a host of rivalries between the choral society, the Leeds Madrigal and Motet Society, the Leeds Choral Union and several others, in which personal jealousy and social tension between wealthy patrons, less wealthy members and professional musicians all played a part, these societies became the basis of the choral works in the first Leeds Music Festival of 1858 and the triennial festivals which were established in 1874.

The building of the Town Hall was a paradigm of the cultural activities of the elite. They resented the view that Leeds was a place of ugly and insignificant buildings. They were irritated by the fact that Bradford had a better concert hall. So, to celebrate their wealth, they went out and bought the biggest town hall, the best artists, the best composers and a massive orchestra, with chorus and audience provided by themselves. The result was a great success.

VI   By the end of the 1850s Leeds was, as it is now, part of a national, even international culture. The industrial revolution did not harm the cultural life of the town, but provided the wealth and contacts that built a cultural life of rich and incoherent profusion. The visits of the Gotts to London and the Continent, the tours of the violin-playing Haddock family, bringing back the scores of Mendelssohn's quartets, or the correspondence and exchange of journals of the Phil. and Lit. with other societies scattered over the globe from Paris to Philadelphia, were all part of this pattern. Leeds never would nor could build a chauvinistic culture distinct and independent of other centres. There were distinctive local features like the choral music, but there was always a danger that the citizens would become merely the purchasers of cultural products, most of them from London, and would gain a passive rather than an active and creative culture, becoming a perpetual audience, always applauding but contributing nothing. The solution to this challenge which had emerged by the end of the nineteenth century involved taking what was wanted from the stream of British and international culture, and laying down the basis for an active participation in that culture through two types of organisation.

In the last quarter of the nineteenth century were laid the foundations of the city's cultural life in the twentieth. The municipal corporation was pushed and pulled by its more imaginative members into becoming a cultural sponsor: first the Town Hall; then, in 1871-72, the Reference and Central libraries; in 1888 the Art Gallery, followed by the laying out of City Square, that palazzio of Colonel Harding, and by the post-war purchase of the Phil. and Lit. museum. Industrialisation brought an inexorable progress from private to public cultural life. In Thoresby's time paintings and fine books had been enjoyed by wealthy men in their own homes. By 1800, and more so by 1850, privately owned works of art like the Farnley Hall Turners and Gott's collection at Armley were increasingly available for public exhibition, and through voluntary organisations, many financed by private wealth, more and more books were being bought for public loan. By the end of the century, publicly owned books and pictures were available for public enjoyment and use.

The founding of the Yorkshire College in 1874 was the other pointer to the direction which cultural life would take in the twentieth century. The college, which became part of the federal Victoria University in 1887 and an independent university in 1904, was carefully grafted on to the soul and mind of Leeds by a small and dedicated group of men, Kitson, Fairbairn, J. D. Heaton and the Nusseys, who were convinced that excellent technical instruction was needed to meet German industrial competition. For the first time, with professorships in chemistry, physics and maths, and geology and mining, a cultural organisation reflected the industrial base of the town. The research interests which now mark a modern university developed slowly. The geologist Green surveyed the strata of the Yorkshire coalfield. The chemists increased scientific knowledge of dyeing and colour chemistry. By the mid-1920s, under the guidance of Sir Michael Sadler, the university began to establish that uneasy balance between loyalty to its host community and responsiveness to the wider world of learning and research which is a true reflection of cultural conditions in twentieth-century industrial society.

Why did the nineteenth-century cultural life sustained by the free market and by voluntary organisations and their wealthy patrons come to an end? The fate of the Philosophical and Literary Society is instructive. Like the economic growth rate, membership of the Society reached a peak in the early 1870s. After that its leaders became dimly aware that things were going wrong. During the 1890s leading members of the Society became convinced that they needed to make better use of their resources, and a committee was appointed to consider '. . . the best means of extending the usefulness of the society'.

Membership was declining. Evening meetings in Park Row were becoming less attractive to a middle class which was retreating to the suburbs and now dined late instead of taking tea at six. Besides, a host of new societies, like the Priestley Club and the Thoresby Society, had been founded since 1870. Cultural interests were becoming more specialised, and energy and attention were being taken from the broad interests of the Phil. and Lit. The council of the Society was worried by the growing pressure of taxation and the increasing cost of maintenance. It knew that the presentation of its crowded museum, the lack of system in its lectures, and the poor salaries and pensions of its employees were falling behind modern standards. Little action was taken in 1895-96, but the same problems, now more acute, were considered in 1905. A confidential report approved by a general meeting of the Society recommended the sale of the museum, with its valuable city-centre site, and the building of a larger one on a cheaper site farther out. At this point the university offered a merger with the Society. The university was attracted by the Society's library, in view of the inadequacies of its own book collection. Just as the scheme was on the point of being approved the town clerk asked that the property and art gallery committee of the corporation be given time to prepare an alternative. Postponement was agreed by the council of the Society, who were aware of their responsibilities to the town, and that many members were deeply suspicious of the Yorkshire College, which, with several professors on the Phil. and Lit. council, seemed to be silently plotting the take-over of resources rightly belonging to the citizens of Leeds. The activists on the corporation failed to get backing, and nothing more happened until 1918, when the Phil. and Lit., now more than ever pressed by the rising costs of wartime inflation, heard the corporation's suggestion that its property should be purchased as part of the municipal plan for a Hall of Fame to commemorate the war dead, with a new building for a museum, library and art gallery. After a little civilised competition between the city and the university, and some indecision by the Society, a tripartite agreement was signed in which the city gained the museum, the university the library. The Society, free of its financial burdens, promoted an active and distinguished lecture programme as a bridge between city and university. The first session was opened on 16 November 1921 by Sir Michael Sadler, vice-chancellor of the university, with a lecture on 'Sandford and Merton'. The cultural organisations of Leeds had been dragged into the twentieth century, albeit trailing clouds of glory from the wealth and luxuriance of the nineteenth.

NOTES

[1] T. S. Eliot, *Notes towards the Definition of Culture* (1948), 21.

[2] *Annual Report of the Leeds Philosophical and Literary Society*, 1838–39.

[3] Mrs Gott's diaries, Brotherton Library MSS 194/3/8.

[4] Philosophical papers of William Hey, in Leeds Phil. and Lit. Papers, Brotherton Library MSS Dep 1975/1, Box 10/207/vii.

[5] *Leeds Guide . . .*, printed for John Ryley by Edward Baines (1808).

[6] Rev. T. D. Whitaker, *Leodis et Elmete* (1816), 86.

[7] Treasurer's papers, New Subscription Library, 1805–11, in the Lupton Papers, item 124, Brotherton Library.

[8] *Leeds Intelligencer*, 9 and 23 March 1801.

[9] T. Wemyss Reid, *A Memoir of John Deakin Heaton, M.D.* (1883).

[10] *Annual Report of the Leeds Mechanics' Insititution*, 1846; Report of the AGM of the Chapel Allerton Mechanics' and Literary Institution, *Leeds Mercury*, 9 September 1848.

[11] *An Answer to a pamphlet in Defence of Stage Amusements entitled 'Further Remarks on the Theatre' by a Churchman* (1817).

[12] *Blackwood's Edinburgh Magazine*, IX (1821), 26.

[13] W. B. Crump (ed.), 'The Leeds woollen industry, 1780–1820', *Thoresby Soc.* (1931), 26.

[14] Gott Papers, Brotherton Library, MSS 194/2/51–52.

[15] *Leeds Mercury, 19 October 1839*.

[16] Diary of a Tour, 20 September 1824, Baines MSS, Leeds city archives.

[17] C. T. Thackrah, *An introductory Discourse delivered to the Leeds Philosophical and Literary Society* (1821).

[18] *Leeds Literary Observer* (1819).

[19] *Annual Report of the Leeds Phil. and Lit.* (1824–25).

[20] P. H. Wicksteed, *Memorials of the Rev. Charles Wicksteed, B.A.* (1886), 37.

[21] On the Elgin Marbles, MSS notes in the Baines Papers.

[22] Part of the following paragraphs has appeared in an article, 'In a glass case', in *New Society*, 7 September 1978.

[23] William Osburn, *An Account of the Egyptian Mummy presented to the Museum of the Leeds Phil. and Lit. Society . . .* (1828).

[24] C. H. Cope, *Reminiscences of Charles West Cope, R.A.* (1891).

[25] *Yorkshire Weekly Post*, 16 September 1916.

[26] B. P. S. Scattergood, *A Short History of the Leeds Musical Soirées, 1848–1931* (1931).

BIBLIOGRAPHICAL NOTE

Emily Hargrave, 'Musical Leeds in the eighteenth century', *Thoresby Soc.* (1928), XXVIII; Frank Beckwith, *The Leeds Library* (1950); Joseph Priestley, *Autobiography* (repr. 1970); John Pearson, *Life of William Hey, F.R.S.* (1822); John Copley, 'The theatre in Hunslet Lane', *Thoresby Soc.*, Vol. 54, Parts 2 and 3 (1974 and 1976); Trevor Fawcett, *The Rise of English Provincial Art, 1800–1830* (1974); *Joseph Gott, Sculptor* (1972); William H. Thorpe, *John N. Rhodes, a Yorkshire Painter, 1809–1842* (1904); R. J. Morris, 'Leeds and the Crystal Palace', *Victorian Studies*, XIII (1970); E. Kitson Clark, *The History of 100 years of the Life of the Leeds Philosophical and Literary Society* (1924); George Haddock, *Some Early Musical Recollections* (1906); Derek Linstrum, *Historic Architecture of Leeds* (1969); P. H. J. Gosden and A. J. Taylor, *Studies in the History of a University, 1874–1974* (1975). Extensive use has also been made of the Gott papers, and the

Phil. and Lit. papers in the Brotherton Library, and of the collection of trade directories, exhibition catalogues and concert programmes in the Local History Room of Leeds Central Library.

W. B. STEPHENS

IX

Elementary education
and literacy, 1770–1870[1]

The view that the British population was largely ignorant and unschooled before the Education Act of 1870 is no longer acceptable, but it is clear that in the period of the industrial revolution and its aftermath the quality of schooling and the availability of education varied greatly from one place to another. Education in the Lancashire cotton towns, for example, was adversely affected by the factory system and population growth, and it seems likely that other industrial towns, such as those in the West Riding woollen area, may have had similar experiences.[2] This chapter examines the extent and nature of elementary schooling in Leeds, the centre of that area, during the century before the advent of the Board schools. For this purpose Leeds is taken to be the parish of Leeds, which in this period embraced a number of townships – Leeds itself, four out-townships agricultural in character (Chapel Allerton, Farnley, Headingley and Potternewton), and six out-townships which were industrial villages (Armley, Beeston, Bramley, Holbeck, Hunslet and Wortley).

I   The only available statistical yardstick of educational standards in eighteenth-century Leeds is the number of brides and grooms able to sign their names on marriage – admittedly a crude measure of only basic literacy, but at least providing comparable evidence from year to year. During the decade 1760-69 the parish registers reveal 46·6 per cent signing (53·4 making marks). Consistently a very much higher proportion of brides than grooms were illiterate (table 18).

Far more brides and grooms reared in Leeds were illiterate over this period (70·1 and 38·2 per cent) than were immigrants from country districts (69·9 and 22 per cent).[3] Although the sample on which this conclusion is based is too small for defiite conclusions, it may point to the same cultural distinction as existed in Lancashire, between urban centres with plenty of job opportunities for children and others, but where educational facilities were unable to keep pace with the growing population or were unwanted, and more rural areas where working-class prosperity might be lower, but where there remained more time and opportunity for a modicum of schooling and self-education. On the other hand immigrants may have represented the more enterprising and better educated of rural youth.

Table 18 Grooms and brides making marks on marriage, 1760–69 (%)

Year	Grooms	Brides	Total
1760	38·7	76·6	57·7
1761	40	71·3	55·7
1762	29·8	70·4	51·1
1763	38·5	77·8	58·2
1764	38·6	75·7	57·2
1765	38·7	70·8	54·8
1766	30·2	62·7	46·5
1767	41·7	70·4	56·1
1768	36·5	67·2	51·9
1769	30·1	60·6	45·4
Average	36·3	70·4	53·4

Source. Calculated from figures in M. Yasumoto, 'Urbanization and population in an English town: Leeds during the industrial revolution', *Keio Economic Studies*, X, 2 (1973), p. 84. My calculations of averages differ from Yasumoto's but always by less than 1 per cent.

Some northern industrial towns suffered a severe collapse of standards of literacy in the later eighteenth and early nineteenth centuries.[4] At Leeds there was some deterioration for brides in the mid and late 1780s and a distinct fall-off for grooms (table 19), and while the first decade of the nineteenth century saw a discernible improvement in the bridal signature rate, grooms' literacy remained lower than in the later 1760s. Since marriage signature figures were for persons in their late twenties they probably reflect the extent of schooling some fifteen years earlier. It thus seems likely that during this period of industrial and population expansion the proportion of children obtaining an education in Leeds did diminish, though the catastrophic experience of places like Halifax and Ashton under Lyne was avoided.

This likelihood is supported by what we know of the availability of schooling at this time.[5] In the latter half of the eighteenth century in Leeds and its townships schools were not numerous, while population was growing fast. Some working-class children no doubt attended dame or other small schools, such as those recorded at Farnley in 1743 and Headingley in 1764, while for the better-off there were the academies and seminaries which were advertised in local newspapers and directories. Leeds Grammar School offered a secondary education throughout this period, but while working-class boys appear to have been admitted up to the early 1850s, few went to the school after that.

Table 19 Grooms and brides making marks on marriage, 1781–1811 (%)

	Year	Grooms	Brides	Total
	1781	34·2	68·5	51·4
	1784	57·7	72·4	65·0
	1787	41·0	76·4	58·6
Average	1781/4/7	44·3	72·4	58·3
	1805	36·4	68·4	52·4
	1808	44·5	54·2	49·3
	1811	50·0	62·0	56·0
Average	1805/8/11	43·6	61·5	52·6

Source. These figures were calculated (from the Leeds parish registers published by the Thoresby Society) by Miss F. Z. Mirza while a student at the City of Leeds College of Education, 1975. I am grateful to her for permission to use them here.

On the other hand a school at Wortley, founded to teach English and Latin, had become an elementary school by the early nineteenth century, teaching the three Rs to a few poor children free and to others for small fees. Other public (as opposed to private) schools were of a charitable nature. The largest charity school was in Leeds township, established in 1705. It admitted children already familiar with the ABC at the age of eight, clothed them and provided instruction in the principles of the established Church and the three Rs, with sewing and knitting for girls and spinning for boys – a superior elementary and craft education. The number on the roll rose from forty in 1705 to 120 in 1757.

Smaller charity schools existed in the satellite townships, though they were not always in continuous existence. In 1743 there were such schools at Bramley and at Hunslet, and by 1764 at Holbeck. There were then no charity schools at Armley, Beeston, Farnley or Headingley, but by the 1790s Beeston and Headingley had acquired one each. Generally these took only a handful of children, though a school at Woodhouse originally founded in the 1650s was revived by middle-class subscriptions in 1775 to teach religion and reading to between twenty and fifty children aged five to nine.[6] Most of these charity schools taught reading, and some taught writing and arithmetic, while a few pauper children in Leeds workhouse were both taught reading and given practical training in textile production.[7] Many children, however, must have had no formal education, especially as population growth increased the pressure on existing schools.

II   This situation was to some extent alleviated by the introduction of Sunday schools into Leeds from 1784.[8] Mushroom growth followed: by 1817 few churches or chapels in the parish were without a Sunday school, and in all these catered for some 5,000 pupils. Expansion continued, and by 1858 there were some 35,000 pupils in over 130 schools. Taking population growth into account, there was a rise in Sunday school attendance from about 5 per cent of the borough population in 1818 to some 17 per cent in 1851.[9]

The impetus of the Sunday school movement nationally has been attributed to middle-class enthusiasm to impose morality and good behaviour on potentially dangerous concentrations of rough working-class communities – all through part-time schooling which would not interfere with the availability of child labour. Out of this developed a sectarian struggle for the souls of the poor. Such influences were evident in Leeds, as indicated by a report of 1795 describing the local Sunday schools as 'an excellent method of restraining the poor from . . . disorderly conduct', and by a Leeds clergyman's claim in 1845 that the teaching of the Sunday schools 'inculcates submission to authority . . . upholds the claim of masters . . . inspires contentment under calamity . . . order will find in this system, its best security, property its safest bulwark, – and law, its truest reverence!'[10]

The Sunday schools[11] were part and parcel of the ferment of Evangelical activity in the town in this period, alongside religious tract, Bible and missionary societies. Initially especially, religious zeal, particularly strict sabbatarianism, seems to have been the chief force motivating middle-class support for Sunday schools. To this was soon added inter-sectarian rivalry. A Leeds branch of the non-denominational Sunday School Union, established in 1816, failed to save the movement from such denominational strife. Leeds Anglicans as early as 1788 had set up a Sunday school management committee, and most Church schools attached themselves to the Parochial Sunday School Society. The Wesleyans established circuit control of their Leeds schools, failed to respond to an invitation to join the Union in 1820, and from 1837 had their own national association. The Unitarians and Roman Catholics likewise kept out of the Union, which was consequently identified with other Nonconformist sects. Most schools, therefore, emerged as strictly denominational, with, by mid-century, the Nonconformists providing rather over two-thirds. In 1858 there were forty-one Church schools, twenty-three Wesleyan, fifteen Methodist Free Church, twelve Independent, seven Methodist New Connexion, four Wesleyan Reformers, ten Primitive Methodist, eleven Baptist, three Roman Catholic, two Unitarian, and five others. The ready response of the working classes in Leeds, as in other large towns, to Sunday schools cannot, however, be attributed solely to middle-class religious zeal or social pressure. Attendance was, after all, voluntary, and there is some evidence in Leeds to support the view that many Sunday schools of this period were products of the working-class communities they served, since they were largely attended and to some extent controlled by the working classes. This is demonstrated quite clearly by the division of outlook between middle-class providers and working-class clients over the curriculum. Many working-class parents were doubtless religiously activated, but a desire for the elementary education of a secular nature available in the Sunday schools was probably equally if not more significant in attracting pupils. For many it was the only chance of even a smattering of education. The earlier Leeds Sunday schools taught both reading and writing. There were early objections to writing, like that of William Hey, a leading Leeds Anglican, who in 1807 was shocked that some Leeds Methodist schools taught 'nothing but writing', and argued that the schools' 'true design is not to make scholars, but true christians'.[12] Most of the schools, however, continued to teach both reading and writing, and some also added arithmetic. In Leeds Wesleyan schools in the first twenty years of the nineteenth century most teachers were unwilling or insufficiently skilled to teach scrip'ure, a subject reserved in 'select classes' for a minority of older pupils, while the majority spent the bulk of their time on secular subjects, using the copy books and slates common in day schools. Some Anglican schools taught only reading, but at least by 1820 writing was often added.

In 1816 the Wesleyan Sunday schools opened four classrooms for the evening instruction of youths over fifteen where secular instruction dominated. This, however, was not a sabbatarian move, for secular instruction for children on Sundays continued, even being advertised in 1820 as an attraction. By then some Anglican Sunday schools, too, provided week night instruction in writing and arithmetic.

An event in the late 1820s demonstrated the connection of working-class support with the secular aspects of the curriculum. In 1827 the national Wesleyan Conference ordered all secular instruction in their

Sunday schools to cease, and reading to be taught only as a means to religious knowledge. The middle-class managing committee of the Leeds Wesleyan schools sought to implement this policy in 1828, but a revolt by the pupils, teachers and local chapel committees of the majority of their sixteen schools followed. An attempt was made to counter this 'clamorous opposition' by 'the introduction of a popular system of instruction on weekday evenings to obviate the prejudices likely to be made in the minds of the poor by the abolition of Sunday writing'. In addition to writing and arithmetic, sewing too was to be offered. This satisfied only six of the Wesleyan schools. All the others appear to have left the association and, presumably dominated by working-class teachers and committees, continued for a while to meet the needs of local parents by providing secular schooling on Sundays. Such instruction seems to have continued in other Leeds Sunday schools, too, particularly in those which might be considered products of working-class self-help. Voluntary teachers at the non-denominational Zion Sunday school in New Wortley, founded by a working-class community in the 1830s, taught writing on Sundays, despite initial opposition, as well as in the week. The New Connexion Methodists and the 'Protestant Methodists', whose leaders were lower in the social scale than the Wesleyans, were also still teaching writing on Sundays in the 1830s, attracting children from those schools which did not.

The working-class ethos of at least some Leeds Sunday schools is exemplified, too, by the increasing replacement of middle-class teachers by local workpeople, particularly as the better-off removed themselves to more salubrious suburbs. By the 1820s the Wesleyans were recruiting their own older pupils as teachers. In the 1830s at Queen Street school, where 70 – 80 per cent of the pupils were factory children, teachers were drawn from their ranks at the age of fourteen or fifteen. By 1847 the *Sunday School Teachers' Manual*, published in Leeds, reported that the schools were 'conducted by working people, earnest young men and women who labour after a hard day's work'.

Sunday schools represented an important part of the social life of the town. In the 1830s and 1840s a large number of their pupils obtained all their education there. In 1851, of some 180 English boroughs and cities, only about thirty had higher proportions of their population than Leeds attending Sunday schools. The actual educational impact is difficult to assess and certainly varied. The hours attended on Sunday were the equivalent of a full weekday's schooling, and children attended over more years than was normal in day-school pupils and probably more regularly. Moreover most Leeds Sunday-school pupils were aged eight to fourteen, older and of a more receptive age than many in day schools. Youths and adults could often continue at evening classes connected with their Sunday schools, so that the Sunday-school organisations formed a network of part-time educational provision for the ambitious and respectable working-class citizens and their children.

On the other hand the educational standards of some teachers was little above that of their pupils, and while some working children, like Alonzo Hargraves, a miner of Little London, could claim in 1833 to have learnt to read and write at Sunday school, many pupils from factories and mines attended infrequently or were too tired from their labours to profit from schooling. In 1842 of boy miners in the Leeds district who had attended Sunday school for two to three years 'fewer than half could read', and only a handful could write their own names. Nor did the schools reach everyone. In the meanest areas of Leeds the attraction of the Sunday school was least evident. In Darley Street, for example, the Methodists later admitted that the schools had 'little hold on the people'.

III From the early 1830s the combination of legal restrictions on child employment, a rise in working-class incomes, and the better provision of day schools gradually decreased the need for Sunday schools as agents of general education. By 1860 no writing was taught in Anglican or Wesleyan Sunday schools in Leeds, and only about a third of the Union schools' pupils were learning to write, most of those in weekday evening classes. The expansion of day schooling in Leeds, between 1810 and 1850, and particularly from 1830, represents a remarkable achievement in a community where the population was expanding so quickly and where opportunities for child labour despite restrictions still abounded. This expansion could not have occurred without a general demand for something more than Sunday schooling and evening classes. Working-class self-enterprise is evidenced by the attendance of working-class children at private schools. Surveys of 1818, 1833 and 1843 all show that the bulk of day schools in Leeds and its townships were private ones supported solely by fees. In 1843 some 8,800 children attended over 300 such schools in the borough. About 3,500 of them were at dame or infant schools, the other private schools educating about as many children as the 'public' or 'voluntary' schools provided by religious bodies. By 1851, however, though 9,000 out of 22,000 day-school pupils were still at private schools, most of the rest attended voluntary schools. This change had been made possible by the efforts of the local middle class and particularly the Anglican clergy and congregations.

The motives of middle-class promoters of day schools were complex. Religion was basic, but the desire to rescue the poor from paganism was quickly subordinated to a bitter interdenominational battle which dominated the Leeds educational scene for much of the century. As with the Sunday schools, a non-sectarian approach proved impossible. The first Leeds voluntary school, the Royal Lancasterian, established in 1812 for 500 boys, was non-denominational, with trustees divided seven to six between Anglicans and Dissenters. The opening of a like school for 170 girls, did not, however, ensure an ecumenical atmosphere. Lectures in Leeds by Joseph Lancaster in 1809 and 1810, which had influenced the establishment of these 'British' schools, as they were termed, found support from the *Leeds Mercury*, the organ of local Dissent, but some Anglicans objected. These, pointing out the dangers of a spread of Dissent, immediately stirred up support for a school linked with the Anglican National Society, to be confined to children who would be instructed in the 'formularies ... of the Church of England'. Such a school, for boys and girls, was opened in Kirkgate in 1813 and the boys from the charity school were absorbed into it.[13] For a few years there was little further development. A tentative Church enquiry of 1815 looked into the possibility of establishing National schools in many Yorkshire parishes, including the Leeds townships, and in 1820 the Nonconformist *Leeds Mercury* opposed a Bill which sought to establish parish schools under Church control. Even by 1833, however, the only new voluntary school added to those already mentioned was a Methodist Sunday and day school.

Dissenters' fears of Anglican domination in schooling came to a head over a Bill of 1843 which would have set up 'factory schools', largely under Anglican control, for child workers in certain industries to attend part-time. Edward Baines, of the *Leeds Mercury*, led a successful opposition, and, though the dispute belongs to national as much as to local history, in Leeds it was made the more bitter by Baines's allegation that the Bill derived from a hole-in-the-corner Anglican conspiracy inspired by W. F. Hook, Vicar of Leeds. In fact Hook's view (doubtless reinforced by the financial difficulties of the Leeds Church schools in the early 1840s) was that the Church could not bear the burden of providing elementary education, and he knew that Leeds workpeople supported National schools for secular reasons. Some State assistance for voluntary schools had been forthcoming since 1833, but Hook's growing advocacy of a more fully State-provided system encouraged some Leeds Nonconformists in the suspicion that Church and State might combine to promote rate-supported day schools controlled by the Church. Thus Baines, this time unsuccessfully, opposed the introduction in 1846 of State grants for pupil teachers, which Hook supported. Baines put himself at the head of the 'voluntaryists' (who wanted schools to be the concern of religious congregations untrammelled by State aid). Hook found support from local Unitarians and Roman Catholics, and out of a group set up in Leeds in 1849 (including W. E. Forster, J. G. Marshall, MP for Leeds, Canon Jackson and one Wicksteed, a Unitarian minister) grew the Leeds Education Society to promote rate-aided schooling.[14] In a series of public meetings in Leeds in the early 1850s the supporters and opposers of a national non-sectarian system of public schools argued their viewpoints.[15]

Meanwhile, however, the Church established an invincible lead in the provision of day schools in the town. Hook and others obtained an Anglican Board of Education for Leeds (1839) and assiduously established National schools with the aid of local subscriptions and grants from the National Society and the government. In these activities the value of education as a weapon against Dissent was often clear. The incumbent of Christ Church wrote in 1840, for example, that it was essential to have a large National school 'as a sort of nursery at a Church in a district where the present generation had to a large extent become Dissenters before the Church was built', and five years later the perpetual curate of St Andrews, catering for a growing working-class district adjacent to St George's, urged the quick setting up of a school because there was no Dissenting voluntary school and, using military terminology, 'the ground is at present unoccupied'.[16]

Many Leeds Nonconformists were determined not to accept State grants, though the Wesleyans did. In the face of the Anglican campaign, however, some Dissenting congregations which had previously concentrated on Sunday schools were from 1840 stimulated to establish day schools. By 1851 there were fifteen Dissenting voluntary schools in the borough, three of them Roman Catholic. Church schools, however, by then numbered thirty-six with almost 7,000 pupils. In comparison the Roman Catholic schools had 500, the two British schools 600, and the Protestant Nonconformist schools 1,700 pupils. Samuel Smiles's claim that voluntaryism had done next to nothing for education in Leeds is not without foundation. Leeds, a town where Dissent was strong, and where voluntaryism was centred, had a higher proportion of its population at Church schools in 1851 than did London, Liverpool, Manchester, Birmingham, Bristol, Bradford, Hull or Newcastle.

In the 1850s and 1860s more Dissenting day schools were opened but the Church maintained its lead, average attendance at National schools in Leeds township almost doubling. By 1869 there were fifty-four Church schools (15,364 on the roll) as against three British and twenty-two Protestant Dissenting schools (together 4,782), and four Roman Catholic schools (1,729). J. G. Fitch, who surveyed education in Leeds in that year, remarked on the 'exceptional apathy and inaction of the Dissenting bodies in Leeds'; 'with the exception of the Wesleyans and the Unitarians I have been unable to find a single Nonconformist congregation in Leeds which is doing anything to help forward primary education or is contributing money or supervision to the permanent maintainance of a day school in any form'.[17]

By 1867 even Edward Baines admitted that a completely unaided voluntary system was not viable. Some Leeds Dissenters were now 'looking forward to the time when the sects should be superseded, not aided, in the work of education', but Baines preferred to support the National Education Union, a largely Anglican body wishing to keep the existing sectarian schools strong through public finance.[18]

Sectarian conflict and religious proselytising were not the only factors at work in the extension of elementary education in Leeds before 1870. Strong too were humanitarian motives and also the belief that the civilising influence of education should mitigate crime and political and social disaffection. Both the Lancasterian and the National schools stressed the object of saving children from a life of idleness and crime, to make them useful and respectable 'in that state of life into which it pleased God to call them'. A desire to use education to perpetuate subordination must not, however, be overstressed. John Marshall, whose factory schools for his workers in Holbeck (see below) were held up as models throughout the country, professed educational motives far from selfish, which his actions supported. The Lancasterian school, too, increasingly moved to a policy of encouraging the young to raise themselves in the world, a sentiment not out of place in a town associated with Samuel Smiles. Oastler and Sadler, the reformers who sought to reduce child labour, were also Leeds men, and it is evident that many who supported the voluntary schools were largely activated by philanthropic motives.[19]

IV   It was in provision of schooling for the lowest elements of society that a social welfare rather than a purely educational purpose was especially evident. The voluntary schools in some areas catered like the private schools for the artisan and shopkeeper class and the respectable better-off labourers who were able and willing to pay fees. Often these were districts where middle-class inhabitants made subscriptions. Other voluntary schools, however, like St James's, York Street, established in a district the 'most dense and degraded in the town', and St Saviour's, in an area whose 6,000 population was allegedly 'almost entirely destitute',[20] had to provide cheap education and did it with difficulty. Yet in these and worse slum areas large numbers of destitute and criminal children, often the offspring of the unskilled Irish and rural immigrants who crowded the insanitary slumland of east Leeds, were not reached by the ordinary day or Sunday schools. In some of the industrial out-townships and the neighbouring manufacturing villages the situation was as bad.[21] The existing charity schools were incapable of coping with the mass needs of the new industrial slums. The largest, the Leeds Charity School, in the first half of the century took but eighty girls at a time, largely over twelve years of age. Small-scale private effort began to meet the extended need only slowly. Around the turn of the century a couple of day 'schools of industry' were founded for the very poor, funded by subscriptions and run by middle-class women. One for fifty girls was established in Beezon's Yard, Briggate, in 1799, and there was by 1817 another at Quarry Hill for thirty girls. Each taught reading, knitting and sewing and prepared for domestic service, and one of these still existed in the early 1830s. Wesleyan ladies began a similar girls' day school in the late 1830s, but it was ill attended, soon becoming the 'industrial department' of St Peter's Wesleyan Day School.[22] But such schemes were a drop in the ocean.

In 1844 the incumbent of St George's pointed out that a high proportion of the children of the lowest class were still receiving no education at all.[23] Their parents' precarious way of life 'and reckless indifference to all but their animal wants' made progress difficult. Nationally the problem was being met by 'ragged schools', partly functioning as educational establishments but mainly as Christian missions to provide the elements of care, particularly food and shelter and general guidance. The government inspector (HMI) for the Leeds area, the Rev. Watkins, suggested that ragged schools should be set up for such children in Leeds, and about that time two of the voluntary schools, Edgar Street British School and St Peter's National School, both serving slum districts, are reported to have assumed some of the characteristics of ragged schools by recruiting the poorest of children. In the later 1840s, too, the board of guardians opened a Moral and Industrial Training School for pauper children – separate from the workhouse – to break the cycle of 'family pauperism'. This was large enough to provide 300–400 children with elementary education and training in craft and domestic work. Until the later 1850s, however, HMIs were critical of the standard of the school's general education, and the industrial training was slow to get off the ground. Moreover the institution was under-used. In 1848, for example, it held only 106 when there were over 3,100 children of paupers receiving relief outside the workhouse in Leeds. The majority of 'out-door' paupers resisted education for their young, even though from 1859 the guardians would pay the school pence.

Only those who fell foul of the law received an enforced education. In 1851 241 children (forty girls) were in Leeds gaol school, and in 1857 the Leeds Society for the Reformation of Juvenile Offenders established a Reformatory School at Adel, taking about forty to sixty young offenders, mainly boys, and receiving a generous annual government grant and money from the West Riding magistrates. The pupils were trained as craftsmen and for agricultural work as well as given elementary education.

The second half of the century saw revived efforts to provide for the ordinary slum child. A ragged school existed in Sussex Street in 1854 but it was not until 1859 that really well organised ragged schools were established, one for boys and girls on Richmond Hill and another for girls in Regent Street. They were as much mission stations as schools, for although they offered the normal elementary education they also provided cheap mid-day meals and distributed free clothing, bedding and food given by the better-off. For the destitute there were night refuges, and some boys who used these were organised into a 'Shoe-Black Brigade' to earn an honest living. About half the rest lived in 'low lodging houses'; many had drunken parents, fathers in gaol, or were ex-gaolbirds themselves. In 1862 the two schools were amalgamated and given accommodation in a new building in Edgar Street, York Road, together with a Certified Industrial School formed under an Act of 1861. Magistrates could now commit to the certified school orphans and children found destitute, begging, vagrant, or frequenting the company of reputed thieves, out of the control of parents or with one parent in gaol, and first offenders under twelve. They were to be taught a trade and apprenticed, 'or otherwise started in life'. The character of the school was thus changed somewhat. In 1860 Hole had pointed out that the pupils 'are drawn thither by kindness'; now, though local pupils still attended voluntarily, the addition of children compulsorily resident by process of law under regulations governed by the Home Office and paid for from public funds introduced a penal atmosphere. Emphasis on 'habits of regular industry' and 'continuous labour' took precedence over religious and moral instruction and an aura of benevolent philanthropy.

The absence of compulsory education made difficult a solution to the problem of the schooling of children whose parents were too indifferent or poor, or of those children who worked.[24] Part-time education filled some of the gaps, although with the growth of Church and Chapel day schools the Sunday schools increasingly dropped their secular instruction in the latter half of the century. Some evening classes were available, and from 1833 legislation ensured that certain factory children received day schooling for part of each week. Evening classes often began in connection with Sunday schools. In 1816, for example, the Society of Friends was supporting two adult schools (one each for men and women) and other religious groups were also running adult classes. By 1858 some 3,600 pupils attended classes in sixty evening institutions. Of these about 1,300 males were in mechanics' and similar institutes, the remainder in institutions connected with religious bodies. Although the original aspirations of the mechanics' and some other institutes were to provide a higher technical education for workmen, in practice only 7 per cent of the 3,600 evening pupils were following instruction above the elementary level.

Other evening schools grew up to meet the needs of factory children, and the same class as the ragged schools. As early as 1802 an industrial school, run by a committee of middle-class women, was providing evening instruction for some thirty factory girls. In the same philanthropic tradition was the Leeds Spitalfields Sewing School, started in 1852, which had some 300 young female factory hands on its books in 1858. An average of 90 to 200 attended two evenings a week to learn dressmaking, sing a few hymns, and hear uplifting stories. Several similar schools were started in Leeds, and others existed about 1860 in Kirkstall, Hunslet, Seacroft and Farnley.

Nevertheless, although only half a dozen of the sixty evening classes of 1858 had paid teachers and only one relied on them, the majority of such teachers were not drawn from the middle class but from the ranks of the better-educated workmen and clerks. Such teachers had little intellectual background or social standing, so that the vast majority of evening classes, like the Sunday schools, must have had a strong working-class ethos and can hardly have been engines of middle-class moral and political pressure.

Yet even in the 1860s, when many night-school pupils had attended day schools, the majority of evening pupils were still factory workers with no formal schooling. One evening school which catered for young factory hands over fourteen was established by John Marshall, the flax spinner, and other mill owners in Holbeck. Marshall, who soon assumed sole responsibility, began in 1825 to send some of his eleven- and twelve-year-old workers to the school during working hours. By 1833 Marshall was sending his eight- to eleven-year-old mill children to the school for half of each day; and over the next thirty years or so some 600 child workers attended the school. Marshall further encouraged education by refusing employment to children not already reaching a certain standard. The school became a model establishment of national esteem, providing schooling not only for the factory children but for other children in the district, and earning praise from the HMIs.[25]

Marshall's school was clearly of great significance in Holbeck, but 'half-time' education of young factory workers introduced by national legislation from 1833 was never on a large scale in Leeds. In 1839 there were only some 360 or 460 children in twenty factory schools in the town, though about 10,000 children were employed in the flax mills alone.[26] Moreover, most of the twenty 'factory schools' were ordinary day schools which factory children attended, like St Peter's Bank National School, where they were given precedence in admission.[27] In 1851 there were two actual factory schools with 963 pupils, and by 1869, when half-time legislation had been extended to cover more trades, and workshops as well as factories, there were but 1,212 'half-timers' employed in forty establishments. Nearly half were in Marshall's school, and only eighty-seven were in woollen mills, where technical improvements rendered 'entirely unnecessary the employment of half-time children'. Indeed, legal restrictions on child labour caused employers to cease to take children in the age groups covered by the educational clauses of the Acts. Unfortunately this did not increase full-time schooling but diverted these children into jobs outside the scope of the Acts, or left them unemployed but still unschooled.[28]

V Leaving aside the completely unschooled, it is difficult to measure in terms of quantity, quality and attainment the extent of all the educational activity in this period. The impression given by various contemporary surveys of schools and pupils is of steady expansion both in raw numbers and in relation to population growth, even though these records contain inaccuracies and, because they cover varying topographical areas or only certain kinds of schools, are not exactly comparable. A return of 1818 revealed over thirty day schools, apart from the grammar school, in Leeds town and liberty with provision for some 1,900 pupils as well as Sunday schools for about 4,400. But while it was felt that there was adequate day schooling in Leeds township itself (seven schools; some 1,150 pupils) it was 'deficient' in the other townships in the parish. In the borough as a whole the 1,900 day pupils represent a proportion of 2·3 per cent of the total population, though this survey clearly omitted some private schools, some of which were certainly as large as the schools included. A Church survey of 1815, for example, shows five day schools at

Chapel Allerton, with an average of thirty pupils in each, whereas the 1818 returns lists only one school, with thirty-eight children.[29]

An investigation of 1833 lists some 130 day schools in Leeds and its townships with about 6,100 pupils. Fifty-eight schools were in Leeds itself (some 3,200 pupils) but this was known to be an incomplete return. The ratio of pupils to population suggested by the return was about 5 per cent (in Leeds township, about $4\frac{1}{2}$ per cent). The town council's own survey of 1839 found 154 day schools in Leeds town, with 6,400 pupils plus 360 half-time factory children, a ratio of about 7·8 per cent of the town population, apparently a very considerable increase over 1833 even allowing for deficiencies in the earlier return.

A few years later, in 1843, Edward Baines in a survey designed to demonstrate the sufficiency of education in the northern manufacturing districts, claimed that in Leeds borough there were by then 353 day schools with 15,155 pupils (206 schools and 9,082 pupils in Leeds township), just less than 10 per cent of the population for the borough, and just over 10 per cent for the township. The education census of 1851, probably the most accurate of all these surveys, showed Leeds borough with 371 day schools and 21,843 pupils – that is, 12·7 per cent of the population. A further survey of 1869 noted some 28,000 pupils on the books of day schools in the borough, 11·2 per cent of the population (for Leeds township also 11·2 per cent). The figures provided by the surveys are certainly insufficiently accurate for fine distinctions to be made, and for 1851 and 1869 are anyway for pupils on the roll rather than in actual attendance. Nevertheless they do suggest for the period to 1851 a considerable expansion both in actual numbers at day school and in the proportion there. For the two decades following 1851, although numbers increased substantially, the proportions at day school may not have kept pace with the enormous increase of population (see table 20).

Table 20 Proportion of population at day school, 1833–69

Population (to nearest 1,000)	*% increase in population*	*% of population at day school*
1821 : 84,000		
1831 : 123,000	47	1833 : 5
1841 : 152,000	23	[1839 : 7·8[a]]
1851 : 172,000	13	1851 : 12·7
1869 : 253,000 (estimated)	47	1869 : 11·2

Note

[a] 1839: Leeds town only.

In comparison with other large towns Leeds may have enjoyed some relative improvement in the 1830s and 1840s. In the 1830s the proportion of the population receiving an effective education was estimated at 1 : 41, compared with 1 : 38 for Birmingham, 1 : 35 for Manchester, and an average of 1 : 24 for fifteen large centres investigated.[30] By 1851 while Leeds, with enrolments at day school equalling 48 per cent of children aged five to fourteen, was below the average of 52 per cent for seventy-one 'principal towns' in England and Wales, it bettered Manchester (with Salford, 32 per cent) and Birmingham (35·5 per cent). It was about the same as Liverpool, but greatly superior to many other industrial towns (as, for example, Oldham 21 per cent, Wolverhampton 30, Coventry 30, Stockport 33, Bolton 36, Sheffield 42, Nottingham 43 per cent). Its neighbour Bradford had 37 per cent of the age range at school. Moreover in a list confined to forty-four larger towns Leeds had a proportion of 1 in 7·9 of its population on the books of day schools, against an average of 1 in 9·4, being bettered by only fourteen of those towns. Birmingham's proportion was 1 in 11·0, Liverpool's 1 in 8·6, Manchester's 1 in 11·6, and Bradford's 1 in 10·8.[31] By 1869, however, the proportion of Leeds's population at school had fallen to 1 in 9·2, comparing with 1 in 9·9 for Birmingham, 1 in 9·8 for Liverpool, and 1 in 10·0 for Manchester.[32]

Statistics of this kind are, however, no indication of the quality of education, and though 'quality' is subjective certain circumstantial evidence may be used to indicate changing standards over the period. Many Victorians, for example, like present-day historians, believed that day schooling was educationally preferable to Sunday-school instruction, that the 'public' voluntary schools were superior to the private schools available to the working classes, and that government-inspected public schools were better than non-inspected ones. Robert Baker, who carried out the Leeds survey of 1839, alleged that many private day schools were 'dame schools only ... more for keeping children out of danger during the employment of the mother, than for the purposes of real education', while many proprietors were 'more fitted to be scholars than teachers'. He estimated that of the 11,300 children under nine in school, only about 6,760 were deriving any benefit.

Thirty years later J. G. Fitch described the thirty-four private schools (with 2,750 pupils on the roll) held in places like church halls (and so mistakenly regarded by parents as Church schools), as 'with scarcely any exception ill-organised and badly taught', with only 'one-fifth of the so-called scholars' able to reach proper standards. The 105 more openly private schools (with some 2,700 on the roll) were, he alleged, even worse. Of those run by men it was 'impossible to exaggerate the dullness and the intellectual stagnation, the badness of the methods, the waste of time'. Those run by women were better, but private schools as a whole were 'very bad', with 'scarcely a good school among them'. The school inspectors, too, preferred the voluntary schools.

If all this is true – and of course it represents the partisan views of those engaged in public education – then any increase of the proportion of schoolchildren attending public schools is an indication of improvement. Of the pupils recorded in the 1833 returns for Leeds some 60 per cent attended private schools; in 1843 it was about 58 per cent, in 1851 some 40 per cent, and in 1869 perhaps 36 per cent.

Even within the public voluntary schools the type of education offered varied. The extension of schooling was enjoyed differently by different social groups, though it is not easy to generalise about the class of children attending different kinds of public schools. Most of the voluntary schools charged fees, more being charged for advanced instruction; some schools expected craftsmen to pay more than labourers. At Darley Street Wesleyan School in the 1840s, where a mixed clientele of children of artisans, labourers and paupers was to be found, advanced arithmetic, mensuration, geography, mapping and drawing were offered for 1s a week, three times the cost of the basic curriculum. Other schools, especially by the 1860s, were geared to the needs of particular working-class groups. The 'better' National schools in the town were by then attended by the children of the lower middle class and superior artisans, who felt they could obtain there a sounder schooling than in the private schools. The Leeds parish National school, for example, had an 'upper department' teaching Latin, geometry and algebra, and at St George's National School in 1848 geography, history, algebra and mensuration were taught and homework was set.

In most voluntary schools, however, the bulk of the pupils were of lowlier status. Thus in 1863, in three National schools in parts of the town where the better-off working class predominated, only 5 per cent of the pupils were of that class, and in most Leeds schools (the cheapest known as 'penny Nashes') the labouring classes were in the majority. The more respectable labourers were not attracted to the National schools for religious reasons, for many of them were Dissenters who yet appreciated the value of the education in the Anglican day schools, even though they preferred the Chapel Sunday schools. The better-off artisans and clerical workers often sent their children to private schools 'of worse instruction, but higher gentility', and as late as 1869 J. G. Fitch found the 'better class of poor' attracted to the dearer private schools because they flattered their vanity and social ambition, the teachers 'calling the children "Master" and "Miss"'. Parents lower in the social scale, too, were able to find private schools at a cost as low as or lower than the voluntary schools, and many did so – some because there was no convenient voluntary school, some because they disliked their size or preferred independence to the taint of charity, but not a few because they disliked the religious atmosphere of the Church and Chapel schools.

It was in the voluntary schools, however, that there was from the beginning an interest in methods of organisation and teaching and where a discernible increase of teachers with some sort of training occurred. Initially the Church of England had encouraged the introduction of the monitorial system in its schools in the area. The parish National school sent its first teacher to learn this system (in which teachers instructed large numbers of pupils with the aid of young monitors) and recruited successors from the National Society's Central School. The Leeds Infants School adopted the monitorial system from the start and also acted from the mid-1830s as a local training establishment for infants' teachers, at first gratuitously and then for payment. By the 1840s some Church schools were using paid monitors on a large scale. The Wesleyans in the early days of their schools in St Peter's Square and the Bank sent their teachers to the training institution in Glasgow to learn the system of teaching and organisation advocated by David Stow, and then arranged their own training system in Leeds for assistant teachers.[33]

It must be admitted, however, that progress was slow. In 1833 many more trained teachers were said to be needed, and in 1838 Hook pointed out, 'we want not systems but masters'.[34] The system of monitors was a stop-gap with many defects. The monitors were often children of eleven or twelve, only a little older than their charges and frequently of low capacity. Classes remained very large. For instance in 1845 at Christ Church there were 250 boys to one master, at Quarry Hill 120, and at St Saviour's 120, with 145 girls under one mistress. Even as late as 1860 at Caroline Street British School 180 girls were taught by one nineteen-year-old teacher aided by two younger colleagues. Nevertheless from the mid-1840s inspectors increasingly noted teachers recruited from well known training establishments. These were augmented from 1847 by government-subsidised pupil teachers. Leeds quickly became 'pre-eminent' in the north-east in the use of these properly apprenticed teachers, with eighty-two in sixteen schools. True, inspectors often complained of low standards, and the best pupil teachers were frequently drawn away into better paid employment, but gradual and satisfactory progress was reported. By 1869 the Leeds day schools had 269 head teachers, 88 assistants, and 171 apprentice teachers, as well as paid and unpaid monitors.

The improvement in the numbers and qualifications of the teaching body was accompanied by a gradual extension of the curriculum. In 1839 reading was the only subject offered in all the 154 day schools in Leeds, 'writing and accounts' being taught in seventy-four. By 1847 all government-inspected voluntary schools (except three for infants) were teaching writing and most children were learning arithmetic, though only a minority were being taught grammar, geography, history or other subjects. Twenty years later grammar and geography were taught to some children in over half the schools, and nearly half also offered history. 'Science' had crept into six schools and there had been a great increase in teaching drawing. Needlework remained significant for girls, who tended to be taught less arithmetic than boys.

The private schools shared the broadening of the curriculum only to a limited extent. By 1869, almost without exception, they taught reading and writing, and needlework for girls (the last said to take up an excessive part of the day). Quite a few, however, even of those taking children aged five to ten, did not teach arithmetic, and a large number taught no other subjects; out of 139 private schools, for example, only fifty-one taught history and fifty-seven geography. Religious instruction, found in all the voluntary schools, was ignored by a large minority of the private schools, probably reflecting parents' tastes.

There is little evidence of improvement in the buildings and equipment of the private schools catering for the working classes in this period. The annual reports of HM inspectors indicate, however, that middle-class philanthropy combined with school fees, and, as far as the inspected voluntary schools are concerned, government financial assistance, to ensure that 'public' schooling was pursued with increasingly good equipment and buildings. The Dissenting voluntary schools, other than the Wesleyan ones, did not accept government grants and were less well equipped and housed.

In the length of time spent at school by Leeds working-class children in the period before 1870, however, there was little if any improvement. Throughout the years 1840 to 1870 shortness of 'school stay' and irregularity of attendance remained a greater hindrance to educational advance than any lack of school places. In 1851 21,843 children were on the books of day schools in the city, but only 18,108 were found at their desks on census day. At Hunslet National School in 1844 the average attendance of 439 enrolled pupils was 241, and in 1845 only 20 per cent of the pupils had full attendance over six months. In 1848 the infants' section, able to take 180 children, had twenty-four. At the inspection of Holbeck and Wortley British Girls' School in 1844 only eighteen of the seventy girls were present. In the early 1850s St Matthew's, Holbeck, with accommodation for over 500, had only eighty-four in regular attendance. Such examples could be multiplied. In 1869, of the 27,509 Leeds children enrolled at day school, only 21,057 were in attendance on the day of the returns, a smaller percentage than in 1851. Attendance at private schools was at a considerably higher rate than at the public schools both in 1851 and in 1869.

The smallness of attendance relative to accommodation perhaps reflects the difference between official and working-class views on the proper length of schooling and regularity of attendance. In the early 1840s most children at school were in the age group three to twelve, though in the poorer areas like Holbeck the range tended to be two to nine. When trade was good children left school for jobs, frequently never to return. Girls were often kept at home for domestic duties. School work was disrupted by a continuously changing body of pupils. At St Philip's, for example, in the year 1850-51 500 children entered the school and 354 left. In a survey of Yorkshire as a whole in 1856 48 per cent had been in their schools for less than a year and only 17 per cent for over two years. In 1845 most children leaving Holbeck National School appear to have had one and a half to two and three-quarter years' schooling. In 1857 the average age of leaving in ten Leeds schools was nine and a half and the average school-life four and three-quarter years. A decade or so later about 72 per cent of day-school pupils were aged ten or below (22 per cent under five), but 23 per cent were aged ten to fifteen. This was much the same as the proportions in Yorkshire generally. An extensive study of Holbeck, one of the poorest areas of Leeds, indicates the likelihood of an improvement in the 1860s. There the percentage of the five-to-thirteen age group at school rose from 52·6 in 1851 to 68·6 in 1861 and 77·1 in 1871 (not including half-timers), and very few children missed school completely.[35]

Statistical evidence of reading and writing abilities in young Leeds factory hands, miners, army recruits and prisoners exists, but the samples are too small to be of great value and are often based on subjective criteria.[36] Like the reports of the HMIs they do suggest a gradual improvement in standards. Other statistics may be calculated from marriage signatures and marks for the years 1842-84 (table 21). Though indicating only a very basic skill, the figures in the table are likely to bear a relationship to higher educational attainments. There is evidence, too, that more Leeds children in this period could read

Table 21 Grooms and brides making marks on marriage, 1842–84 (%)

Year	Grooms	Brides	Average
1842[a]	28·9	61·0	44·9
1843	28·4	60·2	44·3
1844	29·3	59·7	44·5
1845	28·4	59·1	43·7
1846	27·5	55·1	41·3
1855	23·7	43·1	33·4
1856	24·8	47·7	36·2
1857	24·6	44·7	34·6
1858	17·4	33·2	25·3
1859	23·7	42·7	33·2
1860	16·7	31·9	24·3
1861	15·6	30·1	22·8
1862	16·2	30·8	23·5
1863[b]	21·6	40·2	30·9
1864	20·9	39·3	30·1
1865	21·3	39·1	30·2
1866	20·6	38·4	29·5
1867	21·2	36·3	28·7
1868	17·4	35·3	26·3
1869[c]	19·9	36·6	28·2
1870	19·4	37·0	28·2
1871	18·9	35·6	27·2
1872	19·0	34·7	26·8
1873	19·1	34·7	26·9
1874	17·8	34·5	26·1
1875	16·8	30·9	23·8
1876	16·9	30·3	23·6
1877	15·8	30·1	22·9
1878	15·1	29·4	22·2
1879	14·2	26·9	20·5
1880	14·6	27·7	21·1
1881	13·7	24·6	19·1
1882	14·0	25·3	19·6
1883	12·5	22·8	17·6
1884	12·3	19·1	15·7

Notes

[a] 1842–46, 1855–62: figures are for Leeds and Hunslet (Hunslet is distinguished in the reports from 1845 but has been added in here). Horsforth was excluded from 1861.

[b] 1863–68: reports distinguished Leeds, Hunslet, Holbeck, Kirkstall, but they have been conflated here. From 1863 Bramley is also distinguished and its statistics are embraced here, but the marriages were not numerous enough materially to affect the percentages shown.

[c] 1869–84: reports distinguished Leeds, Hunslet, Holbeck (which are conflated here). Kirkstall, however, is not shown separately in the reports. Most of Kirkstall was

than could sign their names, reflecting the greater emphasis on reading in schools. Boundary changes of registration districts render strict comparability throughout the period impossible but the percentages again give the impression of some progress since the late eighteenth and early nineteenth centuries (tables 18 and 19), and a great improvement between the early 1840s (when those who had been of school age about 1825-32 were marrying) and the later 1850s (spouses of school age about 1840-47), reflecting perhaps the great expansion of voluntary schooling in those earlier decades. The apparent rise in illiteracy in the statistics in the 1860s is probably accounted for more by boundary changes than a fall in standards. The reduction from 28 per cent in 1869-70 to 16 per cent in 1884 reflects if anything the achievements of the voluntary school era, since most products of the Board schools established under the Act of 1870 would hardly have reached the marriage market by 1884.

Throughout the period the superior literacy of men over women, common in industrial areas, is evident in these figures, as earlier. The proportion of girls in Leeds schools rose from about a third in 1833 to some 46 per cent in 1851, with more in private than in public schools, but a study of Holbeck for 1851–71 reveals by then little discrepancy between the sexes in any school age group.[37] The differences in the signature statistics were probably due to girls' greater irregularity of attendance, more school time devoted to sewing and knitting, and greater parental indifference and lack of social incentive; more girls than boys were employed in the local textile mills.[38]

On the eve of the Education Act of 1870 there was no overall shortage of school places in Leeds in relation to the numbers seeking schooling; indeed, there was a surplus. On the other hand attendance was very irregular (for 20,000 enrolled in inspected schools the average attendance was 12,400) and some children were on the books of no school. Contemporary official pronouncements based on such estimates[39] exaggerated the size of the problem by failing to point out that children unenrolled at any particular time might have previously attended school, or might later do so. Yet it is clear there would have been a deficiency of places had schooling between the ages of, say, five and thirteen been made compulsory.

A residue of the population was unable or unwilling to educate its

---

allotted to Leeds, Hunslet and Holbeck, but Swillington went to Tadcaster, and Shadwell to Wetherby, and marriages in those two places are not covered for these years in this table.

Source. Based on *Annual Reports of the Registrar of Births, Deaths and Marriages.*

children. In particular a body of Irish immigrants, estimated at 20,000 in 1869, mostly 'from the wildest parts of Connaught', lived a life of 'indigence, squalor and hopelessness, . . . in complete disregard . . . of schools for their children', and could not anyway pay school pence. Free schools for the submerged classes by this time included two ragged schools, two[40] certified industrial schools taking both day pupils and children under detention, schools connected with the Hunslet and Leeds workhouses, and some voluntary homes for orphans, but they were insufficient to alleviate the situation greatly. Moreover lack of school provision was greater in some parts of Leeds than others. The government grant system, based on aid given in proportion to local financial provision, had from its institution worked against poorer areas without well-off residents, and in 1869 National schools in central Leeds were 'sometimes so near as to be in a relation of serious rivalry, while other places are left wholly unsupported'. Thus the proportion of children aged three to thirteen on the rolls of day schools varied greatly between districts – from 24 per cent in Whitkirk, and 39 per cent in Kirkstall and Hunslet, to 61 per cent at Bramley, and 69 per cent at Holbeck.[41]

In the 1850s an HMI had reported of schooling in Leeds and other West Riding towns that 'the machinery for doing the work is . . . on the spot *and in gear*'.[42] That machinery had remarkable success but did not solve the problem. The Act of 1870 added to the existing schools the Board schools, and education in Leeds entered a new phase.

NOTES

No attempt has been made in the references to cite all sources on which parts of the text are based, and readers should look at the Bibliographical Note, particularly for details of general surveys, newspapers, directories and Parliamentary Papers, of which extensive use has been made. In some notes below short references are provided, the fuller reference being found in the Bibliographical Note.

[1] *Nineteenth-century educational development and terminology.* The term 'public school' is used here in the proper sense to mean a school conducted as a public service and not for profit. It embraced free 'charity schools' financed by bequest or subscription, and 'voluntary schools' (so called because run by 'voluntary' societies connected with religious groups or denominations), which usually charged a small fee. The main types of voluntary school were those in association with the National Society (an Anglican body), known as National schools, and the British or Lancasterian schools run in connection with the British and Foreign School Society (a non-denominational religious society originally called the Royal Lancasterian Institution). 'Private schools' were those conducted by individuals for private profit and included 'dame schools', often run by women for infants, and 'common day schools' catering for older children. Private schools were attended by working-class children in large numbers.

State financial aid to the voluntary schools was forthcoming from 1833, though not all voluntary schools sought assistance. From 1839 government inspectors (HMIs), responsible to a committee of the Privy Council (an embryonic ministry of education), were appointed to see that schools seeking aid were sufficiently efficient to deserve it. Grants were usually dependent on a proportion of local financial support. In 1846 the government initiated a scheme to finance the salaries of pupil teachers – older, brighter children following a teaching apprenticeship. The pupil-teacher system gradually replaced the monitorial system where one teacher had taught large numbers of pupils with the help of young monitors.

School attendance was not generally compulsory in the period covered in this chapter. A series of Factory Acts from 1833, however, made part-time attendance at school incumbent on children employed in factories and workshops in certain trades and industries. These children, known as 'half-timers', attended either factory schools provided by their employer or other approved schools. Some factory owners, like the Marshalls, provided schools before 1833.

Apart from workhouse schools and schools of a reformatory type, there were, generally speaking, no 'local authority' schools before the Education Act of 1870, after which public 'Board schools' emerged, controlled by locally elected School Boards (and financed from rates). The voluntary schools continued to exist and today are known as 'voluntary aided' schools, forming with local authority schools, successors to the Board schools, our present system of publicly provided education.

[2] W. B. Stephens, *Regional Variations in Education during the Industrial Revolution, 1780–1870* (1973); M. Sanderson, 'Social change and elementary education in industrial Lancashire, 1780–1840', *Northern History*, III (1968).

[3] M. Yasumoto, 'Urbanization and population in an English town: Leeds during the industrial revolution', *Keio Economic Studies*, X, 2 (1972), 83–5.

[4] W. B. Stephens, 'Illiteracy and schooling in the provincial towns, 1640–1870', in D. A. Reeder (ed.), *Urban Education in the Nineteenth Century* (1977).

[5] The following is based on: *Archbishop Herring's Visitation Returns*; Archbishop Drummond's Visitation Returns; Leeds city archives, Pietas Leodiensis (DB/196/1); Leeds Charity School Minute Books, Accounts, and other records (DB/196/1A; 196/58; 197/5); *15th Rep. Charity Commissioners*; National Society, school files for Headingley, Wortley.

[6] Leeds city archives, Minutes, etc., of Trustees of Woodhouse School, 1784, Norths–Gott deeds, parcel of papers *re* Armley; J. Mayhall, *Annals of Yorkshire*, I, 114; A. C. Price, *A History of Leeds Grammar School* (1919), 131–2; *Education in Leeds, Souvenir Handbook* (1926); M. E. Shaw, thesis, 1975 (see Bibliographical Note), 161.

[7] *Rules and Orders for Relieving and Employing the Poor of the Township of Leeds and for the Government of the Workhouse there* (1771), 8.

[8] *Gentleman's Magazine*, LIV (1784), 377, 410; J. A. Langford, *A Century of Birmingham Life, 1741–1841*, I (1868), 411.

[9] Based on surveys of 1818, 1833, 1839, 1843; Education Census, 1881; Hole (1863); directories; *Rep. Children in Factories* (1833), 462.

[10] *Leeds Mercury*. 30 May 1795; R. W. Hamilton, *The Institutions of Popular Education* (1845), 40–1. Cf. A. Briggs, *Victorian Cities* (1968), 172 (Geo. Heap).

[11] The following is based on newspapers and directories; Langford, *op. cit.*, 411–12; Pearson, *Life of Hey*, Part 2, 110–11, 163 ff., 174, 307, 311, 313; Hole (1863), 31, 35–6; *Rep. Children in Factories* (1833), 401 ff.; 449, 462–3; *Rep. Children in Mines* (1842), 176, App., 929–37; survey of 1839; *Church School Enquiry, 1846–7*; *British and Foreign Schools Soc., Annual Rep., 1839*, 100–1; Leeds city archives, Brunswick Sunday School minutes; Leeds University, Special Collections, MS116, Zion Sunday S. register; *Rules of St. George's Chapel Sunday*

School, Leeds (1833); R. S. Mortimer, 'Zion Sunday School', *Leeds University Review*, III (1952–53), 137; T. W. Laqueur, *Religion and Respectability* (1976), 39, 101, 144–5.

[12] Pearson, *op. cit.*, 307, 311, 313.

[13] *British and Foreign Schools Soc., Annual Rep. 1815*, 72–4, 132; *Philanthropist*, I (1818), 193; *National Society, Annual Rep. 1814*, 33; Leeds Parish Church, Mins. Leeds District National Soc., early entries; Pearson, *op. cit.*, 190–2, 321 ff.; Mayhall, *op. cit.*, I, 240–1; *Leeds Mercury*, 11, 18 February 1809; 17 November, 1, 8 December 1810; S. Frith, 'Socialization and rational schooling: elementary education in Leeds before 1870', in P. McCann (ed.), *Popular Education and Socialisation in the Nineteenth Century* (1977), 73.

[14] Baines, *Life of Baines*, 115–16, 314–15, 330 ff.; Baines, *Social, Educational and Religious State . . .* ; W. F. Hook, *On the Means of Rendering More Efficient the Education of the People* (1846); Stephens, *Life of Hook*, 345–8, 402 ff.; Stranks, *Dean Hook*, 72–82; *Leeds Mercury*, 7 October 1843; Reid, *Life of Forster*, I, 436; Sykes, *Jackson*, 121–2; Leeds Parish Church, Mins. Leeds District National Society, pp. following entry of 18 January 1849.

[15] Leeds newspapers, many entries from 1850; Mayhall, *op. cit.*, I, 586, 630–1.

[16] Stephens, *Life of Hook*, 266–7; National Soc., school files for Leeds and townships, *passim*.

[17] *Return of Schools* (1870) (J. G. Fitch) (cited hereafter as Fitch), 80–9, 98; Leeds city archives, National School Returns.

[18] F. Smith, *The Life and Work of Sir James Kay-Shuttleworth* (1923), 159 n.; *National Education – Address of Edward Baines* (1867); Fitch, 89; *National Education Union, Report of the Education Conference held at Leeds, 8 December 1869*.

[19] Frith, *op. cit.*, 75, 78; W. G. Rimmer, *Marshall's of Leeds, Flax Spinners, 1788–1886* (1960), especially 107 ff.

[20] National Society, school files: St James, letter 16 August 1844; St Saviour, letter 16 May 1848.

[21] Surveys of 1819, 1839, 1841, 1843; *Leeds Mercury*, 15, 30 June 1833; Hook, *op. cit.*, National Society, school files for Upper Armley, New Wortley, Holbeck (St Matthew's), various items.

[22] Survey of 1833; directories; Frith, *op. cit.*, 73; Leeds city archives, Wesleyan Day School Soc., Minute Book, E. Circuit, 1837–46, various entries, 1839–44.

[23] The following is based on: *Minutes, Committee of Council on Education* (henceforth *M.C.C.E.*); *ibid.* (*Schools of Parochial Unions*), vols. 1847–49 to 1857–58); Hole, 96–7, 100–3, 141–6, 164–5; Schroeder, *Annals of Yorks.*, vol. 2, 19–20; *Education Census, 1851*; *Reports of the Leeds Ragged School and Shoe Black Society*; *Ragged School Magazine* (1862), 22; *The Times*, 7 December 1866, leading article; *A Few Plain Facts about the Leeds Ragged and Certified Industrial Schools* (1867). I am indebted to Dr E. A. G. Clark for several of these references.

[24] The following is based on: Hole, 34, 41–51; directories; *M.C.E.E.*

[25] Rimmer, *op. cit.*, 217; A. H. Robson, *The Education of Children Engaged in Industry in England, 1833–1876* (1931), 52–3; *M.C.C.E.*; Fitch, 119–20.

[26] *Journal Statistical Soc. of London*, II (1839–40), 416: '460 scholars of whom 230 are males and 130 are females' (*sic*); *6th Rep. Committee on Factories* (1840), 731.

[27] National Society, St Peter's, Bank, school file, letters from Saunders, HMI of Factories, 26 October, 6 November 1840, *inter alia*; Christ Church school file, statement by W. F. Hook *et al.*, 30 April 1841.

[28] *Education Census, 1851*; Fitch, 116–20; Hole, 23; survey of 1843, 57; *M.C.C.E.*

[29] Borthwick Institute of Historical Research, Day School Returns, 1815. There are similar discrepancies for Headingley, Hunslet and Bramley. Leeds itself is not covered in the 1815 return.

[30] *Rep. Education of Poorer Classes* (1837–38), 164. These figures are, however, dubious; private schools for Leeds were omitted. Cf. *British and Foreign School Soc., Annual Rep., 1839*, 15.

[31] Stephens, 'Illiteracy and Schooling'.

[32] Calculated from Fitch, 6–7. Much of the rest of this chapter is based without further citation on Fitch; *M.C.C.E.;* the surveys indicated in the Bibliographical Note; annual reports of the British and Foreign School Society; records of the Wesleyan Day School Society (Leeds city archives); National Society, school files, Leeds and townships.

[33] College of Ripon and York St John, York Diocesan Education Society, records, various correspondence, 1814–22; *National Society, 23rd Annual Rep.* (1834), 59; *1st Annual Report, Leeds Infant School Society* (1827), 6–7; *Leeds Mercury*, 13 July 1839.

[34] *Leeds Mercury*, 12 October 1833; Stephens, *Life of Hook*, 266.

[35] Shaw, *op. cit.*, 147 ff.

[36] E.g. survey of 1839; *Rep. Children in Mines* (1842), XVII, h34–h41; Robson, *op. cit.*, 51–2; Fitch, 110–11.

[37] Shaw, *op. cit.*, 147–8.

[38] Based on detailed study by Jennifer H. Robson, 'Educational attainment of the working-class female in the West Riding of Yorkshire, 1850 to 1870', M.A. research exercise, University of Leeds, 1976 (copy in my possession).

[39] Fitch, 78–9; *Hansard*, 3rd ser., vol. CLXXXVIII, col. 1351 (W. E. Forster).

[40] One had been detached from the Certified Industrial and Ragged School. The two ragged schools amalgamated *c.* 1873: *School Board Chronicle* (1873).

[41] Calculated from Fitch, 28. Other districts: South East, 54 per cent; North, 48 per cent; Chapeltown, 45 per cent; Bramley, 61 per cent; Wortley, 48 per cent. The high proportion at Holbeck perhaps reflected the Marshalls' efforts there.

[42] *M.C.C.E., 1850–1*, 274. Cf. *ibid, 1852–3*, 484–5.

BIBLIOGRAPHICAL NOTE

Consideration of space have made it impossible for detailed references to the text to be given, but this note will provide an indication of the main sources used.

A number of surveys of Leeds schools (including Sunday schools) exist. The following have been used without extensive citation: T. D. Whitaker, *Loidis and Elmete* (1816 (*sic*) but contains information for 1817), App., 29; *Digest of Parochial Returns on the Education of the Poor*, P.P. (1819), IX (2) (for 1818); *Abstract of Education Returns, 1833*, P.P. (1835), XLII; 'Report upon the Condition of the Town of Leeds ... Oct. 1839', *Journal of the Statistical Society of London*, II (1839–40); R. Baker, *Report on the Condition of the Residences of the Labouring Classes in the Town of Leeds* (1842); E. Baines junior, *The Social, Educational and Religious State of the Manufacturing Districts* (1843; repr. 1969); *Rep. Commissioners for taking a Census of Great Britain on Education*, P.P. (1852–53), XC (cited as *Education Census, 1851*); J. Hole, *The Working Classes of Leeds: an Essay on the Present State of Education in Leeds ...* (1863); and *Return of Schools for the Poorer Classes in Birmingham, Leeds, Liverpool and Manchester*, P.P. (1870), LIV (for 1869, by J. G. Fitch). Other surveys in print include: *Archbishop Herring's Visitation Returns, 1743* (ed. S. L. Ollard and P. C. Walker), I and II (Yorkshire Archaeological Society, Record Series, vols. 71–2, 1928, 1929); *Fifteenth Report of the Charity Commissioners*, P.P. (1826), XIII; *Church School*

Enquiry, 1846–7 (printed, not published; copies at National Society, Department of Education and Science Library, and the College of Ripon and York St John). In addition much information, including numbers of schools, is found in directories and handbooks: particularly useful are T. Haigh, *General and Commercial Directory of the Borough of Leeds* (1839); *An Historical Guide to Leeds and its Environs* (1858), and the directories of White and Baines, of various dates. Unpublished surveys include Archbishop Drummond's Visitation Returns for 1764 (Borthwick Institute of Historical Research); and a return of schools for 1815 covering some Leeds townships (Borthwick I.H.R., Y/DSR).

A great deal of evidence has been culled from the annual reports of the British and Foreign Schools Society and the National Society (both published) and from newspapers, especially the *Leeds Mercury* and the *Leeds Intelligencer*.

The Parliamentary Papers include (as well as those cited above) the annual *Minutes* (later *Reports*) *of the Committee of Council on Education*, a mine of information from 1840 onwards, and, for the years 1847 to 1858, the *Minutes of the Committee of Council on Education (Schools of Parochial Unions)* (for Poor Law schooling). Other useful Parliamentary Papers are the *First Rep. R. Commission into Employment of Children in Factories*, P.P. (1833), XX; *Rep. Select Committee on the Education of the Poorer Classes*, P.P. (1837–38), VII; *Sixth Rep. Select Committee into Act for Regulation of Factories*, P.P. (1840), X; and *First Rep. R. Commission into Employment of Children in Mines and Manufactories*, P.P. (1842) XV. The *Annual Reports of the Registrar General of Births, Deaths and Marriages* have been used for marriage signatures from 1842 (before that marriage signature percentages are derived from the parish registers).

General works containing information on education include J. Mayhall, *Annals of Yorkshire* (n.d.); H. Schroeder, *Annals of Yorkshire* (1852); and the following biographies: E. Baines, *The Life of Edward Baines, late M.P. for the Borough of Leeds* (1851); W. R. W. Stephens, *Life and Letters of Walter Farquar Hook, D.D., F.R.S.* (6th edn., 1881); C. J. Stranks, *Dean Hook* (1954); T. Wemyss Reid, *Life of William Edward Forster* (1888); L. and K. Sykes, *Sketches in the Life of Edward Jackson* [1912]; J. Pearson, *The Life of William Hey, F.R.S.* (1822).

Manuscript collections used include records of the Leeds Charity School, the local Wesleyan Day School Society, Brunswick (Leeds) Sunday School minutes, 'National School Returns' (from 1850) (DB196/19–55) – all in the Leeds City Archives depository; correspondence in the records of the Diocesan Education Society (at College of Ripon and York St John, York): YOS/1/7, Letter Books; the many files on the schools (day and Sunday) of Leeds and its townships at the National Society's depository at Church House, Westminster, and the records of Church schools (especially the Parish school) at Leeds Parish Church. For those interested in educational development in Leeds immediately following the Education Act of 1870 there is much information in the Public Record Office (Kew branch) (references: Ed. 16/366 and 367).

Two unpublished theses covering elementary education in Leeds in this period are: H. Fligg, 'A history of elementary education in Leeds prior to 1870', M.Ed., University of Leeds (1938); and M. E. Shaw, 'The childhood of the working class in Leeds, 1830–70', M.Phil., University of London (1975).

NIGEL YATES

X

The religious life
of Victorian Leeds

The history of the Victorian Church in England has still to be written,' wrote the distinguished Methodist historian, Professor John Kent, in 1969.[1] Since then a good deal has been written on nineteenth-century Nonconformity, though mostly from a sociological or statistical angle, but there are still glaring gaps in other areas. Most striking is the complete absence of any satisfactory study of Roman Catholicism since 1850 or of the Salvation Army, despite the importance of both, and even the established Church of England has received very uneven treatment in recent work. At the local or regional level there are few parts of the country for which significant studies have been attempted. In Leeds only the Baptists, the Quakers, some sections of the Church of England and some aspects of early Methodism have attracted the attentions of recent historians, and many gaps remain to be filled. This chapter must, therefore, be regarded as essentially an interim introduction to the subject, and the author must express the hope that it will lead others to investigate particular aspects much more fully and, almost inevitably, to challenge the preliminary conclusions offered here.

I   'The *de facto* established religion is Methodism,' wrote the new Vicar of Leeds to the future bishop of Oxford and Winchester in 1837.[2] It was hardly surprising. Like many parishes in the north of England, that of Leeds had covered a wide rural area on each side of the town, an area which was entirely urbanised during the eighteenth and nineteenth centuries. The parish church had developed dependent chapelries at Armley, Beeston, Bramley, Chapel Allerton, Farnley, Headingley, Holbeck and Hunslet by the early seventeenth century. Thereafter new churches were built in the town itself: St John, Briggate, in 1634; Holy Trinity, Boar Lane, in 1727; St Paul, Park Square, in 1793. All these churches were in the parish of Leeds and were served only by curates. So were two of the three churches built in 1826–27 as a result of the first grant by Parliament towards the provision of additional churches in populous places. These were Christ Church, Meadow Lane, and St Mary, Quarry Hill. The third church to be financed in this way, St Mark, Woodhouse, was given a separate parish, as was the new church of St Stephen, Kirkstall, consecrated in 1829. The patronage of the vicarage of Leeds and of the new vicarages of Kirkstall and Woodhouse was in the hands of twenty-five trustees, who included in their number the most prominent Anglican laymen in the town.[3] In 1837 the Vicar of Leeds was still pastorally responsible for a parish of some 125,000 people with a chapelry system which had proved unworkable even in the eighteenth century.[4]

The main challenge to the Anglican establishment came from Methodism. None of the older branches of dissent was particularly strong. The chapels at Mill Hill and Call Lane had been established in 1674 and 1691 respectively. The former had become Unitarian in doctrine during the eighteenth century and attracted an intellectually distinguished congregation. Two ministers, Joseph Priestley (1767–73) and Thomas Hinks (1855–69), were fellows of the Royal Society. The trustees included several members of the Kitson and Lupton families and others prominent in the public life of Leeds.[5] Three new Independent congregations were established in the eighteenth century, and the Queen Street chapel, opened in 1825, was the largest Independent chapel in the West Riding at the time.[6] Salem chapel, opened in 1790, could count among its congregation many of the most influential business and professional families in Leeds, including the elder and younger Edward Baines.[7] The Baptists established a congregation at Bramley in 1777 and one in the township of Leeds in 1779. The latter congregation built a new chapel in South Parade in 1826 and counted among its members Sir George Goodman and Sir John Barran, both of whom were mayors of Leeds after 1835 and both of whom later represented Leeds in Parliament.[8] The Society of Friends had a long established meeting in Leeds with a membership of 418 in 1829, and again this number included several important citizens.[9] The political and social influence of the older branches of Dissent, however, far outweighed the size of their congregations. In terms of popular appeal the various branches of Methodism attracted many more adherents than all the other non-Anglicans put together.

Methodist preaching began in Leeds in 1742, and the first chapel was established in 1751. It has been calculated that by 1811 one person in fifteen in Leeds would have been a member of a Methodist society. The Leeds circuit was formed in 1777 and originally stretched from north of Otley to south of Pontefract. The outlying districts were progressively split off as membership grew. The Bramley circuit was formed in 1811 and covered most of the western townships. In 1826 the Leeds circuit was divided into the Leeds East and West circuits, each of which contained a substantial rural area. These two circuits had a membership of 4,160 in 1828, which had increased to 8,079 by 1840; the Bramley circuit had a membership of 1,469 in 1825. There is little doubt that Methodism owed its early and substantial success in Leeds to the weakness of the Anglican chapelry system and the lack of Anglican churches in rapidly growing areas of the town. At Woodhouse a Methodist chapel was opened in 1769, almost sixty years before the Church of England made any provision for that community. In 1809 the society had 372 members; in 1831, five years after the new church of St Mark was opened, membership had fallen to 237. Between 1770 and 1840 no fewer than twenty-two Wesleyan Methodist chapels were opened in the out-townships. The Church of England, which had had only eight existing chapels of ease, could only manage to erect a new church at Kirkstall and acquire control over a chapel erected at Wortley by the lord of the manor largely for his own use. At Meanwood a Wesleyan chapel was opened in 1811, and there was no Anglican competition until 1849. But the story of Leeds Methodism before 1837 was not just one of triumphant advance. Leeds was the scene of two major schisms, that of the Kilhamites or Methodist New Connexion in 1797 and that of the Leeds Protestant Methodists in 1828. The latter schism attracted about a quarter of the Wesleyans in Leeds at the time. The Primitive Methodists were active in Leeds from 1819 and opened their first chapel, at Quarry Hill, in 1822.They drew their support almost exclusively from among the lower-paid workers.[10]

The strength of Nonconformity in Leeds, politically, socially and numerically, posed serious problems for the Church of England. Anglicans had lost control over the improvement commission by 1829 and the town council after the reform of 1835. More serious, they lost control over the vestry, the meeting of the ratepayers that controlled the election of the churchwardens, the making of the Church rate and the financial management of parish affairs. A majority of the churchwardens were Dissenters by 1833. In 1827 the vestry voted against any payments being made towards the building of new Anglican churches. Between 1818 and 1833 the amount raised through Church rates fell from £2,611 to £614 per annum; no rate was levied after 1833 despite an attempt by the vicar, Richard Fawcett, to force a poll on the issue. Dissenters argued against the rate on four main grounds: they made no use of the churches and had chapels of their own to finance; the Church was wealthy and had no need to levy rates; if they were granted the Church would seek to impose a high rate merely to beautify existing buildings; and the establishment, of which rates were a part, was not in the best interests of the Church of England anyway. Thus Dissenters could argue that they were actually doing the Church a service by withholding the rate.[11] The majority of churchmen, including Richard Fawcett, disagreed, but in 1837 the trustees of the parish church elected to the then vacant vicarage someone who took a different view.

II The election of Walter Farquhar Hook to the vicarage of Leeds was one of the most significant events in the religious history of the town.

68   Walter Farquhar Hook, 1798–1875, Vicar of Leeds 1837–59

To begin with, he was a 'High Churchman',[12] whereas the incumbents of all the other major West Riding churches, with the sole exception of Wakefield, were Evangelical in their outlook, as Hook's own predecessor, Richard Fawcett, had been.[13] He was also a man with deep social as well as spiritual concern. He was a strong supporter of factory reform, profit-sharing and popular education. He supported mechanics' institutes, distrusted by many of his fellow clergy who thought they bred political radicalism, and he advocated the breaking down of unnecessary class divisions. He was, in fact, far more in sympathy with the aspirations of the working classes than the Leeds Nonconformist, liberal establishment. The effects of Hook's arrival were immediate and dramatic. By 1839 the number of communicants at the parish church had increased from about fifty before 1837 to an average of between 400 and 500, and within a few months of his arrival two Methodist local preachers had seceded to the Church of England.[14] Unlike Fawcett, Hook took the view that there was little point in trying to force the levying of a Church rate, and he abandoned the attempt, substituting collections at services instead. He felt that the Church should be supported financially by those who actually worshipped in it, and his example was followed in many other town parishes long before the official abolition of Church rates in 1868.

Hook's incumbency at Leeds (1837–59) had two lasting monuments: the development of a new liturigical and pastoral mission for the Church of England in an urban community, and an impressive record of church-building. He was assisted in both respects by the establishment of the new diocese of Ripon, carved out of that of York, in 1836 and the energy of its first bishop, Charles Thomas Longley, whose brief spells at Durham, York and Canterbury after 1856 have made people forget how good a bishop he was in his twenty years at Ripon. Longley established a Ripon Diocesan Church Building Society in 1838 and revived the office of rural dean, always held in Leeds by the vicar of the parish church, in 1847.[15] Hook rebuilt Leeds Parish Church. The new building, consecrated in 1841, was one of the first Anglican churches designed for a surpliced choir and sacramental worship. There were daily choral services and a weekly celebration of Holy Communion. Hook's standards of worship were gradually adopted at many other churches in Leeds and in other parts of the country as well. By the end of the nineteenth century Leeds was predominantly a 'High Church' town in contrast to Bradford, Hull or Sheffield, which were still Evangelical strongholds.[16]

In terms of church-building Hook's contribution to the new diocese of Ripon can best be seen by comparing the growth of the number of

Anglican churches in Leeds between 1831 and 1911 with the growth in the population (table 22). In 1831 there had been one Anglican church for every 6,000 inhabitants. He reduced this to one church for every 5,000 inhabitants by 1851, and the ratio was maintained until 1861. It was a remarkable achievement. In many towns Anglican church-building fell well short of the growth in population, as it did in Leeds after 1861. Between 1838 and 1860 most new churches in Leeds were built with the assistance of grants from the Ripon Diocesan Church Building Society, usually of between ten and thirty per cent of the total cost. The society also made grants towards the endowment of certain churches and towards the building of parsonage houses. Nine churches built between 1844 and 1855 received grants from the Church Building Commissioners financed by Parliament. Relatively few were financed by private individuals, since the majority of wealthy merchants were not Anglicans. St Saviour's (1845), Meanwood (1849) and St John, Holbeck (1850), were notable exceptions. After 1864 the task of building and financing new Anglican churches became the responsibility of the Leeds Church Extension Society. Between then and 1910 a total of twenty-five new churches was built and the inadequate chapels at Armley, Headingley, Farnley, Wortley and Chapel Allerton were replaced by larger and worthier buildings.

Table 22 Growth in the number of Anglican churches compared with the growth in population, 1831–1911

Years	No. of new churches	Growth in number (%)	Growth in population (%)
1831–41	3	14	23
1841–51	11	46	13
1851–61	8	23	20
1861–71	7	16	25
1871–81	8	16	20
1881–91	5	8	19
1891–1901	2	3	17
1901–11	3	5	4
1831–1911	47	224	361

But Hook was not just concerned with church extension. He wanted all the Anglican clergy in Leeds to exercise proper pastoral responsibility over the communities served by their churches. This could only be done by the division of the parish, for which Hook had to promote a parliamentary Bill. Under the Leeds Vicarage Act of 1844 all the chapelries of the ancient parish of Leeds became separate ecclesiastical districts and provision was made for the creation of additional parishes as new churches were built. The Act also made provision for an increase in the number of free pews and for the building of schools and parsonage houses. For Hook the ideal parish unit was one of church, vicarage, school and resident incumbent with assistant curates who knew their parishioners and visited them regularly. It became the standard model for Anglican parish life in the century that followed, not just in Leeds but nationally. The Leeds Vicarage Act was attacked vigorously by Dissenters and by the *Leeds Mercury,* who were fully aware that it would increase the efficiency of the established Church and lead to a diminution in their own ranks. They were singularly unimpressed by the fact, given due prominence in the *Leeds Intelligencer,* that Hook had voluntarily surrendered about a third of his income through the reduction in fees for marriages and burials payable to him as a result of the Act. Whether the pattern of parish administration based on small units was wise in the long run is a moot point, but it was still sacrosanct in 1900 when a commission appointed to examine the general condition of the Anglican Church in Leeds reported to the Bishop of Ripon. It only recommended the closure of three inner-city churches and that three others should cease to be parish churches and become chapels of ease to their respective neighbours. But it also recommended the building of eight new parish and twelve new district churches, so that Leeds would have had a net increase of two parishes and seventeen churches had all the proposals been implemented.

The progress of the non-Anglican Churches between 1839 and 1914 is less easy to record, because of the tendency of congregations to move from one chapel to another, and even for chapels to be sold from one denomination to another. The one denomination that progressed rapidly throughout the period was Roman Catholicism. The mission had begun in 1786, and the Lady Lane chapel was replaced by the rather more ambitious St Anne's in 1838. New churches were built in 1831 (St Patrick's) and 1857 (Mount St Mary's) to serve the large number of Irish immigrants in east Leeds. The Irish formed 12·6 per cent of the population in 1861 but 85 per cent of them lived in that part of the town. Mount St Mary's was also partially set up to attract converts from the neighbouring Anglican ritualist church of St Saviour's. Between 1860 and 1909 nine new Roman Catholic churches were built in other parts of Leeds. In 1878 St Anne's became the cathedral of the new Roman Catholic diocese of Leeds and was rebuilt in the grand manner in 1902–04.[17] The Society of Friends and the Unitarians, on the other hand, suffered a progressive decline. The society replaced its meeting house in 1868 at a time when the membership had fallen to a then all-time low of 294. There was a gradual increase in membership up to 1892, when it totalled 449 and was the third largest meeting in England, after Birmingham and Bristol. But the membership, which was extremely middle-class, fell gradually to 267 by 1921.[18] At Mill Hill Unitarian chapel there was a serious decline in the congregation during the ministry of Charles Hargrove (1876–1912), an ex-Roman Catholic Dominican friar, and the chapel was forced to close its day schools in 1899 and its library in 1907.[19]

The major Nonconformist Churches had rather mixed fortunes between 1839 and 1914. The Independents, later known as Congregationalists, built eighteen new chapels in this period but the membership of most was small. That of Salem, which transferred to East Parade in 1841, rose from 266 in 1833 to 570 thirty years later, but fell steadily after that. In 1891 the active membership was only 320 and the highest communion attendance only 162. In one year alone, 1889–90, the total income of the chapel fell from £1,944 to £1,469 and that from pew rents from £673 to £518.[20] The Baptist chapels seem to have had a violently fluctuating membership (table 23) and it is not unlikely that other Nonconformist chapels, all of which were to a large extent dependent for their success on the preaching ability of the minister, had similar experiences. It should, however, be pointed out that actual congregations in some Nonconformist chapels tended to be rather larger than the technical membership of the chapel might suggest. There was a good deal of membership transference between the different denominations. Between 1834 and 1900 South Parade Baptist chapel gained seventy-nine members, mostly from Congregational and Methodist chapels, but they lost 140 members, more heavily to Congregational than to Methodist chapels, and even twenty-three to the Church of England; Blenheim chapel gained seventy-nine members and lost fifty-six, but here the transference was almost entirely from or to Congregational chapels. Baptist chapels

Table 23 Membership of selected Baptist chapels, 1832–1900

Chapel	1832	1845	1856	1873	1876	1877	1880	1886	1900
South Parade	179	511	351	426	579	412	509	482	554
Bramley Zion	129	226	143	199	206	206	147	192	193
Hunslet	—	93	73	83	119	128	142	230	340
Blenheim	—	—	97	123	182	151	175	201	267
York Road	—	—	—	100	94	90	164	109	80
Armley	—	—	35	79	45	48	80	108	196

Source. Figures in R. J. Owen, *op. cit.*, pp. 543–6.

attracted a very much higher level of working-class support than the other major denominations, with the exception of the Primitive Methodists. Even the important South Parade chapel was financially dependent on a small number of wealthy members, and the congregations at Armley and Hunslet were exclusively working-class.

Leeds Methodism seems to have suffered badly from its internal divisions and the Anglican renaissance of the 1840s organised by Hook. Wesleyan membership dropped from 8,079 in 1840, when Leeds was reorganised into four circuits, to 7,362 in 1849 and to 5,462 in 1854, in effect back to the level of the 1820s. This collapse was not unique. In other towns, such as Bristol and Newcastle, Wesleyan membership was more than halved in the late 1840s and early 1850s.[21] There was no dramatic increase after 1860. In 1871 the number of circuits was increased to six, and there were twelve circuits with sixty-four chapels and thirty-five ministers by 1910. In the same year there were nine Primitive Methodist circuits with twenty-eight chapels and fourteen ministers and four United Methodist (a union of several schisms from Wesleyan Methodism) circuits with thirty-five chapels and twenty-three ministers. The main strength of all these circuits, however, lay not in the centre of Leeds and the old established chapels but in the suburbs and villages and newer missions that the circuits embraced. One contemporary Wesleyan writer regarded the whole period from 1840 to 1885 as disastrous for Leeds Methodism, with only one major new chapel opened, Roscoe Place in 1861. He hoped that the current new phase of chapel-building begun after 1885 would be productive, though the membership figures were not particularly encouraging.[22]

III   It might be supposed that the orgy of church and chapel-building which was such a marked feature of Victorian religious life indicated that the existing buildings were incapable of meeting the needs of eager congregations. Unfortunately this was rarely true. Most Victorian churches and chapels were built for potential rather than actual congregations and many were probably never full at any time in their history. Statistics can be misleading, and none more so than those provided by the religious census returns for 1851, the only such exercise ever conducted on a national as opposed to a local basis. But the returns do indicate a general pattern of poor attendance, especially in urban areas. The specific information which the returns make available is an assessment of the number of sittings available and how many were free, together with an assessment of the adult congregation and number of Sunday scholars present at each of the major services on Sunday 30 March and whether this varied from the normal average over the previous year. Most of the returns were made by the minister or a church official and, although they frequently contain additional comments which are sometimes useful, there is little doubt that some are inaccurate and reflect a not unnatural desire for churches to inflate their congregation figures by various means. The evidence thus provided for churches in the township of Leeds, though of great value, does need to be treated with caution.[23]

It has frequently been assumed that in the provision of free as opposed to rented sittings the various Nonconformist Churches had a better record than the Church of England. In fact this was far from true, and the figures for Leeds bear this out (table 24). There was therefore room in all the churches of Leeds township for only about half the population, and the majority of sittings were rented. Only the Church of England and the Primitive Methodists provided a bare majority of free sittings. This is not entirely surprising. Many chapels were financially dependent on pew rents for their continued existence, but this prevented them from being able, even in theory, to attract working-class congregations. When Mill Hill Unitarian chapel was running at a deficit in 1828–29 the pews were revalued and the rents increased by 50 per cent; between 1829 and 1846 the rents were trebled. Many Nonconformist chapels also relied on pew rents to clear the debts on their buildings, since the level of subscriptions and collections at the opening services were usually insufficient. The collections at the opening of Belgrave Independent chapel in 1836 raised £423 and paid for 8·3 per cent of the total cost of the building. During the second half of the century all denominations made strenuous efforts to abolish pew rents and to raise the money to maintain the buildings and, in the case of non-Anglicans, to pay the minister through collections and fund-raising events. But pew rents at, for instance, Queen Street Congregational chapel were not abolished until 1896, nor those at Richmond Hill Wesleyan chapel until 1905.[24] Because the Church of England was able to rely partly on endowments – never to the extent, however, that its critics imagined, especially for the payment of its clergy – it found it easier to dispense with pew rents at an early stage, and some new churches, such as St Saviour's (1845) and All Saints (1850), had no rented pews at all.

Church leaders in the nineteenth century were particularly concerned that they were providing so few sittings in urban areas like Leeds, but the interesting fact is that so many of the sittings available were not being sat in. There has been a tendency to look at total congregation figures for Sunday 30 March 1851 in an attempt to

Table 24 Number of sittings available in churches and chapels in Leeds township in 1851

Denomination	No. of churches	Total No. of sittings	Free	Rented
Church of England	16	14,900+	7,164+	6,884+
Wesleyan Methodists	10	12,202	4,452	7,750
Wesleyan Methodist Association	3	2,444	780	1,664
Methodist New Connexion	3	1,225	242	983
Primitive Methodist	2	1,540	780	760
Independents	5	6,275	1,330	4,945
General Baptists	3	1,690	404	1,286
Particular Baptists	3	1,800	700	1,100
Roman Catholics	2	1,220	400	820
Other denominations	10	3,330+	930+	1,300+
Total	57	46,626+	17,182+	27,492+

Note. One Anglican church, the Wesleyan Reformers and several of the minor sects made no return of the number of sittings available.

compare one denomination with another, but this can be misleading. Many of those who went to church attended both morning and evening services, and the numbers attending are therefore even smaller than some commentators have assumed. In table 25 the numbers attending both morning and evening services have been supplied and where possible expressed as an approximate percentage of the sittings available. Afternoon attendances, which were negligible, since most Leeds churches had abandoned afternoon services in favour of evening ones, have been ignored. Only 3,698 adults attended such services, one being a special Society Meeting at Wesley Chapel, Meadow Lane, and another being a love feast at the Wesleyan Methodist Association chapel in Lady Lane.

The congregation figures include only adult attenders; Sunday scholars were counted separately and have been excluded, but overall they added about 25 per cent to the figures given in the table. In other words less than half the available sittings were actually occupied at either the morning or evening service. The best attended were Leeds Parish Church, where some 350 people were customarily obliged to stand through the evening service and people had even to be turned away on occasion, and St Patrick's Roman Catholic church, in the heart of the Irish quarter, which was full for three morning Masses and the evening service; even so this only represented less than 20 per cent of the known Irish population of Leeds in 1851. St Anne's Roman Catholic church, which had pew rents, though children and 'old infirm people' could apply for a free ticket to the services, was less well attended. Many of the most fashionable of the Nonconformist chapels were more than half empty at both the morning and the evening service. They included both Brunswick and Oxford Place Wesleyan Methodist chapels, South Parade Baptist chapel, and all the Independent chapels, clearly a change from the period between 1814 and 1848 when R. W. Hamilton's preaching had attracted vast congregations to the Albion and Belgrave chapels.[25] The worst attendance was at the Inghamite chapel in Duke Street, which attracted a grand total of twenty-eight adults and nineteen Sunday scholars to three services in a building with 200 sittings, all free. The Inghamite chapel survived until the early 1890s, the remnant of a sect once powerful in Yorkshire, whose leader had had links with both the Moravians and the early Methodists.

Table 25 Number of attenders at morning and evening services in Leeds township on 30 March 1851

| Denomination | No. of churches | Attendance and % of sittings occupied | |
		Morning	Evening
Church of England	16	5,789 (39%)	7,242 (49%)
Wesleyan Methodists	10	4,352 (36%)	5,362 (44%)
Wesleyan Methodist Association	3	590 (24%)	922 (38%)
Wesleyan Reformers	1	650	750
Methodist New Connexion	3	376 (31%)	612 (50%)
Primitive Methodists	2	358 (23%)	743 (48%)
Independents	5	2,205 (35%)	1,932 (31%)
General Baptists	3	535 (32%)	636 (38%)
Particular Baptists	3	330 (18%)	546 (30%)
Roman Catholics	2	2,682	1,000 (82%)
Unitarians	1	305 (38%)	No service
Society of Friends	1	363 (33%)	No service
Other denominations	8	398 (28%)	859 (60%)
Total	58	18,933 (41%)	20,604 (44%)

Among the other minority sects the Mormons attracted good congregations, being popular nationally at the time, but less so after 1852 when their position on polygamy proved too much for sensitive Victorian morality. The Swedenborgians, who had been established in Leeds since 1816 and who purchased the Albion chapel from the Independents in 1849, had a struggle to manage on a small and poor membership and were without a minister for a total of forty-seven years.[26] The Jews had opened their first synagogue in 1846 but had only eighteen paying seat-holders in 1853. New synagogues were opened in 1860 and 1869, but only after the Russian pogroms of 1881 did the main immigration take place, and there were about a dozen synagogues by the turn of the century.[27] After 1851 several new religious bodies established themselves in Leeds: the English Presbyterians in 1856, with three churches by 1900; the Catholic Apostolic Church, which mixed extreme ritual with a belief that the end of the world was at hand, by 1880; and the Salvation Army, which had ten missions in Leeds by 1900. In that year there was also a Labour Church and a branch of the Free Church of England but both had disappeared by 1910.

Two interesting general trends can be detected in the 1851 religious census returns for Leeds. One is the respective strengths of Anglicanism and Nonconformity, especially Methodism. The Church of England was rather stronger than it was in Bradford, Hull or Sheffield, and Methodism comparatively weaker. One suspects that had a census been taken five or ten years earlier the position would have been somewhat different, and that Methodists, who, put together, only just outnumbered Anglicans in 1851, would have done so much more substantially. How much of this was due to Hook's influence and how much to the tendency towards schism within Methodism it is difficult to assess. The second trend can be seen in the generally better figures for evening than morning attendances at the majority of churches and chapels. Evening services tended to attract a much higher proportion of working people, especially servants and shop assistants, and the figures suggest that most denominations had a fair sprinkling of working-class support. There is some indication that the evening congregation on 30 March was below average; both St Andrew's church and Call Lane Baptist chapel recorded a 20 per cent drop as a result of bad weather. Generally disappointing attendances at both morning and evening services at Salem Independent chapel were blamed on sickness among the congregation, and those at Woodhouse Wesleyan Methodist chapel on dissensions within the society. The incumbent of St Paul's, Park Square, took the view that his congregations would have been higher if all the seats in his church had not been private property, but the figures show clearly that even free seats were not being occupied.

IV   Two significant trends that can be detected within the development of Victorian religion were the moves in one direction towards liturgical formality and increased ritual, and in another towards temperance. To a greater or lesser degree all denominations were affected by both trends. Within the Church of England there was a clear move towards sacramentalism (table 26). All Leeds Anglican churches had at least a weekly communion service after the closure of St Paul's, Park Square, where it had been twice monthly until the end, in 1905. This move towards sacramentalism was an important aspect of the moderate brand of High Churchmanship of Hook and his successors at the parish church. Neither the Evangelicals nor the extreme ritualists, or Anglo-Catholics as they were later known, were particularly strong within Leeds Anglicanism. There was one major ritualistic controversy involving the new church of St Saviour's between 1845 and 1851.[28] The Victorian dread of popery, or anything that remotely resembled it, could and did reach hysterical proportions. Attacks on St Saviour's were led by both Anglican and Nonconformist clergy. The Baptists opened a schoolroom in the area in 1847 and the Wesleyans a new chapel at Richmond Hill in 1849, both avowedly to counteract the obnoxious influence of St Saviour's in east Leeds.

Table 26 Frequency of communion services in Anglican churches, 1837–95 (%)

Churches with	1837	1856	1895
Monthly communion	29	60	3
Fortnightly communion	—	7	5
Weekly communion	—	9	85
Daily communion	—	—	7

The moves towards liturgical formality and even sacramentalism can be seen within the Nonconformist Churches as well. At South Parade Baptist chapel there was a proposal in 1903, though it was rejected, to introduce a weekly communion service. At other Nonconformist chapels the main moves were in the direction of a more structured liturgy. At Mill Hill Unitarian chapel, sumptuously rebuilt in 1847–48 to look like a miniature replica of Leeds Parish Church, there were stained glass windows, a proper chancel with the pulpit to the side of the chancel arch, and the liturgy consisted of five services compiled largely from the Anglican Book of Common Prayer. Whereas the liturgical changes in the Church of England probably contributed to the increase in its congregations in Leeds during the 1840s, the move towards liturgical formality among the Nonconformists may have had the reverse effect. In the 1830s the success of Leeds Methodism clearly lay in 'a noisy meeting and a love-feast', which according to one contemporary constituted 'a great portion of their ordinances', and presumably attracted a considerable degree of working-class support.[29] The implication of the decision to hold a special monthly evening service at East Parade Congregational chapel in the 1870s for those 'to whom the term *working classes* is commonly applied', and to set up an invitation committee 'having for its chief object to superintend and stimulate the invitation of street passengers and loungers ... to our services', is that liturgical formality may have been limited in its appeal to the ministers and to the more middle-class members of chapel congregations.[30]

Certainly conflict within Methodism was generally over liturgical rather than purely doctrinal matters. Methodism, especially Leeds Methodism, was particularly prone to schism. Within six years of John Wesley's death the Kilhamite schism had taken place at the Leeds Conference in 1797 and Leeds became one of the principal centres of the new sect, known as the Methodist New Connexion. At that time the division had been over whether Methodism should remain what it was, a pressure group within the Church of England, or become what it eventually became, a proper denomination with its own ministerial and sacramental structure. Leeds was always a hotbed of radical Methodism, and conservatives were distrusted as quasi-Anglicans. The Bramley circuit was so anti-Conference that the superintendent suggested its division in 1837 as the only way to defeat the radicals. A second major schism took place in 1828 when twenty-eight local preachers, seven exhorters, fifty-six leaders and 900 members seceded from the two Leeds Wesleyan circuits to form the Leeds Protestant Methodists. Various conflicts within the two circuits were brought to a head by a proposal to install an organ in the new and fashionable Brunswick chapel. An organ could only be introduced with the consent of Conference after investigation and approval by a district meeting. The trustees of the Brunswick chapel were divided eight to six in favour of an organ, with one neutral. The leaders' meeting, however, viewing the organ as certainly a middle-class and possibly a popish status symbol, opposed its introduction by a majority of more than twenty to one and were upheld by the district meeting. Conference was persuaded by Jabez Bunting, who represented the most conservative tradition within Wesleyan Methodism and who was regarded as a would-be pope by his opponents, to support the trustees, and a special district meeting was held, with Bunting in attendance, at which large numbers of the more radical members were expelled. The Leeds Protestant Methodists linked up after 1835 with the supporters of the Warrenite Secession to form the Wesleyan Methodist Association.[31] Another schism took place in 1849 when the Wesleyan Reform Committee was established. Wesleyans who joined this body were expelled, but within three months the committee was drawing congregations of more than 500 to services held in the Albion Street stock exchange.[32]

Despite their relatively small numbers the Leeds Baptists also suffered from internal divisions during the nineteenth century. They were, in any case, divided into General and Particular Baptists, the former being moderately less rigid in their doctrine and discipline than the latter. Most of the schisms seem to have taken place from Particular Baptist churches. Blenheim chapel was founded in 1848 when the minister and eighty-four members withdrew from South Parade chapel because of its insistence on closed communion. The Regent Street chapel was formed by the secession of the minister and his supporters from York Road chapel in 1869, though it had collapsed within a few years. There was a brief schism at Armley between 1873 and 1879. At Bramley the minister and seventy-four members seceded from Zion chapel in 1877 after months of internal strife, and the relations between the two congregations were so hostile that transference of members between them was not recognised until 1881. The role of ministers in these secessions has been attributed to the tendency of congregations to appoint ministers simply because of their preaching ability and without any proper regard for their capacity for pastoral work and spiritual leadership. Baptist chapels imposed a rigid discipline on their members. At South Parade one girl was expelled for fornication, as was her father for trying to conceal what had happened. At Blenheim the congregation resolved that any member who failed in business or who got into any sort of financial difficulty should hold no office in the chapel. At Hunslet the deacons were so violently opposed to theatrical entertainment that one member who advertised a theatrical performance in his shop window was expelled. In Leeds the Baptists were very slow to permit open communion, favoured by Congregationalists and Methodists, and indeed by most Baptists elsewhere. Communion was closed at South Parade chapel until 1868, and at the Bramley chapels until well into the present century.[33]

The Leeds Baptists were in the forefront of the local temperance campaign, which united most Nonconformists and even attracted Anglican Evangelicals, like T. S. Fleming of St Clement, Sheepscar, who was also a promnent campaigner for the rescue of fallen women. The Leeds Temperance Society, one of the earliest in England, was founded by Edward Baines the elder in 1830. In 1847 the Band of Hope, which encouraged young people to pledge themselves to total abstinence from alcohol, was launched at a meeting in South Parade Baptist schoolroom and had pledged more than 4,000 Leeds children between the ages of six and sixteen within two years.[34] The temperance movement had a profound impact on all the Nonconformist denominations, not just socially, but liturgically as well, as congregations debated whether they should use fermented or unfermented wine at the communion services. Most decided in favour of the latter. At East Parade Congregational chapel two communion services were held each month, one with fermented and the other with unfermented wine. At South Parade Baptist chapel fermented wine was used until 1849, when one cup with unfermented wine was provided for those who preferred it, but in 1892 it was decided to use unfermented wine exclusively, under pressure from the temperance deacons.[35]

V   How important was religion to those who lived in Victorian Leeds? We have already seen that the figures for church attendance show that many people clearly did not bother to go to church, but the influence of the Churches was considerably greater than the level of their numerical support. This was largely because religious observance was much more in evidence among the upper and middle than among the working classes. As we have seen, many churches could count among their congregation men who were the leaders of political and commercial life; put the other way round, there were very few men in this category who did not go to church, and although some may have done so for social reasons many Victorian politicians and businessmen, both national and local public figures, were committed Christians. This meant two things. It meant that the lay members of Churches were effectively controlling the secular life of the nation and its towns. And it meant that the clergy had a high social standing, and therefore social influence, because of the power exercised by members of their congregations.

We have to remember as well the important influence of the Churches in the field of education and welfare. The work of Hook in establishing day schools attached to many Anglican churches meant that the religious influence in the education of many Leeds children was particularly strong. The contributions made by the various denominations to the improvement of social conditions and the development of welfare services was a feature of all Victorian urban communities, but one can think in Leeds particularly of the work that many clergymen did, at personal risk to their own lives, in the cholera epidemics of the 1840s. Indeed, during the nineteenth century the changing concepts of the pastoral nature of the clergyman's role in society increased the specifically religious influences that were exerted in the general field of social reform.

On the other hand there was the role, which later came to be denigrated, of the Churches in improving the morals of society. In fact it is unhistorical to see these attempts as reactionary. They sprang from a genuine desire to improve the quality of life and not, as is sometimes asserted, merely from an unhealthy obsession with preventing people from enjoying themselves. The temperance campaign was motivated substantially by the appalling suffering caused by easy access to cheap alcohol. The influence of religion on society was such that enormous changes did take place in moral attitudes, and the successes they enjoyed misled some campaigners into adopting those puritanical positions that later came to be so despised.

One can conclude, therefore, by saying that although not everybody in Victorian Leeds went to church, most of those who held an important political, commercial or social position in the town would have done so. They and the clergy of the churches they attended were able to use their position in secular society to influence most aspects of other people's lives. Christian moral values were almost universally accepted, even among those who may not have gone to church, and forthright campaigns for their practical implementation were bound to attract considerable public support.

NOTES

[1] In *Pelican Guide to Modern Theology*, II, 307.

[2] W. R. W. Stephens, *Life and Letters of Walter Farquhar Hook* (1878), I, 403.

[3] R. J. Wood, *Church Extension in Leeds* (1964), 1–6.

[4] R. J. Wood's 'Leeds church patronage in the eighteenth century', *Thoresby Soc.*, XLI (1954), 103–13, and L (1968), 193–211.

[5] W. L. Schroeder, *Mill Hill Chapel* (1924).

[6] W. L. Wade, *West Park Congregational Church* (1972), 1–3.

[7] C. Binfield, *So Down to Prayers* (1977), 73–6.

[8] R. J. Owen, 'The Baptists in the borough of Leeds during the nineteenth century', unpublished M.Phil. thesis, University of Leeds (1970), 1–6, 110–11, 258.

[9] W. Allott, 'Leeds Quaker Meeting', *Thoresby Soc.*, L (1966), 58–9.

[10] B. Greaves, 'Methodism in Yorkshire, 1740–1851', unpublished Ph.D. thesis, University of Liverpool (1968), 75–9, 85, 88, 91–2, 111, 117–21, 130–4, 235–6.

[11] C. M. Elliott, 'Social and economic history of the principal Protestant denominations in Leeds, 1760–1844', unpublished D.Phil. thesis, University of Oxford (1962), 180–203. See also D. Fraser, 'The Leeds churchwardens, 1828–1850', *Thoresby Soc.*, LIII (1971), 1–22.

[12] A member of that group within the Church of England that stressed her historical continuity with Catholic Christianity and hence upheld a 'high' conception of the authority of the Church and its ministers. Evangelicals had a 'low' conception of this authority, which they regarded as unscriptural.

[13] A. M. G. Stephenson, 'Formation of the See of Ripon and the episcopate of its first bishop, Charles Thomas Longley', unpublished B.Litt. thesis, University of

Oxford (1960), 76, 177.

[14] W. R. Ward (ed.), *Early Victorian Methodism: the Correspondence of Jabez Bunting, 1830–1858* (1976), 198–9.

[15] Stephenson, *op. cit.*, 113, 157.

[16] W. N. Yates, 'Leeds and the Oxford Movement', *Thoresby Soc.*, LV (1975), 14–16, 18–24, 65.

[17] N. Waugh, *Short History of St. Anne's Cathedral and the Leeds Missions* (1904); T. Dillon, 'The Irish in Leeds, 1851–61', *Thoresby Soc.*, LIV (1974), 1–7.

[18] Allott, *op. cit.*, 59, 64–5, 74.

[19] Schroeder, *op. cit.*, 72–7.

[20] Binfield, *op. cit.*, 73–6, 95–6.

[21] W. R. Ward, *Religion and Society in England, 1790–1850* (1972), 261–2, 268.

[22] J. Elsworth, in *Wesleyan Methodist Magazine* (1906), 201–8.

[23] All that follows is based on the returns in the Public Record Office, H.O. 129/501.

[24] Wade, *op. cit.*, 7; W. E. Treen, *Methodism in East Leeds* (1947), 25.

[25] J. G. Miall, *Congregationalism in Yorkshire* (1868), 308.

[26] *Centenary Souvenir of the Leeds Society of the New Church* (1918).

[27] E. Krausz, *Leeds Jewry* (1964), 2–10.

[28] W. N. Yates, *The Oxford Movement and the Parishes: St. Saviour's Leeds, 1839–1929*, Borthwick Paper No. 48 (1975), 2–16.

[29] Ward, *Early Victorian Methodism*, 92.

[30] Binfield, *op. cit.*, 75–6.

[31] *Early Correspondence of Jabez Bunting, 1820–9*, ed. W. R. Ward, Royal Historical Society, Camden Fourth Series, IX (1972), 7–8, 156–92, 207–8; see also Ward, *Religion and Society in England*, 144–7.

[32] Greaves, *op. cit.*, 113.

[33] Owen, *op. cit.*, 83, 213, 238, 300, 311, 340, 492–4, 499, 508, 522.

[34] Binfield, *op. cit.*, 71; see also B. Harrison, *Drink and the Victorians* (1971), 192.

[35] Owen, *op. cit.*, 53, 55; Binfield, *op. cit.*, 97.

BIBLIOGRAPHICAL NOTE

1. *Primary sources.* A substantial amount of ecclesiastical material has been deposited in recent years in the Leeds City Archives Department; it includes records of about forty Anglican parishes, those of the Brunswick, Headingley and Leeds West Methodist circuits, incorporating records of individual chapels, a separate deposit by the trustees of Oxford Place Chapel, and the records of the Yorkshire Congregational Union, which contain material for seven chapels in Leeds. Local Baptist records have been mostly deposited at the West Yorkshire Record Office in Wakefield, and Roman Catholic records are the responsibility of the diocesan archivist (details in *Catholic Directory*). The major ecclesiastical collections still in the custody of their owners are those of Leeds Parish Church, Mill Hill Unitarian Chapel, and the Leeds Society of Friends. The major collections of contemporary pamphlet literature will be found in Leeds Central Reference Library and there is substantial coverage, in particular, of the Brunswick organ case and the ritualist crises at St Saviour's.

2. *Secondary studies.* The most significant and useful local studies have been cited in the footnotes. The fundamental introduction to the national background is W. O. Chadwick, *The Victorian Church* (2 vols., 1966–70). K. S. Inglis, *The Church and the Working Classes in Victorian England* (1963), needs to be treated with caution and has been perceptively criticised in D. Bowen, *The Idea of the Victorian Church*

(1968). E. R. Wickham, *Church and People in an Industrial City* (1952), is a useful comparative study of Sheffield from a quasi-sociological viewpoint. Recently the study of Victorian Church history has benefited considerably from statistical analysis in A. D. Gilbert, *Religion and Society in Industrial England* (1976), and R. Currie, A. D. Gilbert and L. Horsley, *Churches and Churchgoers* (1977). The best introduction to both national and local religious censuses is by H. Macleod in *Sociological Year Book of Religion in Britain*, VI, ed. M. Hill (1973), which discusses the previous work in this area by K. S. Inglis, D. M. Thompson and others. J. Kent, *Hold the Fort* (1978), is a splendid study of Victorian revivalism.

DEREK FRASER

Politics and society
in the nineteenth century

XI

Political party feeling prevails to a mischievous extent at Leeds – the parties are nearly balanced and it is scarcely possible to take any step in Leeds Township without exciting strong party feeling.[1]

I   Politics was an important part of the life of Leeds citizens in the nineteenth century. Indeed, until the late Victorian era, when sport began to take priority as the great national pastime, more local interest was devoted to politics than to any other activity. It was politics that injected great issues into workaday lives, and Leeds was a town where rapid population growth multiplied problems whose solution acquired much political significance. Moreover the term encompassed a far wider range of institutions and issues than it does today. For urban Victorians, unlike ourselves, politics began at the front gate, not at Westminster. What has so often today become routine administration could be a highly charged issue. Politics in Leeds thus ran through many superficially 'non-political' channels. There were four main reasons for this diversity.

First, the primary areas of politics – Parliament and municipal elections – were initially closed to its citizens. Until the Great Reform Act of 1832 Leeds was not separately represented in Parliament. It had no MPs of its own and therefore no elections took place in the town. Though there was a corporation it was self-elective, through co-option, which meant that favoured merchants and gentlemen could be invited to become members without any reference to the citizens at large. It also meant that the corporation was quite immune from any popular influence. We may regard those who dominated the town as a traditional elite of 'insiders'. When new families or 'outsiders' wished to challenge the authority of this elite they were forced to look not to parliamentary and municipal elections, which were non-existent, but to other institutions through which they could assert rivalry in the competition for authority. These alternative institutions accessible to the 'outsiders', such as the parish vestry or the improvement commission, became a political counterweight to a closed corporation.

The second reason concerns the minor institutions themselves. Politics is the pursuit and exercise of power, and these institutions exerted quite considerable power over the town's affairs, for instance the running of the Church, the relief of the poor and the question of the urban environment. The middle class was bitterly divided by both religion and politics, and to Whig Dissenting 'outsiders' the power of these institutions and the status of their offices seemed attractive when alternative avenues to power were closed. Where a new manufacturer could not aspire to become alderman, mayor or magistrate it was understandable that he might wish to act as churchwarden or improvement commissioner, in order to improve his status and exercise some control over the life of the town. Because the middle-class economic elite was so divided, Leeds politics never fully polarised along class lines, and between about 1825 and 1875 the working class was involved largely in supporting the contending middle-class protagonists – as Whig radicals or Tory radicals. Yet whenever the working-class movement tried to develop an independent political existence and assert its distinctive position, it too began its political campaign in the minor institutions of parish and township.

The power exercised by these minor institutions raised important issues of policy, and of course disputes over policies are also an integral part of political activity. They constitute our third reason. Many superficially non-political topics in fact generated great political excitement and so widened the field of political debate. Religion was a potent source of conflict, for the established Church of England enjoyed a position of legal predominance in a town where, numerically, Anglicanism was overwhelmed by Methodism and Dissent (see Chapter X). The religious grievances of militant Nonconformists were throughout the nineteenth century a subject of continual political debate, and so we shall find the politics of religion central to the political system of Leeds. Social questions too, such as the relief of poverty or the provision of water, took on a political importance in a town where power was fiercely contested and extensions of public intervention into the free market were viewed with deep suspicion. Social utilities that are now taken as common sense might in the nineteenth century be regarded as novel infringements of individual liberty or as an extension of jobbery and patronage.

That we may designate certain areas as essentially non-political social administration suggests the existence of a system of categorisation which Victorians would not have recognised. Theirs was, in a sense, a one-class political system in which all issues could be related together on a common political scale, and this is the fourth reason for the diversification of Leeds politics. Political activists had no difficulty in relating disparate factors to an overall political context, since, for them, there was a political dimension to all facets of the urban experience. The microcosm of city life was but part of the macrocosm of the national political culture. This was neatly illustrated by one who saw the links between his ward activity and the wider political nation and who warned that 'the Whigs of North West ward were part and parcel of a mighty power which was at work in the British Dominions that was attempting the separation of Church and State and the ultimate destruction of the Protestant Religion'.[2]

There is a danger that any attempt to describe such a diversified political system will be overwhelmed by the sheer plethora of political activities. How are we to make sense of a political system which encompassed both suburb and nation? The difficulty is resolved if we view the town's political system in terms of an archaeological image. We may regard the different areas of municipal politics as archaeological strata, each with an identity of its own but closely connected to the others. There are four levels in this structure. The first, and lowest, stratum of political life was parochial and township administration, comprising the vestry institutions, the Poor Law authorities and the highways and improvement commissions. The next level up was municipal government, closed to popular participation until 1835 but thereafter constantly widening its functions and responsibilities. The third was that of parliamentary elections and their associated political organisations. This was the most open arena of politics, where periodic public declarations of faith would be made and where symbolic identification of interests was important. Finally the highest level of political activity, though one which often originated in the lowest, was that of political agitation. This involved the attempt to persuade Parliament itself to adopt some cherished political, social or economic objective. In this layered system political issues acted as boreholes penetrating each level in turn, thus allowing the political gas of one stratum to explode with often damaging effects in another.

The political activities of Dissenters and the issue of Anglican predominance provide a good example of its working. Dissenters, anxious to reduce *de facto* the power of an established Church which they could hardly defeat *de jure*, began their campaigns in the vestry. As soon as it became possible legally they entered municipal government both to secure their social and political position and to use municipal authority in support of their views. They took part in parliamentary elections, forcing candidates to take note of their opinions and even on a celebrated occasion in 1847 splitting their own party. Finally they campaigned incessantly for Parliament to relieve Dissenters of their civil and religious disabilities and eventually to disestablish the Church. Dissenters were not unique in playing a system which is unfamiliar to twentieth-century eyes. They operated in a political world which was distinctively urban and Victorian. We can recreate that political world with the help of this fourfold model, which will be utilised throughout the chronological survey that follows.

II   At the end of the Napoleonic wars that Tory oligarchy of gentlemen merchants described in Chapter II was still firmly in control. Within a generation it had been supplanted by a rival Liberal elite in all the political institutions of the town. The economic growth of Leeds had attracted migrants with entrepreneurial talents and had thrown up new manufacturing, commercial and professional families to challenge the authority of the traditional elite. Most of these 'outsiders' were Dissenters in religion and Whig Liberals in politics, and they looked for an outlet for their views not to the venerated *Leeds Intelligencer* but to the *Leeds Mercury*. It had been a consortium of these newly risen families which in 1802 had established Edward Baines as editor of the *Mercury*. Baines transformed the paper into the leading provincial Liberal organ of opinion of its day.

It was through Baines and the *Mercury* that the rival elite challenged the authority of the Anglican oligarchy entrenched in the corporation, and the battle was joined in the parish vestry. Each of the townships of the borough elected churchwardens to administer the affairs of the Church, and in Leeds township there were eight such offices. The most important function of the churchwardens was to levy a Church rate upon the property of the town for the running costs of church administration. Dissenters and Anglicans alike paid rates, and they were seen as a galling injustice by religious groups who derived no spiritual benefit from the Church of England and who maintained their own chapels by voluntary contributions. In 1819 Baines began a prolonged battle for economies in parish expenditure, to reduce the level of Church rates, and the Easter vestry meeting to approve the annual accounts became a noisy confrontation between the establishment and its challengers. Liberal control of the vestry crowd ensured reductions in expenditure and began to make possible the election of churchwardens pledged to economy. In 1827 Liberals elected half the wardens and in 1828 secured six of the posts, so gaining a majority. Led by John Armitage Buttrey, a Liberal Anglican wool stapler, a regime of strict economy was embarked upon which reduced parish expenditure from £1,500 to £500 per annum within five years.

This was an important accession of power for the Liberal 'outsiders' which offered the promise of *de facto* abolition of Church rates in the town. Moreover the complex system of Poor Law administration meant that control of the churchwardens also secured control over the so-called workhouse board. Strictly speaking, the administration of the Poor Law was in the hands of overseers appointed by the magistrates, but during the previous century a system had evolved to share out the duties among a wider section of citizens. The board comprised a roughly equal number of appointed overseers and trustees elected by the vestry, together with the churchwardens. Hence the normally Tory overseers appointed by a Tory bench of magistrates were matched by normally Liberal trustees elected by the vestry, and so the churchwardens held the balance of power. Up to 1828 that balance lay with the traditional oligarchy but Buttrey's Liberal regime deprived the Tories of control of the Poor Law and transferred a second institution to the Liberal camp.

A third followed with the improvement commission. The corporation had few administrative functions, and such environmental powers as existed devolved upon the improvement commission established by local Act in the eighteenth century. By far the most important Improvement Act was that of 1824 which granted powers to demolish the famous moot hall in Briggate. The passage of this Act coincided with the politicising of the vestry, so that selections for the commission took on a new political importance. Whereas earlier the commission had been an arm of the corporation, it now became a Liberal-dominated body. The Royal Commission on Municipal Corporations noticed how in Leeds the improvement commission had acquired an acute political significance.

> In cases where the election is popular as in the choice of the Commissioners under the Local Acts the persons selected are all of one political party, professing the opposite opinions to those entertained by the majority of the corporation: which is accounted for by the necessity of balancing the influence of the corporation ... This choice of Commissioners exclusively from one party is admitted to be undesirable but is justified as being resorted to in self defence.[3]

The inaccessibility of the corporation drove Liberal activists into the vestry, and the absence of parliamentary elections drove them into the country. Yorkshire politics were dominated by the great county families who regarded any interference by townsmen as an invasion. Nevertheless Earl Fitzwilliam had been happy enough to call on the support of Baines and the *Mercury* party of the West Riding in the gladiatorial contest of 1807 between the great houses of Wentworth Woodhouse and Harewood. In 1826 the county families were willing to allow a townsman, John Marshall, the flax spinner, to take one of the four seats, though this honour rested more upon his long purse than anything else: even this uncontested return cost him £27,000. In 1830, however, Leeds asserted its independence by imposing the Whig politician Henry Brougham upon an unwilling county, a great triumph for Baines and the anti-slavery groups of the West Riding towns.

Brougham was appointed Lord Chancellor in the 1830 Whig government, which was committed to parliamentary reform, and the question of reform was at the forefront of Leeds politics for the next two years. The temporary organisation hastily put together to secure the election of Brougham established itself in December 1830 as the Leeds Association, led by Baines and two wealthy Dissenting woollen merchants, John Clapham and George Rawson. The Association organised support for the Reform Bill, acting behind the scenes to sponsor petitions, initiate meetings and encourage propaganda. The most public demonstrations were the work of the Leeds Political Union, led by Joshua Bower, a wealthy but uncouth glass manufacturer from Hunslet. Bower, with his racy Saxon language, was popular with the crowds but he could not prevent the launching of a separate Leeds Radical Political Union which rejected the leadership of Baines and the middle class. While Baines and Bower supported the Whig Reform Bill, the leading radicals, James Mann, a bookseller, and John Foster, editor of the radical *Leeds Patriot*, argued for the ballot, universal suffrage and annual Parliaments.

Moreover the Radical Union looked to factory rather than parliamentary reform to ameliorate working-class conditions. It was to the *Leeds Mercury* that Richard Oastler had addressed his famous letters on 'Yorkshire Slavery' which had launched the Short Time or Ten Hours Movement. When Oastler's invective against heartless manufacturers exploiting child labour became too controversial for the *Mercury's* middle-class readership Oastler switched to the *Intelligencer*, and the support of the *Patriot* confirmed the existence of a Tory–Radical alliance. Thus there were two important parliamentary Bills in 1831–32 which affected Leeds politics: the Whig Reform Bill, by which the town would be enfranchised, and the Ten Hours Bill, which would reduce the hours of labour for children and which was sponsored by a Leeds citizen, Michael Thomas Sadler. These two issues, the factory question and parliamentary reform, became inextricably linked in the first election of 1832.

The candidates in what was to be the town's most exciting and long-drawn-out contest in the nineteenth century personified the issues of the campaign. John Marshall junior, son of the founder of the largest flax-spinning firm in Europe, was a natural Liberal first choice. He was a Unitarian from Mill Hill chapel, a reformer, a townsman and a great employer of labour who could represent the town's economic interest in Parliament. The second Liberal candidate knew nothing at all about Leeds or its trades. He was Thomas Babington Macaulay, a writer and career politician, later noted as probably the most famous historian England has produced. Just as Baines had imposed Brougham upon the county so he imposed Macaulay upon the town, and for similar reasons – that he was a distinguished reform politician who would grace Leeds as its MP. Though there were two seats to fill the Tories put up only one candidate, Michael Sadler, again an obvious choice. Sadler had been an MP since 1829 and the seat he had won in 1831 was to be disfranchised under the Reform Act. Leeds was a natural haven for him. He was a linen merchant, a member of the corporation and a well known Evangelical paternalist. Brought up as a devout Methodist, he identified himself publicly with the extreme Tory–Anglican interest.

Liberal strategy in the eighteen-month campaign from the summer of 1831 was to fight the election squarely on the parliamentary reform question. The Marshall family had a proven record on reform and some of the best speeches in the Commons in support of the Bill had been made by Macaulay. Sadler, on the other hand, had opposed the Reform Bill and if his view had prevailed in Parliament Leeds would have had no votes to cast at all. Yet he was less of a politician than a social philantropist, and on the social question of factory reform he could attract wide support. Indeed, the whole panoply of party labels was meaningless in the context of real social distress, as one imaginary protagonist explained:

> Why talk about Toaries and Redigals and such like while Oastler and Sadler and them'll stand up for us, I care nowt about what colour they wear; its not blue nor yellow at makes 'em either better or warse.[4]

Looked at as a 'factory election', the Leeds contest personified three strands in the factory question itself – economic self-interest (Marshall), ideological commitment to *laissez-faire* (Macaulay) and paternalistic philanthropy (Sadler).

Though Sadler gained radical support by adopting factory reform he forfeited perhaps more important allies. Many of the factory owners such as J. R. Atkinson, a flax spinner, and the great cloth manufacturers the Gotts were themselves Tories, and Marshall predicted, 'the Factory Bill does not promise popularity to Sadler, [whose] coquetry with the Radicals will fling him out of his Tory saddle'. Similarly the adoption of one moral issue, child labour, left Sadler vulnerable on another, slavery, and the leading Methodist theologian of the day concluded that 'on the great question of slave emancipation ... we cannot for a moment hesitate to give the influence we may have with the people connected with us'. Methodists were angered by Sadler's 'ambition which has made him court the high church and despise us' and he noted that though Sadler had never spoken on slavery, to Macaulay's 'venerable father, that great, that sacred cause of negro liberation owes more perhaps than to any other man in the empire'.[5]

The election campaign was hard fought, producing much propaganda, and there were many lively political meetings of great excitement. It was also a bitter personal battle involving not only the candidates but also their leading local allies. Stories of beer, bribery and bludgeons in the later stages do not change the general picture of an election where serious arguments were fought out. It did, however, have its lighter side, with doggerel verse and dramatic satire, much of which derived from the question of a personal canvass. Sadler believed it reasonable to solicit votes personally and was much pilloried for this fawning approach to the electorate: his opponents preferred public meetings where the electorate could be persuaded by argument. Macaulay stoutly defended this approach.

> The practice of begging for votes is, as it seems to me absurd, pernicious and altogether at variance with the true principle of representative government ... seats in the House of Commons ought not to be given, like rooms in an almshouse, to urgency of solicitation ... I hope to see the day when an Englishman will think it as great an affront to be courted and fawned upon in his capacity of elector as in his capacity of juryman ... equally shocked at the thought of voting for a candidate for whose public character he felt no esteem, merely because that candidate had called on him, and begged very hard, and had shaken his hand warmly.[6]

The attack upon Sadler's personal canvass was not always so high-minded, and one anonymous squib, noting that Sadler had grown a beard to please his Jewish constituents, enquired what other rites of the Jewish religion he was prepared to undergo in order to capture the Jewish vote. This brought a reply of righteous indignation against an allusion 'intended to turn the attention of his readers to a certain part of the human body to which it has hitherto been thought in a civilized society indecent to allude'. The wives and daughters of Leeds were equally being outraged by a song entitled 'I'll kiss in public, if you please, an operative's backside'. Liberal politicians must not be allowed to 'proceed in their disgusting filthy and obscene career or they will soon destroy the finest feelings of our nature and disarm the female character of its best protection – modesty'.[7]

The personal canvass was not enough to save Sadler from defeat but it was Oastler who best explained the 1832 result when he remarked, ' "The People" don't live in £10 houses.' The Reform Act granted the suffrage to £10 householders, a broadly middle-class franchise, and Sadler's popular support came mainly from non-voters. Marshall and Macaulay were victorious, and Leeds returned two sound Liberals as its first MPs. Yet Sadler's 44 per cent of the vote was a respectable achievement and within a year the Tories had a chance to redeem their position, for in December 1833 the impecunious Macaulay resigned in favour of a lucrative post in India. Baines, who had been talked of in 1832, was an obvious choice, though rather ungratefully Macaulay confided to his sister,

> I do not think they have chosen well. He is a highly respectable man, – liberal, moderate, honest, intelligent; and these qualities have made him very powerful and very useful in his own town. But he has not quite so much polish or literature as the persons among whom he will now be thrown . . . His newspaper, which is now decidedly the best and most widely circulated provincial paper in England, will, I fear, lose its influence, when it is considered not as containing the sentiments of a disinterested spectator of public affairs but as a plea of an interested party for his own proceedings.[8]

The newspaper aspect was easily dealt with by assigning full editorial control to his son, Edward Baines junior, who had been writing leaders for the *Mercury* for some time. More serious, Baines senior faced the prospect of a Whig–Radical schism at the 1834 by-election. The leaders of the Political Union, Bower and Joseph Lees, the secretary, had been offended by the arrogance of the exclusive Leeds Association, which had apparently thrown them over after they had served their purpose in 1832. Bower decided to go to the polls as an independent radical candidate, and much of Sadler's popular working-class support now went to him. The Tories skilfully slid Sadler off to Huddersfield and brought out a respectable right-wing candidate unencumbered by social radicalism – Sir John Beckett of the local banking family. Bower got only twenty-four votes, which could have been crucial, since Baines was returned with a majority of only thirty-four.

With the electorate so closely divided, any new party advantage was certain to be decisive and the Tories discovered one in the registration of voters. By cleverly objecting to Liberal compounders (tenants whose rates were paid by their landlord) at the 1834 revision of voters the Tories made a gain of some 250 votes. The Liberals were not unduly worried, for they expected to reverse the position at the next revision, but the dismissal of Melbourne provoked an unexpected general election in January 1835. It was clear that Beckett was safe, favoured by the registration advantage, and it was a hapless William Brougham who was hastily brought up from London to contest the second seat along with Baines. Beckett now topped the poll by over a hundred votes, with Baines in second place. It was a remarkable Tory victory, representing a swing of about 8 per cent in the two years since Sadler's defeat, and it illustrates the importance of organisation in Leeds politics. Registration was all-important, for the 1835 contest was evidence that elections could be won not in the polling booth but in the revision courts.

The capture of one parliamentary seat at the beginning of the year was some compensation for a major Tory reverse at the end of it. Vigorously though it fought to avoid reform the corporation was forcibly remodelled by the Municipal Reform Act of 1835. At the first municipal election there was a resounding defeat for the traditional governors of the town, who won only six of the forty-eight contested seats. As one Liberal enthusiast correctly forecast, the first election established a Liberal ascendancy on the town council that was to last for sixty years. Exultantly the new political masters, identical to the old elite socially but differing in politics and religion, shared in the spoils of office. The mayoral chain, the aldermanic robe and the magisterial seat were now in the Liberal gift, and these honours went as political rewards to Liberal partisans. Baines and Son got the printing contract, a Liberal solicitor, Edward Eddison, soon became town clerk, and another active in registration, James Richardson, became clerk of the peace. It was, as Baines explained, 'a transference of local power beyond all calculation', and a local Whig peer, speaking at a dinner to celebrate the reform of local government, congratulated Liberals who were 'sharing in the first fruits of that system in all possible prosperity and credit'. Yet there was some truth in the plaintive cry of those dispossessed — 'it was the robbery of one party in order to pamper another party with the spoils'.[9]

Nothing upset the Tory elite more than being removed from the bench of magistrates, and former mayors, aldermen and justices were incensed at their exclusion from the list of council nominees. The much maligned 'Russell Justices' of 1836 comprised nineteen Liberals but only three Tories. But there was more than offended pride in the

Tory opposition to an exclusively Liberal bench of magistrates. A Liberal bench would once more remove Poor Law authority from Tory control and complete a Liberal monopoly of local power. Following the 1832 election defeat the Tories had made a determined effort to regain control of the vestry. In 1833, 1834 and 1835 there was a strong Tory bid to recapture the office of churchwarden, in the last year by a full-scale town poll. When this failed the Tories resorted to law, arguing that the workhouse board had no legality and that the Poor Law was the sole responsibility of the overseers. Counsel's opinion supported this assertion, as Robert Baker explained.

> The Board room has long been a sort of arena for party politics on a small scale— ... of late politics have run high with us, the Trustees and Churchwardens chosen by the people in Vestry have been a little opposed to the overseers chosen by the magistrates and to such a pitch has this feeling been carried that public poor law business has been very much neglected and very bad feeling has existed. The affair has ended in the overseers taking Sir John Campbell's and Sir F. Pollock's opinion as to the legality of the votes of the Churchwardens and Trustees both of whom have decided in favour of the overseers. The confusion consequent on the latter decision which came a few days ago may be imagined.[10]

The Tories were jubilant and levied the next poor rate themselves, symbolically and with 'domineering insolence' taking possession of the board minute book.

It was, of course, a short-lived victory. Once a Liberal bench had been confirmed in office, it in turn appointed Liberal overseers. Hence a Liberal Poor Law was added to a Liberal vestry, Liberal churchwardens, Liberal improvement commissioners, a Liberal council and a Liberal bench of JPs. The only Tory crumb of comfort was the borough's Conservative MP but his victory was ascribed to electioneering trickery. Within a decade the political system had registered the replacement of one elite by another as the outsiders supplanted the insiders.

III   This 'Liberal empire' which seemed so all-embracing on Victoria's accession was subject to much strain during the next decade. The challenge came on three fronts. First, at all levels of Leeds politics a revived Toryism manifested itself and the Liberal hold on total local power was forcefully challenged. Second, the problems of maintaining the Whig–Radical alliance, forged at the time of the Reform Bill, became increasingly obvious. Liberals came under the threat of independent radical and working-class activity which culminated in Chartism. Third, internal disagreements within Liberalism appeared during the 1840s and seriously divided the middle-class Liberal elite.

High Anglican Toryism received a great boost by the appointment of W. F. Hook as Vicar of Leeds in 1837. In time he was to champion the cause of moderation but in his early years he inspired Conservatives with his uncompromising Anglicanism and flayed Liberal Dissenters with his High Church propaganda. His appointment led to a determined attempt to regain the office of churchwarden, and the 1837 election was described by the *Leeds Times* as 'one of the most turbulent vestry meetings ever held in this town'. Indeed, a near riot occurred and tempers were scarcely less frayed in August 1837 when Hook demanded a Church rate which a crowded vestry meeting rejected. The rebuilding of Leeds Parish Church, set in train by Hook in 1838, was a symbolic rebirth of militant Toryism in the town and under his aegis Anglican fortunes revived (see Chapter X).

Nevertheless Liberals retained the churchwardens' posts, Church rates were not levied, and Hook's rebuilding had to be financed by voluntary subscriptions. The Tories were more successful in the improvement commission, where a four-year Conservative regime began in 1837. The issue of a new waterworks politicised the improvement question. After several abortive attempts to get a new scheme going the Liberals had suggested the idea of a united committee composed of magistrates, councillors and improvement commissioners. It will be noticed that Liberals controlled all three offices, and to displaced Tories this seemed a bid for yet another sphere of influence. As Robert Perring, editor of the *Intelligencer*, explained, 'the Town Council and the Town Commissioners clutch the whole thing. They are in search of power—power, patronage—patronage.'[11] The Tory alternative was a joint-stock company financed by the income from water consumers. Thus the political system distorted the normal ideological position. Free-market Liberal individualists favoured public control while paternalistic Tories looked to private enterprise.

The Tories contested the 1837 improvement commission election on the water question, firmly committed against the collectivist scheme. They were now better equipped to deal with noisy and crowded public meetings by virtue of the Leeds Operative Conservative Society, launched by William Paul, a flax spinner at J. R. Atkinson's factory. This society replaced Sadler's Tory–Radical alliance based on factory reform with an uncomplicated deferential Church-and-Crown Toryism. Independent working-class radicals found this somewhat anomalous:

why a poor devil depending on his day's work and obliged to give a portion of that to the support of the Church and other Institutions should rank himself as a Conservative Operative is rather astonishing . . . the society consists of overseers who do the dirty work of their masters and who act as crimp sergeants to kidnap those whom machinery make dependent upon the owner for subsistence. If the market for labour was open we should have no such nondescript animals as poor men, professing to support a system which produced their 'poverty' and causes their 'destitution'.[12]

Whether through duress of Tory employers or genuine commitment, these Operative Conservatives acted as the storm troops of the Tory cause, and with good effect. In 1837, 1838 and 1839 the Tories had a majority of the improvement commissioners, breaking a Liberal tenure that stretched back to 1824. It was the Liberal hold on power elsewhere which made the commission an institution worthy of political interest. As Perring admitted in 1840, 'some persons may think the improvement commission is not worth contending for', but he warned that the Liberal attempt to win back control was 'part of a plan to get possession of all local offices . . . the object of which is the acquirement of local power'. Again in 1841 he asserted, 'the prize contended for is of no value in itself . . . the question is shall the Whigs and Whig-Radicals be permitted to monopolize everything'.[13] Through a technicality the Tory commission elected in 1839 actually remained in office throughout 1840, until defeat on a poll in January 1841.

By then the Tories were within sight of control of the town council. As table 27 shows, municipal elections had gone strongly against the Liberals in the late 1830s. After the 1839 election Conservatives had more councillors than the Liberals, whose hold on power was dependent upon the aldermanic vote. After the 1840 election the council was exactly divided and in practice better attendance by Tory councillors effectively weakened Liberal control. This Tory success was the result of popular resentment at increased municipal expenditure, superior party organisation and the local effects of a declining Whig government. It brought into the council Tory partisans of the old corporation such as Richard Bramley, a wool merchant, and Ralph Markland, a corn merchant, as well as newer activists including a leading solicitor, John Atkinson, ironfounders in John Cawood and his son Martin, a Methodist carpet manufacturer, John Howard, and the pugnacious doctor Adam Hunter. Another Tory doctor, William Hey III, linked the council to the oldest and most distinguished medical family in Leeds. It was from these Conservatives that the anticipated first Tory mayor since reform

Table 27 Political composition of Leeds council, 1835–81

Year	Councillors		Aldermen		Whole council	
	Liberal	*Tory*	*Liberal*	*Tory*	*Liberal*	*Tory*
1835–36	39	9	12	4	51	13
1836–37	37	11	12	4	49	15
1837–38	33	15	12	4	45	19
1838–39	27	21	16	0	43	21
1839–40	20	28	16	0	36	28
1840–41	16	32	16	0	32	32
1841–42	23	25	16	0	39	25
1842–43	26	22	16	0	42	22
1843–44	31	17	16	0	47	17
1844–45	34	14	16	0	50	14
1845–46	38	10	16	0	54	10
1846–47	36	12	15	1	51	13
1847–48	33	15	16	0	49	15
1848–49	35	13	16	0	51	13
1849–50	39	9	16	0	55	9
1850–51	41	7	16	0	57	7
1851–52	40	8	16	0	56	8
1852–53	40	8	16	0	56	8
1853–54	39	9	16	0	55	9
1854–55	35	13	16	0	51	13
1855–56	32	16	16	0	48	16
1856–57	34	14	16	0	50	14
1857–58	39	9	16	0	55	9
1858–59	41	7	16	0	57	7
1859–60	41	7	16	0	57	7
1860–61	41	7	16	0	57	7
1861–62	42	6	16	0	58	6
1862–63	40	8	16	0	56	8
1863–64	36	12	16	0	52	12
1864–65	32	16	16	0	48	16
1865–66	31	17	16	0	47	17
1866–67	34	14	16	0	50	14
1867–68	36	12	16	0	52	12
1868–69	37	11	16	0	53	11
1869–70	37	11	16	0	53	11
1870–71	37	11	16	0	53	11
1871–72	31	17	16	0	47	17
1872–73	25	23	16	0	41	23
1873–74	18	28	16	0	34	28
1874–75	25	23	16	0	41	23
1875–76	33	15	16	0	49	15
1876–77	35	13	16	0	51	13
1877–78	37	11	16	0	53	11
1878–79	36	12	16	0	52	12
1879–80	37	11	16	0	53	11
1880–81	38	10	16	0	54	10

would be chosen. The first five mayors of the reformed council had demonstrated the social similarities but religious and political differences between the old corporation and the new. The first reform mayor was the Baptist wool stapler George Goodman, who was succeeded by the Independent doctor James Williamson and then by the respected Unitarian solicitor T. W. Tottie. Next came reputedly the first Roman Catholic mayor in England since the Reformation, the silk spinner James Holdforth, who was followed by the Wesleyan William Smith, a cloth merchant. The Tories had high hopes of choosing their own mayor, for 1841 was a year of aldermanic elections and in the parliamentary contest of that year the local banker William Beckett had been returned for the Conservatives at the head of the poll. Yet in a desperately close municipal election, in which four seats were won by a total majority of only twelve votes, the Liberals just managed to hang on to power. Municipal Conservatism, as though exhausted by this effort, fell back rapidly and not for another thirty years was there to be the prospect of a Tory town council.

There was some compensation for municipal failure in the 1840s, however, within the Poor Law. The Tory strategy of restricting sole control of the Poor Law to the overseers, noticed earlier, had indeed proved a misguided ploy. The Liberal JPs appointed Liberal overseers, and so the Operative Conservative influence in vestries was of no value here. In 1842 Peel's government removed one area of Tory grievance by appointing nine Tory magistrates, and the bench thereafter decided that the overseers should be appointed from all parties. This truce was short-lived because in 1844 the New Poor Law was belatedly applied to Leeds, an earlier attempt in 1837 having ended in electoral fiasco. Pious hopes about a non-political contest for the board of guardians soon evaporated, and, as expected, the first guardians election in Leeds township in December 1844 was fought on party lists. The Tories won fifteen of the eighteen seats and for the rest of the decade were comfortably in control of the board. Now came an opportunity for the vanquished of the mid-1830s to become the political masters of the mid-1840s. Two relieving officers, two registrars of births, marriages and deaths, and the clerk were all dismissed and replaced by Tory partisans. John Beckwith, a reporter on the *Intelligencer* and scourge of the Liberals at vestry meetings, was appointed clerk to the guardians and Edward Auty, a Tory party agent, was rewarded with the post of registrar. To complete a symbolic transfer of power the *Intelligencer* office was awarded the printing contract for the board. With unconvincing innocence, displaced Liberals complained that 'no other than political motives' influenced appointments which were all 'referred solely to political considerations'.[14] The Leeds Poor Law stood out as a Conservative island in a sea of Liberalism.

The three non-Tory guardians in 1844–45 were not Liberals but Chartists, whose activities deprived early Victorian Leeds Liberalism of some of its radical flank and whose existence was the second threat to Liberal power. Bower's refusal to stand down in the 1834 election had been a warning that radicals would not always toe the Liberal line, and in 1836–37 independent radical activity, especially in the southern out-townships, forced the Whig-Liberal elite to concede one parliamentary seat to the radicals. Many wealthy Liberal supporters were unhappy about supporting the eccentric radical aristocrat Sir William Molesworth but they did so in order to preserve the Whig–Radical alliance, which held firm and returned Baines and his radical partner in the 1837 election. During the next two or three years radicals, inspired by the newly established *Leeds Times*, could hardly be contained within the Liberal fold. Many of them supported the People's Charter when it was launched in the summer of 1838, and Leeds was an important centre of Chartist propaganda, as O'Connor's *Northern Star* was published in the town. With a strong radical tradition, and as a centre of ideology and propaganda, the town was an important Chartist stronghold. Yet it lacked what in many towns was the backbone of Chartism – a class of depressed handworkers. Leeds Chartism was decidedly non-proletarian, appealing to artisans and craftsmen, shopkeepers, teachers and writers and a fair number of lower middle-class sympathisers. Its social composition encouraged hopes that a link could be forged between middle and working-class radicalism, and in 1840 the 'new move' was launched. Samuel Smiles, doctor and editor of the *Leeds Times*, the cloth merchant Hamer Stansfeld and the wealthy flax spinner James Garth Marshall were the leading lights in the Leeds Parliamentary Reform Association. Their splendid festival in Marshall's new mill in January 1841 drew an audience of 7,000 and attracted radicals from all over the country. O'Connor, however, dubbed it 'the Fox and Goose Club', and from the other side it was condemned by Baines and the *Mercury* Liberals.

It soon withered away and Leeds Chartists pursued an independent line, seeking power, just as the proscribed Liberals and the displaced Tories had done, in the minor parochial and township institutions. It was to Chartists that Liberals finally relinquished control of the churchwardens when the printer Joshua Hobson proposed a Chartist list to the vestry in 1842. For the next five years the High Church Vicar of Leeds was served by a board of Chartist wardens and so long as no Church rates were levied Liberals were happy to leave this humble post to the humble. In 1842 also Hobson and his followers captured the improvement commission, having been frustrated by a legal quibble in 1840 and having shared control with Liberals in 1841. It was Chartists, led by the grocer William Brook, who first politicised the board of highway surveyors in 1843 when they captured control of that most minor of minor institutions. For ten years Brook and the Chartists were in total and unchallenged control of the body which gave Robert Meek Carter, a prominent radical of the 1860s, his first experience of local government. As already noted, Chartists sat on the first Leeds board of guardians in 1844–45.

Of all these accessions of power by far the most important was the improvement commission, for Hobson assumed control just when a major new improvement Bill was under consideration. He decided to make it the occasion for an experiment in real local democracy, and the Chartist control of the vestry in 1842 enabled the Bill to be drastically remodelled. Under it powers were granted to commissioners elected direct by the vestry, with no role for magistrates or councillors; there was to be a residential but no financial qualification for commissioners; separate authority from ratepayers would be required for every scheme costing more than £500; all meetings were to be held at seven o'clock instead of the normal noon; houses under £10 were to be assessed at one-third the rate of houses above £50. Here was an attempt to democratise local government. Popular control would be maintained by direct election; working men would not be debarred by a financial qualification; financial control would be maintained by the £500 limit; working-class participation would be facilitated by evening meetings; progressive taxation would lay the burdens on the wealthy. Not surprisingly the bench, the council and the influential interests previously supporting the Bill recoiled from this radical transformation. In the event Parliament merged the improvement commission with the council in 1842, which, as the next chapter shows, extended municipal functions considerably. It also deprived Chartists of an area of influence.

Chartists were in fact able to enter the town council during the 1840s but could never aspire to gain a majority there. It had been a radical, John Jackson, who had advised working men in 1838 to choose their own municipal candidates and 'make the Municipal Council of Leeds in miniature what we want the Commons House of Parliament to be'.[15] From 1842 this strategy began to pay off and Chartist councillors were elected, though the designation 'Chartist' was a fluctuating one. All these men had to be rated at £30 or above (when the parliamentary franchise was £10) and some of them were able to swear that they owned £1,000 worth of real property in the borough. One, Thomas White, was a gentleman of independent means, another, James Dufton, owned much slum property in Kirkgate. They reinforced the non-proletarian image of Leeds Chartism. Since they took their place alongside many radicals in the council and often voted with them, the idea of a separate and united Chartist group on the town council is somewhat misleading.

Chartist councillors were, however, a thorn in the Liberal side and were always on the look-out for police scandals and evidence of secret committee deals. Contrary to the received picture, Chartists did not always vote for economy, nor did they always vote together. Jackson voted against a major drainage scheme in 1844 but in favour of enlarging the courthouse and altering the market in 1845–46. Another Chartist, George Robson, voted with Jackson on the former but not on the latter, and William Brook voted against Jackson on both. In the first six votes on the building of the Town Hall Chartists were split every time. They were by no means arch-economists. In 1845 Joshua Hobson urged a major redevelopment of Boar Lane in order to lay out 'a new street of shops in first rate style to serve as a model street for the town', while in 1846 Brook, a great advocate of sewerage, reminded the council that the working class 'dread the doctor's bill more than the rate'.[16] What gave consistency to municipal Chartism was belief not in economy but in democratic control. Brook was in favour of municipal expenditure in 1846 or 1850, relatively prosperous years, but advocated economy and delay in 1848–49 when his constituents would have been embarrassed by rate increases during a depression.

Chartism was a movement full of internal division and it should not therefore surprise us to find Leeds municipal Chartists divided among themselves. Their voting in the council was characterised by that same dissension which plagued Liberal councillors the 1840s. Indeed, it was on the town council that this third threat to Liberalism, internal disunity, first began to show itself. Paradoxically it derived partly from the strength of municipal Liberalism. Nothing secured party unity more than a rampant opposition, and once the Tory challenge had withered away in the 1840s Liberal party discipline perforce relaxed and fragmentation ensued. On the surface all was well. As table 27 shows, Liberals had an overwhelming majority of aldermen and councillors. The succession of Liberal Dissenting mayors continued, and no fewer than four mayors within five years came from Mill Hill Unitarian chapel, earning it the title 'the mayors' nest'. These four were all cloth merchants connected by family and business: Hamer Stansfeld, Darnton Lupton, J. D. Luccock and Francis Carbutt. It was such men who gave Leeds Unitarianism a political influence beyond its modest numbers. Municipal Liberalism ensured that corporate offices would still go to partisans, and when the town clerk, Eddison, retired through ill health in 1843 he was replaced by John Arthur Ikin, Liberal Party secretary in the West Riding.

Beneath the surface, however, Liberal control was weakening. Party spirit itself was sapped somewhat in the 1840s. The 1842 Chartist Plug Riots, though less serious in Leeds than in places to the west, convinced some that the threat to property and order made party differences between middle-class protagonists irrelevant. The passing of the 1842 Improvement Act, which extended the duties of the council, reduced party tension, for as one Tory councillor explained, 'in proportion as the important duties of the members are increased by their new functions in the same proportion the war of words will be diminished'.[17] In this atmosphere the Liberal solicitors T. W. Tottie and John Hope Shaw argued that municipal honours ought to be shared out, and when they secured in 1846 the election of one Tory alderman at the same meeting that voted on a drainage scheme it was hailed as

> a moral sewerage . . . a first step towards draining off that accumulation of party feeling which has hitherto suffered to infect and paralyse party bodies. Mad political party hate is beginning to be an old fashioned vice. It is unavoidable it should be so, the moment there springs up a real earnestness about the public good.[18]

Threatened from above by this moderate Liberalism which wished to reduce party control, municipal Liberals were challenged from below by radicals and Chartists who also refused to play a straightforward Liberal game. Furthermore public fears over the extension of the powers and the increased costs associated with the Improvement Act led to a form of ratepayers' revolt which sent to the council a group of 'economists' to attack Liberal extravagance. The great hero of Leeds sanitary reform, Robert Baker, was driven from the council and the new popular saviour was John Yewdall, a Wesleyan tea dealer in Briggate. He proclaimed that 'the people were more solicitous about draining rates from their pockets than draining the streets'.[19] This was contrary to the Chartist view, expressed by William Brook, in favour of expenditure on public health and it was equally opposed to the sanitary plans of H. C. Marshall, third son of the flax-spinning family and Liberal mayor in 1842–43. When Yewdall had first emerged as a parochial economist in the vestry dispute of the 1820s he had been at the heart of the Liberal campaign led by Baines. As a municipal economist in the 1840s he was a symbol of Liberal fragmentation.

Much more significant were the threats to Liberal unity which derived from the field of political agitation. The great agitational issue of the 1840s, corn law repeal, challenged the basis of the Whig–Liberal alliance in the county. Richard Cobden, leader of the Anti-Corn Law League, was anxious for Leeds Liberals to break away from the county Whigs led by Earl Fitzwilliam and set up an independent free-trade organisation for the riding, based on the towns. Edward Baines junior parried this mercantile thrust at landed domination, for Baines senior could trace his support for the county Whigs back to 1807. Baines junior skilfully married the League's invasion of the West Riding with traditional social leadership in the county and it was a triumph for him that a free-trade majority on the register of electors, secured by League money and effort, was placed at the disposal of Lord Morpeth from Castle Howard, who was elected unopposed for the West Riding in 1846. Yet ironically it was Baines junior himself who was to be responsible for a major Liberal schism in both town and county in the 1840s.

When education emerged as a serious political issue in the proposed factory Bill of 1843 it did so in terms which allowed Liberals of all shades of opinion to unite behind the banner of civil and religious liberty. An arrogant Anglicanism seemed to be demanding the sole right to educate children in the manufacturing districts, and Anglican control of the prospective publicly financed schools was an affront to the Nonconformist conscience. In a remarkable display of political feeling over two million signatures were presented in petitions against the Bill, which was soon dropped. It was this agitation which gave Baines junior a national reputation, for he published a series of letters and tables claiming to show that the manufacturing districts were already providing enough education by voluntary means. He defined a rigorous new philosophy of 'voluntaryism' which argued that the State had no right to interfere with schooling and that Dissenters must not be tainted by the receipt of State grants. It was Bainesite voluntaryism which was to wreak havoc in Leeds Liberalism in the years 1846 to 1848.

Though, as Chapter IX has shown, most Nonconformist groups did not follow Baines's Congregationalists in refusing State grants, all were united with him in 1843 in resisting Anglican State indoctrination. Once Anglicanism had moderated its tone, many Liberals were receptive to the idea of increased State aid if it was free from the taint of Church domination. Leeds was to be the scene for a display of such Anglican moderation from none other than Hook himself. By the mid-1840s he had accepted that the Church of England had no moral claim to favoured treatment by the State and in a celebrated pamphlet suggested in 1846 a system of rate-aided schools

69   Edward Baines, 1800–90 (knighted 1880)

which would treat all denominations fairly.[20] Many Liberals who had reservations about Baines's extreme position, and who doubted whether voluntaryism could ever adequately supply the educational needs of great cities, welcomed Hook's olive branch. Baines, however, reacted strongly and used all the *Mercury's* influence to attack the scheme and to proclaim the virtues of voluntaryism. Education thus became a major issue during 1846 and began to divide Liberalism when the great free-trade victory of that year ought to have united it.

From the voluntaryist point of view worse was to follow, and in 1847 Parliament adopted Kay Shuttleworth's pupil-teacher scheme, involving increased government grants and greater State intervention. Baines and the voluntaryists refused to accept defeat quietly and the State education question polarised Leeds politics in 1847. Originating in political agitation, education permeated the other levels of the political system. Francis Carbutt, who deserted his fellow State educationists from Mill Hill in favour of voluntaryism, raised the education question on the town council, which was split in half by this issue. By a narrow majority, twenty-seven to twenty-three, the council petitioned against State education, with the Liberals split two to one in favour of voluntaryism. Ominously the defeated twenty-three comprised thirteen Liberals and ten Conservatives. When aldermanic and mayoral nomination came round in November 1847 the education question determined the division of the spoils. It had been expected that Joshua Bateson, a long-standing Anglican Liberal activist, would become mayor, but he had been a State educationist and so the voluntaryist majority chose Carbutt, the acknowledged deputy to Baines. Similarly prominent Liberals, including Stansfeld and Lupton, were, in the language of the day, 'dispossessed of their Aldermanic dignity' for their support of State education.

Voluntaryism thus took on the guise of a municipal vendetta and showed itself equally unforgiving at the parliamentary election of 1847. Since Liberals were united on all issues except education, it seemed sensible that the town's two MPs should consist of one Liberal educationist and one Liberal voluntaryist on a joint platform. This Hamer Stansfeld proposed to Baines. Baines could not stomach so unprincipled an arrangement, which had in fact merely been a variation on the shared representation traditional in Leeds politics. His conscience would not be sullied by any alliance with State education and he insisted that Dissenting Liberals must stand alone on 'pure voluntaryism'. He adopted the family ploy so effectively used by his father in Reform Bill days of bringing a distinguished stranger to the town. As Edward Baines senior had imposed Brougham upon the county in 1830, and Macaulay upon the borough in 1832, so his son sought to do the same with Joseph Sturge, a radical Quaker from Birmingham and a leading voluntaryist. As some Liberals pointed out, Sturge had supported universal suffrage, which had previously earned the *Mercury's* disapproval. Now all was forgotten and education was the sole consideration. Other suffrage reformers in Leeds such as Stansfeld, J. G. Marshall and Smiles were now State educationists and they opposed Sturge.

It was James Garth Marshall whom the educationists nominated as their candidate, and in other circumstances he would have been an ideal choice. A radical, a free-trader, an active political campaigner, a large employer, a great philanthropist – what more could an urban constituency ask of its MP? Yet the shibboleth of the election was voluntaryism, and because of this alone he was *persona non grata* with Baines. Since the 'great oracle of voluntaryism' made the whole election turn on education, Liberal educationists, in a minority in their own party, looked to Tory educationists for salvation. The sitting MP, William Beckett, had voted with Peel in 1846, thus dividing local Conservatives, but the education issue reunited them, and on education if on little else they could coalesce with Marshall. In religious terms this was an alliance mainly of Anglicans, Unitarians, Wesleyans and Roman Catholics in favour of State education against Congregationalists, Baptists and individuals of all denominations pledged to voluntaryism. Though two Liberals could easily have been returned in 1847, the voluntaryist schism prompted a Liberal–Conservative coalition which returned Beckett and Marshall. The latter commanded perhaps a quarter of the Liberal vote and would have been defeated without Tory help. Sturge's three-quarters of the Liberal vote was not sufficient to match the combined State education total. Baines had sacrificed a safe Liberal seat to his conscience.

In 1848 he repeated the process in the West Riding. Lord Morpeth succeeded to the family title as Earl of Carlisle, thus creating a vacancy. There was still a free-trade register, and Cobden and Morpeth had been returned unopposed in 1847, so all seemed set fair for an easy Whig–Liberal return. Baines, however, injected the poison of voluntaryism as before. Earl Fitzwilliam's youngest son Charles was too inexperienced to cope with the demands of the riding, and when he was forced to withdraw as a candidate Baines produced a quite impossible contender. He was Sir Culling Eardley, an extreme Dissenter from London, for whom not even the town Liberals had any love. The Tories, scenting Whig–Liberal disunity, contested the seat with E. B. Denison, who had sat as MP for the riding from 1841 to 1847 and who was closely related to the Becketts of Leeds. Baines had one advantage: the party's electoral machine was on his side, for the party agent, the Leeds accountant Thomas Plint, was a voluntaryist. With so poor a candidate voluntaryism did well to get some 12,000 votes, about 3,000 behind Denison's total. The key facts of the election were that over 4,000 known Liberal voters abstained and nearly 2,000 changed sides because of Baines. A safe seat in the borough had been sacrificed in 1847 and now a safe seat in the county had been conceded in 1848. Baines and voluntaryism had indeed sapped the strength of local Liberalism.

IV   Only time could heal the wounds inflicted in 1847–48. In the county Carbutt became chairman of the party organisation, Thomas Plint was appointed paid secretary and the county Whigs refused to join them. In the borough education continued to divide Liberals into 1850. It was not until 1852 that the quarrels were patched up when Baines and Carbutt sought a reconciliation in Leeds and the West Riding. The voluntaryists were now willing to accept that shared representation which they had rejected in 1847 and it was agreed that at the next election Carbutt and Marshall should stand. In fact at the 1852 general election neither stood. Carbutt was too much identified with past divisions and was replaced by George Goodman, first reform mayor and recently knighted for his work on the Great Exhibition. J. G. Marshall retired because of business problems and was succeded by Matthew Talbot Baines, Edward's brother but, unlike him, an Anglican and a State educationist. The two Liberals had an easy victory, especially as the contest was fought on free trade, which helped to unite the party. Similarly the free-trade issue preserved Cobden's seat in the county, where Baines and Carbutt had been able to resurrect the urban–rural connection with the help of Sir Charles Wood, MP for Halifax and go-between for the county Whigs.

There was another reconciliation in 1852 which had much significance in Leeds. In January 1852 Baines, Carbutt and J. G. Marshall joined forces with three former Chartists, David Green, William Brook and R. M. Carter, to press for further suffrage reform. This reunification of middle and working-class radicalism had a dual effect. It committed many middle-class leaders such as Baines to moderate parliamentary reform, which strengthened Liberalism and secured Baines's election as MP in 1859, 1865 and 1868. It also affected the very lowest levels of the political system by giving Liberal support to Chartist control over the board of highway surveyors. When in 1852 William Brook and his Chartist surveyors faced a Tory challenge for the first time, Liberals strongly supported the Chartists in the town poll which was called. The same thing happened in 1855, and these two polls echoed at the township level that alliance which had been forged in the field of political agitation. Though the Chartist designation was dropped in the 1850s, ex-Chartists like Carter or ex-Chartist councillors like Brook or William Parker, owner of a temperance hotel, continued to predominate. Until its demise in 1866 the board was the political resort of the humble.

A major Improvement Act of 1866 amalgamated all the townships' surveyors with the town council, whose powers were once more enlarged. In the 1850s there had been much municipal activity, supported by many improvement societies in the borough, the most important of which was led by Dr J. D. Heaton. The sewerage scheme had progressed, Hope Shaw had finally persuaded the council to take over the water supply, and despite many setbacks the Town Hall had been built. Asa Briggs has shown elsewhere how many issues entwined themselves round the latter question, and its completion was indeed a monument to civic pride and municipal achievement.[21] When Queen Victoria opened the Town Hall in 1858 she knighted the mayor, Peter Fairbairn, and the accolade crowned a political career which well illustrates the Leeds political system itself. Fairbairn, a self-made engineering magnate, had first established a foothold in politics at the lowest level of parish and township. He served his apprenticeship as a churchwarden in the 1830s. Moving upward, he became a councillor and served between 1836 and 1842, when he withdrew to concentrate on his business. He was a prominent Liberal activist in parliamentary elections and was one of Sturge's main supporters in 1847. Though an Anglican he was an ardent voluntaryist, and he also participated in the movements for free trade and suffrage reform. His career epitomises the political structure of Leeds, and his distinctions in the 1850s (alderman in 1854, mayor in 1857 and 1858, knighted in 1858) also reflected his success in business.

During Fairbairn's mayorality the Conservative share of council seats was only one-eighth, and it was not until the early 1870s that Liberal control was again threatened. By then the Liberals were once more being scourged by their own radical economists. The 1866 Improvement Act was followed closely by another major water scheme under which the Lindley Wood, Swinsty and Fewston reservoirs were constructed. This took the borough debt up to £800,000, and the purchase of the gas companies and of Roundhay Park in 1870 and 1871 added a further £900,000. As some argued, this was more like a mini-national debt than a borough debt. G. A. Linsley, a pawnbroker, and the flamboyant fruit merchant Archie Scarr – later 'the mayor of the masses' – led the ratepayers' revolt and argued for economy inside the council chamber. This fear of extravagance, together with an alliance of 'beer and church' (hostile to Gladstone's licensing and Irish policies), launched a revival of Conservatism. The capture of one seat at the 1868 election and a more vigorous ward organisation put the Tories within sight of municipal control in 1874, again a year of aldermanic elections. As in 1841 a parliamentary election victory was not reflected in municipal success and, needing to win by at least eleven to five in the 1874 local elections, the Conservatives actually lost in that exact ratio.

The more disciplined and organised municipal politics of the 1870s, a feature of many other towns as well, was based upon the so-called 'caucus' system. Some found this politicising of municipal affairs a novelty, but of course it had been traditional in Leeds for half a century, as one contemporary explained:

> a member of the Leeds Town Council is seldom returned on the simple grounds of personal fitness; he must be pronounced and definite in his party views and sympathies to be acceptable to the ratepayers and so the struggles which are gone through each November are fought under the rival flags, sometimes with a bitterness and always with an intensity of effort which the Municipal interests of the ratepayers alone will scarcely account for . . . this habit . . . has obtained the strength and force which long continuance in any habit whether good or bad does obtain; and it appears today to be as likely to last as in any by-past period.[22]

This more systematic form of politics also expressed itself in the minor institutions, notably the Poor Law.

We noticed earlier that the board of guardians had been safely Tory in the later 1840s. A major Poor Law Board enquiry in 1852 had revealed extensive corruption in Poor Law elections in Leeds, and a shocked Liberal party gained control for two years in 1853. Liberals also did well in 1859 and 1860, but for the most part during the mid-Victorian years the board was the one bastion the Tories held against the Liberals. In 1869 the Leeds Union was extended to include the northern suburbs, and in the consequent increased political interest further accusations of corruption were made. A second Poor Law inquiry of 1870 again revealed fabrication and destruction of voting papers. This stimulated the Liberals to greater efforts, and in 1874 they secured a prestigious conquest. William Middleton, a retired pawnbroker, who had been a guardian for twenty years and chairman for fifteen, was defeated and two years later Liberals gained control of the board by winning twenty-one of the thirty-one seats at the annual Poor Law elections. During the 1870s Poor Law elections were once more overtly political and the same was true of the new institution of the decade, the School Board.

The first election of a School Board in Leeds again put to the test pious demands for the removal of politics from local government. There were plans to avoid a contest but John Barran, a wealthy clothier, twice mayor and Liberal MP from 1876 to 1885, announced that the Liberals would put up an official list organised by Frederick Spark, proprietor of the radical *Leeds Express*. It was above all because of the religious policy to be pursued by the Board that political interest concentrated upon the elections, which were fought on grounds partly political and partly religious. Indeed, the composition of the Board is best understood in terms of religious policy, as indicated in table 28. The table analyses the composition of the Board after each triennial election, using the categories which make most sense. The Church party was predominantly Conservative, though its leader and the first chairman of the Board was Sir Andrew Fairbairn, son of the mayor knighted in 1858 and a Liberal. The Dissenters and official Liberal candidates tended to coalesce together in support of a policy of unsectarian or secular education, while those designated Denominational were openly supporters of their own schools (two Roman Catholics in each election, joined by two Wesleyans in 1879). The Independents were a real entity only in 1879, when Wesleyans refused to work in harmony with other Dissenters and there was considerable political fragmentation.

Table 28 Composition of the Leeds School Board, 1870–85

Year	Church	Liberal/ Unsectarian	Denominational	Independent
1870	7	6	2	
1873	5	8	2	
1876	5	8	2	
1879	5	3	4	3
1882	5	8	2	

Perhaps inevitably, the opening up of a new area of public experience was followed by accusations of extravagance. Again Archie Scarr was in the forefront, accusing the Board of purchasing costly sites and building magnificent schools. The confused election of 1879 produced a Board which was inhibited by cries for economy, and the non-sectarian Board schools were somewhat starved of funds. In general, however, considerable educational progress was made by the School Board:

It has not treated the children of the working classes as paupers and criminals for whom the barest and most tasteless sustenance would suffice. On the contrary, it has sought to equip them fully for the battle of life so that even the poorest and humblest among them might have a fair start in the race of existence.[23]

Great issues were often the concern of minor political office. The minor institutions of Leeds were always related to that wider political world of Victorian England which is fully explored in Chapter XIII. It is worth enquiring here by way of conclusion what overall political judgement is suggested by the town's election data. Leeds was always a bastion of Liberalism, yet Conservatives won eleven out of the thirty parliamentary seats contested between 1832 and 1880. No election in that period failed to return at least one Liberal MP, yet only five contests failed to return a Conservative. The voting figures also indicate a Liberal predominance, but not an overwhelming one. As table 29 shows, only in 1852, 1868 and 1880 did the Liberal share of the vote exceed 60 per cent. The Conservative one-third share of parliamentary seats is roughly comparable with the 29 per cent of council seats won at municipal elections between 1835 and 1880. By virtue of both their annual occurrence and their ward basis, municipal elections were more sensitive indicators of political strength within the town. Table 30 shows the share of seats won by Conservatives in each ward, with a comparison of the ward's economic status. It reveals some wide variations in political support within the borough. The contiguous industrial wards south of the river, South, Hunslet and Holbeck, were overwhelmingly Liberal. Within the township of Leeds north of the river, West and North West also voted heavily Liberal in municipal contests. On the other side Headingley was solidly Conservative, remaining so into the present century. There appears to

Table 29 Conservative share of the poll in parliamentary elections, 1832–80 (%)

1832	44·11	1847	53·80	1865	51·42
1834	49·56	1852	32·57	1868	37·19
1835	51·84	1857(i)	48·99	1874	49·13
1837	46·45	1857(ii)	50·07	1876	45·24
1841	50·39	1859	49·56	1880	35·09

Notes. The method of computing share of poll has been devised to cope with the two- or three-member seat where parties do not always put up the same number of candidates nor voters use both their votes. Leeds and other large constituencies were in this position between 1832 and 1885. The present method *assumes* that the contest was in fact for a single seat (which was true in any case in 1834, 1857(ii) and 1876) and compares leading Liberal with leading Conservative, thus giving in percentage terms a comparison between the best totals achieved by each party. Only 1847 may not be effectively treated by this method because of the quirk of a cross-party vote of over 50 per cent.

Table 30 Municipal elections: voting and wealth

Ward	Conservative share of municipal seats (%)	Ratable value per capita (£)	
		1841	*1871*
1. Mill Hill	46·94	11·94	23·69
2. Kirkgate	66·00	7·52	11·21
3. Headingley	82·00	6·27	4·39
4. South	6·12	3·82	3·94
5. West	19·39	3·67	3·33
6. Bramley	22·68	2·82	2·78
7. North West	12·24	2·78	2·37
8. North	33·33	2·24	2·16
9. Hunslet	8·16	2·23	1·92
10. Holbeck	3·09	2·11	2·20
11. East	30·61	1·83	1·67
12. North East	39·58	1·49	1·38

be some correlation between wealth and voting, for the three wealthiest wards, Mill Hill, Kirkgate and Headingley, were the three most Conservative ones. Yet we must beware of assuming too strong a link, since there was no great difference in Conservative support (still below 50 per cent) between the richest ward, Mill Hill, and the poorest, North East). Class never became a powerful determinant of political behaviour in mid-Victorian Leeds. In the competition for power and authority the main contenders could always call on rich and poor alike. It was not always to be so, and when, as Chapter XIV explains, Labour established itself as a separate and independent political interest the political system described in this chapter began to crumble.

NOTES

[1] C. Mott, Assistant Poor Law Commissioner, 24 April 1841, P.R.O. M.H. 12/15225

[2] *Leeds Intelligencer*, 1 December 1838.

[3] *R.C. Report on Municipal Corporation*, P.P. (1835), XXIII, Leeds Report, 6.

[4] *The Factory System*, 12 (University of London White Slavery Collection).

[5] J. Marshall, junior to Lord Brougham, 4 September 1832 (Brougham Papers, University College, London); R. Watson to J. Anderson, 16 September 1831, quoted by W. R. Ward, *Early Victorian Methodism* (1976), 17.

[6] T. B. Macaulay to J. Lees, 2 August 1832, in T. Pinney (ed.), *The Letters of Thomas Babington Macaulay*, II (1974), 162–3.

[7] *To the Electors of the Borough of Leeds From a Hater of Indecency and Cant* (printed at the Patriot Office by John Foster), Oastler and the Factory Movement, 562(3) (University of London Library).

[8] Pinney, *Letters of . . . Macaulay*, II, 361.

[9] *Leeds Mercury*, 2 January, 3 September 1836; *Leeds Intelligencer*, 2 January 1836.

[10] R. Baker to Poor Law Commission, 18 March 1836, P.R.O. M.H. 12/15224.

[11] *Leeds Intelligencer*, 1 October 1836.

[12] *Northern Star*, 21 April 1838; cf. W. Paul, *History of the Rise and Progress of the Operative Conservative Societies* (1838).

[13] *Leeds Intelligencer*, 4 January 1840, 9 January 1841.

[14] G. M. Bingley to Poor Law Commission, 13 January 1845; C. Naylor to Poor Law Commission, 21 January 1845, P.R.O. M.H. 12/15226.

[15] *Leeds Times*, 13 October 1838.

[16] Council Minutes, Improvement Act, I, 348; *Leeds Mercury*, 16 August 1845; *Leeds Intelligencer*, 20 June 1846.

[17] *Leeds Mercury*, 6 August 1842.

[18] *Leeds Intelligencer*, 20 June 1846.

[19] *Leeds Mercury*, 2 March 1844.

[20] W. F. Hook, *On the Means of Rendering More Efficient the Education of the People* (1846).

[21] Cf. A. Briggs, *Victorian Cities* (1963), 137–84.

[22] J. S. Curtis, *The Story of the Marsden Mayoralty* (1875), 1.

[23] *Leeds Mercury*, 17 November 1879.

BIBLIOGRAPHICAL NOTE

The major source for a study of mid-nineteenth century Leeds politics is undoubtedly the Leeds press, references to which are made in the textual notes. The *Leeds Mercury* was the main Liberal paper and the *Leeds Intelligencer* the main Conservative source: both are available in the Central Reference Library. These may be supplemented by the *Leeds Times*, the *Northern Star* and the *Leeds Express*. Leeds is well endowed with poll books, and a complete run exists for every contested election between 1832 and 1868. The town is less well off for family papers, very few of which exist apart from the rather patchy Baines family collection in the city archives. Pamphlets, handbills and cartoons abounded at election time, and much of this material may be found in the Reference Library and in the library of the Thoresby Society. For municipal and parochial politics valuable records are held at the Civic Hall, including extensive administrative archives.

Local antiquarian publications of value include J. Mayhall, *Annals of Yorkshire* (3 vols, 1875), R. V. Taylor, *Biographia Leodiensis* (1865), J. Wardell, *The Municipal History of the Borough of Leeds* (1846), and H. Schroeder, *Annals of Yorkshire* (2 vols, 1852). Valuable biographical data may be gleaned from E. Baines junior, *The Life of Edward Baines* (1851), J. T. Barker, *The Life of Joseph Barker* (1880), T. Mackay, *The Autobiography of Samuel Smiles* (1904), W. R. W. Stephens, *The Life and Times of Walter Farquhar Hook* (1880), J. S. Curtis, *The Story of the Marsden Mayoralty* (1875), and H. Yorke, *A Mayor of the Masses* (1904). Modern works with Leeds material include C. Driver, *Tory-Radical: the Life of Richard Oastler* (1946), J. T. Ward, *The Factory Movement* (1962), E. P. Thompson, *The Making of the English Working Class* (1963), A. Briggs, *Victorian Cities* (1963) and *Chartist Studies* (1959), E. P. Hennock, *Fit and Proper Persons* (1973), and D. Read, *Press and People* (1961).

Many of the themes touched on in the present chapter are explored more fully in the author's essays in *Publications of the Thoresby Society* (1970) and in *Northern History* (1972 and 1977). Leeds developments are placed in the wider framework of Victorian cities in the author's *Urban Politics in Victorian England* (1976 and 1979) and *Power and Authority in the Victorian City* (1979).

B. J. BARBER

Aspects of municipal government, 1835–1914

XII

The council of the reformed corporation of Leeds which met for the first time in December 1835 had been assigned a very limited role in the community, and was responsible for little more than the finance and management of the police. The principal motives of the government in reforming the corporations were political, in particular the desire to remove corruption and allow greater participation in local government by the middle class through the creation of elected assemblies. There was no intention of establishing authorities which were equipped to govern the evolving urban society of nineteenth-century England. Indeed, it has been argued that one of the intentions of the reformers was to reduce rather than to increase local government expenditure, and certainly many of the new corporations inaugurated their regimes with acts of ostentatious parsimony. Despite such inauspicious beginnings, over the subsequent eighty years the range of activities of the Leeds borough council progressively grew wider until by the early twentieth century it had come to exert a major influence over many facets of urban life. By 1914 the corporation provided the gas, water and electricity supply, operated the tramways, was responsible for environmental health, had created parks, libraries, markets and other amenities, and was beginning to tackle the problems of the slums. As in other large towns, the initiative to add these services to the municipal agenda had come not from central government, but from local decisions, given effect through the promotion of local Acts of Parliament. Between 1835 and 1914 Leeds acquired nearly two dozen of these local Improvement Acts, and in the process endowed itself with what was virtually its own constitutional history.

Within the limits imposed by this chapter we can scarcely examine the whole spectrum of municipal affairs, so we shall consider three major aspects and relate them to issues of wider historical importance. As Professor Flinn has observed, in the history of public health 'the two chronologies – the legislative and the mortality scales – moved forward with only a substantial time lag between them'.[1] National legislation began in the 1840s, but falling death rates came only in the 1870s. Similarly, in Leeds more than thirty years separate the major local Act of 1842 and the beginning of the sustained downward trend in crude mortality rates in the late 1870s. Chapter III discusses public health in detail; here we are concerned only with the contribution the council made.

Slum clearance was the last major responsibility the council assumed before 1914. Up to the 1890s virtually nothing was done, but in the middle of the decade the council began one of the largest clearance projects in the country. A similar chronology — inertia before the last decade of the century and then a sudden quickening of activity — has been noticed as a national feature, but not satisfactorily explained. As far as Leeds is concerned the principal cause of the change in policy seems clear, and it may also have been an important factor in other towns. Municipal ownership of public utilities came to be of increasing significance in the second half of the century. In 1852 the council acquired the waterworks, in 1870 the two gas companies, and a generation later took over the tramways (1894) and the electricity supply (1898). We shall inquire into the motives which justified these incursions into the domain of private enterprise, and relate them to the contemporary debate over 'municipal socialism'.

I   The first in the series of municipal local Acts was obtained in 1842, and it endowed the council with major powers to improve public health conditions. According to the historian of private Bill legislation, the Act was 'one of the most comprehensive and complete which had then been obtained by local authorities'.[2] Yet the council failed to sustain the expectations the Act had raised, and by the end of the following decade the sanitary condition of Leeds was beginning to cause considerable disquiet. In 1858, 1865, 1870 and 1874 the town was visited by officers of the Medical Department of the Privy Council, and their findings led John Simon to declare unequivocally that the administration of public health 'in proportion to the importance of the town may perhaps be deemed the worst that has ever come to the knowledge of this department'.[3] Criticism centred on four aspects of municipal policy: the sewerage system, refuse disposal, the water supply and building regulations. The history of the water supply is considered in the next section, and here we need only note two features of its development. One was the rapid growth in the number of houses supplied in the middle decades of the century. In 1842 only 3,000, less than 10 per cent, consumed water supplied by the company. By 1852 nearly 23,000 houses, almost two-thirds, drew their water from the mains, and by the mid-1860s about 95 per cent did so. The other feature is less complimentary to municipal enterprise. In 1854 the council decided to draw water from the river Wharfe, despite warnings about pollution. By the beginning of the 1860s these fears had been realised, and in the 1870s the council was obliged to spend large sums to obtain a pure supply from other sources.

The construction of a comprehensive sewerage system for the central urban area, in the townships of Leeds, Hunslet and Holbeck, was one of the most important provisions of the 1842 Act. Initially there was considerable delay in making definite plans, and work on the first contract did not begin until 1850. This, however, was far from being wholly the fault of the council. Technical, legal and financial obstacles conspired to prevent any positive action from being taken before 1849, and then for a short time the council hesitated to approve an item of massive, if pressingly necessary, expenditure in a period of severe economic depression. Nevertheless, when work began it did so in earnest, and between 1850 and 1862 the council spent £211,155 on its sewerage network. Unfortunately, for several decades the network had little opportunity of achieving the object for which it had been planned. In December 1854 the streets and sewerage committee noted that the contractor was receiving very few applications for house drains to be installed, and in 1857 the inspection sub-committee, after a tour of the drainage district, noted with regret 'the very large number of streets either wholly or inefficiently drained, notwithstanding the excellent outlet which has been in almost every instance been brought close to them by your main sewers'.[4] In the face of passive resistance by landlords the council took no action to compel them to connect their property to the main sewers — indeed, in 1857 the streets committee decided that it would only sewer streets where two-thirds of the owners had voluntarily made a prior arrangement to do so. The majority of the population continued to rely upon the privy-and-ashpit for the disposal of human and household refuse. Before 1859 the removal of domestic wastes was solely the householder's responsibility, but in that year the council decided to provide a cleansing service in the drainage district only. At first the work was done by direct labour, but in 1862 it was put out to contract, with catastrophic results which unfortunately coincided with the arrival of Dr Hunter from the Privy Council in 1865. The alternation between contractors and direct labour characterised the service over the next twenty-five years, forming a saga of sordid inefficiency in which cost was the only criterion the council applied. It was not until 1890 that it finally accepted that the contract system was not an appropriate way of providing a vital sanitary service and decided to create a permanent municipal cleansing department. By this time the council had overcome its earlier prejudice against the water-wasting water closet. In the 1870s the sanitary committee began a systematic campaign against 'the abominable middenstead and cesspool', or at least the most offensive examples, and this, combined with the rising standards of new housing, had already led to a considerable increase in the number of w.c.s by the end of the 1880s.

Table 31 Number of water closets, 1856–89

Year	No. of w.c.s
1856	1,005
1860	1,628
1865	3,221
1870	6,348
1875	approx. 8,500
1884	20,281
1889	27,990

In the same period the sewerage system was being gradually extended to the whole of the borough. The planning of the first major extensions in the late 1860s, which involved the creation of a main drainage network for Armley, Wortley, Headingley, Chapel Allerton and Potternewton, led to serious opposition from riparian landowners downstream from Leeds. In 1869 a Chancery injunction prevented the corporation from discharging raw sewage into the river Aire, and serious attention had to be given to devising an efficient purification process. The problem took eight years to solve, during which time a succession of ingenious and inept entrepreneurs came forward to try to realise the council's hopes that the plant might be a source of profit. From 1877 to 1900 nearly £600,000 was spent on sewerage and drainage, and in the 1880s and 1890s approximately 120 miles of sewers were being built in each decade, more than doubling the size of the pre-injunction network. This greatly increased the problems of sewage disposal, and by the turn of the century it had become clear that additional works were necessary. In 1900 the council took up a scheme which had originally been suggested by the borough surveyor in 1868 but rejected on the grounds of expense. About two thousand acres of land were purchased near Selby, but the Bill to allow its use for sewage disposal was defeated in the House of Lords. Nothing further was done until 1907, when the council was again provoked into activity as a result of legal action, this time by the West Riding Rivers Board. As a result of the providential death of the owner of the Temple Newsam estate, who had strenuously resisted proposals to sell land for sewage works, the council was able to purchase 600 acres from the new owner for the purpose and in 1908 it acquired an Act to allow it to spend £1,277,600 on land and purification plant.

The power to enforce minimum standards in the construction of new streets and houses was another important feature of the 1842 Act, but for twenty years after, until the creation of the building clauses committee in 1863, the council took little action to ensure that builders complied with them. In 1866 one informed observer claimed that 'if the cottage speculator chooses to disregard such regulations he may do so with impunity. No summons has been issued for many years for any breach of building regulations. The authorities are great friends of "moral suasion" pure and simple.'[5] Indeed, there are only three recorded instances of the sanctions of the 1842 Act being invoked. One reason for the council's unwillingness to enforce the statutory penalty was probably its severity, for the only remedy was to order the offending building to be demolished. This difficulty could have been removed by having the building clauses amended, but no alteration was made until the Improvement Act of 1866. In the intervening years more than 12,000 houses were added to the housing stock of the borough, an increase of over a third. There is of course no reason to suppose that the motives of the speculative builders and the consequences of their activities were any different in these decades from those of an earlier generation castigated by Robert Baker in the 1840s.

The formulation of a detailed code of building bye-laws in 1866 showed that in at least two important respects the council was not prepared to interfere with the established practices of the local building trade, however deleterious they might be. The council refused to prohibit back-to-back houses, but introduced a slight departure from existing practice by enacting that they were to be built in blocks of no more than four pairs, with each block separated by a space 'free from any erection above the level of the ground, excepting privies'.[6] Later regulations increased the minimum air space between blocks, and improved the ventilation requirement for the houses, but the standards laid down in 1866 remained essentially unmodified for over forty years. The council even persuaded the Commons select committee which examined its improvement Bill of 1893 to allow a clause which safeguarded its powers to allow the continued building of back-to-backs in the face of strenuous opposition from the Local Government Board and protests from its own medical officer, who in his evidence had condemned the building of such houses as 'utterly wrong'. The council had indeed, as one MP complained in the House in 1901, 'obtained power to set aside the almost universal law of this country against the erection of back-to-back houses'.[7] The council remained the unabashed apologist for this type of house: as will be seen later, it hoped to rehouse some of its slum clearance evacuees in purpose-built back-to-backs, and later petitioned against the section in the Housing and Town Planning Act, 1909, which prohibited further building of them.

The LGB had no greater success in the 1870s when it tried to persuade the council to forbid the use of the privy-and-ashpit system in new houses. Following the Public Health Act, 1875, the Board, on receiving the annual submission of the council's bye-laws, asked it to adopt the 'model' clauses then being prepared. In reply the council asserted its right to make bye-laws under its local Acts and was 'so alarmed at the suggestion that their position as an ancient corporation should be made subservient to a Central Authority' that the clerk was

70   View from Rope Hill, *c.* 1840

instructed to gain a personal interview with the Board. There was a slight unbending when the council realised that it could benefit from the Board's technical expertise over minor matters, but it was not prepared to acknowledge the 'necessity for the revision of the entire series' for which the Board was pressing. In particular, as one official noted, the bye-laws 'contemplate in fact, the perpetuation in Leeds of a form of privy-and-ashpit which has again and again been shown to be the prime source of some of the greatest sanitary evils in Leeds'. If the revised version of the bye-laws which emerged in 1878 was, as an official minuted, 'such as the town council will accept and the Board may safely confirm'[8] the concessions had come from the latter rather than the former. The failure to proscribe the privy-and-ashpit in the building bye-laws produced an anomalous situation once the sanitary committee's campaign of conversion began. Whilst the committee was abolishing privies in the poorest areas of the town, houses were being built in the suburbs provided only with privy middens, and the building clauses committee felt powerless to intervene. It was not until the Improvement Act of 1899 that the council obtained for itself the power to require that all new buildings should have water closets.

Nevertheless, by the turn of the century considerable advances had
been made, as can be seen from table 32. As might be expected, there
was a pronounced contrast in this respect between cottages, and
houses with a ratable value of more than £10. In 1902 slightly more
than a fifth of the tenants in cottage property were dependent upon
the privy-and-ashpit, compared to less than a twelfth in the case of
house tenants. But as can be clearly seen, the proportion of cottage-
property dwellers so dependent had fallen by as much as a third
between 1900 and 1902. Leeds was at last finally abandoning the
practices which several generations of investigators had believed to be
a primary cause of its poor sanitary record.

Table 32 Provision of water closets, 1900–02

Year	Total No. of tenants supplied with water	No. with no w.c.	% of total	Tenants of cottages without w.c. as % of total	Tenants of houses without w.c. as % of total
1900	96,425	22,979	23·8	19·8	2·9
1901	99,103	18,205	18·4	15·4	2·1
1902	100,894	15,517	15·4	12·7	1·9

The probable reasons why the death rate remained disturbingly
high until the late 1870s should be clear from the evidence presented
in the preceding pages. The recurring inefficiency of public cleansing
continued for forty years, from the 1850s, when the service began, up
to the 1890s. The sewerage system had little impact upon sanitary
conditions from its inception in the 1850s up to the late 1870s, when it
seems likely that the considerable increase in the number of water
closets could have made a contribution to the diminution of the death
rate. The council's spirited defence of the privy-and-ashpit system did
nothing to hasten this. In many respects Leeds was perhaps not very
different from other municipalities, and it is not difficult to
understand why the aims of the public health propagandists of the
1840s took so long to realise.

II   By the time the council nominally assumed some responsibility for
regulating building standards in 1842, the town already possessed a
considerable stock of sub-standard housing. The activities of several
generations of small-scale speculative builders, working without co-
ordination or the constraint of building bye-laws, had left a legacy of

high-density back-to-back housing, often without sanitary facilities of any kind, built in a jumble of closed courts, yards and narrow streets which were usually unpaved and undrained. The passage of time added decrepitude to this catalogue of defects and ultimately the only solution to the problem of the deteriorating housing stock was demolition. The council first obtained powers for this in its Improvement Act of 1870, the provisions of which were explicitly modelled on those in the pioneering Liverpool Act of 1866. The medical officer of health quickly took the opportunity to suggest areas where the powers to carry out demolition could be exercised most advantageously. In April 1871 the council approved a scheme to demolish buildings in East Lane, the Old Post Office Yard and Wellington Yard, which formed a half-acre site near Kirkgate market. They comprised sixty houses and twenty-one cellar dwellings which housed about six hundred, most of whom the medical officer thought were 'migratory characters'. The clearance was completed by 1874. Six months after it had agreed to the first scheme the council, in October 1871, approved a second, involving the demolition of 163 houses and forty-six cellar dwellings, with a population of about a thousand. The property was in courts in the Union Street area, among the houses which Professor Beresford has identified as the town's first back-to-backs, built in the 1780s. The total cost of both these projects was under £40,000. In 1884–85 a further £1,130 was spent in acquiring twenty-four cottages unfit for human habitation and a foundry in Meadow Lane, Holbeck. These were the only three occasions on which these provisions of the 1870 Act were put into operation. Indeed, they were such isolated incidents that when, early in this century, the chairman of the Unhealthy Areas Committee surveyed the council's work in slum clearance he missed the significance of the Union Street clearances, believing them to have been made 'under the ordinary provisional orders for street improvements',[9] and failed to mention the other two, presumably because he was unaware of them.

Another aspect of the housing problem, later to assume greater importance, also came to the attention of the council in the 1870s. Demolition alone merely exacerbated the problem of the slums. The crux of the matter was that the buildings could be demolished but the slum dwellers remained and unless alternative accommodation was made available the result was simply to increase overcrowding in neighbouring areas. But rehousing raised questions about the proper sphere of municipal activity, for here was a source of potential conflict between public policy and private enterprise. Thus when in 1851 Parliament allowed local authorities to provide common lodging houses the *Leeds Mercury* observed unenthusiastically:

> We do not say that a municipal corporation or a local board of health might not erect one or two common lodging houses if no one else could be induced to make the experiment, but we would much rather they distributed widely the information ... that well-constructed lodging houses will pay better than lodging houses of another description. As to their becoming builders to such an extent as to provide 'substitutes' for a large proportion of existing lodging houses, we apprehend no body of ratepayers will ever permit such a use of their money.... The true parties to provide houses for the poor, as well as for the rich are private capitalists.[10]

A more subtle and realistic approach was adopted by the town clerk when he reported on the provisions of the newly enacted Artizans and Labourers Dwellings Act in 1876.

The report was made in response to an appeal from the Poor Law guardians. They claimed that the scarcity of working-class accommodation was so severe as to force people to apply for admission to the workhouse in the absence of any alternative, and consequently urged the council to adopt the 1875 Act. The town clerk recommended the purchase of land on the outskirts to build houses for the 'very poor', whom he defined as those earning between 25*s* and 30*s* a week. Such a scheme, he believed, would be financially viable, since four-room cottages built on suburban land could be let for low rents which would more than cover the rate of interest on a local authority loan. In answer to the argument that this would interfere with private builders he asserted that rents from the houses, whilst sufficient to cover the cost incurred by the corporation, would not be high enough to yield an attractive rate of return on private capital. The council accepted these recommendations, and included in its Improvement Act of 1877 the power to buy land and build houses 'for the labouring classes'. Nothing, however, was done to implement these provisions, and the question of the council's role in the housing market did not re-emerge until the end of the century.

The tentative manner in which the council approached the problem of the slums in the 1870s and 1880s changed completely in the following decade. In the last twenty-five years of our period it inaugurated two major and several lesser clearance schemes and had spent more than three-quarters of a million pounds. This clearly indicates that some new element had appeared to influence municipal policy-making. One conceivable influence is perhaps to be found in the political motive. Since 1835 municipal government had been, with only the briefest of interludes, under the control of the Liberals, but by the early 1890s the Conservatives were emerging as serious rivals. The two parties vied with each other to present themselves as the party of effective reform, and at the head of the list in 1893 the Liberal manifesto promised 'the immediate clearance of insanitary areas, with due regard to the provision of accommodation for persons displaced by demolitions'.[11] This was probably an important factor then, but the sanitary committee's preparation of a comprehensive scheme antedates the appearance of such election promises, although the threat to their hegemony may have strengthened the political nerve of the Liberals when the time came to make the decision to implement it. Another contributory factor may have been financial. The scale of municipal expenditure and the growth of ratable values would have made the slum clearance programme seem less of an impossibly costly venture in the context of the total municipal budget. For example, the Improvement Act of 1893 proposed new capital expenditure on gas and water works, street improvements and sewerage to a total of over a million pounds. But it seems that the decisive influence was the changes in the law of land purchase brought about by the Housing of the Working Classes Act, 1890, under the sanction of which the council's clearance programme was carried into effect. If we accept the usual verdict on the 1890 Act this would seem a mistaken claim, since it is usually regarded as being little more than a consolidating measure. But in fact there is clear evidence that the statute was regarded in Leeds, and elsewhere, as enacting a most important advance. The reason was that it revised the law of compulsory purchase, which had hitherto inhibited local authorities from acquiring property for slum clearance projects.

Compulsory purchase law, developed out of the common law procedure of *ad quod damnum*, became formalised in private Bill legislation dealing with street improvements and canal promotion in the later eighteenth century, and as a result of the railway-building boom of the 1840s had been codified in the Lands Clauses Consolidation Act, 1845. Under these procedures the law allowed infringements of the rights of property but in return insisted that considerable concessions were made to the dispossessed owners. The most sanguine estimate of the value of the property was awarded to them, as well as liberal compensation for the forced deprivation of their rights. Whilst these conventions might be legitimate where the purchaser was a business enterprise, such as a railway company, they could not have any but an inhibiting effect upon any scheme to buy land where commercial criteria were inapplicable. For this reason the council failed to adopt the national slum clearance Acts of 1868 and 1875. In a discussion on the former, one councillor observed that 'the value of the property was to be arrived at under the Lands Clauses

Consolidation Act. Everybody knew that was a tedious and expensive process . . . corporations buying under it generally had to pay double the value of what they purchased.'[12] Similarly, on the subject of the 1875 Act, the town clerk wrote to the Home Secretary informing him that 'practically the present measure was valueless because of the enormous cost involved'.[13] The 1890 Act remedied this situation by extensively revising compulsory purchase law where property was to be acquired for slum clearance. Arbitrators were explicitly directed to base their estimates upon the 'fair market value' and to discount enhanced rentals which were caused by overcrowding and to allow for defective sanitation and dilapidation. Nor were owners to receive the hitherto customary allowance for compulsory purchase.

The fact that this revision of the law was of crucial importance was attested many times at the hearings held at the various stages through which the council's schemes progressed before receiving parliamentary approval. The chairman of the sanitary committee made it explicit that 'as to dealing with the properties . . . under the Lands Clauses Act, such a course would mean the "killing" of the scheme on account of the enormous additional cost that would be entailed'.[14] The property owners who petitioned against the schemes also testified, by implication, in support of this and similar statements, in claiming that their own properties should, for various reasons, be taken under the 1845 rather than the 1890 Act. F. M. Lupton believed that the total cost of purchasing the sixty-seven acres within the council's two principal slum clearance areas was between 10 and 20 per cent more than their market value, and there is every reason to believe that these were far more favourable terms than would have been obtained under the Lands Clauses Acts.

The inception of the council's two major clearance schemes, the only ones we have space to consider here, can be dated from an outbreak of typhus fever in the east end of Leeds township in 1890. The outbreak, which began in April and continued into June, produced only forty-six cases altogether, but there were two disturbing features about it. The first was the nature of the disease itself. As the medical officer of health observed in exculpating his colleagues in private practice from any charge of negligence, 'there seems to be a certain amount of difficulty on the part of many medical men in recognising typhus fever. This is not very much to be wondered at, considering how improved sanitary conditions have almost banished this disease from England.'[15] In the second place, all the victims lived in the North East ward, and a third lived in Allison's Buildings, Quarry Hill. The medical officer reviewed the history of epidemics in this area since 1867 for the benefit of the sanitary committee and concluded that 'infectious diseases are more or less habitually present' in the neighbourhood. Only two years before, the streets and sewerage committee had actually visited Allison's Buildings and had advised the sanitary committee that demolishing the property would be a significant improvement for the area, but no action had been taken. Dr Cameron now proposed a slightly more ambitious venture, but the sanitary committee was prepared to consider something larger, and instructed him to report on all the property bounded by Quarry Hill on the north, Mabgate beck on the east and Marsh Lane on the south, 'with recommendations as to what property should be demolished for sanitary improvement'.[16] This was presumably to be done under the powers in the local Acts of 1870 and 1877 and it was probably not until September 1890 that the committee first became aware of the powers bestowed by the new Housing Act. The sanitary committee approached its decision cautiously, hoping that the area might be covered by Part II of the Act, which dealt with minor clearances, but prolonged examination convinced them that the whole district would have to be acquired. Considering the sheer size of the area involved it is not surprising that it took the committee some time to acclimatise to the implications. Here, perhaps, political considerations exerted an influence. In January 1892 the mayor broached the subject cautiously in public, observing that:

> the time might come, though he did not think that it would come just yet, when the corporation would see its way to apply for powers to purchase the insanitary property . . . pull it down, and provide for the erection of habitations fit for people to live in. In doing this, however, it must not be forgotten that those who might enter upon the enterprise would require a fair return for money invested.[17]

But, as we have already noted, just over a year later the promise of immediate action figured prominently in the Liberals' municipal manifesto. Even so, it was some time before planning preparations were completed, and the council was not finally presented with a scheme for approval until October 1895. This scheme, known as the York Street insanitary area, contained a population of just under 4,000 and was a sixteen-acre segment in the south-west corner of the area specified for the medical officer's survey in 1890. The council applied to the Local Government Board for the necessary local inquiry, and the Board accepted the council's project. The confirming Act became law in August 1896, and four years later arrangements had been completed to purchase all the property involved. The evidence available substantiates Lupton's claim over the cost of acquisition. Of the transactions with the 152 owners involved, financial details are available in eighty-three cases. The aggregate amount initially claimed by the seventy-three who eventually settled without arbitration was £91,342 and that offered by the council £55,221. The total amount finally agreed upon came to £65,322, or about 30 per cent less than the total demands of the owners and about 20 per cent more than the council's offer. The ten who took their cases to arbitration fared less well. They claimed compensation to a total amount of £21,854, in contrast to the council's offer of £12,160. The Local Government Board's arbitrator, however, awarded only £12,970 in all, so endorsing the council's own assessments of values. By the time all the negotiations were completed in June 1900 plans were already under way to acquire the far larger part of the remaining area investigated in 1890. The sanitary committee had realised that it would be impossible to produce a coherent design for the whole if it were to be bought in sections, and so recommended the council to apply for powers to take the district of about fifty acres designated the Quarry Hill insanitary area. The same procedure of local inquiry, provisional order and confirming Act took place, but in the Commons the Bill encountered some opposition, for reasons we shall consider shortly. Purchasing began in 1902, and the council succeeded in buying the greater part by agreement, with only twenty-four of the 555 owners resorting to arbitration.

The council now owned about sixty-seven acres of the worst slums in the city, and was faced with the problem of what to do about them. In 1902 the chairman of the insanitary areas committee declared that its policy was not 'to make a tremendous clearance all at once. [He] . . . computed that twenty-five or thirty years would be required for the completion of the scheme.'[18] This gradualist approach entailed the removal of only those houses in an irremediable condition and the renovation of the others. By 1914, on the basis of the number of residents displaced, three-quarters of the York Street area and half the Quarry Hill area had been cleared.

Once the council was launched on its clearance schemes, the question of how it was to fulfill its rehousing obligations under the 1890 Act came into prominence. In approving the York Street scheme the Local Government Board had specified that it was to be carried out in four stages, with a proportion of 2,000 working-class inhabitants of the area rehoused after each, so that none should be homeless by the time it was completed. This stipulation resurrected a problem which had first been considered in Leeds in the 1870s, namely the proper sphere of municipal enterprise in the housing market. Initially the council decided in 1897 to build fifty houses to plans approved by the Board on the Ivy Lodge estate, about a mile from the insanitary area. A few months later the decision was reversed, and it was resolved to sell the land by auction to builders who were prepared to build to the agreed specifications. This brought conflicting ideas about municipal enterprise into the open. The supporters argued that the corporation was already a 'great trading concern' and that no new departure would be initiated by building houses for the slum dwellers. Against this Alderman Lupton the chairman of the insanitary areas committee claimed that 'it was not the duty of the corporation to compete with private traders; that they had no right to use public money for such purpose, even if it could be shown to produce a profit to the city'.[19] As we noted earlier, the town clerk has countered this objection twenty years previously when he argued that there would be no unfair competition, since the council would only be providing houses for those whose incomes were too low to be a source of effective demand in the private sector. But there was now a new twist to the problem. The houses that were built on the Ivy Lodge estate were, by contemporary standards, well designed and soundly constructed but the rents they commanded – 5s 4d to 5s 6d including rates – were much higher than most of the inhabitants of the insanitary area could afford. In the mid-1890s, of 500 houses in one area of Quarry Hill, only three were let for 5s 4d or more. This was not, however, the result of private builders' costs, but of the high standards set by the LGB, which meant that 'the lowest rent of a house complying with the central authority's requirements was 5s 6d a week'.[20] To find a way out of this impasse, in November 1898 a deputation went to the LGB to try to persuade it to allow back-to-back houses to be built on the York Street site when it was cleared; predictably the Board refused to consider this. Some cheaper accommodation became available when in 1900 the council approved the building, again by private enterprise, of a tenement block containing two and three-roomed flats to house 198 people in the York Street area. Nothing, however, was done to meet the trades council's sensible request to the council to adopt Part III of the 1890 Act and build working-class lodging houses. The redoubtable Alderman Lupton argued that private enterprise had proved superior in this area of the housing market as well, pointing to the success of Lord Rowton's company. By the turn of the century the council had apparently provided alternative accommodation for 1,104 of the tenants of the York Street area. Of these, houses for 906 had been constructed at Ivy Lodge, but they 'did not provide for a single person displaced by the clearance'[21] and the remainder were catered for by two blocks of tenements. We can well imagine that many of the area's residents were put to some hardship by this first stage in the slum clearance programme.

The issue was taken up again when the council applied for a provisional order to deal with the Quarry Hill area. On this occasion opposition to its proposals came not from local groups but from some members of the House of Commons. The confirming Bill proposed the rehousing of two-thirds of the area's 9,000 working-class residents, and the remainder were expected to move into the 500 empty houses within a mile radius of the area. When the Bill was brought up for its second reading, several MPs questioned the decision to allow the demolition of property, containing 1,000 residents, before any rehousing was obligatory, which comprised the first stage of the scheme. Their opposition failed either to obtain a revision of the text of the Bill or to prevent its passage, and on its second reading it was voted through by 307 to 52. In 1906 the LGB issued a modified order which increased the number who could be displaced to 2,000 at the first stage, and in 1908 to 4,000. As we have seen, in one sense it was paradoxically fortunate that the council did not adopt a more vigorous approach to slum clearance. For inhabitants of the insanitary areas it would have involved considerable upheaval, leading to even higher densities in adjacent districts, or considerably higher rents for those able to move away from the East End. The only way in which the council could have provided alternative accommodation would have been through subsidised municipal housing, which it was not prepared to contemplate. During the council debates in 1897, when this possibility was discussed, one speaker claimed that 'the town clerk would tell them that they could not carry out the Socialistic idea of the corporation remaining the landlord', and another 'objected to . . . people being benefited at the expense of the rest of the community. The scheme proposed was Utopian, and he hoped the council would not adopt it.'[22] It was not until after 1914 that Leeds Corporation came to adopt the 'Socialistic idea' urged upon it at the end of the nineteenth century.

III   The municipal ownership of utilities began in 1852, with the purchase of the waterworks. Since 1837, when its management had been resigned by the improvement commission, it had been vested in a joint-stock company with a board composed of equal numbers of shareholders' directors and councillors. Under the terms of the 1837 Act the council, furthermore, had the right to buy out the company at any time after twelve years had elapsed. What stimulated certain councillors to urge the council to take advantage of this right was that in the early 1850s the company found itself in a similar predicament to that which had created the crisis which had precipitated the 1837 Act. On both occasions the managing body had failed to anticipate the growth of demand and so were confronted by a dilemma over where to obtain adequate supplies for the future. On the other hand, there were councillors who looked askance at the proposal for municipalisation. One alderman, for example, urged that

> there was a broad distinction to be drawn between the supply of water to a town and administering the ordinary duties of a town council, such as sewerage, police matters, lighting, paving etc. A parallel had been attempted between the water supply and the sewerage; but there was this wide distinction that the idea of profit had never been entertained as derivable from the construction of town sewers.[23]

How then did John Hope Shaw, the leading proponent of municipilisation, convince those opposed to his scheme that 'the town council was the proper body to manage the supply of water and that no principle of trade would be violated by their management of such works'? There were, he contended, four possible methods of solving the problem of the water supply. The council itself might apply for an Act to give it independent powers to supply water. This was not tactically feasible, since a complaint against the management of the existing works would be self-incriminating. The present company could be allowed to make the new capital investment necessary, yet it could not do so as cheaply as the council, which, backed by its superior financial security, could borrow at a lower rate of interest than a private firm. Another possibility was to leave the issue to be resolved by the classic free-market solution, the establishment of another private company. This, it was argued, would produce the worst of both worlds. Resources would be needlessly duplicated, nor could a second company achieve an extension of supply more cheaply than the original one. Furthermore, recent evidence given to the Royal Commission on Large Towns, and the experience of the metropolis, provided a considerable body of evidence to substantiate the view that the existence of two companies would be less likely to benefit the consumer through competition than to lead to collusion in order to protect profits. This left the fourth choice, public ownership, as the only acceptable solution. Whilst Shaw stressed the importance of pure water supply in the improvement of public health, he did not invoke criteria other than strictly commercial ones. The council was not being advised to take on the subsidising of a public service, 'but if it would only bear its own expenses, and pay its own way, then upon grounds of policy and public duty the council ought to undertake it'.[24] His advocacy prevailed and in November 1852 the purchase was completed at a cost of £227,417.

The mere transfer of ownership did not solve the problem of how the much-needed additional water supplies were to be obtained. Two rival schemes were canvassed; one, backed by Shaw, was gravitational, making use of the river Washburn, the other entailed an extension of the existing practice of pumping water from the river Wharfe. Although the choice between the two was complicated by technical questions, the fundamental difference was financial. The waterworks committee calculated that the Wharfe pumping scheme would produce a profit, whereas the gravitational project, because of the cost of land purchase and reservoir-building, would produce considerable losses, at least for the first decade. The council decided in favour of the former, and in 1856 obtained an Act to authorise the pumping of 2·5 million gallons a day from the river, increased by an Act of 1862 to 6·0 million gallons daily. But by this time there was growing concern over the purity of this source, as predicted by the pro-Washburn group of a decade before. The solution the council was forced to adopt was basically the same as that which it had then rejected. The borough engineer proposed the impounding of water from the Washburn in a series of reservoirs along its valley, and this became municipal policy, embodied in the Leeds Waterworks Act, 1867. The scheme was undertaken in three stages: the Lindley Wood reservoir was built between 1869 and 1875, that at Swinsty between 1871 and 1877, and the Fewston reservoir, begun in 1874, was completed in 1879, at a cost of £508,173. By the 1880s, then, planning and investment in the waterworks had completely overcome the effects of the myopic policy of the 1850s. But by this time, if the water supply had ceased to be a contentious issue, the policy of the gas committee was giving cause for public concern.

As we have seen, one of the arguments in favour of municipal purchase of the waterworks was based upon contemporary experience of private companies in London. To find evidence of collusion between companies insulated from competition the councillors of Leeds did not need to look as far afield as London. It could be found, almost literally, on their own doorsteps. The town's gas was supplied by two companies, the Leeds Gas Light Company, dating from 1818, and the Leeds New Gas Company of 1835. The activities of these two were of direct importance to the council, since it was itself a large consumer through its responsibility for street lighting. The 1842 improvement Bill had originally contained powers to enable the council to manufacture gas but they had been abandoned after the two companies had threatened opposition. The issue re-emerged later in the decade when it was proposed that Leeds should follow the example of Manchester, where a municipal gasworks provided profits to subsidise other municipal services. Further support came in 1850 from a parliamentary return on gas company statistics, which showed that the Leeds companies compared unfavourably with those in other parts of the country. The *Leeds Mercury* was moved to object that 'a joint stock company had no right to calculate on deriving large profit out of a public rate'[25] and this view was echoed in the vestry and in the council. But, after preliminary soundings, no further action was taken, probably because other projects, in particular the sewerage system and the water supply, had prior claims on the council's budget.

It was not until 1868 that purchase was considered again, this time with tangible results. By this date the council had absorbed the functions of the highway surveyors and was buying out the bridge and turnpike trusts in the borough, so establishing an absolute control over the highways. In one respect the merging of the two companies under municipal ownership was a logical extension of its policy, since 'there would not be that breaking up of the roads and streets which now prevailed for the purpose of laying pipes first by one company and then by another'[26]. The most important reason, however, remained the prospect of supplying cheap gas at a healthy profit. It could not be said that the proposal would offend against economic orthodoxy by supplanting the benefits of competition, for

> there was virtually no competition between the gas companies at present, nor had there been since the new company had obtained for itself a firm footing in Leeds. Those who were connected with the lamps committee would know very well that the price charged by one company was exactly what was charged by the other; in fact the two companies seemed to have an understanding as to what they would charge all around the town.[27]

Negotiations were completed in late 1869, and ratified by an Act obtained the following year. The transaction cost the council £763,245.

Apart from the considerable losses made by the works in 1873 and 1874, when a meteoric rise in coal prices and a statutory limitation on prices charged to gas consumers led to a deficit of £27,000, the new municipal utility was financially sound. Indeed, by 1877 the losses of the 'coal famine' years had been liquidated, and £32,324 had been paid from the gasworks' profits into the borough fund. But from the late 1870s the gas committee adopted a new objective for the enterprise, that of producing the cheapest possible gas so as to 'give the gas consumer the benefit of the profit'.[28] Before 1870 the gas companies were charging 3s 6d to 4s 6d per thousand cubic feet, but from 1877 the price was progressively reduced until it had reached 1s

10*d* by 1881. But by that time consumers were becoming concerned
not over the price but over the quality of the product: 'the gas
supplied, though undoubtedly cheap, has been decidedly nasty',[29]
remarked the *Leeds Mercury*, a judgement in which others concurred.
The twin problems of purity and illuminative strength were the direct
result of the gas committee's new policy. When in 1885 the committee
asked its harassed engineer to explain why the yield of gas per ton of
coal was low in Leeds compared to other towns, he pointed out that the
committee chose coal giving high yields of tar and ammonia but which
had 'almost contemptible' gas-making qualities. But, given the cheap
gas policy, the choice of coal was a logical one, since the by-products
from a given weight of coal produced more income than the gas
obtained from it. We can see here an obvious parallel between the
council's approval of cheap but poor-quality gas in the late 1870s and
1880s and its decision to opt for a cheap but inferior water supply in
the 1850s.

Two of the motives which influenced the council's decision to
purchase the gas companies – the need for undivided control over the
highways and public ownership of renumerative utilities – also
appeared in the initial discussions over the introduction of tramways.
Discussion was stimulated by the news the council received in October
1869 that a private company intended to promote an Act to enable it
to operate tramways in Leeds. The council decided to oppose the
application to Parliament, and to promote a Bill on its own account if
it was found to have public support. The arguments in favour of this
course of action were compendiously expressed by Alderman George,
who maintained that

> if there was a great benefit derived from laying down tramways, and if
> there was to be great profit derived from tolls for the passage of carriages,
> the inhabitants of Leeds ought to have the benefit. The Corporation had
> spent £60,000 in the purchase of the tolls, and had expended a good deal
> of money in the improvement of the streets; they were at present asking
> Parliament for powers to take over the gas companies, so that the streets
> might be under no control but their own, and it would be hardly
> consistent to allow the promoters of these tramways to assume the powers
> over the highways which they wanted.[30]

Further action, however, was forestalled by the government's
Tramway Act of 1870. This gave local authorities powers to construct
tramways and lease the right to operate them, or to approve a private
company's plans to build and run a tramway. But it expressly forbade
any local authority to provide the service itself, although the track and
rolling stock could be purchased from the private operators after
twenty-one years. In November 1870 the council voted to support a

private application to construct and manage a service in the town. No reason for this change of heart was made explicit, and a plea for municipal ownership by one councillor went unanswered. After initial difficulties a limited company was incorporated in 1872.

In the early 1890s, as the twenty-one-year veto on municipal ownership was coming to an end, a familiar problem drew the attention of the council to the company's activities. The culprit was 'that most objectionable of urban complaints – the steam tram',[31] which, introduced on lines designed to carry the lighter horse-drawn vehicles, was making road surfaces hazardous. Despite repeated admonition the company did nothing to improve the 'shameful state of repair' of its permanent way, and in late 1892 the council finally decided that it had no option but to exercise its right of purchase. After arbitration the council paid £112,226 to the company and came into formal possession in February 1894. The highways committee created a sub-committee to manage the undertaking temporarily, for at this time the council certainly had no intention of doing so on a permanent basis. Nevertheless, in November 1894 the council decided to apply for an Act to allow it to operate the tramways, but in the debate it was stressed that this was simply a permissive measure and did not imply a conversion to the idea of public ownership. In the event, however, it proved impossible to find a suitable lessee, and the council was obliged, unwillingly, to move from provisional to permanent management.

To the tramway workers municipalisation meant a considerable improvement in wages and reduction in hours: the immediate effect was an increase in wages by a fifth and a shortening of the working week from eighty-one to sixty-seven hours. To passengers, it meant a progressive reduction in fares – by about 60 per cent over the first decade of public ownership – made possible by the cheaper operating costs which came with electrification. Lower fares led to more passengers. In 1895 10·5 million were carried, and by 1914 the number was 93·7 million. Nevertheless, the tramways still catered for the suburbanite rather than the working man. It was only towards the end of our period that fare concessions were introduced which noticeably increased the proportion of workmen in the tramways' clientele, despite the city engineer, in 1895, drawing the council's attention to 'the sanitary or health aspect of the question, the enabling of the artisan to live in more airy surroundings than he does at present'.[32] Workmen's cars were run every morning up to 5.45, but workers returning home in the evening had to pay the same fare as other passengers. Transfer ticket facilities were also restricted, and it was not until 1911, when more generous terms were introduced, that the percentage of workers using the trams showed a marked increase.

Even so, only slightly more than 7 per cent of passengers were availing themselves of workmen's fares in 1914.

Electrification had first appeared in 1890 when the council made an agreement with the Thomson-Houston International Electric Company to run electric cars on a corporation-built line from Sheepscar to Roundhay. Once the council had bought out the tramway company, electric traction was introduced on to other routes. By 1914 the twenty-two miles of track the council had acquired in 1894 had become 114 miles and capital expenditure had reached £1·5 million. The financial return was unmistakably healthy, for the net surplus of under £5,000 had grown into £70,000 by 1914. Apart from the record on workmen's fares, municipal trams were an unquestionable success, essentially because the opportunities offered by electric power were recognised and fully exploited. But in contrast, the council was far more hesitant in its attitude towards the potential of electricity as a source of lighting. During the early 1880s there was a national boom in the promotion of electric lighting companies, and in August 1882 the council was asked to support a private application to the Board of Trade to obtain a provisional order under the Electric Lighting Act, 1882, to authorise a firm to begin business in the city. A committee set up to consider the matter reported that there were eight applicants in all with hopes of supplying electricity, and suggested that the council should seek a provisional order itself. In May 1883 the electric lighting committee was allowed by the council to begin experimental lighting. Six years later it felt sufficiently confident to recommend to the council that it should be allowed to obtain plant and equipment to light town-centre properties as a beginning. The committee urged the council to retain control over 'what may prove eventually a very important business'.[33] It reiterated the argument that no other body should be allowed to interfere with the streets and contended that consumers would benefit from a municipal supply, since it would be about half the price that would be charged by a private firm. The report, presented in July 1889, was firmly rejected. The venture was regarded as highly speculative, and one speaker, doubtless voicing the opinions of many council members, pithily remarked that 'they need not have any fear that the town would not be provided with electric light. As certain as the summer brought them new potatoes, there would be fools who would invest their money in electric lighting.'[34]

The committee reported again in the following year, but failed to move the council from its earlier scepticism, and in April 1891 the council gave its assent to a Board of Trade order in favour of the Yorkshire House-to-House Electricity Company. To the *Leeds*

Mercury the council's decisions were deplorable, and tantamount to 'declaring itself incompetent to take upon itself an essentially municipal responsibility'.[35] It is true that in the 1880s the development of electric lighting was indeed uncertain in both commercial and technological terms. But, as far as technology was concerned, the committee seems to have taken a perverse pride in neglecting to make use of professional advice, in a situation where it was very much needed, in order to keep its costs to a minimum. In its first report it informed the council that it was 'buying the engines, dynamos, and other materials in the open market, and employing ordinary workmen on the installation, thus avoiding not only excessive trade profits on the material, but all profit on the labour, as well as high professional charges'.[36] At the very same time a leading professional journal, putting a different gloss on the committee's claim, dryly expressed the hope that 'the forthcoming installation . . . may give as much satisfaction to the inhabitants, in a practical sense, as the confidence which the committee have in their own ability, without the aid of professional assistance, to carry out the same successfully, does to that body. Something must have been learned in six years.'[37]

Indeed, as events proved, the council had taken a short-sighted attitude, and in 1897 the question of public ownership was reopened. The speculative element which had created wariness eight years before had disappeared, and an old complaint was raised when one councillor observed that 'no one . . . could have observed the state of the public thoroughfares along which the House-to-House Company had recently laid wires without feeling that the entire control of the streets should be vested in the corporation'.[38]

The council paid dearly for its earlier lack of nerve. Under the terms of the Board of Trade order of 1891, if the council purchased the company before ten years had elapsed, substantial compensation was to be paid in addition to the value of the capital assets. The capital value of the works in 1895 was estimated as £154,409, but the price paid was £217,420, or 40 per cent more. In the following years the scale of operations expanded rapidly. By April 1914 capital expenditure had reached just over £1 million and the number of consumers had risen from 980 to 12,900, or slightly less than 2 per cent of the total population, which was about average for the early twentieth century.

IV   The purchase and management of public utilities described above is often referred to as 'municipal socialism', and in the history of urban government this is sometimes interpreted as a new departure in municipal policy which occurred in the later decades of the century. When used with reference to a period in which no socialist party had control of any municipality, some care obviously needs to be used over the precise meaning of the expression. It was given wide currency by Sidney Webb in his book *Socialism in England,* and in this context 'socialism' means little more than the extension of public, at the expense of private, ownership. In a well known passage Webb described the 'unconscious permeation' of municipal councillors by 'socialist' ideas in several paragraphs of heavy-handed humour which mock intellectual inconsistencies unconsciously revealed by the shallow-minded 'Individualist Town Councillor'.[39] But, as we have seen, the reasons for the council's incursions into the private sector were clearly articulated and consistent ones which had first been formulated as early as the 1850s. The basic reasons for municipalisation were substantially the same in all four cases. One was the existence of a local monopoly of supply, obvious or disguised. Another was that the activities of all four utilities interfered with the council's statutory duty of maintaining the highways. The importance of this prosaic motive ought not to be underrated. By 1914 the council had incurred capital expenditure of £2·94 million on street improvements, highways, bridges and the abolition of tolls – more than its total capital spending on education and slum clearance combined.

Financial considerations were a subsidiary but significant motive. The prospect of acquiring an additional source of revenue was as persuasive in Leeds as it was, for example, in Manchester and Birmingham. Up to the late 1870s the council treated profits from the water and gas utilities in the conventional manner, but with the Improvement Act of 1877, which included detailed provisions for the financial management of the gas and water works as well as powers to fund the borough debt, municipal policy abruptly changed. From that time until they lost their majority in 1895 the Liberals operated the utilities for the benefit of the consumer rather than the ratepayer. Profits were passed on in the form of lower prices rather than being transferred to the borough fund. It is not clear why this reversal took place. Several of the financial reforms of the 1877 Act were the work of W. L. Jackson, later created Baron Allerton, and it may have been his influence which brought it about. If so, it is an indication of the mediocre quality of the Liberal leadership that they were dependent on a Conservative councillor for their financial policy. It would also be ironic, for when the Conservatives captured the council they revived the policy the Liberals had abandoned twenty years before. Despite their opposition at the time, the Liberals did not interfere with the arrangement when they later returned to power, and profits from gas, water, tramways and electricity continued to flow into the borough fund.

NOTES

[1] A. P. Stewart and E. Jenkins, *The Medical and Legal Aspects of Sanitary Reform*, with an introduction by M. W. Flinn (1969), 7–8.

[2] F. Clifford, *The History of Private Bill Legislation* (1885), I, 493.

[3] R. Lambert, *Sir John Simon, 1816–1904, and English Social Administration* (1963), 434.

[4] Streets and Sewerage Committee Minutes, 22 May 1857.

[5] J. Hole, *The Homes of the Working Classes* (1866), 1. 29.

[6] *Bye-laws as to New Streets and Buildings, etc.*, 1870, No. 8.

[7] *Parliamentary Debates*, 4th Ser., XCV, 14 June 1901, col. 392.

[8] These four quotations come from the letter books of the Local Government Board, P.R.O. M.H./12/15247–8.

[9] F. M. Lupton, *Housing Improvement: a Summary of Ten Years' Work in Leeds* (1906), 11.

[10] *Leeds Mercury*, 22 November 1851.

[11] Quoted in E. P. Hennock, *Fit and Proper Persons* (1973), 254.

[12] *Leeds Mercury*, 26 March 1867.

[13] *Ibid.*, 3 January 1876.

[14] *Yorkshire Post*, 20 March 1896.

[15] Sanitary Committee Minutes, 6 May 1890.

[16] *Ibid.*

[17] *Yorkshire Post*, 15 January 1892.

[18] *Leeds Mercury*, 4 December 1902.

[19] *Ibid.*, 2 September 1897.

[20] *Ibid.*, 4 December 1902.

[21] *Yorkshire Post*, 5 September 1901.

[22] *Leeds Mercury*, 8 July, 2 September 1897.

[23] *Ibid.*, 16 August 1851.

[24] *Ibid.*, 16 August 1851.

[25] *Ibid.*, 26 October 1860.

[26] *Ibid.*, 2 January 1868.

[27] *Ibid.*, 2 January 1868.

[28] *Report of the Select Committee on the Electric Lighting Bill*, P.P. (1882), X, evidence of the Town Clerk of Leeds, q. 814.

[29] *Leeds Mercury*, 14 August 1879.

[30] *Ibid.*, 10 February 1870.

[31] Leeds Electric Tramways, *The Electrical Review*, XLI (1897) 275.

[32] Report Book, January 1895.

[33] *Ibid.*, July 1889.

[34] *Leeds Mercury*, 4 July 1889.

[35] *Ibid.*, 7 October 1890.

[36] Report Book, July 1889.

[37] *The Telegraphic Journal and Electrical Review*, XXV, Part 2, 19 July 1889, 71.

[38] *Leeds Mercury*, 2 September 1897.

[39] S. Webb, *Socialism in England* (1890), especially 116–17.

BIBLIOGRAPHICAL NOTE

This chapter is based on sections of the author's doctoral thesis, 'Leeds Corporation, 1835–1905: a history of its environmental, social and administrative services' (unpublished Ph.D., University of Leeds, 1975) in which the intrepid will find a more detailed and fully documented account of municipal government than has been possible here. The research depended heavily upon the records of the corporation, currently held in the Civic Hall, Leeds, and I am most grateful to the officers of the corporation for being allowed free access to these records over a period of several years. The principal records comprise the proceedings of the council (from 1835), the report books (from 1842), the minutes of committees, and the series of annual reports of committees which begin in 1879. Council proceedings were not printed until 1897, but the annual reports of committees were printed from the start. Annual abstracts of accounts appeared in print regularly from 1870, but apart from those for 1867, 1870–1872, 1875 and 1877, the medical officer's annual reports appear annually only from 1890. All these printed sources are held in the reference department of Leeds City Library.

Volumes 263–265 of the Webb Local Government Collection, housed in the British Library of Economic and Political Science (at LSE), contain the research on Leeds Corporation done by the Webbs and their research assistants around 1900 as part of their projected but unwritten history of modern English local government. The letter books of the Local Government Board which contain the correspondence between the Board and Leeds Corporation between 1871 and 1896 are to be found in the Public Record Office, M.H. 12/15244–74. The House of Lords Record Office possesses the minutes of evidence occasioned by local Bills promoted by the corporation.

In addition to the works already cited in the footnotes, two which bear directly on the subject of this chapter are, A. Ravetz, *Model Estate: Planned Housing at Quarry Hill, Leeds* (1974), and G. C. Dickinson and C. J. Longley, 'The coming of cheap transport – a study of tramway fares on municipal systems in British provincial towns, 1900–1914', *Transport History*, VI (1973), 107–25. The author is preparing a short study of the Lands Clauses Consolidation Acts and the law of compulsory purchase *c.* 1770–1919 for the Standing Conference for English Local History to substantiate the claim made in section II of this chapter.

E. D. STEELE

Imperialism and Leeds
XIII *politics, c. 1850–1914*

I   Imperialism, understood as an amalgam of interest and sentiment, of trade, politics and religion, bolstered the hegemony of the urban patriciate by counteracting the divisions of class, sect and race within Leeds. Moreover, in Leeds as elsewhere, empire deeply affected the entire local community's relationship with the historic rulers of the nation, the landed class, whose primacy proved so enduring. Landed leadership was successfully adjusted to new political and social demands. The land-owning politicians, Gladstone included,[1] understood and employed the appeal of imperialism. It helped to contain the resentment and perpetuate the deference simultaneously felt towards them by the small number of wealthy and influential citizens who dominated the political life of Leeds, along with its economic and cultural life, until after 1914. These citizens constituted the patriciate, and were thought to be more prominent than their counterparts in other big towns.

Their influence was particularly evident in a near-monopoly of the town's parliamentary representation. Between 1832 and 1868 Leeds sent two members to the House of Commons under the Great Reform Act, and three from 1868 to 1885 after the Act of 1867 had introduced household suffrage and a lodger qualification to vote. The Redistribution of Seats Act, 1885, raised the number when it divided the town into five single-member constituencies. The foremost Liberal patrician of that epoch, James Kitson, did not like to see his town split up under the Act. 'It was something,' he grumbled, 'to fight a doubtful Leeds, but to win a couple of wards has no political significance. It is not a community that you represent but only a vote.'[2] Only seven of the twenty-five MPs who represented Leeds from 1850 to 1914 could not claim to be townsmen by family, if they had not made a career there. The patriciate furnished the majority of representatives with the preferred local background. The enlargement of the parliamentary franchise in 1867 not unexpectedly made little difference to patrician domination. It followed a generation's experience of the municipal ratepayer franchise that dated from 1835. The municipal electorate prior to 1868 had never shown much desire to loosen the leading families' hold upon civic business. It was a hold shared with others, some of whom aspired to equality, and also with petty bourgeois who seldom forgot that they were junior partners. The Leeds patriciate was an 'open aristocracy', resembling the landed interest but with greater social mobility. The origins and standing of the three MPs it provided at both general elections in 1910, the last in the period covered by this chapter, were typical of their predecessors. If their progressive Liberal views were rather less typical, they were still friends of empire. Rowland Barran (North Leeds) was managing director of his family's well known clothing firm and son of Sir John Barran, MP for undivided Leeds in 1876–85. Robert Armitage (Central Leeds), a substantial ironmaster and Lord Mayor in 1904–05, drew the electors' attention to his local lineage. The supporters of Edmund Harvey (West Leeds) did the same for him. He was the grandson of the Quaker pharmaceutical manufacturer and nationally respected humanitarian, Thomas Harvey.

Writing in 1848, the third Earl Fitzwilliam, an eminent Whig and a West Riding territorial magnate familiar with the complexities of political activity in one of the most industrially advanced regions of the country, recognised the ruling class in Leeds. Indeed, he made a nice distinction between 'the inferior aristocracy' and 'the high aristocracy of that great city'. It is significant that Fitzwilliam used the term 'aristocracy' of the uppermost layers of the middle class. He did so in a functional sense, for their position in urban society was comparable to that of the nobility and gentry in the countryside. He did not consider the 'high aristocracy ... Becketts ... Benyons ... Browns ... Gotts ... Marshalls ... families which have allied with some of the noblest in England' to be the equal in rank of those with whom they had contracted marriage alliances. The 1840s were years of sometimes acute tension between the landed class and that section, more especially, of the industrial middle class designated as 'inferior aristocracy' by Fitzwilliam. At the 1841 general election Dr Hook, the redoubtable High Church Vicar of Leeds, cut short a Continental trip to support in person William Beckett, of the Leeds banking house of that name, as Tory candidate for the constituency. Hook proclaimed that they were fighting for 'the cause of the Queen, the cause of the aristocracy, above all the cause of the poor, and', he added for good measure, '. . . the cause of God'.[3] The meaning of 'aristocracy' here was the usual one of titled landowners. It is important to remember that they had in the troubled second quarter of the century a very strong body of political adherents, in the Whig/Liberal as well as the Tory camp. The conviction that aristocratic government responsive to the pressure of a variety of interests served the country best was widespread. From the early 1850s many middle-class radicals of the previous decades noticeably began to moderate their opposition. They uttered stock criticisms of the landed grasp of national institutions with dwindling assurance. A general prosperity justified the late Sir Robert Peel's hope that his economic policies would render threats to his order ineffectual. Radicals whose wealth and authority had established them in the urban patriciate showed a conspicuous tendency to welcome the growing stability.

The relaxation of social tensions ran through all classes. The radical mayor of Leeds in 1858–59, Sir Peter Fairbairn, symbolised the quite altered mood before the end of the 1850s by two public acts at the start and close of his mayoralty. Speaking to the West Riding Trade Protection Society in October 1858, he censured John Bright for the language of speeches on parliamentary reform delivered in the course of his agitation of 1858–59. (The great demagogue was attempting to force the pace in the context of the first Derby–Disraeli reform Bill, then impending.) Fairbairn was a rich, self-made machine maker whose works had become one of the sights of Leeds. He displayed extreme sensitivity to the risk that attacking the landed interest might jeopardise the climate of confidence he appreciated by arousing hostility to large property of all kinds. Fairbairn's reply to Bright, and more specifically to his attack of 27 October at Birmingham upon traditional institutions, earned him the relieved gratitude of Queen Victoria and Prince Albert, no less. The Whig statesman Lord Clarendon wrote to his brother-in-law, '. . . the Royal Pair . . . were still more pleased, however, with the speech of their friend Fairbairn, the Mayor of Leeds, who, though a radical and risen from the ranks, pitched handsomely into J. Bright . . .'. On his side, Fairbairn was delighted with the honour the Queen had done him by conferring a knighthood when she visited Leeds earlier that year to open the new Town Hall. He told the businessmen of the West Riding Trade Protection Society, meeting at Barnsley, that 'the great object of Bright seemed to be to set class against class – the worst course . . . a politician could possibly adopt. He had seen this in every speech . . . Mr Bright had made for the last few years . . . since the repeal of the Corn Laws his occupation had gone.'[4]

Bright warmly admired the working democracy of the United States, and was given to comparing it with Britain under a reactionary landed oligarchy. Unlike Bright, Sir Peter had been in America, and like so many mid-Victorian businessmen had formed a highly unfavourable estimate of the political habits of Britain's main trading partner and the principal destination of British emigrants. He referred to the phenomenon of lynch law, profoundly shocking to almost all Englishmen, and to such notorious incidents as the savage personal assault in the Senate on Charles Sumner, an acquaintance of his, by an opponent who was also a member of Congress. Fairbairn denied that an American was freer than an Englishman when the expression of unpopular opinions might cost a man his life. While he was, of course, exaggerating, the reality of American politics on the eve of the civil war and in the decade that had seen the Know Nothing party's crude appeal to prejudice was sufficiently repellent to confirm the feelings of mingled superiority and apprehension on which he called. 'He could not sit silent,' declared Fairbairn, 'without answering that speech as one of the most mischievous ever uttered in an assembly of Englishmen.' Bright sought 'to set the working classes against the middle classes, and the middle classes against the aristocracy', but he, Fairbairn, wished his countrymen of different classes 'to be one family and live together in brotherly love'. His fellow radical, Edward Baines,[5] moved in the same direction during the '50s, and broadly aligned the editorial policy of his family newspaper, the *Leeds Mercury*, with the Palmerstonianism of *The Times*. For this he was taken to task by Richard Cobden, whose association with Bright needs no explanation. Baines, he wrote charitably or with unwonted tact, 'was *quite unconsciously* under the influence of an *immoral* clique which has the control of the *Times*'. In fact a famous journalist on the *Mercury*, Wemyss Reid, recorded that Edward Baines was, from about this time, 'very much disturbed when he found that the *Leeds Mercury* took a directly opposite view . . . to that of "the leading journal" '.[6] Besides, Baines had always been mindful of the political weight possessed by 'the great landowners . . . powerful and respected Liberals' of the West Riding, reeling off their names to Cobden in a letter of 1844. There were the Dukes of Devonshire and Norfolk, the Earls of Scarborough, Burlington and Thanet, Sir Edward Vavasour, Bart., Fawkes of Farnley Hall and, at their head, the third Earl Fitzwilliam. Yet Fitzwilliam resented Baines's intrusion into political management in the riding, despite the obvious usefulness to the landowners of such a persuasive voice as the *Mercury's*. The paper reached many more than those citizens of Leeds qualified to participate in a county election as 40*s* freeholders.[7]

Fairbairn ended his mayoralty on a high note with a civic banquet to Fitzwilliam's son, the fourth earl, who was, as his father had been, Lord Lieutenant of the West Riding, and a numerous attendance of landowners. It was conceived as a feast of goodwill to mark improved relations between landed and business wealth in the riding and to encourage their cordial co-operation in future. 'He believed,' said Sir Peter to his guests from town and country

> that they would do everything in their power to cement this union, and that the little prejudices – he did not say the antipathies – which had previously existed would be entirely obliterated. With this feeling he had invited the Lord Lieutenant as the head of the nobility and gentry of the Riding . . .

The fourth Earl Fitzwilliam was an inflexible aristocrat, and made it clear that he did not propose to admit business to equality with land in his part of Yorkshire, notwithstanding the concentration of industry there. '. . . although they met together on that occasion', he replied, 'they still maintained their own peculiar views, for that was a social meeting, intended to promote the harmony . . . good, and . . . benefit of all classes alike . . . They must educate themselves,' he observed pointedly, 'so as the better to understand their relative positions . . .' Swallowing the rebuff, Fairbairn persisted when he rose to speak again:

> . . . the Corporation rejoiced to see the aristocracy of the West Riding present . . . he hoped this would not be the last of such gatherings, but, on the contrary . . . the beginning of a new era, and that his successors would follow in his footsteps and endeavour to bring about similar gatherings of the Corporation of the Borough and the gentry of the . . . Riding.[8]

Fitzwilliam could afford his cool attitude. Edward Baines and the *Mercury* far outdid Fairbairn in the contemporary courtship of aristocracy, evincing little inclination to dispute their national and regional leadership.

The visits to Leeds in 1858 of two former Cabinet Ministers, Lord Monteagle, a connection by multiple intermarriage of the Marshalls, and Lord Carlisle, drew fulsome and revealing comments from the *Mercury*. Monteagle and Carlisle lectured to the Philosophical and Literary Society and the Mechanics' Institute respectively. '. . . even in England', the newspaper enthused, 'our fathers would not have dreamed of peers and statesmen . . . coming from their ancestral halls to deliver lectures to popular audiences in provincial towns, and exposing themselves to burgher criticism (except, indeed, when they wanted thereby to get into Parliament) . . .'. 1861 saw the advent of Lord Stanley, the Tory leader's son, and himself a likely future head of the party on his showing as Secretary of State for India in his father's short-lived administration of 1858–59. The event elicited the purest satisfaction from the *Mercury*:

> A STANLEY in Leeds Town Hall addressing a Mechanics' Institute, presents a combination of the *aristocratic* and the *popular* altogether in accordance with the spirit of our constitution. Few other countries could witness such a spectacle: no other age of our history has witnessed it: yet ... we believe the intertwining of the two elements ... makes the strongest social and political fabric in the world.

The most radical of mid-Victorian Leeds politicians, Councillor R. M. Carter, first elected as a Chartist, fell in with the prevailing mood, seconding the motion in the town council for an address to Lord Carlisle, whose benevolence and Yorkshire connections made him a favourite with the citizens. The compliment to distinguished visitors, said Carter, was a matter of form but certainly worth while in Carlisle's case, 'if ... only as an encouragement to other noblemen to imitate his example'. To Baines's paper, Carlisle personified the disposition of 'the highest class [to] devote themselves with such energy, such goodwill, such kindliness ... to the education of the lowest, and ... the improvement of all'. Therein probably lay, the *Mercury* declared, the secret of 'the genuine love of the aristocracy, deeply rooted among the English ...'[9]

When Dr Hook remarked in 1851 that 'the commercial interests ... represented by Cobden and his friends ... are ... as unpopular among the working class as the aristocrats', he was thinking of the Leeds working men who had been attracted to Chartism. As the 1850s wore on, and it became clear that the social atmosphere was fast changing for the better, comfortable middle-class radicals, like, of course, urban Whigs and Tories, remained apprehensive of the mass of the working class. The *Mercury* rejected the idea of household suffrage in 1859 with harsh candour: it would embrace 'classes so little qualified morally or mentally for its exercise'. Leeds Toryism, on the other hand, did contain an underrated element of populism advertised in the slogan of Christopher Kemplay, owner and editor of the *Leeds Intelligencer*, under whom the Tory paper stood for 'the Altar, the Throne, and the Cottage'. They were the sentiments of Richard Oastler, the Yorkshire factory reformer.[10] The teaching of Hook and the Evangelical vicar of St George's, the Rev. William Sinclair, was instrumental in developing this aspect of Toryism in the town. Thus, when Palmerston visited Leeds as Prime Minister in 1860, the collective mind was more sympathetic than might be supposed to the unambiguous statement of his views on domestic policy. The town council, with its majority of Liberals, Whiggish and radical, ventured to hint at the hope of some instalment of parliamentary reform.

> ... rapid and pen-stroke improvements [he answered] may suit despotic countries where ... the nation is compelled to obey ... impulses which

proceed from above, yet in a country like this, where public opinion is as powerful as . . . edicts of the governing authority, time and delay are often essentially necessary for the accomplishment of good, sound and useful legislation.

The growth of literacy had, in his view, only reinforced

the one peculiarity, perhaps, more than another, that belongs to the British character . . . the sentiment of gradations of rank . . . There is a general consciousness that in human society there must be degrees, and . . . preservation of that gradation is essential to the welfare of the country.

Commenting on this speech, the *Mercury* admitted that public opinion in Leeds and elsewhere was, to all appearances, predominantly with Palmerston in resisting a Reform Bill such as the paper favoured. The *Mercury* advocated a measure to strengthen the towns and their middle-class rulers but one 'so limited as not in the slightest . . . to warrant . . . fears of democracy'.[11]

Palmerston would not have enjoyed the success he did without creating a novel consciousness of empire. The community of feeling that quickly evolved as a result caused some well publicised alarm by its vigour, but it plainly fostered social solidarity. Near the end of the Crimean war Baines had attempted to excuse his increasing Palmerstonianism in a letter to Cobden: 'I would follow you through evil report and good report in the noble scheme for a general reduction of armaments . . . But . . . events of the last . . . years have compelled me to change my opinion – not of the desirableness of your scheme – but of its practicability . . .' How thoroughly he had revised his thinking was illustrated by the *Mercury's* leading article of May 1858 on the disputes between Britain and a minor European State, the kingdom of Naples:

There are two ways of making a request. The one is the whining manner of the English beggar; the other is the manner of the Spanish beggar in *Gil Blas*, which though modest in tone, was rendered formidable by a loaded blunderbuss. This is the way in which it becomes a great nation to make its requests . . .

There was no trace here of the inhibitions felt by the Tory Foreign Secretary of the moment, Lord Malmesbury, who considered that 'a gentleman might as well strike a woman as fire upon Naples'.[12] At the general election of 1865, Palmerston's final victory, G. S. Beecroft, Tory MP for the town since 1857 and formerly a partner in Kirkstall Forge, gave expression to the unease that was felt in Leeds, as generally, over the Prime Minister's methods with foreigners: 'He disapproved of England bullying small states, and currying to large powers.' It was a fair criticism of Palmerston's policy, but Beecroft's other speeches showed that it implied no fundamental disagreement. With few exceptions, the citizens of Leeds acquired a keen appreciation of the economic value of empire in the 1850s and '60s. This was true whether they thought that value should be realised through the triumphant imperialism of free trade, to which the *Mercury* committed itself, including the judicious use of force to open markets where appropriate, or through the discarded protectionism from which the *Intelligencer*, renamed the *Yorkshire Post* in 1866, was never wholeheartedly converted. Cobden, as member for the West Riding in 1847–57, watched the businessmen of Yorkshire's self-styled capital paying more attention to markets that were unlikely to be opened, or widened, except by means detestable in his eyes. 'I confess I look with suspicion and dread to all such projects,' he wrote to Baines about a Leeds meeting in 1849 on the economic penetration of Japan. 'Disguise it as they may, *force* is at the bottom of the plans for extending commerce through government interference . . .' He was quite right. Before long, the *Mercury*, at times, discussed even the giant dependency of India in terms that were a negation of the Cobdenite ideal of universal progress by the civilising agency of unfettered industry and trade. 'India,' the newspaper maintained in August 1860,

> is not a military position, nor a benevolent undertaking, it is a great commercial adventure . . . our main object, as a people, is not to civilize or to Christianize . . . We hold India, as a nation, for the sake of opening up its commerce, and so of extending and benefitting our own.[13]

The town council's address to Palmerston that same year saluted his imperial achievements with an allusion to his 'Civis Romanus sum' speech of 1850 in the House of Commons. By contrast, his speeches at Leeds were of 'a thoroughly practical kind'. At the Mechanics' Institute he did no more than remind hearers that they were reckoned amongst 'the people of the united empire'. At the local Ragged School Society he dwelt with compassionate realism on the subjection of a huge minority in Britain to 'the pinching effects of poverty, and all those afflictions which arise from such a condition'. He laid it down, justifiably in the free economy of the day, that 'The greater the community, the greater the development of industry . . . the greater the accumulation of population, the more will this class exist.' His recommended method of social control over the minority in irredeemable poverty was simple religious and moral instruction in youth: 'Teach them betimes the . . . importance of rules, regulations and order.' But Palmerstonianism and later imperialism to 1914 accepted that religion was not enough to keep the poverty-stricken from breaking out in desperation. There had to be a high level of economic activity to minimise destitution and avert the recurrence of so politically formidable an attempt to incite the working class, from the artisanate downwards, as Chartism. Although China persistently disappointed after and in spite of the Anglo-Chinese wars of 1856–60, India fulfilled the post-Mutiny expectations of her. In 1858, with the Mutiny not yet extinguished, the Bradford mill owner and radical W. E. Forster, then much involved in Leeds politics, informed the educated and prosperous membership of the town's Philosophical and Literary Society; 'India is to England as a large prize attached to a small schooner, which will . . . perhaps even sink her, unless manned and handled by a well chosen prize crew . . .' The analogy with successful commerce-raiding on the high seas was a singular one for such a God-fearing man to use shamelessly. Everybody nevertheless understood why imperial and quasi-imperial markets must be held and won in the era of free trade as in that of mercantilism. For political reasons Britain was far better placed in them than she found herself to be in genuinely independent foreign countries. Palmerstonianism drove the point home, and contrived to make it morally palatable by reference to a comprehensive national superiority upheld by the approval of Providence. A generation after Forster's lecture of 1858 another God-fearing man, W. L. Jackson, subsequently the first Lord Allerton, employed similarly resolute – if less startling — language at the 1885 election: 'England needs to say boldly . . . that nothing but the destruction of the empire itself shall see the severance of India from this country . . . India . . . was of the utmost importance to manufacturing England.' The embodiment of Toryism in the town, he represented it as an MP for over twenty years. He exemplified the combination of religious faith, patriotism and the economic virtues characteristic of someone who built up in Leeds the largest British firm of tanners.[14]

II The links between religion and empire seemed natural and right to most Englishmen in the last century and were not seriously queried before the 1914–18 war. The excesses of imperialism were more frequently and severely condemned by Nonconformity than by the established Church: but the Dissenting sects likewise took pride in British expansion, believing in its necessity and righteousness. Edward Baines was a devout Dissenter. So too was James Kitson, an avowed imperialist and the recipient of a baronetcy from Gladstone and of Leeds's second business peerage from Campbell-Bannerman —

W. L. Jackson's from the Tories being the first. Other prominent Dissenters who spoke up for empire may be picked out. They were John Barran, made a baronet by Lord Rosebery, and his son Rowland, both Liberal MPs for Leeds. Kitson, like the Barrans, was an industrial magnate in the town and, like Baines, a notable figure in the Liberal Party, locally and nationally. Kitson, indeed, reorganised the party in Leeds and long remained the power in it. He kept Leeds Liberalism mostly loyal to Gladstone during the party turmoil of 1886 and, as president, took the same line with the National Liberal Federation. A Unitarian, he belonged to the 'aristocracy of Dissent', whose significance derived from their quality, not from their numbers. Kitson's spiritual guide was the Rev. Charles Hargrove, minister of Mill Hill chapel from 1876 to 1912. The Unitarian ethic, as interpreted by Hargrove to his select congregation, diverged from the sect's old type of radicalism. Historically a self-conscious elite, the Unitarians were drawn to imperialism by its emphasis on duty and example. 'Your men and women,' wrote Kitson to Hargrove in 1896, 'have done a good deal at Leeds for the commerce which supports the people . . . social life which betters their lot, and . . . the political life which makes for manhood and . . . patriotism . . .' Reproving a friend who had doubts about the social outlook of their mutual creed, Hargrove held that 'the man of business, the politician, the town councillor, the striving tradesmen are of more importance to the world than the thieves and drunkards . . .'.[15] Leeds Protestants – Anglicans and Dissenters at all social levels – pursued a different approach to the responsibilities of empire, dictated by their unavoidable preoccupation with numbers, with the led as much as with the leaders.

This is not to suggest that the established Church, Wesleyans, Congregationalists and lesser denominations deliberately exploited imperial feeling for their own sectarian purposes. Protestantism was so completely integrated with the country's social and political fabric that the overall health of the nation indicated Divine satisfaction to those – and they were the rule – who looked for His blessing in the nation's fortunes as in their individual lives. 'There was no old age for a nation if only it preserved its religion, its industry, its social, its domestic virtues,' said the Rev. William Sinclair at the conclusion of his lengthy presidency of the Philosophical and Literary Society. National prosperity and greatness were held to testify to the God-given advantage of British Protestantism over a Catholicism associated with Continental reaction and Irish rebelliousness. Religious and political unreason, it was asserted, were bound to succumb to the ordered progress demonstrated by Britain. In the same way, Nonconformists felt themselves superior to the undisciplined

71   James Kitson, 1835–1911, first Baron Airedale (1907)

proliferation of sects in the United States, which seemed all of a piece with her turbulent politics. Lastly, the disarray of the organised unbelief that had appeared on the extreme wing of Chartism and in the 1848 revolutions on the Continent was a source of relief, though not of complacency. Dr Hook gave his Church most of the credit for a satisfactory state of affairs:

> Let it be . . . understood that England and the Church of England stand forward as a model to foreign nations and churches. As in our civil institutions we are an example to all continental governments, so is the principle of our Reformation . . . a model to all other communities of Christians.

The aristocratic Evangelical Sinclair, who cultivated and enjoyed particularly good relations with Dissent, was more tactful, comparing political corruption in France and America, and the results, with 'the noble condition of all our public men of all parties in this free and enlightened country'.[16] Churchman and Dissenter united in the determination to combat what he called 'the late outburst of anarchical and infidel opinions throughout Europe'. Cardinal Wiseman brought down upon himself the indignation of the Leeds and London press when he deplored this Protestant triumphalism to the town's Catholic Institute: '. . . humility is a social and national virtue, quite as much as . . . an individual one'. He specified 'the tone of those . . . who address the masses . . . flattering . . . almost . . . fawning . . . to make them exalt themselves above all other races . . .'.[17] He spoke, of course, as someone who was virtually an alien. The global spread of British authority and interests did not want for clerical encouragement and justification. The inhabitants of Leeds learned that their status as an imperial people transcended differences in home politics, and that the glorious prospect unfolding before them should diminish those differences. The Protestant clergy's inculcation of a popular imperial consciousness was achieved through the continuous exposition of shared obligations and benefits. They contributed to a mentality which the politicians at Westminster, and not least Palmerston, soon found a cause of recurring embarrassment, because of the public inclination to overestimate Britain's strength. When the middle classes, metropolitan and provincial, perceived her limitations as a great power they did not lose their enthusiasm for empire, but were concerned to make the most of what their country had and could hope to have.

A borough meeting to protest against 'Papal Aggression' in 1851 heard Dr Hook say, 'During the last three hundred years of Protestant ascendancy this little island had become the foremost nation in all the world. It possesses an empire upon which the sun never sets.' Speaking to the jubilee celebrations of the Society for the Propagation of the Gospel, he gave out a theme that was to run through Victorian and Edwardian imperialism: '. . . practical Christians', he said, '. . . are directing their minds to the one great point which is perhaps for the next fifty years to engage the attention of mankind — the more extended diffusion of the comforts of life'. Education, housing and sanitary reform would all better the existence of the poor in Britain, but 'It is for . . . this, that God has given us our colonial empire and our Indian empire.' Ten years passed, and W. E. Forster told a gathering of the unenfranchised at Bradford, 'India showed how the prosperity of the working classes of this country rested upon the good government of our Indian empire, and the absolute necessity, therefore of having all classes represented in Parliament.'[18] An imperial people might reasonably expect to be admitted to the pale of the constitution. The Australian colonies demonstrated the compatibility of manhood suffrage, the ballot and security of property, except for the very large holdings of the squattocracy. Councillor Carter presided in the Town Hall when the New South Wales radical, Henry Parkes, pointed out that his colony had all these recommendations. Even Baines's *Mercury* had conceded in 1858, writing about Victoria, that the operation of a popular electoral system there by men who 'received their political training in England, furnishes a strong argument in favour of reform here'. But what was possible in a new land, the paper contended, could not readily be adopted in a very old country. One of the constellation of dukes in Palmerston's administration, the Peelite Colonial Secretary, Newcastle, talked in 1862 of the loyalty and profitability to England of Australian democracy, and the *Mercury* followed cautiously in his wake. Its editorial acknowledged the inescapable relevance to Britain of 'peaceful revolution' in colonies of settlement, although echoing the duke's disapproval of the 'socialist democratic spirit' visible in several measures enacted by Australian parliaments. The paper had no reservations about endorsing Newcastle's claim that the British had attained a new perfection in the art of colonisation:

> While other nations – including that which declares most conspicuously the doctrine of popular sovereignty – are striving by force of arms to maintain a hated sway over protesting peoples, England keeps a vast colonial empire attached to her by the simple force of 'mutual affection and interest'.[19]

Religion reinforced ethnic and economic ties with British settlers, and it did more. Canon Worlledge, head of the Leeds clergy school, defended the Church of England at the 1885 general election, when disestablishment overshadowed other issues before the town's electorate, by citing its role in a Divine plan. The national Church, he said, 'affects the respect in which a vast ring of colonies and native races, dependent upon us, look at the Kingdom of God'. The unveiling of Queen Victoria's statue in Leeds moved the Vicar, Dr Bickersteth, to see in it 'not only a memorial of Imperial expression, but also . . . of missionary enterprise'. He optimistically viewed the recent Anglo-Japanese alliance as proof that 'the Empire had been raised by God to do for the Far East in the twentieth century what our islands did for Northern Europe in the eighth century'. The Church's success in the colonies of settlement during the preceding half-century had been offset by its failure to make anything like the hoped-for impression in India and China. Its still relatively undimmed confidence went back to the Palmerstonian epoch. A previous Vicar of Leeds, John Gott (1873–86), remarked, when instructing his wife to paste the newspaper report of a speech by Forster into their copy of J. R. Seeley's imperialist classic *The Expansion of England*, 'It is a sign of GOD's grace in England that He trusts us with a great mission and with the men to do it . . .'[20] Gott's predecessor, Canon Woodford (1868–73) thought the Church should tackle the education of the broad middle class between rich businessmen and small shopkeepers 'not . . . in the . . . narrow spirit of proselytising, but . . . to . . . qualify them for the imperial work which, in the providence of God, they were called to do'. The action of this class on the constituencies was indeed growing, if not 'with startling rapidity'.[21]

Solidarity in support of empire lessened but did not by any means overcome the divisions among Protestants. Alderman John Hope Shaw, a Whig three times mayor of Leeds between 1848 and 1852, was sanguine that the obligations of missionary work would do something to heal the rifts within the Church of England herself. The deep theological disagreements between Hook and Sinclair were mitigated by their zeal for the missions. These two, but especially Sinclair, combined with Dissenters to demand for Protestant missionaries in India, Anglican and Nonconformist, the greater freedom and official backing which the East India Company withheld, and which the home government, after terminating the company's rule in 1858, declined to grant in full. From the chair at a meeting to set up a Leeds branch of the Christian Vernacular Education Society, attended by leading Evangelical, Wesleyan and Congregationalist clergymen in the town, Edward Baines complained about the Palmerston administration's deliberately discouraging policy on the Christianisation of India. The Indian Mutiny had convinced statesmen of the terrible danger of exciting the religious fears of Hindu and Moslem. Uncomprehending, Baines argued that 'during the late Mutiny not a single native . . . converted to Christianity had . . . joined the Sepoys'. Moreover, he alleged, Western secular education had made 'deists or atheists' of those Indians exposed to it, and several had fought with the mutineers. 'If,' he finished, 'they were to attach the natives of India to this country by an enlightened sense of the supreme value of being attached to a great Christian country, they must give them a Christian education.' An awareness of the material rewards of empire was never far from the minds of these Leeds worthies as they talked about the missions. Alderman Hope Shaw reflected that solicitude for the welfare of souls in southern Africa 'might have an important influence on the commercial condition of Leeds'. The local branch of the interdenominational British and Foreign Bible Society heard Sinclair refer fervently to the Deity's intentions on the outcome of the second Anglo-Burmese war: 'Every day new causes arise for gratitude to God. A . . . kingdom . . . falls into our power.'[22] To some extent the success or failure of Christian endeavour abroad mattered less than its internal impact, described by Lord Shaftesbury to loud and prolonged applause from the Bible Society in Leeds. 'It might please God,' he surmised, '. . . to bless the agent instead of those to whom he was sent . . . to turn their missionary efforts rather to the good of England than of the heathen world, but he was sure of this . . . the secret of the greatness of our empire, that we have been called to this . . . work.' He exulted in a Christian imperialism, saying, 'we will bring him [an enemy] to meetings such as this and let him behold the vigour of the empire and the spiritual and intellectual muscle of old England . . .'.[23]

Dissenters did not want a godless empire: it was inconceivable to them. Increasingly, however, they were impatient of the established Church's legal and social privileges at home. The compromise in the Elementary Education Act of 1870, and the whole series of Gladstonian reforms designed to placate Nonconformity and stave off disestablishment in England, allayed but could not dissipate the swelling resentment of the Dissenting middle class. The 1902 Education Act intensified their discontent. Two Leeds Liberal MPs forcibly expressed the activists' temper. They were T. R. Leuty, a linen manufacturer, mayor in 1893–94 and member for East Leeds 1895–1900, and Rowland Barran, who captured bourgeois North Leeds from the Tories in the by-election of 1902 after they had held the seat since 1885. Dissent, always strong in Leeds, was now more confident and less deferential as the middle-class element in the chapels grew with the advance of the economy. 'Our forefathers would not be penalized out of existence,' said Leuty in the Commons, 'and Nonconformists would not be bribed out of existence . . .' His radical father's baronetcy did not restrain Rowland Barran from averring in the 'constitutional crisis' of 1909–11 that 'it is the abolition of the hereditary principle . . . the country is interested in'. For Anglicanism and aristocracy still stood or fell together in contemporary opinion. None of this meant any loss of faith in the empire. On the contrary, Barran suggested in his constituency that a reformed second chamber should have representatives from the colonies of settlement. '. . . then', he added, 'the radicals in the . . . Commons would have to look to their laurels, lest those in the second chamber were more radical than they were in the other'.[24] The most progressive of the Leeds patriciate to sit for the town, the Quaker Edmund Harvey, concerned himself with the other empire, the dependent territories inhabited by coloured peoples. His only objection to the Liberal government's boldly imperialist initiative in purchasing a controlling shareholding in the Anglo-Persian Oil Company was that the company did not operate in a colony. A nominally sovereign State, Persia was an arena for the dangerous rivalry of great powers.[25]

Outside the ranks of English Protestantism were two politically significant minorities, at once religious and racial. The first to arrive and the bigger, the Irish, took decades to accept, in some degree, that the empire might be theirs too. In contrast to the second minority, the Jews, they found it extremely hard to rise above the lowest occupational levels. Yet their electoral weight was appreciable. From necessity and choice they tended to congregate in certain neighbourhoods. Their history had politicised the race to an extent not matched by the English at or near the bottom of the social scale. The deep-seated unpopularity of their religion and country of origin perpetuated a comparative isolation inexplicable by economic tensions alone. They could not even count on the sympathy of their English co-religionists. The influx of Famine Irish in the late '40s and early '50s disturbed English Catholics. J. D. Holdforth was the son of James Holdforth, mayor in 1838–39 and England's first Catholic holder of the office since the Reformation. A silk manufacturer, the elder Holdsforth did his Christian duty by the poor Irish in and around his factory. By 1862 the son was writing to the *Mercury* to dissociate English Catholics 'of any respectability' from the pervasive Irish nationalism of the immigrants and their children. Soon the Fenian conspiracy and its itinerant clerical propagandist, Father Patrick Lavelle, president of the National Brotherhood of St Patrick, a front for Fenianism on both sides of the water, worked up this expatriate nationalism.[26] In 1867 Leeds beheld an imposing and effective show of force. Regular infantry and artillery, yeomanry cavalry and special constables sworn in for the emergency overawed the local Irish. The latter had been summoned by mysterious placards to stage a demonstration against the execution of the 'Manchester Martyrs'. The Leeds Irish afterwards conformed to the national pattern of these immigrants in politics following the setback to revolutionary nationalism in Britain and Ireland. They changed to constitutional methods. The small majorities frequent in Leeds elections compelled Liberals and Tories to treat them circumspectly. Gone were the days when Sinclair forecast, publicly and mistakenly, that 'the power of the priesthood was about to fall like that of Brahminism in India'. The enmity between English and Irish stayed close to the surface. It flared up memorably in 1885–86, embroiling the Irish first with the Liberals and then with the Tories as Parnell ordered his immigrant voters to switch from one English party to the other and back again. The Irish held the balance in the newly created working-class constituency of East Leeds. In obedience to Parnell, they secured the election of a Tory for a national Liberal seat at the 1885 general election, and put him out next year. The notice he was obliged to take of the Irish sorely tried James Kitson when he ran the Liberal Party in Leeds. He disliked and distrusted them, but needed to make common cause with them. His letters to Herbert Gladstone, MP for Leeds and West Leeds (1880–1910), speak of 'Irish malice' in his allies.[27] 'I do not wonder,' he confessed, 'at the Irish being oppressed; their tone raises the worst part of the English nature.' Kitson's conversion to Home Rule was decided by Gladstone's insistence that the safeguards devised to protect British interests would be adequate.[28]

The Leeds Irish eventually came to terms with Liberal imperialism. Leeds Jewry had no difficulty in doing so. The Jewish vote was a factor in Central Leeds. The rich Ashkenazi banker Sir Samuel Montagu fought the constituency for the Liberals in 1900 primarily, he said, 'to defend Jewish interests'. Recent immigrants, like most of those in other provincial cities affected and in the East End of London, the Jews of Leeds were the target of a prolonged agitation, partly economic and partly racial, which led to the Aliens Act of 1905. It was Sir Samuel's intention to show them that they could rely on the help and protection of the older Jewish immigration, successful in business and politics. He stressed his position as a Liberal supporter of the Tory government in the current South African war, desiring to make 'loyal British subjects' of the Afrikaners. Sir Samuel did not win the seat, but his fight was a milestone in the achievement of recognition and security by Leeds Jewry. Campaigning for Robert Armitage at the second general election of 1910, Rabbi Manson of the New Briggate synagogue pointed to the presence of three Jewish Ministers in the Liberal government. Their selection enhanced the standing of the minority locally.[29]

III Late Victorian and Edwardian imperialism was only the Palmerstonian kind under pressure. When a young MP, Lord Salisbury sharply criticised Palmerston's conduct of British external policy and thereby got the reputation of being somewhat of a 'Little Englander', which he has never quite lost. When he was about to become Prime Minister for the third time, his realistic speech on empire and trade at Bradford in May 1895 affirmed, in sombre vein, that profit and power were more than ever inseparable. He frankly recognised that the country's fate lay with its businessmen and the political will of a mass electorate non-existent in Palmerston's day. James Kitson said in 1887 at the dinner to celebrate his baronetcy, 'the time had come ... when captains of industry ... had a right to these honours'. Perhaps he really believed that 'a new order of men will rule', nationally, as he observed with private relish to Herbert Gladstone.[30] But such aspiring rulers did not only blunt the edge of their determination by eagerness to obtain hereditary titles from landed Prime Ministers like W. E. Gladstone and Salisbury. They were as fundamentally interested as the landowners in the collaboration of classes throughout English society. Salisbury could safely tell businessmen that the crucial decisions which he and his kind would implement depended upon them and the industrial working class. Political disagreements might be heated. They were about means rather than ends. Empire was the proof of this. Notwithstanding their acrid discussions over the reintroduction of protective tariffs, Tory and Liberal imperialists dealt efficiently with the apparent threat from the Labour movement. James O'Grady, from 1906 Leeds's first Labour MP, was not at all exceptional in being impelled to state: '. . . the expansion of Empire and the acquisition of markets . . . I have not a word to say against that.'[31]

Salisbury spoke as a free-trader. The party which he headed did not revive protection in earnest until after his retirement in 1902. He reminded his audience how England had defeated Napoleon I's European blockade by expanding her trade with other continents. 'Many men,' he remarked, 'have dreamt that it would be a pleasant thing ... to close the capital account of ... empire and to add no further to its responsibilities.' He proceeded to dismiss their illusions: '. . . that is not the condition which fortune or the evolution of the world's course has assigned to the development of our prosperity'. Faced with the rising tariff barriers of Europe and America, he continued, 'we must be prepared to take the requisite measures to open new markets for ourselves among the half-civilized or uncivilized nations of the globe, and . . . not be afraid if that effort which is vital to our industries should bring with it new responsibilities of Empire and government'. These conditions should constantly inform and guide the actions 'of the great captains of industry in towns such as this, where the forces of industry are created and strengthened'. But he warned those provincial leaders that the freedom to act in accordance with his counsel was conditional upon 'an adequate popular power behind'. Finally, he besought them not to think of empire as 'a mere question of sentiment'. 'It is,' he said with palpable sincerity, 'a question that involves our prosperity and . . . commercial existence to the last extent . . . a question upon which the deciding voice of the commercial and industrial classes will have to pronounce, whether our prosperity is to go on . . . increasing, or . . . to decline.' Only thus might the maintenance and betterment of working-class living standards be ensured without an unacceptable degree of State intervention.[32]

The realisation that Africa and the Far East, the two areas to which Salisbury called attention in his Bradford speech, could not fulfil the hopes of them pushed the Tories towards tariff reform instead. Not before Leeds Liberals had attacked Toryism at the 1900 general election for failing, through preoccupation with the South African war, to seize the opportunities presented as the great powers bargained over a moribund China.[33] Leeds Toryism displayed a stubborn fondness for protection, from Lord Derby's time through Disraeli's to its reappearance in the forefront of politics. Gladstone chose Leeds for a speech to counter the slowly reviving issue in 1881, when the contemporary recession produced a demand for some defensive moves against imports. W. St J. Wheelhouse, the Leeds Tory barrister and municipal politician returned to Parliament for the town in 1868–80, was a persistent sceptic with regard to free trade. He resurrected the idea of an imperial customs union after Disraeli had dropped the notion, aired in his Crystal Palace speech, as not being practical politics. W. L. Jackson, who displaced Wheelhouse as Tory member for Leeds, was no enthusiast for 'Fair Trade', the current euphemism for protection. Jackson, however, told the Commons that he could not ignore a petition signed by 25,000 people in Leeds. Believing that no one seriously wished to revert to a system of tariffs, he nevertheless concluded that 'if we did not occasionally speak out and make it known that we intended, if need be, to protect ourselves, we should find ourselves left behind in the commercial race'. The prospective imposition of a 400 per cent duty on nine-tenths of the leather exported to France evidently prompted his cautious protest. He also mentioned the troubles of the Leeds engineering employers, 'some of the most eminent . . . in England', with the protectionism written into French patent law.[34] Jackson's place in Leeds Toryism almost rivalled Kitson's in the town's Liberalism. His reluctance to come out for tariff reform embarrassed its proponents. The declaration in the midst of the heated campaign preceding the election of January 1910 that 'Leeds was honoured by having two Lords' commanded practically universal assent.[35] Their townsmen, of either party, listened respectfully to Allerton (Jackson) and Airedale (Kitson). Allerton's late conversion was attributable to party pressure and to foreign competition where it was least expected in his own business. India was the main source of supply for the firm's raw material. 'Germany,' complained Allerton to an election meeting in December 1909, 'bought hides in Calcutta which we could not afford ... but she was enabled to do so because German manufacturers started with protection.' As for Kitson, whose extensive interests were concentrated in iron, steel and engineering, he conceded that some sectors of those trades had been hard hit by imports. He ascribed their plight to lagging behind in 'the progress of invention'. He cited the wages paid to his own workers as evidence of their, and his, ability to prosper under free trade. In another contribution to the debate he argued that two-thirds of exported iron and steel products went outside the formal empire.[36]

His case was in no sense anti-imperialist. He opposed Chamberlain's plans, among other reasons, because of their preoccupation with the colonies of settlement. He classed India with Argentina, noting that the former provided one-third of the imperial market for iron and steel products. Liberal imperialists, in fact, continued to put their trust and money in the exploitation of 'half-civilized or uncivilized nations'. During the general election of 1909–10 Lord Airedale treated the voters of West Leeds to a lucid exposition of the relationship between industrial and finance capital in Anglo-Argentine trade, taken as an example. In part, the financing of Argentine purchases of locomotives built in the town was effected in Leeds herself. 'They thus got their capital back,' he commented, 'and all he could say was that the more capital ... sent out of this country, the better ... for England. At present ... the Argentine was practically keeping some ... English workshops going.' He was afraid the flow of capital would not stop the South American republic from preferring German competitors for orders in the event of a British duty on her wheat. Winding up with a heartfelt plea, 'he begged his hearers to stick to Free Trade, reject the dangerous Tariff Reform scheme, and return Harvey'. The Unitarian minister of Holbeck was on the platform to signify the concurrence of religion.[37] Kitson and Co. employed a good number of West Leeds voters. With the business doing well, they had a sufficient incentive to heed Lord Airedale's advice. The same was true of Robert Armitage's employees at the Farnley Ironworks. The many Jewish immigrant hands in Rowland Barran's clothing firm voted Liberal, irrespective of the state of trade, if they had the vote. The verdict of Leeds in the three general elections of 1906 and January and December 1910 favoured the Liberals, who, by arrangement with Labour in East Leeds, thrice excluded the Tories from all five seats. The losing but substantial Tory vote reflected the deepening fears for national and imperial welfare and the anxieties of businesses that were not doing so well. As the Liberals persuaded a decisive majority of voters in Leeds that they could still make the hallowed economic formula work, so they vindicated their record on the integrity of the empire and its defences.

72   W. L. Jackson, 1840–1917, first Baron Allerton (1902)

Rowland Barran ridiculed Tory attempts to depict the Liberals as lacking in enthusiasm for the empire. He instanced reconciliation with the Afrikaners in South Africa, and the self-governing colonies' greater willingness to help with the cost of 'the Imperial Navy'. The often explicit fear of Germany was something different, on which the Tories tried to capitalise. The following exchange between Lord Allerton and a working man occurred in the 1909–10 campaign. 'You can't shout Rule Britannia on eighteen bob a week,' cried the humble critic, to whom his lordship replied crushingly, 'You had better shout Rule Britannia on eighteen bob a week than Rule Somebody Else.' The Liberals met this line of attack by the naval programme for which the Lloyd George budget of 1909 made provision. The coming of war in 1914 was natural in the mental climate that had developed from the late 1870s, if not earlier. By 1910 a leading engineering employer, R. H. Fowler, chairman of the family firm, the big Leeds Steam Plough Works, was telling his workpeople, 'Commerce is war . . .' He sent out an open letter warning them to vote for tariff reform if they cared about their wages and jobs.[38] J. D. Birchall, Tory candidate for North Leeds in the Edwardian general elections and son of an important cloth manufacturer in the town, typified the apprehensiveness. He joined to his fears, again typically, the old Tory dread of Irish liberty. He quoted an appeal by the extreme Irish nationalist, Major John MacBride, who had fought with the Boers in South Africa. The Major, Birchall asked the electors to remember, wanted to discourage Irishmen from enlistment in 'the "degraded" British Army' because their boycott 'would be making the path smooth for the conquest of England by Germany'. Nothing divided Leeds politicians and voters more clearly than the Irish question, which raised the problems of empire in an acute form. Ireland was emphatically seen as an imperial issue. The Irish then seemed incorrigibly alien. The *Mercury* of 1895 reported, with perceptible astonishment, a Marian festival in a working-class suburb of Leeds: 'As the procession wended its way along the principal streets, the Rosary was recited . . . Hymns . . . sung, and we felt for the time being as if a sudden transformation into a Roman Catholic country had taken place.'[39]

The Liberals reckoned with the ineluctable truth that 'most of the masses in this district . . . judge all Irishmen far too much by the standard of those alongside . . . whom they work . . . Their dislike to Irishmen often amounts to bitterness, and blinds them, or, rather, makes them indifferent about . . . Irish affairs.' This was the expert opinion of J. S. Mathers, one of Kitson's two chief associates in the reorganisation of their party in Leeds. A grave complication of the difficult situation was the articulate hostility of the immigrants to everything British. It lent credibility to such attacks on the Liberals and the Irish as those at the Leeds Conservatives' rally to set their campaign going in 1880. R. M. Tennant, a very wealthy brewer in the town and its junior Tory MP since 1874, struck the right chord in claiming that 'had Lord Palmerston lived now, he would have been far more a Conservative than a Liberal . . .'. Beneath the rhetoric, the greatest difference between Palmerstonian and Gladstonian Liberalism consisted in their attitudes to Ireland. Councillor George

Irwin, a Protestant businessman of Ulster origin long settled in Leeds, indulged a style which the *Yorkshire Post* allowed to have been 'a little florid'. Let them not,' he exclaimed, 'with sacrilegious hands . . . tear the red and white cross of St. Patrick . . . emblazoned . . . on . . . the Union Jack.' He specially urged the Anglican clergy 'to remember that the gowns they wore did not prevent them from being Englishmen'. If Irwin had 'the poetic Irish temperament', he was a talented political organiser – the Tory equivalent of Mathers – whose work for the party earned him a knighthood.[40] Religion and nationalism were a potent mixture for the English too. The Rev. John Gott, in his almost episcopal post as Vicar of Leeds, could not be an unashamed partisan. Everyone knew, however, where his sympathies lay. While incumbent at Bramley in 1869 he had said to the local Conservative Working Men's Association, as legislation disestablishing his Church in Ireland went through Parliament: '. . . Conservatism was the great thing that would save this country, but only if they supported it with the whole of their understanding, intelligence and energy of character.'[41]

In 1880 the Tory alarm seemed overdone. Not so in 1886, when Lord Salisbury delivered a keynote speech in the town. He played on the working-class antagonism to Irish competition for employment in a recession. Tory tactics drove Liberals and Irish closer to each other. First the Irish nationalists of Leeds turned fiercely on the Labour movement, itself strongly Irish, when it threatened the common front against Toryism and its Liberal Unionist allies. H. H. Champion, the ex-army officer prominent in the early Labour movement, vented his shock and disgust in a letter to *The Times* testifying how Labour's Irish candidate in the South Leeds by-election of 1892 fared at the hands of Irishmen. 'As I have never had an opportunity,' he wrote, 'of seeing political meetings of Hottentots, I cannot say how far it would be a libel on those inhabitants of Africa to compare them to . . . Leeds Irishmen.' The candidate did not go to the poll. Then it appears that the Irish were gratified in 1900 by the adverse reactions of many Liberals to their party's endorsement of Rochfort Maguire in East Leeds. He was a renegade nationalist and a trusted colleague of Cecil Rhodes.[42] From 1906 the constituency returned in O'Grady a Labour man with Liberal support who declared himself an Irish nationalist.[43] Leeds Jewry had an easier time because it was never anti-British. The Jewish vote rose as immigrants from Tsarist Russia took out naturalisation papers. The response of both Tories and Liberals to popular anti-semitism was uncomfortable and evasive, although the Tories promised and at length instituted control of immigration and the Liberals left the Aliens Act on the statute book when they came to power. 'Let them vote for . . . the greatest lovers of the Jews,' a speaker, himself a Jew, candidly advised a Jewish public meeting before the 1906 election. The Liberals got and kept the Jewish vote, by and large. The Jews had good friends in Leeds, such as the Barrans, who employed these late Victorian and Edwardian immigrants very profitably.[44] The immigrants quickly gave proof in trade of their legendary resourcefulness. Jews and Irish alike had to adapt to the political and economic realities of a town in which, an authoritative witness before the Royal Commission on Education of 1886–87 agreed, 'the population is very much more divided between men of large property and the working classes than in many parts of the kingdom'.[45]

NOTES

[1] E. D. Steele, 'Gladstone and Ireland', *Irish Historical Studies*, XVII (1970), 86 and n. 118.

[2] J. Kitson to H. J. Gladstone, 21 February 1885, B.L. Add. MSS, 46027.

[3] Earl Fitzwilliam to Sir C. E. Eardley, 25 November 1848, quoted in F. M. L. Thompson, 'Whigs and Liberals in the West Riding, 1830–1860', *English Historical Review*, LXXIV (1959), 234; *Leeds Intelligencer*, 3 July 1841.

[4] Lord Clarendon to Sir G. C. Lewis, 5 November 1858, in Sir H. Maxwell, *The Life and Letters of George William Frederick, Fourth Earl of Clarendon* (1913), II, 162–4; *The Times*, 2 November 1858.

[5] Throughout this chapter the Edward Baines in question is the younger of that name.

[6] *Ibid.*; R. Cobden to E. Baines, 19 May 1860, B.L. Add. MSS, 43664; S. J. Reid (ed.), *Memoirs of Sir Wemyss Reid* (1905), 170.

[7] E. Baines to R. Cobden, 12 November 1844, B.L. Add. MSS, 43664.

[8] *Leeds Intelligencer*, 3 September 1859.

[9] *Leeds Mercury*, 16 January 1858; 19, 17, 18 October 1861.

[10] Dr W. F. Hook to Sir W. Page Wood, December 1851, in W. R. W. Stephens, *The Life and Letters of Walter Farquhar Hook* (1878), II, 351; *Leeds Mercury*, 8 January 1859; *Yorkshire Post*, 28 May 1872.

[11] *Leeds Mercury*, 27 October 1860; E. Baines to Alexander Ritchie, Baines Papers (Leeds city archives), 45/15.

[12] E. Baines to R. Cobden, 19 January 1856, B.L. Add. MSS, 43664; *Leeds Mercury*, 29 May 1858; Lord Malmesbury, *Memoirs of an Ex-Minister: an Autobiography*, new edn. (1885), 384, diary entry for 12 November 1856.

[13] *Leeds Intelligencer*, 11 July 1865; R. Cobden to E. Baines, 4 April 1849, B.L. Add. MSS, 43664; *Leeds Mercury*, 16 August 1860.

[14] *Ibid.*, 27 October 1860, 14 April 1858; *Yorkshire Post*, 22, 25 September 1885.

[15] See A. W. Roberts, 'Leeds Liberalism and late Victorian politics', *Northern History*, V (1970), on the activities of figures mentioned in this paragraph; J. Kitson to the Rev. C. Hargrove, 1896, in L. P. Jacks, *From Authority to Freedom: the Spiritual Pilgrimage of Charles Hargrove*, (1920), 306; the Rev. C. Hargrove to L. P. Jacks, 1896, *ibid.*, 298.

[16] *Leeds Intelligencer*, 23 March, 5 October, 3 August 1850.

[17] *Ibid.*, 30 November 1850, 5 February 1853.

[18] *Ibid.*, 29 March, 6 December 1851; *Leeds Mercury*, 9 February 1861.

[19] *Ibid.*, 22 November 1861, 18 December 1858, 14 February 1862, where the

northern states of the USA are the aggressive democracy cited.

[20] *Yorkshire Post*, 19 November 1885, 28 November 1905; the Rev. J. Gott to his wife, 16 March 1885, in A. J. Worlledge (ed.), *The Letters of Bishop Gott* (1919), 101.

[21] *Yorkshire Post*, 20 November 1873.

[22] *Leeds Mercury*, 13 October 1860; *Leeds Intelligencer*, 5 February, 22 October 1853.

[23] *Leeds Mercury*, 23 October 1858.

[24] Hansard (4th ser.), XLVII, cols. 979–80 (18 May 1897); *ibid.* (5th ser.), XVI, cols. 955 ff. (11 April 1910); *Leeds Mercury*, 24 November 1910.

[25] Hansard (5th ser.), LXIII, cols. 1206–8 (17 June 1914).

[26] *Leeds Mercury*, 12 February 1862; Archbishop Cullen to Dr P. F. Moran, 3 July 1864, Cullen Papers (Dublin diocesan archives), on Fr. Lavelle in Leeds; E. D. Steele, 'The Irish presence in the north of England, 1850–1914', *Northern History*, XII (1976), 229–32.

[27] *The Times*, 13, 14, 16 December 1867; *Leeds Intelligencer*, 29 November 1851; J. Kitson to H. J. Gladstone, 11 May 1881, B.L. Add. MSS, 46027.

[28] J. Kitson to H. J. Gladstone, 2 May 1881, *ibid.*; *Leeds Mercury*, 4 May 1886.

[29] *Ibid.*, 1 October 1900, 28 November 1910.

[30] *Yorkshire Post*, 24 May 1895; *Leeds Mercury*, 3 February 1887; J. Kitson to H. J. Gladstone, 20 March 1883, B.L. Add. MSS, 46027.

[31] Hansard (5th ser.), II, cols. 1708 ff. (23 March 1909).

[32] *Yorkshire Post*, 24 May 1895; compare A. J. P. Taylor, *Essays in English History*, paperback edn. (1976), 122–28.

[33] *Leeds Mercury*, 25, 26, 28, 29 September 1900; Leeds does not seem to fit Dr Henry Pelling's generalisations about this election in *Popular Politics and Society in late Victorian Britain* (1968), ch. 5.

[34] D. W. R. Bahlman (ed.), *The Diary of Sir Edward Walter Hamilton* (1972), I, 174, 11 October 1881; Hansard (3rd ser.), CCL, cols. 1604 ff. (13 February 1880); *ibid.*, CCLXIV, cols. 1765 ff. (12 August 1881).

[35] *Yorkshire Post*, 13 January 1910, the speaker was J. R. Flitch, a leather manufacturer, at a Tory meeting in Central Leeds.

[36] *Ibid.*, 14 December 1909; Hansard (4th ser.), CXXIX, cols. 801 ff. (9 February 1904); *ibid.*, CLIII, cols. 949 ff. (12 March 1906).

[37] *Leeds Mercury*, 31 December 1909.

[38] *Ibid.*, 17 December 1909; *Yorkshire Post*, 31 December 1909, 14 January 1910.

[39] *Ibid.*, 4 January 1910; *Leeds Mercury*, 11 May 1895.

[40] J. S. Mathers to H. J. Gladstone, 10 June 1881, B.L. Add. MSS, 46039; *Yorkshire Post*, 17 March 1880, 12 June 1899, Sir George Irwin's obituary.

[41] Nigel Yates, 'Leeds and the Oxford Movement', *Thoresby Soc.*, LV (1975), 11; *Yorkshire Post*, 18 March 1869.

[42] *Leeds Mercury*, 19 June 1886; *The Times*, 19 September 1892; *Yorkshire Post*, 29 September 1900.

[43] Hansard (5th ser.), XXXIX, col. 943 (12 June 1912).

[44] *Yorkshire Post*, 10 January 1906; J. Thomas, 'A history of the Leeds clothing industry', *Yorkshire Bulletin of Economic and Social Research*, Occasional Paper No. 1 (1955), 10, and E. Krausz, *Leeds Jewry: its History and Social Structure* (1964), 13.

[45] *Second Report of the Royal Commission on Education*, P.P. (1887), XXIX, 815, q. and a. 37, 705, evidence of Wesley Lee, clerk to the Leeds School Board. I am grateful for the ready assistance of Mr D. Cox, the University Librarian, and Mr P. S. Morrish, Sub-librarian, at Leeds, without whom this essay could not well have

been written. I have also to thank those institutions which allowed me to use the MSS consulted.

BIBLIOGRAPHICAL NOTE

The main source, unquestionably, for nineteenth-century Leeds history is its newspaper press. Editorial comment, although certainly important, is much less informative than the reports of the proceedings at meetings of every kind. The two famous papers used in this short essay, the *Leeds Mercury* and the *Leeds Intelligencer* (from 1866 the *Yorkshire Post*), may be supplemented, very selectively, by other journals published in the town, particularly the *Leeds Times* and *Leeds Express*. Microfilms or original copies of the *Mercury* and the *Intelligencer/Yorkshire Post* are available between the Central and University Libraries in Leeds. Complete series of the minor publications are less easy to come by; failing the Leeds libraries, a reader must have recourse to the newspaper collection of the British Library kept at Colindale in north-west London. The utterances of Leeds MPs in the Commons, infrequent but sometimes revealing, are of course preserved in Hansard. Several manuscript collections have proved valuable. While the Kitson and Baines papers in the Leeds City Archives are fragmentary, the (W. E.) Gladstone papers, the Viscount (Herbert) Gladstone papers and the Cobden papers in the Department of Manuscripts of the British Library all contain correspondence – extensive in the case of the Viscount Gladstone papers – that is relevant. The *Bibliography of British History*, 1851–1914 (1976), edited by Professor H. J. Hanham, lists a good selection on pp. 112–15 from the massive literature on imperialism in this period. The index should be consulted under 'Leeds' for books and articles on the town, which appear under a variety of headings scattered through the volume. Professor Hanham's bibliography does not include the latest work indispensable to a student of Leeds history, notably Dr Derek Fraser's essay on Edward Baines junior, in Patricia Hollis (ed.), *Pressure from Without in early Victorian England* (1974), and his authoritative monograph *Urban Politics in Victorian England: the Structure of Politics in Victorian Cities* (1976).

T. WOODHOUSE

XIV   *The working class*

One of the most exciting developments in the writing of history over the past twenty years has been the growing interest in labour history, or more broadly in social history, often in the form of local or regional studies.[1] Yet there is no comprehensive or systematic social history of Leeds, and the history of the working-class community has failed to receive the attention it merits.

This chapter aims only to review the major features of labour history up to 1914. In particular, it looks at the politics of the labour movement between 1880 and 1914 in order to analyse the crucial development of that period, the emergence of a distinct Labour Party.

The main question is: how and why did working-class politics change between 1880 and 1914? Before it can be answered a number of other tasks have to be undertaken. First, a general survey of working-class history, highlighting Chartist activity in the first half of the nineteenth century and, in the third quarter, the developing dominance of the Liberal Party over the labour movement. Liberal dominance came under threat from the mid and late 1880s, a process to be seen in the pattern of parliamentary and municipal election results. What emerged was a new and politically independent labour movement which by 1914 had established an important influence on the city's politics. An attempt is made to understand the nature of the new movement, particularly in three areas: the role of socialist ideas, personalities and organisations in the labour movement between 1880 and 1914; the relationship between socialist and non-socialist activity in the labour movement, and the persistence of everyday trade union attitudes on pay, conditions and unemployment to the exclusion of broader socialist objectives centred on the struggle between the classes for power; and living conditions, that is, the day-to-day reality in which any scheme of politics that was to be relevant to working people had to be rooted.

I   According to Harrison, there were distinctive economic and social factors at work in Leeds which tended to make its working class different from comparable communities in other parts of the West Riding. The most usual distinction is that a rapidly expanding commercial and manufacturing community helped to produce a relatively well protected working class which, except in periods of acute trade depression, was normally prosperous. Thus George Goldie, the medical officer of health, in evidence to the Royal Commission on Housing, attributed what he regarded as the good housing conditions of the city to

> the opulence of the working classes in Leeds, there are a great many trades and we never suffer from a panic . . . They are all well to do people, all people earning good wages . . .
> There is no substratum that is not pretty well off? – Not of that poverty of which I have seen cases twenty years ago in the East End of London; we have not that wretched squalor . . .[2]

A moderate standard of living, according to contemporary opinion, produced a tendency towards moderate politics. Radicalism and socialism displayed an early paradox: Leeds, 'second only to Manchester as a centre of Radical and working class movements in the north . . .',[3] was nevertheless a place where Chartism failed to achieve the mass involvement experienced in Bradford and other parts of the West Riding.

Despite working-class intellectuals of the quality of John Francis Bray[4] searching for alternative social values, and the existence of a flourishing radical press, Leeds remained unadventurous and moderate. Fraser, in a more recent study, has significantly deepened and developed Harrison's account and in paying closer attention to the impact of Chartism on local politics has established its significance as a precursor of experiments in local democracy. For Fraser much of the significance of Chartism lay in its fundamental acceptance of parliamentary government. Participation in local administration, as in Leeds, provided an opportunity to demonstrate responsibility and respectability, and this in turn laid the foundation of renewed agitation for the extension of the parliamentary franchise in the 1860s. Leeds had an influence not in pioneering the revolutionary side of Chartism (even though the 'physical force' leader, Feargus O'Connor, and his paper, *The Northern Star*, operated from the town) so much as in consolidating faith in liberal democracy among working people.[5]

When we come to the political events of the 1880s the same paradox emerges. The labour movement consisted, on the one hand, of a radical and dynamic group with strong socialist convictions and vision, and on the other, of working-class organisations cautious and slow to move. The Socialist League, set up by Tom Maguire, became from 1885 a centre for discussing the ideas associated with William Morris and the *Commonweal* newspaper. Indeed, the League spread its influence throughout the West Riding. Yet 'Leeds was to provide a remarkable example of arrested development'.[6]

What were the barriers the labour movement faced? What informed and directed its activities? The Leeds labour movement, as it developed in the 1880s, can be adequately understood only in the context of its political and cultural experience during the previous thirty years. Paramount in that experience was the power of Leeds Liberalism.

II   Politically there was no independent labour movement in Leeds from mid-century; the fundamental rejection of capitalism, the search for alternatives characteristic of Bray and the co-operators in the 1830s appear to have receded completely. There was a failure to sustain either an alternative view of society, or a movement acting, or aspiring to act, for and with the working class as a whole.

There has been much controversy about the process by which the working class was accommodated within the framework of liberal capitalist values. It is clear that in Leeds middle-class cultural and political dominance was very important. Harrison describes the general aim of the strong Nonconformist middle class as being to break up the old popular culture (considered undisciplined and wasteful) and to provide instead a formal, literary, instructed one based on the three Rs.[7] The mechanics' institutes, for example, were intended *inter alia* to inculcate sound principles of liberal political economy, especially the idea that the worker should be enabled to look after his own interests and to advance by education, temperance and moral restraint.

Marxists have used the concept of the labour aristocracy to explain why working people in Victorian and Edwardian England failed to develop a full revolutionary consciousness. In pointing to the emergence of a 'respectable' upper stratum it clearly has some relevance to Leeds. Edward Baines gave his opinion that it would be safe to allow the franchise to 'the better portion of the working classes ... earning good wages ... skilled and educated men ...', amounting to one-tenth of the town's working class, that is, 'the better portion of the working classes' who had proved themselves by participation in the 'twenty-three mechanics' institutes, the savings banks, friendly societies, temperance, building, and church and charitable societies'.[8]

In the 1860s and 1870s the labour movement consisted largely of skilled trades organised in small societies, a good proportion of whose membership participated in the range of 'improving' activities of which Baines approved. It is important to understand the political function of this group, and we must disagree with the little that has been written about it.[9] Steele has misunderstood the concept of the labour aristocracy as used by Marxist historians:

> What Marxist historians have taught us to call — it is hyperbole — the 'aristocracy of labour' . . . expected to have political debate directed at them . . . to know that their employers felt it a duty to keep them in work. If he was broadly satisfied in these respects the 'labour aristocrat' – and still less the ordinary labourer – was not the intensely political animal that some Marxist historians would have him be. . . .[10]

John Foster, in the best account of the formation of a labour aristocracy, has shown how it served to embed respect for liberal authority systems and values among working people and among the institutions of the labour movement.[11] For Marxist historians the labour aristocracy is not the most advanced political section of the working class, although it may be the most active politically. A labour aristocracy was well entrenched in 1880, and continued to resist socialist and independent labour ideas well into the twentieth century. But resistance to socialist ideas cannot be explained adequately by applying the concept of the labour aristocracy as it has been used so far. Complex processes of social control were at work. The effect of popular leisure and cultural activities, the role of the family, sexual roles, the effect of the State education system, and the influence of socialisation within the workplace are all subjects needing research at the local and regional level.[12]

Clear evidence of working-class assimilation of liberal political values may be seen in the way the labour movement and Liberal politics drew together in the third quarter of the nineteenth century. By the mid-1850s the remnants of the Chartists were operating as the Advanced Liberal Party. The labour movement as it existed before the socialist revival of the 1880s and 1890s considered itself, and was considered to be, part of the political world of Liberalism. In the late 1860s, after the second Reform Act, J. Hales and S. Brighty visited Leeds to assess the state of Liberal electoral organisation. They reported:

> The increase . . . in Leeds is enormous. The old register was only 8,480, whilst the new one will be a little over 38,000. This extraordinary addition is principally composed of mechanics and factory workers, or as they are termed here 'mill hands'. There has been no gauge taken of their opinion, but they are believed to be liberal . . . The Trades Societies are both numerous and strong, and will be useful for working . . .[13]

In the 1880s the Liberals still felt secure in their working-class support, and moreover looked optimistically to the future. James Kitson, as an engineer among the town's largest employers of labour, advised Herbert Gladstone, son of the Liberal Prime Minister and later to be responsible for negotiating an electoral pact with the rising Labour Party, to choose West Leeds as his constituency:

> South and west, which are south of the River, are both working class constituencies . . . of the two, the west, which includes Holbeck (where is the Co-Operators Society and Mill, and many evidences of solid institutions) . . . is the one I should take . . . I am a member of the 200 of the West, my works are in the division . . .[14]

In fact working-class communities generally, south of the river Aire, were regarded as Liberal strongholds.[15] Given the predominantly Liberal loyalties of working-class wards and constituencies, and the presence of a labour aristocracy, the reality which socialists had to confront in the 1880s was a hard core of Lib-Lab sympathy in the labour movement whose dogged resistance to any attempt at independence of the Liberals has been underestimated.

Yet having made this point we must also insist that the record between 1880–1914 is also one of important change. Both skilled and unskilled workers did go over to socialist and independent labour politics and it is this change which needs to be emphasised and understood. The Liberal Party, having dominated affairs for much of the nineteenth century,[16] found Labour capable of offering the main alternative to the Conservatives before the first world war. The transition was due to the growth of the labour movement's aspirations well beyond the capacity of the Liberal Party to satisfy them. Hales and Brighty in the late 1860s described the labour movement in Leeds as composed of twenty-eight trade unions accounting for approximately 3,500 members, all believed to be Liberal. In 1909 forty-seven different trade unions and a total of sixteen political associations (including ward Labour representation committees, ILP and socialist clubs, and Women's Labour League branches), representing a total membership of 11,232, were affiliated to the Leeds Labour Representation Committee. Such figures help to quantify the extent of the development of the labour movement away from Liberal influence.

III It is not entirely clear why national politics changed as they did between 1880 and 1914. There has been lively debate about the reasons for the emergence of a Labour Party as distinct from a more avowedly socialist organisation, on the one hand, or the development of a progressive Liberal Party, holding the working-class vote, on the other. How and why did Labour emerge as it did, and why did the Liberals decline?

Three explanations have been offered. The first is that the Liberal Party could have retained the working-class vote by adopting a new and progressive programme, a development which was prevented largely by the impact of the first world war.[17] The second argues that there would have been no need of a Labour Party had the Liberals been more flexible, more adept in their use of local labour leaders, and their whips less muddled and confused.[18] The third, put forward by a number of socialist commentators, sees the emergence of Labour as regrettable because the party was a shadow of what a socialist party should be, devoid of 'the cutting edge of serious theoretical analysis'.[19] In this view it was preoccupied with the politics of parliamentary compromise, confused social reform with socialism, and put a populist appeal to civic and national interest above class interest. How does the experience of the labour movement in Leeds fit these interpretations?

This chapter proposes a fourth view. It argues that what emerged in Leeds was a Labour Party containing not only the strands of parliamentary and municipal reform and popular appeal but also the influence of a serious and theoretically acute group of socialist leaders whose views were directed by the resurgence of Marxist ideas from the mid-1880s. The Labour Party as it existed in Leeds by 1914 rested on the politics firstly of populism, secondly of reform, and thirdly of a combative working-class-based Marxian socialism. Although by the outbreak of war the third factor was overlain by the other two, it was still important, indeed in the early years it was the decisive influence in the continuing success of Labour and the noticeable decline in Liberal fortunes in working-class areas. The demise of the Liberal Party was not, therefore, the outcome of Liberal politicians' mistakes, or external 'accidents' (like the war), but a result of the policy developed by working-class socialists in the 1880s and 1890s. Their aim was to break the Liberal Party in Leeds and replace it with an independent political party of the labour movement and the working class.

Parliamentary election results do not provide much evidence to support this claim. Of the five constituencies into which the town was divided by 1885, Labour had captured only East Leeds, won by James O'Grady in 1906.[20] Even this success was due to the absence of Liberal opposition, since the seat was one of those covered by the Gladstone–MacDonald pact under which Herbert Gladstone as Liberal chief whip and Ramsay MacDonald as leader of the new

Labour Representation Committee (LRC) had agreed not to oppose Liberal and Labour candidates in certain constituencies.[21]

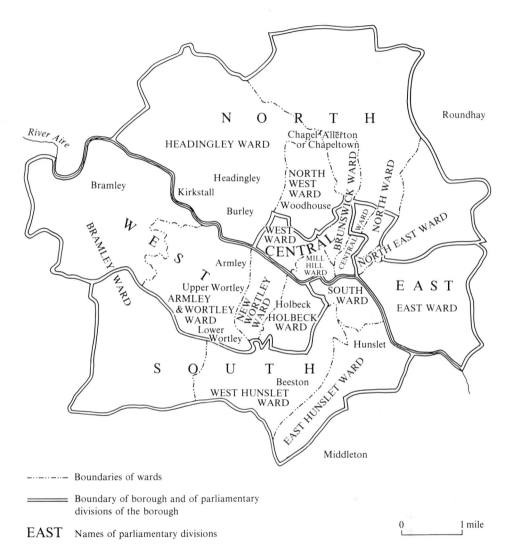

73 Electoral constituencies of Leeds, 1885; simplified version of the original map in *P.P.*, 1884–85 (4287–1, XIX, p. 297)

Of the others South Leeds remained Liberal throughout our period, despite Labour campaigns in 1906, 1908 and 1910. Leeds West, the stronghold of Liberalism, remained uncontested by Labour throughout the period up to 1914.

Table 33 Municipal elections, 1891–1913

Wards	1891	'92	'93	'94	'95	'96	'97	'98	'99	1900	'01	'02	'03	'04	'05	'06	'07	'08	'09	'10	'11	'12	'13
Mill Hill	C	C	C	C	C	C	C	C	C	C	C	C	C	C	C	C	C	C	C	C	L	C	C
West	L	L	C*	L*	L	L*	L	L	L	C	L	L	L	L	L*	L	C	L*	L	C*	C*	C†	L†
North West	C	C	C	C*	L	L	C	L	C	L	L	C*	L*	L	C*	C*	C*	C	L	L	C	C	L*
Brunswick	C	C	C	C	C	C	C	C	C	C	L	C	L	L	L	C	C	C	C	L	L	C	C
Central	C	C	C	L	C	C	C	C	C	C	C	C*	C	C	L	C	C	C	C	C	C	C	L
North	C	C	C	C	C	C	C	C	L	C	C	L	L	C	C	C	C	C	C	C	C	C	C*
North East	L	L	C	L*	L*	L	L	L*	L	L	L	L	C	L	L	C*	L*	C*	La	C*	La	C*	La
East	L	L	L	L	L	L	L	L	L	L	L	L	C	L	La	C*	C*	In*	C*	La	La	La	La
South	C	C*	C*	C	C	C	C	C	C	C*	C*	L	C*	L	C	C	C	C	C	C	C	C	C*
East Hunslet	L*	L	L*	C	L	L	L	L*	L	L	L	L	L	L	La	La	L*	La	La	La	La	L*	La
West Hunslet	L	L*	L	L	C	L	L	L	L	L	L	L	L*	L*	La	La	L*	L*	L*	L*	L*	La	L*
Holbeck	L	L	C*	L	C*	L*	L	L	L	L	L	L	L	L	L	L*	L*	L*	L*	La	L*	La	La
New Wortley	L	C	L	L	C	L	L	C*	L	L	C	L	La	La	La	La	La	C*	L†	L†	La	L*	L*
Armley and Wortley	L	L	C	L	C	L	L*	L	L	L	L*	L*	L*	La	L*	L*	C*	L*	L*	C*	C*	La	
Bramley	L	L	C	L	C*	C	L	C	C	L	C	L	L	L*	L*	L*	L*	C*	L*	L	C*	La	L*
Headingley	C	C	C	C	C	C	C	C	L	C	C	L	L	L	C	L	C	C	L	L	L	C	C

Key. *La* Labour victory. *C* Conservative victory. *L* Liberal victory. *Wards contested by ILP and Labour Party. †Wards contested by the Social Democratic Federation and the British Socialist Party.

In the field of municipal politics, however, the picture is entirely different. Liberal strength in Leeds West depended on control of the municipal wards which made up the constituency. Table 33 illustrates the effect of the Labour challenge in the local elections. Armley and Wortley, Bramley, Holbeck, and New Wortley, which together formed Leeds West, were all under heavy Labour challenge. Herein lay the difficulty for the Liberals. It was all very well to try and forge an alliance at parliamentary level between the Liberal Party and the LRC; as Herbert Gladstone recognised, this was one way 'to establish the Liberal Party as the best available instrument of progress'.[22] But what if the labour and socialist movement was engaged in a furious assault on Liberalism locally, an assault aimed at totally replacing the Liberals as a power in municipal politics? In that event the Liberal Party would have no base to operate from, and its parliamentary strength would soon decline. P. F. Clarke has argued that a progressive Liberalism was not only possible but actually established in Lancashire by 1910. He contends that Liberalism and the political structure as a whole had undergone changes that would have kept the party relevant and electorally successful. Against the argument that grass-roots pressure for independence prevented Labour from being gathered into the progressive fold, he suggests that the ambit of politics had changed from the local to the national; and against the claim that Liberalism was ideologically bankrupt he posits the intellectual synthesis of Liberalism with socialism, to form the attractive policies of progressivism.[23] In Leeds, however, there is no evidence of any synthesis that might have brought Liberals and

Labour together. Such efforts as there were to accommodate Labour had less to do with ideological reorientation than with tactics to inhibit the growth of independent politics within the labour movement. In 1892, for example, J. S. Mathers, a Liberal Party organiser, wrote to Herbert Gladstone to say that he had met Marston and Bune (president and secretary of the trades council):

> Our object was to find a common platform — ... *to stop, before it took any definite form, the Labour Party from going off* ... [it was decided to run Bune as a municipal candidate] ... if you succeed with Marston in the matter of the bench we shall all but capture the Labour Party ...[24]

Here was a clear attempt to win over influential Labour leaders by holding out the prospect of advancement through the Liberal Party. William Marston in fact became a JP and a long-serving Liberal councillor.

If allowing James O'Grady a free run in East Leeds is seen as an example of progressive Liberalism, it must be observed that the concession was opposed as damaging by local Liberal activists. The reason was that the Labour Party in Leeds simply did not respect the policy of *rapprochement*. Given its head in East Leeds, it was all the more ready to attack the other Liberal seats. Joseph Henry, watchdog of Liberal interests in their stronghold of West Leeds, pointed out the effects of the policy: 'I hope the party is not going to do as it did at the last election – leave the Labour man at liberty to fight a Tory and then allow him to fight a Liberal whenever he likes ...'[25]

The tendency among Leeds Liberals was rather to consider alliances with the Tories, and from 1913 onwards the Tory alderman Charles Wilson periodically proposed an alliance against socialists at local elections. The suggestion was formally repudiated by Joe Henry as chairman of the Leeds Liberal Federation, but there was said to be some support for it among Liberal businessmen and from F. Kinder, chairman of the Liberals on the council. A Tory–Liberal alliance had actually come to pass in Armley and Wortley in 1907, but in future years Henry opposed this strategy too.

Clearly, then, Liberalism was under severe electoral stress well before the first world war. Under pressure its natural inclination was to the right, finding Labour ideologically and politically hostile. At the national level Herbert Gladstone persisted with the politics of accommodation. Joe Henry, in the thick of a battle to retain West Leeds, decided that the only course was to fight, for locally the political labour movement was refusing to enter into any bargains. In November, 1904, for example, he had offered the New Wortley municipal ward without a contest if the LRC would allow the Liberals

West Hunslet. 'They would not agree. They are most difficult to deal with, and nothing but a beating will do them good . . .'[26]

Although it is true that Labour had achieved only the limited success of one parliamentary seat by 1914, this should not be attributed to any ideological development that enabled the Liberals to hold off the Labour Party. In Lancashire the outlines of progressive Liberalism owed much to a vigorous radical press. In Leeds the Liberal press proved incapable of breaking new ground: thus 'although the *Mercury* perceived the political world in general to be in a state of transformation it was incapable of seeing that Labour's role was, in this situation, to be a dynamic one', and the *Mercury* continued to adhere to 'the orthodox Liberal creed of individualism'. Similarly the *Leeds Express*, although aimed explicitly at the needs of the urban working class, had a proprietor whose solutions to industrial problems were 'superficial' and 'conventional'.[27]

By 1914 Labour had fourteen elected councillors, one more than the Liberals, and was only prevented from being the main opposition party to the Conservatives by a disproportionately high allocation of aldermanic seats to the Liberals. Whatever Clarke's findings in Lancashire, and despite his claim that the ambit of politics had changed from the local to the national, local politics remained supremely important in Leeds. Not only was municipal success a good indicator of parliamentary election results but local politics raised important ideological and policy issues.

The emergence of a politically independent labour movement can perhaps best be understood by observation at a local rather than national level, primarily because up to the first world war capitalism was locally based. The bourgeoisie was *visible*, entrenched alike in local industry and local politics. Thus 'the investment resources of Leeds were largely self-generated and the predominant form of business organisation at the end of the Victorian era, as at its beginning, was the family business or partnership'.[28] This industrial and commercial elite also constituted the largest single occupational group on the council: manufacturers, businessmen and managers formed 45·6 per cent of the total of all who served between 1888 and 1905.[29]

Those among them who as employers also claimed to represent through the Liberal Party the political interests of the working people of the town found themselves in a difficult position when a coherent socialist group willing to exploit their dilemma emerged. It is illustrated by an early warning from James Kitson to Herbert Gladstone about the dangers of Gladstone's attempts to retain the loyalty of the labour movement with political concessions. We have seen that Mathers was confident of keeping Labour in check by offering positions of status to leaders of the trades council. This policy,

Table 34 Political composition of Leeds council, 1882–1913

Date Nov.	Councillors			Aldermen			Total		
	Cons.	*Lib.*	*Lab.*	*Cons.*	*Lib.*	*Lab.*	*Cons.*	*Lib.*	*Lab.*
1882	11	37	—	—	16	—	11	53	—
1883	13	35	—	—	16	—	13	51	—
1884	15	33	—	—	16	—	15	49	—
1885	14	34	—	—	16	—	14	50	—
1886	11	37	—	—	16	—a	11	53	—
1887	12	36	—	—	16	—	12	52	—
1888	16	32	—	—	16	—	16	48	—
1889	16	32	—	—	16	—	16	48	—
1890	18	30	—	—	16	—	18	46	—
1891	24	24	—	—	16	—	24	40	—
1892	21	27	—	—	16	—	21	43	—
1893	24	24	—	—	16	—	24	40	—
1894	28	20	—	—	16	—	28	36	—
1895	30	18	—	8	8	—	38	26	—
1896	25	23	—	9	7	—	34	30	—
1897	25	23	—	9	7	—	34	30	—
1898	22	26	—	16	—	—	38	26	—
1899	22	26	—	16	—	—	38	26	—
1900	21	27	—	16	—	—	37	27	—
1901	20	28	—	16	—	—	36	28	—
1902	18	30	—	16	—	—	34	30	—
1903	18	29	1	16	—	—	34	29	1
1904	13	32	3	7	8	1	20	40	4
1905	12	29	7	7	8	1	19	37	8
1906	14	26	8	7	8	1	21	34	9
1907	21	18	9	7	8	1	28	26	10
1908	29	15	3	7	8	1	36	23	4b
1909	27	15	5	7	8	1	34	23	6b
1910	24	18	5	7	8	1	31	26	6b
1911	19	20	9	7	8	1	26	28	10
1912	26	15	10	8	8	1	34	33	11
1913	25	12	14	9	6	2	34	18	16

Notes

  a Party affiliation of the aldermen elected for this year is not given in the press but it is likely that all sixteen were Liberals.

  b One independent councillor served for these three years.

Source. Leeds Official Year Book; Morrison's Leeds 'Blue Book' and City Record; Leeds Mercury.

developed early in Leeds, was eventually to reach its logical conclusion in the Gladstone–MacDonald agreement. Kitson, speaking as a businessman, was not so confident about its wisdom:

> If I am correct in believing that a certain possible appointment might be made having in mind that Tom Mann would be an acceptable candidate for the vacancy and that thereby I should at a future election be placed in a more favourable position in a contest . . . after much reflection I desire to say that I am very sensible of the kindly thought for myself. But as I should consider it a calamity if Tom Mann had a direct interest in organising labour in Leeds for the purpose of combatting capitalists, I should not wish to see him in Leeds. My interests and those of my partners have suffered by his action. Today we are almost without work . . . I ask you therefore not to consider me in any transactions – I see a great contradiction of enterprise is upon us as far as our efforts are involved.[30]

74   Tom Maguire

IV   The realignment that took place between 1880 and 1914 cannot be explained simply in terms of political and electoral activity. New ideological dimensions were being opened up and discussed by the labour movement. *Political* accommodation was no longer enough. More important, and far more difficult for Liberalism, the ideological challenge of a resurgent socialism had to be met.

The labour movement was harder to contain because it was demanding more than just economic or social reform. Its leadership sought to develop a class consciousness that would insist on *independent* political action. Thus when Clarke suggests that Liberal progressivism aimed at social reform to be given to, and not gained by, the working class, he is ignoring one of labour's cardinal principles in the years before 1914. This is certainly true of Leeds, where the most active working-class socialists insisted that no policy that had not been developed and fought for by the working class itself was of any value. The central concern of the pioneers from the 1880s was to overthrow Liberal hegemony so as to create a new context in which policies and priorities could be informed by working-class need. The first step was to question Liberal domination of the labour movement.

A serious defect of Leeds Liberalism was its failure to offer a convincing framework to explain the social and industrial problems of the day. An alternative was put forward mainly by two men: Tom Maguire (1864–95) and John Lincoln Mahon (1865–1933). Maguire was described as a photographer's assistant, Mahon was a skilled engineer, and both were among the leaders of political activity at a crucial transitional point.

Writing of this period, Edward Thompson has asked; 'In what sense did the new socialist theory (and its strategies) constitute a critical break, or rupture, not with this or that point of Liberal Victorian thought, but with the organising ideas of bourgeois Liberalism?'[31] There is no space here for a survey of Liberal social theory, but the concept of individualism, especially the principle of *laissez-faire* in the domestic, social and economic spheres, was certainly prominent in it.[32] One of the first preoccupations of the socialist revival was to project an image of social cleavage based on the opposition of working-class and capitalist interests. A small group of socialists appeared in the early 1880s who counterposed to the Liberal attack on the land an attack on industrial capital, whose owners were often also the political leaders of the town. The business and professional grip on local government made municipal politics a key area for demonstrating the incompatibility of interest between the working classes and their employers. This challenge to the traditional alignment based on loyalties that ran across class boundaries, and was characterised largely by working-class delegation of political responsibility to middle-class representatives, heralded a critical break with the recent past. We must now turn to the personalities, organisations and ideas responsible for the break.

The socialist revival in Leeds can be traced back to the activities of Tom Maguire, and its ideas were first defined in radical circles. Alfred Mattison, a young Hunslet-born engineer who was drawn into socialist politics by the influence of Maguire, recalled in later years the memories of one of the pioneers:

> I was a frequenter to Vicars Croft (Leeds) in the years 1883–1884. At that time I was a follower of Charles Bradlaugh and the Radical School . . . there was an S.D.F. branch in Leeds. I remember Tom Maguire and a few friends and I believe they came mainly from St. Anne's Roman Catholic Church. Finn, Kelly and others.[33]

The Social Democratic Federation had emerged in the early 1880s under Henry Mayers Hyndman, himself much influenced by the little that was available on Marx's work. It had its origins among radicals in the Liberal Party, who formed the Democratic Federation. It became the SDF in 1883–84, when a more comprehensive and socialist programme was adopted, attracting in the process the support of disgruntled personalities like William Morris in search of alternatives to what they considered the limited vision of Victorian liberalism.

One important element in the socialist revival, then, was the intellectual ferment at the radical edge of the Liberal Party. Another, often underestimated, was the experiences and activity of the largest immigrant group in the town, the Irish. Maguire was the son of Irish parents and was raised among the Catholic community of East Leeds. The stimulus to socialist ideas came from a small group[34] who followed the debates about Ireland in the Secular Society and in the pages of the *Christian Socialist*, where the doings of the Democratic Federation received attention. Significantly, the Federation was beginning to see connections between the land question, the Irish problem and the troubles of labour in England. There was a confused period in which radical Liberalism and socialism mingled, finding common ground in a belief that land appropriation was one of the main cause of social problems in both countries. Leeds socialism, however, had gone beyond the land and Irish questions, and beyond tolerance for many Liberal standpoints.

In September 1884 Tom Maguire spoke on 'The Aims of Socialism' in Vicars Croft to about 300 people. Later in the month John Lincoln Mahon, making one of his earliest appearances in Leeds, gave an address on 'The Method of Robbing the Workers'. That evening, at 16

Henbury Street, a branch of the Social Democratic Federation was formed, with Tom Maguire as its secretary.[35] Next came the decision to follow William Morris in seceding from the Federation. A meeting of the Leeds SDF in March 1885 at the Royal Sovereign Inn, Vicar Lane, decided to dissolve the branch and declare themselves members of the Socialist League, thus signifying their 'renunciation of the political opportunism and State Socialism of the S.D.F., and a full endorsement of the purely revolutionary propaganda to which the Socialist League was pledged'.[36] The Socialist League had been formed by a group (prominent among it William Morris) which had broken away from the SDF earlier that year. The split was partly due to dislike of Hyndman himself but arose also from a different view of socialism, one hostile to parliamentary and municipal involvement and to ameliorative reforms in general. The League's propaganda called for full conversion to socialism, scorning half-measures. Implicit in its approach was the expectation of capitalism's imminent collapse.

In its early phase up to 1885–86 Leeds socialism was preoccupied with developing a rich vision of the future socialist society, taking much from the inspiring ideas of William Morris and the *Commonweal*. Yet the working class did not turn to the Socialist League in significant numbers. There are indications that after their secession from the SDF the Socialist Leaguers soon grew dissatisfied with the purist revolutionary ideas advocated by Morris and the *Commonweal*. Nevertheless the years from 1884 to 1887 saw an important advance in the level of theoretical discussion, socialist ideas being taken into debating clubs, Liberal clubs, trade unions and the Secular Society as well as public meetings in Vicars Croft. It was during the 1880s that the relationship of socialist ideas to the realities of working-class life came to be better understood. And although active membership remained pitifully small, the League in general and Tom Maguire in particular accumulated invaluable experience.

Yet important changes were taking place in the political attitude of the Leeds Socialist League, highlighted by the upsurge of strikes between 1889 and 1892. The same socialists who in 1885 had declared themselves revolutionaries, adverse to parliamentary and municipal reforms and sceptical of the effectiveness of trade union action, were found in the late 1880s and early 1890s leading a new political labour movement based on trade union support and demanding just such reforms. This movement was to lead to the formation of the Independent Labour Party at Bradford in January 1893; the ILP in turn encouraged the emergence in 1900 of the Labour Representation Committee, eventually to become the modern Labour Party. The switch from revolutionary purism to active engagement has not been adequately accounted for. Events in Leeds can help to explain why effort became centred on building a party of Labour.

The change was not as short-sighted and ill-considered as some commentators have claimed. It was not, in Leeds, a case of abandoning revolution for reformism, but rather of fusing socialist vision with practical politics. Maguire was particularly concerned that socialism should be able to counter the assumptions of *laissez-faire* Liberalism. It has been argued, for example, that Liberals were couching their radicalism in terms of the need for land reform. Maguire, on the other hand, warned that concentrating on land nationalisation might divert attention from the more urgent task of tackling the centres of capitalism. The catchwords of Liberalism were irrelevant to the needs of the working class. Against Liberal emphasis on individual advancement he counterposed the idea of collective action: 'we working men, although divided by politics and religion, are socially one . . . can the political differences of a Whig and a Tory be really the political differences of a plasterer and a bricklayer?'[37] The socialists also raised the first criticism of Liberal notions of social responsibility. The *Mercury* believed that attempts to alleviate social problems by government intervention were bound to fail because they offended the laws of political economy; Maguire attacked the Charity Organisation Society for complacency in regarding widespread unemployment as normal in winter. Public responsibility for unemployment was a basic tenet of the Independent Labour Party. Despite the Chamberlain circular allowing the council to bring forward public works in times of depression, little action was taken and the ILP had to mount special campaigns for the unemployed in the winters of 1891, 1892 and 1898. The Leeds campaigns specifically sought to establish the principle that the council had a responsibility for the whole community, not only the business sector. The way was opening up for a justification of working-class participation in welfare politics. A welfare programme was essential because 'neither the Liberals nor the Tories are prepared to deal with the terrible problems of poverty and unemployment' and neither could answer the question of 'why machinery, instead of making labour easier, is in reality taking the place of labour'.[38] Public provision for the economically disadvantaged continued to be among the foremost socialist demands in future years, clashing with orthodox opinion. At a conference in 1908 the Lord Mayor, the Vicar of Leeds and the Bishop of Wakefield all emphasised the need for 'moral regeneration' and 'charitable measures' as a solution to unemployment, in the face of the Yorkshire Federation of Trades Councils' demand for 'either useful remunerative employment, or healthy maintenance' *as a right*.[39]

The Liberals came late and somewhat opportunistically to support measures of social reform. But even if they had been more enthusiastic they could not have kept the support of the labour movement on that basis alone; neither the ILP nor the LRC saw welfare legislation as an end in itself. Hence O'Grady regarded Lloyd George's 'People's Budget' as 'aimed only to mitigate the chafing of economic fetters, not to break them'.[40]

Socialists' tactics grew more sophisticated between 1884 and 1890. Maguire questioned the relevance of the League's revolutionary purism when the need was for immediate reforms, and the move towards trade union struggle and political activity was signalled with the historic handbill written by Maguire in the autumn of 1887.[41]

> A definite step is now being taken towards the formation of a Socialist Labour Party in Leeds . . . The objects of socialism are, briefly, . . . to put a stop to the mad competition for existence, which is the cause of poverty . . . and to establish a co-operative commonwealth . . .[42]

The switch from purist detachment to active participation can be clarified by considering the contribution of John Lincoln Mahon.[43] With Maguire he fashioned a strategy for the movement which had a decisive impact on its development well after he had left Leeds. Much maligned, he has not been treated as sympathically as Maguire, yet the two were close politically and his importance in Leeds needs to be reassessed. Above all, Mahon recognised the need to intervene in the organisation and running of the labour movement: 'Socialism is simply the most advanced stage of the labour movement . . . Trades Unionism means securing to the workers a larger share in the fruits of their labour; socialism means securing to the workers the full fruits of their labour . . .'[44] He consolidated his theory of socialist politics in *A Labour Programme* (1888), which did much to elucidate the strategy of the ILP tradition in Leeds. In 1889 he promoted a scheme for a Labour Union, advocating the formation of an independent Labour party. As we have seen, the town's socialists had in any case been moving along similar lines, Mahon's arrival in 1890 simply giving the movement a sharper edge.

By 1890 the labour movement in Leeds was set for rapid development. The socialists had made contact with the wider working-class movement, having been instrumental in the formation of the local branch of the Gas Workers' and General Labourers' Union, composed initially of stokers from the corporation's New Wortley and Meadow Lane works. Tom Paylor, secretary of the Socialist League, became organising secretary of the union. But this socialist-inspired union was opposed by the trades council, whose leaders' ideas of what constituted legitimate trade union activity were limited. The story of labour and socialist politics in the city over the next decade is comprehensible only in terms of the relationship between these two groups, for while the members of the union had accepted a socialist leadership, most of the labour movement decisively rejected any such influence. This was the reality that had to be faced, and if the path to socialism lay through working-class organisations, tactics had to be adapted accordingly. The GGLU intensified political debate and activity. While John Bune of the trades council saw its object as no different from any other union's — to make its members better off 'financially, physically, and morally' — Maguire set for it the political aim of making the town council more amenable generally to the needs of labour. The socialists deliberately used conflicts between corporation employees as GGLU members and the councillors who employed them to symbolise the conflict between capital and labour. This was the crux of the famous gas strike of 1890,[45] and its political significance overrode its importance as a trade union matter. Maguire spelled out the lesson: ' . . . if [the Gas Committee] persisted in the course they had adopted nothing was more certain than that the LIBERAL PARTY IN THIS TOWN would get such a knockdown blow as they would never recover from'.[46] The strike and its aftermath saw the beginning in earnest of the campaign for an independent Labour Party, and the break-up of the old Socialist League. Maguire explained:

> . . . perhaps the real issue . . . is which of the two courses is the correct one to take bearing in mind the events of the gasworkers struggle . . . [we] considered a Labour Electoral League should be formed . . . Our anarchist friends . . . finally told the people that no policy should be entertained but physical force . . . I admit the Labour Electoral move is not all to be desired, but it seemed to be the next immediate step to take in order to keep the labour unions militant, and to emphasise the conflict between the workers and the employers.[47]

The attempt to establish a lasting independent Labour Party proved difficult, and went through three early phases. A Labour Electoral League was inaugurated at the Central Cocoa House on 9 July 1890; when it collapsed the decision was taken to try and politicise the trades council. The GGLU joined the council and Mahon, Paylor and Cockayne represented the union as delegates. After bitter wrangling (caused by attempts to eject Mahon) the delegates forced through a resolution forming a 'Leeds Trades and Labour Council Electoral Union' in May 1892. The LEU, as it was more commonly referred to, miserably failed its first test when Lib–Lab sentiment in the trades council vetoed a proposal to run an independent Labour candidate against a Liberal in the South Leeds by-election. Mahon decided not to accept the veto, campaigned as a candidate himself, and suffered a great deal of slander and physical violence. This ended the second phase of independent politics, and in the third the socialists, having experienced the intransigent hostility of Liberalism in the trades council, decided to work outside it again. Later in 1892 Maguire, Mattison and Mahon transformed the club rooms of the old LEU into a home for the East Hunslet Independent Labour Club. Soon there were seven such clubs, and late in November 1892 forty delegates met at the West Ward Clubrooms, Sale Street, to form the Leeds Independent Labour Party. At the first General Conference of the ILP in Bradford Leeds had six delegates, Maguire and Mahon among them.

Recapitulating, it may be seen that socialist politics had a complicated and difficult birth in Leeds. Out of a combination of radical discontent with the Liberal Party and immigrant unrest about Ireland and social problems, a small group of socialists began to raise a conception of politics incompatible with the concerns of the Tory and Liberal parties. The Socialist League emerged as the organisation which would educate, agitate and organise for a society based on the reality of joy in work and the abolition of wage slavery, and derived from the ideas of Marx and Morris. Confronted by the tougher reality of life in working-class Leeds in the 1880s, the League collapsed in 1890, yet those who had served in it learned a good deal. They had adapted their politics to make contact with working people. In the summer of 1890 the first independent political organisation of labour had been formed. When it collapsed they had tried to make the trades council support independent labour politics. Fierce opposition from Lib-Labs frustrated this effort, and the third attempt had to be made outside the council — outside, that is, the main labour organisation in the town. The Independent Labour Party, set up in 1892–93, had still to capture the support of the labour movement.

If we wish to understand the nature of the ILP and of the early Labour Party, we must try to appreciate the problems facing those who were involved in setting up both organisations. Edward Thompson, for example, has written that the essence of the ILP was its socialism.[48] Yet there are difficulties here. Maguire and Mahon, soon after the ILP had been formed, somewhat paradoxically seemed to be playing down the socialist rhetoric of the new organisation, and indeed for long periods up to 1914 socialist policies failed to win the support which the euphoric years of early 1890s had suggested they might. Thompson ascribes this arrested development to structural features of the Leeds economy, as well as to a more subjective cause, the failure of leadership locally. Maguire, out of personal modesty and the onset of an illness which was soon to kill him, allowed Mahon, 'vain, incurably quarrelsome, and given to intrigue', to assume the leadership of the movement.[49] Similarly Pierson, in a recent analysis of the socialist revival of the 1880s and 1890s, describes Maguire as a disillusioned man, retiring into the background, drinking and reminiscing.[50]

However, qualities of political wisdom linked to socialist theory were a far stronger feature of their leadership than has been realised. When Mahon argued at the Bradford conference that the ILP should declare itself independent and not socialist his amendment was not an opportunistic quirk but a reflection of policy in Leeds since 1891, for the rules of the Leeds ILP, written before the conference, did not include a collective ownership clause.[51] Maguire and Mahon were painfully aware of the strength of Liberalism within the organised labour movement, a reality they could not ignore even during the period of unskilled militancy. The years 1889–93 were merely the beginning of a political process, and maximum advantage was taken by tactically well prepared socialists. To insist on the use of the word 'socialism' could have been meaningless, even damaging. What were coming to be described as socialist objectives in the 1890s often derived from a misplaced idealism propagated by people in the 'intermediate strata', from white-collar and professional occupations. Such idealism altered the conception of the role of the working class in politics, seeing it not as an agency of social change but as an object of social policy.[52] For Maguire and Mahon the priority was not to push the word socialism to the fore but to define its content, and the element both of them settled on was activity generated within the working class itself — a critically important notion, especially in a period when that class was emerging from an extended phase of political dependence. It was central to Maguire's work between 1880 and 1914, a period which represented not a disillusioned retreat but a tactical development, and which saw a demonstration of the need for combined industrial and political action in pursuit of independence from Liberalism. Above all, the objectives in Maguire's view of socialist activity are expressed in the statement: 'To the workers, however, any gain coming indirectly, and not achieved by their own organised effort, is not worth the having'.[53]

The ILP was not deeply rooted in Leeds in the 1890s, as we realise when we cut away the euphoric language of the socialist press, for its membership was confined to sections of the GGLU and individuals from other unions: it excluded the wider labour movement and the trades council. A white-collar leadership was influential in the ILP of the 1890s, a situation which highlighted the weak position of the manual working class and its failure to become actively involved, as a class, in socialist politics. In a world beset by economic insecurity it was easy for socialism to become a matter of quantity rather than quality, so that people from the manual working class who were interested in politics were more concerned with trade unionism (and economic betterment) than theories of power relationships in society. We shall return to the question of living conditions later, for this did have an important bearing on the nature of working-class politics.

Maguire was concerned, then, to develop a strategy that took account of the weaknesses of the movement, and he was particularly concerned about the socialist enthusiasm of the new leadership:

> we grow exasperated and curse the thirty millions, mostly fools . . . That *we* are all right goes without saying. And here I beg . . . to differ. We are not all right . . . we [define socialism as the collective ownership and control of the means of production,] which is as true as it is beautiful and as vague as it is both. The people don't doubt the truth and desirability of socialism; but they do doubt themselves and their ability to attain it . . .[54]

The priority was not to talk vaguely of socialism but to build an organisation of labour that would 'widen their bonds of union from particular trades to their whole class'.[55]

The ideas of Maguire and Mahon were kept alive, after the death of the one and the departure of the other, by the GGLU leadership. Walter Wood became involved with the Leeds socialists in 1890 when he was a gas stoker at York Road, and was instrumental in raising independent political ideas within the mainstream of the labour movement, leading the fight against the Liberal Party. J. E. Smith became secretary of the union about 1895, came from an Irish background, was a member of the Catholic Club in Briggate and of the Irish Nationalist League, and was instrumental in securing Irish support for James O'Grady in East Leeds. Both were resolutely committed to the principle of independence, which by 1914 had become so much a feature of the labour movement's ideas generally that the Liberal Party was forced to consider an alliance with Leeds Toryism.[56] Maguire had shown in 1890, during the gas strike, the possibilities of combined political and industrial action: heightened periods of industrial militancy generally also brought more active political conflict on the town council, accentuating the differences between Liberalism and Labour. Two phases illustrate this point: the engineers' lock-out of 1897–98, and the industrial unrest of 1911 and 1913. The Amalgamated Society of Engineers was a stronghold of labour aristocracy attitudes. Typical was James Tetley, born in 1841;

an engineer and trade unionist of the old school, he remained loyal to the Liberal Party when so many others had broken away. He was Liberal councillor for East Hunslet until his defeat in 1909 by a Labour candidate; a member of the ASE No. 9 branch, founder member of the trades council, a JP in 1905, and president of the Co-operative Society on a number of occasions. Socialists had been hard at work in the 1890s, pointing out that engineers' pay was lower in Leeds than in other towns, overtime more common, unemployment frequent, and that James Kitson, the Liberal industrialist, was one of the worst offenders.[57] Yet calls for an eight-hour day and political action were staunchly opposed by the local ASE branches.[58] This attitude changed abruptly in 1898 when thirty-four engineering companies locked out their employees. The chairman of the lock-out committee, on the return to work, drew out the lesson of the conflict: '. . . they must reorganise their society and make it a powerful political force'.[59] The lock-out had an effect on politics as significant as the gas strike of 1890, for it brought one of the most important groups of workers into closer sympathy with independent labour politics. Walter Wood of the gas workers' union and the ILP had advised the engineers throughout the dispute, and immediately after the lock-out there was an influx of ASE members into the ILP clubs. The ASE was among the strongest unions on the trades council, and once it began to change so too did the council.

Late in 1897 the trades council decided to increase its fees in order to pay for union representation on public bodies, so it experienced little difficulty in affiliating in June 1900 to the Labour Representation Committee.[60] It will become apparent that the decision to engage in political action in 1900 did not necessarily mean a break with the Liberal Party, since a number of influential trade unionists on the council considered that it was possible and desirable for labour to be politically independent *within* the Liberal Party. Important battles remained to be fought between this group and the socialists of the ILP. Nevertheless the policy Maguire had laid down in 1890 of using local industrial conflict to detach the loyalty of working people from the Liberal Party was the most successful single factor in the emergence of an independent political party of labour. It decisively shifted the ASE in 1898, and was to be effective at another stage in the advance of the Labour movement between 1911 and 1914, when it became clear that any hope the Liberals might have had of accommodating the labour movement was finally lost. Again the catalyst was a major industrial dispute. The corporation strike of 1913 confirmed the process of decline in the local Liberal Party. Given the chance to side with the trades council and the GGLU, and stand out

CARTOON.

THE SOCIALIST SOWER.

Sower, Scatter thy Seed.

The face of the earth is furrowed deep,
  By share and harrow riven,
The sun in the morning seems fain to sleep,
  And the moon comes late at even;
But the sun shall smile, and the clouds shall weep,
  And the pitiful moon shall plead —
New life to bring in the Spring, the Spring!
  Sower, scatter they seed.

Silently, aimlessly into the clod
  Falleth the seed; in gloom
It quickens, and cleaves to the nourishing sod
  Till it bursts into light and bloom,
A product fresh from the hands of God,
  A mystery none may rede,
The awakening of the Spring, the Spring!
  Sower, scatter thy seed.

Scatter thy seed with a lavish hand,
  Though foes behind thee follow,
For what they spoil will return to the land
  Through their bodies rank and hollow;
And cleansed of their carrion presence, and
  From touch of their tallons freed
Sweet life it will fling round the Spring, the
  Spring!

For the seed will grow to a mighty crop,
  And the sower shall reaper be,
And the receiving rooks will be fain to stop
  When their wondering eyes shall see
Each blade and shoot with a thinking top,
  And ears and eyes to heed —
So hurrah for May! and the Labour Day!
  When the sower scatters his seed.
                     BARDOLPH

75   Cartoon illustrating May Day verses by Maguire ('Bardolph'), from the *Labour Leader*, 5 May 1894 (whose printer omitted the refrain from the third stanza)

against the aggressive anti-union stance of Charles Wilson, the Liberals in the event were seen to side with Wilson, since their members on the town council agreed to the formation of a special committee to deal with the strike consisting of three Tories and two Liberals but no Labour councillors. Wilson spoke of the strike as having symbolic importance, representing the excesses of an overgrown labour movement. As the *Leeds Weekly Citizen*, the paper of the Labour Party, commented; 'The Liberal position we can well understand. They realise how hopelessly they have lost touch with the working class.'[61]

The Leeds Labour Party represented a confident and united movement in the years up to 1914, its strengths going deeper than electoral success. In 1913 the Marxist British Socialist Party was allowed to affiliate, despite an announcement that it could not accept the authority of the Labour Party nationally, and Harold Clay, a member of the BSP, was president in 1913–14. The Socialists had a newspaper of good quality, the *Leeds Weekly Citizen*, and were strongly based in the working-class community. The West Leeds BSP, for example, had set up a retail co-operative, and its club, with Sunday school, choir, dramatic and debating societies, was regarded as 'a centre for social life and fellowship'.[62]

V   Although by 1914 the Leeds Labour Party represented a labour movement stronger and more confident than at any time since the Chartist era, the level of political understanding and the development of a critical theory of socialism were both constrained by the inequalities of living standards among the working-class community. It is difficult to present an accurate account of wage rates, since the city's industries were varied, the occupational structure within each industry was complex, and there was marked fluctuation in the level of wages at different times of the year. It is useful, however, to present official estimates for the major occupations, to convey some general idea of the changes from the 1880s into the early twentieth century.

Using material published by the Board of Trade it is possible to compare the standard of living with conditions in other industrial centres. Giving London prices and wages in 1905 an index of 100, the comparison in table 35 can be made. It is clear that Leeds enjoyed a slightly higher standard of living, at least in these occupations, than its other West Riding counterparts Bradford and Huddersfield. The comparison with major industrial centres outside the West Riding is less favourable.

There is evidence that wages were improving significantly

Table 35   Selected industries: wages for one week in 1905 as a percentage of wages in London

	Building		Engineering				Rent and price index[a]
Town	Skilled	Labourers	Skilled	Labourers	Furnishing	Printing	
Birmingham	98	100	91	83	86	88	85
Bradford	83	85	87	96	83	85	88
Huddersfield	81	85	77	—	81	87	90
Leeds ·	87	94	85	—	87	91	86
London	100	100	100	· 100	100	100	100
Liverpool	98	78	93	81	87	94	86
Manchester	95	92	91	83	88	90	86
Newcastle	90	89	89	89	90	90	94

Note

 [a] The rent and price index is based on assumed consumption of a fixed amount of the following commodities per working class family: tea, sugar, bacon, eggs, cheese, butter, potatoes, flour, bread, milk, meat, coal.
Source. *Report of an Enquiry by the Board of Trade into Working Class rents, Housing and Retail Prices together with the Standard Rate of Wages . . . in the Principal Industrial Towns of the U.K.*, P.P. (1908), CVII, Cd. 3864.

throughout the period which saw the formation of the Labour Party. In engineering and boilermaking, for example, the Board of Trade estimated that there had been an overall increase of 25·9 per cent between 1886 and 1906. This figure must be treated with some caution, since 1886 was a bad year for trade, while 1906 was a busy one, but the Board considered that there was a general upward movement over the period.[63]

One final set of figures, presented in table 36, provides evidence of the level of wages in the major industries in Leeds itself. The rates refer to a full week in October 1905, and reflect official estimates of remuneration for work particularly in the more skilled occupations. They ignore disparities in income between the skilled and the unskilled, and estimates of wage rates from the *Yorkshire Factory Times*, the paper of the Yorkshire trade unions, put actual earnings at a much lower level than official or employers' estimates.

In the eyes of trade unionists Leeds was notorious for its low wages and for its poor union organisation. The working class was far from homogeneous, and there was much diversity of economic fortune. Table 36 highlights the role of women as cheap labour in key industries, a situation which highlights a problem never satisfactorily confronted by the labour movement. The role of women in the domestic and industrial economy had important consequences for the level of union organisation and of class consciousness.

Over a third of the adult women of the borough went out to work up to 1914, yet the dominant cultural stereotype saw the ideal woman as home-based, a stereotype which ignored the reality of the importance of women in the economy. The *Yorkshire Factory Times* advised men

Table 36 Wage rates in major industries in Leeds, 1905

Trade and principal occupations	Weekly rate of wages
Building	
Bricklayers, masons, plasterers	39s 2d
Carpenters and joiners and plumbers	37s 1½d
Painters	33s 4d
Labourers	26s 10d – 28s 10½d
Engineering	
Fitters and turners	33s
Smiths	34s
Patternmakers	37s
Printing	
Compositors	35s 6d
Furnishing	
Cabinetmakers	35s 1d – 39s 4½d
Upholsterers	37s 2d
French-polishers	35s
Woollen and worsted	
Weavers, one loom (women)	10s – 16s
Ready-made clothing	
Cutters (men)	28s, 30s, 32s
Machine sewers (women) +	11s – 16s
Finishers (women) +	8s – 14s
Boot and shoe	
Clickers, lasters and finishers	28s
Pressmen	25s

Source. The table is a summary of the original in *Report of an Enquiry, op. cit.*, table 34.

not to marry mill girls, since home life suffered: 'the best wives for working men are those drawn from the ranks of domestic service'.[64] Again in an editorial of 1904: 'Men should set their wits to work to get more wages for women, and for married women a chance to stay at home to be what nature intended them to be – viz housewives.'[65] The refusal to admit that married women in particular should work naturally inhibited the growth of trade unionism among them, and was an attitude itself based on a firm idea of what men should be: 'there was a large number of lazy loafers in Lancashire and Yorkshire who lived off their wives' work. This robbed children of love and was a danger to the State.'[66] It was from Tom Maguire, and more consistently from Isabella Ford,[67] that the push towards women's trade unionism came. Ford attacked the attitude of the men whose chivalry disguised their real intentions, which were not the admission of women into men's trade unions on equal terms but rather were expressed in the idea 'Let us so restrict women's labour by kindly legislation that eventually women will be driven from the field altogether'.[68] This attitude was not confined to a few manual trade unionists but dominated the male mind in general. Robert Baker, the liberal-minded Leeds doctor, saw female labour as 'pre-inducing the causes of pauperism and disease' and 'reversing the order of nature',[69] implying a view of women's role which remained insufficiently challenged throughout the period of independent labour politics. At its first General Conference the ILP drew up a programme aimed at 'the abolition of overtime, piecework, and child labour', and a Mr Slaithwaite moved to insert 'and the employment of married women', regarding it as 'one of the greatest curses in the country'.[70] His amendment was rejected by a surprisingly narrow majority.

Given these views, the exploitation of women at work was general and trade union organisation almost non-existent. While it may be considered that Leeds did not have a large casual labour force, or a sub-stratum, it may equally be that such a group existed but was ignored because it was female. Although some attempt was made to discuss male and female economic roles and relationships,[71] this did not become a major theoretical question in British socialism, and was left aside as socialists narrowed their concerns to the attack on the Liberal Party. The failure to confront and define the needs of women as part of the labour force damaged the strength of the movement as a whole. For example, one of the city's largest industries, ready-made clothing, remained effectively unorganised, its workers in four main unions divided by sex, by race and by skill, and a weak trade union presence characterised most other industries.

We have seen unemployment to be an ever-present problem in the early and mid-nineteenth century. There are no indications that it was less important between 1880 and 1914. In 1893 there was an 'exceptional depression', with a total of 12,000 people out of work, and between 1896 and 1904 unemployment ran at between 2 per cent and 5 per cent, figures based only on the most skilled and best organised groups of workers. In the annual report of the trades council for 1910 the secretary, Owen Connellan, claimed that increasing prices and the frequent short-time working between 1906 and 1910 meant that real wages were lower than they had been in the 1890s.

There was, then, a considerable degree of insecurity and hardship, which was as likely (and more normally) to result in competition for work among working people as to produce united and militant class action. The role of socialists, as conceived by Maguire and Mahon, was to produce working-class unity where the reality was fragmented political experience and economic insecurity.

VI   This chapter has emphasised the critical role played by a socialist leadership in the politics of the labour movement. It is necessary, however, to look more closely at what exactly socialism meant in the Leeds Labour Party, what ideas and values it conveyed, and how deeply these ideas penetrated the labour movement and working class.

Clearly working people were not always in a constant state of political excitement and activity. Neither can we speak of a working class already formed and eager to act as one politically. Politics and political abstraction were not at the forefront of working people's minds. Thus Richard Hoggart in an observation based on experience in Leeds, although at a later period, described the 'core of working-class attitudes' as being defined by a 'predominant sense of the personal, the concrete, the local: it is embodied in the idea of first, the family, and second, the neighbourhood . . .'.[72] The mother is the pivot of the home, and the 'working-class neighbourhoods are small worlds, each as homogeneous and well defined as a village'.[73] Working-class culture was neither revolutionary nor subversive. Aside from trade unionism its focal points were not politics and education but entertainment, sport and leisure-time activity.[74] Life itself was a constant struggle, not to raise the status of the working class against other classes, but for different occupational groups within the working class to maintain their status against other groups.[75]

Thus Ben Turner, the Yorkshire textile trade unionist, could dismiss the ideas of the syndicalists and industrial unionism in 1910:

> class snobbishness in the mills is against it . . . the warper looks down on the weaver . . . the twister is a superior person . . . and the man at two shillings a week more than the woolcomber is a little God Almighty in his own estimation . . .[76]

Stedman Jones has pointed out that historians have neglected to examine the relationship between working-class culture and the development of the labour movement.[77] The two areas have been treated as separate domains, not only by historians but also in the historical experience of the labour movement, which failed to connect politics, education and culture. Thus the persistence of working-class conservatism (reflected, for example, in the strength of nationalist feelings, support for the Empire, and the primacy of male authority in politics and the family) has not been well understood or analysed. The inability of the labour movement to develop an awareness of attitudes rooted in popular culture resulted in a form of socialism which was in many ways shortsighted and ignorant of a range of issues concerning power relationships in society, and this situation was in turn related to the material divisions and insecurities which characterised working-class life.

This chapter cannot attempt to touch on the popular culture of the Leeds working class, as reflected in, for example, music hall and public house life, in the popular press and literature, in clubs and societies, and in attitudes to sport, music, theatre and other pursuits. Attitudes to education and religion, in particular the effect of the 1870 Education Act, would also be rewarding areas of study. Lack of space, and the undeveloped nature of research into working-class cultural patterns in Yorkshire, make it possible merely to point to the importance of the relationship between popular culture and the labour movement.

Throughout the period 1880–1914, despite the strong influence of socialist ideas, the aggressive activity of the Labour Party, and the widespread use of a socialist vocabulary, one must not underestimate the continued persistence of a concern with what socialists would now refer to as economistic activity, or what labour movement activists then would have understood as the bread-and-butter issues of day-to-day trade unionism. The trades council, although it was important, as we have seen, as a political centre of the labour movement, was essentially an organisation to protect the interests of working people organised in particular trade unions. By far the greatest part of its time was devoted to mutal aid and support in the almost endless series of local strikes and lock-outs; to the collection and publication of lists of local businesses which paid union rates; and to the protection of the legal position of trade unions. It was concerned at least as much with the politics of trade unionism as with the politics of socialism.

At a more explicitly political level there was a remarkable tenacity of Lib–Lab conviction among leading sections of the labour movement. The struggle of socialists to commit the trades council and labour movement to independent political action was a much more protracted affair than is often realised. William Marston, trades council president for much of the 1890s, tried to channel the political needs of the labour movement by developing the work of the Labour Electoral Association, which itself tried to promote labour candidates through the Liberal Party. Marston, and two other trades councillors, Maundrill and Buckle, were all officials of the Leeds LEA from 1895. Even when the trades council affiliated to the LRC in 1900 a number of trade unionists did not regard the LRC as necessarily opposed to the Liberal Party. Owen Connellan saw the LRC as a body which would work in co-operation with it. Thus while Connellan represented Leeds at the Manchester conference of the LRC in 1901 he continued to represent the East ward as a Lib–Lab councillor. It was only after insistent pushing by members of the ILP that the Leeds LRC established itself as an alliance which included all trade union and socialist organisations but which excluded the Liberal Party.[78] Further, the socialists developed the LRC in Leeds so that it became distinct and separate from the trades council, as opposed to the ideas of Connellan, who, it seems, would have preferred the LRC to be a sub-committee of the trades council and under its control. The developing autonomy of the LRC was important, since the socialists on it had a vision of it developing as a mass political organisation, whereas under the guidance of Lib–Labs like Connellan, Kennedy and Buckle it might not have developed into anything more than a pressure group on the Liberal Party. By 1903, despite the reluctance of Connellan, the Leeds LRC had won the right to speak politically for the labour movement.

> That it be a standing order of this Council that [in any political action] the Leeds Trades Council take action with the Leeds LRC . . .[79]

Though a number of skirmishes with Connellan were still to come, the outlines of the battle had been won. With the splitting of William Marston's vote at the municipal elections of 1912 by a BSP member, and Connellan's acceptance by 1904 of the virtues of independent politics, the potential local leadership of a progressive Lib–Lab alliance was removed.

Recognising the basic weaknesses and insecurities in working-class economic and political life, where fragmentation and not unity was the norm, Maguire's socialism, taken up after his death by the Leeds ILP and LRC and others, became a matter of working for class unity rather than awaiting the 'objective' collapse of capitalism. The political potential of 1890–93, demonstrated by Maguire in the call to independent action, was developed through the critically important periods of 1897–98 and 1900–04, and consolidated in local election successes from 1906 to 1914. It is not sufficient to say merely that a reformist Labour Party developed, since this ignores those 'Socialist priorities expressed at local levels',[80] and the political realities the socialists confronted – that is, not a 'pure' working class but one deeply affected by the influence of strong middle-class political moulding. In Leeds a local socialist leadership won the support of the labour movement in the LRC and excluded the option of developing the LRC and the trades council within the Liberal Party.

It cannot be claimed that a mature socialist theory was formed in this period, fully adequate to the building of a socialist society. Many important questions were not asked – we have already referred to the way women were stereotyped. Industrial democracy and co-operative production were largely ignored. Another area of confusion stemmed from the relationship between white-collar/intellectual and manual labour. The existence of widespread poverty among the manual working class had a number of important consequences; firstly, the most creative theoreticians and activists of the movement in Leeds were often forced out of key positions by poverty. It killed Tom Maguire in the winter of 1895;[81] and John Mahon had to leave the city, being too well known to get work. Given this situation, the leadership which came to be institutionalised in the local Labour Party often came from more secure backgrounds and occupations; the man who emerged as full-time secretary of the Leeds Labour Party in 1912, D. B. Foster, had been a cloth merchant, buying his own business in 1887. His became an important voice in the Leeds movement, defining the content and objectives of socialist ideas and policy; we are aware at once that important changes have been made. There is a narrowing of socialist definitions to the point where socialism becomes *only* the amelioration of poverty by welfare measures, and the original preoccupations, concerned as they were with socialist production relationships and working-class self-activity, become subdominant. The class struggle too is rejected;

> The unfortunate thing about the class war is that it produces a very one-sided man. The members of the working class and the master class have both their special qualities . . . .[82]

Public service and citizenship are thus placed above class loyalty, since both transcend class to produce a higher 'social consciousness'. Hence the controlling ideas of socialism in Leeds by 1914 put national above class identity, society being a harmonious interrelationship of classes carrying out specialised functions. Even the left-wing BSP in Leeds regarded 'national feeling' as an important part of socialism, supported an increase in armaments, and not only acquiesced in the war but helped with the local recruitment campaigns.

For those who had developed their ideas in the Socialist League the creation of a political party of labour engaging in electoral contests for specific ameliorative measures was only a beginning: by 1914 dominant people in the Leeds Labour Party regarded an electoral majority in local and national government as an end in itself. In the narrowing down of the ideas of the labour movement in this way, ideological issues were confused or neglected. Socialists like Maguire were confronted with the hardships of working-class life, the insecurity and the competition between, and lack of unity among, members of the manual working class. The political domination of leading parts of the labour movement by Liberalism did little to challenge this division and perhaps much to sustain it. That was why political independence became a prerequisite of socialist strategy. We may conveniently summarise the objectives of Leeds Liberalism before 1914 with the following comment on the death of James Kitson: 'Sir James objected to the Labour Party's attempt to make themselves a separate class with distinct interests'.[83] Tackling the organisational principles of Liberalism and creating the context in which collective political action and responsibility could thrive against competitive individualism was the primary objective of the socialists in this period, an objective which involved greater struggle, and was characterised by a greater degree of theoretical coherence, than has often been realised. The labour movement did indeed free itself from Liberal hegemony during 1880–1914, and perhaps to have shed the old Liberal Party was a prerequisite for being able to ask theoretical questions which until then had been neglected.

NOTES

[1] See the review of developments in social history in E. Hobsbawm, 'From social history to the history of society', in M. W. Flinn and T. C. Smout (eds.), *Essays in Social History* (1974).

[2] *Royal Commission on the Housing of the Working Classes*, P.P. (1885), XXXI, 325. Evidence of G. Goldie, Leeds M.O.H.

[3] J. F. C. Harrison, 'Chartism in Leeds', in A. Briggs (ed.), *Chartist Studies* (1959), 65.

[4] *Ibid.*, 68–70, for biographical details of Bray.

[5] D. Fraser, *Urban Politics in Victorian England* (1976).

[6] E. P. Thompson, 'Homage to Tom Maguire', in A. Briggs and J. Saville (eds.), *Essays in Labour History* (1960), I, 302.

[7] For further discussion of these ideas see E. P. Thompson, 'Time, work discipline, and industrial capitalism', in Flinn and Smout, *op. cit.*

[8] Quoted in E. D. Steele, 'Leeds and Victorian politics', *University of Leeds Review*, XVII, 2 (1974), 260–1.

[9] Steele, *op. cit.*

[10] *Ibid.*, 282.

[11] J. Foster, *Class Struggle and the Industrial Revolution* (1974).

[12] For a discussion of the use of the concept of the labour aristocracy see H. Moorhouse, 'The Marxist theory of the labour aristocracy', *Social History*, III, 1 (1978).

[13] See the report on Leeds by Hales and Brighty for the Reform League, George Howell Collection, Bishopsgate Institute.

[14] J. Kitson to H. Gladstone, 4 April 1885, Viscount Gladstone Correspondence, B.M. Add. MSS, 46027. *James Kitson*, first Baron Airedale, 1833–1911. Iron and steel manufacturer, Lord Mayor of Leeds 1896–97. President of the Leeds Liberal Association 1880. President of the National Liberal Federation 1883–90. Colne Valley MP 1892–1907. *Herbert John Gladstone*, 1854–1930. Leeds MP 1880–85,

and subsequently MP for West Leeds until 1910. Chief Liberal whip 1899; Home Secretary 1905–10. Governor General of the Union of South Africa 1910.

[15] See, for example, A. Roberts, 'Leeds Liberalism and late Victorian politics', *Northern History*, V (1970).

[16] See D. Fraser, 'Areas of urban politics, Leeds, 1830–1880', in H. J. Dyos and M. Wolff (eds.), *The Victorian City* (1973), II, especially 779.

[17] P. F. Clarke, *Lancashire and the New Liberalism*, (1971).

[18] See, for example, H. Pelling, *Origins of the Labour Party, 1880–1900* (1965), 222, and R. Douglas, *History of the Liberal Party, 1895–1970* (1971).

[19] S. Pierson, *Marxism and the Origins of British Socialism* (1973), 276. See R. Miliband, *Parliamentary Socialism* (1973), for a socialist critique of the politics and history of the Labour Party.

[20] For a biography of James O'Grady see J. Saville and J. Bellamy (eds.), *Dictionary of Labour Biography* (1974), II.

[21] For details of this agreement see F. Bealey and H. Pelling, *Labour and Politics* (1958), especially ch. VI.

[22] 13 March 1903, Visct. Gladstone Correspondence, B.M. Add. MSS, 46106, Memo. on the Liberal–Labour pact marked 'Secret, Labour and Liberalism'.

[23] Clarke, *Lancashire and the New Liberalism*, especially ch. 15.

[24] J. S. Mathers to H. Gladstone, 20 November 1892, Visct. Gladstone Correspondence, B.M. Add. MSS, 46039.

[25] J. Henry to H. Gladstone, 9 April 1909, Visct. Gladstone Correspondence, B.M. Add. MSS, 46037.

[26] Henry to Gladstone, 2 November 1904, Visct. Gladstone Correspondence, B.M. Add. MSS, 46036.

[27] D. Jones, 'The Liberal press and the rise of Labour', unpublished Ph.D thesis, University of Leeds (1973), 93.

[28] A. J. Taylor, 'Leeds and the Victorian economy', *University of Leeds Review*, XVII, 2, 302.

[29] See B. M. Powell, 'A study of the change in social origins, political affiliations, and length of service of members of Leeds City Council, 1888–1953', unpublished M.A. thesis, University of Leeds (1958), 158.

[30] Kitson to Gladstone, 27 April 1893, Visct. Gladstone Correspondence, B.M. Add. MSS, 46028.

[31] E. P. Thompson, *William Morris* (1977), 76.

[32] A good survey of the ideas held by Leeds liberals is provided by Jones, *op. cit.*

[33] A. Mattison, *Notebook 3*, 76–7.

[34] The names appearing on the foundation certificate of the Leeds Socialist League show a proportionally high number of Irish surnames: C. Connell, F. Corkwell, J. Ferns, J. Finn, T. Hunter, F. Kelly, T. Maguire, P. Malone, J. Malone, J. O'Reilly, C. MacHal, S. Wooley, D. Wormald, J. Wormald, Williamson. *Socialist League Certificate*, February 1885 (Leeds city archives).

[35] *Justice*, 27 September 1884.

[36] John Lincoln Mahon MSS, 8 February 1885, Socialist League Collection.

[37] *Justice*, 13 September 1884.

[38] *Yorkshire Factory Times* (*Y.F.T.*), 12 July 1895.

[39] *Y.F.T.*, 19 December 1908. The first ILP municipal candidate in Leeds stood for an advanced welfare programme (*Y.F.T.*, 31 October 1890). For trade unions, welfare reforms and socialism were frequently directly equated. See, for example, the 'Yorks. Federation of Trades Councils Report', *Y.F.T.*, 20 January 1905.

[40] *Y.F.T.*, 4 November 1909.

[41] Thompson, in 'Homage to Tom Maguire', dates the handbill as 1888 but Mattison in *Leeds Weekly Citizen* (*L.W.C.*), 14 January 1918, and *Commonweal*,

15 October 1887, both indicate that the handbill came out in 1887.

[42] *L.W.C.*, 14 January 1918.

[43] *John Lincoln Mahon.* Born Edinburgh 1865. Irish parents. Father a skilled engine fitter, and this was Mahon's trade also. Arrived London 1884; toured the north of England 1887–88. Arrived in Leeds 1890; was blacked in Leeds and between 1895 and 1900 travelled in an attempt to resume work as an engineer. In Dublin 1900 as commercial salesman; returned to London 1904 and died there 1933. Joined BSP towards the end of the war but never as politically active as in the period 1884–95. For more details of his political career see E. P. Thompson's *William Morris*.

[44] *Commonweal*, 27 August 1887.

[45] See the account in Thompson's 'Homage to Tom Maguire'.

[46] *Leeds Evening Express*, 30 June 1890.

[47] Maguire to Edward Carpenter quoted in I. Ford (ed.), *Tom Maguire: a Remembrance* (1895).

[48] Thompson, 'Homage to Tom Maguire', 311.

[49] *Ibid.*, 303–4.

[50] S. Pierson, *Marxism and the Origins of British Socialism*, 248–9.

[51] *Y.F.T.*, 13 January 1893.

[52] See, for example, G. Stedman Jones, *Outcast London* (1971), E. Hobsbawm, 'Fabians reconsidered', *Labouring Men* (1964). J. Whelan, 'The working class in British socialist thought', unpublished M.Phil. thesis, University of Leeds (1974).

[53] *Labour Leader*, 1 September 1894.

[54] *Ibid.*

[55] J. L. Mahon, *Labour Programme* (1888).

[56] *Y.F.T.*, 26 February 1914.

[57] *Ibid.*, 7 January 1890.

[58] *Ibid.*, 3 April 1896.

[59] *Ibid.*, 21 January 1898.

[60] *Ibid.*, 8 June 1900.

[61] For a more detailed account of the strike see J. E. Williams, 'The Leeds Corporation strike of 1913', in A. Briggs and J. Saville (eds.), *Essays in Labour History, 1886–1926* (1971).

[62] *L.W.C.*, 23 January 1914.

[63] There is further evidence on wage rates in important Leeds industries in *Report of an Enquiry by the Board of Trade into Wages in the Engineering Industry in 1906*, P.P. (1911), LXXXVIII. *Report of an Enquiry . . . into the Textile Industry in 1906*, P.P. (1909), CCVI, and into *Building and Woodworking*, P.P. (1910) LXXXIV.

[64] *Y.F.T.*, 5 December 1890.

[65] *Ibid.*, 18 March 1904.

[66] Ben Tillett in *Y.F.T.*, 28 December 1894.

[67] Ford was a member of a prominent Quaker family at Adel, Leeds. She was a founder of the Tailoresses' Union, a member of the ILP and an active suffragette.

[68] *Y.F.T.*, 17 March 1893.

[69] See Baker's comments in his *Report on the Residences of the Labouring Classes in the Town of Leeds* (1842).

[70] Independent Labour Party, *First General Conference Report* (1893).

[71] See the discussion of Edward Carpenter's ideas in S. Rowbotham and J. Weekes, *Socialism and the New Life* (1977), and A. Marles's interesting discussion of prostitution in *Hypnotic Leeds* (1894).

[72] R. Hoggart, *Uses of Literacy* (1957), 33.

[73] *Ibid.*, 59.

[74] G. Stedman Jones, 'Working class culture and working class politics in London, 1870–1900', *Bulletin of the Society for the Study of Labour History*, No. 27 (autumn 1973), 29.

[75] R. Roberts, *The Classic Slum* (1971), especially ch. 1.

[76] *Y.F.T.*, 9 June 1910.

[77] Stedman Jones, 'Working class culture', 29.

[78] *Y.F.T.*, 12 September 1902.

[79] *Ibid.*, 27 March 1903.

[80] Thompson, *William Morris*, 775.

[81] See the account of Maguire's death in A. Mattison, *Notebook 1*, 8 March 1895.

[82] D. B. Foster, *Life Story* (1924).

[83] *Yorkshire Post*, 17 March 1911.

BIBLIOGRAPHICAL NOTE

This bibliography is composed of material already mentioned in footnotes and of additional references intended as a guide to further reading and research.

The labour movement and social history. There are several accounts of the history and politics of the labour movement nationally, offering different interpretations. Among these are H. Pelling, *The Origins of the Labour Party, 1880–1900* (1965); R. Miliband, *Parliamentary Socialism* (1973); W. Kendall, *The Revolutionary Movement in Britain, 1900–1921* (1969). Trade union history is covered by H. Pelling, *History of British Trade Unionism* (1963), and more critically by T. Lane, *The Union makes us Strong* (1974). A good social history of the working class covering the period of this chapter is provided by S. Meacham, *A Life apart: the English Working Class, 1890–1914* (1977). For the earlier period see A. Briggs (ed.), *Chartist Studies* (1959). An account of the emergence and politics of the SDF and the Socialist League, with much reference to Leeds, is contained in E. P. Thompson, *William Morris* (1977).

The politics of the Leeds labour movement: sources. A fascinating but regrettably brief glimpse of the nature of the Socialist League in Leeds, and of the personality of Tom Maguire, may be gained from the *Correspondence of John Lincoln Mahon and Tom Maguire (1885–1888), Socialist League Collection*, International Institute of Social History, Amsterdam. Indispensable guides to archive and source material appear in the *Bulletin of the Society for the Study of Labour History*. Additionally, see G. B. Woolven, 'Publications of the Independent Labour Party', *Society for the Study of Labour History*, Aids to Research, No. 2 (1977). There is also a great deal of personal reminiscence combined with a chronicle of Leeds labour events in the *Journals, Notebooks, Newspaper Cuttings* and *Scrapbooks* of Alfred Mattison, from his early involvement with the Socialist League and then the ILP and the Labour Party until his death in 1944. The Labour Party in Leeds is covered by the following: *City of Leeds Labour Party: Leeds Labour Representation Committee, General Ledger and Memoranda Book, 1911–31. Leeds Labour Representation Committee, Minutes of General Executive, and Executive Group Meetings, 1912–16, Leeds Labour Representation Committee, Yearbooks, 1908–16.* The most relevant of the reminiscences of labour and socialist pioneers are *Tom Maguire, a Remembrance: being Selections from the Prose and Verse Writings of a Socialist Pioneer* (1895), with memoirs by E. Carpenter and A. Mattison, containing a short biography of Tom Maguire and a collection of his poems which deal with the varieties of everyday experience of working class life. D. B. Foster's *Life Story* (1924) provides an account of the career and political ideas of an influential figure within the early Labour Party, while Mary Gawthorpe's *Up Hill to Holloway* (1962) has a good account of the social background and political involvement of a woman active later in the suffragette movement.

Newspapers. Yorkshire Factory Times (weekly, 1889–1926), for information on trades unionism in Leeds and Yorkshire. *The Labour Chronicle* and the *Labour Champion* were two pro-ILP newspapers published by Maguire, Mattison and others in May and June, and October and November 1893. The *Labour Leader*, the paper of the ILP, containing frequent reports on Leeds with articles by Maguire ('Gurth') which give a good insight into the political ideas of the Leeds ILP. *Commonweal*, the paper of the Socialist League, with reports on the affairs of the Leeds branch in the mid-1880s. The *Leeds Weekly Citizen*, the paper of the Labour Party, which has run continuously since 1911.

Secondary sources. E. P. Thompson, 'Homage to Tom Maguire', in A. Briggs and J. Saville (eds.), *Essays in Labour History* (1960), considers the role of Maguire in the emergence of independent labour politics, while J. E. Willaims, 'The Leeds Corporation strike of 1913', in Briggs and Saville (eds.), *Essays in Labour History, 1886–1926* (1971), describes the impact of a strike which did much to confirm the separation of the labour movement from the Liberal councillors. For information prior to the period 1880–1914 see J. F. C. Harrison, 'Chartism in Leeds', in A. Briggs (ed.), *Chartist Studies*, and *id.*, 'Social reform in Victorian Leeds: the work of James Hole, 1820–1895', *Thoresby Soc.*, Monograph No. 3 (1954). G. D. H. Cole, *Attempts at General Union, 1818–1834* (1953), contains information on early Yorkshire trade unionism. Very little has been published on the experience of the Leeds labour movement in the middle of the nineteenth century, between the decline of Owenism and Chartism and the socialist revival of the 1880s, although D. Fraser, *Urban Politics in Victorian England* (1976), analyses general political developments.

Social and economic conditions, 1880–1914. The *Yorkshire Factory Times* provides a good source for day-to-day wages and conditions in the main trades. There is no general analysis of standards of living but sources include *Report of an Enquiry by the Board of Trade into Working Class Rents, Housing, and Retail Prices, Together with the Standard Rate of Wages . . .*, P.P. (1908), CVII [Cd. 3864]; *Report of an Enquiry by the Board of Trade into Wages in the Engineering Industry in 1906*, P.P. (1911), LXXXVIII; *Report of an Enquiry by the Board of Trade into Working Class Rents and Retail Prices Together with the Rates of Wages in Certain Occupations in Industrial Towns of the U.K. in 1912* (1913), LXVI [Cd. 6955]. More general accounts of social conditions may be gained from D. B. Foster, *Leeds Slumdom* (1897); A. Marles (ed.), *Hypnotic Leeds* (1894), and the Leeds Fabian Society and the ILP, *Leeds and the Unemployed* (1905). For the earlier part of the century see R. Baker, 'Report on the condition of the town of Leeds and of its inhabitants', *Journal of the Statistical Society of London*, II (1839–40). Finally there is a good bibliography covering conditions in early and mid-nineteenth-century Leeds in J. F. C. Harrison, *Living and Learning* (1961).

ARTHUR J. TAYLOR

XV

Victorian Leeds: an overview

I   In 1870 Leeds was first among English provincial towns in terms of area, fourth in population. In area the town was more than four times as large as either Liverpool or Manchester, in population it was less than three-quarters the size of either.

Comparisons of this kind may be significant for the light they throw on the practice of local government, but they mislead in their implications for urban topography. Leeds in 1870 was still a town with its population heavily concentrated in a narrow heartland bordering the river Aire. Three-quarters of its inhabitants were housed in little more than an eighth of its area, together with all its factories, workshops, warehouses and offices. The later suburbs of an expanding city – Headingley, Chapeltown and, even more, Bramley and Farnley – still retained much of their village character; Horsforth, Adel, Alwoodley and Roundhay as yet lay outside the borough boundary. During the next half-century this situation changed not so much by a thinning out of the population in the old area of intensive settlement – though there was some movement away from the central districts – as by the transfer of the burden of growth to the outer areas: Potternewton, for example, increased its population from 9,000 to 26,000 in the course of a single decade between 1891 and 1901. The main agent of this expansion was the tramcar, which first made its appearance in 1870,[1] but this powerful instrument of change was abetted by no less potent forces of social discrimination making for territorial differentiation between the classes. A distinction, familiar to politicians, has long been made between north and south Leeds. It was to the higher and healthier ground of the north and west that the middle classes retreated from the smoke and congestion of the growing industrial town, while industry and its attendant working population clung to the river valleys of the Aire and the Meanwood beck and spilled out to the south on to the coalfield at Beeston and beyond.

In the second half of the nineteenth century the population had grown, partly by a high rate of natural increase, partly by immigration. Between 1870 and 1900 the town gained on balance 36,000 citizens by migration – all but 6,000 of whom it lost as the flow was reversed in the next decade.[2] The ebb and flow of migrants which these figures indicate was largely short-distance in character. In 1911, as forty years earlier, two-thirds of the population had been born in the town and half the remainder elsewhere in Yorkshire. Twice in the course of the nineteenth century, however, Leeds experienced the shock waves of expulsive migratory forces overseas. By the end of the century there were perhaps 20,000 people of Irish descent in the town, and from 1880 it played host to a steadily increasing number of Jewish immigrants from Russia and from Russian Poland.

Leeds, unlike Manchester and Liverpool, had only a small community of Jews before 1880. Thereafter, however, in the wake of the Russian pogroms the number grew rapidly. The census of 1891 recorded 4,540 inhabitants as born in Russia or Poland – less than a sixth of the number suggested two years earlier before the Select Committee on Emigration and Immigration by Alderman Scarr, but consistent with the figure of 5,000–6,000 which Rabbi Moses Abrahams presented as his estimate of the Jewish population to the same enquiry.[3] Twenty years later, in 1911, the number had increased to 6,422. If allowance is made for the children and grandchildren born to these Russian expatriates, it seems probable that upwards of 15,000 Jews were living in Leeds on the eve of the first world war.

Their significance on the life of the city, therefore, was less numerical than social and economic. The ghetto-like existence to which they had been condemned in Russia was imposed upon them again by force of circumstance and habit. Poor, if not wholly penurious, the immigrants settled in a triangle of land immediately to the north of the city centre bounded to west and east by North Street and Regent Street, with its apex at Sheepscar – the district known by its proximity to the Meanwood beck as the Leylands.[4] Within two decades the immigrants had come to monopolise the housing in this district. There they formed a tightly-knit community, excluding from its territory the indigenous population but encroaching little on the areas outside these narrow confines. Even as late as 1914 the immigrants had pushed only marginally out of the area westward towards Camp Road and northward towards Chapeltown and Harehills. Directory evidence suggests that only a handful of Jewish families had established themselves outside the Leylands and its immediate vicinity. As yet in residential terms there was no more than the beginning of the social differentiation which was to become as much the characteristic of the Jewish community as of the Leeds population at large.

Like every alien community, particularly one recently and quickly established, the Jews attracted varying degrees of interest, suspicion and antagonism from the wider citizen body. At its worst, antagonism could mean social ostracism or even physical molestation; at a lower level there were complaints about the condition of Jewish houses and workplaces, and accusations that Jewish workmen undercut the wages and prejudiced the employment of native workers. While the immigrants were praised for their personal morality and orderly behaviour, they were said to work excessive hours and to indulge in sharp commercial practices.[5]

The early settlers found employment largely in the tailoring and shoe-making industries. Of 2,600 Jews whose occupation can be clearly traced through the 1891 census over 70 per cent were employed in tailoring and almost half the remainder in boot and shoe-making.[6] Over the next quarter-century there was some shift from manufacturing industry into trade but there is little evidence of penetration beyond the narrow range of industrial and trading occupations into the wider fields of commerce, administration and the professions. As late as 1910 Jewish doctors and lawyers in Leeds could be counted on the fingers of one hand; and though Jewish children were winning more than their proportionate share of places in the new local authority secondary schools, they had scarcely penetrated into the independent Grammar and High schools.[7]

On the value of the contribution which the immigrants made to the town's expanding economy there were divergent views. Alderman Scarr, himself an immigrant – from Burnley – considered that immigration had 'contributed to the commercial prosperity of the town' and that it would be a misfortune to 'limit labour of any kind'. By contrast, William Clayton, the chairman of the board of guardians, thought it a pity that foreigners were admitted to England while Englishmen were 'walking about the streets in want of work'.[8] In this he would seem to have echoed an increasing volume of trade union opinion.[9] Jewish workmen undoubtedly put in long hours and to that extent their presence arguably was destructive of employment opportunity; but the Jew was an easy scapegoat for more general changes that were affecting the prosperity of the older craft industries in Edwardian England. The bespoke tailoring craftsmen who were particularly vocal in their criticism of Jewish working practices were as much the victims of new machinery and the concomitant division of labour as of the competitive zeal of the Jewish workmen.

II   In its occupational structure the Jewish workforce was untypical of the working community at large – even of that part of it which was concentrated in the more distinctively working-class areas of the south and east of the town. By 1891 tailoring had become the largest single industry in Leeds but even at its pre-war peak twenty years later it employed barely a fifth of the labour force. Moreover, while for Jews tailoring was primarily a male occupation, the industry in general depended on women and girls for its main source of labour.[10]

In 1871 cloth-making, engineering and tailoring employed respectively one-fifth, one-seventh and one-tenth of the adult labour force. Forty years later the roles of cloth-making and tailoring in the industrial economy had been reversed, as also had their proportionate contributions to the provision of working-class employment. Tailoring was a fast-expanding and cloth manufacture, once the Leeds staple, a stagnant industry. But it was engineering, capital-intensive and male-dominated, that had established itself as the backbone of the city's industrial economy.

Within these three major industries, as indeed outside them, there was great variety in the nature and form of manufacture and enterprise. From the city's engineering workshops came products so diverse as textile machinery, agricultural implements, railway locomotives and machine tools; even in decline the textile industry produced not only traditional woollens and worsteds but also cotton yarn and linen cloth; and this diversity brought with it variety in the form and size of business operation. Nowhere was this more evident than in tailoring, where, side by side with the large factory-based concerns of John Barran and John Hepworth, there existed numerous small workshop enterprises run by Jewish entrepreneurs working either independently or under contract to one of the larger factory concerns.[11]

Industry, however, by no means exhausted the employment opportunities of the citizens of late Victorian Leeds. Between 1870 and 1914 tertiary employment gained greatly in significance, as in other large towns. The proportionate increase in such employment between 1861 and 1911 has been calculated at over 40 per cent – from 18·6 per cent of the employed population in 1871 to 26·7 per cent in 1911. There were increases in the proportion of the labour force engaged in transport from 4·0 to 7·9 per cent, in commerce from 1·6 to 5·6 per cent and in the professions from 2·5 to 3·6 per cent – though on the other side of the ledger employment in domestic and other forms of service declined from 9·3 to 7·0 per cent.[12] By comparison with other large industrial centres, Leeds by 1911 was second only to Manchester in the proportion of workers engaged in the professions and in the higher branches of commerce, but the city was inferior to Manchester and Liverpool and also, significantly, to Bradford in the employment of business and commercial clerks.[13]

At a more immediately obvious level, the increasing sophistication of commercial life at the turn of the century was manifest in the development of the central shopping area, with the widening of major arteries like Briggate and Boar Lane and the virtual sterilisation of the town centre as a residential area. To this period belong the creation of the shopping arcades and the new market, with its elaborate Vicar Lane facade, and also the advent of the multiple shop and the department store. It was in Leeds in January 1881 that Thomas Lipton, the Scottish pioneer of the multiple grocery trade, opened his first English shop, soon to be followed by competitors both from outside and from within the town.[14] The department stores were in the main indigenous growths, developments from modest drapery establishments. By 1914 such stores were strategically placed in and around the commercial heart of the city – Matthias Robinson in Briggate in the east, Snowden Schofield in the Victoria Arcade and Upper Headrow to the north, Marshall and Snelgrove to the west and Monteith Hamilton and Monteith, trading under the name of the Grand Pygmalion, in Boar Lane to the south. Their location would seem to have had a significant influence on the quality of their trade and the social class of their customers. In addition the Leeds Industrial Co-operative Society, with its central premises in Albion Street, was at once multiple shop and department store, while on opposite sides of Briggate F. W. Woolworth and Marks and Spencer, 'the original Penny bazaar' of the Kirkgate Market, had already staked out their long-term positions.[15]

III   Viewed from the higher ground towards Woodhouse moor, where the dwellings of the prospering middle class were appearing in increasing numbers, the central core of Leeds in the river valley presented itself in 1870 as a thriving modern town. The smoke rising from hundreds of factory chimneys and thousands of tightly packed houses told of a community large in numbers and busily engaged in the production and distribution of industrial wealth. Crowning this urban agglomeration the resplendent dome of Broderick's Town Hall testified to civic pride, achievement and aspiration.

In the valley where the majority of its citizens lived, and where the wealth was created, perspectives could be different. As recently as 1866 the Medical Officer of the Privy Council, Dr John Simon, had described public health provision as 'in proportion to the importance of the town ... perhaps ... the worst which has come to the knowledge of this department'. The town presented 'a surprising sight, bringing to remembrance the condition of many English towns of twenty years ago'.[16] Three years later, in 1869, J. G. Fitch, the assiduous investigator of the Schools Inquiry Commission, spoke of Leeds as 'one of the most benighted towns, educationally, in the country'.[17]

In its failure to meet adequately the problems of nineteenth-century industrialisation and urbanisation Leeds was by no means unique. No large town was without its central area where overcrowding, disease and premature death went hand in hand. Leeds, however, was both tardy in facing up to its problems and spasmodic in the pursuit of remedies. It needed catastrophic events like the visitation of the cholera in the 1840s, the abnormal death rates and the government inquiry of the '60s, and the Headingley typhoid epidemic of 1889 to stir the municipal authority into thought and action, but reforming zeal tended to evaporate as soon as the immediate crisis was past.

This failure of will, most important in its consequences for public health, extended to the whole field of local government. For this, blame has been laid on a town council which for a crucial twenty years between *c.* 1870 and *c.* 1890 was in the hands of a group of men who were by vocation small tradesmen, by political persuasion Liberal and by religious affiliation Nonconformists.[18] These predispositions bred a belief in the principle of self-help. They encouraged a sense of responsibility in the individual citizen and no less promoted a jealous rejection of the intervention of central government in municipal affairs. A virtue was made of economy, reflected in the modesty both of the demands placed upon the ratepayer's pocket and of the rewards paid to the authority's servants. As a result, in 1870 the council's expenditure outside the field of law and order amounted to no more than £22,000, of which less than a fifth went in the payment of salaries to its officials.[19] It is hardly surprising that an authority which ran its affairs on so tight a shoestring should in 1872 have baulked at the prospect of offering its incoming medical officer of health the £500 it had paid his predecessor while at the same time, out of a misguided sense of principle, refusing to accept the subvention which the central government offered it to maintain the former level of payment. The price of this civic cheeseparing was paid in the typhoid epidemic of 1889.[20]

The record of the '70s and '80s, however, was not wholly one of inaction. At the most basic level, the middens and ashpits of the central area which had been a prime cause of the high death rates of earlier decades were gradually replaced by communal water closets and, in part as a result of this, the death rate fell sharply after 1875. Roundhay Park was acquired in 1872, largely on John Barran's initiative; to it went the trams which contributed not only to the town's economy but also to its health. Until 1892, however, the tramway system was allowed to remain in private hands and gave by no means general satisfaction. The council was more enterprising in buying out the two companies supplying gas in 1870 and, after some initial alarms, ran this service both to the satisfaction of consumers and to its own profit. Other positive acts were the taking of powers under the Public Libraries Act in 1868 and the building, eighteen years later, of a municipal art gallery, the construction of New Briggate and the widening of Leeds bridge, and the tentative beginning of a programme of slum clearance. Yet beneficial as were these and other similar acts, they compare unfavourably with the more substantial achievements of Chamberlain's Birmingham and even with those of the less strongly directed councils of Manchester and Liverpool.[21]

This lack of civic ambition and aspiration derived in part from social and even sectarian causes; but it also had economic roots. A clue to these is provided by the returns of the tax inspectors, details of which exist for the single year 1877–78.[22] The amount charged in income and property tax in that year was less than a third of that in either Liverpool or Manchester and little more than two-thirds of the amount levied in Birmingham. Even when allowance is made for differences in size of population, Liverpool and Manchester, and to a lesser degree Birmingham, emerge as markedly wealthier towns than Leeds. A *per capita* comparison indeed gives Bradford also – but not Sheffield – a higher income. Generalisations based on the experience of single years may, of course, mislead, but the size of the differentials – paralleling those in ratable values – suggests that the difference in wealth was more than ephemeral. Moreover the cost of educational provision under the Act of 1870 fell more heavily on Leeds ratepayers in these years than on those of other large towns and no doubt encouraged economies in other areas of public welfare.

A pronounced change in the attitude and performance of the municipal authority came in the 1890s. Though it coincided with the end of the long sixty-year reign of the Liberal Party in Leeds, it is an over-simplification to explain the change of policy wholly in party-political terms. The shift in political control following the aldermanic elections of 1895 and the general change in the political climate of the town undoubtedly influenced the outlook and policies of the council but it would be facile to interpret this simply as a victory for Conservative munificence over Liberal parsimony. In the parallel field of educational provision it was the Liberals who, albeit for sectarian reasons, showed a disposition to spend and the Conservatives to economise. The change in party fortunes after 1890 was part of a more fundamental movement in the public life of the borough which outlasted the town's return to its old political allegiance in the early years of the new century. Alongside the shift in party representation went a change in the personnel of the council, bringing with it, on the one hand, a decline in the numbers and influence of the shopocracy and, on the other, both a revival in the active participation in council affairs of representatives of professional and more substantial business interests, and the arrival of labour as an effective pressure group both outside and within the council. These forces inside the town itself were reinforced by the increasing involvement, both legislative and financial, of central government in local affairs and the development of a public opinion more favourable to welfare provision and to 'gas and water socialism'.

Under these pressures the city council, as it became from 1893, sought to repair the neglect of the preceding century. The council set out to improve the deficient water supply, embarked on a major programme of clearance in the older central areas, replanned much of the city centre, took over and extended the tramway system and made a modest beginning in the creation of an electricity supply. Much the heaviest commitment, however, came with the Education Act of 1902 and the designation of the council as the authority responsible for the provision of education at both the primary and the secondary level. As a result of these extensions of its activities the city council by 1914 was itself raising and spending over £400,000 annually. Of this sum almost half went to the support of the education services, in respect of which the city also received over £200,000 from the Board of Education and £30,000 from pupils' fees. The main items on the income side of the account, apart from these Exchequer subventions, were rate receipts of £225,000, and £100,000 drawn as a share of the profits of the city's trading concerns. Outside education, the maintenance of the police force, the courts and the gaols still took the major part of civic expenditure, but the parks committee alone disposed of more money than had sufficed the borough council for all its operations apart from law and order in 1870; and the total salary bill for the council's officials, less than £5,000 in 1870, had now reached £80,000.[23]

IV   Before 1870 the Leeds Corporation had had no responsibility for the provision of education. Elementary education in so far as it was not wholly in private hands was a matter solely between the denominational societies and the State – an arrangement in which the representatives of God and Caesar neither needed nor desired the services of any local intermediary. On the adequacy of this provision in qualitative terms there is room for differences of judgement; on its quantity the investigations made by Joshua Fitch throw much valuable light.[24]

In 1869 there were 58,000 children between the ages of three and thirteen in Leeds and 29,000 children on the registers of schools in the town, of whom no more than two-thirds were in regular attendance. Though the greater proportion of school places were in inspected schools, up to one-third of the children were in one of the many one-man – or, more commonly, one-woman – schools, each offering instruction to a handful of pupils. The majority of children were without regular educational provision of any kind and what was offered to the minority was frequently of poor quality.

Differences in the numbers on the rolls of schools in the main sub-divisions of the Leeds area indicate wide variations in educational provision. In Holbeck there were places for two-thirds of the three-to-thirteen age group, in Hunslet for only 40 per cent; in the centre of the town Fitch found National schools 'so near as to be in a relation of injurious rivalry, while other places [were] left wholly unsupplied'.[25]

In terms of the availability of places in grant-aided schools Leeds in 1870 compared unfavourably with all other large provincial towns except Sheffield. Liverpool, for example, had twice as many grant-aided school places. This deficiency was in part the result of the relative smallness of the Catholic population in Leeds, in part the consequence of the powerful hold which the voluntaryist movement exercised on local Nonconformist opinion.[26] Edward Baines, for long a strong opponent of State involvement in elementary education, had by 1870 tempered this opposition but the outcome of his long-pursued campaign against State aid was a situation in which the number of pupils in Anglican schools outnumbered those in Nonconformist schools by almost four to one, with detrimental consequences not only for the education of Nonconformist children but for Leeds elementary education in general.

Beyond the elementary level Leeds had little to offer in educational opportunity. In 1870 the long-established Grammar School had no more than 200 boys on its register. The school's pupils were drawn largely from among the sons of the wealthier business and professional men of the town.[27] The Leeds Commercial and Mathematical School, established in 1845 by and under the management of the committee of the Leeds Mechanics' Institute and Literary Society, was distinguished from the Grammar School as 'a school where the sons of tradesmen, clerks and middle or lower middle classes [might] obtain a good, sound and thorough education at reasonable cost'.[28] This boys' school had been joined in 1854 by a girls' school of equal size and ambition. Between them in 1870 these two schools offered education to upwards of 400 boys and girls. Parallel to them and equally class-oriented were the Leeds Church Middle Class Schools, Victorian foundations attached to the parish church of St. Peter's.[29]

The 1870s were in many respects a climacteric decade in the developing life of Leeds, but, whereas in the more general stream of civic activity the forward movement tended to lose some of its impetus with the passing of time, in education the advance begun in 1870 was not only substantial but long-lasting. The developments of the decade were in part a response to central government prompting, in part a consequence of local enthusiasm and initiative. Leeds in 1870 was among the first towns to establish a School Board under the provisions of Forster's Education Act; in 1874 the Yorkshire College was established to promote the study and teaching of science and technology in Leeds and more generally in the West Riding; and in 1876 the combined efforts of the Yorkshire Ladies' Council of Education and the Leeds Ladies' Educational Association brought into existence the Leeds Girls' High School.

The newly elected School Board inherited a deficiency of at least 20,000 school places and a situation in which only one-fifth of the three-to-thirteen age group were attending a school under government inspection. It also fell heir to the controversy, part sectarian, part political, which had raged throughout the preceding thirty years. From 1870 the struggle between the two parties was institutionalised in the triennial elections to the School Board and in the Board's proceedings, but whereas the voluntaryists had effectively limited school-building by their refusal of State aid, it was now the policy and interest of Liberal Dissent to promote the establishment of Board schools. Since the representatives of Dissent were commonly in a majority on the Board, the only brake on development was provided by the pressure exerted in the early years by the Ratepayers' Protection Society and by the Liberal predisposition to economy. In general, however, the Dissenting element on the Board was vigorously expansionist – to the extent on at least one occasion of defying the Board of Education by building in excess of authorised accommodation standards – and it was only during the short period of Liberal eclipse between 1879 and 1882 that economy became the watchword of Board policy.[30]

By 1876, when elementary education became compulsory, the

Board had already provided over 15,000 places in sixteen new schools. Within a further four years the number of schools was doubled and the places increased beyond 28,500. Thereafter, as demand and supply came more closely into balance, the pace of building slowed. Nevertheless thirteen new schools with 12,000 further places were provided in the '80s and eleven schools with 11,500 places in the '90s. By 1902, when the Board reluctantly handed over its responsibilities to the city council, it passed on fifty-seven schools with places for 52,564 pupils. By 1914 a further 11,600 places had been made available, comfortably accommodating the 57,760 pupils then on the local authority registers. In the voluntary schools the margin was much slimmer. Places in the local authority schools outnumbered those in the voluntary schools by more than two to one, and the surplus of over 6,000 in the local authority area compared with one of less than 200 in the private sector.[31]

The establishment of the public school system was a prodigious achievement in financial and physical terms and in the response to the demands that were placed upon both teachers and administrators; but it was also significant for the new partnerships which were established between central and local authority and between public and private enterprise. It is not surprising, therefore, that, when the early obstacles had been overcome so successfully, the pioneers of the new educational order should have sought out further areas of conquest. They found them in the growing need and demand for education beyond the elementary level.

The Grammar School, which Fitch had praised in 1869 as much for the excellence of its teaching as for the commodious stateliness of its new buildings, now came under more critical scrutiny. In 1895 A. P. Laurie, acting for the Bryce Commission, castigated the school as badly directed and poorly run.[32] Its governing body was dominated by Anglican and Conservative interests, its curriculum gave too little weight to science and too much to languages, its masters were 'sleepy' and there was 'a general want of smartness and briskness about the way in which the classes [were] conducted'. Educational excellence is no doubt, in part at least, in the mind of the observer. Laurie was himself a scientist – and also, one suspects, a Liberal and a Dissenter. He was certainly no friend of the old order. His strictures were excusably and, on the evidence, to a degree justifiably resented. But the school's numbers had in fact declined in recent years and with this had come a narrowing of the already limited social range from which its pupils were drawn. Justified or not, the criticisms of Laurie and others provided a stimulus to change, and the Grammar School charted a reformed course into the new century.[33]

More appealing to Laurie than the Grammar School was the Central Higher Grade School – 'the most interesting school in Leeds in many ways'.[34] The school had emerged clandestinely out of the School Board system. Coincidentally with its establishment in permanent buildings at the lower end of Woodhouse Lane in 1885 it had acquired a new and vigorous headmaster in D. A. Forsyth. From the outset Forsyth had superimposed an organised senior science school on the elementary forms. By 1894 there were over 2,200 pupils on the register of a school whose official capacity was no more than 1,000. The school had acquired a reputation extending far beyond the city, but its success made it the more vulnerable to the charge that State resources were being used to undertake activities beyond those proper for a Board school. Nevertheless the school survived and prospered along with the older Mathematical and Commercial Schools (renamed the Leeds Modern Schools in 1897) and two later constituted Higher Grade schools – Cockburn and Thoresby – to provide the springboard for the development of public secondary education after 1902. Along with the Grammar and Girls' High schools and more recent Catholic foundations, the local authority secondary schools had by 1914 established the system of secondary education which was to serve the city until the end of the second world war.[35]

In its early years the Yorkshire College of Science, destined to become in 1904 the University of Leeds, was in many respects more secondary school than university. The vacuum which existed in the teaching of science before 1870 had been filled only to a very limited degree by the creation of the Mathematical and Commercial Schools and the Leeds Church Middle Class Schools. The initial spur to the development of the Yorkshire College was provided by the needs of local industry, but such were the limitations of the school system that the college had in its early years to undertake science teaching of a most elementary kind and with a distinctive industrial application. From the outset, however, the capacity and ambition of the college's teachers – its three foundation professors were all elected to the fellowship of the Royal Society – far outran the ability of its students. To ambition was soon added the desire to emulate the achievements of sister institutions in Manchester and Liverpool. The college broadened its structure by adding first medicine – through a marriage of mutual convenience with the longer-established Leeds Medical School – and then the arts to its curriculum, and by creating a department for the training of teachers to complement the provision made by the civic authority in the City of Leeds Training College. In 1887 it became the third partner in the Victoria University, and when in 1904 Manchester and Liverpool had both gone their separate university ways the Yorkshire College also reluctantly assumed the status of a separate university.[36]

This reluctance was born out of a sense of inadequacy, itself the result of financial undernourishment. Despite the early munificence of local philanthropists like Edward Baines and John Barran, and still more the support of the London Clothworkers' Company, the Yorkshire College was, by Lancashire or Birmingham standards, under-financed. As Baines himself expressed it, 'We cannot get such donations as they got at Manchester and at Birmingham; we are a quieter, slower town and our neighbourhood is quieter'.[37] It is to the credit of the city council that what its citizens as individuals failed to offer the authority corporately in part made good by the provision of an annual grant greater than that offered to their local universities by the city councils of either Manchester or Liverpool. Notwithstanding this, in financial terms Leeds remained in 1914 significantly the weakest of the three successor universities of the old Victoria University. Yet with more than a thousand students, an eminent vice-chancellor in Sir Michael Sadler and a distinguished physicist, William Bragg, soon to be a Nobel prizewinner, among its professoriate, the university had fully established itself at the head of the educational pyramid in its city and its region. The creation of the total edifice was perhaps the most impressive achievement of the civic community in the half-century between 1870 and 1914.

V   Through the close fabric of civic life in the nineteenth century ran the twin threads of religious and political division and controversy. At the middle of the century Leeds had been pre-eminently, if by no means exclusively, a Dissenters' town. Of its churchgoers only a third were Anglicans, almost 60 per cent Nonconformists. In spite of the vigorous creation of new parishes and the erection of new churches and schools by Dr Hook and his successors at St Peter's, this predominance, though declining, persisted to the end of the century: as late as 1872, when the main work of new church-building was over, the established Church provided only 36 per cent of the church sittings in the town.[38]

Among the Dissenters were prominent Congregationalists like Baines, and the still influential members of the Mill Hill Unitarian congregation, but in 1851 the Methodists outnumbered all other Nonconformists by more than two to one, and there is no indication that they had surrendered this numerical primacy by the end of the century. Among the Methodists the Wesleyans in their turn enjoyed a clear predominance. Whereas in much of north-eastern England

Primitive Methodism was particularly strong and drew its adherents substantially from among the working classes, in Leeds, as elsewhere in the West Riding, Wesleyanism was the largest Methodist sect, and its following was as much made up of members of the middle as of the working class. Wesleyanism was also, both in religious and in political terms, the most conservatively inclined of the Nonconformist sects. Nevertheless the association between Dissent and Liberalism was always close, and more particularly so among political activists. As late as 1891–92, when the links between political and religious radicalism were beginning to weaken, only four of twenty-seven Liberal councillors whose denominational affiliations can be traced were Anglicans. The remaining twenty-three were all Nonconformists, and fifteen of these were Methodists.[39] Notable exceptions like Sir Andrew Fairbairn, a prominent and influential member of the School Board in the early years, only point the general rule. Fairbairn was both a Liberal and an Anglican, but his influence on the Board derived in part at least from the uniqueness of his dual allegiance.

For sixty years from the creation of the new corporation in 1835 until 1895, when a Conservative majority finally materialised, the Leeds authority was in the hands of a Liberal majority. The Liberal dominance of the borough's parliamentary representation was never equally effective. In six out of nine general elections between 1832 and 1865 Conservatives shared the electoral spoils in the two-member constituency, though the Conservatives never won both seats and only once was a Conservative candidate able to head the poll. The Liberals' failure to exercise in parliamentary affairs the total dominance they enjoyed at municipal level was in fact as much a consequence of Liberal division as of Conservative strength. The Liberals in Leeds were a many-sided party, frequently at odds among themselves and in no way reticent in airing these internal disputes in the public arena. For many years before 1870 the party had been in the play of the forces of voluntaryism and teetotalism, which, while they appealed to and indeed largely sprang from the interests of radical Dissent, were less welcome to those of more moderate persuasion.

The second Reform Act of 1867 increased the town's parliamentary electorate fivefold and, by giving a preponderance to working-class voters, provided the basis for renewed Liberal dominance. But although at the next three general elections a Liberal candidate was always at the head of the poll, the party managed the elections in the new three-member constituency so ineptly that they never took all three seats and in 1874 held only one. From the mid-1880s new pressures, largely of national origin, were brought to bear on Leeds

Liberalism – the Home Rule question and the Chamberlainite secession; the new imperialism and the challenge of Fair to Free Trade; the electoral redistribution measure and the emergence of the single-member constituency; and the awakening of organised labour as an economic and political force. Underlying these developments was a basic shift in Britain's international economic status and with it the onset of profound economic and social changes in the life of the nation.

Meeting these forces called for flexibility and adaptability on the part of the Liberal Party. Redistribution suggested a division of the borough's five seats still favourable to Liberal interests, but in 1885, in the wake of the redistribution measure and the immediate aftermath of the Home Rule crisis, the Liberals found themselves divided and in a minority in the borough's representation. The threat of more permanent division, however, was quickly contained. After a brief initial hesitation the *Leeds Mercury*, now under the editorship of Wemyss Reid, rallied strongly to Gladstone, and the local Liberal leadership was no less solid in its support. Leeds indeed, with Sir James Kitson now installed as chairman of the National Liberal Federation, seemed set to take the place which Birmingham had surrendered as the focal point of official Liberalism. Though the opportunity was allowed to pass, the town, often in the past a source of embarrassment to the national Liberal leadership, now emerged as a model of loyal rectitude.

Nevertheless there was a steady seepage from the Liberal Party of members of the older commercial and industrial families. In North Leeds – the constituency covering Headingley, Chapeltown and Harehills – the Conservatives increased their share of the poll in every election between 1885 and 1900, and in Central, where redistribution had created a seat in which declining numbers of the working class were joined in electoral wedlock to a substantial body of business and property-owning voters, the Conservatives narrowly won at each of the five elections in these years. Liberal strength now clearly lay south of the river, where there was a heavy concentration of working-class voters in each of the three divisions. Leeds South and Leeds West were bedrock Liberal constituences, Leeds East only less so because of the ambivalence of the Irish vote, which from 1886 tended to be Liberal when Home Rule was at issue but Conservative when education came to the fore.

That the old alliance between Liberalism and Nonconformity was not wholly dead, however, was amply demonstrated in the controversy at the end of the century over the government of the Grammar School and, still more, in the furore which surrounded the passing of the

Education Act in 1902. The Liberals won a famous by-election victory in North Leeds in 1902, fought largely on the educational issue. Thence-forward to 1914 Liberalism in the city wore two faces. North of the river the appeal was to the older Liberal interests of Dissent and free trade; in the south the emphasis was on the new Liberalism with its message of welfare and social reform. This dual approach served the Liberals well, as it did in other large towns. Four of the five Leeds divisions – including North and Central – were won at the general election of 1906 and held at the two elections of 1910. The fifth, Leeds East, had been voluntarily ceded to the Labour Party as part of the pact between Herbert Gladstone and Ramsay MacDonald. The Labour Party, faced with the problems of the wayward Catholic voters, neatly solved its own Irish problem by nominating a Nationalist, James O'Grady, as candidate. This was, however, the limit of Labour's parliamentary achievement in the city. Though, in the town of Tom Maguire and John Mahon, socialist thinking and propaganda were much in evidence, the candidates who offered themselves in the name of Labour on three occasions in Leeds South between 1906 and 1910 were unable to offer any serious challenge to the sitting Liberal member.

Municipal politics ran a more wayward course. This may have reflected the electorate's greater sensitivity to local issues but it was also a consequence of the difference in structure between parliamentary and municipal elections. Municipal elections were held annually – though on each occasion for only one-third of the councillors – and on a ward basis. This, together with the practice of six-yearly aldermanic appointments covering a quarter of the council, produced a pattern of representation significantly different from that of the House of Commons. Between 1896 and 1905 the Conservatives held power in the city council as they held it at Westminster – though from 1899 their tenure of office was wholly dependent on their monopoly of the aldermanic seats. After 1905, when the parties agreed to a division of the aldermanic spoils, changes in control of the council became much more frequent.

The Liberal position was made increasingly tenuous by the arrival of Labour as a significant third force in local politics. The system of annual ward elections provided fertile ground for Labour advance. Except in 1908, when both Liberal and Labour suffered as a result of Conservative resurgence, the new party of the working class increased the number of its councillors from year to year, and after the election of 1913 its representation was for the first time greater than that of the Liberals. It was a portent and, for the Liberals, a warning of more permanent change ahead.

VI   The nineteenth century was the age of the great provincial town. In the course of the century Leeds exercised an increasing authority in national affairs through its size, the strength of its industry and the contribution it made to the moulding of national opinion. Though the city never held quite the position of dominance in West Yorkshire that Manchester enjoyed across the Pennines – the proximity of Bradford, Wakefield, York and even Ripon in different ways and in different degrees precluded this – it nevertheless came increasingly to occupy a position of leadership in regional affairs. By 1914, however, there were already signs that, like other great northern towns, the city had passed the zenith of its influence. In all the great northern conurbations the rate of population growth was slackening and the balance of economic power was shifting from north to south and from the provinces to the capital; and with this change of emphasis provincial influence was beginning to lose its force.

These changes, however, were not readily perceived by contemporaries. In absolute terms Leeds was larger in area and numbers, wealthier and, if the growth of its educational institutions is taken as guide, wiser in 1914 than it had ever been before. The city had, moreover, achieved for itself a measure of balance – in the variety of its industry, in the interplay of its public and private affairs and, not least, in the development of its social and cultural institutions.

Balance did not necessarily mean harmony, still less synthesis. Leeds in 1914 was no less two cities than England was two nations. The sharp division between areas and classes had been exposed at the time of the corporation strikes in 1890 and in 1913. Culturally the two main sections of the population also went their separate ways. Significantly, however, the longer-established middle-class institutions increasingly had their working-class counterparts. Where the middle class had its Music Festival, the workers had their brass bands, the Grand Theatre was matched by the Music Hall, the clubs by the pubs.

And if the emphasis was on separation, points of contact and common purpose both existed and tended to increase. Such unity of interest and effort was to be found in politics and religion, in the use of public libraries and in other civic amenities. Equally interesting were developments in the world of sport. At Headingley, deep in middle-class territory, a thriving outpost of the new professional working-class rugby of the rebel Rugby League established itself, while on the neighbouring cricket ground Yorkshire county cricket with its curious but successful amalgam of aristocracy and plebeianism, of amateurism and professionalism, also struck deep roots.

More fundamentally the city had achieved a balance between its private and public sectors. This found material expression in its schools, its hospitals and its public and commercial buildings: it was epitomised in Victoria Square, where the Town Hall and its adjacent municipal buildings to the north looked across a generous open space to the elegant banking and commercial houses of Park Row and East Parade. After the headlong, often unbalanced progress of a century Leeds had at last found a breathing space and was coming to terms with itself.

NOTES

[1] G. C. Dickinson, 'Passenger transport developments', in M. W. Beresford and G. R. J. Jones (eds.), *Leeds and its Region* (1967), 168–9.

[2] A. K. Cairncross, *Home and Foreign Investment, 1870–1913* (1953), 80.

[3] *Report of the Select Committee on Emigration and Immigration*, P.P. (1889) X [265], qq. 927, 1189.

[4] E. Krausz, *Leeds Jewry* (1964), 4 ff.

[5] *Rep. S.C. on Immigration* (1889). Evidence of Alderman Scarr, John Talbot and William Clayton, *passim*.

[6] *Reports on Immigration from Eastern Europe*, P.P. (1894), LXVIII [341], 156.

[7] A. S. Diamond, 'A sketch of Leeds Jewry in the nineteenth century', in A. Newman (ed.), *Provincial Jewry in Victorian Britain*, published privately for the Jewish Historical Society of England (1975), 171.

[8] *Rep. S.C. on Immigration* (1889), qq. 953, 978, 1143.

[9] *Report of the Royal Commission on Alien Immigration* (1903), IX [Cd. 1743], William Marston's evidence.

[10] W. G. Rimmer, 'Occupations in Leeds, 1841–1951', *Thoresby Soc.*, L (1968), tables 2 and 3.

[11] On the tailoring industry see especially J. Thomas, *A History of the Leeds Clothing Industry* (1955).

[12] Rimmer, *op. cit.*, table 1.

[13] Census (1911), vol. X, P.P. (1913), LXXVIII [Cd. 7018], table 22, 502–3.

[14] P. Mathias, *Retailing Revolution* (1967), 98.

[15] *Kelly's Directory of Leeds, 1914.*

[16] *Eighth Report of the Medical Officer of the Privy Council*, P.P. (1866), XXXIII [3645] 23, 233.

[17] Cited by G. Taylor, 'Education in Leeds', in Beresford and Jones, *op. cit.*, 288.

[18] E. P. Hennock, *Fit and Proper Persons* (1973), 214 ff.; but see the comment by D. Fraser, *Northern History*, XI (1976), 255.

[19] *Abstract of Monies Received and Expended in Municipal Boroughs, 1870*, P.P. (1871), LVIII [453], 4–5.

[20] Hennock, *op. cit.*, 231.

[21] *Ibid., passim.*

[22] *Return of Duty Charged as Property and Income Tax*, P.P. (1878–79), XLII [390], 4–7.

[23] Hennock, *op. cit., passim*. City of Leeds Annual Financial Accounts, 1913–14, *passim*.

[24] *Return . . . of Schools for the Poorer Classes of Children*, P.P. (1870), LIV [91], 77–111.

[25] *Ibid.*, 77.

[26] *Ibid.*, 88.

[27] *Schools Inquiry Commission*, P.P. (1867–68), XXVIII, Vol. XVIII [3966–XVIII], 167 ff.

[28] *Ibid.*, 657.

[29] E. K. Scott, *Leeds Church Middle Class School: Records from 1870 to 1927* (1927), *passim*.

[30] M. A. Travis, 'The work of the Leeds School Board, 1870–1902', *University of Leeds Institute of Education, Research and Studies*, VIII (1953), 89.

[31] Based on City of Leeds Education Committee, *Official Handbook* (1914), 236–43.

[32] *Report of the Royal Commission on Secondary Education*, Vol. VI, P.P. (1895), XLVIII [C. 7862 v.], 136–41.

[33] A. C. Price, *A History of the Leeds Grammar School* (1919), 260 ff.

[34] *R.C. on Sec. Educ.* (1895), 159.

[35] L. Connell, 'A study of the development of secondary education in Leeds, 1895–1921', University of Leeds Ph.D. thesis (1960), *passim*.

[36] A. N. Shimmin, *The University of Leeds: the First Half-century* (1954), *passim*. P. H. J. H. Gosden and A. J. Taylor (eds.), *Studies in the History of a University, 1874–1974* (1974), *passim*.

[37] *Royal Commission on Technical Instruction*, P.P. (1884), XXX, 50.

[38] *Census 1851*, P.P. (1852–53), LXXXIX [1690], 102; *Nonconformist*, 8 January 1873, cited by H. Pelling, *Social Geography of British Elections 1885–1910* (1967), 291.

[39] Hennock, *op. cit.*, 221.

MODERN LEEDS

The years of political transition, 1914–39

XVI

I   Leeds entered the Great War with its political affairs unresolved. The last months of 1913 had seen a big upsurge in Labour's electoral support – 50 per cent up on the poor results of the previous year – and the beginning of a full-scale strike of the council's workpeople that was to end in defeat for the strikers one month later.[1] Labour had the capacity to compete successfully with the other parties at the polls, and even to overtake the Liberals in elected representatives, though not in votes, but not the industrial strength to succeed in a confrontation. Labour's thorough preparations in 1914 for local and parliamentary elections[2] were vitiated by the outbreak of the war and the suspension of elections, but the party kept its political machine in being despite the constrictions of war and the constant drain of able-bodied men into the forces.

The Conservative and Liberal parties agreed to work together to encourage recruitment for the forces but Labour would not join in officially at first and only agreed to Labour members taking part as individuals by a narrow majority. The party issued instructions that, if the Lord Mayor moved a patriotic motion at the city council meeting, Councillor Arnott was to make a noncommital speech.[3] Leeds Labour Party contained a significant number of pacifists, so much so that a leading party member complained in 1918 that all the party's prospective parliamentary candidates were pacifists. The one notable exception was Labour's only MP, James O'Grady, whose unopposed return in South East Leeds caused suspicions to be voiced that he had the support of the coalition as a result of recruiting Irishmen into the forces. Another leading Labour member, Percy Horner, resigned from the city council in 1918 in anticipation of his imprisonment as a conscientious objector.[4]

The Liberals of West Leeds faced a similar problem of conscience. They had considered themselves fortunate to secure T. Edmund Harvey as the successor to Herbert Gladstone as their member of

Parliament in 1910. Harvey had an impeccable Liberal and Leeds family pedigree but his uncompromising Quakerism was bound to lead him into conflict with the local party as soon as war broke out. The local Liberal leaders were firmly – and outspokenly – committed to the war but were as firmly devoted to their member. They were prepared to allow him his beliefs as long as he did not act upon them, but quiescence over such a crucial matter was impossible for Harvey and the inevitable split between him and his constituency came in late 1917. He was not a natural rebel and preferred to avoid unpleasantness, but having determined the correctness of his position he put personal considerations behind him and followed the consequences of his pacifism, both in actively supporting pacifist causes in Britain and also in involvement with Quaker relief work in France and Belgium.[5]

Despite the serious and embarrassing political consequences of the break with their MP the Liberals retained genuine admiration and respect for Harvey,[6] and he returned to the House of Commons, briefly in 1923 as Liberal member for Dewsbury, and from 1937 to 1945 as the Independent Progressive member for the English universities.

However, although the problems of individual conscientious objectors regularly occupied both Labour and Liberal parties, and the tribunals, they had little effect on the city as a whole. Leeds set to with, in hindsight, alarming enthusiasm. In the eight months to July 1915 36,000 recruits signed on, and the Leeds 'Pals' and 'Bantams' were formed. A training camp was set up at Colsterdale with Alderman Charles Wilson, the Conservative leader and a man of considerable size and personality, as quartermaster until he fell off his horse in June 1915 and 'retired with the honorary rank of Captain'.[7]

Munitions factories were established at Armley, Hunslet and Newlay, and aircraft were built at Roundhay Road. At Barnbow, between Crossgates and Garforth, 400 acres of farm land was acquired and a huge shell-filling factory built, which eventually employed 16,000 workers and despatched over half a million tons of ammunition overseas. Barnbow was a dangerous place and was the scene of three fatal explosions, the first of which on 5 December 1916 killed thirty-five women.

Beckett Park Teacher Training College was requisitioned as a military hospital – with 3,200 beds, compared with its present-day complement of 400 residents – and Temple Newsam House became a Voluntary Aid Detachment hospital, at which, together with VAD hospitals in other historic houses, over 50,000 patients were treated. Rationing was introduced in late 1917 and the Art Gallery became the food control office. Aliens were imprisoned at the Town Hall, Boy Scouts helped to guard the reservoirs, and amateur wireless stations were dismantled.

Air raids were liable to come via the Zeppelins, which travelled so slowly that there was sufficient time from the first warning of distant approach to put an effective blackout into operation. The nearest any Zeppelin came to Leeds was Collingham, and unlike Hull, the city escaped bombs completely.

However, there was no way of escaping the carnage in Belgium and northern France. The city had almost 90,000 men in the fighting forces, and of these 9,640 were killed in action. The men served in a number of different regiments, but it was the formation of the Leeds 'Pals' and Leeds 'Bantams' battalions that particularly drew volunteers together in separate units. This apparently innocent way of building on the camaraderie of local pride and identification had disastrous results. The appalling trench warfare of 1914–18 depended on units covering a specific section of the line, so that as an advance was called those emerging from the forward trenches took the full force of the enemy's fire. Consequently when any city battalion was thus involved the casualties struck that city in a single shattering blow.

This experience came to Leeds following the Somme offensive on 1 July 1916. In just ten minutes C and D companies of the Leeds Pals were destroyed. One officer, no sergeant-majors, and only forty-seven of the 800 NCOs and men survived the attack. The official history of Leeds in the Great War sums it up in a style that must remain inimitable:

> One of the darkest weeks of the whole war for Leeds was undoubtedly that at the beginning of July 1916, when news arrived of the battle of the Somme – the British Armies' first great onslaught on the German lines. It was a glorious victory, but at what a cost! Foremost in the fight were the Leeds 'Pals'. They acquitted themselves like true sons of Britain and were nearly all killed facing the enemy.[8]

Perhaps the most macabre sequel to this debacle came six months later when the new Pals returned to the same spot and 'came across grim reminders of the previous July 1st, in the shape of the remains of a number of officers and men who fell in that struggle, and whose bodies could not be recovered at that time'.[9] Leeds men won nine VCs in the war; most of them happened to be working men from south or west Leeds.

News of the armistice reached the city shortly after 11 a.m. on 11 November 1918, and, given the horrors and sacrifices of the past four years, it was no wonder that 'the phlegmatic reputation of Leeds was entirely swept away by the torrent of enthusiastic rejoicing which deluged the city'.[10] The war had forced changes in social structures and attitudes, not least in the attitude towards women, who had formed over 90 per cent of the factory workforce. The need to concentrate on the work of reconstruction ensured the acceptability of a greater level of public activity and expenditure. There was no question now of a return to pre-war methods and attitudes.

Paradoxically, however, the most remarkable home event of the war had no directly attributable long-term effect. This was the Leeds Convention of 3 June 1917, called by the Independent Labour Party and the British Socialist Party, following the first Russian revolution in March of that year, to express solidarity with the workmen and soldiers of Russia and to press for the emulation of the revolution in Britain. The Cabinet discussed whether to prohibit the meeting and decided that because it was already widely known it would be 'undesirable' to do so. The city fathers were successfully lobbied, apparently by the British Empire League, and cancelled the booking of the Albert Hall and refused to permit an open-air assembly arranged for the Victoria Square. Even the hoteliers were pressed into cancelling the delegates' bookings.[11]

In consequence the party members organised a reception committee at the station and directed delegates to the houses of colleagues, who provided hospitality. The convention met at the Coliseum in Cookridge Street, scene of many famous meetings, with Keir Hardie, Asquith and Lloyd George among others. Fred Jowett of Bradford was one of the convenors, and the 1,150 delegates included Ramsay MacDonald, Philip Snowden, Robert Smillie, Tom Mann, Bertrand Russell, Herbert Morrison and Ernest Bevin, who introduced one of the rare moments of controversy by attacking the ILP's pacifism. Leeds Labour Party was overwhelmingly in favour of sending a delegate, but the trades council voted for representation by only thirty-seven to thirty. In the event the Leeds delegates were D. B. Foster and Bertha Quinn.[12]

The convention debated and carried four resolutions in an atmosphere of emotion and enthusiasm. It congratulated the Russian people on the revolution, declared for an international agreement for world peace, demanded a charter of civil liberties, and, most significantly, called upon 'the constituent bodies at once to support in every town, urban and rural district, Councils of Workmen and Soldiers' Delegates for initiating and co-ordinating working-class activity ...'. It was this last resolution, 'put to the meeting, and carried amid enthusiasm with only two or three dissentients', that alarmed the establishment. The alarm was, however, unnecessary: the national co-ordinating committee met a few times but the momentum quickly dissipated, and the second Russian revolution of October 1917 and the separate Russo-German peace treaty of the following March discouraged any revival of the extremist spirit.

During 1918 there was talk of a wartime general election, and the result of the vote in Parliament on the Maurice affair,[13] in which, on a vote of confidence, Liberal MPs voted in different lobbies, meant that from May onward the speculation increased. In the event the election was announced on 14 November – three days after the armistice. The following night Sir Rowland Barran persuaded the Leeds Liberals to enter into an arrangement with the Tories, who were prepared to give Coalition Liberal candidates a free run against Labour in the four Liberal-held seats provided the Liberals kept out of the 'new' North East division.[14] Overwhelmingly, and with only the North East Liberals speaking against it, the executive committee supported the agreement. Those who might have carried on the fight were discouraged by the resignation of the Liberal candidate for North East Leeds. As it happened the coalition saved the four Liberals' seats, which would probably have gone equally to Conservative and Labour on the evidence of the subsequent local election results.

Labour fought all six constituencies for the first time and professed themselves satisfied with their vote although, in proportion, it was considerably down on their municipal vote at the last elections in 1913. A minor consolation was the announcement just before polling day of six new Labour magistrates, thus trebling the number of socialists in this much coveted position. These appointments, following upon the signing of a concordat with the other parties to allocate the lord mayoralty to each party in turn, ensured that Labour had arrived socially by the end of the war.

In 1919 Leeds was on the brink of the great changes in civic enterprise and social acceptance that were later taken for granted. Only 50 per cent of the population had the vote (as opposed to 65 per cent with full adult suffrage twenty years later). For the first time women had the parliamentary vote, but the 70,000 women under thirty were not enfranchised until 1928. Because of the different qualifications involved, over a quarter of parliamentary electors were denied a vote at municipal elections. The implications of electricity and of the internal combustion engine were beginning to exercise the minds of the city fathers, and the whole question of transport, by road, rail and eventually air, had serious consequences for town planning. Only the established Church appeared to ignore the recognition of the cities as the natural centres of their regions, rejecting the forceful claims for a Bishopric of Leeds.[15]

The city council was a more obvious focal point of the city's life than it is now and, by force of personality, Charles Henry Wilson was the ideal man to grasp the opportunity of the early post-war years. More than any other individual he epitomised the spirit of the time and had the energy and political skill to initiate and carry through many of the projects that are today almost commonplace. The ideas were not always his but the execution of them was his particular forte.

Charles Wilson replaced the more patrician John Gordon as Conservative leader in 1904, and the change in style represented a tacit acknowledgement of a new century and a new political era, with socialism officially represented in the council for the first time. An accountant, Wilson led the city council from 1907 to 1928 (with the single exception of 1911–12) and represented the Central division in Parliament from 1923 to 1929. He was knighted in 1923 and died in 1930. He was tough and outspoken but not vindictive and had a particular skill in political wheeling and dealing that was essential to the smooth transition from Liberal to Labour dominance. In only three of his twenty years in office did the Conservatives have a majority of council seats, but the dominant political influence during the whole period was Conservatism – and Wilson's particular brand of Conservatism at that.[16] The Liberals were too weak politically to be able to combat both the other parties successfully, so that Wilson's careful fostering of Liberal over-representation on the aldermanic bench and in committee places, plus quiet collusion over seats fought, effectively ensured that the Liberals were in no position seriously to challenge the Conservatives' 'control' of the council.

However, if the Liberals maintained the semblance of a presence on the city council they ceased to be a force at parliamentary elections by the 1923 general election, thereafter failing to secure a second place in a three-cornered contest and even to put forward a single candidate in the 1935 election. Labour made steady progress, adding Leeds South to James O'Grady's South East seat in 1922, and then the West and Central divisions in 1923 and 1929 respectively. In 1931, as in virtually every other area following the Ramsay MacDonald National Government, Labour lost a quarter of its electoral support in the city, losing three seats in the process. Labour made a swift local recovery, gaining control of the council in 1933 and putting its vote at the 1935 parliamentary election back almost to its 1929 peak, although only one seat, South, was regained.

II   A theme that runs with variations throughout Wilson's post-war time in office is that of boundary extensions. He was a municipal imperialist, stating publicly that his long-term aim was for Leeds to control everything from the Pennines to the sea. Such an attitude hardly endeared him to neighbouring authorities, who spent much of the time between 1919 and 1928 battling against incorporation into the city. Before the war, in 1911, Shadwell, Roundhay, Crossgates and Seacroft had been added and in 1919 Middleton was incorporated. Then began the struggle to bring in all the adjacent towns. The Leeds Corporation Bill was thrown out by the House of Commons in May 1922, mainly owing to the opposition of the county MPs. Reference was made in the House to 'Alderman Wilson's passion for aggrandisement', no doubt referring to his most famous remark when, at the boundary extension enquiry in 1921, he had said in reply to a question about how Leeds could promote such efficiency and ruthlessness, 'I am Leeds.'[17]

A further Bill was promoted in 1927 and in the meantime, in 1924, the parish of Adel had voluntarily opted for incorporation. The new Bill included Gildersome, Temple Newsam, Alwoodley, Eccup and Austhorpe, and had an easier passage. Gildersome was excluded at the committee stage but the rest were incorporated on 30 March 1928. The other townships of Sir Charles Wilson's 1920 proposals remained independent until the total reorganisation of local government in 1974.

The practical difficulties faced by the city council in relation to its boundaries were clearly seen when the ring road was planned. By mid-1921 work was in progress on a number of sections, but of the thirty miles planned only slightly over half was within the city's boundary, and there were serious problems of obtaining ownership. The result was that by August 1924 only seven miles were completed, including Otley Road to Weetwood Lane, Harrogate Road to King Lane and pieces at Swinnow, Whitehall Road and Middleton.

III   At the same time as the ring road was planned to provide 'good cross-routes leaving the centre more traffic free'[18] steps were taken to enhance the arterial routes for public transport. By 1920 there was considerable criticism of the existing tramways, and the city council took steps to develop rapid transit routes along the centre of specially wide and straight roads. Liverpool had already integrated such routes into its new housing developments, and Leeds Tramways Committee had been favourably impressed with the scheme on a visit just before the end of the war. By mid-1921 the first two express routes, to Middleton and to Roundhay, were under way.

76   'I am Leeds!' Alderman Sir Charles Wilson, MP, 1859–1930

Within a short time the council realised that further steps were needed to deal with the rapidly increasing traffic in the city centre. The only east–west route, Boar Lane, was becoming jammed. In May 1924 Alderman Charles Lupton, chairman of the improvement committee, announced that an 80 ft wide thoroughfare was to be constructed between the Town Hall and Mabgate at an estimated cost of £500,000. Although much of the property was owned by Wade's Charity, which was sympathetic to the scheme, there was a multiplicity of land ownership which, together with other practical problems, delayed the commencement of the work on site for more than two years. Originally the road was to be called 'Kingsway' but in October 1929 it was decided to name it 'The Headrows', thus preserving the link with the Upper and Lower Headrows that had been demolished to make way for the road, and which were themselves a link with a pre-industrial past when the name referred to the heads of rows of arable land. By the time the road was completed three years later the final 's' had been dropped.

Alderman Lupton and his improvement committee were concerned not only about the utilitarian purpose of the new road but also with the aesthestic potential provided by its construction. Sir Nikolaus Pevsner comments, 'The Leeds Corporation in 1924 made a praiseworthy gesture for the monumentality of Inner Leeds by insisting on a unified frontage all along the N. side of The Headrow Garden to Cookridge Street.'[19] Other influential voices, including that of the *Yorkshire Post*,[20] urged the modernisation of the space in front of the Town Hall and Municipal Buildings. This took a further five years to accomplish: in October 1937 the Lord Mayor opened the Headrow Garden, and the Vicar of Leeds rededicated the war memorial, which had been moved from City Square.

Efforts to improve the rail service to the city were being made at the same time. The 1921 grouping of the railways into four large companies was a stimulus to rationalisation, but in 1925 the companies declared against a scheme for a new single joint station in place of the adjacent Wellington and New stations, and it was only the threat of a major hotel development on the north side of the Headrow in 1933 that spurred the LMS to rebuild the Queen's Hotel and, with it, a single new station. The new hotel was opened by the Earl of Harewood in November 1937, and by the following July the new station entrance and concourse were in use. The threatened hotel in the Headrow never materialised.

The prospect of air travel on a reliable scheduled basis began to be taken seriously in the late 1920s. In October 1928 the Air Ministry wrote to all major local authorities urging the establishment of aerodromes. Sir Charles Wilson, MP, declared himself in favour of an airport for Leeds, and the chamber of commerce supported the idea – even suggesting Soldiers' Field, by Roundhay Park, as a possible location! Early the following year began the search for a suitable site in conjunction with Bradford. Sir Alan Cobham was employed as consultant and his report strongly recommended Whinmoor. This site, to the east, was geographically unacceptable to Bradford and the report admitted that Yeadon was 'undoubtedly . . . the only possible Municipal aerodrome site within the environs of Bradford'.[21] The first flights took place in the summer of 1931 but scheduled flights, between Heston, Yeadon, Newcastle and Edinburgh, did not commence until April 1935. The development of a municipal aerodrome was a clear indication of civic faith in changing transport means, in sad contrast to the decline of the waterways, despite occasional efforts to promote the idea of a ship canal from Hull to Leeds.[22]

IV   The back-to-back house is synonymous with Leeds and other northern towns. Although sophisticated versions continued to be built up to the early 1930s, steps to clear the worst of the slums had begun in the 1870s and continued, at a fairly low level, until the outbreak of war. Alison Ravetz says in her book on Quarry Hill:

> After the first world war the Leeds housing problem was exacerbated by the large influx of wartime munition workers, many of whom stayed and founded families, and by a birthrate which jumped from 17·6 to 25·0 per thousand between 1919 and 1920. The pre-war surplus of houses had gone for ever and all parties on the council were resigned, if not positively enthusiastic, about building council estates.[23]

The first council houses were built under the 1919 Housing Act at Hawksworth, Wyther Park, Meanwood, Cross Gates, Middleton and York Road. More were built on these sites, and at Hollin Park, under the 1923 and 1924 Acts. By 1926 over 5,000 houses had been erected at an average cost of £750 each. Because of the shortage of bricklayers over a third were built of concrete, and it was some of these that, by 1978, had deteriorated to the stage where demolition was proposed.

In the same period private housing development accelerated. In early 1923 private estates were being built at Gipton Wood, Gledhow Wood, Oakwood, Weetwood Lane, Armley Grange, St Martins, Newton Park and north of Street Lane in a generic style recognisable as typical of the inter-war years. The issue of houses to rent or to buy sharply divided Conservative and Labour parties, and Alderman Sir

Charles Wilson made no attempt to hide the reason: 'It is a good thing for people to buy their houses. They turn Tory directly (laughter). We shall go on making Tories and you [the Socialists] will be wiped out (renewed laughter).'[24]

77   Councillor the Rev. Charles Jenkinson, 1887–1949

In 1930 the Conservatives gained control of the city council and cut the modest proposal to clear 3,000 houses over a five-year period by a third. A new Labour member of the council that year was Charles Jenkinson, a clergyman from the East End of London who had been appointed Vicar of Holbeck only three years before. In a strange way Jenkinson, from a completely different political standpoint, was the successor to Sir Charles Wilson. He had the same characteristics of drive and leadership and could, at times, be similarly intolerant of opposition. Just as Sir Charles left his mark on Leeds with the Headrow and Temple Newsam, so the later housing estates, in particular Quarry Hill, were Jenkinson's legacy. In February 1931, within three months of his election, he tabled a motion calling for a survey of the slums. It had an inauspicious beginning – he had to agree to withdraw it because of the lateness of the hour. Two months later it was put again and was defeated, with only the Labour and Liberal members in support. A special sub-committee was set up, but its official report was unacceptable to the Labour and Liberal members. Although recognising that 33,500 houses would have to be cleared sooner or later, it recommended that '. . . at the present juncture slum clearance should be limited to those cases the Medical Officer of Health considers the most vitally urgent'.[25]

Three months later in March 1933, the minority report[26] was published. It proposed the clearance of 16,000 houses by 1938, and approximately 30,000 more by 1948. In addition to estates it also urged the building of blocks of not less than 500 flats to last 'for a century'. It further proposed a bye-law against overcrowding and a housing director responsible to a housing committee. The opportunity to act on these proposals came in November when Labour gained control of the council, established a housing committee and appointed Jenkinson its chairman. By January 1934 he had published plans for the clearance of 3,000 houses in the first year, 5,000 in the second and 5,500 in each of the following four. Thirty thousand new houses were to be built – 2,500 of them at Gipton – and the whole plan would cost £12 million. The estate roads that carried trams would be 150 ft wide and were 'to be planned with an eye not only to safety but also to beauty – as, indeed, we hope, will be the whole'.[27] In case all this was not enough to antagonise the Conservatives, he next announced plans for the introduction of differential rents, with some very poor tenants paying none at all, started a furniture hire-purchase scheme for rehoused tenants and planned Shaftesbury House, a 500 room municipal lodging house.

The clearance plan was dubbed the 'Red Ruin' by its opponents, but the differences between the parties were mainly over the pace of demolition. Jenkinson's own pace was formidable and his outspoken and independent style, which sometimes embarrassed his colleagues almost as much as his opponents, ensured that housing policy would be a crucial matter of debate. His impact was so great that it is hard to realise that he was on the council initially for only two three-year terms, losing his Holbeck seat to a Liberal in 1936 on the local issue of bringing housing back to Sweet Street, Holbeck, to which he was opposed. He was offered a seat on the council immediately as party leader, but he refused, and did not return to active politics until 1943, becoming housing committee chairman again in 1945 and Labour Party leader in 1947, a position he retained until his sudden resignation from the council just before his death in 1949.

Jenkinson's target of 30,000 dwellings in the seven and a half years from 1934 was a brave one, but even he could not overcome the limitations of the building industry, nor could he have anticipated that the contractor responsible for the Gipton estate would go bankrupt. Consequently, even had Labour remained in control they could not have reached their target. But, as Alison Ravetz states, 'they went far to redeem the poor record of Leeds in the 1920s, as well as setting the style in which Leeds municipal housing has operated ever since'.[28] Even so, one aspect of the policy that was never repeated was the Quarry Hill complex of flats. Within fourteen months of Labour's taking control the details of the development had been published, and three years later, early in 1938, the first section was occupied. Eventually it had 938 flats, housing 3,300 people, five playgrounds, laundry, shops, bowling greens and tennis courts. The different blocks were named after famous citizens: a long list of approved names was published for Quarry Hill and later, unbuilt, developments.[29]

V   The attempt in 1936 to bring Charles Jenkinson back on to the council as Labour leader may well have been a conscious attempt to change the style of the party's local leadership. Previously the tendency had been to match the Conservatives, which posed the stark problem of finding a leader to cope with Charles Wilson. John Arnott had become Labour leader in 1917; although much respected for his sincerity and intelligence, he was altogether too quiet and serious in comparison to Wilson. Labour's problem was even aired publicly in its own newspaper: '. . . since John Badlay left he [Alderman Wilson] has had the happiest time making fools of the Labour Party in all manners possible'.[30] Labour had the man for the job in the person of Bill Armstrong, a tough, humourless but able councillor from Middleton, but the problem for his colleagues lay in the enemies his brusqueness had made within the party. He appears to have become leader for two years, 1920–22, after which the party reverted to Arnott. However, in 1925 Arnott became the third Labour Lord Mayor and Armstrong again replaced him, retaining the position through the first brief period of Labour control from 1927 to 1930,[31] until July 1931, when he resigned the leadership because 'he could not get the party to discipline itself, even during council meetings'.[32]

Labour's problem, in Leeds as elsewhere, was the conflict between maintaining a radical socialist position – and incurring considerable hostility from the established parties – and becoming respectable and participating in the traditional city council processes. John Badlay,

Labour's leader before the war, was temperamentally a radical but his successors wanted the party to be judged 'by its administrative wisdom and capacity, and not by its powers of denunciation'.[33] So successfully did Labour make the transition that in 1929 the Conservative leader, Alderman Leslie Owen, could say of the first Labour-controlled council, 'the Socialists have had a majority for twelve months and here we are asked to vote for rates which are certainly not in any sense revolutionary for the simple reason that not one of the things you said you would do have been done. There is nothing in that financial statement which has a vestige of Socialism in it.'[34]

Labour attitudes to the lord mayoralty show a parallel sea change. Before the war the Labour group would not even take tea with the Lord Mayor after the council meeting but went to a near-by coffee house. In 1912 Tom Duncan, a leading Leeds socialist, attacked the decision to pay the Lord Mayor £1,250 per annum:

> ... the action of the [Labour] Group in supporting the exceedingly high salary was incomprehensible. The idea of upholding the dignity of the Lord Mayor was absurd. He thought we, as working people, ought to strenuously oppose functions of the sort of type provided by the Lord Mayor, and insist on the provision of adequate productive relief works instead of civic functions.[35]

In 1918 Labour signed a concordat with the other parties to allocate the mayoralty to each party in turn. A year later Tom Duncan became the first Labour Lord Mayor, at a salary 50 per cent higher than in 1912! He was a popular, respected and non-political incumbent, and, like all his Labour successors, provided the refreshments that the earlier socialists had spurned![36]

Sir Charles Wilson died at the end of 1930 and his successor as Conservative leader, R. C. (later Sir Charles) Davies, although effective was not an initiator. Consequently Labour were now free to elect a different type of leader. Alf Dobbs, a union official and party worker of long standing, was a respected leader and a sound and capable politician but, like his opposite number, not an initiator. He remained as leader until appointed national organiser for the National Union of Boot and Shoe Operatives in October 1936, when he was succeeded by George Brett. Alf Dobb's political career came to a tragic end when he was killed in an accident on the A1 on his way back from the count at which he had been elected member of Parliament for Smethwick in 1945. Davies resigned unexpectedly from the council in April 1935, having taken on a position in the management of the Leeds Permanent Building Society. His successor was C. V. Walker, who had been the party's whip for ten years.

The Liberals' leadership, such as it was, depended on George Ratcliffe from 1919 to 1932.[37] A sweet manufacturer and a lifelong and loyal Liberal Party man, Ratcliffe lacked both the interest and the capacity for philosophic initiative. He revelled in the petty battles of municipal politics but, despite long and respected service, was regarded as a political lightweight. During his period as leader the Liberal vote dropped from 30 to 10 per cent, although of course this was in line with the national trend. The biggest single blow to Ratcliffe personally, and to the Liberal cause in Leeds, came in June 1926 when the two Liberal whips and three other Liberal councillors defected to the Conservatives.[38] At the municipal elections the following November the Liberals lost a third of their 1925 vote and the party slumped from eighteen to eight council representatives in five months. The influence of the party had been in decline since the establishment of an independent Labour presence ten years before the war but the secessions of June 1926 marked the visible end of that influence.

Unlike many other towns Leeds had no formal Liberal–Conservative alliance but, to safeguard their council positions, and even seats, the Liberals clearly co-operated informally with the Tories.[39] This enabled Wilson to remain in office, but he became impatient with the restraints the balance of power imposed on him and, from 1922, with the growing strength of Labour. He therefore approached individually most of the Liberal group in 1926, offering political inducements for them to join the Conservatives. It was an opportune time, particularly with the Lloyd George–Asquith split having been publicised anew, and five Liberals took the bait. With supreme irony it proved to be Wilson's downfall. The Liberal Party was more radical than many of its council representatives, and its angry response was to fight thirteen of the seventeen wards, so enabling Labour to win ten in the consequent three-cornered contests and become the largest party.

These were not the only defections from the Liberals in the inter-war years. Of those who were Liberal candidates at one or more elections six joined Labour[40] and four others the Conservatives. The party lacked a recognisable identity and its leaders were incapable of appreciating that need and of meeting it.

Of the other parties the Communists sought affiliation to Labour, both collectively and individually, and, when denied it, fought sporadically and inconsequentially. The fascists established a club in Albion Street in 1926 but were barely noticed until a rally on Holbeck moor in September 1936 ended in disorder with fourteen people injured and three arrested. They then announced parliamentary candidates for Leeds and Bradford and put up token municipal candidates in Armley and Burmantofts in 1937 and 1938.

Table 37 Political composition of Leeds council, 1913–1939

Year	Conservative	Liberal	Labour	Independent
1913	34	18	16	—
1919	29	17	22	—
1920	30	18	19	1
1921	29	20	18	1
1922	30	23	13	2
1923	30	21	14	3
1924	31	18	16	3
1925	30	18	17	3
1926	29	8	31	—
1927	27	8	33	—
1928	27	5	36	—
1929	27	5	36	—
1930	63	5	36	—
1931	63	6	35	—
1932	57	4	43	—
1933	49	1	54	—
1934	50	1	53	—
1935	54	1	49	—
1936	60	3	41	—
1937	57	2	45	—
1938	54	2	48	—

Notes

a The figures are as at the end of November each year, i.e. following the annual elections, any aldermanic elections and consequent by-elections.

b There was an electoral truce for the duration of the 1914–18 war which allowed the parties to re-elect, or replace, their council representatives without electoral contests.

c The Labour totals for 1919, 1920 and 1921 include two 'Co-operative' councillors, and those for 1922 and 1923 one 'Co-operative' councillor, who were not opposed by Labour candidates and were indistinguishable from Labour representatives.

d The Liberal defections of June 1926 made the council composition: Conservative 35, Liberal 13, Labour 17 and Independent 3 until the November elections.

e In anticipation of new ward boundaries and the consequent election of the whole council in 1930 the three parties agreed an electoral truce in 1929 which only two Communist candidates 'spoilt'.

A short-lived independent organisation, the Citizens' Municipal Movement, appeared briefly on the scene in the 1920s. Composed largely of Liberals, it succeeded in winning Headingley ward in 1922, 1923, 1925 and 1926. One of its policy planks was concern about the financial involvement of members of the council in council contracts, and it was as a result of questions in council from them, followed up in the courts by an ex-Liberal councillor, that two Conservative aldermen, Braithwaite and Penrose-Green, resigned in September 1924. The adverse court verdict was subsequently reversed on appeal, but neither returned to the council.[41]

Overlapping with the contracts issue was the Dr Fernandez affair, in which the political parties found themselves in a highly embarrassing situation. Dr Fernandez was an Indian doctor who had worked at the Leeds Tuberculosis Clinic for some years but who in 1924 was not promoted to Chief Tuberculosis Officer when the other four candidates on a short list all withdrew. Amidst allegations of racialism he was appointed 'on probation' for twelve months. Any thoughts that he would then quietly continue in the post indefinitely were shattered when it was advertised again and an outsider appointed. In March 1927 the health committee asked the Ministry of Health to undertake an 'enquiry into matters appertaining to the work of the Tuberculosis Dispensary'.[42] The subsequent report criticised Dr Fernandez, who immediately resigned. The Labour group supported the council motion on his resignation and was severely criticised for doing so by a section of the party. Dr Fernandez was subsequently elected Labour councillor for Richmond Hill ward and served on the city council until just before his death in 1961.

December 1937 saw the resignation of the city treasurer, W. J. Ball. In the previous June the council had approved the mechanisation of the accounts. By the end of the year there were three months' arrears of work, and many ratepayers had received no requests for payment since the beginning of the financial year in April. The treasurer was invited to resign and did so, leaving behind a deficit of £109,000 attributable to the delay. An outside firm of accountants was brought in to advise, and the new treasurer did not take over his duties until September 1938.[43]

VI   In the inter-war years a number of buildings were bought by the council for public use. In some cases the private owners were unable to sustain the heavy cost of maintenance and looked to the city council to take over the burden. One such building was the Philosophical and Literary Society Hall at the corner of Park Row and Bond Street. In 1921 it was 'given' to the council in return for £1,500 per annum for twenty-five years, and became the City Museum. Damaged by bombs in the second world war, it was eventually demolished, and the site is now occupied by a modern bank.

A year later the council took over one of the most impressive stately homes in Britain. Temple Newsam House belonged to the Halifax family, who could no longer afford to maintain it. In November 1921 it was offered to the council for £35,000 and the purchase was completed in September 1922. The council set up a standing committee to run the house and its grounds – the only example of a council committee set up to administer a place rather than a service. The house was developed as a museum and, together with the surrounding park, soon became a popular leisure attraction. It did not escape controversy, as in 1925, when the Liberals called a special council meeting over allegations that Sir Charles Wilson had attempted to hush up financial information, including the purchase of bulls and overcharging for milk![44]

In 1924 Abbey House was bought, ostensibly to be judges' lodgings when the Assizes were sitting at Leeds. The neighbouring field was bought for £5,000 from Colonel T. W. Harding, who promptly gave the money back to the council for the purchase of art treasures. Property in Hyde Terrace continued to be used by the judges, and Abbey House was eventually developed as a folk museum. The question of accommodation for the judges was not resolved until the end of 1937, when Carr Manor was bought from Lord Moynihan for just over £17,000.

The city did not, however, only acquire existing buildings, and there were two significant additions to the skyline that date back to the 1920s. In 1925 the university launched an appeal under the patronage of the Duke and Duchess of York for £500,000, with the aim of building a new library, medical school, six new departmental buildings and a student union. Lord Brotherton of Wakefield, who had been Lord Mayor in 1913–14, gave £100,000 and promised his valuable collection of books. By early 1934 the new main buildings in University Road were completed, as was the medical school and two residential hostels. The Brotherton Library was opened by the Archbishop of Canterbury in October 1936, but the central block and clock tower, named after Frank Parkinson, who had given gifts totalling £250,000, was not completed until 1951.

The second new building of the period was the Civic Hall. Since 1858 the council had met in the Town Hall, but over the years, with the expansion in local government work, more and more council offices were moved into separate offices. This was clearly inefficient and unsatisfactory and, with the impending increase in the size of the city council from sixty-eight to a hundred members, it was imperative that the whole question of accommodation be considered. A special sub-committee was set up at the beginning of 1929, and it was eventually decided that an entirely new building was required. In mid-

1930 Alderman Armstrong and Councillor (later Alderman Sir) George Martin, respectively the Labour and Conservative chairman and deputy chairman of the finance and parliamentary committee, went to see what goverment grants would be available under the unemployed relief works programme. They received a sympathetic reception from the Minister, and, as they were leaving, were called back by a senior official who urged them to get a scheme costed and submitted in detail within weeks, as the government was liable to fall at any time. The two Leeds men, leader and whip of their respective parties, decided that in the circumstances, despite having no formal authorisation from the council, they would take the initiative whilst in London. They ascertained the home address of an architect who had recently designed buildings in Leeds, arrived on his doorstep the same evening, and asked him to recommend an architect! He enquired why he himself was unacceptable, only to be told, in Armstrong's typically blunt manner, that there had been criticism of his work in Leeds. The man then went on to recommend Vincent Harris.

The next morning Armstrong and Martin arranged to see Harris and asked him whether he would be able to prepare all the necessary drawings and quantities within a matter of weeks. Harris satisfied them that he could do the work, and they returned to Leeds to sell the deal to the council. There was immediately criticism that a London architect had been appointed, and a short hiatus ensued when Harris refused to design a building for the council's preferred site in the Headrow. Harris insisted that the new building had to be on a higher site than the Town Hall, and got his way. Work began just before October 1930, only slightly more than three months after the initial approval. Different teams of workmen were employed in the construction for set periods of time in order to spread the work among the unemployed.[45]

The new enlarged city council was elected in November 1930 and met in the university Great Hall pending construction of the new Civic Hall. However, the acoustic was unsatisfactory and the council met there on only three occasions. Alterations were made at the Town Hall and, by cutting the public gallery down to fifty-five seats, the council squeezed into the old council chamber for a further two and a half years until the opening of the Civic Hall by King George V and Queen Mary on 23 August 1933, seventy-five years after the king's grandmother had opened the Town Hall. The new building had been completed six months ahead of schedule, utilised 5,000 tons of stone, had the public rooms finished in walnut and oak and incorporated a 2,500 sq. ft staff dining room that was never used for its intended purpose. The two 7 ft high gold-leafed owls reached 170 ft from the ground and prompted the *Yorkshire Post* to wax eloquent: 'We have set up over [the Civic Hall] the owls we share with Athens and, for all our difficulties in these harsher days, we feel towards our city that devotion out of which the Greeks built their civic pride and joy.'[46]

VII   The inter-war years were also a period of innovation in other, less grand, ways. In May 1925 the Liberal councillor A. E. Wilkinson proposed that a municipal wash-house be built at Stocks Hill, Holbeck, to serve his ward. It was agreed without opposition to borrow the £17,800 necessary, and the first wash-house opened in February 1928. The wash-house era just failed to reach its jubilee – the last remaining one (in Armley) being closed in 1977.

In the mid-1920s a clean air committee was established. Its report, published in July 1926, pointed out that as much as half the natural daylight can be lost through dirt in the atmosphere. The committee produced figures to demonstrate the wide differences between areas of the city in relation to atmospheric pollution. Whereas in Roundhay only 25·7 tons of solid impurities were deposited per square mile per year, in central Leeds the figure was almost ten times more, at 242·6 tons. At Beeston Hill the figure was 448·1 tons, and at Kirkstall Forge it reached 539 tons. It was the work of this committee and its successors, backed up by legislation, that led to the smokeless zones that now cover virtually all of Leeds.[47]

Headlines such as 'Car Hits Robot' could occasionally be seen in Yorkshire newspapers of the 1930s, to the puzzlement of southerners and, probably, most of today's northerners. It simply referred to the automatic traffic lights that were introduced in the period. The very first automatic traffic lights in England were installed at the corner of Park Row and Bond Street on 16 March 1928. The numbering of postal districts, the forerunner of today's post codes, also began about the same time, and the first twelve districts were 'launched' on 28 November 1932.

Another 'first' for Leeds was the establishment of a physical education college for men. The Carnegie United Kingdom Trust defrayed the capital costs of the new college, built on the campus of the teacher training college at Beckett Park. It was opened in October 1933 by Lord Irwin, president of the Board of Education. It was later amalgamated with the City of Leeds College of Education to unify the colleges on the Beckett Park site. Both are now part of the polytechnic.

Two initiatives that failed were the establishment of a zoo and the building of an underground railway. Many years of speculation about a zoo culminated in a parks committee resolution of April 1937 approving the establishment of one, but the three party leaders opposed it, and the full city council threw the idea out by a two-to-one majority. Early in 1939 a Conservative councillor, Allan Bretherick, proposed a tube railway for Leeds. His proposal was for twelve and a half miles of track connecting the city with its suburbs at a cost of £6¼ million. The scheme was examined with a view also to its relevance to air raid precautions but never proceeded with.

VIII   Leeds always prided itself on the scale and diversity of its manufacturing industries and on the fact that a large proportion of their products were exported.[48] Even in 1928 the Civic Week handbook singled out nine different manufacturing trades[49] but made no mention of the city's growth as a commercial centre, even though it drew attention rather delicately to the decline in both the engineering and boot and shoe trades. The census of occupations demonstrates the trend clearly (table 38). In 1921 47 per cent of all the working population were employed in manufacturing, compared with 20 per cent in white-collar occupations. By 1931 the proportion in manufacturing had declined to 38 per cent and the white-collar sector had increased to almost 23 per cent. By 1951, the year of the first postwar census, the gap had narrowed still further: 36 per cent in manufacturing to 30 per cent white-collar.

Table 38 Employment in occupational sectors, Leeds: percentages of those in employment

Sector	1921	1931	1951
All manufacturing	47·0	38·1	35·9
Agriculture	0·9	1·0	0·7
Mining and quarrying	2·9	1·7	1·0
Other manual (skilled and unskilled)	13·4	19·4	16·5
Transport and communication	7·4	7·0	6·8
Personal service (including hotels, etc.)	7·6	9·4	9·1
Other, miscellaneous	0·5	0·6	0·4
White collar	20·2	22·7	29·6

Source. Official census, 1921, 1931 and 1951.

During the 1930s Leeds was beginning to emerge as a regional centre, and by 1938 branches of five government departments had been established in the city: Home Office factory inspector, Inland Revenue stamp office, Ministry of Health insurance department, Ministry of Labour divisional controller and Ministry of Transport traffic commissioners. A look at Park Row in 1938, compared with 1913, shows the disappearance or amalgamation of six small local banks and the beginning of the dominance of the 'big five'.[50] The trend towards the concentration of regional administrative and financial institutions in Leeds was already well established before the beginning of the second world war.

Overshadowing all the events and activities of the 1920s and 1930s was the hardship of mass unemployment and the precarious position of industry. It is difficult accurately to compare the figures of unemployed year by year, owing to the differing definitions used in the published statistics, but it is clear that from the high point immediately after the 1914–18 war that the numbers steadily declined until by 1927 only half as many men were registered as unemployed compared with 1921.[51] Thereafter the numbers began to rise rapidly, more than doubling in the two years 1929–31, after which the position began to improve, and by 1937 the figure of unemployed men and women stood at 16,236, roughly the same as in 1929.[52] Approximately one in eight of the registered unemployed were women, and up to a fifth of the total were described as 'temporarily stopped'. In 1928 it was reported that 34,000 men had been employed at one time or another in approved schemes of relief work, but, commendable though such efforts were, the situation appeared to be worsening in 1938 and 1939, until the whole population was caught up in military service and war work.

The 1926 general strike did not have the catastrophic effect on the city and its services that was expected. A state of emergency was proclaimed on 1 May, and Captain D. H. Hacking, an under-secretary at the Home Office, was appointed civil commissioner, with an office at 13 King Street. Volunteer service committees were set up, and the First Police Reserve and the Special Constabulary called up. Some tramcars were attacked, and about a dozen men and women jailed, but the picketing was 'by and large peaceful'.[53] By the fourth day there were 3,725 volunteers for strike-breaking and some fifty trams were running. In all 10,000 volunteers came forward, of whom 2,000 were used.[54] Alderman Sir Charles Wilson called a special meeting of the city council for 10 May and, trying to repeat his successful tactics of 1913 against the municipal workers, proposed a special committee with delegated powers, comprising five Conservatives and three Liberals. The Liberal leader, Alderman Ratcliffe, explained the exclusion of Labour members: '[they] could not work on the Committee, they were not free members of the Council'. The Liberals were not united, and Councillor Dr Hawkyard opposed the motion. Wilson realised that with some Liberals joining Labour in opposition his position was precarious and adjourned the council meeting for one week. The strike ended two days later, and the motion was never put.[55]

In October the Labour magistrate and miner William Hemingway was fined £30 and removed from the commission of the peace, for intimidating six youths returning to work. The Labour Party pressed for his reinstatement but it was not until May 1931 that he was readmitted.[56] For three weeks in February and March 1936 9,000 workers at the giant Burton clothing factory went on unofficial strike in sympathy with a hundred coat fitters who had come out, also against union advice, over a pay grievance. By the third week three more factories were involved but a third of the strikers had returned to work. The management threatened those still on strike with the loss of their jobs, and after demonstrations and processions the strikers accepted the union's advice and called off the strike.[57]

IX   The years between the wars were a time of struggle and disappointment. The lofty idealism of 1918 and the inspiring rhetoric of Lloyd George promised more than could be delivered. But there were many significant changes in Leeds society. Politically the situation was considerably clearer in 1939 than in 1919. Labour, despite its parliamentary disaster in 1931 at the hands of Ramsay MacDonald and the National Government, was in good shape locally and polled its highest-ever municipal vote in 1933. By 1939 the political battle was clearly a two-party one, with the Liberals reduced to two representatives and their traditional newspaper, the *Mercury*, ignominiously swallowed up by the *Yorkshire Post*.

By 1939 town planning was accepted as the norm and roads were being deliberately built to a pattern, with sections of the ring road and, most important, the Headrow completed. The new Civic Hall had been built, 20,000 council dwellings constructed, and a municipal aerodrome established. Street lighting was slowly switching to electricity, trams were being supplemented by buses, and the city's boundaries had extended by 50 per cent since 1918. It was possible to mark civic progress over the two decades, and, with unemployment slowly reducing, and service industries providing increasing white-collar work, even to be optimistic about the future. But from late 1938 the preparations for war were obvious, with gas masks issued to every man, woman and child, plans for evacuating 100,000 children, teachers and mothers, 5,000 free air raid shelters for the poor, and sirens tested. For the second time in a generation the life of the country was disrupted by world war.

APPENDIX

1. *Party leaders, 1919–40*

Conservative	Liberal	Labour
C. H. Wilson 1906–28	G. Ratcliffe 1919–27	J. Arnott 1917–20
Leslie Owen 1928–29	Dr. Hawkyard 1927–28	W. J. Armstrong 1920–22
C. H. Wilson 1929–30	G. Ratcliffe 1928–32	J. Arnott 1922–25
R. C. Davies 1930–35	A. E. Wilkinson 1932–33	W. J. Armstrong 1928–32
C. V. Walker 1935–41	B. W. Goodall 1933–36	A. J. Dobbs 1932–36
	A. E. Wilkinson 1936–37	G. Brett 1936–40
	E. J. Morrish 1937–40	

2. *Freemen of the city, 1919–40*

Field Marshal Earl Haig, 23 January 1920
General Foch, 8 June 1922
Admiral Beatty, 18 October 1922
Rt. Hon. David Lloyd George, MP, 21 October 1922
Rt. Hon. E. F. L. Wood, MP, 5 March 1923
Ald. Charles H. Wilson, 5 March 1923
Rt. Hon. Stanley Baldwin, MP, 13 March 1925
Rt. Hon. Lord Oxford and Asquith, 13 March 1925
Sir Berkeley Moynihan, 6 October 1926
Sir Edward Brotherton, 6 October 1926
Sir William Middlebrook, 6 October 1926
Alderman Charles F. Tetley, 6 October 1926
Alderman Charles Lupton, 6 October 1926
John Rawlinson Ford, 6 October 1926
Henry C. Embleton, 6 October 1926
Rt. Hon. Philip Snowden, MP, 11 September 1930
Rt. Hon Arthur Greenwood, MP, 11 September 1930
Alderman George Ratcliffe, 11 September 1930
Hon. Rupert Beckett, 3 December 1930
HRH. The Princess Royal, 6 July 1932

NOTES

[1] J. E. Williams, 'The Leeds Corporation strike in 1913' in A. Briggs and J. Saville (eds.), *Essays in Labour History*, II (1971); *Report of Special Committee on the Strike of Municipal Workmen, 11 December 1913 to 13 January 1914* (Leeds Corporation, 1914); E. P. Hennock, *Fit and Proper Persons* (1973), 272–3.

[2] John Arnott and Bert Killip had been engaged as full-time organisers but were released from this commitment when elections were suspended (see Leeds Labour Party Minutes, LP3, 234, Leeds city archives).

[3] Leeds Liberal Federation, Executive Committee Minutes, 8 September 1914, Leeds city archives; Leeds Labour Party Minutes, LP3, 244, 251–3; Labour joined within six weeks. W. H. Scott, *Leeds in the Great War*, (1923), 312.

[4] *Leeds Weekly Citizen*, 24 May, 5 July and 30 August 1918; also K. Dugdale,

'Conservatives, Liberals and Labour in Yorkshire, 1918–1929', unpublished M.A. thesis, University of Sheffield (1976).

⁵ J. Henry to H. Gladstone, 26 November 1916, 30 December 1917, Gladstone Papers, B.L Add. MSS, 46038 and 46039; G. Ratcliffe to H. Gladstone, 6 September 1917, *ibid.*, 46083; T. E. Harvey to W. Harvey, 24 May 1915, 4 and 29 August, 8 December 1916, 6 and 12 February 1918, and W. Taylor to T. E. Harvey, 24 July 1916 (MSS in care of E. H. Milligan, Librarian, Friends' House, London).

⁶ G. Ratcliffe, *Sixty Years of it* (1935), 175–8.

⁷ Scott, *op. cit.*, 114.

⁸ *Ibid.*, 39 and 40.

⁹ *Ibid.*, 119.

¹⁰ *Ibid.*, 67.

¹¹ *British Labour and the Russian Revolution, The Leeds Convention: a report from the Daily Herald* (1977). F. Brockway, *Socialism over Sixty Years* (1946), 88; C. Cross, *Philip Snowden* (1966), 264; B. Donoughue and G. W. Jones, *Herbert Morrison: Portrait of a Politician* (1973), 40; D. Marquand, *Ramsay MacDonald* (1977), 208, 209; R. Miliband, *Parliamentary Socialism* (1961), 55; B. Webb, *Diaries, 1912–1917* (1948), 88; S. White, 'Soviets in Britain', *International Review of Social History*, XIX (1974); F. Williams, *Fifty Years' March* (1969), 264.

¹² Scott, *op. cit.*, 56, trying to depict Leeds Labour as respectable and to play down the convention, suggested that it 'had nothing to do with organised labour in Leeds'.

¹³ Early in May 1918 Major-General Sir Frederick Maurice, who had recently been deposed from the post of Director of Military Operations, sent a letter to the press in which he contended that certain public statements of Lloyd George and Bonar Law on the subject of British military strength in France were false. Asquith moved for a select committee to investigate but Lloyd George defended the government against the charges themselves. The government won the division by 295 votes to 108. Seventy-one Liberals voted for the government and ninety-eight against. This vote had some bearing on who received the coupon at the subsequent election. See R. Douglas, *The History of the Liberal Party, 1895–1970* (1971), 113–31.

¹⁴ The city's parliamentary boundaries had been redrawn to provide a sixth constituency. North East was the only constituency without a retiring member of Parliament contesting and was therefore regarded as the 'new' constituency, although, strictly speaking, all were new. Leeds Liberals' support of the coalition lasted only until late 1920 – see Leeds Liberal Federation, General Council Minutes (1920).

¹⁵ *Yorkshire Post*, 23 December 1919.

¹⁶ *Ibid.*, 31 December 1930, for obituary.

¹⁷ *Ibid.*, 12 May 1922, 29 March 1968.

¹⁸ *Ibid.*, 11 April 1921.

¹⁹ Nikolaus Pevsner, *The Buildings of England: Yorkshire, West Riding* (1967), 317. From the context he appears to mean Woodhouse Lane, not Cookridge Street.

²⁰ *Yorkshire Post*, leading article, 4 November 1932.

²¹ *Ibid.*, 10 January 1930.

²² *Ibid.*, 2 January 1929, 24 January 1935.

²³ A. Ravetz, *Model Estate* (1974), 23.

²⁴ Speech in City Council, *Yorkshire Post*, 7 October 1928.

²⁵ *Ibid.*, 29 November 1932.

²⁶ *Ibid.*, 3 March 1933; a third report, from the Liberals, was promised but, if ever produced, has not survived. The minority report was called *Housing Policy in the City of Leeds* and was presented on 23 February 1933 and later adopted as official

Labour policy. For a biography of Charles Jenkinson see H. J. Hammerton, *This Turbulent Priest* (1952).

[27] Councillor the Rev. Charles Jenkinson, in *Yorkshire Post*, 13 January 1934.

[28] Hammerton, *op. cit.*, 30.

[29] For a number of reasons outside the scope of this chapter Quarry Hill never lived up to its promise and was eventually demolished in 1978. The full account can be read in Ravetz, *op. cit.* See also *Yorkshire Post*, 18 June 1938, for list of names.

[30] Letter from 'Socialist', *Leeds Weekly Citizen*, 11 July 1919.

[31] Labour became the largest party in 1926 but did not take office in the council until 1927; it did not have an overall majority until 1928. See M. J. Meadowcroft, 'Transition in Leeds City government, 1903 to 1926', unpublished M.Phil. thesis, University of Bradford (1978), 123 and 124.

[32] *Yorkshire Post*, 27 February 1950. He had apparently fallen out with the Leeds Labour Party executive, who, in any case, wished to get rid of him as leader.

[33] Meadowcroft, *op. cit.*, 155–8; Rev. David Stewart, former chairman, Leeds Labour Party; and candidate, Leeds North, 1922, quoted in Leeds Labour Party, *op. cit.*, LP4, 404, April 1929.

[34] *Yorkshire Post*, 5 March 1929.

[35] Leeds Labour Party, *op. cit.*, LP2, 45, 18 April 1912.

[36] Ratcliffe, *op. cit.*, 316; see also Meadowcroft, *op. cit.*, 202–6 and 216, reference 37.

[37] Except for 1927 to 1928, when he was Lord Mayor and Dr Hawkyard acted as leader. See George Ratcliffe, *Sixty Years of It* (1935).

[38] See Ratcliffe, *op. cit.*, 261–4, and Meadowcroft, *op. cit.*, 206–12.

[39] See C. Cook, *The Age of Alignment, 1922–29* (1975), 49–87; G. Peele and C. Cook (eds.), *The Politics of Reappraisal, 1918–1939* (1975), 166–88; and Meadowcroft, *op. cit.*, 143–51.

[40] One of whom, David T. Barnes, later rejoined the Liberals.

[41] Meadowcroft, *op. cit.*, 189.

[42] *Ibid.*, pp. 190–1.

[43] *Yorkshire Post*, 11, 14, 16, 17 and 23 December 1937, 6 January, 3 March, 2 September 1938.

[44] *Ibid.*, 27 October 1928.

[45] Background information from interview with Sir George Martin, 29 October 1975.

[46] *Yorkshire Post*, leading article, 23 August 1933.

[47] *Ibid.*, 17 July 1926.

[48] A Leeds Chamber of Commerce report in 1914 showed the following percentages for exports: engineering and machinery, 75; locomotives, 95; traction engines, 80; textile machinery, 50; ready-made clothing, 33.

[49] *Leeds Civic Week Handbook* (1928), 67–82.

[50] *Kelly's Directory of Leeds*, 1913 and 1938.

[51] *Yorkshire Post*, 14 March 1928.

[52] *Ibid.*, 6 July 1937.

[53] *Ibid.*, 6 May 1926.

[54] *Ibid.*, 5 May 1976, and *Leeds Mercury*, 10 May 1926.

[55] *Leeds Weekly Citizen*, Special Strike Bulletin, 11 May 1926.

[56] Hemingway was elected to the Hunslet Board of Guardians in 1913; councillor 1915–25; alderman 1926–67; freeman of the city 1956; knighted 1965. He was the longest-serving council member of all time.

[57] *Yorkshire Post*, 22 February, 3, 13 and 14 March 1936.

BIBLIOGRAPHICAL NOTE

The material available for a study of inter-war Leeds is substantial but patchy. The Archives Department of City Libraries has the minute books of the Leeds Labour Party, the Leeds Liberal Federation and, less comprehensively, the City of Leeds Conservative Association. It also has a considerable amount of financial and related material, such as the rating valuation lists.

There are three sets of personal papers extant: the Herbert Gladstone papers are available at the British Library, London, the T. Edmund Harvey papers are in the care of E. H. Milligan, the Librarian of the Society of Friends, Euston Road, London, and the Alf Mattison diaries are in the Brotherton Collection of the University of Leeds Library.

The Local History Library, at the Leeds Central Reference Library, has the *Leeds Mercury, Yorkshire Post, Yorkshire Evening Post, Yorkshire Evening News* and certain weekly papers on microfilm, together with the Labour Party's official paper, *The Leeds Weekly Citizen*, which is a valuable source of political material. The Local History Library also has numerous press cutting books, including the Matthewman collection of cuttings on Leeds municipal affairs. The Director of Administration, Leeds Civic Hall, has charge of all the council's official papers, yearbooks, etc., and there are also official handbooks for the tercentenary celebrations in 1926 and for the Civic Week in 1928.

Four different yearbooks cover all or part of the period: Morrison's 'Blue Book' and *Leeds Record*, 1903–31, Kelly's *Directories of Leeds* for each year, Robinson's *Directory of Leeds*, 1904–30, and *Yorkshire Post Year Books*, 1936–38.

Amongst the sparse published material E. P. Hennock, *Fit and Proper Persons* (1973), covers the period to 1914 and W. H. Scott, *Leeds in the Great War* (1923), deals with the first world war in the typical official style. The Leeds Convention of 1917 has recently been reprinted in *British Labour and the Russian Revolution* (1977) with an introduction by Ken Coates. There are two books of political memoirs: George Ratcliffe, *Sixty Years of it* (1935), and Mary Gawthorpe, *Up Hill to Holloway* (1962), and two biographies: H. J. Hammerton, *This Turbulent Priest* (1952), on Charles Jenkinson, and E. Kitson Clark, *Kitsons of Leeds* (1938). Alison Ravetz, *Model Estate* (1974), recounts the history of the Quarry Hill flats.

Finally there are four unpublished theses containing political material on Leeds: Brenda Powell, 'A study of the change in social origins of members of Leeds City Council, 1888–1953' (Leeds M.A., 1958); C. P. Cook, 'The Liberal Party in decline' (Oxford D.Phil., 1973); K. Dugdale, 'Conservatives, Liberals and Labour in Yorkshire, 1918–1929' (Sheffield M.A., 1976), and my own 'Transition in Leeds city government, 1903–1926' (Bradford M.Phil., 1978), which contains a fuller bibliography and an index. R. E. Finnigan's thesis on Leeds municipal housing policy is due to be completed in 1980 (Bradford M.Phil.), and he has written an essay on this subject in J. Melling (ed.), *Housing, Social Policy and the State* (1979).

OWEN HARTLEY

XVII

The second world war
and after, 1939–74

Although the range of its concerns was wider in 1939 than in 1974, the activities of the city council were central to the affairs of Leeds throughout this period. Other perspectives are possible, but all have at some point to turn to the council, its officials and its policies. Its responsibilities ranged from art galleries to waterworks,[1] and in carrying them out the council acted through, and pursued policies devised by, professional officers of its own choosing, mobilising interest and enthusiasm among the public at large. What were the problems that had to be faced in these years, and how much continuity was there up to the radical reorganisation of 1974?

I   To understand the city council it is important to understand the political system in which it played a central role. City politics is city *council* politics. Constituency politics has been highly predictable in Leeds. In 1929 Labour had four of the six parliamentary seats and the Conservatives the other two. By 1935 Labour had only two but had real hopes of taking two others (one was held by National Labour) and in the 1945 election did in fact take them both, with the bonus of the only unexpected win in the period, Leeds North East. In 1950 and 1951 there were seven parliamentary seats, Labour taking five and the Conservatives two, and thereafter, of the restored six seats, Labour and Conservative were certain of their four and two respectively.

The politics of other organisations are interesting but usually eccentric. The two bodies that in other cities could have been expected to be Labour strongholds were held by opponents – the local co-operative society until 1965 by 'Non-politicals' (i.e. Liberals and Conservatives) and the trades council by Communists and those of similar convictions. Equally, the local Conservatives had no continuing support or sympathy from the chamber of commerce or even the local 'Conservative' press. Political activity outside the parties and the city council was either unintegrated with the general structure of political activity and without wide support, or occurred in a spontaneous *ad hoc* fashion without continuing effect.

Secondly, though parliamentary elections are uninteresting in Leeds, *national* politics are not. The sheer size of the city means that its doings are nearly always of some concern to the country at large: its leaders automatically become national figures in such bodies as the Association of Municipal Corporations, as well as within their own parties, and there is a continuous interplay between 'Leeds' policies and 'national' policies. The Labour Party's municipal election manifesto of 1945 urged the electorate to 'Forge the Link' between Town Hall and Westminster by voting Labour. The Conservatives have never been quite so explicit, yet the local Conservative magazine *Leeds Searchlight* continuously exhibited such links between local and national issues.

Council politics was dominated by political parties which were a local expression of national parties. The major battle was between Labour and Conservative, with Liberal intervention. The Conservatives controlled the city in 1935–45, 1951–53 and 1967–72; Labour in 1945–51, 1953–67 and 1972–74. The Leeds Metropolitan District Council, which sat in 1973–74 as a parallel body to the city council until April 1974, when local government reform ended the old council and transferred its powers to the new one, was controlled by Labour in 1973–75, though without an overall majority because of the size of the Liberal group.

Party politics in Leeds was not a clash of ideologies. It was not even a debate about the distribution of civic goods and services to persons or areas. Party politics provided a framework for individuals to practise their skills and fulfil their ambitions.

When the local Conservative magazine in May 1972 wanted to praise the Conservative administration of 1967–72 it listed the achievements as: rate increases kept to a minimum; Project Leeds initiated – creating more jobs; pedestrian precincts provided; government backing secured for Leeds as host to the Commonwealth Games; private housing development brought back inside the city by the sale of council-owned land; council rents kept steady for the past eighteen months; the lodger charge abolished; the first housing information centre in the provinces; over 1,000 council tenants enabled to buy their own houses; the slums attacked; housing development unsurpassed; concessionary fares for old people extended; the Fastway bus services (and one-man buses); initiated the first all-electric buses in the country; bus shelters provided; social services reorganised; the Grand Theatre saved; the Town Hall cleaned and the organ renovated; the clean air programme almost completed. The *only* items in this formidable list with which the Labour group dissented were selling council houses and cleaning the Town Hall. To be fair, the Conservatives did not list their reorganisation of education, due to begin in September 1972, which was disputed. But, to be equally fair, it was the Labour Party who implemented the education plans in 1974.

Thus the degree of policy differentiation on any ground has always been small and is most evident in two areas, housing and education, which will be examined later. The politics of ideology being weak, the politics of distributing civic goods and services was not significant either. Neither Labour nor Conservatives worried unduly about providing special services for 'their' voters, except perhaps slightly, in that Labour tried to keep council house rents down harder than the Conservatives did, and vice versa with bus fares and parking charges. The politics of distribution between areas was suppressed in the Labour group by the fact that councillors were not expected to be closely attached to their wards, Conservatives were expected to try to be but rarely succeeded, while the Liberals did genuinely make an effort to be eager ward representatives but failed because in the end area differentiation was difficult to sustain.

Party politics was the necessary framework for the politics of personal conflict that was at the centre of the local political battles. The debate between the parties was rarely about measures to be undertaken, it was about the style and the personal credit that was to be earned by being associated with measures. Within the parties the debates were plainly and publicly those of personal conflict.

Party was needed to provide, through the idea of 'party loyalty', some of the essentials aspiring politicians without personal wealth, connection or fame needed. It created safe electoral havens, produced a group of colleagues from whom a degree of support was available in return for the right verbal gestures, and had machinery in group meetings and the convention of party voting as a single bloc for ensuring the success of particular policies once they had been decided on. Without party organisation no individual could win and maintain electoral support, partly because support was always difficult to generate and in a very large council – 104 councillors and aldermen up to 1951, 112 up to 1968 and 120 up to 1974 (and ninety-six councillors on the Metropolitan District Council after 1973) – some organisation was needed if meetings were not to be entirely without shape or consequence.

Personality politics produced the larger-than-life charismatic figure. The model for the two best examples of the 1939–74 period, the

Rev. Charles Jenkinson and (Sir) Frank Marshall, was the earlier figure of Sir Charles Wilson. Jenkinson was to some extent created as an answer to the Conservative Sir Charles by Labour activists, Marshall was a more direct imitation. Both specialised not so much in actual achievements as in presenting their special characters. Both became national figures with a reputation for expertise, Jenkinson in housing and Marshall in city government, and both obtained the due reward of such distinction, governmental patronage into difficult jobs, Jenkinson to the chairmanship of Stevenage New Town Corporation and Marshall to the third London airport. Both 'thought big' and had considerable gifts, especially for self-publicity.

The charismatic figure was the special outcome of personality politics, but many other political leaders played more routine roles as and when the opportunity arose. In consequence the policy direction of the city's activities fell into the hands of the professional officers. With party ideological direction weak and political leaders only slightly interested in policy, the competent local officials happily undertook the devising of policies which parties and leaders would be willing to accept. These policies were invariably expansionary and involved more expenditure, but expansion was acceptable to all political parties and, while the innovations may have been devised by officials, both could claim the credit for successful results. Councillors and officials were allied in their interests and the benefits were mutual.

The alliance was not merely over policies but also on the general structure of local decision-making. A partial consequence of having a large council was that the number of committees expanded to the point where every councillor could sit on at least one and every leader of the majority party could have a chairmanship. The number of committees remained fairly constant at about twenty-seven from 1939 to 1966. In a similar fashion, the number of separate departments into which the activities of the council were divided stayed around thirty, as each committee wanted its own department, and the professional concerns of the officials sought just such a separate status. This stability in numbers disguised major changes, such as the loss of gas and electricity as local services, and those consequent on the creation of the National Health Service and the setting up of new departments like the city architect's in 1946, but it was a workable system of a common type.

The widespread feeling of the 1960s that local government could be made more efficient by creating stronger central co-ordinating machinery at the local level posed a problem for Leeds. Central co-ordination meant more power to a smaller group of councillors and officials. The innovations of Marshall's new Conservative administration of 1967, which were accepted by Labour in 1972, created two sets of central machinery. A policy committee consisting of a few senior councillors reigned over a smaller number of committees (eleven in 1967, sixteen in 1972). A management team of three officers led by a town clerk, renamed chief executive officer, in parallel with the centralisation of politicians reigned over only eleven departments. Senior councillors and senior officials benefited: the losers were the junior members of both groups and those who lost the personal arguments that inevitably accompanied the change of structure.

The pattern of local politics to be understood in this period is, then, a party political system organisationally strong but intellectually weak, centred on the city council, wherein councillors manoeuvred for office and prestige in association with policy-inventing officials, who themselves manoeuvred for office and prestige.

II   The first priority in 1939 was to survive the war. It is common for historians to attribute to its impact major changes in social, political and economic life. At the local level in Leeds it is hard to detect any shifts of attitude. The war certainly involved social and economic dislocation, but the overwhelming impression is of a happy return in 1945 to the concerns of 1939 without any noticeable changes of attitude or direction.

The social dislocation was greater than anything known before. At the personal level, people were moved to jobs thought essential to the national interest, called up to the forces and sent to distant parts, conscripted into tasks like fire-fighting additional to their ordinary duties and interests, urged and bullied in campaigns for National Savings and Digging for Victory, and subjected to the rationing of essentials like food and clothing. At work things changed too: clothing factories produced uniforms, printers produced forms, engineering works the weapons of war; conditions deteriorated and traditional activities were disrupted. Leeds itself was threatened with direct enemy action, and the conflict elsewhere produced floods of refugees that, with the billeting of war workers and troops, led in effect to the rationing of another essential, housing. Dislocations of this order might be expected to have had *some* consequences: did not much smaller ones in the industrial revolution lead to significant change? The problem is to explain why the effects were so negligible. The explanations can be summarised as: a fairly solid refusal by the mass of the population to be panicked about the war, its conduct or its consequences; the deliberate efforts that were made to conciliate society so as to lessen social tension, and the fact that at no point did the strain become immediate and particular rather than general.

When war was declared on 3 September 1939 Leeds was ready for it. The corporation's air raid precautions and civil defence committee had made many sensible arrangements since 1936, and after 1938 local businesses had also taken air raid matters seriously. As an industrial and commercial centre the city could expect to be bombed in the early stages of a European war, and precautions in the shape of casualty, fire, decontamination and rescue services were well in hand. Efforts by local Communist and Labour leaders to make 'lack of preparation' an issue both before September 1939 and afterwards failed miserably: the population refused to panic and moreover the facts did not warrant a scare. Even the opportunity to evacuate children to areas of the North Riding and Lincolnshire, where bombs were unlikely to fall, was accepted by the parents of less than a third of the schoolchildren. So although some 18,000 children were evacuated on 1 September 1939, and on 2 September some 8,000 mothers, expectant mothers, children, and blind and disabled people went, in a real feat of administration, it was few compared to the numbers possible. A further evacuation in October 1939 moved only 732 of a registered 1,889 children, and most of those evacuated returned after Christmas to join their fellows who had enjoyed the privilege of missing school for a whole term. It seemed that if disaster were to strike, then the citizens of Leeds wanted their children with them.

If there was next to no panic at the personal level, in politics the citizens were not tempted to vote for an end to the war. In a parliamentary by-election in the North East ward in March 1940 the truce between the major parties held, and the only opponent of the Conservative was a British Union of Fascists candidate who advocated an immediate peace settlement and gleaned only 722 votes (2·9 per cent). The formation of a coalition government in 1940 led two Communist sympathisers in the ranks of the local Labour Party to protest and imply that the war effort was being misdirected. The Labour group disowned them both in October 1940, and there is no sign of their having had any real public support for their radical stance.

There is on the contrary evidence of strong willingness to contribute to the war effort. This can be illustrated by looking at the Home Guard, raised quickly from volunteers in May 1940 to three battalions (later four). Having attaining standards of modest competence, after February 1942 men could be directed to Home Guard duties. As a candid officer of one Leeds battalion put it, 'Directed men who wholly refused to do any HG duty whatever largely "got away with it" by pleading medical unfitness, hours of work, and all sorts of excuse,' but noted equally, 'Throughout the period when compulsion was applied to the HG, fully 90 per cent of the work done by an even moderately keen HG was in excess of what he could, in practice, have been compelled to do.'[2]

The conciliation of all social groups was considered important. Competing organisations were treated as equals for the duration of the war. It could be symbolised in small matters like the distribution of tickets for mass meetings: equal allocations went to the Church of England, the Free Churches, Jews and Roman Catholics, to property owners and to the Co-operative Society, to the trades council, chamber of trades, chamber of commerce, the university and the British Legion. Only in the case of political parties was there discrimination: Labour and Conservatives were regarded as equal, but the Liberals always got 70–80 per cent less. Social dislocation did not lead to disorder because no organisation or group was left out.

The final reason is more specialised. There was no point at which the strain moved from being general to being immediate and particular. It had been feared that the exposure of civilians to modern warfare, particularly aerial bombardment, would lead to a collapse of morale and then of social order. Even areas that were bombed more heavily suffered only a little in this respect, and Leeds had a comparatively quiet war. The city was raided by aircraft nine times, only six of which were serious. The first, in August 1940, killed four and injured thirteen and led to some minor panic, as those who had not previously applied for air raid shelters now did so urgently and met with a cool response from the city authority. The worst raid was on 14 March 1941, when shortly before midnight high explosives and incendiaries were showered over the city. The telephone system was put out of action immediately, the waterworks and gas supplies were affected, there was some panic, a lot of courage, some damage to the City Museum and the Town Hall, 4,600 houses damaged (100 of them beyond repair) and – depending on whether you take the contemporary emergency committee report or the medical officer of health's post-war report – sixty-five or sixty-four dead, and fifty-six or fifty-seven seriously and 202 or 203 slightly wounded. The emergency committee's private report exudes an air of quiet confidence that Leeds had withstood a severe test with honour. Throughout the war seventy-seven people were killed by bombing, seventy-one seriously and 249 slightly wounded by enemy action, and seven injured by the shell fragments of the anti-aircraft defence system. The mobile emergency services were used to assist Hull, York, Sheffield and later London in their time of need.

Hostilities over, the city happily returned to its 1939 problems. The war left no sense of having endured a great test, no feeling that anything other than a regrettable interruption of business as usual had occurred. Even the arrival of the Labour Party to local and national power in 1945 was not unexpected; local Labour leaders and many Conservatives were convinced it was going to happen in 1940, so the war had merely delayed the inevitable.

III   A further example of the continuity of life from 1939 can be seen in the following list of the projects that were 'alive' in 1939 as something the city council wanted to have done, and showing what had happened to them by 1974.

'Live' projects in 1939	Situation in 1974
1 Roads:	
(*a*) Eastgate–Headrow–Westgate.	Completed 1958–59.
(*b*) Outer ring road.	Northern section completed but southern section superseded by motorway schemes of 1960s.
2 Yeadon Airport expansion.	Expansion in 1960s. Future uncertain.
3 Seacroft housing and industrial estate development.	Completed 1960s.
4 Slum clearance programme.	1930s completed plan in 1960s.
5 New housing estates (various sites).	Most completed by 1960.
6 New wholesale market and abattoir.	Opened 1966.
7 New fire and police stations.	New fire brigade HQ 1972, new police HQ 1965.
8 New central library, art gallery and museum.	On central site 1967 but not in new buildings.
9 New central baths.	Opened 1967.
10 New central bus station.	Still being planned.
11 Central college site for art, commerce and technology.	Centrally sited by 1963, became Polytechnic 1970.
12 New school building programme.	Completed in 1950s.
13 Extension of new civic centre.	Phase I completed 1969, phase II postponed indefinitely.
14 Health and hospital developments:	
(*a*) St James's extensions.	Completed 1940 as planned.
(*b*) New children's hospital.	A major unit at Seacroft 1950.
(*c*) Seacroft Hospital developments.	Infectious diseases reduced, hence never completed as planned.
(*d*) Radium institute and cancer hospital.	Built at Cookridge after 1956.
(*e*) Central laundry.	Still awaited.
(*f*) Central ambulance station.	Opened 1954.
(*g*) Public mortuary.	Opened 1948.

It is clear that for at least twenty years Leeds was occupied in fulfilling a programme of public works that in 1939 had been seen as the task of the next decade. It is notable that any additions date almost entirely from the 1960s: motorways, new slum clearance, more housing estates, further education colleges, school building and reorganisation, the development of St James's Hospital, and the expansion and rebuilding of the university and the infirmary. The 1960s projects will be substantially completed by 1980, that is, somewhat more quickly than the 1939 plans.

There is another list to be considered. This records the matters which were lost from council control in 1939–74 and became the responsibility of a new authority:

Services lost to the city council	New authorities	
1 Gas.	North Eastern Gas Board.	1949
2 Electricity.	Yorkshire Electricity Board.	1948
3 Public assistance.	National Assistance Board.	1948
4 Hospitals.	Leeds Regional Hospital Board.	1948

It cannot be said that the loss of the first three items created discontent amongst councillors. All three services, while still generating plans for expansion of facilities and improvements in detail, had become the preserve of professional officers where ordinary councillors could offer little in the way of initiative and support and where even the chairmen of the committees concerned seemed slightly bored with their responsibilities. The National Health Service after 1948 did generate some stronger feelings. In 1939 Leeds was responsible not merely for environmental health but, since in 1934 the corporation had taken over the old Poor Law hospitals, for a wide range of general medical matters. The creation of the NHS took away the council's potential role in developing public health, especially hospitals, while leaving the city with a scattering of underdeveloped minor health activities. Being allocated a small role was perhaps more frustrating than complete nationalisation might have been. However, with the remaining health functions the council continued the expansionary and dynamic development that had been characteristic of its efforts before 1939.

There was, then, a strong continuity between the Leeds of 1939 and that of 1974. To pursue this theme through all the council's activities would be a lengthy matter, so the following pages concentrate on four major activities.

IV   The council's interest in health and hospital matters was the achievement of the medical officer of health, Dr J. J. Jervis, who was in office from 1916 to 1947. He generated enthusiasm among councillors and gathered a team of gifted subordinates who were equally adept at winning political approval for specific fields of endeavour. Under him, and to a great extent because of him, the health record improved: infectious diseases diminished in frequency and impact, and the life expectancy of all, and especially of children, improved dramatically. Jervis moved from efforts to create a great hospital out of St James's, the old Poor Law hospital, to nurseries and the prevention of atmospheric pollution without losing his sense that all health matters were closely connected. By convincing councillors as well, he could associate them with the numerous tributes of outside observers. The Ministry of Health surveyors, for example, in 1945 commented very favourably on the city's hospital services and especially singled out St James's: 'The Surveyors feel it is their duty as well as their pleasure to express their very high appreciation of the work done at this hospital and the breadth of outlook possessed by the Health Authority in charge.'[3]

The breadth of outlook could not survive the creation of the National Health Service. Under I. G. Davies (1947–58) and D. B. Bradshaw (1958–73) as medical officers of health, the city's health department put great efforts into the special responsibilities left to the council: maternity and child welfare, home nursing, ambulances and mental health. In so far as finance and a persistent shortage of skilled manpower permitted, these services were maintained at a high level, but they did not allow of a broad view either by the medical officer or by councillors. Each section of the health services developed independently at the initiative of its head, but with support from the council in each case. The council was always ready to create 'health centres' where general practitioners and health and welfare activities could be commonly situated. After rebuffs from various quarters, the first was created in 1969, and the council thereafter took to building two a year. But this was the only major opportunity it had of taking a broad view.

Enthusiasm had to be channelled into support for individual schemes. The most creative individual was J. Goodfellow, the chief sanitary (later chief public health) inspector. Goodfellow's role has been insufficiently appreciated, since each of his initiatives was in itself small, but, when backed by organising skill and enthusiasm, the results were significant and, cumulatively, very important. His role in housing will be examined below, but in health matters his ridding the town of atmospheric pollution, or 'smoke' as it was more popularly known, and his strict enforcing of food, shop and office legislation, made a substantial contribution to improving the quality of life.

An interesting feature of the National Health Service in Leeds after 1949 was the persistence of the city council's plans and attitudes. The two management committees that dealt with hospitals under the Regional Hospital Board contained many people with local council experience, and they continued most of the plans drawn up by Jervis for expansion, especially at St James's. Even in such small matters as issuing clear annual reports the council's practices were followed. Eventually the weight of the medical profession, and of professional managers on the committees themselves, reduced outside knowledge and involvement to the point where public or party support for any proposal could not be aroused. Management committees were composed of selected people, without the necessary skill in dealing with contentious or 'political' issues, and it is hard to believe that the council would have left quite so many problems for the reorganised National Health Service to deal with in 1974.

V At first sight housing appears to be one area of intense political debate: the parties clashed in the 1930s over slum clearance, the building of new estates and the sale of council houses, and similar conflicts as well as new ones on compulsory purchase for housing improvement were to be found after 1945. But it is important to see each as on the fringe of basic agreement. It was accepted policy that the council should build houses for letting to general applicants who simply wanted somewhere to live; that slums should be cleared as quickly as they could; and that houses should be improved, with council financial assistance, wherever possible. The debates about slum clearance and compulsory purchase were over the principles of compensation; those about new estates were over the proper balance between local authority and private building; and the debate on the sale of council houses to sitting tenants was argued from abstract principles, since no party actually thought many tenants would take up the option to purchase.

This being so, the history of housing in 1945–74 was one of benevolent politicians encouraging the efforts of their professional officers, even when the latter disagreed among themselves. There was in fact not one housing policy but at least four, each supported by a professional officer. The city architect argued for house and flat building; the medical officer of health and chief public health inspector wanted slum clearance; the health inspector had his favourite policy of house improvement as well; and the housing manager wanted to place all applicants in appropriate council housing, which meant argument sometimes with the architect and sometimes with the health inspector.

The priority was to provide as many houses as possible. In April 1943 the housing committee foresaw a post-war programme that was more a continuation of the 1934 target of clearing 30,000 slum houses than a realistic attempt to fulfil the growing demand from new families, but its expectation of the rate of house-building that might be possible was optimistic. The committee planned for 53,000 council houses over twenty years, basing the figure on pre-war experience. For seven consecutive years after 1933–34 new houses exceeded 3,700 a year, and for three years after 1936–37 over 2,379 houses each year were built for the corporation. But despite its best efforts new construction passed 3,700 in only three post-war years (1960, 1966, 1967) to 1974, and council house building exceeded 2,379 in only six years, although it was a larger part of the total programme than before the war.

Throughout the period 1945–74 council house building always lagged behind demand. The waiting list was always inflated but was always substantial enough to justify more building. The council's commitment to clearing the slums increased the pressure, and the same level of new building was maintained by both Labour and Conservative administrations. Labour preferred to build for general letting and the Conservatives for slum clearance, but both built as much as they thought they could manage.

The directing genius behind the building programme was R.A.H. Livett. He had come to the city in 1934 as housing director. His interests lay more in constructing houses, and especially flats – in which he had a fervent belief based on a personal aesthetic preference – than in managing council housing. He became city architect in 1946, while J.W. Burton became chief officer of a housing department concerned mainly with tenancy matters. It is noteworthy that the building of flats coincided with major slum clearance projects, despite their higher cost as against ordinary houses. Thus Livett's aesthetics were never tested against the wishes of the people who were being rehoused. Under him city architecture became associated with multi-storey flat developments and a large-scale building programme, and his successors after 1959 continued this tradition.

Since Livett had come to Leeds to assist in a slum clearance housing policy, and only in clearance schemes did flats seem possible, he was never hostile to the continual promptings of the housing committee by the medical officer of health and chief public health inspector to make slum clearance a priority. It never really ceased, for even at the height of the post-war housing shortage in 1945–54 individually unfit houses were swept away. The return in the middle 1950s of clearance as the city's main housing policy led to the completion of the 1934 programme around 1964. Though 'slum clearance' continued, the committee was clear that what it was doing away with was not houses 'unfit for human habitation' but only ones that needed repair and modernisation.

It was this that troubled the chief public health inspector. Indeed, Goodfellow might well have believed that many of the 'slums' already declared were capable of being improved. Once he had demonstrated in a series of experiments in 1955 that back-to-back houses could be ventilated there were usually no grounds for demolition, since irremediable structural defects were rare. He did not explicitly challenge the clearance programme but instead promoted his own policy of house improvement. It became nationally known as 'the Leeds method', but was wholly his invention. It involved selecting a small area for 'treatment' and, using persuasion and the threat of compulsory purchase, having all the houses brought up to a better standard. The controlling Conservative group on the council disliked the threat of compulsory purchase, and in the very month (March 1970) that Goodfellow retired the council abandoned the area method. Haltingly and in other terminology it had to be reintroduced, since it was found to be so effective elsewhere.

The remaining policy was that pursued by the housing manager in dealing with tenancies. The system devised after 1946 was a strongly decentralised one, with area offices operating within fairly loose guidelines. The policies pursued in this field, though closely supervised by councillors, especially in 1946–50, when there was a desperate housing shortage, were devised by the professional staff and carried through with skill and sympathy, as outside observers were quick to detect.

What then was the role of the councillors and especially the chairman of the housing committee? It would seem to have been the task of the chairman to have enormous technical knowledge of the subject, to be a dedicated party man, and to use his political skills to keep the councillors away from the officers so that they could get on with their job. This was possible because the councillors' objectives were clear and, despite the rhetoric of party strife, not very different between the parties. Building, slum clearance, improvement and fairness in council house allocation were agreed matters. In the hands of someone as competent as the long-serving Labour chairman of the housing committee, Sir Karl Cohen, political direction might seem self-evident. But Sir Karl's skill was to keep all his officers happy and his own colleagues in their supporting roles. Parties could and did make choices about housing policy, but innovation and development were firmly in the hands of the officers who served them.

VI   Educational provision in 1939 could be characterised thus: a reputable university that had strong associations with local industry and its problems; a considerable range of advanced technical training institutions intended to form a central college complex in the near future; a range of maintained grammar schools of high quality and a reputation to equal if not surpass the well endowed private Leeds Grammar School; generally weak secondary education, since the education committee and chief education officers had taken a sceptical view of the demand for 'Secondary education for all'; a healthy basic provision of primary and 'all-age' schools; and an unusually effective system of nursery education by the local authority. The achievements of 1939–74 were to see a much expanded but nationally oriented university, a well developed polytechnic emerging from the central colleges concept, further technical colleges, and a twice reorganised school system (from which the maintained grammar schools and nursery education had been eliminated) whose efficacy was yet to be demonstrated.

The causes of these changes must include national trends and dispositions, especially in the growth of the university, where the resources were provided by central government. Central resources were crucial to other local developments too, but the options available to the city council were somewhat wider than those open to the university. It would be tempting to attribute the changes in secondary education to the effect of party political choices, especially in view of the national debate of the 1960s between the parties on the subject. But at least from the time of the 1946 education committee's Education Development Plan the creation of a stronger secondary sector including 'multilateral', that is, mixed grammar, technical and general secondary, schools was common ground between the local parties. The final Conservative reorganisation scheme for all Leeds schools was implemented by Labour after 1972 with only small differences of emphasis.

The primary role of education committee chairmen like Aldermen Walsh and Crotty, the two leading figures from the Labour and Conservative groups respectively, was similar to that of housing committee chairmen. Technical competence in the intricacies of the education system, allied to the ability to keep the officers happy and their own colleagues from making education a party issue, was what was required of them. This they achieved, leaving innovation to three separate stimuli. The first was the sheer need to cope with the demand for education. The second and third were the professionals, the chief education officer and the teachers.

A substantial part of the work was coping with the numbers of children to be educated. In 1939–40 there were 53,188 children between the ages of five and fourteen. In 1971–72, before the second raising of the leaving age, there were 79,397 children aged five to fifteen. Moreover there was also the pressure of numbers from children reaching school age and from those staying on after fifteen, especially to acquire further and technical education. Providing the accommodation and the teachers was an annual problem. It is easy to overlook the achievement involved in actually managing the system, but it was nonetheless real. It was, however, an achievement with two consequences. In order to cope, the excellent nursery education system disappeared shortly after the end of the war. And with no spare teachers or classroom capacity, plans for school reorganisation had to be drawn within very narrow limits.

The chief education officer was responsible for managing the education system. At least one of the occupants of this office, George Taylor (1950–65), was accorded by the education committee, and later claimed for himself, a leading innovative role. The chief education officer could indeed encourage new developments and be creative about existing problems. Taylor, faced with a shortage of teachers, created a special college (James Graham) for the training of mature students; faced with the growth of degree-level work in the central colleges, he devised the branch colleges to continue real technical education; faced with the problems of selecting children for different sorts of secondary education at eleven years of age, he pressed for 'comprehensive' secondary schools. Chief education officers in Leeds were expected to respond to circumstances with concrete proposals. He ran the educational organisation and was expected to produce organisational answers.

Education, however, is fundamentally not about structures of educational provision, but about the content. Taylor was able to encourage individual schools to experiment with musical education and the early introduction of language teaching, but head teachers and teachers generally remained free to teach what they liked how they liked with a degree of competence chosen by themselves. Neither the education committee nor the chief education officer could challenge the views of the professional educators and, at one remove, their professional organisations about the content and direction of the education provided.

The power of the professionals, it was to be found, extended beyond simple control of the content of education. The effort to create comprehensive secondary education in Leeds became channelled into a reorganisation of all the city's schools for the benefit of the teaching profession. Since the political parties did not contest the desirability of comprehensive secondary education, the means of implementing it became a technical matter which was left to the chief education officer and the teachers' professional organisations to resolve.

They faced three problems: accommodation, parental choice, and security for teaching staff. Whatever scheme of reorganisation was proposed had to fit in with the existing stock of accommodation, which had no surplus available for some of the more interesting schemes. The major post-war school-building effort had gone into creating sufficient secondary schools by 1965 that no all-age five-to-fifteen schools remained. It had produced many small schools, and 'proper' comprehensives needed to be larger. Nothing, short of a twenty-year building and adaptation programme, could have allowed this and created suitable schools for eleven-to-eighteen-year-olds.

Parental choice was a problem of a similar kind. If parents were genuinely free to choose their children's schools, the ones regarded as better or enjoying more prestige would be swamped with applicants and selection would be unavoidable in any case. Some form of 'guided' choice was necessary to make the system work if selection was to be abandoned.

It was agreed from the outset that any reorganisation should be designed to cause the 'minimum disruption of the teaching staff of the schools',[4] and as the discussions developed this was taken to include in effect the proviso 'unless teachers benefit professionally from the disruptions'.

The impulse towards comprehensive schools was present in the 1946 Education Plan. It was given effect in newly built-up areas in the 1950s but became something more of a cause, partly as a result of national debate, partly through local opportunity after 1965, when the last all-age school was divided, and partly because since 1958 local authority education had been financed not by a percentage grant but by a block grant out of which education had to take its share. The consequence was that for the first time education had to justify its high cost to those concerned with running other local services. With a Labour council, a 'socialist' education policy that cost money was a useful tactic for the education committee to adopt. It was, however, made more difficult because the local Conservatives showed an equal concern for social justice and also wanted to end selection at the age of eleven. They refused to play the role allocated to them by the Labour Party and so the impulse of political advantage died an early death.

The first schemes were discussed by councillors without much reference to the problem of accommodation, but three successive schemes devised between 1963 and 1965 fell at this hurdle when they were passed to the professional educators for comment. The consequence was that the whole business was remitted to a working party of fourteen teachers and six department of education officials. Its proposals of 1966 suggested a building programme to create by 1981 proper eleven-to-eighteen comprehensive schools while running an interim 'comprehensive' system with eleven-to-thirteen and thirteen-to-eighteen schools between 1970 and 1981. The proposals solved the accommodation problem but admitted of only limited parental choice.

The Conservative group were disturbed at the lack of parental choice, and when they came to local office in 1967 they reviewed the whole scheme. Their suggestion was for a reorganisation of the entire school system into schools for children aged five to nine, nine to thirteen, and thirteen to eighteen, with 'guided parental choice'. The matter was, however, remitted again to a working party of teachers and officials which in 1969 produced a rationalisation of these proposals in appropriate language. The crucial element in winning teacher approval for this major reorganisation was the nine-to-thirteen school. Head and other senior teachers' salaries were determined with reference to the age of the eldest children in the school. If the eldest children were twelve, then the salaries were on the lower 'primary' scale, while if they were thirteen they were on the higher 'secondary' scale. By creating another tier of schools the proposals also created an extra school for every two existing ones. Thus in September 1969 there were 846 posts of the rank of head of department and above; under the proposals the *minimum* number of such posts would be 1,307.

The reorganisation that took place in September 1972 was based on Conservative acceptance of the proposals but was actually implemented by the Labour group. It was satisfactory as far as accommodation and teacher satisfaction went. The question of parental choice was, however, unresolved. The Labour group tried in 1973 to abolish it altogether, but failed in practice, and the position settled down to parental choices that depended on the obduracy of parents in insisting on having a choice against the prevailing guidance – a situation that in practice suited both the main political parties. The new system was the creation of professional educational administration and the professional self-regard of teachers.

VII   Town planning legislation from 1909 onwards gave local authorities considerable powers to determine the physical nature of the environment and, through the manipulation of physical land use, affect the social and economic life of their areas. It might therefore be expected that the parties' different views of what constituted the most desirable social and economic structure would find an outlet in the debate about planning. In Leeds, however, party and even councillor interest was low. Major proposals were made and implemented without arousing more than the faintest political interest. This reflected the general lack of public concern with planning, except for property owners adversely affected by new schemes. It also reflected the view of councillors that planning was a technical matter best left to professionals, who only had to observe two principles which the whole town seemed to share: that Leeds should be 'improved' into a pleasanter place to live in, and that all changes would merely be developments of an already satisfactory state of affairs.

Until 1945 town planning was part of the multifarious activities of the improvement committee. Since 'in broad outline, Town Planning is defining on a plan the areas to be used for industrial, business and residential purposes respectively, the principal roads and open spaces, the number of buildings to the acre and similar matters',[5] it was a natural adjunct to such important matters as bridges, new streets and street widening, slum clearance, and private street works. The city had a long tradition of 'improvement', and control over zoning, density and road planning was a useful addition to existing powers, which were strongly based on local attitudes. By 1940 town planning schemes covered almost the whole of suburban Leeds but only half the central area. In the suburbs they were designed largely to regulate shop and office development so as to minimise inconvenience to residents. In 1945 the name of the committee was changed to Town Planning and Improvements, a matter more of tone than of substance, since the old sewerage committee's functions were also included within its remit, and in 1947 the architect's and civil defence departments were also added. The actual policies pursued by the committee were much the same as before the war. However, the 1947 Act required a survey and plan for the whole of Leeds, and work on this began promptly in 1948 when the Act came into force. The first stage was the publication in 1951 of a survey with a draft written statement. A full Development Plan was published later in 1951 but had to wait until 1955 for Ministry approval – a delay that was highly inconvenient for the city in considering appeals by private citizens against some of its provisions. The Ministry considered the plan a very good one of its kind, even featuring it in its own annual report.

The 1951–55 plan had two characteristics. Most of it was devoted to beautifying the city centre, while the other subdivisions of the city were neglected. The whole scheme was strongest on physical dispositions and gave negligible consideration to social and economic consequences. The centre was to have new roadworks, new civil buildings and university and hospital extensions. The removal of existing housing would make more space for shops, offices and hotels. Other areas received cursory treatment: forty-nine 'residential units' ranging in population from an estimate for 1971 of 26,370 to 1,650 were identified with the comment 'The neighbourhoods will be combined later into communities'.[6] How, why and when was not mentioned. This lack of concern for social considerations was paralleled by a complete absence of any economic reasons for the expansion of central facilities and of any precise quantification of the extra space to be allocated to shops, offices and hotels.

Implementation was mainly a matter of approving or disapproving particular projects submitted by other city services or by private individuals and companies. The plan provided a plausible basis on which to take complex decisions, even though it was regularly modified and entirely miscalculated the consequences of increased car ownership, higher birth rates, greater pressure for housing and the demand for better recreational and cultural activities. It seemed to be in no one's interest to observe that the plan was incoherent. That it existed and had professional defenders seemed enough to make it a technical rather than a political matter.

Review began in 1965 and the plan that was, with little modification, to be accepted by the Department of the Environment in 1972 was completed in 1968. The same two characteristics of the earlier one reappeared. The city centre was the focus of attention and the fifty-six 'neighbourhoods' were accorded scant regard. The social and economic consequences of concentrating shops and services in the centre were treated as problems in their own right rather than as symptoms of the weakness of the case for concentration. Thus traffic control and parking, in which Leeds had made some nationally interesting experiments in the 1960s, were treated as something quite separate from the causes of the traffic. Indeed, since the city's economy had come to depend on service industries rather than on manufacturing, the council, eager for new office developments, was prepared to increase congestion by encouraging such building in the central area. In this it was very successful. By 1975 Leeds had 5·5 million of the total 14 million square feet of offices in the whole of West Yorkshire. The social and economic arguments for or against the wisdom of it were never debated.

The professionals of the city council were thus able to draw plans which were to have a serious impact on the lives of the citizens without any debate among councillors being thought necessary or desirable.

VIII   At least three different concepts of 'Leeds' were held by local people in this period. What we may for convenience designate 'Leeds 1' was the historic city centre. 'Leeds 2' was the area that was called Leeds for political, administrative, economic, social or geographical reasons, and was sometimes a little beyond the political and administrative boundaries. 'Leeds 3' was a region as described by the city council in its evidence to the Royal Commission on Local Government in 1966. 'Leeds is the regional centre of a socio-economic region with a population over 3,000,000 covering most of Yorkshire from Northallerton in the North to Barnsley in the South, and from the Pennine watershed in the West to the Yorkshire and Lincolnshire coast in the East.'[7]

The existence of these distinct outlooks was a source of much confusion within Leeds and made the most perceptive of observers uncertain in their assessments. Thus W. L. Andrews, editor of the *Yorkshire Post*, was quoted in 1954 as saying, 'Leeds is in many ways a collection of villages. The patriotism of the village within the city still flourishes.'[8] We have to note the balance here between a 'collection of villages' and the qualifications 'in many ways' and 'within the city' (there is only one city of Leeds but there are many villages).

Similarly, in an entertaining and perceptive book Brian Thompson observed, 'It may well be that the idea of an organic community the size of Leeds is an impossibility – cities might once have had a single corporate life, but no longer ... Leeds is much more a generalised concept place name in inverted commas, it is the city but it also is the commuter villages and the region as well.' But a few pages further on: 'The place is huge but it is all one community.'[9]

Perhaps more significantly, in the actual working of city administration 'districting' became essential, and while the districts that were chosen tended to follow very different sorts of patterns it was not held that the unity of 'Leeds' was in question as a result. By 1974 many services were organised on a district basis: education, housing, social services, environmental health, public works, cemeteries, estates and developments, parks, baths and sports centres, libraries and museums.

There was a gap between the formal political and administrative arrangements of a unitary Leeds and the actual pattern of separate districts, just as there was a gap between the single 'Leeds' insisted on by intelligent observers and the diverse shapes of a real 'Leeds' which they also noted. Almost inevitably, anyone trying to describe the place as a single entity soon found himself talking in terms of 'Leeds 1'. 'Leeds 2' plainly existed in people's minds and 'Leeds 3' also had an existence, but these concepts meant accepting a different sort of picture from the city-centre-dominated one and were not 'real' in quite the same way.

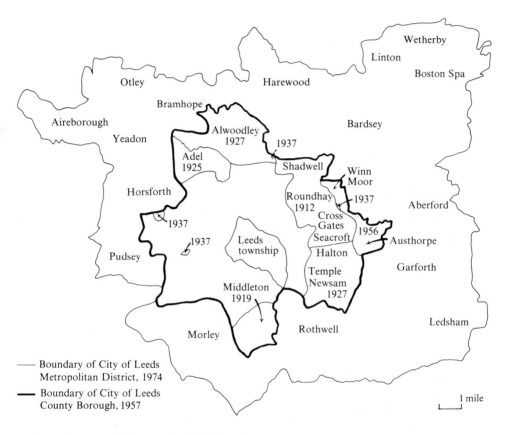

78   The growth of Leeds, 1912–74. The dates are those of acquisition

The problem of defining 'Leeds' in this period, however, was a question not of distinguishing between 'Leeds 1' and 'Leeds 2' but of the extent to which the latter should expand to include parts of 'Leeds 3'. The council, having seen 'Leeds' grow by some 77 per cent in area between 1912 and 1937, took the view that further boundary extensions were desirable. To provide for overspill housing a Greater Leeds plan was devised in 1944–45 which would have doubled the acreage of the city, but it was abandoned in 1946 for a proposal to add a mere 3,000–3,500 acres so that housing developments could be completed.

This proposal was put to the Local Government Boundary Commission, but the commissioners did not report on it before their own demise in 1949. The council then 'agreed' with the West Riding County Council that the city's claim be 'allowed' in return for a promise not to raise the question of boundary extensions again. The city incorporated 2,321 acres in 1957 under a private Act of 1956 passed with the virtual assent of the West Riding, and kept its part of the bargain in 1960 by suggesting to the new Boundary Commission only that there be some mutually beneficial adjustments with Pudsey and that some more building land *might* be allocated to Leeds. The commission did award it some new acres in 1962 but the proposal was not put into effect.

The city council continued its mild policy by telling the Royal Commission on Local Government in 1966 that it would quite happily take over any areas it was given but not suggesting any particular ones. It was rewarded in 1967 when the West Riding agreed that the city might take over the acres allocated in 1962 without opposition from the county.

The Royal Commission reported in 1969 in favour of the establishment of 'unitary authorities' covering very large areas. The powers of a 'unitary authority' would be similar to those the city already enjoyed, but the commission's proposals would create a new Leeds with a population of 840,000 and an area of 317,000 acres, stretching far into the Yorkshire Dales. The city council welcomed the principle of unitary authorities, since it feared the creation of a two-tier system of local government in which Leeds might be only a district with reduced powers in a larger West Yorkshire entity. But it was not enthusiastic about the size of the new authority.

The Labour government's White Paper of 1970 envisaged a metropolitan county structure for West Yorkshire in which the Leeds proposed by the Royal Commission would be a mere metropolitan district. The city council was furious. The Association of Municipal Corporations, led by Alderman Frank Marshall, proposed in reply a two-tier system of provinces and 'most purpose' authorities. This would have created a Yorkshire Province, but also a larger Leeds with its powers intact. The Conservative government's White Paper of 1971, however, retained the idea of a metropolitan West Yorkshire county with Leeds as a district. The size of the proposed district was smaller, at 835,000 population, than in the Royal Commission's scheme.

Without exception at some stage in the next year all the local authorities to be included wholly or partly in the new Leeds District protested, demonstrated, invented more or less plausible alternatives and generally indicated their distaste for the idea of joining the city. Marshall's reaction, that they ought to 'broaden their minds',[10] had exactly the right degree of condescension to infuriate their councillors. His own personality seemed to epitomise the things about Leeds that its neighbours detested: 'arrogance' was the term most commonly used.

The Leeds District proposed in the local government Bill of 1971 took account of much of this criticism. The new Leeds would have a population of 748,000, cover 138,916 acres, and incorporate the boroughs of Morley and Pudsey, the urban districts of Aireborough, Garforth, Horsforth, Otley and Rothwell, and parts of the rural districts of Wetherby (including Wetherby itself) and Wharfedale. During the passage of the Bill many of these authorities fought to stay independent, none more desperately than Rothwell, which was finally included in the Bill's last stages.

The metropolitan district had an elected council for a year before the new Leeds came into being on 1 April 1974. The district council tried to persuade the new West Yorkshire Metropolitan County Council to set up its headquarters at Leeds in fulfilment of the idea of 'Leeds 3', that the city was the centre of a large area. The county council chose instead to go to Wakefield, confirming by this decision the extent to which the pretensions of Leeds were resented by its neighbours.

No one wanted the new Leeds that came into being in 1974. For the old city council, the metropolitan district had too few powers. For the areas incorporated, resentment emphasised the difference between 'Leeds 1' and 'Leeds 2' in a way that had not come to the surface while the debate was on the relation between 'Leeds 2' and 'Leeds 3'. The new Leeds would have to find ways of living with West Yorkshire and at the same time resolving the problems of internal differentiation. Councillors might manage this, especially by continuing old political habits, but whether the new Leeds could have a place in the sentiments of those who live there was as yet unknown.

NOTES

[1] Specifically, for most of the period: art galleries, baths and wash-houses, cemeteries, cleansing, education, environmental health, fire, highways, housing, libraries, lighting, markets, museums, parks, police, sewerage, town planning, transport, waterworks, weights and measures, and welfare services. In 1939 they

also included electricity, gas, general health services, some hospitals, and public assistance.

² H. K. Boyle, 'History of the 9th West Riding (Leeds) Bn. Home Guard (19 May 1940 to 15 August 1945)' (1946), typescript, 6, 7.

² H. Eason, R. Veitch Clark and W. H. Harper, *The Hospital Services of the Yorkshire Area* (1945), 33.

⁴ Leeds City Council, Education Department, *First Report of the Working Party – The Reorganisation of Secondary Education in Leeds* (1966), para. 13.

⁵ Leeds City Council, *Annual Reports of Committees, 1938–39, Improvement Committee* (1939), 3.

⁶ Leeds City Council, *Development Plan, Survey 1951* (1951), Part II.

⁷ Royal Commission on Local Government in England, *Written Evidence of County Borough Councils* (1968), 87.

⁸ *Picture Post*, 12 June 1954.

⁹ B. Thompson, *Portrait of Leeds* (1971), 171, 181.

¹⁰ *Yorkshire Post*, 10 March 1971.

BIBLIOGRAPHICAL NOTE

The major source for the period must be the material generated by the City Council. The council *Proceedings* are the minutes of the committees; the *Annual Reports of Committees* until 1965/66 provided committes with an opportunity for reviewing their labours; and the *Agenda and Verbatim Reports* since 1947 contain an exact record of what was said at council meetings. For 1973/74 the Leeds Metropolitan District Council sat as a parallel but powerless body to the City Council and produced its own *Proceedings* and *Verbatim Report*. This is formal tip to a mountain of departmentally generated paper ranging from duplicated sheets for press announcements to large volumes of newspaper cuttings, while the Archives Office holds a good collection of 'dead' administrative files from all departments. It is best to be aware that, with committee reorganisation and changes in political control, the history of 1966–74 is very difficult to put together. The ending of *Committee Annual Reports* and the obscurantist minuting practices of the *Proceedings* (which continue after 1974) are to be much deplored.

The second major source are the newpapers. The morning daily *Yorkshire Post* is published in Leeds and always records major city news. Its evening stablemate, the *Yorkshire Evening Post* (*Evening Post* after 1969) is much more the city newspaper. The cuttings collection maintained by the two papers is invaluable, and some effort ought to be made to preserve it. Until 1963 the *Yorkshire Evening News* provided an alternative evening newspaper. Until 1958 the *Leeds Guardian*, with its area editions such as *North Leeds News*, provided a weekly commentary, while the Labour Party's *Leeds Weekly Citizen* still continues. The local Conservatives published in 1946–70 a monthly *Leeds Searchlight* which continued on alternate months after 1970. The chamber of commerce produced a monthly *Leeds Journal*. There was also an enormous variety of other papers, often community-based, as with the *Chapeltown News* since 1972, and some crusading, as with *The Other Paper*, 1969–70.

There is a scattering of books that are interesting and useful. P. Nuttgens and A. Rutherford, *Leeds Old and New* (1976), record the changes in the city pictorially, and B. Thompson, *Portrait of Leeds* (1971) is the best contemporary impressionistic account. A formalistic picture of the City Council is contained in H. V. Wiseman, *Local Government at Work* (1967).

The education service in George Taylor's conversations is described in M. Kogan and W. van der Eyken, *County Hall* (1973), the 'Leeds method' in housing in S.

Pepper, *Housing Improvement: Goals and Strategy* (1971), and general housing policy in C. Duke, *Colour and Rehousing* (1970).

The City Library has a good collection of pamphlets, directories, handbooks and some annual or periodic reports, such as those from the Leeds hospitals, but, inevitably, there is still a great deal to be done from them, even at the level of establishing a chronology of events, before this period can be understood outside the City Council framework employed in this chapter.

DEREK FRASER

XVIII

Modern Leeds: a postcript

Leeds is usually a dull, spiritless and inert town. It is awanting in social as well as political activity and energy. It is an inert mass always difficult to be moved. It wants the enthusiasm of Manchester, the enterprize of Glasgow, the volatile gaiety of Liverpool, the intense feeling of Birmingham and the power of London. [*Leeds Times*, 16 December 1843]

This remark, prompted by the waning of a political movement in the early Victorian years, has been echoed through the generations as promoters of clubs, pioneers of good causes, theatrical and musical impresarios and purveyors of new fashions have bemoaned the fickleness of the Leeds public. Leeds folk are hard to win over, and at the height of the Revie era, when United did more to give the city an international reputation than ever its suits had done, it was bitterly remarked that the citizens responded less warmly and in fewer numbers than the followers of Manchester United or Liverpool. Yet the evidence in this book hardly sustains the picture of a city lacking in vitality or enterprise.

In the long term there has been one fundamental geographic factor which has exerted a profound influence upon its development. What is now the Leeds region was regarded in Anglo-Saxon times as a border area, and in a real sense Leeds has remained thus for a thousand years. Its situation places it at the barrier between contrasting regions midway between the Pennine uplands and the Vale of York. To the east and north lie rich agricultural land and open vistas: to the south and west lie heavily industrial regions of coal, textiles and iron. There is a West Riding conurbation, but unlike Greater Manchester its principal city is at the periphery rather than the centre. It remains as true today as in the Victorian era that the traveller from Leeds experiences this contrast by taking different routes out of the city. Yorkshire takes on a vastly different appearance ten miles west of Leeds than from ten miles east.

This permanent feature of the geographic setting has acted

reciprocally with developments in the town and has thus vitally affected its growth and nature. It may be seen in a number of ways, all of which have featured in previous chapters. First, and most obviously, Leeds has always acted as a place of exchange for the commodities of contrasting regions. As a Victorian observer noted, 'with a vast manufacturing district on one side and a rich agricultural district on the other Leeds is calculated to form the most advantageous depot for the commodities which they respectively produce'. At the simplest level Leeds was where the cloth produced to the west was traded for the corn produced to the east. It has meant that, though it may legitimately be classed as one of the pioneering industrial cities of the nineteenth century, Leeds has always been equally a place of commerce. The town's control of the West Riding cloth trade was established not because its manufacturers dominated woollen production but because its merchants controlled the commerce of wool. The human and the environmental reacted with each other as men of entrepreneurial talent exploited and hence reinforced Leeds's geographic position as a natural market place.

This commercial dimension of its economy meant that Leeds never became a staple industrial town. Its commerce always provided alternative forms of employment, and indeed its industry was immensely varied. It boasted a variety of employment possibilities unrivalled in the West Riding. Leeds grew as the woollen cloth trade grew but was never solely a wool town. Engineering, chemicals, pottery, leather, printing and paper, brick-making and many others integrated with woollen textiles and later ready-made clothing to provide a varied economic base. Consequently though Leeds was never immune to trade cycle depressions it never suffered the mass depression of single-industry towns, for a slump in one trade might be offset by a boom in another. The development of the local leather industry well illustrates the effects of geography. Leeds was ideally situated to make use of the hides of the cattle to the north and east to serve its own needs and those of the towns to the west. The growth of substantial tanning and boot and shoe trades in Victorian times is testimony to the relationship of entrepreneur and environment.

Commerce and a variety of industries in turn assisted in establishing a position of regional dominance. Though never the religious or administrative seat of the county and always rivalled by its neighbour Bradford, Leeds established itself as the real capital of the West Riding. It is clear that the town crossed a series of thresholds in the course of its development, steps that marked the stages of its growth. The first, when Leeds became a recognisable town, had already been passed by the seventeenth century. In the last quarter of

the eighteenth it crossed a further threshold when its huge
population growth marked it as an industrial and commercial town of
major importance. Like all large towns, it crossed a third in the mid-
nineteenth century when its sheer size (well over 100,000 population)
meant that an ever-increasing proportion of its citizens worked to
serve the needs of the town in food, accommodation, services and
shops. The really big provincial metropolises with which Leeds is
usually compared – Manchester, Liverpool and Birmingham – all
shared the characteristic of having a large tertiary or service sector.
The final threshold has been the twentieth-century development
which has formalised the city's role as a regional capital. Regional
commercial offices and government departments have arrived in
increasing numbers and Leeds has become the commercial and
administrative capital of the West Riding. The 1974 local government
changes extended the very concept of Leeds to a metropolitan district
far beyond its historic boundaries, much to the annoyance of the
citizens of Otley or Wetherby.

Yet dominance has never been manifested in political terms,
only in the light of the functions Leeds performs for its natural
hinterland. For historical reasons Wakefield has always been the
centre of county government and the new West Yorkshire
Metropolitan County has its headquarters there. But Wakefield is in
no real sense a rival as the economic and social hub of a complex
regional network. And that network has grown partly through
important transport changes. In the seventeenth century Leeds was
largely landlocked, with poor road communications. Now it is at the
heart of an effective communications system and it was no mere
chauvinism that gave rise to the slogan 'Motorway City of the
Seventies', for Leeds stands at the crossroads of the main north–south
and east–west transport axes of the country. From the Aire and
Calder Navigation of the late seventeenth century to the motorway
developments of the 1970s Leeds has been strengthened as a regional
centre by improvements in communications and now has better
transport facilities than at any time in its history. For this reason the
city has become a distribution centre for much of northern England –
a place from which goods are delivered as much as a place where they
are made.

For all these reasons – its role as a market, its variety of industry
and its regional dominance – Leeds is qualitatively a different sort of
place from other West Riding towns. There are of course important
variations of trading specialisation, tradition and topography which
differentiate Bradford from Halifax, Dewsbury from Batley and
Brighouse from Heckmondwike. However, it is mainly size that marks

Bradford out from Huddersfield or Halifax, and them in turn from Batley or Dewsbury. There is a sense in which the towns of the woollen district to the west and into the Pennines are all of a piece. They are wool towns by origin, tradition and development. Their diversification into engineering, chemicals or electricals has not altered the fact that they are wool towns, still recognisable as the outgrowth of the industrial villages from which they sprang. Leeds is different. Bigger in size than any other in the riding, it is not solely or even mainly a wool town. It has always been far more cosmopolitan, far more dependent on migrants and hence perhaps far more anonymous than its neighbours. It is people as well as goods that pass through Leeds, and this has made it a place of mobility. In Edwardian Bradford the vast majority of citizens (some 75 per cent) had been born in the town, and it was this stable population that gave substance to J. B. Priestley's characterisation of it as an overgrown village. Leeds could never boast so many native-born and has always been much more a place of 'comers and goers', and perhaps it is this which makes its citizens slow to loyalty. The more Leeds has taken on the role of a commercial, distributional, administrative and managerial regional centre, the more people move in and out during their working career and the more cosmopolitan it has become. It is not just the Irish and Jews of the nineteenth century who have made it a 'melting pot' in miniature but the British themselves. As an American citizen was one who had crossed the Atlantic, so a Leeds citizen was one who had come there. The 'Loiner' claimed his place in the town by birthright, the citizen by residence. It is perhaps noteworthy that of the present authors who have spent a good part of their lives studying its history only a couple were actually born in the town, though all have lived there at some time.

The continuities in its history must not obscure the fact that modern Leeds has also been the product of dynamic changes. Its emergence as a major town was the direct result of a revolutionary growth in its population. It doubled during the first quarter of the century, doubled again between 1831 and 1871, and the population was some eight times bigger in 1901 than it had been a century earlier. Associated with this population growth were changes in methods of production which radically altered modes of living and working. Many technical innovations either originated or were developed in Leeds itself. Steam engines multiplied, factories abounded and the town burst out of its historic ground-plan. Many individuals carried along these social and economic changes and so left their mark on the life of the place. In manufacturing Benjamin Gott pioneered factory organisation in wool as John Marshall did in flax. Engineers such as

Matthew Murray, Peter Fairbairn or James Kitson were peers in their field, while John Barran exploited the band knife to establish the town's control over the ready-made clothing industry, to be followed by such household names as Hepworth's and Burton's. The country's high streets still display the name Stead and Simpson, whose Leeds origins ought not to be forgotten, while even Marks and Spencer have tenuous links, since it was from Leeds market that the well known retail chain first grew.

Leeds public life too threw up its great individuals. In the mid-nineteenth century the town was often referred to as the seat of the 'Bainesocracy' as a result of the influence of the Baines family and their newspaper, the *Leeds Mercury*. The Baineses' great religious rival was W. F. Hook, Leeds's most distinguished vicar, who did so much to revitalise the Church of England in a city dominated by Methodism and Dissent. Twentieth-century municipal life has been marked by great individuals too. The Conservative leader Alderman Sir Charles Wilson was said to have claimed, 'I am Leeds,' while the Rev. Charles Jenkinson made housing a real social issue in the 1930s. In the post-war years Sir Frank Marshall achieved a national reputation in the field of local government after his work on the city council, while in 1979 Lord Bellwin (formerly Irwin Bellow) found municipal achievement in Leeds a springboard straight into parliamentary government.

These people, and many more, shaped aspects of Leeds affairs in the context of the major forces of industrialisation and urbanisation which have transformed both the city and the nation at large during the last two centuries. And the most profound effect of these changes has been evident in the social structure of modern Britain. It has been argued that before the industrial revolution Britain was a one-class society which was vertically structured: industrialisation changed it into a horizontally class-structured society. Some argue that this new urban industrial society was built around class conflict, others around class consensus. On either argument industrialisation produced *separate* classes which had to find some means of coexistence.

This separation of classes can hardly be better illustrated than in nineteenth and twentieth-century Leeds. In Leeds the gulf between Disraeli's 'Two Nations' can be vividly seen, for perhaps more than elsewhere class manifested itself in physical terms. Industrialisation brought with it a fundamental shift in the residential pattern. Historically Leeds has had an east–west axis, with the older, poorer areas around the parish church and the newer, better-class housing to the west. However, at least until the late eighteenth century, it had been common for rich and poor to live in close proximity, and many fine merchant houses in the centre of the town were also places of business with warehouse or workshop attached. The smoke of industrial Leeds changed all that. The prevailing axis became north–south as the middle classes fled the dirt and smoke to the higher ground to the north. The West End of fine Georgian squares, like Park Square, were doomed by Gott's factory at Bean Ing, which transformed the vista down to the river and whose smoke and soot were carried over the town by the prevailing westerly winds. At the end of the eighteenth century began that sharp residential zoning which became so characteristic a feature of Victorian and Edwardian days. The teeming population was herded into crowded streets of back-to-backs or insanitary cottages and courts. The back-to-backs, making the most of limited space, were popular with speculative builders and multiplied rapidly, giving Leeds its distinctive image of the red-brick terrace with blue slate roof. To the south, west, east and even north-east of the township these streets spread farther and farther, while the wealthier citizens moved out beyond Woodhouse Ridge into Headingley and Chapel Allerton, some even to Roundhay. Now for the middle class workplace and residence were separated as merchants, manufacturers and professional men sought refuge literally 'above the smoke'.

All British cities shared this pattern of zoning in the nineteenth century. Indeed, the great urbanist Lewis Mumford argued that it was one of the defining characteristics of industrial cities throughout the world. Where Leeds differs somewhat is in the rigid separation of 'better' middle-class housing in outer areas from the inner suburbs. In London and Birmingham, for instance, it is common for rich and poor districts to alternate on the journey out from the centre. In the capital this is merely reinforced by changes in fashion which lead 'trendy' people to move into working-class areas. In Birmingham, Edgbaston neatly illustrates the situation. Leave Warwickshire County cricket ground by one gate and you enter tree-lined avenues of large houses with ample grounds: leave by another and you are confronted by decay and squalor in mean terraced streets. In Victorian and Edwardian Leeds no such contrast existed side by side, though it certainly abounded in the borough at large. The whole of the town south of the river, particularly in Hunslet and Holbeck, was heavily industrialised, and former farming areas like Beeston or Farnley became crowded settlements of workers. To the west towards Kirkstall street after street of back-to-backs were developed, while to the east housing remained of poor quality as it had always been. By the turn of the century the march of low-quality bricks and mortar had penetrated Harehills and Potternewton. It was beyond these areas to the north that the middle classes had fled, and this pattern has largely persisted despite municipal attempts to create more mixed housing districts. It is interesting to note how Jewish immigrants soon adopted this pattern. Like all poor arrivals they first crowded into cheap and insanitary housing in the Leylands. Their commercial success and social mobility soon reflected itself in residential choice. The more successful, often second-generation settlers, moved out of the ghetto in the Leylands, only to create in the inter-war years a new ghetto in Chapeltown. In the post-war period the next generation moved farther north into Moortown and Alwoodley. It was a classic Leeds residential pattern as much as classic Jewish social mobility.

The middle classes in their suburbs of villadom viewed with growing concern the alienation of the working-class districts. It was the physical separation of classes that worried the middle-class observer far more than the classic Marxian conflict between capital and labour in the course of production. Many regretted that there were so few opportunities for personal contact between the classes, so few shared activities, so few institutions which catered for a wide social spectrum. Some utilised charitable visiting as a mode of connection, a ploy always tinged with the patronising air of Lady Bountiful. Others sponsored institutions aimed at social control, such as mechanics' institutes or Sunday schools, which would inculcate the right sort of values among the humble. Yet the very pattern of social segregation forced the working class to look to itself for salvation, and so there developed co-operative societies, building clubs, penny banks, friendly societies, evening institutes, trade clubs and temperance groups manned and led by working people themselves. Residential zoning bred residential loyalty, and neighbourhood relationships in the streets where no middle-class face was ever seen strengthened the ties of class consciousness.

Leeds thus had the potential for a strong and radical Labour movement. The paradox of its modern history is that it never fully developed this potential and never became a working-class Labour town such as Bradford or Sheffield. Leeds was indeed always a source of radical ideas, and its vibrant and combative press made it a natural centre of propaganda throughout the nineteenth century. Yet neither during the Chartist period nor during the rise of socialism in the 1880s and 1890s did it become that centre of militant working-class activity that so many believed it might. The ILP was born in Bradford and the great Keir Hardie stood for Parliament there in 1896, for its Labour movement was more firmly rooted than in Leeds. Though James O'Grady was elected as Leeds's first Labour MP in 1906, at the same time as F. W. Jowett was returned in Bradford, Labour's success in the city was due to the tactical association of the Irish and Labour movements in Leeds East.

The failure to realise this Labour potential fully has much to do with the economic structure, previously discussed. The great variety of trades meant that only in exceptional times was unemployment a threat to a large section of working men at the same time. Those who shared the same physical location did not necessarily share the same income, either in amount or regularity. That common experience, far more of a prerequisite for class consciousness than a common relationship to the means of production, was not always generated even in solely working-class districts by an economy with a varied employment base and a large service sector. Divisions within the working class were always as important as the gulf between it and the middle class. There were many large-scale enterprises in which workplace loyalty bred a labour identity: there were also very many small businesses where the gulf between master and men was narrow. Trade unions grew in the fertile ground of large factories but withered in the sweat shops, and the large number of skilled workers distanced themselves socially from the unskilled labourers. Indeed, Leeds was more a town of respectable artisan than of industrial proletariat. And the artisan culture of Leeds was supported by service workers, clerks, small shopkeepers, all often on working-class incomes but aspiring to middle-class manners. All this tended to blur class lines and made for a much more fragmented social structure than a rigorous class stratification which residential zoning would suggest.

Of course it could be said that Leeds did become politically a Labour town, since Labour controlled the city council in the 1930s and for much of the post-war period. Again the social geography of Leeds politics makes it a city where parliamentary seats rarely change hands. During the 1979 election a leading political commentator quipped that one might as well stop having elections in Leeds, so secure were the majorities. One must, however, ask what the character of municipal rule was and what sort of representation these secure majorities have produced. Jenkinson's concern for radical social engineering did not transform what was essentially a moderate Labour Party in Leeds. So lacking in ideological commitment was Labour control in the post-war period that, it is argued in the previous chapter, Conservative accession in the late 1960s marked no shift in municipal policy. That housing pattern which awards Labour four safe seats (with due acknowledgment to the Liberal challenge in Leeds West) provides further evidence of the lack of political extremism in the city. It is surely significant that the prominent Labour politicians who have represented Leeds seats since 1945 have all been middle-of-the-road. Alice Bacon, Charles Pannell, Merlin Rees, Denis Healey and above all Hugh Gaitskell have nailed Leeds's colours to the moderate Labour mast.

If the Labour consciousness of the working-class areas of the city, particularly south of the Aire, has not provided the stuff of revolution, it has helped to sustain a township identity which originated before Leeds itself. It is always important to remember that Leeds borough comprised Leeds township and the ten out-townships of Headingley, Chapel Allerton, Potternewton, Holbeck, Beeston, Hunslet, Armley, Farnley, Wortley and Bramley. If some, like Armley or Potternewton, have been swallowed by the urban swarm, others like Hunslet or Bramley have retained something of their own identity in the face of the metropolis. Bramley and Hunslet still have their own Rugby League teams which, independently of Leeds, take on the might of Wigan or St Helens. Holbeck and many others still have their own feasts which link the township to its dimly remembered pre-industrial past. A firmer link with the past is the open spaces which have survived the onslaught of brick and mortar. Some have been formal acquisitions such as Roundhay Park or Temple Newsam; others remain green areas for topographical reasons, such as Meanwood and Gledhow Valleys; still others survive through historic right of common such as Hunslet and Woodhouse Moors. These open spaces, which thankfully remain so today, also represent the continuity in Leeds's history. The scenes of commotion, entertainment, commerce and political enthusiasm which they have witnessed through the ages deny the image of a dull town. Moderate Leeds may have been, inert never.

INDEX